Revenue Statistics in Latin America and the Caribbean 1990-2017

Estadísticas tributarias en América Latina y el Caribe 1990-2017

Please cite this publication as:
OECD, et al. (2019), *Revenue Statistics in Latin America and the Caribbean 2019*, OECD Publishing, Paris.
https://doi.org/10.1787/25666b8d-en-es

Por favor, cite esta publicación de la siguiente manera:
OECD, et al. (2019), *Estadísticas tributarias en América Latina y el Caribe 2019*, OECD Publishing, Paris.
https://doi.org/10.1787/25666b8d-en-es

ISBN 978-92-64-83946-5 (print/impresa)
ISBN 978-92-64-82603-8 (pdf)

Revenue Statistics in Latin America and the Caribbean/*Estadísticas tributarias en América Latina y el Caribe*
ISSN 2410-4728 (print/impresa)
ISSN 2410-4736 (online/en línea)

Photo credits/Fotografías: Cover/Portada © some of the graphic elements in the main cover illustration were adapted from Freepik.com.

Corrigenda to OECD publications may be found on line at: *www.oecd.org/about/publishing/corrigenda.htm.*
Las erratas de las publicaciones de la OCDE se encuentran en línea en: www.oecd.org/about/publishing/corrigenda.htm.

Foreword

Revenue Statistics in Latin America and the Caribbean *is a joint publication by the OECD Centre for Tax Policy and Administration, the OECD Development Centre, the United Nations Economic Commission for Latin America and the Caribbean (ECLAC), the Inter-American Center of Tax Administrations (CIAT), the Inter-American Development Bank (IDB) and for the first time with the support of the European Union Regional Facility for Development in Transition for Latin America and the Caribbean (LAC). It presents detailed, internationally comparable data on tax revenues for 25 Latin American and Caribbean economies, two of which are OECD members. Its approach is based on the well-established methodology of the OECD Revenue Statistics database, which is an essential reference source for OECD member countries. Comparisons are also made with the average tax indicators for OECD economies.*

The term "taxes" in this publication is confined to compulsory, unrequited payments to general government. As outlined in the Interpretative Guide to Revenue Statistics, taxes are "unrequited" in the sense that benefits provided by government to taxpayers are not normally in proportion to their payments. The OECD methodology classifies a tax according to its base: income, profits and capital gains (classified under heading 1000), payroll (heading 3000), property (heading 4000), goods and services (heading 5000) and other taxes (heading 6000). Compulsory social security contributions paid to general government are treated as taxes and classified under heading 2000. Much greater detail on the tax concept, the classification of taxes and the accrual basis of reporting is set out in the Interpretative Guide in Annex A.

Extending the OECD methodology to Latin American and Caribbean countries enables comparisons of tax systems on a consistent basis both across this region and with OECD countries. In a few cases this methodology differs from the approach used by ECLAC, CIAT and IDB; these differences are noted in the text and in the tables, either with a footnote or an extra row.

The report provides an overview of the main taxation trends in Latin America and the Caribbean. It examines changes in both the level and the composition of taxation plus the attribution of tax collection by sub-level of government between 1990 and 2017.

Presentación

La publicación Estadísticas tributarias en América Latina y el Caribe *ha sido elaborada conjuntamente por el Centro de Política y Administración Tributaria de la OCDE, el Centro de Desarrollo de la OCDE, la Comisión Económica de las Naciones Unidas para América Latina y el Caribe (CEPAL), el Centro Interamericano de Administraciones Tributarias (CIAT), el Banco Interamericano de Desarrollo (BID) y por primera vez con el apoyo del Fondo Regional para el Desarrollo en Transición para América Latina y el Caribe (ALC) de la Unión Europea. Esta publicación presenta datos detallados comparables a escala internacional sobre los ingresos tributarios de 25 economías latinoamericanas y caribeñas, dos de las cuales son miembros de la OCDE. Su enfoque se basa en la metodología contrastada de la base de datos* "Revenue Statistics" *de la OCDE, que se ha convertido en un referente esencial para los países miembros de la OCDE. Se presentan también comparaciones con la media de medidas tributarias de la OCDE.*

En la presente publicación, el término "impuestos" se circunscribe exclusivamente a los pagos obligatorios sin contraprestación efectuados al gobierno general. Tal y como lo subraya la Guía de Interpretación de Revenue Statistics, los impuestos carecen de contraprestación en el sentido en que, normalmente, las prestaciones proporcionadas por el gobierno a los contribuyentes no guardan relación directa con los pagos realizados por estos. La metodología de la OCDE clasifica los impuestos según la base sobre la que recaen: renta, utilidades y ganancias del capital (categoría 1000); nómina (categoría 3000); propiedad (categoría 4000); bienes y servicios (categoría 5000); y otros impuestos (categoría 6000). Las contribuciones obligatorias a la seguridad social abonadas al gobierno general se tratan aquí como impuestos (categoría 2000). Para mayor detalle sobre el concepto de impuesto, su clasificación y su registro según el criterio de devengo, véase la Guía de interpretación que figura en el Anexo A.

Aplicar la metodología de la OCDE a América Latina y el Caribe posibilita la comparación de sistemas tributarios a partir de una base coherente en la region, entre los países latinoamericanos, y con los países de la OCDE. Sin embargo, en algunas ocasiones, esta metodología difiere de la empleada por la CEPAL, el CIAT y el BID; en esos casos, las diferencias se han indicado en el texto y los cuadros, sea con una nota a pie de página, o en una línea adicional.

El informe ofrece un panorama general de las principales tendencias en materia tributaria en América Latina y en el Caribe. A tal efecto, examina los cambios registrados entre 1990 y 2017 en el nivel y la composición de la tributación, así como en la atribución de la recaudación tributaria a los diversos subsectores de gobierno.

Acknowledgements

Revenue Statistics in Latin America and the Caribbean was jointly produced by the Organisation for Economic Co-operation and Development (OECD) Centre for Tax Policy and Administration, the OECD Development Centre, the United Nations Economic Commission for Latin America and the Caribbean (ECLAC), the Inter-American Center of Tax Administrations (CIAT), the Inter-American Development Bank (IDB) and for the first time with the support of the European Union Regional Facility for Development in Transition for Latin America and the Caribbean (LAC). The staff from these organisations with responsibility for producing the publication were: Emmanuelle Modica and René Orozco of the OECD Centre for Tax Policy and Administration under the supervision of the Director, Pascal Saint-Amans, Deputy Director, Grace Perez-Navarro, the Head of the Tax Policy and Tax Statistics Division, David Bradbury and the Head of the Tax Data and Statistical Analysis Unit, Michelle Harding; Sébastien Markley of the OECD Development Centre under the supervision of the Director, Mario Pezzini, the Head of Latin America and the Caribbean Unit, Sebastian Nieto Parra, and the Co-ordinator of Revenue Statistics for the Development Centre, Alexander Pick; and Michael Hanni and Juan Pablo Jiménez of the Economic Development Division of UN-ECLAC under the supervision of chief of Fiscal Affairs, Noel Perez and of the Director, Daniel Titelman; and Julio Alberto López from the CIAT Tax Studies and Research Directorate, under the supervision of Director Santiago Díaz de Sarralde; and Luis Fernando Corrales Lara under the supervision of the Principal Technical Leader in Fiscal Economics, Alberto Barreix of the IDB.

The authors would like to thank other staff at the OECD Development Centre and the Centre for Tax Policy and Administration for their invaluable support in completing and improving the 2019 edition of this publication. Elizabeth Nash and Delphine Grandrieux from the OECD Development Centre's Communications and Publications team and Damian Garnys, statistical editor from the OECD Publications and Communications Directorate, ensured the production of the publication, in both paper and electronic form. Michael Sharratt from the OECD Centre for Tax Policy and Administration, Vararat Atisophon from the OECD Development Centre also assisted production and Stephanie Coic produced the cover.

Finally, the Centre for Tax Policy and Administration and the Development Centre are also very grateful to our colleagues working in national entities with whom we have consulted regularly. These institutions include the finance ministries and national tax agencies of Argentina, Barbados, Belize, Bolivia, Brazil, Chile, Colombia, Costa Rica, Cuba, Dominican Republic, Ecuador, El Salvador, Guatemala, Guyana, Honduras, Jamaica, Mexico, Nicaragua, Panama, Paraguay, Peru, Uruguay and Venezuela. In addition, CIAT would like to thank their Network of Tax Studies and Research. In particular, we are grateful to Jeferson Luis Bittencourt from the Ministry of Finance of Brazil; Jorge Richard Nuñez of Costa Rica´s Ministry of Finance; Mariam Ortiz from the Dominican Republic Finance Ministry; José Patricio Almeida from the Internal Revenue Service of Ecuador; Luis Antonio Campos from the Ministry of Finance of El Salvador and Gerardo Perez from the Embassy of El Salvador in

France; David Antonio Alvarado from the Secretary of Finances in Honduras; Andrea Gregory and Patrika Chambers from Jamaica's Tax Administration and Customs agencies; Pedro Galeando from Paraguay's Finance Ministry; Jorge Rivera Calderón from Peru's Ministry of Economic and Finance ; María Pedro Apezteguia, Valentina Cancela and Victoria Magallanes from the Uruguayan General Taxation Directorate and the Office of Planning and Budget.

This document was produced with the support of the European Commission. The opinions expressed and arguments employed herein do not necessarily reflect the official views of the OECD member countries or the European Union.

Agradecimientos

La publicación *Estadísticas tributarias en América Latina* y el Caribe ha sido elaborada conjuntamente por el Centro de Política y Administración Tributaria de la Organización para la Cooperación y el Desarrollo Económicos (OCDE), el Centro de Desarrollo de la OCDE, la Comisión Económica de las Naciones Unidas para América Latina y el Caribe (CEPAL), el Centro Interamericano de Administraciones Tributarias (CIAT), el Banco Interamericano de Desarrollo (BID) y por primera vez con el apoyo del Fondo Regional para el Desarrollo en Transición para América Latina y el Caribe (ALC) de la Unión Europea. Las personas de esas organizaciones responsables de redactar la presente publicación han sido: Emmanuelle Modica y René Orozco del Centro de Política y Administración Tributaria de la OCDE, bajo la supervisión del director, Pascal Saint-Amans, la sub-directora Grace Perez-Navarro y el Jefe de la División de Políticas y Estadísticas Tributarias, David Bradbury y la Jefe de la Unidad de Análisis de Datos Tributarios y Estadísticas, Michelle Harding; Sébastien Markley del Centro de Desarrollo de la OCDE, bajo la supervisión del director, Mario Pezzini, del Jefe de la Unidad de América Latina y el Caribe Sebastian Nieto Parra y el coordinador de Estadísticas tributarias Alexander Pick; Michael Hanni, Juan Pablo Jiménez, Ignacio Ruelas y Miguel Angel González de la División de Desarrollo Económico de la CEPAL, bajo la supervisión del jefe de asuntos fiscales Noel Perez y del director Daniel Titelman; Julio Alberto López de la Dirección de Estudios e Investigaciones Tributarias del CIAT, bajo la supervisión del Director Santiago Díaz de Sarralde; y Luis Fernando Corrales Lara, bajo la supervisión del Líder Técnico Principal en Economia Fiscal del BID, Alberto Barreix.

Los autores desean agradecer a otras personas del Centro de Desarrollo de la OCDE, del Centro de Política y Administración Tributaria de la OCDE por su invaluable contribución a la mejora y finalización de la edición 2019 de esta publicación. En particular, Elizabeth Nash y Delphine Grandrieux, del equipo de Comunicaciones y Publicaciones del Centro de Desarrollo de la OCDE, y Damian Garnys, editor estadístico del equipo de Publicaciones y Comunicaciones de la OCDE, que aseguraron la producción de la publicación, tanto fisica como en formato electrónico. Michael Sharratt del Centro de Política y Administración Tributaria, Vararat Atisophon del Centro de Desarrollo de la OCDE también colaboraron en la traducción y producción de esta publicación. Asi mismo, Stephanie Coic produjo la portada.

Por último, El Centro de Política y Administración Tributaria y el Centro de Desarrollo de la OCDE hacen partícipes de su agradecimiento a nuestros colegas de entidades nacionales, a los que hemos consultado con frecuencia. Entre esas instituciones, se cuentan los ministerios de finanzas y las agencias tributarias nacionales de Argentina, Barbados, Belice, Bolivia, Brasil, Chile, Colombia, Costa Rica, Cuba, Ecuador, El Salvador, Guatemala, Honduras, México, Nicaragua, Panamá, Paraguay, Perú, República Dominicana, Uruguay y Venezuela. Asimismo, CIAT también desea agradecer La Red de Estudios e Investigaciones Tributarias. En particular, estamos agradecidos con Jeferson Luis Bittencourt del Ministério da Fazenda de Brasil; Jorge Richard Nuñez del Ministerio de Hacienda de Costa Rica; José Patricio Almeida del Servicio de Rentas Internas de Ecuador; Luis Alberto Canjura y Luis Antonio Campos del Ministerio de Hacienda de El Salvador y Gerardo Perez de la Embajada de El Salvador en Francia; David Antonio Alvarado de la Secretaria de Finanzas de Honduras; Andrea Gregory y Patrika Chambers de la Administración Tributaria y la Agencia de Aduanas de Jamaica; Pedro Galeando del Ministerio de Hacienda Paraguayo; Jorge Rivera Calderón del Ministerio de Economía y Finanzas del Perú; Mariam Ortiz del Ministerio de Hacienda de la República Dominiana; Pedro Apezteguia, Valentina Cancela y María Victoria Magallanes de la Dirección General de Impuestos de Uruguay y de la Oficina de Planeamiento y Presupuesto.

Este documento fue producido con el apoyo de la Comisión Europea. Las opiniones expresadas y los argumentos aquí empleados no reflejan necesariamente las opiniones oficiales de los países miembros de la OCDE o de la Unión Europea.

Table of contents

Indice

LIST OF TABLES/LISTA DE CUADROS

Chapter 1/Capítulo 1
Tax revenue trends, 1990-2017/Tendencias tributarias, 1990-2017

Chapter 2/Capítulo 2
Special feature/Sección especial

Chapter 4/Capítulo 4
Tax levels and tax structures, 1990-2017/ Niveles impositivos y estructuras tributarias, 1990-2017

Chapter 6/Capítulo 6

**Tax revenues by sub-sectors of general government/
Ingresos tributarios por sub-sectores de gobierno general**

LIST OF FIGURES/LISTA DE GRÁFICOS

Chapter 1/Capítulo 1

Tax revenue trends, 1990-2017/Tendencias tributarias, 1990-2017

Chapter 2/Capítulo 2

Special feature/Sección especial

Chapter 3/Capítulo 3
Special feature/Sección especial

Executive summary

The Report provides internationally comparable data on tax levels and tax structures for 25 Latin American and Caribbean (LAC) countries: Argentina, the Bahamas, Barbados, Belize, Bolivia, Brazil, Chile, Colombia, Costa Rica, Cuba, the Dominican Republic, Ecuador, El Salvador, Guatemala, Guyana, Honduras, Jamaica, Mexico, Nicaragua, Panama, Paraguay, Peru, Uruguay, Trinidad and Tobago and Venezuela.

In this publication, "taxes" are defined as compulsory, unrequited payments to general government. Taxes are "unrequited" in the sense that benefits provided by government to taxpayers are not normally in proportion to their payments. Compulsory social security contributions (SSCs) paid to general government are classified as taxes. More information on the tax classification and the basis of reporting is set out in the Interpretative Guide in Annex A.

Tax-to-GDP ratios in the LAC region in 2017

In 2017, the average tax-to-GDP ratio in the LAC region (measured as tax revenues, including SSCs paid to general government, as a proportion of GDP) was 22.8%. The LAC average represents the unweighted average of 24 Latin American and Caribbean countries included in this publication and excludes Venezuela due to data availability issues.

Tax-to-GDP ratios ranged from 12.4% in Guatemala to 40.6% in Cuba in 2017. All LAC countries had a tax-to-GDP ratio below the OECD average of 34.2%, except for Cuba. Countries in Central America and Mexico typically have lower tax-to-GDP ratios, with a sub-regional average of 21.0% in 2017, whereas countries in the Caribbean sub-region had higher tax-to-GDP ratios and a sub-regional average of 25.6%. The average for South America was the same as the LAC average at 22.8%.

Between 2016 and 2017, the average LAC tax-to-GDP ratio increased by 0.2 percentage points, as did the OECD average. This increase in the LAC region was driven by large increases in four Caribbean countries as well as Uruguay. The increase in the tax-to-GDP ratio in the LAC region reflects in part the recovery in the overall economic environment in the region in 2017 after a two-year recession, driven by improvements in global demand, increased trade and higher commodity prices.

Between 2016 and 2017, 12 countries reported an increase in their tax-to-GDP ratios while 10 recorded a decrease and two saw no change. Over this period, Guyana and Barbados recorded the largest increases (of 2.6 and 2.2 percentage points respectively) whereas Bolivia recorded the largest decrease (of 2.0 percentage points). In both Guyana and Barbados, an increase in revenue from taxes on goods and services was the main contributor to the higher tax-to-GDP ratios and was mainly explained by tax policy and tax administration reforms.

Evolution of tax-to-GDP ratios in the LAC region since 1990

Between 1990 and 2017, the average tax-to-GDP ratio in LAC countries rose almost continuously, increasing by 7.3 percentage points from 15.5% to 22.8%, and converged towards the OECD average. The difference in the average tax-to-GDP ratio in the LAC and the OECD decreased from 16.4 percentage points in 1990 to 11.4 percentage points in 2017.

South America recorded the fastest growth between 1990 and 2017 and the sub-regional average for South America reached the LAC average in 2005 (at 20.0% of GDP). South America's average tax-to-GDP ratio was consistently higher than the LAC average between 2010 and 2016. In contrast, the growth of the tax-to-GDP ratios for Central America and Mexico and for the Caribbean has been more gradual. The tax-to-GDP ratio of Central America and Mexico was consistently below the LAC average across the period, whereas the Caribbean's average tax-to-GDP ratio was consistently higher.

The main contributors to the increase in tax revenues in the LAC region were value-added taxes (VAT) and taxes on income and profits. VAT revenue as a percentage of GDP in LAC countries increased by 3.7 percentage points between 1990 and 2017, trending to the OECD average level (6.0% and 6.8% of GDP respectively in 2016). Since 1990, nine out of the 25 countries (especially Caribbean countries) introduced a VAT and additional efforts were made in most countries to improve the mobilisation of VAT revenue (through an increase of VAT rates, expansion of the taxable base and strengthening of the VAT collection system). Revenues from taxes on income and profits increased by 2.8% of GDP over the same period, mainly driven by the boom in commodity prices.

Tax structures in the LAC region

The average LAC tax mix shifted towards VAT and taxes on income and profits between 1990 and 2017. In 2017, the LAC average tax mix exhibited a relatively high share of revenue from taxes on goods and services, which made up about half of total tax revenues compared with a third in the OECD (2016 figure). At 27.9% of total tax revenues, VAT was the biggest source of revenue on average in the LAC region in 2017, followed by revenues from taxes on income and profits (27.1%) and from other taxes on goods and services (21.8%).

On average, 44% of tax revenues in LAC countries came from taxes on income and profits and SSCs, compared with 60% in the OECD in 2016. Within taxes on income and profits, the revenue share of corporate income tax (CIT) was higher in the LAC region compared to the OECD while the revenue share of personal income tax (PIT) was lower. In 2016, CIT and PIT accounted for 15.4% and 9.6% of total tax revenues respectively, compared with 9.0% and 23.8% in the OECD. Similarly, the average share of SSCs in total tax revenues was about 10 percentage points lower in the LAC region than the OECD average (16.5% versus 26.2%).

Environmentally related taxes play an increasingly significant role in many countries. In the 22 LAC countries for which data are available, environmentally related tax revenues amounted to 1.1% of GDP on average in 2017, a lower level than the OECD average of 1.6% of GDP. Tax revenues from energy, most commonly from excises on diesel and petrol, represented the highest share of environmentally related tax revenue in the LAC region (0.7% of GDP on average), around two-thirds of environmentally related tax revenue. These were followed by revenues from motor vehicle and transport services taxes, which represented most of the remainder. Tax revenues levied on other environmentally related bases were negligible in the LAC region. In recent years, Chile, Colombia and Mexico have introduced significant green tax reforms. These include the introduction of carbon taxes mostly levied on fossil fuels and/or motor vehicles, based on their carbon content.

Special features

The Report contains two special features. The first identifies trends in fiscal revenues from non-renewable natural resources for a selection of countries in the LAC region in 2017 and 2018. These revenues stabilised in 2017, after falling sharply between 2014 and 2016. A favourable global oil market allowed hydrocarbon revenues to remain at their 2016 level of 2.3% of GDP, with increased non-tax revenues offsetting a decline in tax revenues. Meanwhile, revenues from mining as a proportion of GDP increased to 0.37% on average in 2017 from 0.28% in 2016. Revenues from mining and hydrocarbons are estimated to have strengthened further in 2018 despite a sharp correction in prices over the second half of the year.

The second special feature examines recurrent taxes on immovable property in Latin America. These revenues are a critical means of supporting local governments in providing basic services but in Latin America they are low relative both to other sources of revenue and to average revenues in OECD countries. There is wide variation in terms of the revenues generated through these taxes between the countries examined, from 0.1% of GDP in Ecuador to 0.9% of GDP in Uruguay in 2016. The OECD average level was 1.1% of GDP in 2016. The special feature examines these taxes in greater detail for Argentina, Brazil and Colombia to identify the constraints and enablers of higher revenues.

Resumen ejecutivo

La publicación *Estadísticas tributarias en América Latina y el Caribe* proporciona datos comparables a nivel internacional sobre los niveles y estructuras de recaudación tributaria de 25 países de América Latina y el Caribe (ALC): Argentina, Bahamas, Barbados, Belice, Bolivia, Brasil, Chile, Colombia, Costa Rica, Cuba, República Dominicana, Ecuador, El Salvador, Guatemala, Guyana, Honduras, Jamaica, México, Nicaragua, Panamá, Paraguay, Perú, Uruguay, Trinidad y Tobago y Venezuela.

En este informe, el término "impuestos" se refiere a pagos obligatorios, sin contraprestación, al gobierno general. Los impuestos carecen de contraprestación en el sentido de que normalmente los bienes y servicios brindados por los gobiernos a los contribuyentes no son proporcionales a sus pagos. Las contribuciones a la seguridad social (CSS) pagadas al gobierno general se clasifican como impuestos. Se provee información sobre la clasificación de los impuestos y su criterio de registro en la Guía en el Anexo A.

Proporciones de recaudación tributaria sobre PIB en 2017

En 2017, el promedio de recaudación tributaria sobre el producto interno bruto (PIB) en la región ALC fue de 22.8%. La proporción de recaudación tributaria sobre PIB se mide como los ingresos tributarios, incluyendo CSS pagadas al gobierno general, como proporción del PIB. El promedio de ALC representa el promedio no ponderado de 24 países de América Latina y el Caribe incluidos en esta publicación y excluye a Venezuela debido a problemas de disponibilidad de datos.

La recaudación tributaria sobre PIB osciló entre el 12.4% en Guatemala y el 40.6% en Cuba en 2017. Todos los países de ALC, excepto Cuba, tuvieron unas contribuciones tributarias con respecto al PIB inferior al promedio de 34.3% de la OCDE. Los países de América Central y México típicamente tienen ratios más bajos, con un promedio subregional de 21.0% en 2017, mientras que los países de la subregión del Caribe tuvieron una recaudación tributaria más alta y un promedio subregional del 25.6%. El promedio para América del Sur fue el mismo que el promedio de ALC de 22.8%.

Entre 2016 y 2017, la recaudación tributaria como proporción del PIB en ALC aumentó en 0.2 puntos porcentuales, al igual que el promedio de la OCDE. Este aumento en la región de ALC se debió principalmente a grandes aumentos en cuatro países del Caribe y en Uruguay. El aumento en la relación de impuestos sobre PIB en la región de ALC refleja en parte la recuperación en el entorno económico general en 2017, después de una recesión de dos años, impulsada por mejoras en la demanda global, un aumento del comercio y el aumento de los precios de los productos básicos.

Entre 2016 y 2017, 12 países reportaron un aumento en sus tasas de recaudo tributario con respeto al PIB, mientras que 10 registraron una disminución y dos no vieron ningún cambio. En 2017, Guyana y Barbados registraron los mayores incrementos (de 2.6 y 2.2 puntos porcentuales respectivamente), mientras que Bolivia experimentó la mayor disminución (de 2.0 puntos porcentuales). Tanto en Guyana como en Barbados, un aumento en los ingresos por impuestos sobre bienes y servicios fue el principal contribuyente a los mayores índices de impuestos sobre el PIB y se explicó principalmente por las políticas tributarias y las reformas de la administración tributaria.

Evolución de la recaudación tributaria en la región de ALC desde 1990

Entre 1990 y 2017, los ingresos tributarios como proporción del PIB en los países de ALC aumentaron casi continuamente, pasando del 15.5% al 22.8%, disminuyendo la brecha con el promedio de la OCDE. La diferencia en la recaudación tributaria sobre PIB entre ALC y la OCDE disminuyó de 16.4 puntos porcentuales en 1990 a 11.4 puntos porcentuales en 2017.

América del Sur registró el crecimiento más rápido entre 1990 y 2017, y el promedio subregional de América del Sur alcanzó el promedio de ALC en 2005 (20.0% del PIB). La tasa promedio de impuestos sobre el PIB de América del Sur fue consistentemente más alta que el promedio de ALC entre 2010 y 2016. Por lo contrario, el crecimiento de la recaudación tributaria para América Central y México y para el Caribe ha sido más gradual. La recaudación tributaria como proporción del PIB de América Central y México estuvo consistentemente por debajo del promedio de ALC durante todo el período, mientras que la relación promedio de impuestos sobre el PIB fue siempre más alta en el Caribe.

Los principales contribuyentes al aumento de los ingresos tributarios en la región de ALC fueron los impuestos al valor agregado (IVA) y los impuestos sobre los ingresos y ganancias. Los ingresos por IVA como porcentaje del PIB en los países de ALC aumentaron 3.7 puntos porcentuales entre 1990 y 2017, tendiendo al nivel promedio de la OCDE (6.0% y 6.8% del PIB, respectivamente, en 2016). Desde 1990, nueve de los 25 países (especialmente los países del Caribe) introdujeron un IVA y se realizaron esfuerzos adicionales en la mayoría de los países para mejorar la movilización del ingreso del IVA (a través de un aumento de las tasas de IVA, la expansión de la base imponible y el fortalecimiento del sistema de recaudación). Los ingresos por impuestos sobre la renta y las ganancias aumentaron un 2.8% del PIB en el mismo periodo, principalmente debido al auge de los precios de los productos básicos.

Estructuras tributarias en la región

En ALC, la participación en la estructura tributaria (tax mix) del IVA y de los impuestos sobre la renta aumentó entre 1990 y 2017. En 2017, en promedio ALC tiene una proporción relativamente alta de ingresos por impuestos sobre bienes y servicios, que representaron aproximadamente la mitad de los ingresos tributarios totales en comparación con un tercio en la OCDE (cifra de 2016). Con un 27.9% de los ingresos tributarios totales, el IVA fue la mayor fuente de ingresos en promedio en la región ALC en 2017, seguido por los ingresos provenientes de los impuestos a la renta, utilidades y las ganancias (27.1%) y de otros impuestos sobre bienes y servicios (21.8%).

En promedio, en 2016 el 44% de los ingresos tributarios en los países de ALC provinieron de impuestos sobre la renta y utilidades y las CSS, en comparación con 60% en la OCDE. La proporción del impuesto sobre la renta de sociedades, dentro de la categoría de impuestos sobre la renta y utilidades, fue más alta en la región de ALC que en la OCDE, lo que significa que la participación del impuesto sobre la renta de personas físicas en los ingresos del impuesto a la renta fue menor. En 2016, la proporción de los ingresos del impuesto sobre la renta de sociedades y sobre personas físicas fue respectivamente de 15.4% y de 9.6% del recaudo tributario total comparado con 9.0% y 23.8% en la OCDE. De igual forma, las CSS como proporción de los ingresos tributarios totales fue más baja de 10 puntos porcentuales que el promedio de la OCDE (16.5% comparado con 26.2%).

Los impuestos relacionados con el medio ambiente desempeñan un papel cada vez más importante en muchos países. En los 22 países de ALC para los que se dispone de datos, los ingresos fiscales relacionados con el medio ambiente ascendieron a un promedio del 1.1% del PIB en 2017, un nivel inferior al promedio de la OCDE del 1.6% del PIB. Los ingresos fiscales provenientes de la energía, más comúnmente de los impuestos especiales sobre el diesel y la gasolina, representaron la mayor proporción de ingresos fiscales relacionados con el medio ambiente en la región de ALC (0.7% del PIB en promedio), alrededor de dos tercios de los ingresos fiscales relacionados con el medio ambiente.

A estos les siguieron los ingresos por concepto de impuestos sobre vehículos de motor y servicios de transporte, que representaron la mayor parte del resto de este tipo de ingresos. Los ingresos tributarios recaudados en otras bases relacionadas con el medio ambiente fueron insignificantes en la región de ALC. En los últimos años, Chile, México y Colombia han introducido importantes reformas fiscales verdes. Estos incluyen la introducción de impuestos al carbono principalmente a los combustibles fósiles y / o vehículos motorizados, en función de su contenido de carbono.

Secciones especiales

Este Informe contiene dos secciones especiales. La primera identifica tendencias en los ingresos fiscales provenientes de recursos naturales no renovables para una selección de países en la región de ALC en 2017 y 2018. Estos ingresos se estabilizaron en 2017 después de caer bruscamente entre 2014 y 2016. Un mercado global favorable del petróleo permitió que los ingresos por hidrocarburos se mantuvieran en su nivel de 2016 de 2.3% del PIB, con un aumento de los ingresos no tributarios que compensan una disminución en los ingresos tributarios. Mientras tanto, los ingresos de la minería como proporción del PIB aumentaron a 0.37% en promedio en 2017 desde 0.28% en 2016. Se estima que los ingresos de minería e hidrocarburos se han fortalecido aún más en 2018 a pesar de una fuerte corrección en los precios durante la segunda mitad del año.

La segunda sección especial examina los impuestos recurrentes sobre bienes inmuebles en América Latina. Estos ingresos son un medio fundamental para ayudar a los gobiernos locales a proporcionar servicios básicos, pero en América Latina son bajos en relación con otras fuentes de ingresos y con respecto al promedio en los países de la OCDE. Existe una amplia variación en los ingresos generados a través de estos impuestos entre los países examinados, desde el 0.1% del PIB en Ecuador, hasta el 0.9% del PIB en Uruguay en 2016. El nivel promedio de la OCDE fue de 1.1% del PIB. en 2016. La sección especial examina estos impuestos con mayor detalle en Argentina, Brasil y Colombia para identificar las restricciones y las acciones hacia mayores ingresos.

Chapter 1

Tax revenue trends, 1990-2017

Capítulo 1

Tendencias tributarias, 1990-2017

Chapter 1

Tax revenue trends, 1990-2017

Tax ratios

The fiscal capacity of Latin America and the Caribbean (LAC) must increase for countries to develop in a sustainable and inclusive manner and to achieve the Sustainable Development Goals. Mobilising domestic resources sustainably and fairly is a prerequisite for countries in the region to accelerate the development process, promote long-term growth, and reduce inequality and vulnerability.

The tax-to-GDP ratio is a key measure of domestic resource mobilisation. It reflects the collection of taxation revenue by governments to finance public goods and services and to invest in infrastructure. Raising revenue through taxes is important to ensure a country's economic emergence (OECD, 2014[1]). Taxation provides a predictable and sustainable source of government revenue, in contrast with development assistance and volatile non-tax revenues generated by commodities.

This report presents internationally comparable data on the tax revenues of 25 Latin American and Caribbean countries. This chapter discusses several key indicators in these countries: the tax-to-GDP ratio, the tax structure and the share of tax revenue by level of government. The discussion supplements detailed country information found in Chapter 5.

Tax ratios in 2017

The average tax-to-GDP ratio in the LAC region was 22.8% in 2017 (Figure 1.1). The LAC average represents the unweighted average of 24 countries included in this publication and excludes Venezuela due to data availability issues.

The tax-to-GDP ratio is measured as tax revenues (including social security contributions paid to the general government) as a proportion of gross domestic product (GDP). Tax-to-GDP ratios varied widely in the region, ranging from 12.4% in Guatemala to 40.6% in Cuba. With the exception of Cuba, all LAC countries had a tax-to-GDP ratio below the OECD average[1] of 34.2%.

The highest tax-to-GDP ratios in the LAC region were in Cuba (40.6%), Brazil (32.3%) and Barbados (31.8%). The countries with the lowest tax-to-GDP ratios were Guatemala (12.4%), Paraguay (13.8%) and the Dominican Republic (13.9%).

There were important differences in the level of taxation between Central America and Mexico, South America and the Caribbean[2]. Countries in Central America and Mexico typically have lower tax-to-GDP ratios, with an average of 21.0% in 2017, whereas countries in the Caribbean sub-region had higher tax-to-GDP ratios and an average of 25.6%. In contrast, the tax-to-GDP ratios of South American countries were distributed across the whole range of tax-to-GDP ratios and the average for the South America region was 22.8% in 2017, the same as the LAC average.

In 2017, the average LAC tax-to-GDP ratio was 0.2 percentage points higher than the previous year (Figure 1.2). This increase reflects in part a recovery in the overall economic environment in the region in 2017 after a two-year recession: GDP grew by 1.3% (in real terms) between 2016 and 2017, driven by improvements in global demand, trade and higher commodity prices (OECD/CAF/UN ECLAC, 2018[3]).

Figure 1.1. **Tax-to-GDP ratios, 2017**

Total tax revenue as percentage of GDP

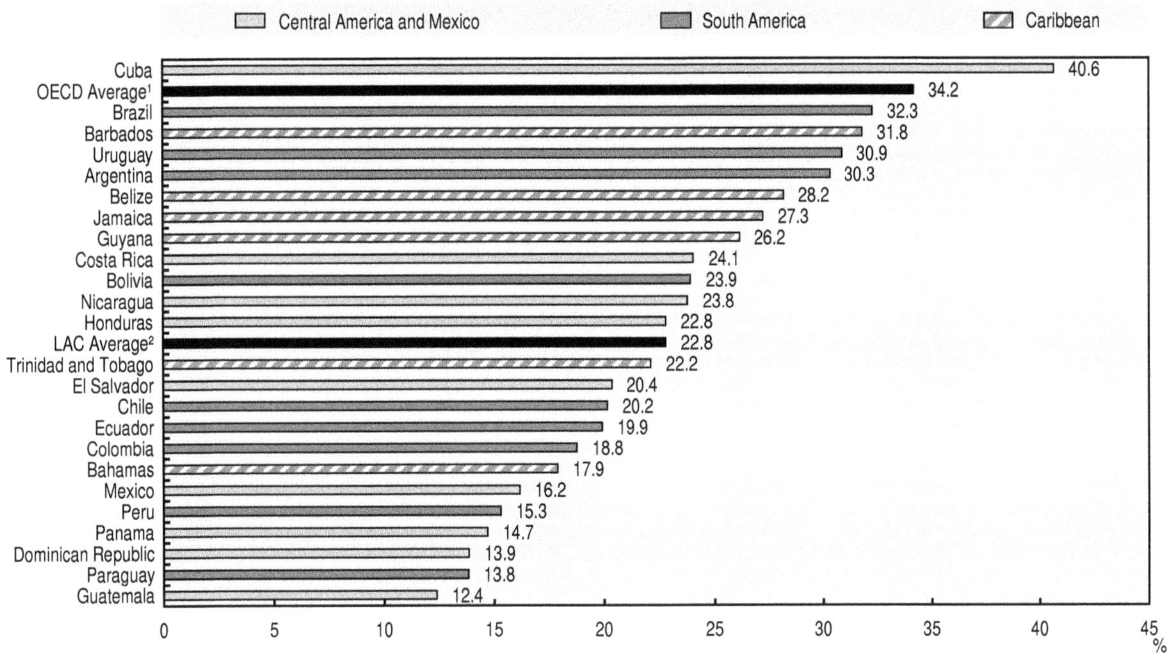

Note: The figures exclude local government revenues for Argentina (but include provincial revenues), the Bahamas, Barbados, Cuba, Dominican Republic and Honduras as the data are not available. Cuba and the Dominican Republic are included in the Central America and Mexico group.

1. Represents the unweighted average of the 36 OECD member countries. Chile and Mexico are also part of the OECD (36) group.

2. Represents the unweighted average of 24 Latin American and Caribbean countries included in this publication and excludes Venezuela due to data availability issues.

Source: (OECD/ECLAC/CIAT/IDB, 2019[2]), Table 4.1.

StatLink https://doi.org/10.1787/888933939883

Figure 1.2. **Changes in tax-to-GDP ratios between 2015-16 and 2016-17**

Percentage points of GDP

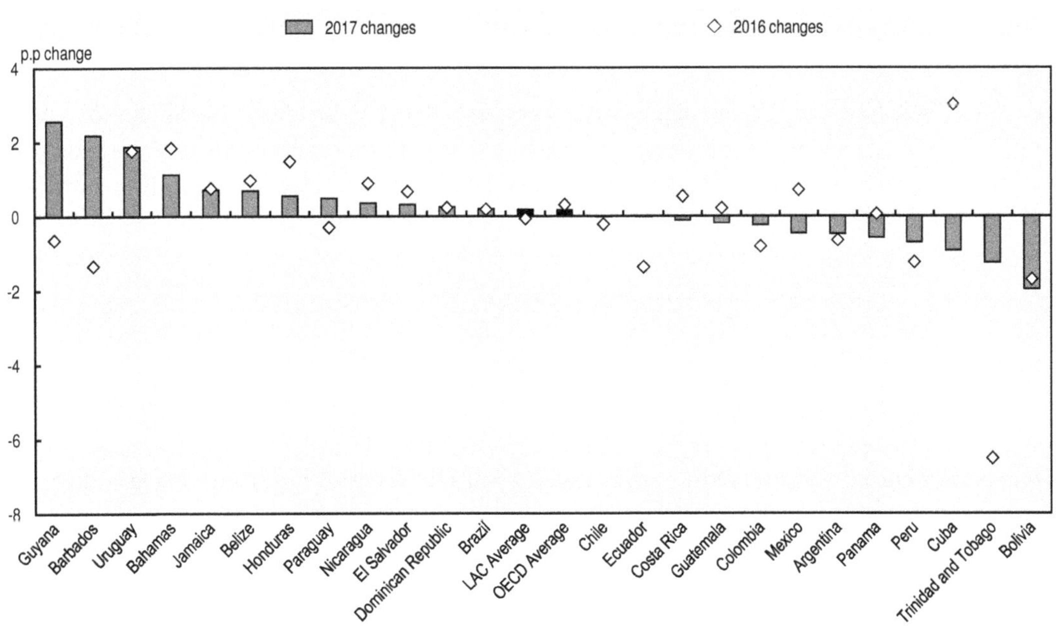

Source: Authors' calculations based on (OECD/ECLAC/CIAT/IDB, 2019[2]), Table 4.1.

StatLink https://doi.org/10.1787/888933939902

There is a range of different situations across LAC countries with respect to tax-to-GDP ratio changes between 2016 and 2017. Twelve countries reported an increase in their tax-to-GDP ratio in 2017 while ten recorded a decrease and two remained stable.

The increases in tax-to-GDP ratios in LAC countries in 2017 were on average larger than the decreases. In 2017, two countries recorded increases in tax-to-GDP ratios of over two percentage points. Guyana reported the largest increase (of 2.6 percentage points) followed by Barbados, whose tax-to-GDP ratio increased by 2.2 percentage points.

Revenues from taxes on goods and services and taxes on income and profits were the main drivers for the increase in the tax-to-GDP ratio for Guyana: they increased respectively by 1.3 and 0.8 percentage points. Revenues from taxes on goods and services (and in particular excise taxes) and from social security contributions were the main contributors to the increase in Barbados (rising by 1.8 and 0.7 percentage points, respectively).

Significant tax and tax administration reforms have contributed to the increases observed in Barbados and Guyana.

- Since 2015, Guyana has made efforts to improve tax administration through the CIAT-SECO Cooperation Program (CIAT, 2017$_{[4]}$): a large taxpayer unit was created; the taxpayer base has increased thanks to implementation of risk models; and tax collection processes were strengthened. In addition, Guyana reformed its value-added tax (VAT) system in 2017 by reducing the VAT standard rate and expanding the VAT base. These changes contributed to a 0.8 percentage point increase in VAT revenue as a percentage of GDP between 2016 and 2017 (IMF, 2018$_{[5]}$).
- Barbados increased the rate of the National Social Responsibility Levy[3] (an excise tax) from 2% to 10% in July 2017, which contributed significantly to the overall increase in the tax-to-GDP ratio. Barbados also increased excise tax rates on gasoline and diesel (IBFD, 2017$_{[6]}$).

By contrast, only Bolivia had a decrease of over two percentage points between 2016 and 2017 and the decreases in most countries were of less than one percentage point. In Bolivia, declines were recorded in all main categories of tax revenue in 2017 as a proportion of GDP. Revenues from taxes on goods and services had the largest decrease of 1.1 percentage points, driven by a decrease in VAT revenues equivalent to 0.7% of GDP. The second highest decrease in Bolivia occurred in income tax revenues (0.6 percentage points).

Between 2016 and 2017, Bolivia's GDP rose more than tax revenues in nominal terms (8% versus 2%). The main sector that triggered this growth was the agricultural sector (due to better climatic conditions and an increase of cultivated lands), followed by the hydrocarbons sector. The lower increase in tax revenues as a percentage of GDP in Bolivia may reflect the fact that agriculture is a challenging sector to tax. In developing economies, most people working in this sector receive low incomes and many are not registered for tax purposes (EPS-PEAKS, 2013$_{[7]}$). Numerous tax exemptions for this sector and a high level of informality in the agricultural sector also cause difficulties in taxation (Ministry of Foreign Affairs in The Hague, 2018$_{[8]}$).

Conceptually, and as seen for Bolivia, changes in the tax-to-GDP ratio are driven by the relative size and direction of change in nominal tax revenues and nominal GDP. If tax revenues rise more than GDP (or fall less than GDP) the tax-to-GDP ratio will increase. Conversely, if tax revenues rise less than GDP, or fall further, the tax-to-GDP ratio will go down. Therefore, a higher tax-to-GDP ratio does not necessarily mean that the amount of tax revenues has increased in real or even nominal terms.

Among the 12 LAC countries that increased their tax-to-GDP ratio in 2017 relative to 2016, annual growth in GDP was positive, although to a lesser degree than tax revenue growth.

Of the ten LAC countries that experienced a decline in their tax-to-GDP ratio in 2017, nine had higher levels of nominal tax revenues than in 2016, although to a lesser degree than growth in nominal GDP levels. Trinidad and Tobago had positive nominal GDP growth and negative tax revenue growth. No countries experienced a decline in nominal GDP (Figure 1.3).

Figure 1.3. **Relative changes in nominal tax revenues and nominal GDP, 2016-17**

Percentage

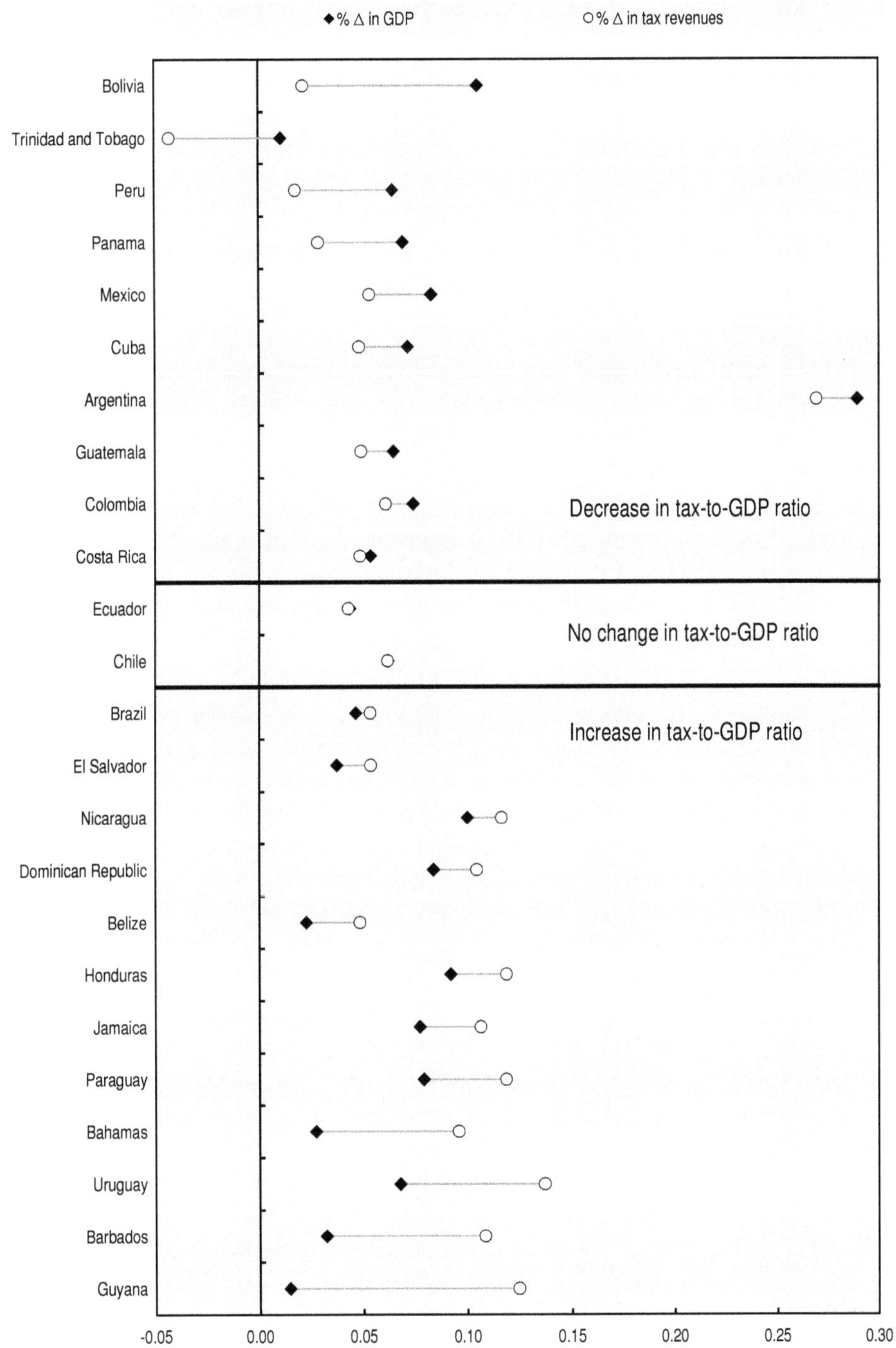

1. Data for Mexico in 2017 show an estimate, including expected revenues collected by state and local governments.
2. Argentina's nominal tax revenues and GDP increased by more than 25% between 2016 and 2017, due to inflation.

Source: Authors' calculations based on (OECD/ECLAC/CIAT/IDB, 2019[2]), Chapter 5 (tax revenues) and Table 4.15 (GDP).

StatLink https://doi.org/10.1787/888933939921

Evolution of tax ratios since 2000

Enhancing domestic resource mobilisation, particularly through increased tax revenues, is critical for LAC's sustainable development, as reflected by its prominent role in the Development in Transition agenda (see Box 1.1). With the exception of 2008, 2009 and 2016, the average tax-to-GDP ratio in LAC countries has risen steadily since 1990 (Figure 1.4). It increased by more than seven percentage points, from 15.5% in 1990 to 22.8% in 2017. This growth reflects favourable macroeconomic conditions, changes in tax system design and strengthening of tax administrations. This trend contrasts with that in the OECD area, where the ratio has been relatively stable; the tax-to-GDP ratio reached 34.2% in 2017, 2.1 percentage points above its level in 1990. The difference between the LAC and OECD average tax-to-GDP ratios fell between 1990 and 2008 and then remained relatively steady (Figure 1.4).

Box 1.1. ***Revenue Statistics in Latin America and the Caribbean* and Development in Transition**

This edition of Revenue Statistics in Latin America and the Caribbean is the first to be produced with the support of the EU Regional Facility for Development in Transition for Latin America and the Caribbean (LAC). This facility is an EU-led initiative, developed with the support of the Organisation for Economic Co-operation and Development (OECD) and its Development Centre, and the Economic Commission for Latin America and the Caribbean (ECLAC).

LAC economies are confronting persistent and new domestic and global vulnerabilities that call for critical transformations to maximise opportunities for development. Most LAC countries have achieved middle-income status but confront profound structural challenges that constrain their continued progress. Four main traps hinder successful transformation and transition to sustainable development. These are the productivity, social vulnerability, institutional and environmental traps, which interact with each other in self-reinforcing dynamics to limit the region's sustainable development opportunities (OECD/CAF/ECLAC/EU, 2019[9]).

Development in Transition embraces an approach to design better policies, practices and partnerships both at home and internationally. Ever-more complex issues require development strategies with more sophisticated policy mixes and greater co-ordination and coherence. Ambitious efforts must be made to overcome the traps and turn vicious circles into virtuous ones. At home, domestic capacities, including tax collection, must be strengthened to better address development challenges. At the global level, international co-operation should act as a facilitator to support countries transitioning towards sustainable development by participating in policy partnerships, as equal partners, and address common concerns, putting LAC national strategies front and centre, strengthen countries' domestic capacities and expand the toolbox of international co-operation modalities and instruments (OECD/CAF/ECLAC/EU, 2019[9]).

Fiscal policy is essential to build capacities, address development traps and ensure inclusive and sustainable development in LAC countries. Revenue Statistics in Latin America and the Caribbean represents an invaluable resource for governments as they look to strengthen fiscal policy. By providing harmonised and detailed tax data across the region, it allows for in-depth tax-policy analysis, identifying not only how the level of tax revenues varies by country but also which instruments generate these revenues, reflecting the fact that how tax revenues are collected can be as important as how much is collected. Revenue Statistics in Latin America and the Caribbean also represents a common starting point for knowledge-sharing and capacity development between countries, as well as with the broader international community.

Reflecting the critical relationship between effective taxation and effective public spending, the DiT Facility brings Revenue Statistics in Latin America and the Caribbean together with ECLAC's work on public expenditure, and social spending in particular. The objective is to provide unprecedented insights and invaluable tools for the development of fiscal policy in the region, thereby unlocking its capacity to fulfil its commitment to the Agenda 2030 and implement long-term development strategies.

Figure 1.4. **Tax-to-GDP ratios, LAC and OECD averages, 1990-2017**

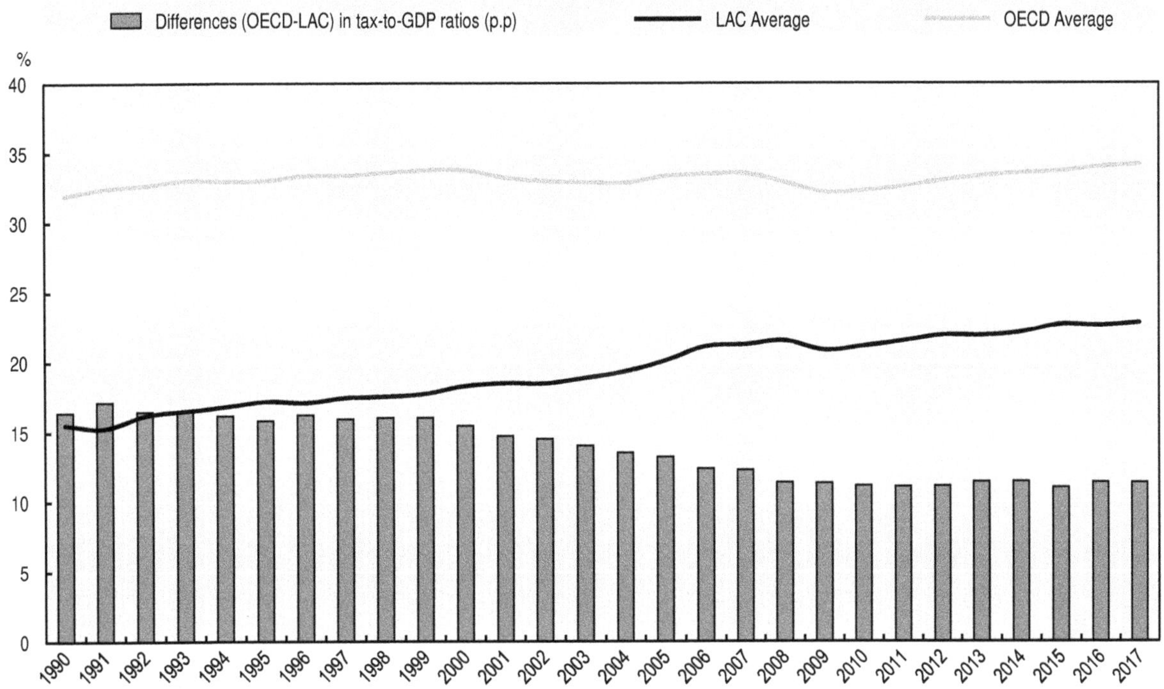

Source: (OECD/ECLAC/CIAT/IDB, 2019[2]), Table 4.1.

StatLink https://doi.org/10.1787/888933939940

Figure 1.5 shows how the average tax-to-GDP ratios for the three sub-regions of Latin America and the Caribbean have evolved since 1990. While all three sub-regions have shown an upward trend in tax levels between 1990 and 2017, their evolution shows notable differences between sub-regions. On average, South America recorded the fastest growth over the period and reached the LAC average in 2005 (at 20.0% of GDP). After 2010, South America's tax-to-GDP ratio exceeded the LAC average until 2016. In contrast, the increase in the tax-to-GDP ratios for Central America and Mexico and for the Caribbean has been more gradual. Throughout this period, the tax-to-GDP ratio of Central America and Mexico remained below the average for the LAC region as a whole, whereas the Caribbean's average tax-to-GDP ratio was consistently higher than the LAC average. Since 1990, the Caribbean average has been slowly trending towards the LAC average whereas the reverse is observed for Central America and Mexico.

Tax-to-GDP ratios in LAC countries increased in the early 1990s after a period of macroeconomic instability during the previous decade. During the 1980s, countries ran large fiscal imbalances and some resorted to alternative ways of financing expenditure (borrowing or printing money). This caused rapid inflation across the region, which eroded the real value of countries' tax revenues. Reforms in the 1990s focused on price stability, trade liberalisation and fiscal discipline. Most LAC governments both reduced spending and implemented policies aimed at increasing tax revenues; budget management and fiscal balances improved considerably. Policy makers implemented reforms to tax policy and administration to reinforce tax systems against inflationary episodes by shortening collection lags and indexing tax liabilities (ECLAC, 2018[10]).

Figure 1.5. **Average tax-to-GDP ratios, LAC and sub-regions, 1990-2017**

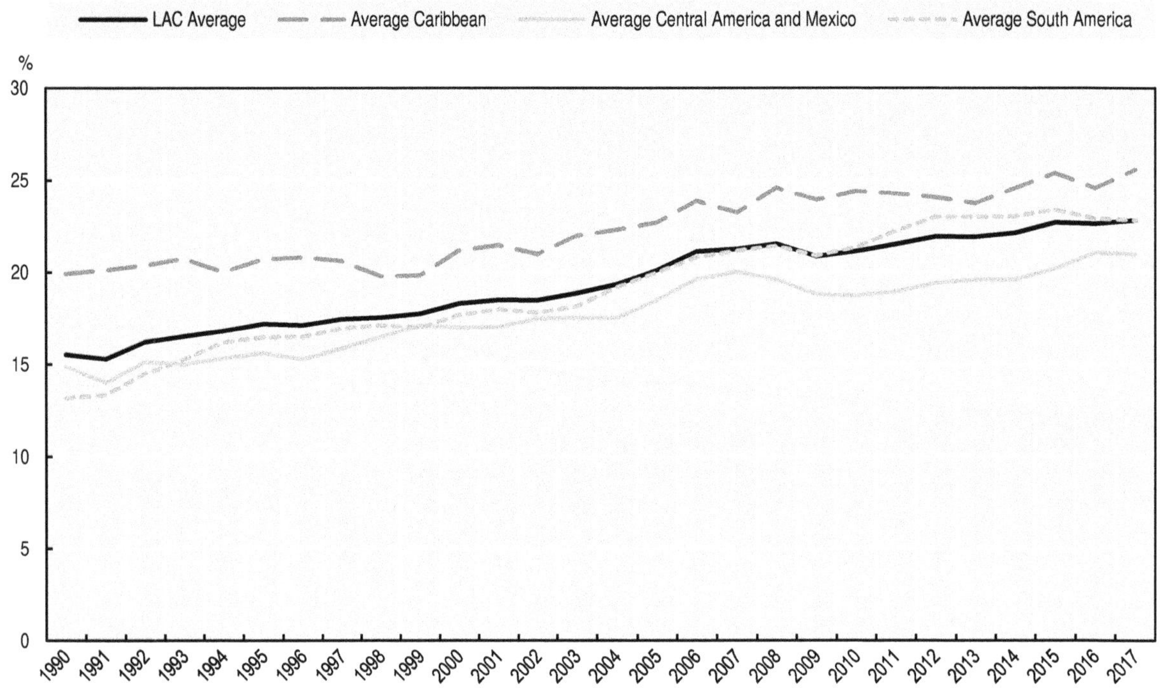

Note: The LAC average represents the unweighted average of 24 LAC countries included in this publication and excludes Venezuela due to data availability issues.

The Caribbean includes six countries (Bahamas, Barbados, Belize, Guyana, Jamaica and Trinidad and Tobago), Central America & Mexico nine countries (Costa Rica, Cuba, Dominican Republic, El Salvador, Guatemala, Honduras, Mexico, Nicaragua and Panama) and South America nine countries (Argentina, Bolivia, Brazil, Chile, Colombia, Ecuador, Paraguay, Peru and Uruguay).

Source: Authors' calculations based on (OECD/ECLAC/CIAT/IDB, 2019[2]), "Revenue Statistics in Latin America and the Caribbean: Comparative tables", *OECD Tax Statistics* (database), *http://dx.doi.org/* 10.1787/data-00641-en.

StatLink *https://doi.org/10.1787/888933939959*

LAC countries have undertaken significant efforts to modernise tax administrations and tax systems over the last two decades. Over this period, new information technology systems have been implemented, the structures of tax administrations were rationalised, tax collection systems became more efficient and staff gained in expertise (IDB, 2013[11]). In addition, some LAC countries simplified their tax systems by broadening their tax bases, which has contributed to the increase in tax receipts. They reduced the number of exemptions and tax incentives granted to certain activities and sectors principally to incentivise foreign investment. Tax reforms included the introduction or development of simplified regimes for small taxpayers and the taxation of property based on presumed incomes. These measures had a positive effect on revenues in a number of countries thanks to the expansion of taxation to labour and capital income, including dividends (e.g. Colombia, Dominican Republic, Guatemala, El Salvador, Nicaragua, Panama and Peru). Reforms have also included the establishment of minimum taxes, taxes on financial transactions and the gradual reduction in the real income level taxed at the top marginal rate (ECLAC, 2013[12]); (ECLAC, 2018[10]).

The introduction of VAT was the most significant tax reform in LAC in the 1980s; twelve[4] countries implemented a VAT system in 1980 and almost all had implemented VAT by the early 1990s. After this period, VAT reforms have increased the tax rate, widened the tax base and strengthened its collection. Reforms also focused on the simplification of VAT systems, with most countries reducing the number of items with zero or reduced rates, moving towards single-rate VAT schemes in several countries (ECLAC, 2018[10]).

Between 1990 and 2017, revenue from VAT as a percentage of GDP more than doubled for LAC countries on average, from 2.3% of GDP in 1990 to 6.0% in 2017 (Figure 1.6). Over the same period, revenues from other taxes on goods and services (excises, customs and import duties) in LAC decreased as a percentage of GDP. This decline was associated with trade liberalisation, as a result of which LAC countries changed the way they taxed imported and exported goods as well as specific goods and services. These changes included a reduction of import tariffs, narrowing the base of products and services subject to excises and the elimination of taxes on exports. One important exception is Argentina, where taxes on exports were re-established in 2002; however, the government established in December 2015 has abolished export taxes on almost all agricultural products (IMF, 2016[13]); (World Grain, 2016[14]).

Figure 1.6. **Revenue from taxes on income and profits, VAT and other taxes on goods and services, 1990-2017**

Percentage of GDP

Source: Authors' calculations based on (OECD/ECLAC/CIAT/IDB, 2019[2]), "Revenue Statistics in Latin America: Comparative tables", *OECD Tax Statistics* (database), *http://dx.doi.org/* 10.1787/data-00641-en.

StatLink https://doi.org/10.1787/888933939978

Since 1990, the increase in the average tax-to-GDP ratio in the LAC region has been driven by increases in income tax revenues and VAT, in roughly equal proportions. Increases in these two sources of revenue have largely tracked each other (Figure 1.6). Between 1990 and 2002, VAT contributed more to the increase in tax revenues (2.0 percentage points compared to 1.0 percentage point for taxes on income and profits). Between 2002 and 2017, revenue from taxes on income and profits and from VAT both increased respectively by 1.8 percentage points and by 1.7 percentage points. The increase in income taxes is partly explained by the commodity price boom after 2003, which drove up corporate income tax (CIT) revenue from companies in the natural resources sector (ECLAC, 2014[15]) (Barreix, Benitez and Pecho, 2017[16]). In several countries, it was also a result of tax policies that reduced tax incentives in free-trade zones, the introduction of minimum taxes for corporations, reforms in international taxation and agreements between countries to fight tax evasion. The decrease in 2016 can mainly be explained by the drop in CIT revenue from non-renewable commodities, especially in Trinidad and Tobago (OECD/CIAT/IDB/ECLAC, 2018[17]). In 2017, revenues from income taxes remained at the same level as in 2016 (6.1% of GDP).

Since 2007, CIT revenues as a percentage of GDP have declined whereas revenues from personal income tax (PIT) have steadily increased. In 2017, the LAC averages for the CIT and PIT revenues stood at 3.4% and 2.2% of GDP respectively (Figure 1.7).

Figure 1.7. **Revenue from taxes on income and profits, CIT and PIT, 2007-17**

Percentage of GDP

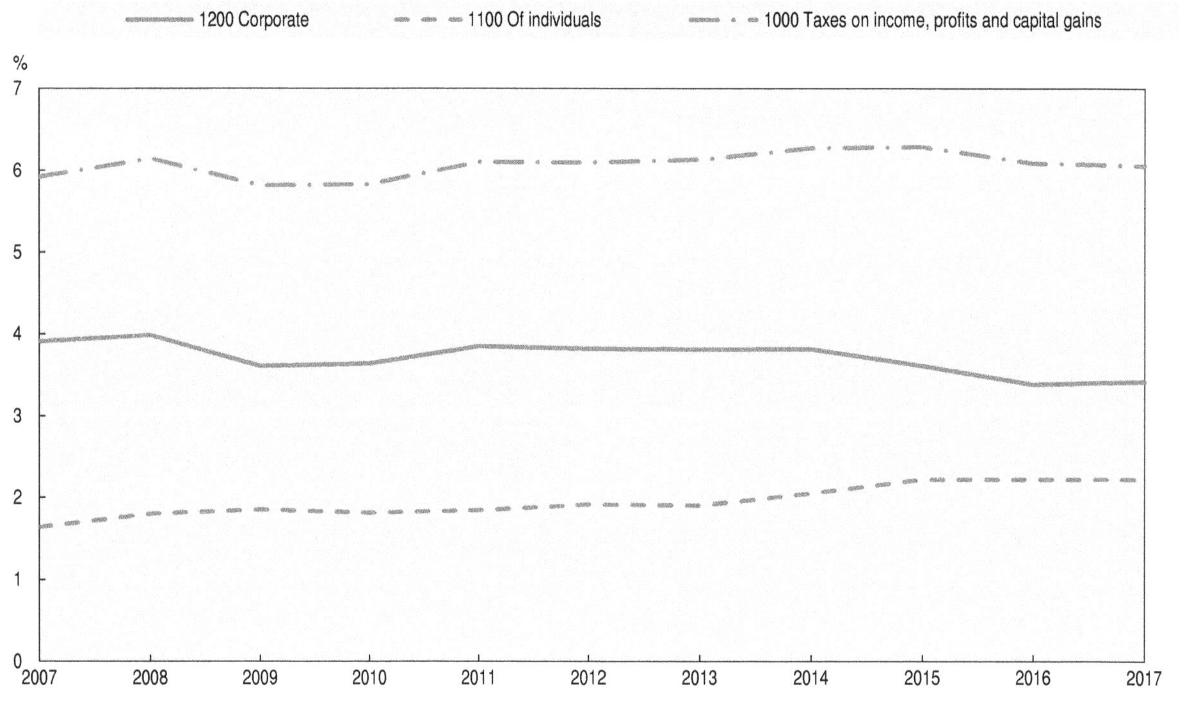

Note: The LAC corporate income tax revenue and personal income tax revenue as a percentage of GDP should be interpreted with caution as Ecuador, Nicaragua and Venezuela are excluded from the calculation. The LAC averages excludes Venezuela due to data availability issues. Ecuador and Nicaragua are excluded from the LAC averages for CIT revenue as a percentage of GDP and PIT revenue as a percentage of GDP as more than a third of their revenue from taxes on income and profits cannot be allocated to CIT revenue (1200) or PIT revenue (1100).

Source: (OECD/ECLAC/CIAT/IDB, 2019[2]), "Revenue Statistics in Latin America and the Caribbean: Comparative tables", *OECD Tax Statistics* (database), *http://dx.doi.org/10.1787/data-00641-en.*

StatLink *https://doi.org/10.1787/888933939997*

There are some notable differences between the three LAC sub-regions when considering the changes in the main tax categories between 1990 and 2017 (Figure 1.8).

- On average, the Caribbean showed – as a percentage of GDP – the largest increase in VAT revenue (6.1 percentage points) and the lowest increases in revenues from income taxes and social security contributions. Five of the six Caribbean countries implemented[5] a VAT system over the period, later than most countries in Central America and Mexico and South America.

- In Central America and Mexico, and in South America, the largest increases between 1990 and 2017 were due to taxes on income and profits (over 3.5 percentage points in both sub-regions), followed by VAT (over 2.8 percentage points in both sub-regions) and social security contributions (less than 2.5 percentage points). Revenues from taxes on income and profits (and indirectly the increase from VAT) were influenced by the large increases in mineral and oil prices between 2003 and 2010.
- In South America, the average increase in social security contributions revenues as a percentage of GDP was much larger than in the other two sub-regions (2.5 percentage points in South America compared to less than 1.6 percentage points in the other sub-regions). In contrast, South America is the only sub-region that did record a minor fall in revenues from other taxes on goods and services, on average. Nonetheless, South America still has the lowest level of revenues from other taxes on goods and services on average (at 3.9% of GDP).

Figure 1.8. **Changes in revenue from taxes on income and profits, VAT, social security contributions and other taxes on goods and services by sub-region, 1990-2017**

Percentage of GDP

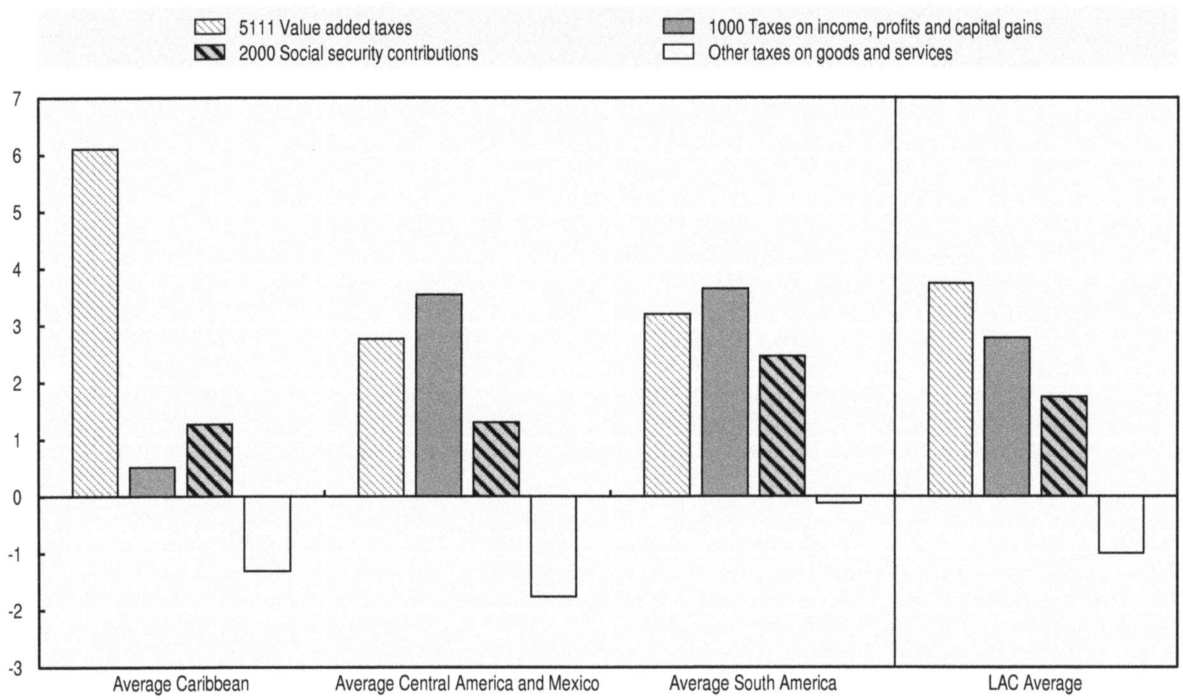

The LAC average represents the unweighted average of 24 LAC countries included in this publication and excludes Venezuela due to data availability issues.

The Caribbean includes six countries (Bahamas, Barbados, Belize, Guyana, Jamaica, and Trinidad and Tobago), Central America & Mexico nine countries (Costa Rica, Cuba, Dominican Republic, El Salvador, Guatemala, Honduras, Mexico, Nicaragua and Panama) and South America nine countries (Argentina, Bolivia, Brazil, Chile, Colombia, Ecuador, Paraguay, Peru and Uruguay).

Source: Authors' calculations based on (OECD/ECLAC/CIAT/IDB, 2019[2]), "Revenue Statistics in Latin America: Comparative tables", *OECD Tax Statistics* (database), *http://dx.doi.org/* 10.1787/data-00641-en.

StatLink https://doi.org/10.1787/888933940016

Factors influencing tax-to-GDP ratios

Differences between the LAC and OECD average tax-to-GDP ratios are consistent with the tendency for higher income countries to have higher tax-to-GDP ratios. The data implies a positive correlation between GDP per capita (a measure of the level of income of a country) and tax-to-GDP ratios (Figure 1.9). In general, OECD countries have higher average incomes than LAC countries and collect higher tax revenues as a proportion of GDP. Argentina, Barbados, Brazil, Trinidad and Tobago and Uruguay show similar tax-to-GDP ratios and levels of income to some OECD countries. Empirical analysis suggests that stronger tax collection, accompanied by better institutions, education and skills, and economic diversification allowed many OECD countries to evade sustainably the middle income trap, in contrast to LAC (Melguizo et al., 2017[18]).

Figure 1.9. **GDP per capita in PPP (USD) and tax-to-GDP ratios for countries in the LAC region, the OECD, and a group of African, Asian and Pacific economies, 2016**

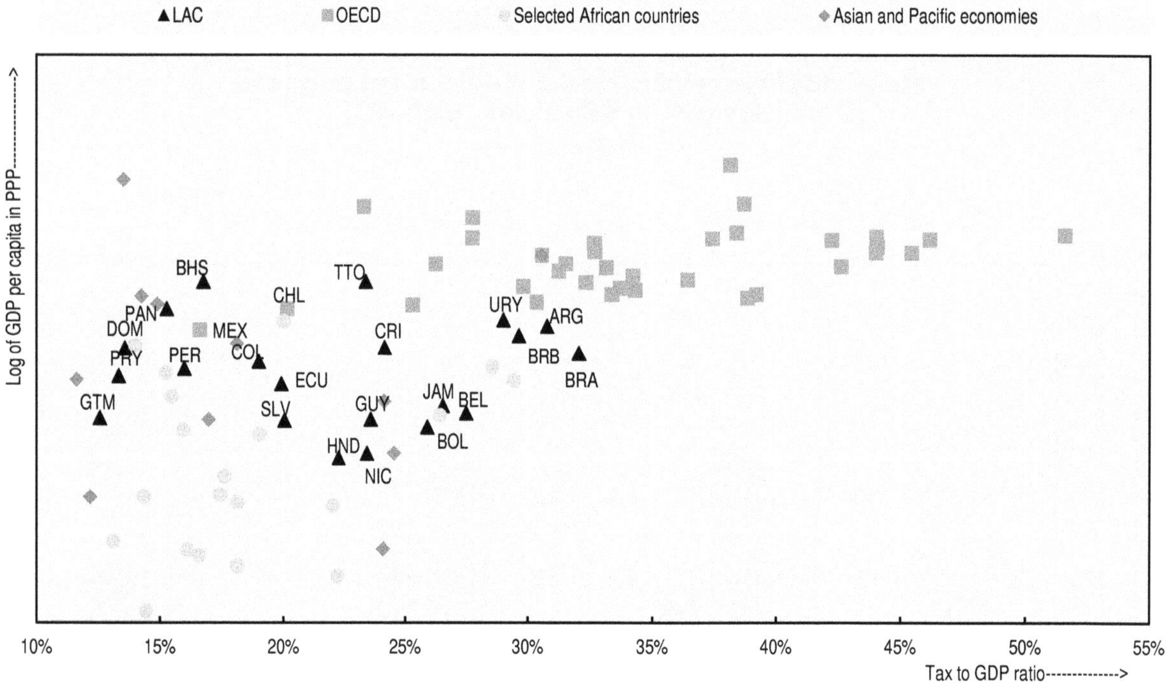

Note: The year of comparison is 2016 as the 2017 data for the tax-to-GDP ratios are not available for the selected African, Asian and Pacific economies. The purchasing-power-parity (PPP) between two countries is the rate at which the currency of one country needs to be converted into that of a second country to ensure that a given amount of the first country's currency will purchase the same volume of goods and services in the second country as it does in the first. The implied PPP conversion rate is expressed as national currency per current international dollar. An international dollar has the same purchasing power as the U.S. dollar has in the United States. An international dollar is a hypothetical currency that is used as a means of translating and comparing costs from one country to the other using a common reference point, the US dollar

Source: (IMF, 2018[19]) for figures of GDP per capita. Tax-to-GDP ratios are sourced from the regional Revenue Statistics publications (*www.oecd.org/tax/tax-policy/revenue-statistics-comparable-tax-revenue-data.htm*).

StatLink https://doi.org/10.1787/888933940035

Tax-to-GDP ratios are influenced by a range of economic and structural factors. GDP per capita, openness to trade, the extent of the informal economy, natural resource endowments and the importance of agriculture in the economy are all factors that can influence tax-to-GDP ratios. Socio-demographic determinants are also key, such as the level of education or the level of female participation in the labour force. The power of tax administrations, the levels of corruption and tax morale (or willingness of people to pay taxes) are also strongly linked to the level of tax revenues (OECD, 2014[20]). Finally, geographic location and historical factors can also influence tax-to-GDP ratios: for example, landlocked countries are less able to impose taxes on goods and services at the port of entry than coastal countries. In addition, international factors, including the tax policies of other countries, can impact tax-to-GDP ratios.

The extent of state participation in financing social security is another important factor underlying the level of tax ratios in the LAC region. From the 1980s onwards, many LAC countries privatised healthcare, pension and social security to greater or lesser degrees. Chile, El Salvador and Mexico, for example, have shifted their public pension programme to a mostly privately fully funded pension system. In Colombia and Peru, private and public programmes compete and employees opt for one of them (OECD/CIAT/ECLAC/IDB, 2015[21]); (OECD/IDB/The World Bank, 2014[22]). On the other hand, Argentina, Brazil and Uruguay follow a model where the public and private systems are complementary. In these three countries, substantial reforms were undertaken to extend coverage of social security systems to those previously excluded. This has also been instrumental in the increase of tax revenues (ECLAC, 2014[15]).

Informality constrains tax collection in LAC countries as it significantly reduces the taxable base. The IMF estimated that the informal economy accounted for 40% of GDP on average in the LAC region during 2010-2014 (Medina, Jonelis and Cangul, 2017[23]). The level of informality was higher in the 1990s, prompting governments to introduce simplified tax systems for small taxpayers that were to some extent successful in integrating informal workers into the formal sector. These simplified systems varied greatly in success depending on the type of taxpayers covered and the capacity of tax administrations (ECLAC, 2014[15]); (OECD/IDB/CIAT, 2016[24]).

Tax structures

The tax structure (defined as the share of major tax types in total tax revenue) depicts the composition of tax revenues by different tax types. It is an important indicator for understanding the economic and social effects of the tax system in the LAC region.

Evolution of tax structures

In the LAC region, taxes on goods and services provide the largest share of total tax revenues, representing half of total taxation in 2017. Between 1990 and 2017, the average LAC tax mix shifted towards VAT and taxes on income and profits and away from other tax on goods and services:

- The share of VAT revenues reached 27.9% of total tax revenues in 2017, corresponding to an increase of 12.3 percentage points between 1990 and 2017, whereas the revenue share of other taxes on goods and services (excise, customs and import duties) declined by 19.3 percentage points over the same period (Figure 1.10).
- The share of revenues from taxes on incomes and profits grew by 6.9 percentage points (from 20.1% to 27.1% of total tax revenues) between 1990 and 2017.
- The share of social security contributions in total tax revenues has increased by 3.8 percentage points over the last 27 years, reaching 16.9% in 2017.

Figure 1.10. **Average tax structure in the LAC region, 1990 and 2017**

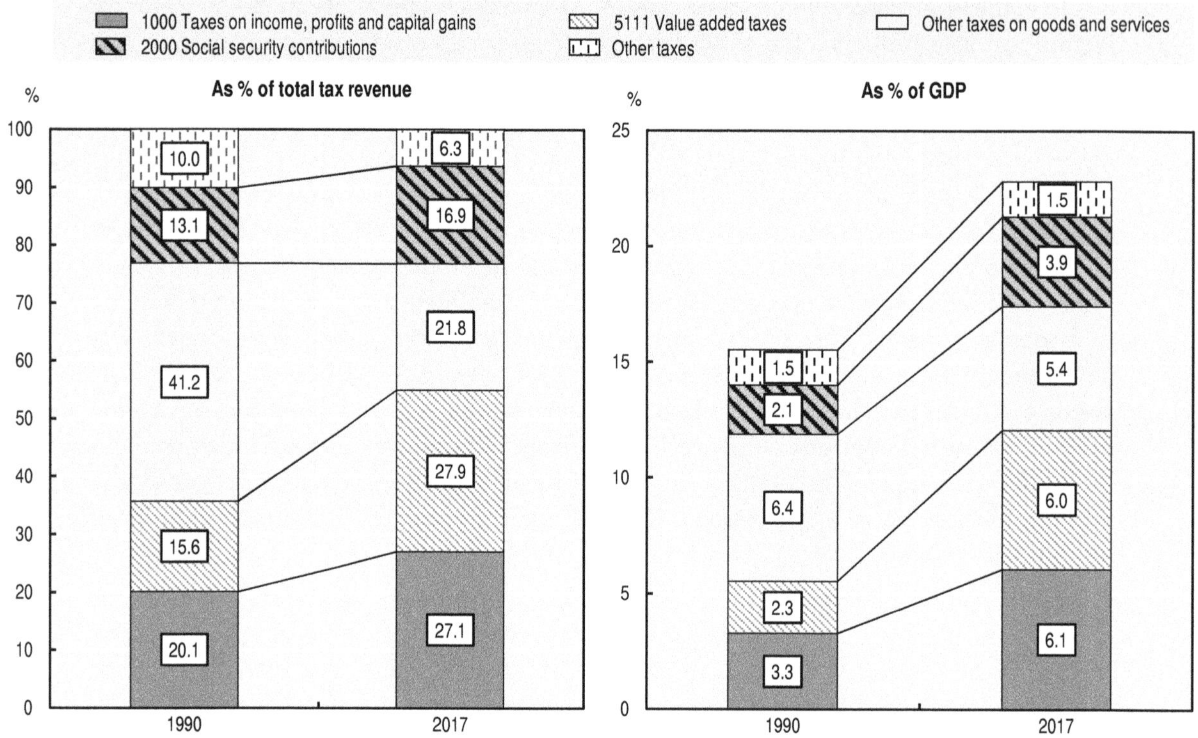

Source: Authors' calculations based on (OECD/ECLAC/CIAT/IDB, 2019[2]), Chapter 4.

StatLink https://doi.org/10.1787/888933940054

Since 2007, the LAC average tax structure shifted towards a greater revenue share from PIT and a lower revenue share from CIT, although revenues from CIT remained higher than PIT revenues in 2017 (15.5% of total taxes versus 9.5%) (Figure 1.11).[6]

The share of PIT revenues grew between 2007 and 2017 in part due to increases in personal incomes. However, the share of PIT revenue remains low in LAC countries on average despite some countries implementing reforms to expand their tax base. After the global financial crisis, several countries established flat rates on capital income that had previously been exempt and implemented progressive rates on labour income (ECLAC, 2014[15]). However, there are relatively few taxpayers, given the concentration of income earners at low income levels: only 10% of the population in Latin America are registered taxpayers (IDB, 2013[11]). Moreover, several other factors continue to limit PIT revenues: a limited taxable base that is comprised primarily of wages, as tax privileges are granted to returns on capital, and high levels of evasion (Barreix, Benitez and Pecho, 2017[16]), (ECLAC, 2014[15]). (IDB, 2013[11]) estimates that "about half of potential revenue from PIT is lost through evasion" in Latin American countries.

The share of social security contributions in total tax revenues increased by 3.8 percentage points from 1990, reaching 16.9% in 2017. Two major factors have influenced the trajectory of social security contributions in the region. Rising personal incomes have led to higher collections but this was counter-balanced by the full or partial privatisation of social security that occurred in many countries.

Figure 1.11. **Average tax structure in the LAC region, 2007 and 2017**

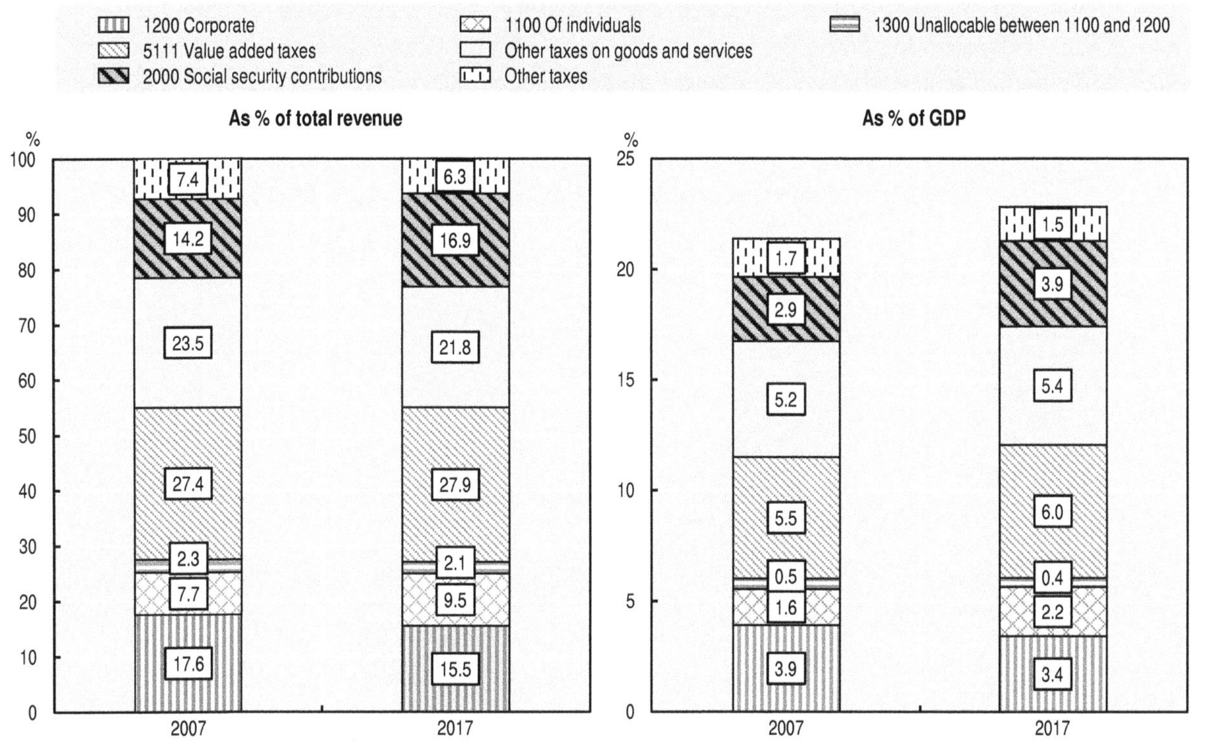

Note: Average CIT revenue and PIT as a percentage of GDP should be interpreted with caution as Ecuador, Nicaragua and Venezuela are excluded from the calculation. The LAC averages excludes Venezuela due to data availability issues. Ecuador and Nicaragua are excluded from the LAC averages for CIT revenue as a percentage of GDP and PIT revenue as a percentage of GDP as more than a third of their revenue from taxes on income and profits cannot be allocated to CIT revenue (1200) or PIT revenue (1100).

Source: Authors' calculations based on (OECD/ECLAC/CIAT/IDB, 2019[2]), "Revenue Statistics in Latin America: Comparative tables", *OECD Tax Statistics* (database), *http://dx.doi.org/* 10.1787/data-00641-en.

StatLink *https://doi.org/10.1787/888933940073*

In 2017, there were notable differences in tax structure across the sub-regions, on average. The Caribbean in particular shows a very different average tax structure to the other sub-regions.

- In 2017, the largest share of revenue was derived from other taxes on goods and services in the Caribbean, on average, representing 30.1% of total tax revenues. These taxes contributed 16.5% in South America and 21.7% in Central America and Mexico.
- In contrast, South America had the highest share of VAT revenue in 2017 at 31.4% on average, compared to the other two sub-regions (27.0% in the Caribbean and 25.1% in Central America and Mexico).
- Social security contributions were lowest in the Caribbean, at 10.3% of total tax revenues on average in 2017, nearly half of the average for the other sub-regions (18.4% in Central America and Mexico and 19.4% in South America).
- All three sub-regions generated higher CIT than PIT revenues.[7]

Average tax structure in LAC and the OECD

The average LAC tax mix exhibits relatively low revenues from income taxes and social security contributions, relative to the OECD average (Figure 1.12). In particular, LAC countries on average rely heavily on taxes on goods and services, which make up more than half of overall tax revenues compared with around one-third in OECD economies on average. However, as a percentage of GDP, revenue from taxes on goods and services in the LAC and OECD regions stood at a similar level in 2016, at 11.2% and 11.0% respectively.[8] The level of VAT revenue as a percentage of GDP was also similar, at 6.0% for the LAC average and 6.8% for the OECD.

Figure 1.12. **Tax structure in the LAC and OECD regions, 2016**

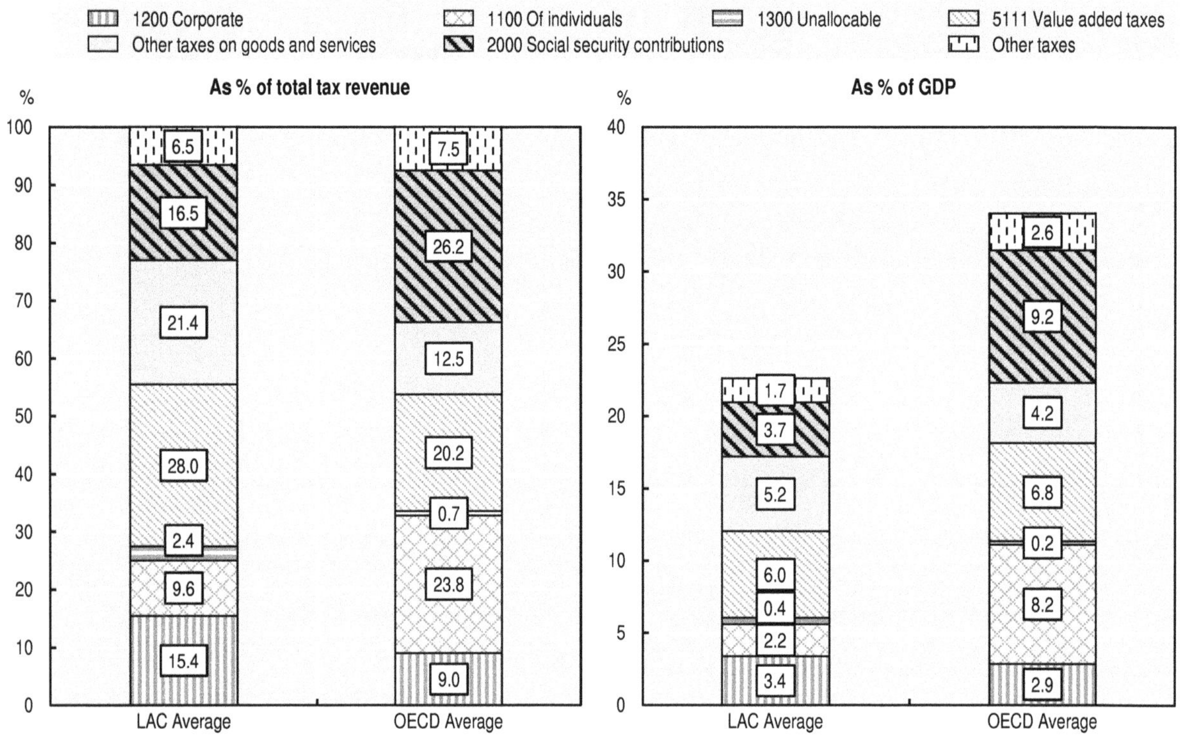

Note: The year of comparison is 2016 as the 2017 data for the OECD average are not available.
The average CIT revenue and PIT as a percentage of GDP for LAC should be interpreted with caution as Ecuador, Nicaragua and Venezuela are excluded from the calculation. The LAC averages excludes Venezuela due to data availability issues. Ecuador and Nicaragua are excluded from the LAC averages for CIT revenue as a percentage of GDP and PIT revenue as a percentage of GDP as more than a third of their revenue from taxes on income and profits cannot be allocated to CIT (1200) or PIT (1100).

Source: Authors' calculations based on (OECD/ECLAC/CIAT/IDB, 2019[2]), "Revenue Statistics in Latin America: Comparative tables", *OECD Tax Statistics* (database), *http://dx.doi.org/10.1787/data-00641-en.*

StatLink *https://doi.org/10.1787/888933940092*

By contrast, the combined share of taxes on income and profits and social security contributions were lower in the LAC region than in the OECD (43.9% relative to 60.0% in 2017, on average). As a percentage of GDP, these two categories amounted to 9.8% in the LAC region, less than half the average OECD level (20.5%). The tendency towards private provision of social security in many LAC countries explains some of the difference in this category.

On average, CIT generated 15.4% of total tax revenue in the LAC region compared to 9.0% in the OECD area (respectively 3.4% and 2.9% as a percentage of GDP) (Figure 1.12). The most striking difference between the regions relates to revenues from PIT, which contributed 23.8% of total tax revenues, on average, in the OECD area in 2016 and 9.6% of total tax revenues in the LAC region. PIT revenues were equivalent to 2.2% of GDP in the LAC region on average, versus 8.2% for the OECD average.

Taxes on immovable property and payroll (contained within the category "other taxes") are less important sources of revenue for the LAC region on average than in the OECD, although there are challenges with data availability for this category. As discussed in Chapter 3, property taxes are generally the main source of revenue for local governments in the LAC region but are operating below their potential.

Tax structures in LAC countries

Taxes on goods and services are the main source of revenue for all LAC countries except for Trinidad and Tobago, Mexico and Panama. For Mexico and Trinidad and Tobago, revenue from taxes on income and profits represented the largest share whereas for Panama revenue from social security contributions was the most important source of tax revenue (Figure 1.13).

The contribution of VAT to total tax revenues ranged from 16.1% in Panama to 41.6% in Chile. There is no VAT system in Cuba. The wide variation across countries is partly a result of differences in the design of VAT as rates, tax bases and the number of VAT exemptions differ significantly across the region.

Figure 1.13. **Tax structure in LAC countries, 2017**

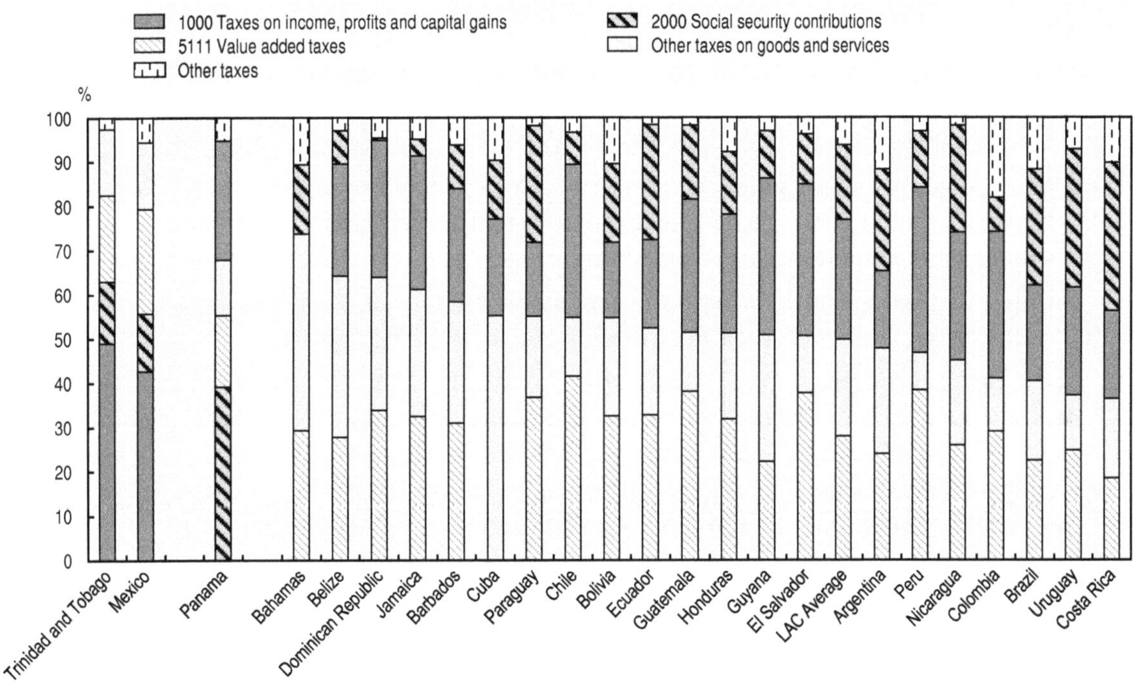

Note: Countries are grouped by the main share of tax revenues between 1000 taxes on income and profits, 2000 Social Security contributions and 5000 Taxes on goods and services. The Bahamas does not tax income. There is no VAT system in Cuba.

Source: Authors' calculations based on (OCDE/CEPAL/CIAT/BID, 2019[2]), Chapter 4.

StatLink https://doi.org/10.1787/888933940111

In 2017, social security contributions varied widely, from 0.5% of total tax revenues in Dominican Republic to 39.2% in Panama. The level of these revenues across countries reflects choices made by governments on how to finance social security schemes: in countries with public or mixed social security schemes (including Argentina, Brazil, Costa Rica, Panama, Paraguay, and Uruguay), social security contributions reach a more significant share (over 20% of total tax revenues).

Environmental tax revenues

Environmentally related taxes, and price-based policy instruments more generally, are playing an increasingly significant role in many countries. By incorporating a price signal into consumer decisions, these taxes implement the polluter-pays principle and encourage businesses and households to consider the social costs of their actions.

An environmentally related tax is a tax whose base is a physical unit (or a proxy of a physical unit) of something that has a proven, specific harmful impact on the environment regardless of whether the tax is intended to change behaviours or is levied for another purpose (OCDE, 2005[26]). In many countries in LAC and the OECD, the largest source of environmentally related tax revenue derives from excise taxes on fuels for road transport. In recent years, a few LAC countries have introduced significant green tax reforms, including Chile, Mexico and more recently Colombia.

Although environmentally related tax revenues cannot be identified in the standard OECD classification of tax revenues, they can be identified through the detailed list of specific taxes included for most countries within this overarching classification. It is on this basis that they are included in the OECD Policy Instruments for the Environment (PINE) database.

The PINE database classifies environmentally related taxes under three main revenue sources[9]:

- Energy: This covers taxation of energy products such as fossil fuels and electricity also including fuels for transportation such petrol and diesel. All CO_2-related taxes are categorised here.
- Motor vehicles and transport services: This category includes imports or sales taxes on transport equipment, recurrent taxes on ownership, registration or road use of motor vehicles, and other transport-related taxes.
- Other: This category include taxes on ozone-depleting substances, water and wastewater, waste management, mining and quarrying, and unallocated taxes.

A detailed examination of country-specific taxes for 22 LAC countries in this Report demonstrates that, on average, revenue from environmentally related taxes amounted to 1.1%[10] of GDP in 2017, a lower level than the OECD average of 1.6% of GDP (2016 figure) (Cárdenas Rodríguez and Haščič, 2018[27]). Environmentally related tax revenue in 2017 varied from 0.1% of GDP in Trinidad and Tobago to 2.3% in Honduras (Figure 1.14).

Between 2000 and 2017, environmentally related tax revenue as a percentage of GDP in the LAC region has increased slightly (by 0.1 percentage points). Half of the 22 LAC countries included in this analysis recorded increases in environmentally related tax revenues between 2000 and 2017 whereas the other half recorded decreases.

In 2017, tax revenues from energy represented the highest share of total environmentally related tax revenue in the LAC region (0.7% of GDP on average). Revenues from energy products, most commonly, on diesel and petrol, amounted to about two-thirds of environmentally related tax revenue, followed by revenues from motor vehicle and transport services tax revenue, which represented most of the remainder. Tax revenues levied on other environmentally related bases was negligible, at 2%, on average, of environmentally related tax revenues. In the OECD, revenues from energy products represent just over two-thirds of total revenues, whereas taxes on motor vehicles and transport accounted for around one-quarter (Cárdenas Rodríguez and Haščič, 2018[27]).

Taxes on energy products accounted for the largest share of environmentally related tax revenues in all but five LAC countries. In these five countries, (the Bahamas, Jamaica, Ecuador, El Salvador and Guyana) revenue from motor vehicles and transport services were the main source (Figure 1.14).

Figure 1.14. **Environmentally related tax revenue by main source of revenue, 2017**

Percentage of GDP

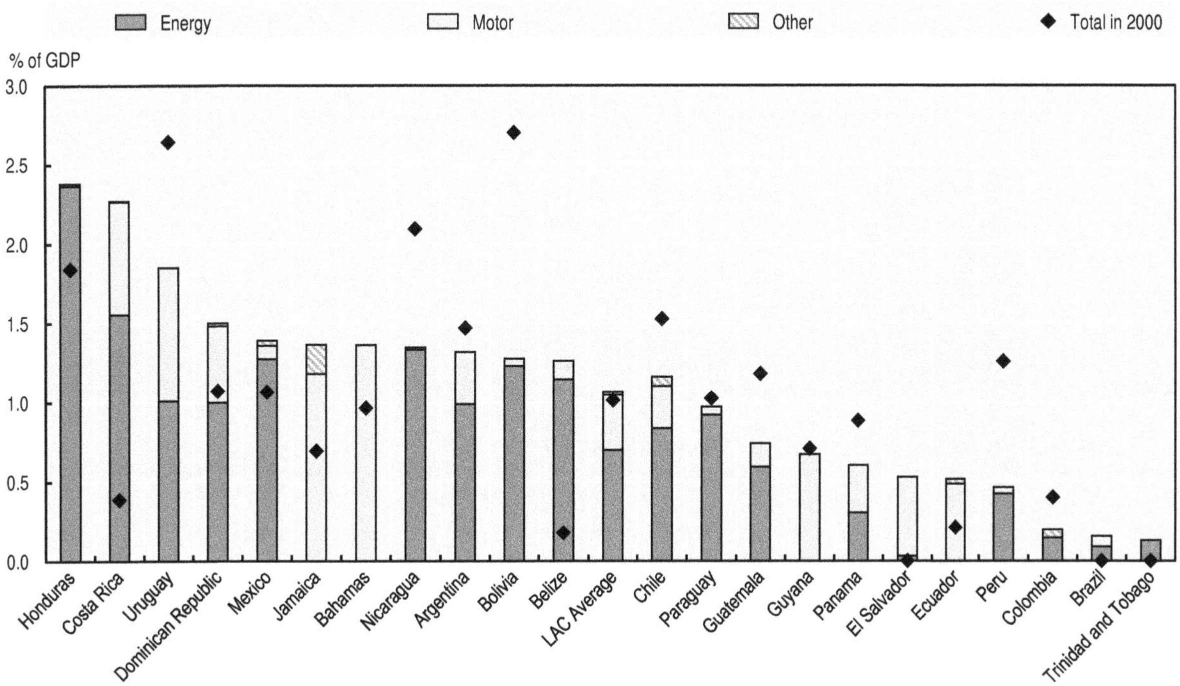

Note: Barbados, Cuba and Venezuela are excluded from the LAC averages. It has not been possible to identify environmentally related tax revenue for Barbados and Cuba. Venezuela is excluded due to data availability issues.

The figures for Chile and Mexico use 2016 data based on the PINE database that presents more comprehensive data on environmental tax revenues.

Source: PINE database for Chile and Mexico and author's calculations based on (OECD/ECLAC/CIAT/IDB, 2019[2]), Chapter 5.

StatLink https://doi.org/10.1787/888933940130

In 2017, taxes on energy were predominantly raised from excises, representing 0.6% of GDP on average in the LAC region. By contrast, revenues from motor vehicles and transport services tax revenue were sourced from three different types of taxes: recurrent taxes on use and ownership of vehicles (0.14% of GDP); taxes on specific services (mainly travel or departure tax, at 0.13% of GDP); and excises on vehicles (0.07% of GDP) (Figure 1.15).

The evolution of these three sources of environmentally related revenues varied between 2000 and 2017. Revenues from taxes on energy decreased from 0.96% of GDP to 0.7%, whereas revenues from the other two sources increased slightly. The decrease in tax revenues from energy was mainly due to declines in revenue from fuels in Bolivia, Chile, Nicaragua, Peru and Uruguay. Through the Paris Agreement of 2016, countries committed to decarbonise their economies by mid-century, implying a shift away from fossil fuels as a source of energy. Revenues from taxes on energy can increase in the medium term, if countries increase effective tax rates on the carbon content of fuels (Marten and Van Dender, 2019[28]). A joint ITF and OECD study (OECD/ITF (forthcoming), 2019[29]) shows how revenues from road transport can be stabilised in the long term through a mix of taxing distance driven, vehicles and fuel.

Figure 1.15. **Environmentally related tax revenue by main tax category and type, 2017**

Percentage of GDP

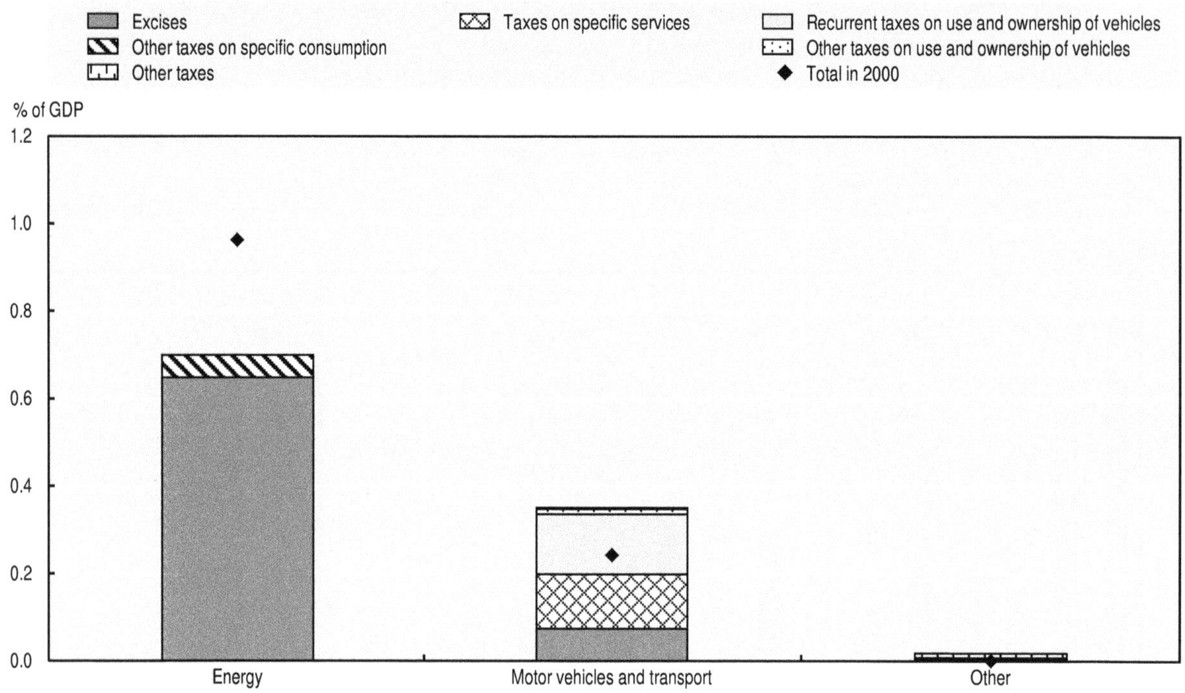

Note: Barbados, Cuba and Venezuela are excluded from the LAC averages. It has not been possible to identify environment tax related revenues for Barbados and Cuba. Venezuela is excluded due to data availability issues.

Source: PINE database for Chile and Mexico and author's calculations based on (OECD/ECLAC/CIAT/IDB, 2019[2]), Chapter 5.

StatLink https://doi.org/10.1787/888933940149

Three countries in Latin America – Chile, Colombia and Mexico – have introduced carbon taxes in recent years:

- In Chile, a major tax reform including new environmentally related taxes was approved in 2014 (OECD/UN ECLAC, 2016[30]). These included a tax on purchases of motor vehicles, which was introduced in 2015 and raised revenues equivalent to 0.03% of GDP in 2017. Motor vehicle tax rates depend on energy efficiency and emissions. In addition, a carbon tax was implemented in late 2017 (to be collected in 2018). This tax applies on emissions of particulate matter, nitrogen oxides, sulphur dioxide and carbon dioxide produced by establishments whose boilers or turbines have a capacity of 50 thermal megawatts or more.
- Mexico introduced a carbon tax in 2014, applied on the sale and import of fossil fuels according to their carbon content. This increased the proportion of emissions that was taxed, although prices remain relatively low compared to other OECD countries and do not reflect the full costs associated with the carbon in these fuels (Arlinghaus and van Dender, 2017[31]). However, the carbon tax significantly increased tax revenues between 2014 and 2015, generating revenues equivalent to 1.2% of GDP in 2015 (OECD, 2018[32]) Mexico further increased tax rates on different fossils fuels in 2016.
- In 2016, Colombia introduced a carbon tax and an excise tax on plastic bags. The carbon tax is levied on fossil fuels (specifically gasoline, kerosene, jet fuel, diesel fuel and fuel oil) depending on the amount of carbon. A price of USD 5 is applied for each ton of carbon dioxide produced by fossil fuel combustion. The revenues are to be allocated to a special fund to

address specific environmental issues (coastal erosion, conservation of water sources, and ecosystem protection) (Monge, 2018[33]). In 2017, this tax generated revenues of 0.1% of GDP.

Effective Carbon Rates (OECD, 2018[34]) provides an overview of carbon prices on all energy-related emissions in 42 OECD and G20 countries including Argentina, Brazil, Chile and Mexico. *Taxing Energy Use* (OECD, 2018[35]) offers detailed information on tax rates, energy use and the base they apply to, for the same set of countries.

VAT revenue ratio

This section discusses the VAT revenue ratio (VRR) in LAC countries in 2016 (Figure 1.16). The VRR "measures the difference between the VAT revenue actually collected and what would theoretically be raised if VAT was applied at the standard rate to the entire potential tax base in a "pure" VAT regime and all revenue was collected" (OECD, 2018[36]).

Figure 1.16. **VAT revenue ratio (VRR) in LAC countries, 2016**

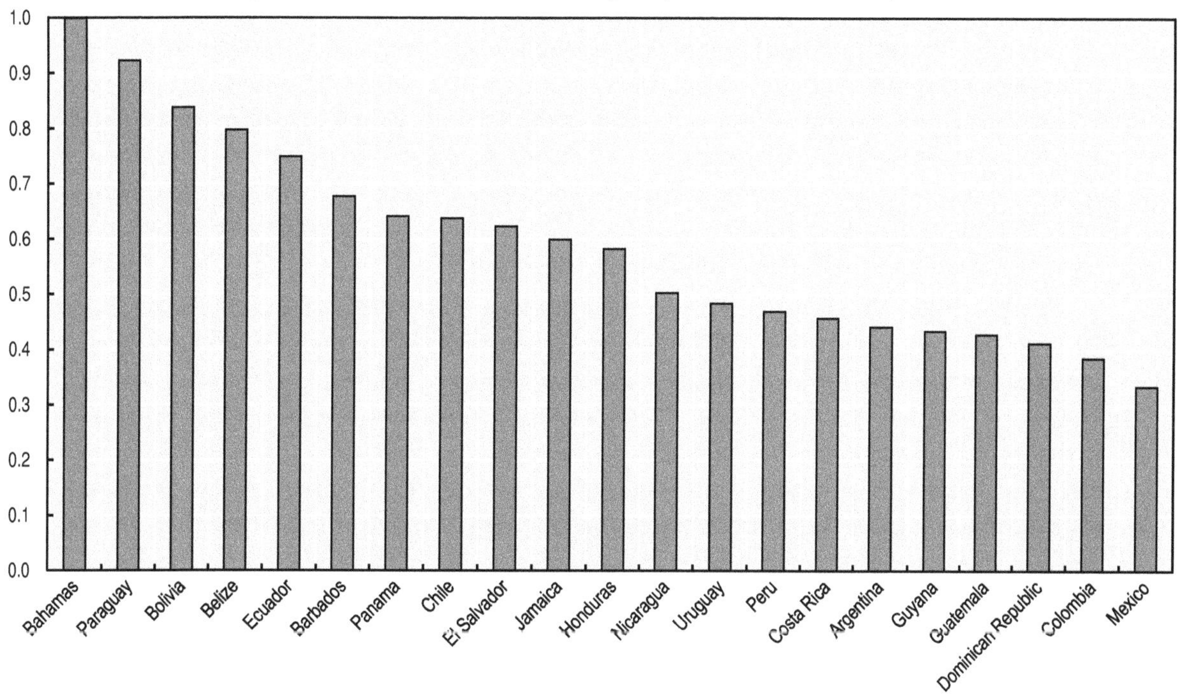

Note: Brazil, Cuba and Trinidad and Tobago are excluded. Brazil operates a multiple-rate system with tax levied at different rates for each sub-national level. Some underlying information was not available for Trinidad and Tobago after 2009; Cuba did not operate a VAT system in 2016.

Source: VAT rates are sourced from the CIAT, Trading Economics and Deloitte websites, the final expenditure consumption figures from the United Nations Statistics Division website and VAT revenues from the country tables in (OECD/ECLAC/CIAT/IDB, 2019[2]), Chapter 5.

StatLink https://doi.org/10.1787/888933940168

- Mexico and Colombia have the lowest VRR ratios, of 0.33 and 0.38 respectively whereas the Bahamas and Paraguay have the highest (of 0.99 and 0.92 respectively).
- The Bahamas introduced VAT in 2015 following international good practices: a broad-based VAT with a low standard rate, a limited number of exemptions and no reduced rates. In the Bahamas the standard rate stands at 7.5% (one of the lowest rates in the LAC region, where the average standard VAT rate stands at 14.4%). VAT revenue in the Bahamas in 2017 was triple the amount raised in 2015 (in nominal terms), in large part due to new systems to collect tax revenues (Schlotterbeck, 2017[37]).

- Paraguay had the second-highest VRR in the selected group of LAC countries in 2016 at 0.92. This is partly explained by improvements in tax administration since 2004 (IMF, 2017[38]). These included measures to broaden the VAT base, a new legal framework for tax and customs which enabled the modernisation of controls and better revenue collection systems (IMF, 2010[39]).
- Several factors may explain the low VRR in Mexico, including the scope of VAT exemptions, the application of a domestic zero rate to numerous goods and services, a reduced VAT rate (11%) in border areas as well as a low compliance (OECD, 2018[36]). A VAT reform implemented in January 2014 replaced the reduced rate of 11% with the standard rate of 16%. It also removed the zero rate on hotels and related services to foreigners, which are now taxed at the standard rate, and adjusted the regime of inward processing arrangements (*maquiladores*) to reduce the risk of fraud. The VRR in Mexico increased by 0.4 percentage points between 2013 and 2014.

Taxes by level of government

In LAC countries, tax revenues are collected predominantly by central or federal entities, with the financing of sub-national activities relying more on a system of transfers from upper to lower levels of government than is the case in OECD countries. Where sub-national data for LAC countries is available, it indicates that tax revenues collected by central government accounted for two-thirds or more of the total collected whereas the corresponding figure for OECD countries was about 60%. Brazil is a notable exception: central government tax revenue amounted to 44% of tax collected in 2016[11] (Table 1.1).

There are two statistical issues to consider when comparing the attribution of revenues for LAC countries with that of OECD members. First, revenues of both groups have been attributed to the different levels of government according to guidelines set out in the 2008 System of National Accounts (SNA). This means that revenues are generally attributed to the level of government that exercises the authority to impose the tax or has the final discretion to set and vary the tax rate. This has implications for situations where one level of government collects tax revenues and transfers them in whole or in part to other levels. Regional examples of this type of mechanism are the Co-participation Law in Argentina, federal participations in Mexico (mandated in the Fiscal Co-ordination Law), and participation funds in Brazil (defined in Article 159 of the Constitution). The second issue is that some LAC countries lack tax revenue statistics at sub-national level.

For the 19 LAC countries for which sub-national data in 2016 is available, the share of sub-national tax revenues as a proportion of total tax revenue is lower than 8% except in Argentina, Brazil and Colombia. In Brazil, states and municipalities collect about 25% of total tax revenues, indicating a significant degree of decentralisation of tax collection. A large part of the VAT (ICMS – *imposto sobre operações relativas à circulação de mercadorias e prestação de serviços de transporte interestadual e intermunicipal e de comunicação*) is collected at the state level. Sub-national tax revenue in Argentina and Colombia represent more than 15% of total tax revenue. Argentina has a significant collection at state level, which is explained in part by the provincial sales tax (*impuesto sobre los ingresos brutos*). Between 2000 and 2016, the share of revenue raised by sub-national levels of government declined in six countries and rose in seven countries. The largest decline was in Uruguay (4.1% of total tax revenue) and the highest increase was in Brazil (1.4% of total tax revenue).

These figures reflect the fact that sub-national governments in LAC countries tend to have a relatively narrow range of taxes under their jurisdiction. The taxes most frequently assigned to sub-national entities are property taxes, motor-vehicle licenses, taxes on specific services and municipal fees. The revenue-generation potential of these instruments is relatively limited compared with the tax bases under central jurisdiction, such as VAT and income taxes. In 2016, the entire subnational tax revenue in Belize, Guatemala, Jamaica, Trinidad and Tobago and more than 50% of tax revenue collected at the sub-national level in Paraguay, Peru and Uruguay was sourced from property taxes (Figure 1.17). All other countries rely principally on revenue from taxes on goods and services. Mexico is the only country that also collected revenue from different tax bases. In 2016, 42% of the sub-national tax revenue in Mexico came from payroll taxes. In OECD countries, sub-national entities tend to have much broader potential tax bases. A substantial proportion of the revenue collection for sub-national governments in OECD countries is through income taxes and profits (representing more than a third of the total collected amount at sub-national level on average).

Figure 1.17. **Tax mix of sub-national tax revenue, 2016**

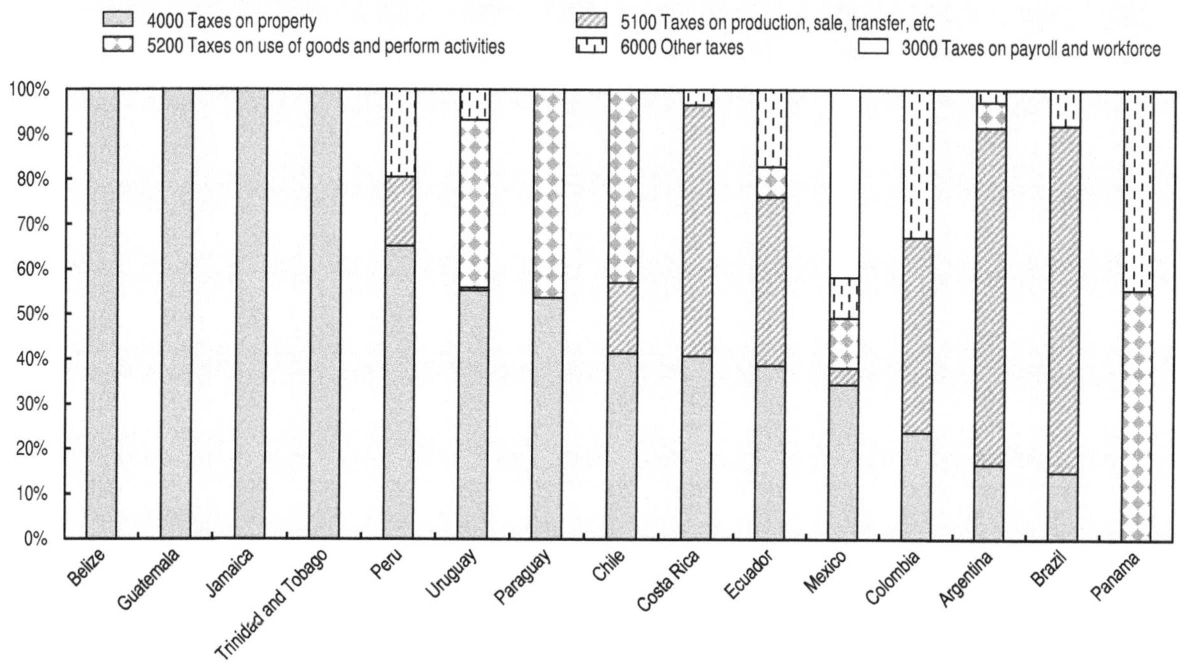

Note: The year of comparison is 2016 as 2017 data for Mexico are not available.

The Bahamas, Barbados, Bolivia, Cuba, Dominican Republic, El Salvador, Honduras, Nicaragua, Paraguay and Venezuela are excluded as either the sub-national tax revenue data or the breakdown of sub-national tax revenue data by the main type of tax category are not available. The figures exclude local government revenues for Argentina (but include provincial revenues).

Source: Authors' calculations based on (OCDE/CEPAL/CIAT/BID, 2019[2]), tables in Chapter 6.

StatLink https://doi.org/10.1787/888933940187

Low tax revenues at the sub-national level in LAC countries may also result from a lack of administrative and technical capacity. Property taxes – a common source of sub-national revenue – require sophisticated systems and information since the collection of this revenue is expensive. In addition, appropriate property registers are lacking in many countries and when they exist they are rarely updated (IDB, 2012[40]). As a result, tax authorities have little access to accurate valuations of lands and buildings and real estate registries are often reluctant to share this information. Property tax also suffers from a high level of informality: buildings are constructed without permits, properties are not registered and reported prices of some real estate transactions are falsified. As property tax is one of the most controversial taxes with citizens and has high political costs, local politicians are often unwilling to invest the appropriate resources to levy this revenue.

Table 1.1. **Attribution of tax revenue to sub-sectors of general government**

Percentage of total tax revenue

	Central government			State or regional government			Local government			Social security funds		
	1995	2000	2016	1995	2000	2016	1995	2000	2016	1995	2000	2016
Federal countries												
Argentina	59.0	66.4	61.1	17.5	17.8	16.8	0.0	0.0	0.0	23.4	15.8	22.0
Brazil	44.7	47.8	43.9	26.8	25.3	24.4	3.7	3.4	5.7	24.8	23.5	26.0
Mexico	73.9	78.3	81.5	2.8	2.7	4.0	1.5	1.0	1.5	21.8	18.0	13.0
Venezuela	94.6	94.6	..	0.0	0.0	..	0.0	0.0	..	5.4	5.4	..
Regional countries												
Colombia[2]	63.2	68.6	73.3	5.5	5.6	4.6	0.0	0.0	0.0	10.9	11.9	15.6
							0.0	0.0	0.0	14.7	15.7	8.3
Unitary countries	89.1	88.1	84.4				0.5	0.7	0.7	6.3	5.8	8.0
Bahamas	85.3	84.3	91.7				5.0	6.3	4.7	0.0	7.3	16.9
Barbados	93.2	93.5	91.4				6.5	7.9	7.8	3.6	4.4	5.7
Belize	95.0	86.4	78.4				1.6	1.9	3.0	33.0	34.8	37.8
Bolivia	89.9	87.8	86.4				0.0	0.0	0.0	11.3	10.4	12.6
Chile	65.5	63.3	59.2				0.0	0.0	0.0	0.7	1.0	0.3
Costa Rica	88.7	89.6	87.4				3.8	1.7	2.6	25.6	12.1	23.8
Cuba	99.3	99.0	99.7				0.0	0.0	1.9	14.1	16.6	11.2
Dominican Republic	70.7	86.2	73.6				0.6	0.9	0.9	15.9	15.5	16.7
Ecuador	85.9	83.4	86.9				0.0	0.0	0.1	7.4	11.4	10.9
El Salvador	83.5	83.6	82.4				4.4	5.5	4.6	9.5	10.0	13.1
Guatemala	92.6	88.6	89.0				0.0	0.7	1.5	0.0	0.0	3.8
Guyana	86.1	84.5	82.3				0.0	0.0	6.5	15.7	19.9	24.1
Honduras	100.0	99.3	94.6				0.0	2.2	1.6	38.0	38.0	38.3
Jamaica	84.5	80.1	69.4				0.0	0.0	4.0	0.0	17.3	18.8
Nicaragua	62.0	59.8	60.1				0.0	1.6	2.9	11.9	12.0	12.5
Panama	100.0	82.7	77.2				2.4	1.9	1.6	3.1	6.4	12.4
Paraguay	88.1	86.4	84.6				8.9	9.4	5.4	30.0	29.3	30.6
Peru	94.5	91.7	86.1				0.0	0.0	0.0	10.9	11.9	15.6
Trinidad and Tobago	61.1	61.3	64.1				0.0	0.0	0.0	14.7	15.7	8.3
Uruguay	59.0	66.4	61.1				8.4	8.4	4.5	30.1	29.6	27.6

Notes:

1. Figures exclude local government revenues for Argentina (but include provincial revenues), the Bahamas, Barbados, Cuba, Dominican Republic, Honduras and Venezuela as the data are not available. Local government revenue data are available from 1994 for Bolivia, 1998 for Jamaica and Panama, 2000 for Peru, 2002 for El Salvador, 2004 for Paraguay, 2010 for Nicaragua and from 1990 for all other countries.
2. Colombia is constitutionally a unitary country with high autonomy of its territorial entities.

Source: (OECD/ECLAC/CIAT/IDB, 2019[2]), Table 4.11.

StatLink https://doi.org/10.1787/888933940529

Notes

1. The figure is provisional and has been calculated by applying the unweighted average percentage change for 2017 in the 34 countries providing data for that year to the overall average tax-to-GDP ratio in 2016.
2. The Caribbean includes six countries (Bahamas, Barbados, Belize, Guyana, Jamaica and Trinidad and Tobago), Central America & Mexico nine countries (Costa Rica, Cuba, Dominican Republic, El Salvador, Guatemala, Honduras, Mexico, Nicaragua and Panama) and South America nine countries (Argentina, Bolivia, Brazil, Chile, Colombia, Ecuador, Paraguay, Peru and Uruguay).
3. A tax imposed on good imported into Barbados and on domestically manufactured goods

4. This includes Argentina; Brazil, Bolivia, Chile, Colombia, Costa Rica, Ecuador, Honduras, Mexico, Nicaragua, Panama and Peru.
5. VAT was introduced in 1991 for Jamaica, 1997 for Barbados, 2006 for Belize (the General Sales Tax), 2007 for Guyana and 2014 for the Bahamas.
6. Around 2.1% of total tax revenue is revenue from taxes on income and profits that cannot be allocated between corporate income tax and personal income tax.
7. For the Caribbean, average revenue from taxes on income and profits hides a wide heterogeneity. The Bahamas does not levy income taxes and Trinidad and Tobago levies half of its tax revenue from this source.
8. The year of comparison is 2016 as the 2017 data for the OECD average are not available.
9. The OECD PINE DB (*http://oe.cd/pine*) collects detailed instrument-level information which is aggregated to produce revenue totals. The database supports the monitoring, design and implementation of effective policies. The OECD PINE database hosts, since 2005, a unique set of detailed information on 3476 policy instruments in 94 countries up from 3200 instruments and 80 countries.
10. Unweighted average of 36 OECD countries.
11. The year of comparison is 2016 as the 2017 data for Mexico are not available.

References

Arlinghaus, J. and K. van Dender (2017), "The environmental tax and subsidy reform in Mexico", *OECD Taxation Working Papers*, No. 31, OECD Publishing, Paris, *https://dx.doi.org/10.1787/a9204f40-en*. [31]

Barreix, A., J. Benitez and M. Pecho (2017), *Revisiting personal income tax in Latin America: Evolution, https://doi.org/10.1787/18151949.* [16]

Cárdenas Rodríguez, M. and I. Haščič, (2018), *The OECD database on Policy Instruments for the Environment: a progress report. OECD document presented at the Working Party of Environmental Information and the Joint Meetings of Tax and Environment Experts., https://one.oecd.org/document/ENV/EPOC/WPEI(2018)7/en/pdf.* [27]

CIAT (2017), , *https://www.ciat.org/as-result-of-the-support-provided-by-the-ciat-seco-cooperation-program-the-tax-administration-of-guyana-progresses-in-key-areas/?lang=en.* [4]

ECLAC (2018), *The Fiscal Panorama of Latin America and the Caribbean*, United Nations, *https://www.cepal.org/en/publications/43406-fiscal-panorama-latin-america-and-caribbean-2018-public-policy-challenges.* [10]

ECLAC (2014), *Tax policy in Latin America: Assessment and guidelines for a second generation of reforms*, United Nations, *https://repositorio.cepal.org/handle/11362/36806.* [15]

ECLAC (2013), *Fiscal Panorama of Latin America and the Caribbean: tax reform and renewal of the fiscal covenant*, United Nations, *https://www.cepal.org/en/publications/3101-fiscal-panorama-latin-america-and-caribbean-2013-tax-reform-and-renewal-fiscal.* [12]

EPS-PEAKS (2013), *Taxation and Developing Countries*, Overseas Development Institute training notes, *https://www.odi.org/sites/odi.org.uk/files/odi-assets/events-documents/5045.pdf.* [7]

IBFD (2017), *IBFD Tax Research Platform, https://online.ibfd.org/.* [6]

IDB (2013), *More than revenues, Taxation as a development tool*, Inter-American Development Bank,. [11]

IDB (2012), *Sub-national Revenue Mobilization in Peru, IDB Working Paper Series No. 299.* [40]

IMF (2018), *2018 Article IV Consultation, IMF Country Report No. 18/220, https://www.imf.org/en/Publications/CR/Issues/2018/07/16/Guyana-2018-Article-IV-Consultation-Press-Release-and-Staff-Report-46083.* [5]

IMF (2018), *World Economic Outlook Database, October.* [19]

IMF (2017), *Paraguay Article IV, IMF Country Report No. 17/233.* [38]

IMF (2016), *Argentina 2016 Article IV Consultation, IMF country report No. 16/346, https://www.imf.org/external/pubs/ft/scr/2016/cr16346.pdf.* [13]

IMF (2010), *Paraguay: Selected Issues", IMF Country Report No. 10/170.* [39]

Marten, M. and K. Van Dender (2019), *(forthcoming), The use of revenues from carbon pricing. OECD Taxation Working Papers*, OECD. [28]

Medina, Jonelis and Cangul (2017), *The Informal Economy in Sub-Saharan Africa : Size and Determinants , IMF Working Paper No. 17/156.* [23]

Melguizo, A. et al. (2017), *No sympathy for the devil! Policy priorities to overcome the middle-income trap in Latin America*, OECD, *http://dx.doi.org/10.1787/26b78724-en.* [18]

Ministry of Foreign Affairs in The Hague (2018), *Doing Business in Bolivia, https://www.nederlandwereldwijd.nl/...in-bolivia.../Doing+Business+in+Bolivia.pdf.* [8]

Monge, C. (2018), *Colombia Puts a Tax on Carbon, https://www.conservationfinancenetwork.org/2018/11/27/colombia-puts-tax-on-carbon.* [33]

OECD (2018), *Consumption Tax Trends 2018: VAT/GST and Excise Rates, Trends and Policy Issues*, OECD publishing, *https://doi.org/10.1787/ctt-2018-en.* [36]

OECD (2018), *Effective Carbon Rates 2018: Pricing Carbon Emissions Through Taxes and Emissions Trading*, OECD Publishing, Paris, *https://doi.org/10.1787/9789264305304-en.* [34]

OECD (2018), *Pine Database, http://oe.cd/pine.* [32]

OECD (2018), *Taxing Energy Use 2018: Companion to the Taxing Energy Use Database*, OECD Publishing, Paris, *https://doi.org/10.1787/9789264289635-en.* [35]

OECD (2014), *Development Co-operation Report 2014: Mobilising Resources for Sustainable Development*, OECD Publishing, Paris, *https://dx.doi.org/10.1787/dcr-2014-en.* [1]

OECD (2014), *Development Co-operation Report 2014: Mobilising Resources for Sustainable Development*, OECD Publishing, Paris, *https://dx.doi.org/10.1787/dcr-2014-en.* [20]

OECD (2005), *https://stats.oecd.org/glossary/detail.asp?ID=6437.* [26]

OECD/CAF/ECLAC/EU (2019), *Latin American Economic Outlook 2019: Development in Transition*, OECD Publishing, Paris, *https://doi.org/10.1787/g2g9ff18-en.* [9]

OECD/CAF/UN ECLAC (2018), *Latin American Economic Outlook 2018: Rethinking Institutions for Development*, OECD Publishing, Paris, *https://dx.doi.org/10.1787/leo-2018-en.* [3]

OECD/CIAT/ECLAC/IDB (2015), *Revenue Statistics in Latin America and the Caribbean 2015*, OECD Publishing, Paris, *https://dx.doi.org/10.1787/rev_lat-2015-en-fr.* [21]

OECD/CIAT/IDB/ECLAC (2018), *Revenue Statistics in Latin America and the Caribbean 2018*, OECD Publishing, Paris, *https://dx.doi.org/10.1787/rev_lat_car-2018-en-fr.* [17]

OECD/ECLAC/CIAT/IDB (2019), *Revenue Statistics in Latin America and the Caribbean 2019.* [2]

OECD/IDB/CIAT (2016), *Taxing Wages in Latin America and the Caribbean 2016*, OECD Publishing, Paris, *https://dx.doi.org/10.1787/9789264262607-en.* [24]

OECD/IDB/The World Bank (2014), *Pensions at a Glance: Latin America and the Caribbean*, OECD Publishing, Paris, *https://dx.doi.org/10.1787/pension_glance-2014-en.* [22]

OECD/ITF (forthcoming) (2019), *Tax revenue implications from the decarbonisation of road transport: scenarios for Slovenia*, OECD. [29]

OECD/UN ECLAC (2016), *OECD Environmental Performance Reviews: Chile 2016*, OECD Environmental Performance Reviews, OECD Publishing, Paris, *https://dx.doi.org/10.1787/9789264252615-en.* [30]

Schlotterbeck, S. (2017), *Tax Administration Reforms in the Caribbean*, "Challenges, Achievements, and Next Steps". [37]

World Grain (2016), *Reforms boost Argentine grain industry, https://www.world-grain.com/articles/6457-reforms-boost-argentine-grain-industry.* [14]

Capítulo 1

Tendencias tributarias, 1990-2017

Proporciones de ingresos tributarios

La capacidad fiscal de América Latina y el Caribe (ALC) debe aumentar para que los países se desarrollen de manera sostenible e inclusiva y logren los Objetivos de Desarrollo Sostenible. La movilización de recursos domésticos de manera sostenible y justa es un requisito previo para que los países de la región avancen en su proceso de desarrollo, promuevan el crecimiento a largo plazo y reduzcan la desigualdad y la vulnerabilidad.

La proporción de recaudación tributaria sobre el producto interno bruto (PIB) es una medida clave para medir la movilización de recursos domésticos. El indicador refleja los recursos disponibles para financiar la provisión de bienes y servicios públicos y la inversión en infraestructura. La movilización de recursos fiscales mediante impuestos es importante para asegurar el desarrollo económico de los países (OECD, 2014[1]). Los impuestos constituyen una fuente predecible y sostenible de ingresos para los gobiernos, en contraste con la asistencia al desarrollo y la volatilidad de los ingresos no-tributarios generada por las materias primas.

Este reporte presenta datos internacionales comparables sobre recaudo tributario para 25 países de ALC. Este capítulo analiza varios indicadores tributarios claves: el recaudo tributario total en relación al PIB, la estructura impositiva y la proporción de ingresos tributarios por nivel de gobierno. Esta discusión complementa la información detallada a nivel de país desarrollada en el capítulo 5.

Proporciones de ingresos tributarios en 2017

El promedio del recaudo tributario como proporción del PIB en los países de ALC fue del 22.8% en 2017 (Gráfico 1.1). El promedio de ALC representa el promedio no ponderado de los 24 países incluidos en esta publicación y excluye a Venezuela debido a problemas de disponibilidad de datos.

La proporción tributaria en relación al PIB se mide como el recaudo tributario (incluidas las contribuciones a la seguridad social) como proporción del PIB. En 2017 el ratio de impuestos con respecto al PIB varió ampliamente en la región, desde 12.4% en Guatemala a 40.6% en Cuba. A la excepción de Cuba, todos los países de ALC tuvieron ingresos tributarios en proporción al PIB inferiores al promedio de la OCDE de 34.2%.[1]

Las proporciones más altas de ingresos tributarios respecto al PIB se dieron en Cuba (40.6%), Brasil (32.3%) y Barbados (31.8%). Los países con los ingresos tributarios como proporción del PIB más bajos fueron Guatemala (12.4%), Paraguay (13.8%) y República Dominicana (13.9%).

Hubo diferencias importantes en el nivel de impuestos entre América Central y México, América del Sur y el Caribe[2]. Los países de América Central y México tienen típicamente proporciones de impuesto respecto al PIB más bajas, con un promedio de 21.0% en 2017, mientras que los países de la subregión del Caribe tienen proporciones de impuesto respecto al PIB más altas y un promedio de 25.6%. En contraste, los impuestos como proporción del PIB de los países de América del Sur fue de 22.8% en 2017, igual que el promedio de ALC.

Gráfico 1.1. **Recaudo tributario (% del PIB), 2017**

Ingresos tributarios como porcentaje del PIB

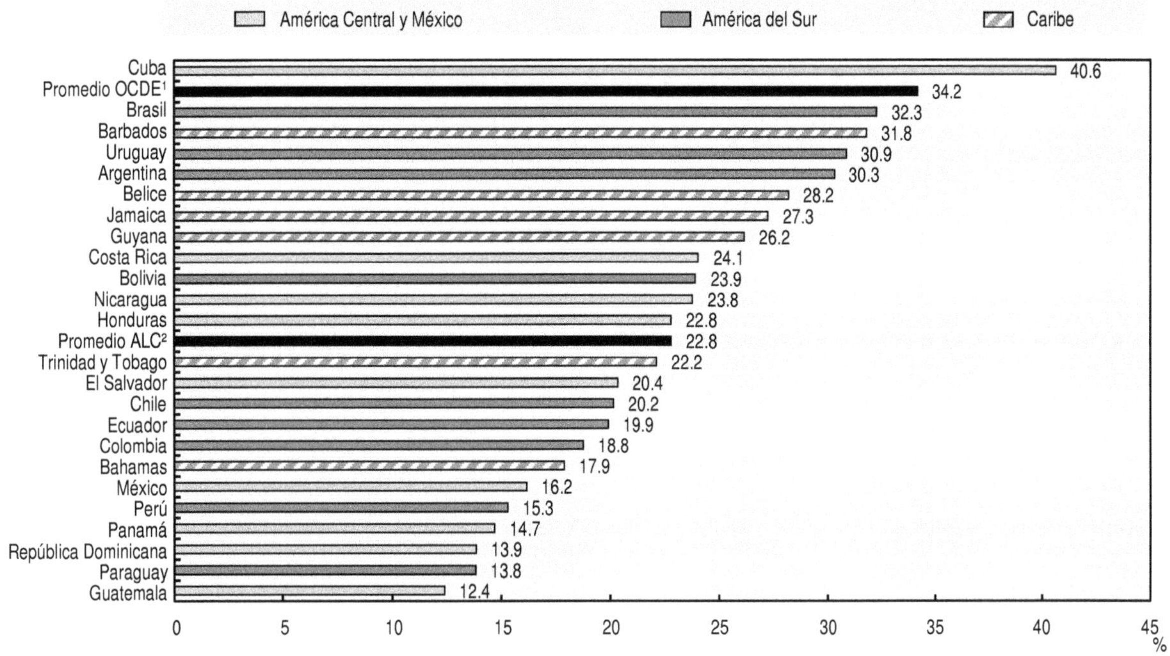

Nota: Las cifras excluyen los ingresos subnacionales de Argentina (aunque se incluyen los ingresos de las provincias), Las Bahamas, Barbados, Cuba, República Dominicana y Honduras dado que los datos no se encuentran disponibles. América Central incluye a Cuba y República Dominicana.

1. El promedio OCDE representa el promedio de los 36 países miembros de la OCDE. Chile y México forman también parte del promedio del grupo de la OCDE (36).

2. El promedio ALC representa el promedio no ponderado de 24 países de América Latina y el Caribe y excluye a Venezuela debido a problemas de disponibilidad de datos.

Fuente: (OCDE/CEPAL/CIAT/BID, 2019[2]), cuadro 4.1.

StatLink *https://doi.org/10.1787/888933940206*

En 2017, el promedio del recaudo tributario sobre PIB de ALC fue 0.2 puntos superior que el año previo (Gráfico 1.2). Este aumento refleja en parte la recuperación en el entorno económico general en 2017, después de una recesión de dos años: el PIB creció al 1.3% (en términos reales) entre 2016 y 2017 impulsado por mejoras en la demanda global, un aumento del comercio y el aumento de los precios de los productos básicos (OCDE/CAF/CEPAL, 2018[3]).

Existe una amplia variación entre los países de ALC en cuanto a los cambios en la recaudación tributaria como porcentaje del PIB entre 2016 y 2017. Doce países registraron un incremento en sus ingresos tributarios como proporción del PIB en 2017, mientras que diez registraron un descenso y dos se mantuvieron estables.

Los incrementos en la recaudación tributaria como porcentaje del PIB en los países de ALC en 2017 fueron en promedio mayores que las disminuciones. En 2017, dos países registraron aumentos de dos puntos porcentuales. Guyana reportó el mayor incremento (de 2.6 puntos porcentuales) seguido por Barbados, cuya recaudación tributaria aumentó en 2.2 puntos porcentuales.

Los impuestos sobre bienes y servicios así como los impuestos sobre la renta fueron los principales motores de crecimiento para Guyana: aumentaron respectivamente en 1.3 y 0.8 puntos porcentuales. Los ingresos de los impuestos sobre bienes y servicios (y en particular los impuestos sobre el consumo) y de las contribuciones a la seguridad social fueron los principales contribuyentes al aumento en Barbados (con un aumento de 1.8 y 0.7 puntos porcentuales, respectivamente).

Gráfico 1.2. **Cambios en 2015-16 y 2016-17 de la recaudación tributaria**

Puntos porcentuales del PIB

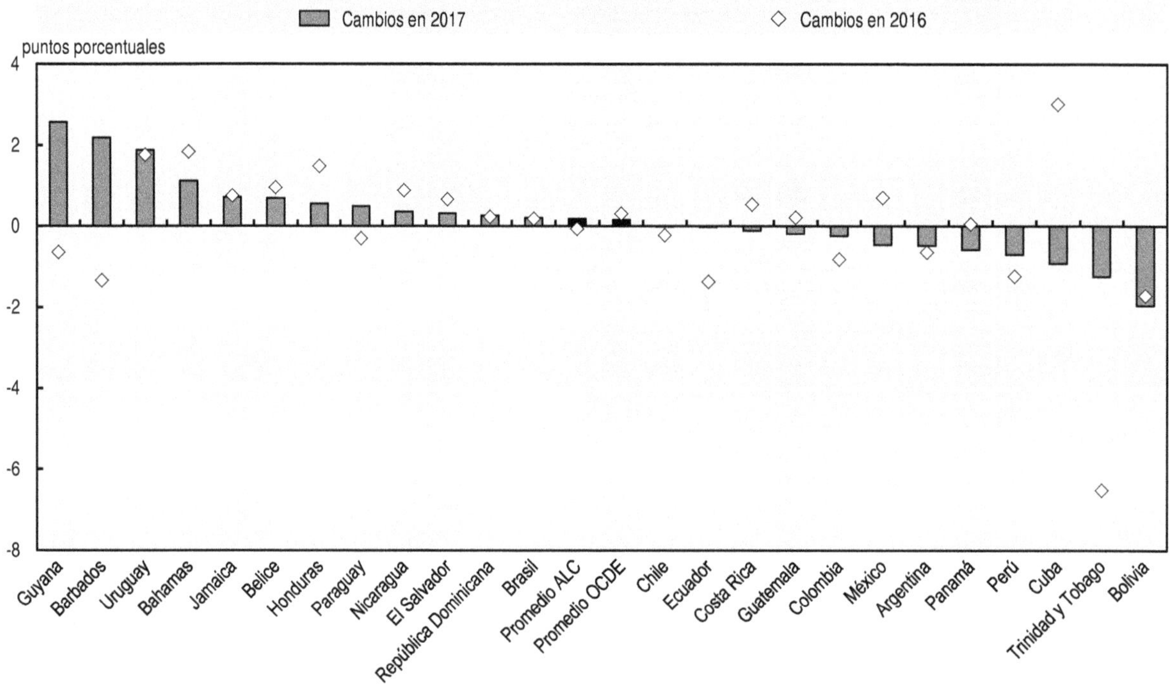

Fuente: Elaboración propia basada en (OCDE/CEPAL/CIAT/BID, 2019[2]), cuadro 4.1.

StatLink https://doi.org/10.1787/888933940225

Reformas significativas han contribuido a los aumentos observados en Barbados y Guyana:

- Desde 2015, Guyana ha realizado esfuerzos para mejorar la administración tributaria a través del Programa de Cooperación CIAT-SECO (CIAT, 2017[4]): se creó una unidad consagrada a los contribuyentes; la base de contribuyentes ha aumentado gracias a la implementación de modelos de riesgo; y se fortalecieron los procesos de recaudación de impuestos. Además, Guyana reformó su sistema de impuesto al valor agregado (IVA) en 2017 al reducir la tasa estándar del IVA y al ampliar la base del IVA. Estos cambios contribuyeron a un aumento de 0.8 puntos porcentuales en los ingresos por IVA como porcentaje del PIB entre 2016 y 2017 (FMI, 2018[5]).
- Barbados incrementó la tasa del Impuesto Nacional de Responsabilidad Social[3] (un impuesto al consumo) de 2% a 10% en julio de 2017, lo que contribuyó significativamente al aumento general del recaudo tributario sobre PIB. Barbados también aumentó las tasas del impuesto al consumo sobre la gasolina y el diésel (IBFD, 2017[6]).

Por otro lado, solo Bolivia tuvo una disminución de más de dos puntos porcentuales entre 2016 y 2017 y las disminuciones en la mayoría de los países fueron de menos de un punto porcentual. En Bolivia, las disminuciones se registraron en todas las categorías principales de ingresos tributarios en 2017 como proporción del PIB. Los ingresos por impuestos sobre bienes y servicios tuvieron la mayor disminución de 1.1 puntos porcentuales, impulsado por una disminución en los ingresos por IVA equivalente al 0.7% del PIB. La segunda disminución más alta en Bolivia se produjo en los ingresos por impuesto a la renta (0.6 puntos porcentuales).

Entre 2016 y 2017, el PIB de Bolivia aumentó más que los ingresos tributarios en términos nominales (8% contra 2%). El sector principal que desencadenó este crecimiento fue el sector agrícola (debido a las mejores condiciones climáticas y al aumento de las tierras cultivadas), seguido por el sector de los hidrocarburos. El aumento relativamente inferior en impuestos en Bolivia puede reflejar el hecho de que cobrar impuestos en el sector agrícola es difícil. En las economías en desarrollo, la mayoría de las personas que trabajan en este sector reciben ingresos bajos y muchas no están registradas con fines fiscales (EPS-PEAKS, 2013[7]). Las numerosas exenciones fiscales para este sector y un alto nivel de informalidad en el sector agrícola también causan dificultades tributarias (Ministry of Foreign Affairs in The Hague, 2018[8]);

Conceptualmente, y como se ve en Bolivia, los cambios en la recaudación tributaria como porcentaje del PIB se deben al tamaño relativo y la dirección del cambio en los ingresos tributarios nominales y el PIB nominal. Si los ingresos tributarios aumentan más que el PIB (o disminuye menos que el PIB), la proporción de impuestos sobre el PIB aumentará. En cambio, si los ingresos tributarios aumentan menos que el PIB, o si caen más, la proporción de impuestos sobre el PIB bajará. Por lo tanto, una mayor proporción de impuestos sobre el PIB no significa necesariamente que el monto de los ingresos tributarios haya aumentado en términos reales o incluso nominales.

Entre los 12 países de América Latina y el Caribe que aumentaron en 2017 con respecto a 2016 su recaudación tributaria como porcentaje del PIB, el crecimiento anual del PIB fue positivo, aunque en menor grado que el crecimiento de los ingresos tributarios. De los diez países de ALC que tuvieron una disminución en 2017, nueve tuvieron niveles más altos de ingresos tributarios nominales que en 2016, aunque en menor grado que el crecimiento en los niveles del PIB nominal. Solo Trinidad y Tobago tuvo un crecimiento del PIB nominal positivo y un crecimiento negativo de los ingresos tributarios. Ningún país experimentó una disminución en el PIB nominal (Gráfico 1.3).

Evolución del recaudo tributario desde el 2000

La mejora de la movilización de recursos domésticos particularmente a través de un aumento de los ingresos tributarios, es fundamental para el desarrollo sostenible de ALC, como lo refleja su papel prominente en la agenda de Desarrollo en transición (Recuadro 1.1). Con la excepción de 2008, 2009 y 2016, el promedio del recaudo tributario como proporción del PIB en los países de ALC ha aumentado, de forma continua desde 1990 (Gráfico 1.4). Durante este periodo se ha incrementado en más de siete puntos porcentuales desde 15.5% en 1990 a 22.8% en 2017. Este crecimiento refleja las condiciones macroeconómicas favorables, cambios en el diseño del sistema tributario y el fortalecimiento de las administraciones tributarias. Esta tendencia contrasta con la de los países de la OCDE donde el recaudo tributario se ha mantenido relativamente estable; los promedios de los ingresos tributarios en relación al PIB alcanzaron 34.2% del PIB en 2017, 2.1 puntos porcentuales por encima del nivel de 1990. La brecha en el promedio del recaudo tributario como proporción del PIB entre ALC y OECD disminuyó entre 1990 y 2009, y luego se ha mantenido relativamente estable (Gráfico 1.4).

Gráfico 1.3. **Cambios relativos en los ingresos tributarios y el PIB nominal, 2016-17**

Porcentaje

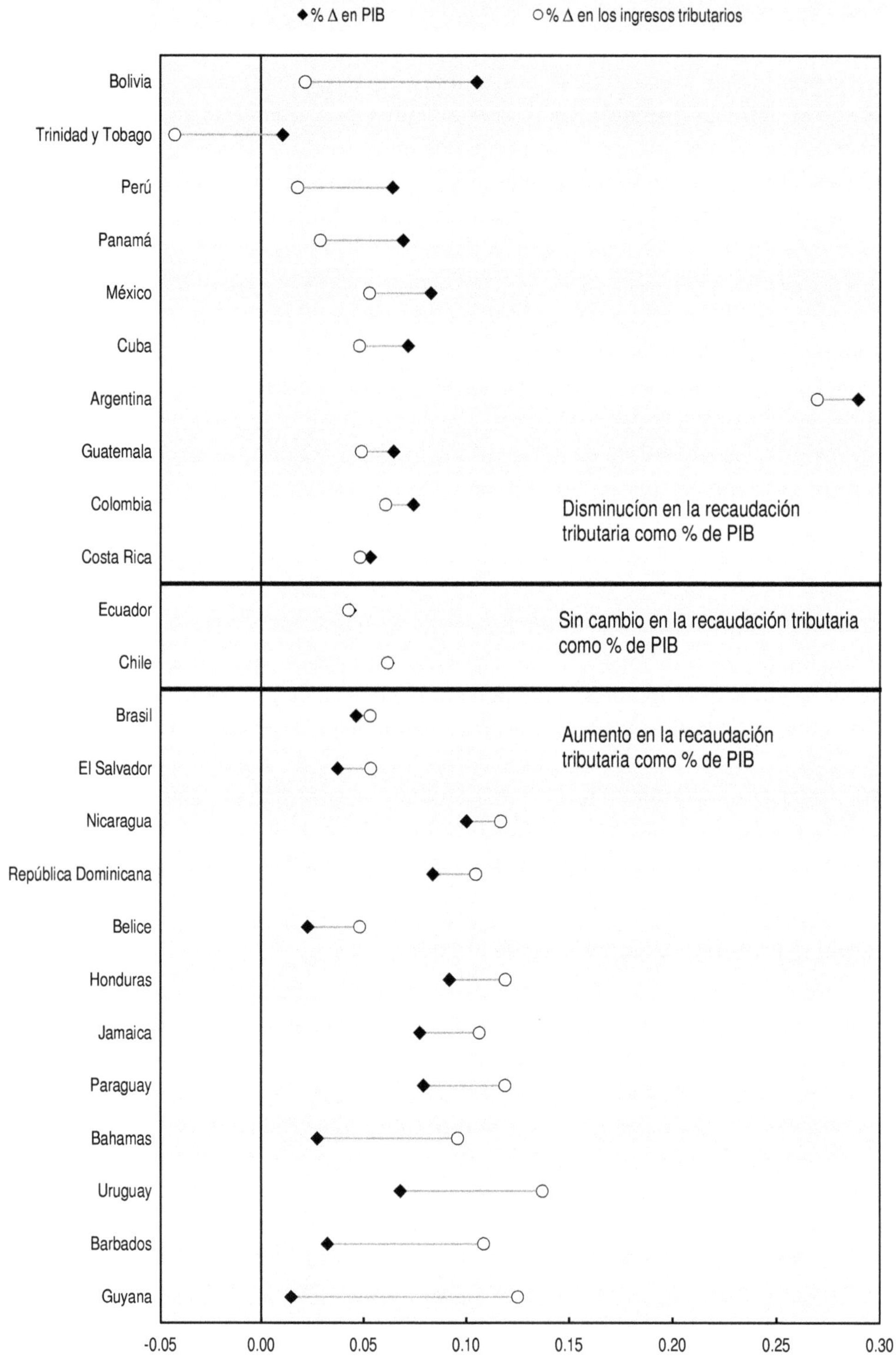

Nota: 1. Los datos de México en 2017 son una estimación, con base a los ingresos esperados recopilados por los gobiernos estatales y locales.

2. Los ingresos fiscales nominales y el PIB de Argentina aumentaron en más del 25% entre 2016 y 2017, debido a la inflación.

Fuente: Elaboración propia con base en (OCDE/CEPAL/CIAT/BID, 2019[2]), cuadros del capítulo 4.

StatLink https://doi.org/10.1787/888933940244

Recuadro 1.1. **Estadísticas tributarias en América Latina y el Caribe y el Desarrollo en Transición**

Esta edición de *Estadísticas tributarias en América Latina y el Caribe* es la primera que se produce con el apoyo de la Facilidad Regional de la UE para el Desarrollo en Transición para América Latina y el Caribe (ALC). Esta facilidad es una iniciativa liderada por la Unión Europea y desarrollada por la Organización de Cooperación y Desarrollo Económicos (OCDE) y su Centro de Desarrollo, y la Comisión Económica para América Latina y el Caribe (CEPAL).

Las economías de ALC se enfrentan a vulnerabilidades domésticas y globales nuevas pero también persistentes que requieren transformaciones críticas para maximizar las oportunidades de desarrollo. La mayoría de los países de ALC han alcanzado nivel de ingreso medio, pero enfrentan profundos desafíos estructurales que limitan su progreso continuo. Cuatro trampas principales dificultan la transformación exitosa y la transición al desarrollo sostenible. Estas son las trampas de productividad, vulnerabilidad social, institucional y ambiental. Cada una de estas trampas interactá entre sí con una dinámica que se retroalimenta para limitar las oportunidades de desarrollo sostenible de la región (OCDE/CAF/CEPAL/UE, 2019[9]).

El Desarrollo en Transición es un enfoque que promueve el diseño de mejores políticas, prácticas y asociaciones tanto al nivel nacional como internacional. Los problemas son cada vez más complejos y requieren estrategias de desarrollo con acciones de políticas más sofisticadas y de mayor coordinación y coherencia. Se deben hacer esfuerzos ambiciosos para superar las trampas y convertir los círculos viciosos en círculos virtuosos. A nivel nacional, las capacidades domésticas, incluida la recaudación de impuestos, deben fortalecerse para enfrentar mejor los desafíos del desarrollo. A nivel internacional, la cooperación internacional debe actuar como un facilitador para apoyar a los países en transición hacia el desarrollo sostenible mediante partenariados en políticas públicas, como socios iguales, y abordar las inquietudes comunes, situando las estrategias nacionales de ALC en el centro, fortaleciendo las capacidades domésticas de los países y ampliando la bateria de herramientas de las modalidades e instrumentos de cooperación internacional (OCDE/CAF/CEPAL/UE, 2019[9]).

La política fiscal es esencial para desarrollar capacidades, abordar las trampas del desarrollo y garantizar un desarrollo inclusivo y sostenible en los países de ALC. Las *Estadísticas tributarias en América Latina y el Caribe* representan un recurso invaluable para los gobiernos, ya que permiten fortalecer la política fiscal. Al proporcionar datos fiscales armonizados y detallados en toda la región, permite un análisis en profundidad de la política tributaria, identificando no solo cómo varía el nivel de ingresos tributarios por país, sino también qué instrumentos generan estos ingresos, teniendo en cuenta que la forma en que se generan los impuestos puede ser tan importante como la cantidad de ingresos que se generan. Las *Estadísticas tributarias en América Latina y el Caribe* también representan un punto de partida común para el intercambio de conocimientos y el desarrollo de capacidades entre los países, así como con la comunidad internacional en general.

Reflejando la relación crítica entre la tributación efectiva y el gasto público efectivo, la Facilidad para el Desarrollo en Transición reune *Estadísticas tributarias en América Latina y el Caribe* con el trabajo de la CEPAL sobre el gasto público, y particularmente el gasto social. El objetivo es proporcionar información sin precedentes y herramientas inestimables para el desarrollo de la política fiscal en la región, y así desbloquear su capacidad para cumplir con el compromiso de la Agenda 2030 e implementar estrategias de desarrollo a largo plazo.

Gráfico 1.4. **El recaudo tributario, promedios ALC y OCDE, 1990 - 2017**

Proporción del PIB

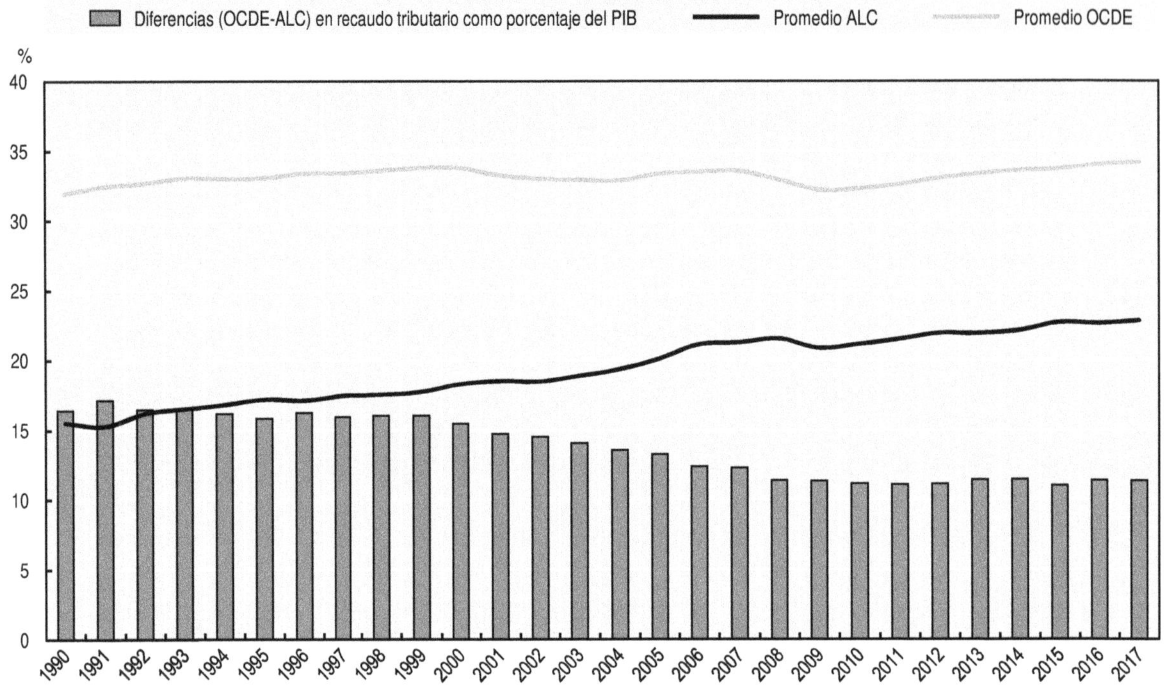

Fuente: (OCDE/CEPAL/CIAT/BID, $2019_{[2]}$), cuadro 4.1.

StatLink https://doi.org/10.1787/888933940263

El gráfico 1.5 muestra cómo la recaudación tributaria como porcentaje del PIB para las tres subregiones de América Latina y el Caribe ha evolucionado desde 1990. Mientras que las tres subregiones han mostrado una tendencia al alza en los niveles de impuestos entre 1990 y 2017, su evolución muestra diferencias notables entre las subregiones. En promedio, América del Sur registró el crecimiento más rápido en el período y alcanzó el promedio de ALC en 2005 (al 20.0% del PIB). Después de 2010, la proporción de impuestos sobre el PIB de América del Sur superó el promedio de ALC hasta 2016. Por lo contrario, el aumento en los impuestos sobre el PIB para América Central y México y para el Caribe ha sido más gradual. A lo largo de este período, la proporción de impuestos sobre el PIB de América Central y México se mantuvo por debajo del promedio de la región de ALC en su conjunto. Desde 1990, el promedio del Caribe ha sido superior al promedio de ALC.

Los ratios del recaudo tributario en los países de ALC aumentaron a principios de los noventa luego de un período de inestabilidad macroeconómica experimentado en la década anterior. Durante los años ochenta, los países mantuvieron grandes desbalances fiscales y al mismo tiempo recurrieron a métodos alternativos para financiar su gasto (vía deuda y emisión de moneda). Lo anterior conllevó a un proceso inflacionario acelerado en la región, lo cual erosionó el valor real de sus ingresos tributarios. Las reformas de los años noventa estuvieron enfocadas a la estabilidad de precios, el libre comercio y la disciplina fiscal. La mayoría de gobiernos de ALC disminuyeron el gasto público e implementaron políticas con miras al incremento del recaudo tributario lo que derivó en una mejora del manejo presupuestario y de los balances fiscales. Las autoridades implementaron reformas de política y de administración tributaria para reforzar los sistemas tributarios durante episodios inflacionarios. Esto se logró disminuyendo los tiempos de recaudo y mediante la indexación de las obligaciones tributarias (CEPAL, 2018[10]).

Gráfico 1.5. **Ingresos tributarios en porcentaje del PIB, promedios ALC y subregiones, 1990-2017**

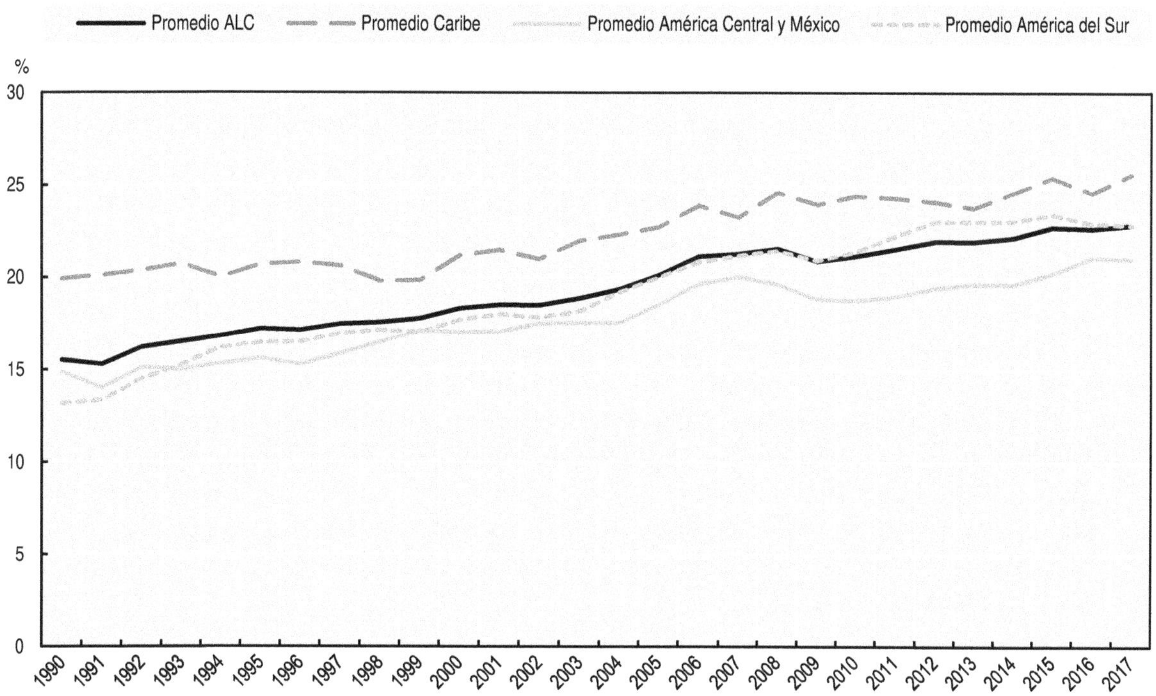

Nota: El promedio de ALC representa el promedio no ponderado de 24 países de ALC incluidos en esta publicación y excluye a Venezuela debido a problemas de disponibilidad de datos.

El Caribe incluye seis países (Bahamas, Barbados, Belice, Guyana, Jamaica y Trinidad y Tobago), América Central y México nueve países (Costa Rica, Cuba, República Dominicana, El Salvador, Guatemala, Honduras, México, Nicaragua y Panamá) y América del Sur nueve países (Argentina, Bolivia, Brasil, Chile, Colombia, Ecuador, Paraguay, Perú y Uruguay).

Fuente: Cálculos de los autores basados en (OCDE/CEPAL/CIAT/BID, 2019[2]), "*Estadísticas tributarias en América Latina y el Caribe*: cuadros comparativos", *Estadísticas tributarias de la OCDE* (base de datos), *http://dx.doi.org/10.1787/data-00641-en*.

StatLink https://doi.org/10.1787/888933940282

Durante las últimas dos décadas se llevaron a cabo esfuerzos significativos para modernizar las administraciones y los sistemas tributarios. Durante ese lapso, se implementaron nuevos sistemas de tecnologías de información, se racionalizó la estructura de las administraciones tributarias y los sistemas de recaudo tributario se convirtieron más eficientes mientras que el personal adquirió mayor experiencia (BID, 2013[11]). Adicionalmente, algunos de los países de ALC simplificaron su sistema tributario y ampliaron su base impositiva, lo que puede haber contribuido al aumento del recibo de impuestos. Similarmente, redujeron los números de las exenciones e incentivos tributarios otorgados a ciertas actividades y sectores, especialmente orientados hacia la atracción de inversión extranjera. Las reformas incluyeron la introducción o el desarrollo de regímenes simplificados para pequeños contribuyentes y la imposición sobre la propiedad basada en criterios de rentas presuntas.

Estas medidas han tenido un efecto positivo en varios países gracias a la expansión del impuesto para que abarque todas las rentas del trabajo y del capital, incluyendo dividendos (por ejemplo. Colombia, República Dominicana, Guatemala, El Salvador, Nicaragua, Panamá y Perú). Las reformas también han establecido impuestos mínimos, impuestos sobre las transacciones financieras, y la reducción gradual del nivel de renta real gravado al tipo máximo marginal (CEPAL, 2013[12]) (CEPAL, 2018[10]).

La introducción del IVA fue la reforma más significativa en los países de ALC en los años ochenta. Doce países[4] implementaron un sistema de IVA en 1980 y casi todos habían implementado el IVA a principios de los años noventa. Despues de este periodo, Las reformas relacionadas al IVA se han centrado en su extensión y fortalecimiento, mediante el aumento de la tasa y la ampliación de su base. Las reformas también se centraron en la simplificación de los sistemas de IVA, y la mayoría de los países redujeron el número de artículos con tasas cero o reducidas, avanzando hacia esquemas de IVA de tasa única en varios países (CEPAL, 2018[10]).

De 1990 a 2016, los ingresos del IVA como proporción del PIB se duplicaron en los países ALC, pasando de 2.3% del PIB en 1990 a 6.0% del PIB en 2017 (Gráfico 1.6). Durante el mismo período, los ingresos tributarios provenientes de otros impuestos sobre los bienes y servicios (los impuestos específicos y los derechos sobre las aduanas y las importaciones) disminuyeron como porcentaje del PIB. Esta caída fue asociada con la liberalización del comercio que trajo consigo un cambio en la forma en la que se gravan los bienes importados y exportados y también los productos y servicios específicos. Estos cambios incluyeron una reducción de los aranceles a la importación, la reducción de la base y de los productos y servicios sujetos a impuestos específicos y la eliminación de los impuestos sobre las exportaciones. Una importante excepción fue Argentina, país en el cual los impuestos sobre las exportaciones fueron re-establecidos en 2002. No obstante, el gobierno establecido en diciembre 2015 abolió este impuesto sobre casi todos los productos agropecuarios (World Grain, 2016[13]) (FMI, 2016[14]).

Gráfico 1.6. **Recaudo de los impuestos sobre la renta, el IVA y otros impuestos sobre bienes y servicios, 1990-2017**

Porcentaje del PIB

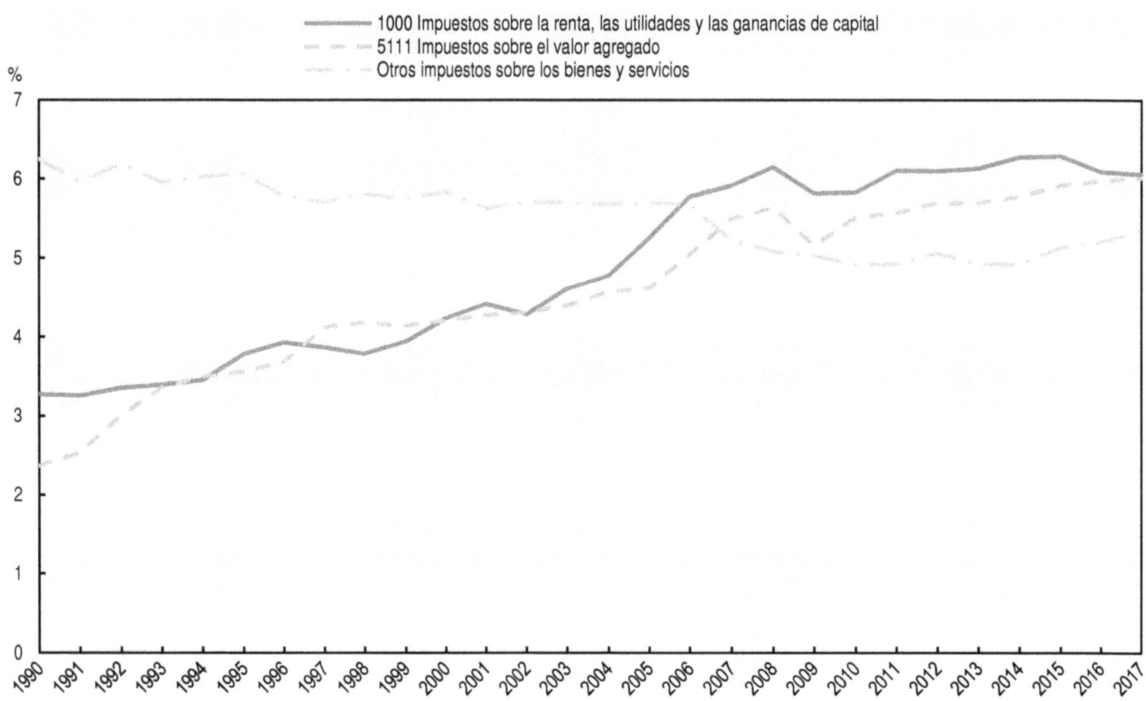

Fuente: Elaboración propia basada en (OCDE/CEPAL/CIAT/BID, 2019[2]), "*Estadísticas tributarias en América Latina y el Caribe*: cuadros comparativos", *Estadísticas tributarias de la OCDE* (base de datos), *http://dx.doi.org/10.1787/data-00641-en.*

StatLink https://doi.org/10.1787/888933940301

Desde 1990, el IVA y los impuestos sobre las rentas y utilidades han sido los principales impulsores del crecimiento en el recaudo tributario en ALC, aproximadamente en igual medida (Gráfico 1.6.). Entre 1990 y 2002, el IVA contribuyó más al aumento de los ingresos tributarios (2.0 puntos porcentuales comparado con 1.0 puntos porcentuales de los impuestos sobre los ingresos y las ganancias). Entre 2002 y 2017, los ingresos por impuestos sobre ingresos y ganancias y por IVA aumentaron en 1.8 y 1.7 puntos porcentuales, respectivamente.

Uno de los elementos que contribuyó a esta tendencia es la recuperación de la actividad económica en ALC y el boom en el precio de las materias primas luego de 2003, que contribuyó al aumento en el recaudo del impuesto sobre las rentas y utilidades de sociedades en el sector de los recursos naturales. (CEPAL, 2014[15]) (Barreix, Benitez and Pecho, 2017[16]). En varios países, también fue el resultado de políticas fiscales que redujeron los incentivos fiscales en las zonas de libre comercio, la introducción de impuestos mínimos para las corporaciones, las reformas en los impuestos internacionales y los acuerdos entre países para combatir la evasión fiscal. La disminución en 2016 se explica principalmente por la caída en los ingresos tributarios de los productos no renovables, especialmente en Trinidad y Tobago (OCDE/CIAT/BID/CEPAL, 2018[17]). En 2017, los ingresos por impuestos a la renta se mantuvieron en el mismo nivel de 2016 (6.1% del PIB).

Gráfico 1.7. **Recaudo de impuesto sobre la renta y utilidades, el impuesto sobre la renta de empresas y el impuesto sobre la renta de personas, 2007-17**

Porcentaje del PIB

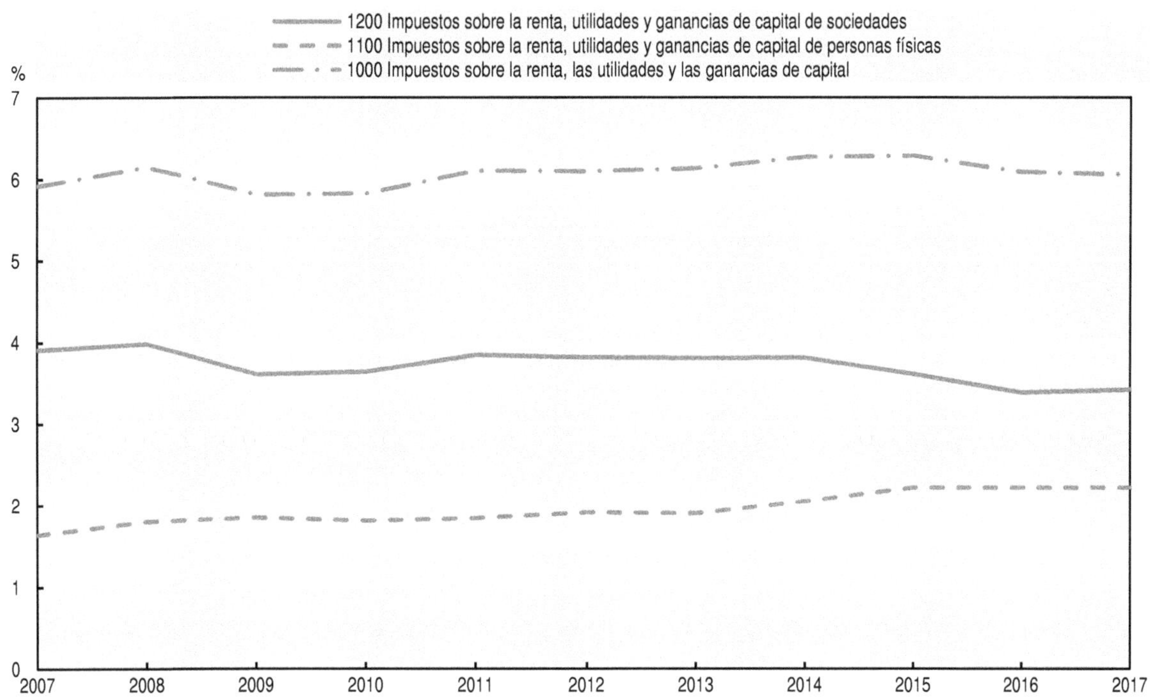

Nota: Ecuador, Nicaragua y Venezuela han sido excluidos de los promedios de los impuestos sobre la renta de empresas y personas físicas. Venezuela ha sido excluido debido a problemas de disponibilidad de datos. Ecuador y Nicaragua quedan excluidos porque más de un tercio de su recaudo no puede ser atribuido a las categorías de renta de empresas (1200) o impuesto sobre la renta de personas (1100).

Fuente: (OCDE/CEPAL/CIAT/BID, 2019[2]), "*Estadísticas tributarias en América Latin y el Caribe*: cuadros comparativos", *Estadísticas tributarias de la OCDE* (base de datos), *http://dx.doi.org/10.1787/data-00641-en*.

StatLink https://doi.org/10.1787/888933940320

Desde 2007, los ingresos provenientes del impuesto sobre la renta y utilidades de empresas se han reducido como porcentaje del PIB mientras que los ingresos provenientes del impuesto sobre la renta de personas físicas han incrementado. En 2017, los promedios de ALC para los recaudos del impuesto sobre la renta y utilidades de empresas y del impuesto sobre la renta de personas físicas se ubicaron en 3.4% y 2.2% del PIB respectivamente (Gráfico 1.7).

Existen algunas diferencias notables entre las tres subregiones de ALC al considerar los cambios en las principales categorías de impuestos entre 1990 y 2017 (Gráfico 1.8).

Gráfico 1.8. **Tasa de cambio anual de los impuestos sobre la renta y utilidades, impuesto sobre la renta de empresas y sobre la renta de personas por subregión, 2017**

Puntos porcentuales del PIB

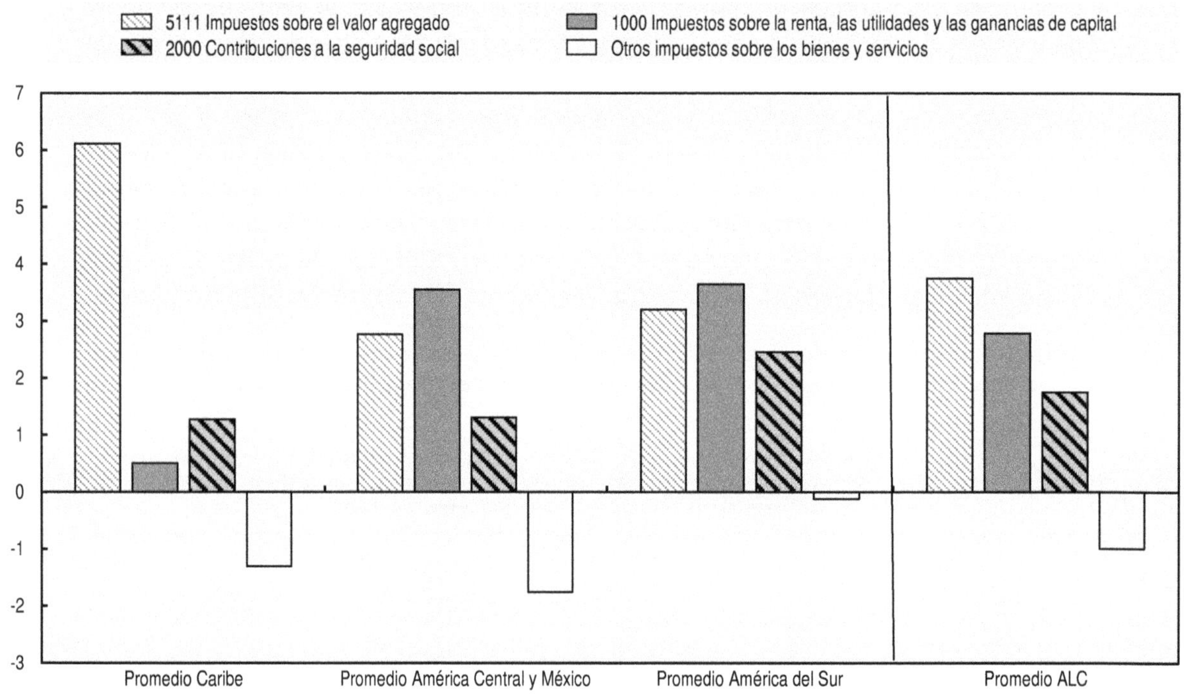

Nota: El promedio de ALC representa el promedio no ponderado de 24 países de ALC incluidos en esta publicación y excluye a Venezuela debido a problemas de disponibilidad de datos.

El Caribe incluye seis países (Bahamas, Barbados, Belice, Guyana, Jamaica y Trinidad y Tobago), América Central y México nueve países (Costa Rica, Cuba, República Dominicana, El Salvador, Guatemala, Honduras, México, Nicaragua y Panamá) y América del Sur nueve países (Argentina, Bolivia, Brasil, Chile, Colombia, Ecuador, Paraguay, Perú y Uruguay).

Fuente: (OCDE/CEPAL/CIAT/BID, 2019[2]), "*Estadísticas tributarias en América Latin y el Caribe*: cuadros comparativos", *Estadísticas tributarias de la OCDE* (base de datos), *http://dx.doi.org/10.1787/data-00641-en*.

StatLink https://doi.org/10.1787/888933940339

- En promedio, el Caribe mostró, como porcentaje del PIB, el mayor aumento en los ingresos por IVA (6.1 puntos porcentuales) y los menores aumentos en los ingresos por impuestos a la renta y contribuciones a la seguridad social. Cinco de los seis países del Caribe implementaron un sistema de IVA durante el período[5], más tarde que la mayoría de los países de América Central, México y América del Sur.
- En América Central y México, y en América del Sur, los mayores aumentos entre 1990 y 2017 se debieron a impuestos sobre los ingresos y ganancias (más de 3.5 puntos porcentuales en ambas subregiones), seguidos por el IVA (más de 2.8 puntos porcentuales en ambas sub-regiones) y las cotizaciones a la seguridad social (menos de 2.5 puntos porcentuales). Los ingresos por impuestos sobre los ingresos y las ganancias (e indirectamente el aumento del IVA) se vieron influenciados por los grandes aumentos en los precios de los minerales y del petróleo entre 2003 y 2010.
- En América del Sur, el aumento promedio de los ingresos por contribuciones a la seguridad social como porcentaje del PIB fue mucho mas importante que en las otras dos subregiones

(2.5 puntos porcentuales en América del Sur en comparación con menos de 1.6 puntos porcentuales en las otras subregiones). Por otro lado, América del Sur es la única subregión que, en promedio, registró una leve caída en los ingresos por otros impuestos sobre bienes y servicios. No obstante, América del Sur todavía tiene el promedio más bajo de ingresos por otros impuestos sobre bienes y servicios (en 3.9% del PIB).

Factores que han influenciado los niveles de recaudo tributario

Las diferencias entre los promedios de recaudo tributario, como porcentaje del PIB, entre ALC y la OCDE son coherentes con la tendencia de que los países con una mayor renta per cápita tienen mayores niveles de recaudo tributario. Los datos arrojan una correlación positiva entre el PIB per cápita (una medida del nivel de ingreso de los países) y el recaudo tributario con respecto al PIB (Gráfico 1.9). En general, los países de la OCDE tienen ingresos más altos que los países de ALC y también recaudan más en impuestos. Argentina, Barbados, Brasil, Trinidad y Tobago y Uruguay muestran niveles de recaudo tributario y niveles de ingreso similares a algunos países de la OCDE. Los análisis empíricos sugieren que una recaudación tributaria más fuerte, acompañada por mejores instituciones, educación y habilidades y una diversificación económica, han permitido a varios países de la OCDE de escaparse sosteniblemente de la trampa del ingreso medio lo que contrasta con la región ALC (Melguizo et al., 2017[18]).

Gráfico 1.9. **PIB per cápita en PPA (USD) y recaudo tributario en países de América Latina y el Caribe, la OCDE y un grupo de países de África y economías de Asia y el Pacífico, 2016**

Porcentaje del PIB

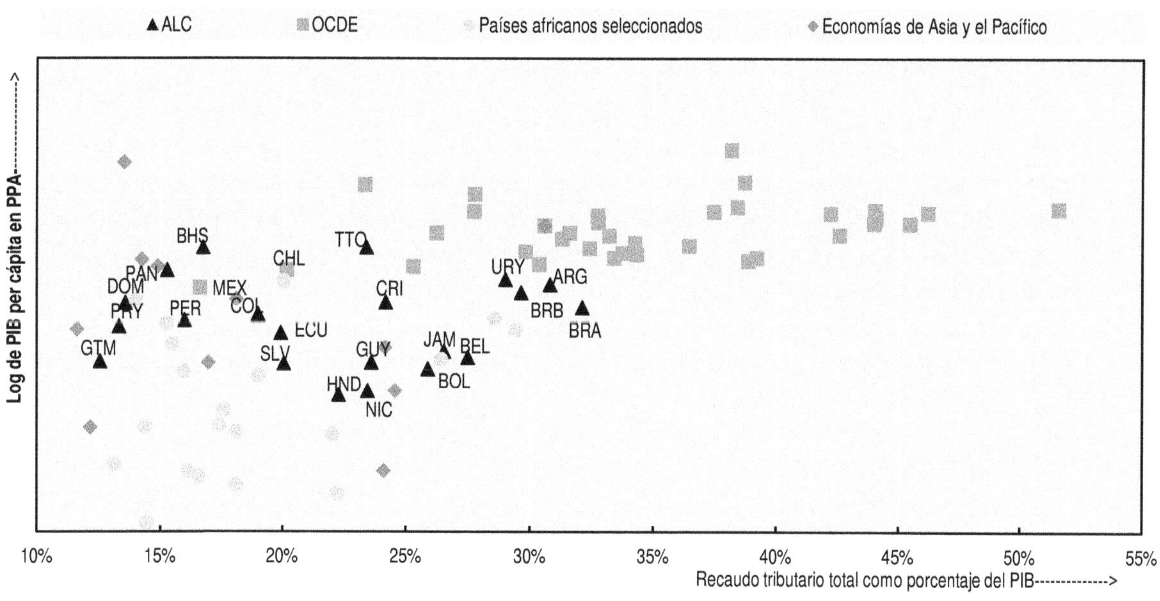

Nota: El año de comparación es 2016 ya que los datos de 2017 en cuanto a los promedios de los ingresos tributarios con relación al PIB no estaban disponibles para los países seleccionados de África y Asia. La paridad de poder adquisitivo (PPA) entre dos países es la tasa a la cual la moneda de un país necesita ser convertida en la de un segundo país para asegurar que el mismo volumen de bienes y servicios puedan ser adquiridos en ambos países. El tipo de conversión PPA implícito se expresa como moneda nacional por dólar internacional actual. Un dólar internacional tiene el mismo poder adquisitivo que el dólar estadounidense en los Estados Unidos. Un dólar internacional es una moneda hipotética que se utiliza como medio para convertir y comparar los costos de un país a otro utilizando un punto de referencia común, el dólar estadounidense.

Fuente: (FMI, 2018[19]) por las cifras del PIB per cápita. Las proporciones entre los ingresos tributarios y el PIB se obtienen de las publicaciones regionales de estadísticas de tributarias (*www.oecd.org/tax/tax-policy/revenue-statistics-comparable-tax-revenue-data.htm*).

StatLink *https://doi.org/10.1787/888933940358*

El recaudo tributario, como porcentaje del PIB, es influenciado por factores económicos y estructurales. El PIB per cápita, la apertura comercial, el tamaño de la economía informal, la dotación de recursos naturales y la importancia del sector agrícola en la economía son todos factores que pueden influenciar el nivel de recaudo tributario. Los determinantes socio-demográficos son también claves, por ejemplo el nivel de educación o el grado de participación femenina en la fuerza de trabajo. El poder de las administraciones tributarias, el nivel de corrupción y la moral fiscal (o la disposición de la gente para pagar impuestos) son todos factores que están fuertemente vinculados al nivel de recaudo (OCDE, 2014[20]). Finalmente, la ubicación geográfica y factores históricos también inciden en la recaudación. Por ejemplo, la posibilidad de gravar bienes y servicios en el puerto de entrada es menor en países sin costa marítima. Adicionalmente, factores internacionales, incluyendo las políticas tributarias adoptadas por otros países pueden tener un impacto en los niveles de recaudo tributario.

El grado de participación del Estado en el financiamiento de la seguridad social es otro factor importante para explicar los niveles de recaudo tributario en la región de ALC. Desde 1980 en adelante, muchos países de ALC privatizaron sus sistemas sanitarios, previsionales y de seguridad social en mayor o menor medida. Chile, El Salvador y México son ejemplos de países que han migrado sus esquemas previsionales a programas de cuentas individuales administrados por el sector privado. En Colombia y Perú, los sistemas públicos y privados compiten y los empleados pueden determinar su afiliación a uno u otro (OCDE/CIAT/CEPAL/BID, 2015[21]) (OCDE/BID/El Banco Mundial, 2014[22]). Por otra parte, Argentina, Brasil y Uruguay siguen un modelo en los cuales los sistemas públicos y privados son complementarios. En estos tres países se han llevado a cabo reformas para expandir la cobertura de los sistemas de seguridad social e incluir a los previamente excluidos. Esto ha sido también un factor importante en el aumento del recaudo tributario (CEPAL, 2014[15]).

La informalidad erosiona el recaudo tributario en los países de ALC dado que reduce la base impositiva significativamente. El FMI estimó que la economía informal representó el 40% del PIB en promedio en la región de ALC durante el período 2010-14 (Medina, Jonelis and Cangul, 2017[23]). El nivel era aún más elevado en los años noventa, lo que llevó a algunos gobiernos introducir impuestos simplificados para pequeños contribuyentes que fueron en alguna medida exitosos en integrar a trabajadores informales dentro del sector formal. Estos sistemas simplificados variaron en cuanto al nivel de éxito alcanzado dependiendo del tipo de contribuyentes cubiertos y la capacidad de las administraciones tributarias (CEPAL, 2014[15]) (OCDE/BID/CIAT, 2016[24]).

Estructuras tributarias

La estructura impositiva (definida como la participación de los principales tipos de impuestos en la recaudación tributaria total) muestra la composición del recaudo tributario por sus diferentes tipos de impuestos. Es un indicador importante para comprender los efectos económicos y sociales del sistema tributario en la región de ALC.

Evolución de las estructuras tributarias

En la región de ALC, los impuestos sobre bienes y servicios proporcionan la mayor parte de los ingresos tributarios totales, lo que representa la mitad de los impuestos totales en 2017. Entre 1990 y 2017, el promedio de la estructura tributaria de ALC se desplazó hacia el IVA y los impuestos sobre los ingresos y ganancias, y se alejó de otros impuestos sobre bienes y servicios.

- La proporción del impuesto al valor agregado alcanzó 27.9% del total de los ingresos tributarios en 2017, lo que corresponde a un aumento de 12.3 puntos porcentuales entre 1990 y 2017, mientras que la proporción de los ingresos tributarios provenientes de otros impuestos sobre bienes y servicios (impuestos especiales, arenceles e importaciones) disminuyó de 19.3 puntos porcentuales durante el mismo periodo (Gráfico 1.10).
- La proporción de impuestos sobre las rentas y ganancias creció en 6.9 puntos porcentuales (de 20.1% a 27.1% del recaudo tributario total) entre 1990 y 2017.
- Las contribuciones a la seguridad social como porcentaje del recaudo tributario total aumentaron en 3.8 puntos durante los últimos 27 años, alcanzando 16.9% en 2017.

Gráfico 1.10. **Estructura tributaria promedio en ALC 1990 y 2017.**

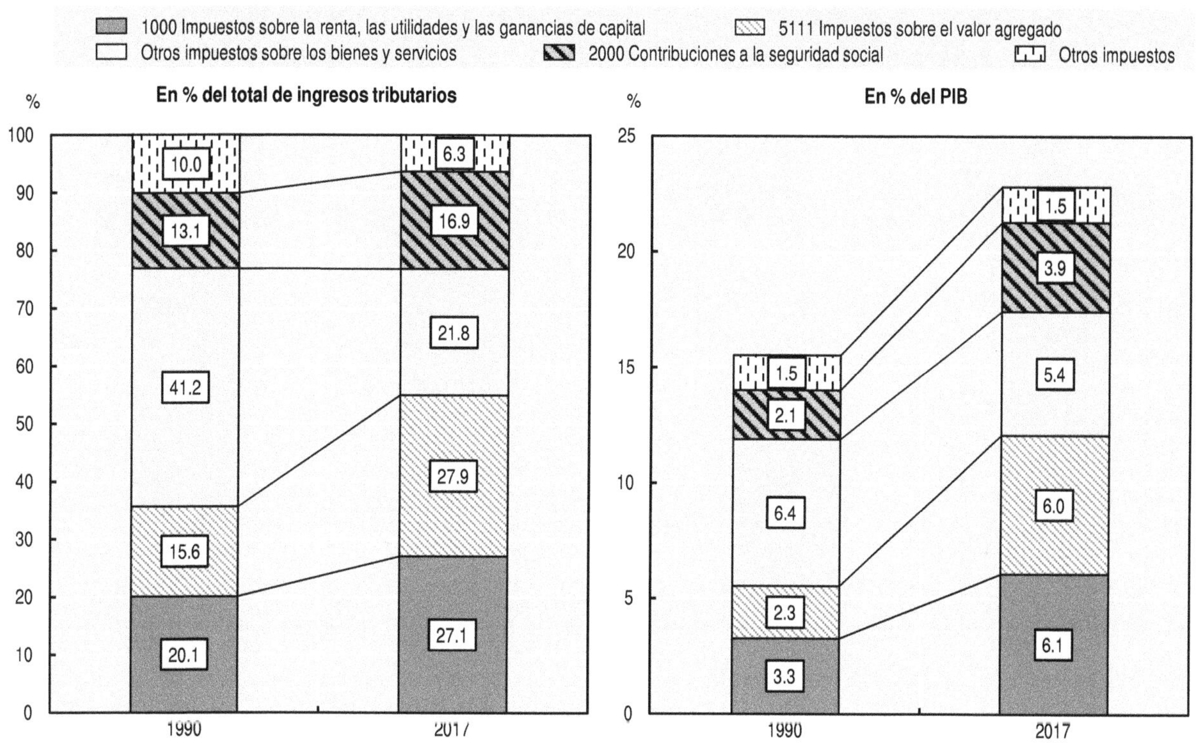

Fuente: Elaboración propia con base en (OCDE/CEPAL/CIAT/BID, 2019[2]), cuadros presentados en el capítulo 4.

StatLink https://doi.org/10.1787/888933940377

Desde 2007, la estructura impositiva promedio de ALC se desplazó hacia una mayor proporcion de ingresos del impuesto sobre la renta de personas y una menor proporcion de ingresos del impuesto a las utilidades, aunque los ingresos del impuesto a las utilidades se mantuvieron más altos que los ingresos del impuesto sobre la renta de personas en 2017 (15.5% del total de impuestos versus 9.5%) (Gráfico 1.11).[6]

La participacion en los ingresos del impuesto sobre la renta creció entre 2007 y 2017, en parte debido al aumento de los ingresos personales. Sin embargo, la proporción en los ingresos del impuesto sobre la renta de personas sigue siendo baja en ALC a pesar de las reformas implementadas por algunos países para ampliar su base tributaria. Depués de la crisis financiera mundial varios países implementaron tasas fijas sobre los ingresos de capital, que anteriormente habían sido exentos, e introdujeron tasas progresivas sobre las rentas del trabajo (CEPAL, 2014[15]). Sin embargo, hay relativamente pocos contribuyentes con obligación tributaria, dada la concentración de personas que perciben bajos ingresos : solo el 10% de la población en América Latina es un contribuyente tributario registrado (BID, 2013[11]). Además, muchos otros factores siguen limitando el recaudo del impuesto a la renta de personas físicas: una base imponible limitada de salarios, ya que los beneficios se otorgan a las rentas del capital, y los altos niveles de evasión (Barreix, Benitez and Pecho, 2017[16]) (CEPAL, 2014[15]). (BID, 2013[11]) estiman que "alrededor de la mitad del potencial de recaudación del impuesto se pierde a través de la evasión" en los países de América Latina.

Gráfico 1.11. **Estructura tributaria promedio en la región ALC, 2007 y 2017**

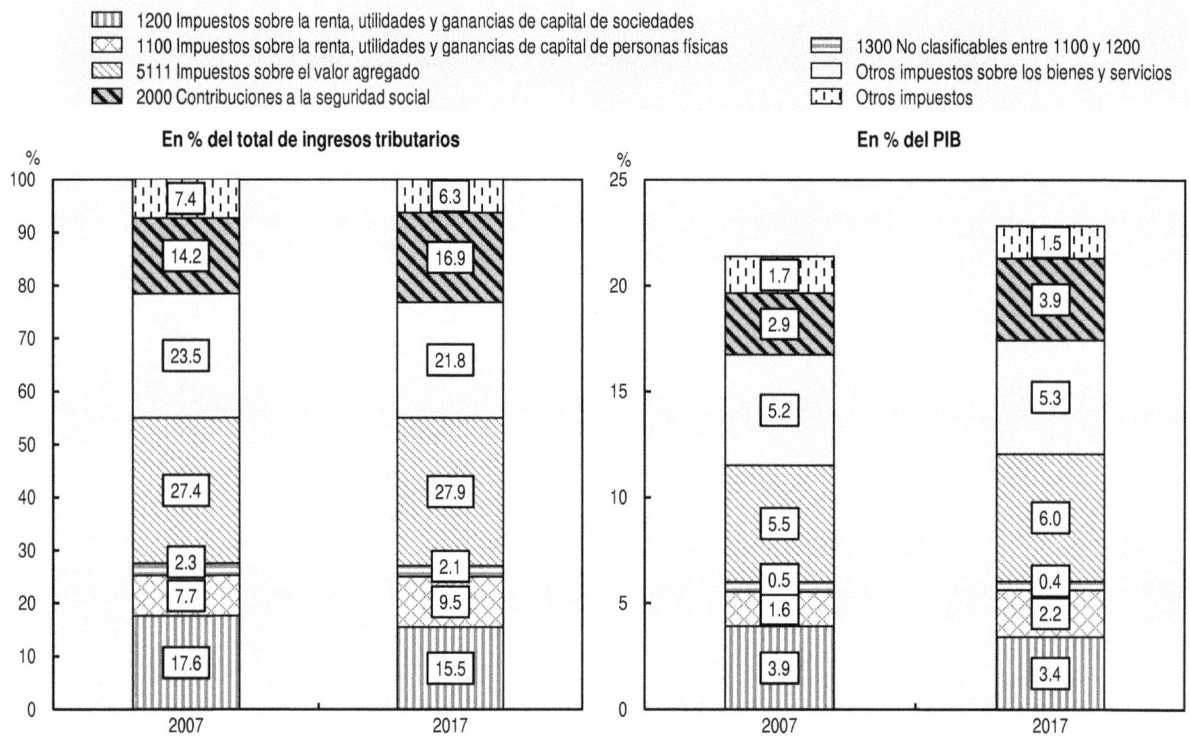

Nota: El ingreso promedio del impuesto a las utilidades y del impuesto sobre la renta de personas como porcentaje del PIB se deben interpretar con cautela ya que Ecuador, Nicaragua y Venezuela están excluidos del cálculo. Los promedios de ALC excluyen a Venezuela debido a problemas de disponibilidad de datos. Ecuador y Nicaragua están excluidos de los promedios de ALC para los ingresos del impuesto a las utilidades y los ingresos del impuesto sobre la renta de personas como porcentaje del PIB, ya que más de un tercio de sus ingresos provenientes de impuestos sobre ingresos y ganancias no pueden asignarse a los ingresos del impuesto a las utilidades (1200) o ingresos del impuesto sobre la renta de personas (1100).

Fuente: Cálculos de los autores con base (OCDE/CEPAL/CIAT/BID, 2019[2]), "Estadísticas tributarias en América Latin y el Caribe: cuadros comparativos", *Estadísticas tributarias de la OCDE* (base de datos) *http://dx.doi.org/10.1787/data-00641-en*.

StatLink https://doi.org/10.1787/888933940396

La participación de las contribuciones de la seguridad social en los ingresos tributarios totales aumentó 3.8 puntos porcentuales desde 1990, alcanzando el 16.9% en 2017. Dos factores importantes han influido en la trayectoria de las contribuciones de la seguridad social en la región. El aumento en la renta per cápita ha llevado a una mayor recaudación, pero esto fue contrarrestado por la privatización total o parcial de la seguridad social que se produjo en muchos países.

En 2017, hubo diferencias notables en la estructura tributaria en las subregiones. El Caribe, en particular, muestra una estructura tributaria promedio muy diferente a las demás subregiones.

- En 2017, la mayor parte de los ingresos se derivó de otros impuestos sobre bienes y servicios en el Caribe, que representan en promedio el 30.1% de los ingresos tributarios totales. Estos impuestos contribuyeron con 16.5% en América del Sur y 21.7% en América Central y México.
- En contraste, América del Sur tuvo la mayor proporción de los ingresos por IVA en 2017 con un 31.4% en promedio, en comparación con las otras dos subregiones (27.0% en el Caribe y 25.1% en América Central y México).
- Las contribuciones a la seguridad social fueron las más bajas en el Caribe, con un 10.3% de los ingresos tributarios totales en promedio en 2017, casi la mitad del promedio de las demás subregiones (18.4% en América Central y México y 19.4% en América del Sur).
- Las tres subregiones generaron ingresos del impuesto a las utilidades de sociedades más altos que los ingresos del impuesto sobre la renta a los individuos.[7]

Estructura tributaria en las regiones ALC y OCDE

El promedio de la estructura tributaria (tax-mix) en los países de ALC muestra ingresos relativamente bajos provenientes de los impuestos sobre la renta, de los impuestos a las utilidades y las contribuciones a la seguridad social, en relación con el promedio de la OCDE (Gráfico 1.12). En particular, los países de ALC en promedio dependen en gran medida de los impuestos sobre bienes y servicios, los cuales constituyen más de la mitad de los ingresos tributarios totales, en comparación con alrededor de un tercio en las economías de la OCDE en promedio. Sin embargo, como porcentaje del PIB, en 2017 los ingresos por impuestos sobre bienes y servicios en las regiones de ALC y OCDE se mantuvieron en un nivel similar en 2016, con un 11.2% y un 11.0% respectivamente.[8] El nivel de ingresos del IVA como porcentaje del PIB también fue similar, con un 6.0% para el promedio de ALC y un 6.8% para la OCDE.

En cambio, la participación combinada de los impuestos sobre los ingresos y ganancias y las contribuciones a la seguridad social fue menor en la región de ALC que en la OCDE (43.9% en comparación con el 60.0% en 2017, en promedio). Como porcentaje del PIB, estas dos categorías representaron el 9.8% en la región de ALC, menos de la mitad del nivel promedio de la OCDE (20.5%). La tendencia hacia la provisión privada de seguridad social en muchos países de ALC explica algunas de las diferencias en esta categoría.

En promedio, el impuesto sobre la renta y utilidades de empresas generó el 15.4% de los ingresos tributarios totales en la región de ALC en comparación con el 9.0% en el área de la OCDE (respectivamente 3.4% y 2.9% como porcentaje del PIB) (Gráfico 1.12). La diferencia más notable entre las regiones se relaciona con los ingresos del impuesto sobre la renta, que contribuyeron con un promedio del 23.8% de los ingresos tributarios totales en el área de la OCDE en 2016 y el 9.6% del recaudo tributario total en la región de ALC. Los ingresos del impuesto sobre la renta y utilidades de personas físicas fueron en promedio equivalentes al 2.2% del PIB en la región de ALC, en comparación con el 8.2% del promedio de la OCDE

Los impuestos sobre los bienes inmuebles y la nómina (agrupados en la categoría "otros impuestos") son, en promedio, fuentes de ingresos menos importantes para la región de ALC que en la OCDE, aunque existen desafíos con la disponibilidad de datos para esta categoría. Como se analiza en el Capítulo 3, los impuestos a la propiedad son generalmente la principal fuente de ingresos para los gobiernos locales en la región de ALC, pero operan por debajo de su potencial.

Gráfico 1.12. **Estructura tributaria en las regiones ALC y OCDE, 2016**

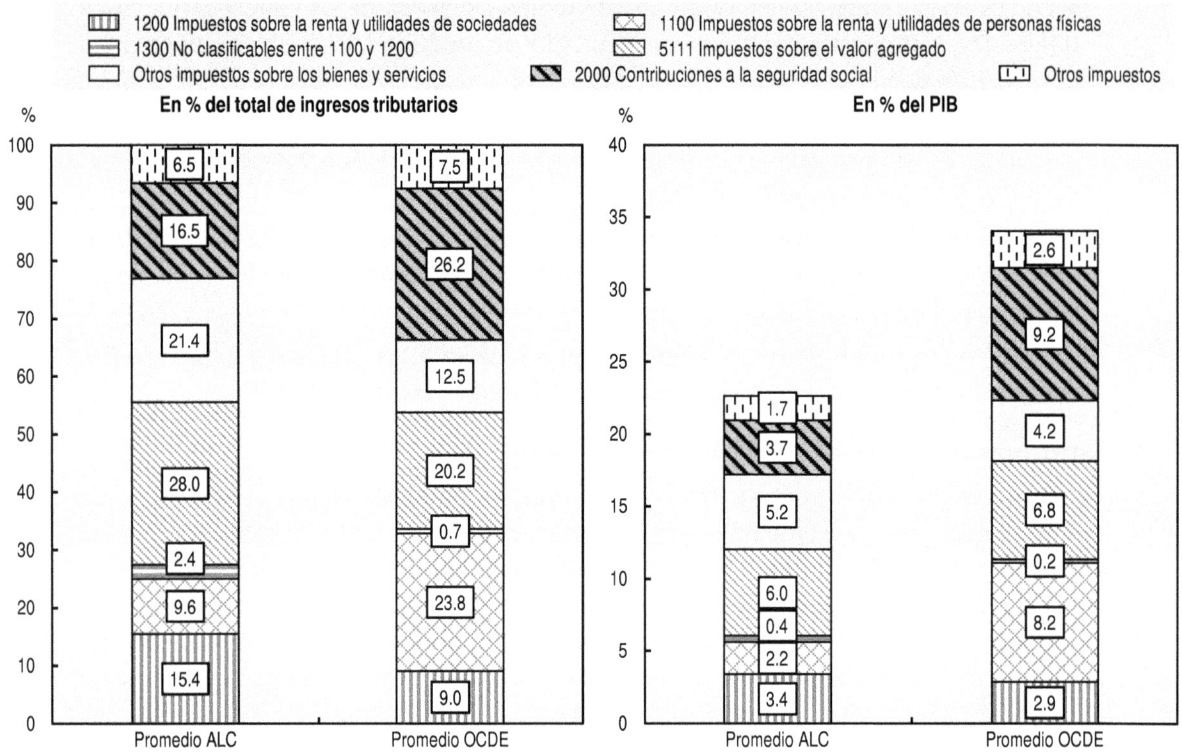

Nota: El ingreso promedio ALC del impuesto a las utilidades y del impuesto sobre la renta de personas como porcentaje del PIB se deben interpretar con cautela ya que Ecuador, Nicaragua y Venezuela están excluidos del cálculo. Los promedios de ALC excluyen a Venezuela debido a problemas de disponibilidad de datos. Ecuador y Nicaragua están excluidos de los promedios de ALC para los ingresos del impuesto a las utilidades y los ingresos del impuesto sobre la renta de personas como porcentaje del PIB, ya que más de un tercio de sus ingresos provenientes de impuestos sobre ingresos y ganancias no pueden asignarse a los ingresos del impuesto a las utilidades (1200) o ingresos del impuesto sobre la renta de personas (1100).

Fuente: Elaboración propia con base en (OCDE/CEPAL/CIAT/BID, 2019[2]), "Estadísticas tributarias en América Latin y el Caribe: cuadros comparativos", *Estadísticas tributarias de la OCDE* (base de datos), *http://dx.doi.org/10.1787/data-00641-en*.

StatLink *https://doi.org/10.1787/888933940415*

Estructura tributaria en los países de ALC

Los impuestos a los bienes y servicios son la principal fuente de ingresos para todos los países de ALC, excepto para México, Panamá y Trinidad y Tobago. Para México y Trinidad y Tobago, los ingresos por impuestos sobre los ingresos y las ganancias representaron la mayor proporción, mientras que para Panamá los ingresos por contribuciones a la seguridad social fueron la fuente más importante de ingresos tributarios (Gráfico 1.13).

La contribución del IVA a los ingresos tributarios totales osciló entre 16.1% en Panamá y 41.6% en Chile. No hay sistema de IVA en Cuba. La amplia variación entre países es en parte el resultado de las diferencias en el diseño del IVA, ya que las tasas, las bases impositivas y el número de exenciones del IVA difieren significativamente en la región.

En 2017, las contribuciones a la seguridad social variaron ampliamente, de 0.5% de los ingresos tributarios totales en República Dominicana a 39.2% en Panamá. El nivel de estos ingresos en todos los países refleja las elecciones hechas por los gobiernos sobre cómo financiar los planes de seguridad social. En los países con esquemas de seguridad social públicos o mixtos (incluidos Argentina, Brasil, Costa Rica, Panamá, Paraguay y Uruguay), las contribuciones a la seguridad social alcanzan una participación más significativa (más del 20% de los ingresos tributarios totales).

Gráfico 1.13. **Estructura tributaria en países de ALC, 2017**

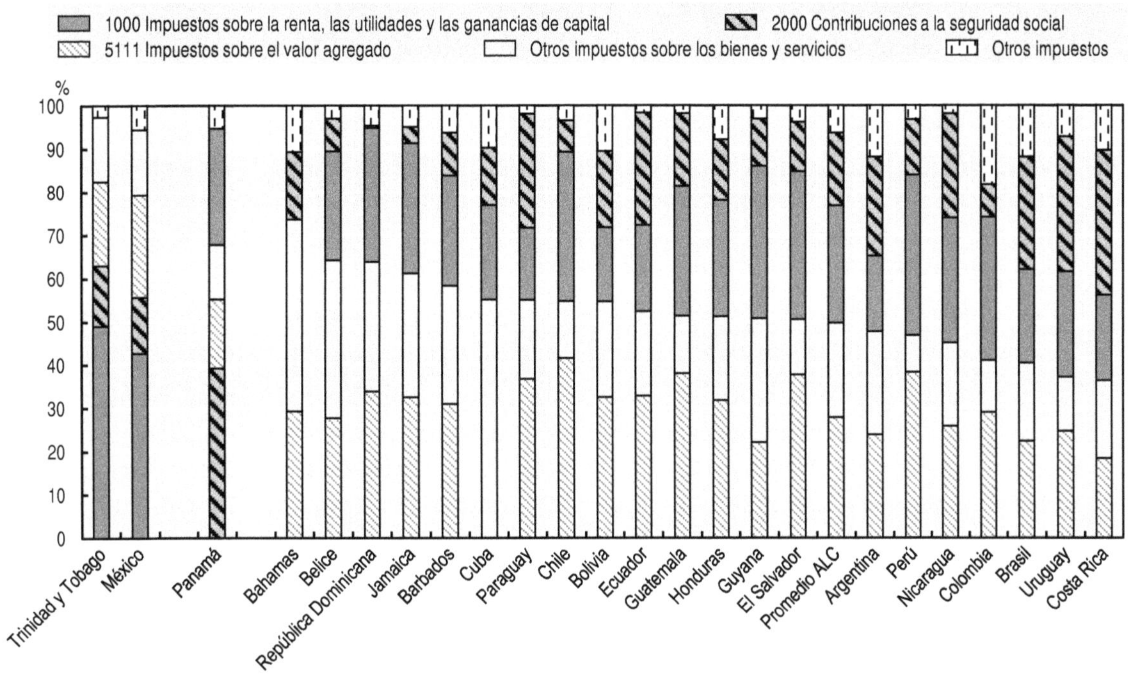

Nota: Los países se agrupan por la parte principal de los ingresos tributarios entre 1000 impuestos sobre ingresos y ganancias, 2000 contribuciones a la Seguridad Social y 5000 impuestos sobre bienes y servicios. Las Bahamas no gravan los ingresos. No hay sistema de IVA en Cuba.

Fuente: Elaboración propia con base (OCDE/CEPAL/CIAT/BID, 2019[2]), cuadros del capítulo 4.

StatLink https://doi.org/10.1787/888933940434

Ingresos por impuestos ambientales

Los impuestos relacionados con el medio ambiente, y los instrumentos de política basados en el precio de forma más general, están jugando un papel cada vez más importante en muchos países. Al incorporar una señal de precio en las decisiones de los consumidores, estos impuestos implementan el principio de quien contamina paga y llevan a que a las empresas y los hogares consideren los costos sociales de sus acciones.

Un impuesto relacionado con el medio ambiente es un impuesto cuya base es una unidad física (o una proxy de una unidad física) de algo que tiene un impacto dañino específico y comprobado en el medio ambiente, independientemente de si el impuesto está destinado a cambiar los comportamientos o se impone por otro propósito (OCDE, 2005[25]). En muchos países de ALC y de la OCDE, la mayor fuente de ingresos tributarios relacionados con el medio ambiente se deriva de los impuestos especiales sobre los combustibles para el transporte por carretera. En los últimos años, algunos países de ALC han introducido reformas fiscales importantes, tales como Chile, México y, más recientemente, Colombia.

Si bien los ingresos tributarios relacionados con el medio ambiente no pueden identificarse en la clasificación estándar de ingresos tributarios de la OCDE, sí pueden identificarse a través de la lista detallada de impuestos específicos incluidos para la mayoría de los países dentro de esta clasificación general. Es sobre esta base que se incluyen en la base de datos de Instrumentos de Políticas para el Medio Ambiente (PINE) de la OCDE.

La base de datos PINE clasifica los impuestos relacionados con el medio ambiente en tres fuentes de ingresos principales:[9]

- Energía: Esto cubre la tributación de productos energéticos como los combustibles fósiles y la electricidad, incluyendo los combustibles para el transporte, como la gasolina y el diesel. Todos los impuestos relacionados con el CO_2 se clasifican aquí.
- Vehículos automotores y servicios de transporte: Esta categoría incluye impuestos a las importaciones o ventas sobre equipos de transporte, impuestos recurrentes a la propiedad, registro o uso de vehículos motorizados en la carretera y otros impuestos relacionados con el transporte.
- Otros: Esta categoría incluye impuestos sobre sustancias que agotan la capa de ozono, agua y aguas residuales, gestión de residuos, minería y canteras e impuestos no asignados.

Un analisis detallado de los impuestos específicos por país para 22 países de ALC en este informe demuestra que, en promedio, los ingresos por impuestos relacionados con el medio ambiente ascendieron a 1.1% del PIB en 2017,[10] un nivel más bajo que el promedio de la OCDE que es de 1.6% del PIB (cifra de 2016) (Cárdenas Rodríguez and Haščič, 2018[26]). Los ingresos tributarios relacionados con el medio ambiente en 2017 variaron de 0.1% del PIB en Trinidad y Tobago a 2.3% en Honduras (Gráfico 1.14).

Gráfico 1.14. **Ingresos tributarios relacionados con el medio ambiente por categoría y tipo de impuesto principal, 2017**

Porcentaje del PIB

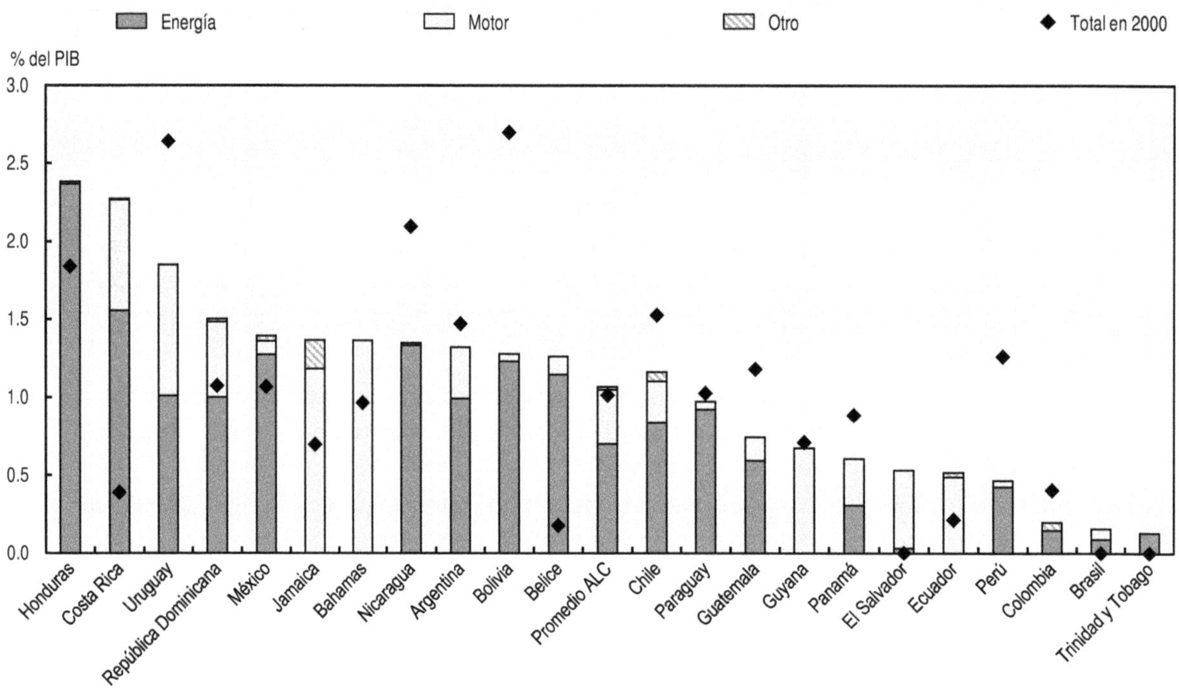

Nota: Barbados, Cuba y Venezuela están excluidos de los promedios de ALC. No ha sido posible identificar los ingresos tributarios relacionados con el medio ambiente para Barbados y Cuba. Venezuela está excluida debido a problemas de disponibilidad de datos. Las cifras de Chile y México utilizan datos de 2016 basados en la base de datos PINE que presenta datos más completos sobre los ingresos tributarios ambientales.

Fuente: Base de datos PINE para Chile y México y cálculos de los autores con base (OCDE/CEPAL/CIAT/BID, 2019[2]), capítulo 5.

StatLink https://doi.org/10.1787/888933940453

Entre 2000 y 2017, los ingresos tributarios relacionados con el medio ambiente como porcentaje del PIB en la región ALC aumentaron levemente (en 0.1 puntos porcentuales). La mitad de los 22 países de ALC incluidos en este análisis registraron aumentos en los ingresos tributarios relacionados con el medio ambiente entre 2000 y 2017, mientras que la otra mitad registró disminuciones.

En 2017, los ingresos tributarios provenientes de la energía representaron la mayor proporción del recaudo tributario relacionada con el medio ambiente en la región de ALC (en promedio 0.7% del PIB). Los ingresos de los productos energéticos, más comúnmente, del diesel y la gasolina, representaron aproximadamente dos tercios del recaudo tributario relacionados con el medio ambiente, seguidos por ingresos de los impuestos sobre vehículos a motor y servicios de transporte, que representaron la mayor parte del resto. Los ingresos tributarios recaudados sobre otras bases relacionadas con el medio ambiente fueron insignificantes, con un promedio del 2% de los ingresos tributarios relacionados con el medio ambiente. En la OCDE, los ingresos por productos energéticos representan un poco más de dos tercios de los ingresos totales, mientras que los impuestos sobre los vehículos automotores y el transporte representaron alrededor de un cuarto (Cárdenas Rodríguez and Haščič, 2018[26]).

Los impuestos sobre los productos energéticos representaron la mayor parte de los ingresos tributarios relacionados con el medio ambiente en todos los países de ALC, excepto cinco. En estos cinco países (Bahamas, Jamaica, Ecuador, El Salvador y Guyana) los ingresos por vehículos motorizados y servicios de transporte fueron la fuente principal (Gráfico 1.14).

En 2017, los impuestos sobre la energía se incrementaron predominantemente de los impuestos especiales, lo que representa un 0.6% del PIB en promedio en la región ALC. Por lo contrario, los ingresos por concepto de impuestos sobre vehículos a motor y servicios de transporte se obtuvieron de tres tipos diferentes de impuestos: impuestos recurrentes sobre el uso y propiedad de vehículos (0.14% del PIB); impuestos sobre servicios específicos (principalmente impuestos de viaje o de salida, a 0.13% del PIB); y los impuestos especiales sobre vehículos (0.07% del PIB) (Gráfico 1.15).

La evolución de estas tres fuentes de ingresos relacionados con el medio ambiente varió entre 2000 y 2017. Los ingresos por impuestos sobre la energía disminuyeron del 0.96% del PIB al 0.7%, mientras que los ingresos de las otras dos fuentes aumentaron ligeramente. La disminución en los ingresos por impuestos provenientes de la energía se debió principalmente a la disminución en los ingresos por combustibles en Bolivia, Chile, Nicaragua, Perú y Uruguay. A través del Acuerdo de París de 2016, los países se comprometieron a reducir las emisiones de carbono de sus economías a mediados de siglo, lo que implica una sustitución de los combustibles fósiles como fuente de energía. Los ingresos de los impuestos sobre la energía pueden aumentar a mediano plazo, si los países aumentan las tasas de impuestos efectivas sobre el contenido de carbono de los combustibles (Marten and Van Dender, 2019[27]). Un estudio conjunto de la ITF y la OCDE (OCDE/ITF (próxima publicación), 2019[28]) muestra cómo los ingresos del transporte por carretera se pueden estabilizar a largo plazo mediante una combinación de impuestos sobre la distancia recorrida, vehículos y combustible.

Gráfico 1.15. **Ingresos tributarios relacionados con el medio ambiente por base imponible y tipo de impuesto, 2017**

Porcentaje del PIB

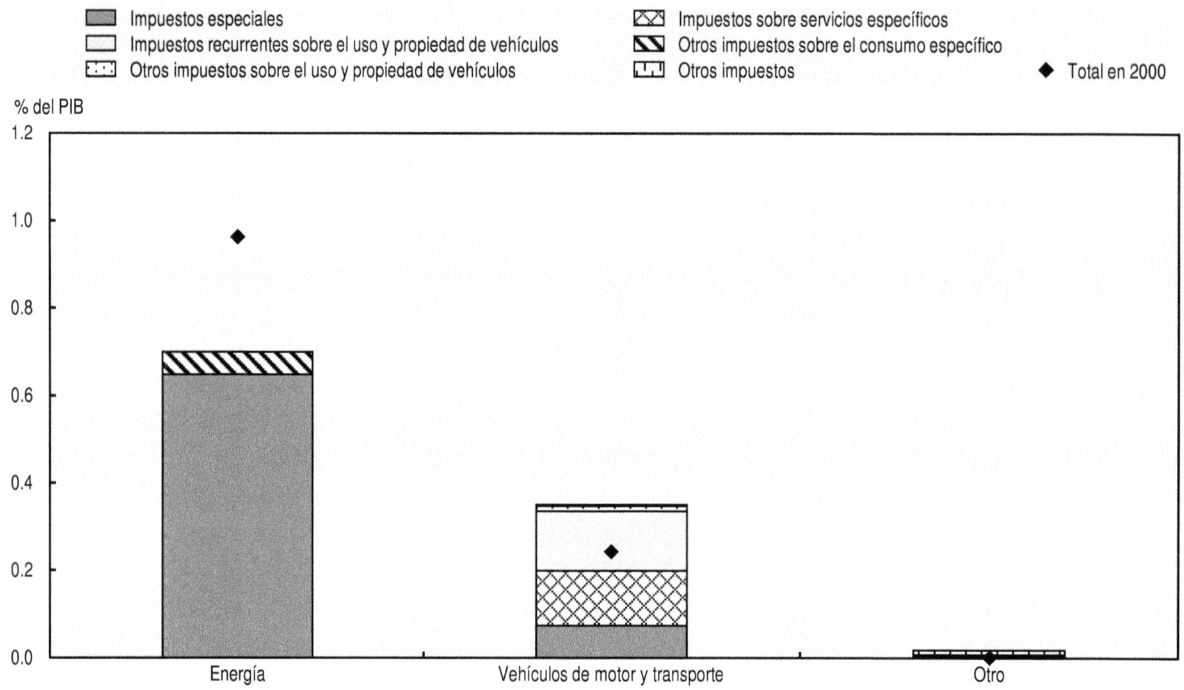

Nota: Barbados, Cuba y Venezuela están excluidos de los promedios de ALC. No ha sido posible identificar los ingresos relacionados con el impuesto al medio ambiente para Barbados y Cuba. Venezuela está excluida debido a problemas de disponibilidad de datos.

Fuente: Base de datos PINE para Chile y México y cálculos de los autores con base (OCDE/CEPAL/CIAT/BID, 2019[2]), capítulo 5.

StatLink *https://doi.org/10.1787/888933940472*

Tres países de América Latina, Chile, Colombia y México, han introducido impuestos sobre el carbono en estos últimos años:

- En Chile, se aprobó una importante reforma tributaria que incluye nuevos impuestos relacionados con el medio ambiente en 2014 (OECD/CEPAL, 2016[29]). Estas incluyen un impuesto sobre las compras de vehículos motorizados, que se introdujo en 2015 y generó ingresos equivalentes al 0.03% del PIB en 2017. Las tasas impositivas de vehículos automotores dependen de la eficiencia energética y las emisiones. Además, a fines de 2017 se implementó un impuesto al carbono (que se cobrará por primera vez en 2018). Este impuesto se aplica a las emisiones de partículas, óxidos de nitrógeno, dióxido de azufre y dióxido de carbono producidos por establecimientos cuyas calderas o turbinas tienen una capacidad de 50 megavatios térmicos o más.
- México introdujo un impuesto sobre el carbono en 2014, aplicado a la venta e importación de combustibles fósiles de acuerdo con su contenido de carbono. Esto aumentó la proporción de emisiones por la cual se cobró un impuesto, aunque los precios siguen siendo relativamente bajos en comparación con otros países de la OCDE y no reflejan los costos totales asociados con el carbono en estos combustibles (Arlinghaus and van Dender, 2017[30]). Sin embargo, el impuesto al carbono aumentó significativamente los ingresos tributarios entre 2014 y 2015, generando ingresos equivalentes al 1.2% del PIB en 2015 (OCDE, 2018[31]). México incrementó aún más las tasas impositivas sobre diferentes combustibles fósiles en 2016.

- En 2016, Colombia introdujo un impuesto al carbono y un impuesto al consumo sobre las bolsas de plástico. El impuesto al carbono se aplica a los combustibles fósiles (específicamente gasolina, queroseno, combustible para aviones, combustible diesel y fuel oil) dependiendo de la cantidad de carbono. Se aplica un precio de USD 5 por cada tonelada de dióxido de carbono producido por la combustión de combustibles fósiles. Los ingresos se asignarán a un fondo especial para abordar problemas ambientales específicos (erosión costera, conservación de las fuentes de agua y protección del ecosistema) (Monge, 2018[32]). En 2017, este impuesto generó ingresos del 0.1% del PIB.

Effective Carbon Rates (OCDE, 2018[33]) proveen una descripción general de los precios del carbono en todas las emisiones relacionadas con la energía en 42 países de la OCDE y el G20, incluidos Argentina, Brasil, Chile y México. Para el mismo conjunto de países, *Taxing Energy Use* (OCDE, 2018[34]) ofrece información detallada sobre las tasas de impuestos, el uso de la energía y la base a la que se aplican, para el mismo conjunto de países.

Ratio de recaudo del IVA

Esta sección analiza los niveles del VRR en América Latina y el Caribe en 2016 (Gráfico 1.16). La medida del ratio de recaudo del IVA (VRR por sus siglas en inglés) mide la diferencia entre el recaudo observado del IVA y el recaudo teórico o potencial del IVA si este fuese aplicado a una tasa única a toda la base impositiva en un régimen de IVA "puro" (OCDE, 2018[35]).

Gráfico 1.16. **Ratio de recaudo del IVA (VRR) en países de ALC, 2016**

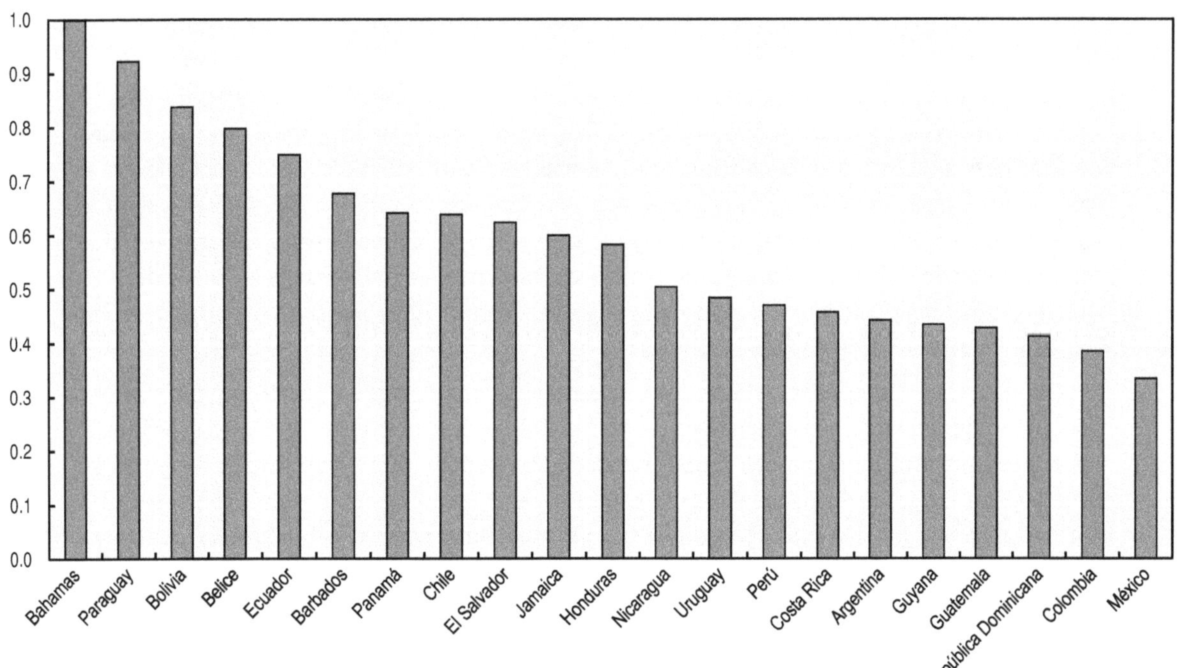

Nota: Brasil, Cuba y Trinidad y Tobago están excluidos. Brasil opera un sistema de tasas múltiples con impuestos cobrados a tasas diferentes para cada nivel subnacional. No se disponía de información subyacente desde 2009 para Trinidad y Tobago. Cuba no tuvo un sistema de IVA en 2016. Venezuela está excluida debido a problemas de disponibilidad de datos.

Fuente: Las tasas de IVA provienen de los sitios web CIAT, Trading Economics y Deloitte, las cifras de consumo final de gastos del sitio web de la División de Estadística de las Naciones Unidas y los ingresos del IVA de las tablas de países del capítulo 5 de (OCDE/CEPAL/CIAT/BID, 2019[2]).

StatLink https://doi.org/10.1787/888933940491

- México y Colombia tienen los índices más bajos de VRR, de 0.33 y 0.38 respectivamente, mientras que las Bahamas y Paraguay tienen los más altos (de 0.99 y 0.92 respectivamente).
- Las Bahamas introdujeron el IVA en 2015 siguiendo las buenas prácticas internacionales: un IVA de base amplia con una tasa estándar baja, un número limitado de exenciones y tasas no reducidas. En las Bahamas, la tasa estándar es del 7.5% (una de las tasas más bajas en la región de ALC, donde la tasa promedio del IVA estándar es del 14.4%) y los ingresos por IVA en las Bahamas en 2017 triplicaron el monto recaudado en 2015 (en términos nominales), en gran parte debido a los nuevos sistemas para recaudar ingresos tributarios (Schlotterbeck, 2017$_{[36]}$).
- Paraguay tuvo la segunda VRR más alta en el grupo seleccionado de países de ALC en 2016 con un 0.92. Esto se explica en parte por las mejoras en la administración tributaria desde 2004 (FMI, 2017$_{[37]}$). Estas incluían medidas para ampliar la base del IVA, un nuevo marco legal para impuestos y aduanas que permitió la modernización de los controles y mejores sistemas de recaudación de ingresos (FMI, 2010$_{[38]}$).

Varios elementos pueden explicar el bajo VRR en México, como el alcance de las exenciones al IVA, la aplicación de una tasa cero nacional númerosos bienes y servicios, una tasa reducida del 11% en zonas fronterizas y también un bajo nivel de cumplimiento. Una reforma al IVA se implementó en enero de 2014 que extendió la tasa estándar de 16% a las zonas fronterizas, eliminando las tasas diferenciadas. La reforma también eliminó la tasa cero sobre hoteles y sobre los servicios provistos a extranjeros, que ahora se encuentran gravados a la tasa estándar, y se ajustó el régimen de las maquiladoras para reducir el riesgo al fraude. El VRR en México se incrementó de 0.4 puntos entre 2013 y 2014.

Impuestos por nivel de gobierno

En países de ALC, el recaudo tributario es recolectado sobre todo a nivel del gobierno central o federal; los gobiernos subnacionales dependen más de un sistema de transferencias de niveles superiores a niveles inferiores de gobierno para su financiamiento que en el caso de los países de la OCDE. Para los países en los cuales se dispone de datos de recaudo subnacional en ALC, los ingresos tributarios a nivel del gobierno central constituyen dos tercios o más de todo el recaudo. El monto correspondiente en países de la OCDE es de 60%. Brasil es una excepción notable dado que el gobierno central recaudó un 44% de todos los ingresos totales en 2016 (Cuadro 1.1).[11]

Existen dos elementos estadísticos que deben considerarse cuando se compara la atribución del recaudo para los países de ALC y el de países miembro de la OCDE. Primero, los ingresos tributarios de ambos grupos han sido atribuidos a diferentes niveles de gobierno de acuerdo a las guías revisadas en la versión final del Sistema de Cuentas Nacionales (SCN). Esto implica que los ingresos son generalmente atribuidos al nivel del gobierno que ejerce la potestad de aplicar el impuesto o tiene la potestad de imponer o modificar la tasa del impuesto. Esto tiene implicaciones en situaciones en las que un nivel del gobierno recauda el impuesto y transfiere lo recaudado parcial o totalmente a otros niveles de gobierno. Algunos ejemplos de este tipo de mecanismos son la Ley de Coparticipaciones en Argentina, y las Participaciones Federales en México (regida por la Ley de Coordinación Fiscal), y la participación de los fondos en Brasil (definida en el artículo 159 de la constitución). El segundo elemento es que los promedios en ALC pueden verse afectados por la falta de datos a nivel subnacional en algunos países.

Para los 19 países de ALC para los que se dispone datos en 2016, el porcentaje de ingresos tributarios totales recaudado por los gobiernos subnacionales es inferior al 8%, exceptuando a Argentina, Brasil y Colombia. En Brasil, los estados y las municipalidades recaudan alrededor de 25% de todos los ingresos tributarios, lo que indica un alto grado de descentralización tributaria. Una gran parte del IVA (ICMS – imposto sobre operações relativas à circulação de mercadorias e prestação de serviços de transporte interestadual e intermunicipal e de comunicação) es recaudado a nivel del estado. El recaudo subnacional en Argentina y Colombia representa más del 15% del recaudo nacional total. Argentina tiene un recaudo sustancial a nivel provincial, el cual se explica en gran parte por el impuesto sobre los ingresos brutos. Entre 2000 y 2016, el recaudo tributario a nivel subnacional disminuyó en seis países y aumentó en siete. La mayor caída de se dio en Uruguay (4.1% del recaudo nacional total) y el incremento más grande fue en Brasil (1.4% del recaudo nacional total).

Estas cifras reflejan el hecho de que los gobiernos subnacionales en los países de ALC tienden a tener bajo su jurisdicción impuestos de bases estrechas. Los impuestos que con mayor frecuencia son asignados a los gobiernos subnacionales son los impuestos sobre la propiedad, sobre vehículos automotores e impuestos sobre servicios específicos y tasas municipales. El potencial de los ingresos tributarios de estos impuestos es mucho más limitado si se compara con los impuestos bajo la jurisdicción de gobiernos centrales o federales, tales como el IVA o los impuestos sobre la renta. En 2016, todo el recaudo subnacional de Belice, Guatemala, Jamaica y Trinidad y Tobago y más del 50% del recaudo subnacional en Paraguay, Perú y Uruguay provino de los impuestos sobre la propiedad (Gráfico 1.17). Todos los otros países dependen del recaudo proveniente de los impuestos sobre bienes y utilidades. México es el único país que utiliza bases tributarias diferentes a las descritas anteriormente. En 2016, el 42% del recaudo subnacional en México procedió de impuestos sobre la nómina. En los países miembros de la OCDE, las entidades subnacionales tienden a tener impuestos cuyas bases son mucho más amplias. Una proporción significativa del recaudo de los gobiernos subnacionales en los países de la OCDE tuvo origen en los impuestos sobre la renta y utilidades (representó más de un tercio del recaudo promedio total a nivel subnacional).

Los bajos niveles de recaudo subnacional en ALC pueden también ser el resultado de una capacidad administrativa y técnica reducida. Los impuestos sobre la propiedad requieren sistemas sofisticados de información, lo que aumenta el costo de recaudo de este impuesto. Además, los registros catastrales están ausentes en varios países y cuando existen rara vez se actualizan (BID, 2012[39]). Como resultado, las autoridades tributarias no pueden acceder a valoraciones precisas de tierras y edificios, aunado a ello, las agencias de bienes y raíces no siempre están dispuestas a compartir esta información. Los impuestos sobre la propiedad también son susceptibles de sufrir altos niveles de informalidad: los edificios son muchas veces construidos sin los permisos adecuados, muchas propiedades no se encuentran registradas y los precios de venta de los bienes inmuebles son muchas veces falsificados. El impuesto sobre la propiedad es uno de los impuestos más controversiales en los ojos del ciudadano y conlleva altos costos políticos, por lo que las administraciones de gobiernos locales rara vez están dispuestas a invertir en los recursos necesarios para recaudar este impuesto.

Gráfico 1.17. **Estructura de los ingresos tributarios subnacionales en países de ALC, 2016**

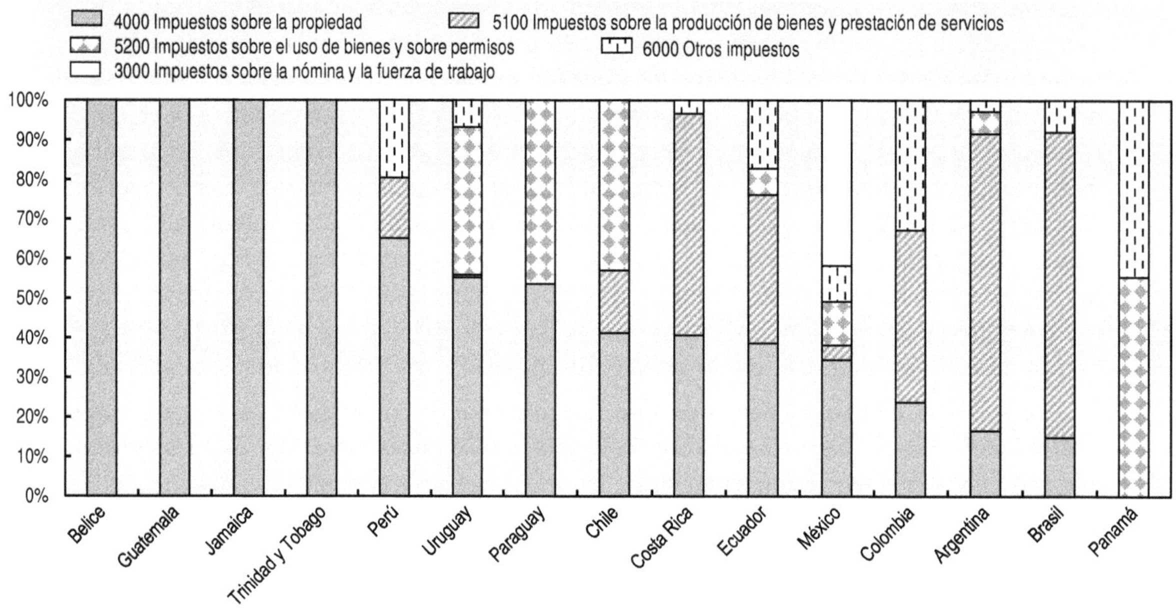

Nota: El año de comparación es 2016 ya que los datos de 2017 no estaban disponibles para México.
Las Bahamas, Barbados, Bolivia, Cuba, República Dominicana, El Salvador, Honduras, Nicaragua, Paraguay y Venezuela quedan excluidos dado que los datos de los ingresos impositivos subnacionales o el desglose de los mismos por tipos de categorías tributarias principales no están disponibles. Las cifras excluyen los ingresos del gobierno local para Argentina (pero incluyen los ingresos provinciales).

Fuente: Elaboración propia con base en (OCDE/CEPAL/CIAT/BID, 2019[2]), cuadros del capítulo 6.

StatLink https://doi.org/10.1787/888933940510

Cuadro 1.1. **Atribución de los ingresos tributarios por subsector del gobierno general, 1995, 2000, 2016**

Porcentaje del recaudo tributario total

	Gobierno central			Gobierno estatal o regional			Gobierno local			Fondos de seguridad social		
	1995	2000	2016	1995	2000	2016	1995	2000	2016	1995	2000	2016
Países federales												
Argentina	59.0	66.4	61.1	17.5	17.8	16.8	..	..	..	23.4	15.8	22.2
Brasil	44.7	47.8	43.9	26.8	25.3	24.4	3.7	3.4	5.9	24.8	23.5	25.9
México	73.9	79.3	81.5	2.8	2.5	4.2	1.5	1.0	1.6	21.8	17.2	13.9
Venezuela	94.6	94.6	..	0.0	0.0	..	0.0	0.0	..	5.4	5.4	..
País régional												
Colombia	63.2	68.6	73.3	5.5	5.6	4.6	0.0	0.0	0.0	22.7	16.4	15.6
Países unitarios	89.1	88.1	84.4				0.5	0.7	0.7	6.3	5.8	8.0
Bahamas	85.3	84.3	91.7				5.0	6.3	4.7	0.0	7.3	16.9
Barbados	93.2	93.5	91.4				6.5	7.9	7.8	3.6	4.4	5.7
Belice	95.0	86.4	78.4				1.6	1.9	3.0	33.0	34.8	37.8
Bolivia	89.9	87.8	86.4				0.0	0.0	0.0	11.3	10.4	12.6
Chile	89.9	87.8	86.9				6.5	7.9	7.6	3.6	4.4	5.6
Costa Rica	68.4	66.8	63.4				..	2.0	3.3	30.0	31.2	33.3
Cuba	88.7	89.6	87.1				..	..	..	11.3	10.4	12.9
República Dominicana	99.3	98.9	99.6				..	..	..	0.7	1.1	0.4
Ecuador	70.5	86.1	73.6				4.0	1.8	2.5	25.5	12.1	23.9
El Salvador	85.9	83.4	87.2				..	..	1.9	14.1	16.6	10.9
Guatemala	83.7	83.6	82.2				0.6	0.9	1.1	15.6	15.5	16.6
Guyana	92.6	88.6	89.6				..	..	..	7.4	11.4	10.4
Honduras	90.1	89.4	85.5				..	..	..	9.9	10.6	14.5

Cuadro 1.1. **Atribución de los ingresos tributarios por subsector del gobierno general, 1995, 2000, 2016** *(cont.)*

Porcentaje del recaudo tributario total

	Gobierno central			Gobierno estatal o regional			Gobierno local			Fondos de seguridad social		
	1995	2000	2016	1995	2000	2016	1995	2000	2016	1995	2000	2016
Jamaica	..	99.3	94.5				..	0.7	1.7	..	0.0	3.8
Nicaragua	84.1	80.0	69.8				..	..	..	15.9	20.0	23.5
Panama	62.0	59.8	61.5				..	2.2	1.6	38.0	38.0	36.9
Paraguay	..	82.7	76.4				..	..	4.0	..	17.3	19.6
Perú	88.1	87.8	85.0				..	..	..	11.9	12.2	12.0
Trinidad y Tobago	61.1	61.3	64.1				0.0	0.0	0.0	14.7	15.7	8.3
Uruguay	59.0	66.4	61.1				8.4	8.4	4.5	30.1	29.6	27.6

Nota. Las cifras excluyen los ingresos del gobierno local para Argentina (pero incluyen ingresos provinciales), Las Bahamas, Barbados, Bolivia (antes de 1994), Cuba, República Dominicana, El Salvador (antes de 2015), Honduras, Jamaica (antes de 1998), Nicaragua, Panamá (antes de 1998), Paraguay (antes de 2004), Perú (antes de 2001) y Venezuela dado que los datos no se encuentran disponibles.
Colombia es constitucionalmente un país unitario con alta autonomía de sus territorios.

Fuente: (OCDE/CEPAL/CIAT/BID, 2019[2]), cuadro 4.11.

StatLink https://doi.org/10.1787/888933940548

Notas

1. Esta cifra es provisional y se ha calculado aplicando el porcentaje de cambio promedio no ponderado para 2017 en los 34 países que proporcionan datos para ese año a la relación entre el impuesto promedio general y el PIB en 2016.
2. El Caribe incluye seis países (Bahamas, Barbados, Belice, Guyana, Jamaica y Trinidad y Tobago), América Central y México nueve países (Costa Rica, Cuba, República Dominicana, El Salvador, Guatemala, Honduras, México, Nicaragua y Panamá) y América del Sur nueve países (Argentina, Bolivia, Brasil, Chile, Colombia, Ecuador, Paraguay, Perú y Uruguay).
3. Un impuesto que se aplica a las mercancías importadas en Barbados y a las manufacturas nacionales.
4. Estos incluyen Argentina; Brasil, Bolivia, Chile, Colombia, Costa Rica, Ecuador, Honduras, México, Nicaragua, Panamá y Perú.
5. El IVA se introdujo en 1991 en Jamaica, 1997 en Barbados, 2006 en Belice (el Impuesto General a las Ventas), 2007 en Guyana y 2014 en las Bahamas.
6. Alrededor del 2.1% del recaudo tributario total son ingresos de impuestos sobre ingresos y ganancias que no se pueden asignar entre el impuesto a las ganancias corporativo y el impuesto a las ganancias personales.
7. Para el Caribe, el ingreso promedio de los impuestos sobre los ingresos y las ganancias oculta una gran heterogeneidad. Las Bahamas no recaudan impuestos sobre la renta y Trinidad y Tobago cobra la mitad de recaudo tributario de esta fuente.
8. El año de comparación es 2016 ya que los datos de 2017 para el promedio de la OCDE no están disponibles.
9. La base de datos PINE de la OCDE (*http://oe.cd/pine*) recopila información detallada a nivel de instrumento que se agrega para generar los ingresos totales. La base de datos soporta el monitoreo, diseño e implementación de políticas efectivas. La base de datos PINE de la OCDE alberga, desde 2005, un conjunto único de información detallada sobre 3 476 instrumentos de política en 94 países, frente a 3 200 instrumentos y 80 países.
10. El promedio no ponderado de los 36 países de la OCDE.
11. El año de comparación es 2016 ya que los datos de 2017 para México no están disponibles.

Referencias

Arlinghaus, J. and K. van Dender (2017), "The environmental tax and subsidy reform in Mexico", *OECD Taxation Working Papers*, No. 31, OECD Publishing, Paris, *https://dx.doi.org/10.1787/a9204f40-en*. [30]

Barreix, A., J. Benitez and M. Pecho (2017), *Revisiting personal income tax in Latin America: Evolution, https://doi.org/10.1787/18151949*. [16]

BID (2013), *More than revenues, Taxation as a development tool*, Inter-American Development Bank. [11]

BID (2012), *Sub-national Revenue Mobilization in Peru, IDB Working Paper Series No. 299.* [39]

Cárdenas Rodríguez, M. and I. Haščič (2018), *The OECD database on Policy Instruments for the Environment: a progress report. OECD document presented at the Working Party of Environmental Information and the Joint Meetings of Tax and Environment Experts., https://one.oecd.org/document/ENV/EPOC/WPEI(2018)7/en/pdf.* [26]

CEPAL (2018), *The Fiscal Panorama of Latin America and the Caribbean*, United Nations, *https://www.cepal.org/en/publications/43406-fiscal-panorama-latin-america-and-caribbean-2018-public-policy-challenges.* [10]

CEPAL (2014), *Tax policy in Latin America: Assessment and guidelines for a second generation of reforms*, United Nations, *https://repositorio.cepal.org/handle/11362/36806.* [15]

CEPAL (2013), *Fiscal Panorama of Latin America and the Caribbean: tax reform and renewal of the fiscal covenant*, United Nations, *https://www.cepal.org/en/publications/3101-fiscal-panorama-latin-america-and-caribbean-2013-tax-reform-and-renewal-fiscal.* [12]

CIAT (2017), *https://www.ciat.org/as-result-of-the-support-provided-by-the-ciat-seco-cooperation-program-the-tax-administration-of-guyana-progresses-in-key-areas/?lang=en.* [4]

EPS-PEAKS (2013), *Taxation and Developing Countries*, Overseas Development Institute training notes, *https://www.odi.org/sites/odi.org.uk/files/odi-assets/events-documents/5045.pdf.* [7]

FMI (2018), *2018 Article IV Consultation, IMF Country Report No. 18/220, https://www.imf.org/en/Publications/CR/Issues/2018/07/16/Guyana-2018-Article-IV-Consultation-Press-Release-and-Staff-Report-46083.* [5]

FMI (2018), *World Economic Outlook Database, October.* [19]

FMI (2017), *Paraguay Article IV, IMF Country Report No. 17/233.* [37]

FMI (2016), *Argentina 2016 Article IV Consultation, IMF country report No. 16/346, https://www.imf.org/external/pubs/ft/scr/2016/cr16346.pdf.* [14]

FMI (2010), *Paraguay: Selected Issues", IMF Country Report No. 10/170.* [38]

IBFD (2017), *IBFD Tax Research Platform, https://online.ibfd.org/.* [6]

Marten, M. and K. Van Dender (2019), *(forthcoming), The use of revenues from carbon pricing. OECD Taxation Working Papers*, OECD. [27]

Medina, Jonelis and Cangul (2017), *The Informal Economy in Sub-Saharan Africa : Size and Determinants , IMF Working Paper No. 17/156.* [23]

Melguizo, A. et al. (2017), *No sympathy for the devil! Policy priorities to overcome the middle-income trap in Latin America*, OECD, *http://dx.doi.org/10.1787/26b78724-en.* [18]

Ministry of Foreign Affairs in The Hague (2018), *Doing Business in Bolivia, https://www.nederlandwereldwijd.nl/...in-bolivia.../Doing+Business+in+Bolivia.pdf.* [8]

Monge, C. (2018), *Colombia Puts a Tax on Carbon, https://www.conservationfinancenetwork.org/2018/11/27/colombia-puts-tax-on-carbon.* [32]

OCDE (2018), *Consumption Tax Trends 2018: VAT/GST and Excise Rates, Trends and Policy Issues*, OECD publishing, *https://doi.org/10.1787/ctt-2018-en.* [35]

OCDE (2018), *Effective Carbon Rates 2018: Pricing Carbon Emissions Through Taxes and Emissions Trading*, OCDE Publishing, Paris, *https://doi.org/10.1787/9789264305304-en.* [33]

OCDE (2018), *Pine Database, http://oe.cd/pine.* [31]

OCDE (2018), *Taxing Energy Use 2018: Companion to the Taxing Energy Use Database*, OECD Publishing, Paris, *https://doi.org/10.1787/9789264289635-en.* [34]

OCDE (2014), *Development Co-operation Report 2014: Mobilising Resources for Sustainable Development*, OECD Publishing, Paris, *https://dx.doi.org/10.1787/dcr-2014-en.* [1]

OCDE (2005), *https://stats.oecd.org/glossary/detail.asp?ID=6437.* [25]

OCDE/BID/CIAT (2016), *Taxing Wages in Latin America and the Caribbean 2016*, OECD Publishing, Paris, *https://dx.doi.org/10.1787/9789264262607-en.* [24]

OCDE/BID/El Banco Mundial (2014), *Pensions at a Glance: Latin America and the Caribbean*, OECD Publishing, Paris, *https://dx.doi.org/10.1787/pension_glance-2014-en.* [22]

OCDE/CAF/CEPAL (2018), *Perspectivas económicas de América Latina 2018: Repensando las instituciones para el desarrollo*, OECD Publishing, Paris, *https://dx.doi.org/10.1787/leo-2018-es*. [3]

OCDE/CAF/CEPAL/UE (2019), *Perspectivas económicas de América Latina 2019: Desarrollo en transición*, OECD Publishing, Paris, *https://doi.org/10.1787/g2g9ff1a-es*. [9]

OCDE/CEPAL/CIAT/BID (2019), *Estadísticas tributarias en América Latina y el Caribe 2019*. [2]

OCDE/CIAT/BID/CEPAL (2018), *Estadísticas tributarias en América Latina y el Caribe 2018*, OECD Publishing, Paris, *https://dx.doi.org/10.1787/rev_lat_car-2018-en-fr*. [17]

OCDE/CIAT/CEPAL/BID (2015), *Revenue Statistics in Latin America and the Caribbean 2015*, OECD Publishing, Paris, *https://dx.doi.org/10.1787/rev_lat-2015-en-fr*. [21]

OCDE/ITF (próxima publicación) (2019), *Tax revenue implications from the decarbonisation of road transport: scenarios for Slovenia*, OCDE. [28]

OECD/CAF/UN ECLAC (2018), *Latin American Economic Outlook 2018: Rethinking Institutions for Development*, OECD Publishing, Paris, *https://dx.doi.org/10.1787/leo-2018-en*. [50]

OCDE/CEPAL (2016), *OECD Environmental Performance Reviews: Chile 2016*, OECD Environmental Performance Reviews, OCDE Publishing, Paris, *https://dx.doi.org/10.1787/9789264252615-en*. [29]

Schlotterbeck, S. (2017), *Tax Administration Reforms in the Caribbean, "Challenges, Achievements, and Next Steps"*. [36]

World Grain (2016), *Reforms boost Argentine grain industry*, *https://www.world-grain.com/articles/6457-reforms-boost-argentine-grain-industry*. [13]

Chapter 2

SPECIAL FEATURE

Fiscal revenues from non-renewable natural resources in Latin America and the Caribbean

Capítulo 2

SECCIÓN ESPECIAL

Ingresos fiscales provenientes de recursos naturales no renovables en América Latina y el Caribe

Chapter 2

SPECIAL FEATURE

Fiscal revenues from non-renewable natural resources in Latin America and the Caribbean

Key findings

Fiscal revenues from non-renewable natural resources in 2017

Hydrocarbon revenues in Latin America and the Caribbean stabilised in 2017 after falling sharply between 2014 and 2016. Favourable global oil market conditions allowed hydrocarbon revenues to remain at their 2016 level of 2.3% of gross domestic product (GDP) on average for the eight countries in the region considered in this analysis. Higher international prices supported an increase in revenues from non-tax instruments as the commercial value of production rose. In contrast, tax revenues dipped marginally as profitability remained weak.

Revenues from mining in the region rebounded in 2017, supported by robust global growth and the spill-over effect of significant fiscal and financial stimulus in China in 2016. A surge in tax revenues lifted overall revenues from an average of 0.28% of GDP in 2016 to 0.37% of GDP. Corporate income tax receipts were particularly strong, boosted by higher prices and a decline in tax refunds arising from financial losses in previous years. The increase in the regional average was due to Chile (0.4% of GDP in 2016 to 0.9% of GDP) and Peru (0.3% of GDP to 0.6% of GDP).

Projected fiscal revenues in 2018

ECLAC projections suggest that revenues from non-renewable natural resources increased in 2018. A rally in crude oil prices translated into the first increase in hydrocarbon revenues since 2012, rising from an average of 2.3% of GDP in 2017 to 2.9% of GDP in 2018. In a similar vein, continued strong growth in minerals and metals prices in the first half of 2018 drove mining revenues from 0.4% of GDP in 2017 to 0.5% of GDP in 2018. This result notwithstanding, a sharp correction in crude oil and minerals and metals prices in the second half of the year put in doubt the sustainability of the increase of revenues registered in 2018.

Fiscal revenues from non-renewable natural resources in 2017[1]

Hydrocarbons

Global oil and gas market trends in 2017 were favourable for the region's hydrocarbons producers. In 2017, the global oil market moved slightly into deficit, as oil demand – including crude oil, condensates, liquid natural gas (LNG) and other sources of non-conventional oil – outstripped supply (International Energy Agency, 2018[1]). Demand for oil, which rose from 96.4 million barrels per day in 2016 to 97.9 million barrels per day in 2017, was largely driven by OECD countries as well as China and India. In contrast, there was little change among developing and emerging markets, excluding developing Asia. This pattern largely reflected global macroeconomic conditions, as economic growth rebounded sharply in industrialised countries after a particularly weak 2016.

Oil supply, in contrast, registered restrained growth during the year, rising from 96.9 million barrels per day in 2016 to 97.5 million barrels per day in 2017. As seen in Figure 2.1, global production of strictly crude oil fell 0.9% in 2017, the first decline since the global economic and financial crisis in 2009 (OPEC, 2018[1]). The key factor behind this downturn was a decline in output among members of the Organization of Petroleum Exporting Countries (OPEC), reflecting reduced production quotas established for the first six months of the year and then subsequently extended to cover the entire year by an agreement in May. Additionally, compliance with OPEC's reduced production quotas was strengthened during the year by the vertiginous decline in output in the Bolivarian Republic of Venezuela. In contrast, rising prices led to higher production in the United States, where drilling activity expanded.

Figure 2.1. **Contributions to year-on-year growth in world crude oil production, 2010-17**

(Percentages and percentage points)

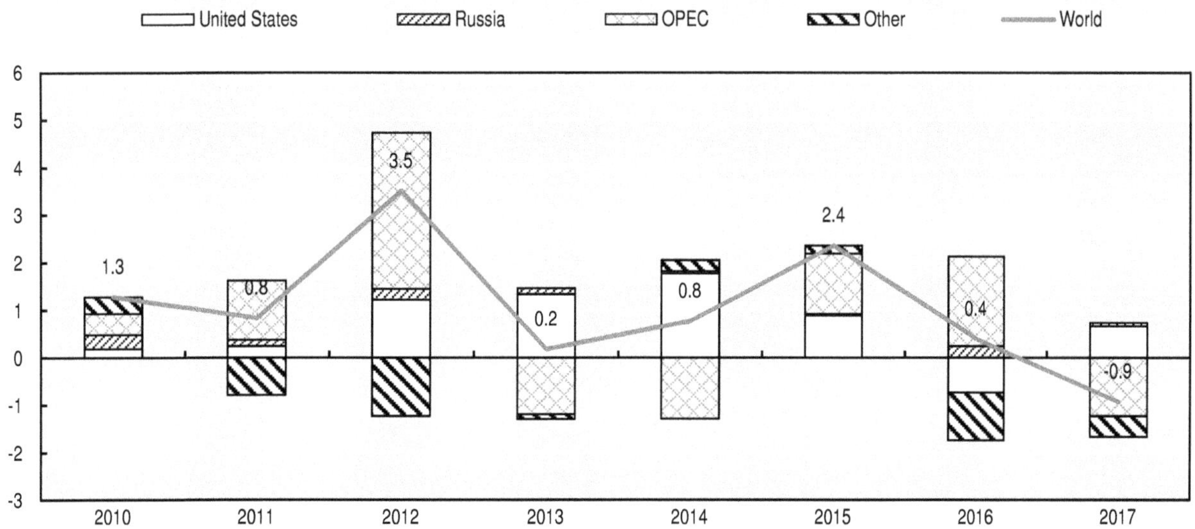

Source: Economic Commission for Latin America and the Caribbean (ECLAC), based on (OPEC, 2018[2]).

StatLink https://doi.org/10.1787/888933940567

As a result of these global trends in supply and demand, the average annual spot price for crude oil increased by 23% in 2017, from USD 43 per barrel to USD 53 per barrel (Figure 2.2). This result notwithstanding, there was significant volatility during the year, as the prevailing spot price slid substantially in the second quarter of the year, only to regain its footing in the third quarter and reach its annual high in the fourth. Geopolitical tensions and climatic factors – such as a particularly cold winter in North America – also helped to drive prices during the year.

After falling precipitously between 2014 and 2016, revenues deriving from the exploration and production of hydrocarbons – up-stream activities – stabilised in 2017 in Latin America and the Caribbean. For the countries under consideration in Table 2.1, average revenues registered no change from a level of 2.3% of GDP in 2016. Tax revenues associated with the sector dipped slightly, reflecting continued weak profitability of the region's principal oil and gas producers, the use of loss carry forward provisions of the tax code to reduce current liabilities and refunds of corporate income tax (CIT) pre-payments that were in excess of final liabilities. Non-tax revenues, however, rose by equal measure supported by higher property rents as the commercial value of production increased.

Figure 2.2. **Crude oil price, January 2013 to December 2017**

In US dollars

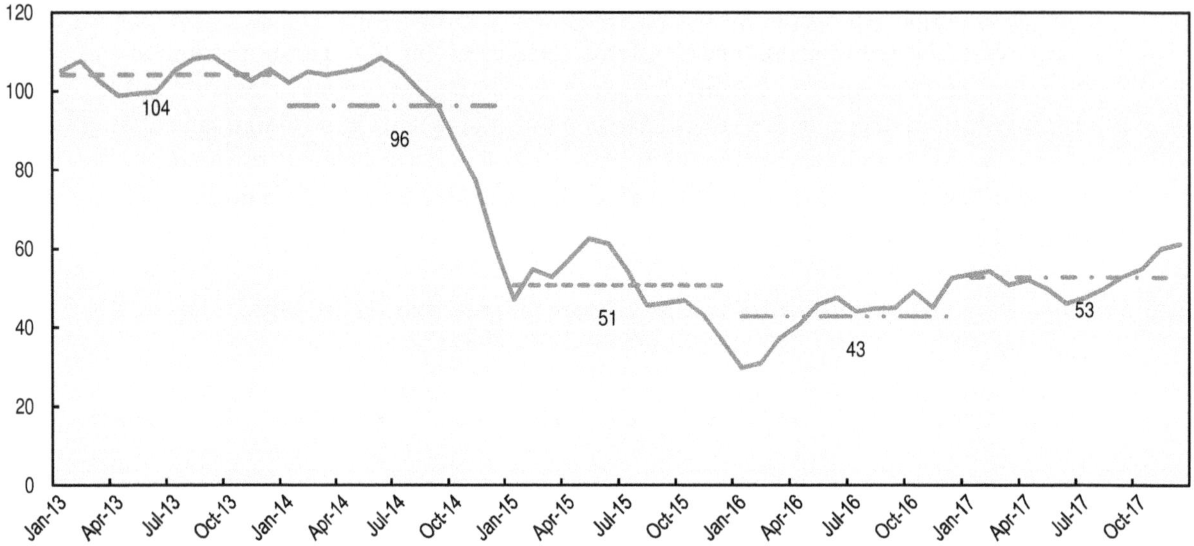

Note: Yearly values correspond to a monthly average.

Source: Economic Commission for Latin America and the Caribbean (ECLAC), based on data from (World Bank, 2018[3]).

StatLink https://doi.org/10.1787/888933940586

Table 2.1. **Hydrocarbon revenues by instrument, 2016-17**

Percentage of GDP

Country	Total		Tax revenues		Non-tax revenues	
	2016	2017	2016	2017	2016	2017
Argentina	0.5	0.4	0.1	0.1	0.3	0.3
Bolivia (Plur. State of)	4.4	4.0	0.3	0.2	4.1	3.8
Brazil	0.3	0.4	0.0	0.0	0.3	0.4
Colombia	0.6	0.7	0.3	0.2	0.3	0.6
Ecuador	5.4	5.6	0.0	0.0	5.4	5.6
Mexico	3.9	3.8	0.0	0.0	3.9	3.8
Peru	0.4	0.5	0.1	0.1	0.3	0.4
Trinidad and Tobago	2.5	2.8	1.4	1.2	1.2	1.6
Simple average	*2.3*	*2.3*	*0.3*	*0.2*	*2.0*	*2.1*

Note: Figures may not sum due to rounding.

Source: ECLAC, based on data from ECLAC's Fiscal Revenues from Non-Renewable Natural Resources in Latin America and the Caribbean database.

StatLink https://doi.org/10.1787/888933940795

Despite the stability of hydrocarbon revenues on average, there was significant heterogeneity at the country level. This reflected the interplay of the evolution of prices, changes in the level of production and country-specific one-off factors that significantly impacted revenues in 2016. In USD terms, oil and gas revenues rose by more than that of the spot crude oil price in Brazil (71% in US dollar terms), Colombia (28%) and Peru (52%) (Table 2.2). In contrast, year-on-year growth in the Plurinational State of Bolivia, Ecuador, Mexico and Trinidad and Tobago was very modest, with rates of 10% or less.

While movement in international prices was the predominant factor behind the evolution of hydrocarbon revenues, variations in production levels also played a role. Average crude oil production declined in 2017, with only Brazil and Peru registering gains (Table 2.2). Extensive exploration and production investments in Brazil during the previous decade have translated into strong gains in output since 2014, although growth has slowed recently. In contrast, rapidly maturing oil fields and limited levels of investment continue to weigh on oil output in Mexico, which dipped by 10% in 2017.

Table 2.2. **Variation in hydrocarbon revenues and production by currency and product, 2016-17**

Year-on-year, percentage change

Country	Revenues		Production	
	National currency	US dollar	Crude oil	Natural gas
Argentina	36	21	-6	0
Bolivia (Plur. State of)	0	0	n.a.	-3
Brazil	57	71	4	15
Colombia	24	28	-3	-7
Ecuador	8	8	-3	n.a.
Mexico	5	3	-10	-12
Peru	47	52	8	-8
Trinidad and Tobago	12	10	0	1
Unweighted average	24	24	-1	-2
Memorandum				
Crude oil		*23*		

Source: Economic Commission for Latin America and the Caribbean (ECLAC), based on data from ECLAC's Fiscal Revenues from Non-Renewable Natural Resources in Latin America and the Caribbean database, production data from (OPEC, 2018[2])and price data from (World Bank, 2018[3]).

StatLink https://doi.org/10.1787/888933940814

The decline in oil output in several countries also led to a reduction in natural gas production, as gas is often a by-product of crude oil production. This phenomenon was especially apparent among larger oil producers such as Colombia, Ecuador and Mexico (Table 2.2). In Bolivia – the largest natural gas exporter in South America – production levels fell due to a decline in export volumes to Brazil (14.2%) as a result of greater generation of hydroelectric power in Brazil during the year (Ministerio de Economía y Finanzas de Bolivia, 2018[3]). Falling gas production in Peru (8%) reflected a decline in domestic demand for gas used in electricity generation (PERUPETRO, 2018[4]).

In Brazil, revenues from oil and gas extraction rose from 0.3% of GDP in 2016 to 0.4% of GDP in 2017, due in large part to a recovery in the government's special participation in production and higher CIT receipts. Revenues from the special participation payment – calculated on the basis of progressive rates on net production revenues adjusted for royalties, exploration investments, operating costs, depreciation and taxes – nearly doubled in 2017 after falling sharply the previous year as companies with concession contracts wrote off exceptionally large investments in exploration.

Hydrocarbon revenues in Peru rose from 0.4% of GDP in 2016 to 0.5% of GDP, despite the aforementioned decline in natural gas production. Higher international prices and an increase in oil production translated into an up-tick in revenues from royalties and hydrocarbon service contracts. The rise in royalty payments was supported by an increase in LNG exports to European markets, where prices are generally higher than in Peru's other traditional markets, such as Mexico (PERUPETRO, 2018[4]). Notably, CIT receipts from the overall hydrocarbon sector doubled during the year, after having reached their lowest level in 2016 – in national currency terms – since 2005.

In Colombia, the increase in oil and gas revenues, which rose from 0.6% of GDP in 2016 to 0.7% of GDP in 2017, was driven largely by a recovery in non-tax receipts. In particular, revenues from the "High Prices" production levy – triggered when the spot price of an international reference price, in this case West Texas Intermediate, exceeds a level established in a company's exploration and production contract – rebounded after falling sharply the previous year (67%) due to exceptionally low oil prices. Dividends received by the central government from EcoPetrol also increased during the year.

In 2017, hydrocarbon revenues in Trinidad and Tobago registered their first increase since 2014. Total revenues rose from 2.5% of GDP in 2016 to 2.8% of GDP, with a dip in tax revenues offset by higher non-tax revenues. Tax revenues remained weak due largely to a substantial decline in receipts from withholdings taxes. Non-tax revenues, in contrast, rose from 1.2% of GDP in 2016 to 1.6% of GDP. Revenues from royalties registered a strong increase as a result of the rise in price and higher-than-expected production, which remained relatively unchanged between years as opposed to a projected decline. Similar factors also bolstered revenues from production-sharing contracts.

In contrast, oil revenues in Mexico slipped in 2017, falling from 3.9% of GDP in 2016 to 3.8% of GDP (although they rose slightly in US dollar terms), despite the boost provided by the rebound in prices. This decline reflected the exceptionally high revenues registered by Petróleos Mexicanos (Pemex) in the previous year thanks to a series of one-off transactions within the public sector. Excluding these inter-governmental transfers, overall oil revenues in 2017 would have risen 20% in US dollar terms. This increase notwithstanding, it would still have lagged that of international oil prices, reflecting the impact of a continued decline in hydrocarbons production in Mexico.

In the Plurinational State of Bolivia, natural gas revenues – especially those from non-tax instruments – registered a significant decline in 2017, falling from 4.4% of GDP in 2016 to 4.0% of GDP. Royalty payments and receipts from the Direct Tax on Hydrocarbons (which, despite its name, is a property rent) were impacted by a decline in sales to Brazil that was not offset by an increase in export volumes to Argentina. The price-fixing mechanism in Bolivia's sales contracts with Argentina and Brazil also played a role in blunting an increase in the commercial value of production during the year. These contracts stipulate that prices are adjusted quarterly based on the average price of a basket of hydrocarbon products in the previous quarter. Therefore, the increase in hydrocarbon prices registered internationally in the fourth quarter of 2017 was only applied from the first quarter of 2018. Tax revenues also trended lower, as lower export volumes and the modest increase in price for Bolivian gas exports weighed on profits and in turn CIT payments.

Mining

Prices for metals and minerals rose in 2017 for the first time since 2011 as strong global macroeconomic fundamentals boosted demand. Key individual factors included a rebound in economic activity in industrialised countries – especially the United States – and the spill-over effect of fiscal and financial stimulus in China in 2016. Strengthened demand for iron ore, for example, was driven in large part by a record-high level of steel production in China arising from global demand for Chinese manufactured goods and large domestic investments in infrastructure and real estate (Vale, 2018[5]).

In contrast, global supply of several key metals and mineral products tightened in 2017. For example, worldwide mine production of copper – a key input for a wide range of activities including construction and the production of electrical components – fell by 0.7% in 2017, led principally by reductions in China and the United States, after posting strong growth in 2015 and 2016 (Figure 2.3). In Chile, the world's largest producer, a 43-day strike at the

Escondida mine, the largest single copper mine in the world, trimmed overall production. Output in Peru, the world's second-largest producer, continued to increase, although its rate of growth slowed significantly, as did its contribution to global growth of copper output.

Figure 2.3. **Contributions to growth in world copper production, 2013-17**

Percentages and percentage points

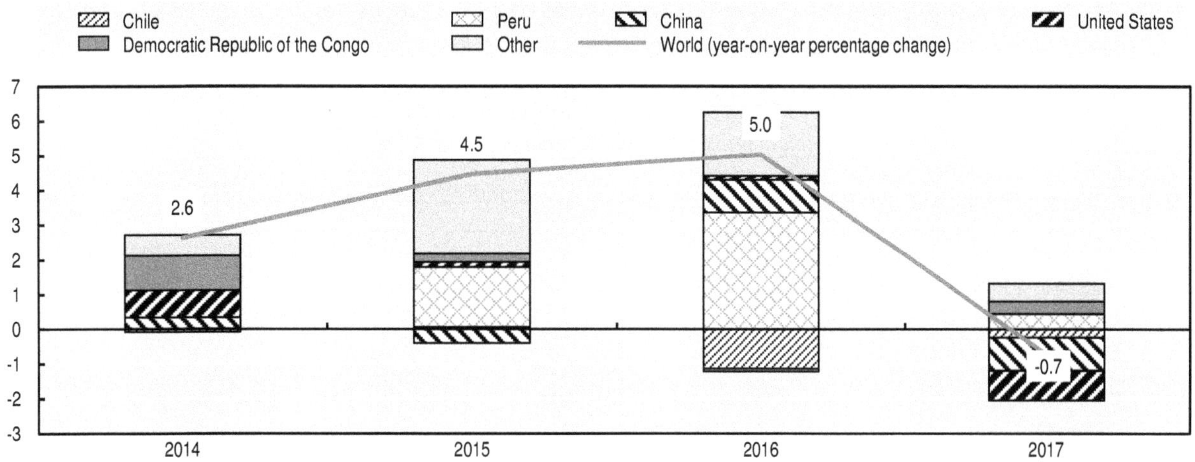

Source: Economic Commission for Latin America and the Caribbean (ECLAC), based on data from (Comisión Chilena del Cobre, 2018[2]).

StatLink https://doi.org/10.1787/888933940605

These factors supported a rally in international prices for a wide range of industrial metals and minerals (Figure 2.4). The increase in the prices for these goods, which had shown greater dynamism over the course of 2016, peaked in the first quarter of 2017 before settling into relatively steady inter-annual growth of 20% during the rest of the year. The prices of some goods, however, experienced significant volatility. Iron ore prices surged in the fourth quarter of 2016 and the first quarter of 2017 on the back of a jump in global steel production but began to give up some of their gains by the end of the year.

Figure 2.4. **Variation of international prices for selected metals and minerals, 2015-17**

Year-on-year, by quarter

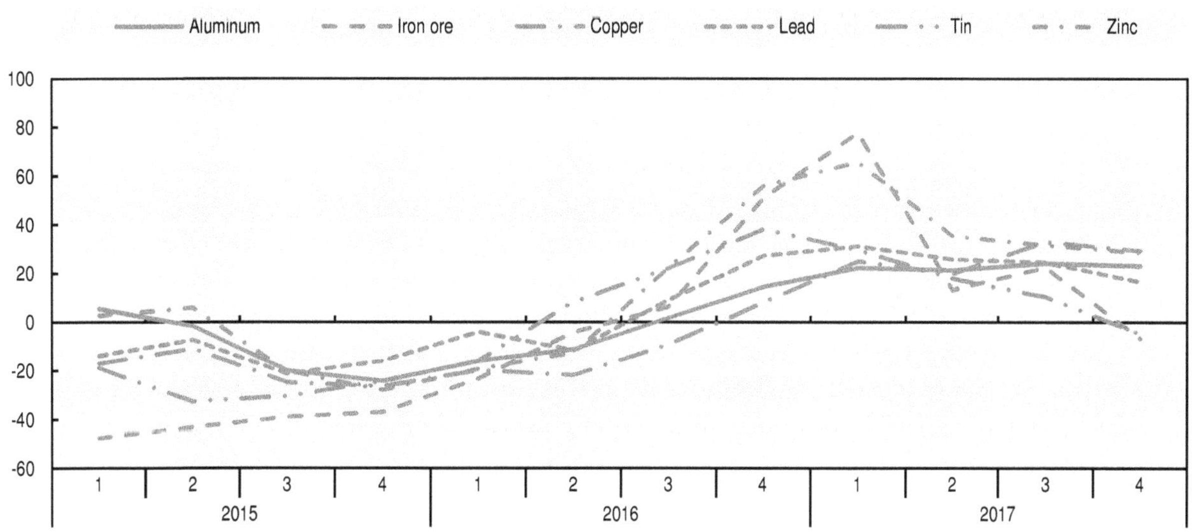

Source: Economic Commission for Latin America and the Caribbean (ECLAC), based on data from (World Bank, 2018[3]).

StatLink https://doi.org/10.1787/888933940624

Mining revenues in Latin America and the Caribbean rebounded in 2017. Rising commodity prices set the stage for the first increase in mining revenues in the region since 2011. While the rebound was modest, from 0.28% of GDP in 2016 to 0.37% of GDP in 2017, it was evident across most countries (Table 2.3). The regional average was most strongly affected by increases in Chile and Peru. Rising revenues were essentially due to higher tax receipts, which rose from 0.12% of GDP in 2016 to 0.20% of GDP in 2017, due in large part to the high elasticity of CIT payments to changes in prices. In contrast, average non-tax revenues– principally stemming from property rents such as royalties – registered little change over the period.

Table 2.3. **Mining revenues by instrument, 2016-17**

Percentage of GDP and percentage points of GDP

Country	Total		Tax revenues		Non-tax revenues	
	2016	2017	2016	2017	2016	2017
Argentina	0.02	0.04	0.01	0.03	0.01	0.01
Bolivia (Plur. State of)	0.79	0.75	0.34	0.26	0.45	0.49
Brazil	0.07	0.07	0.03	0.04	0.03	0.03
Chile	0.38	0.95	0.02	0.46	0.37	0.48
Codelco	*0.37*	*0.49*	*0.01*	*0.01*	*0.37*	*0.48*
Private producers	*0.01*	*0.45*	*0.01*	*0.45*	*0.00*	*0.00*
Colombia	0.27	0.29	0.07	0.06	0.20	0.23
Jamaica	0.14	0.02	0.00	0.00	0.14	0.02
Mexico	0.17	0.19	0.15	0.16	0.03	0.03
Peru	0.30	0.62	0.17	0.46	0.13	0.16
Dominican Republic	0.39	0.43	0.33	0.37	0.07	0.06
Simple average	*0.28*	*0.37*	*0.12*	*0.20*	*0.16*	*0.17*

Note: May not sum due to rounding.

Source: Economic Commission for Latin America and the Caribbean (ECLAC), based on data from ECLAC's Fiscal Revenues from Non-Renewable Natural Resources in Latin America and the Caribbean database.

StatLink https://doi.org/10.1787/888933940833

Viewed in terms of the average inter-annual variation in national currency and US dollar terms – 33% and 35%, respectively – the up-tick in mining revenues was generally in line with movements in prevailing prices for the region's key metals and mineral products (Table 2.4). However, results at the country level were varied, reflecting differences in product specialisation as well as movements in exchanges rates. In contrast to previous years, the currencies of the region's major producers tended to appreciate in 2017 – for example, in Brazil, Chile, Colombia and Peru – reducing the increase in revenues as expressed in national currency and, hence, relative to GDP.

As is apparent from Tables 2.3 and 2.4, some countries in the region registered much greater increases in mining revenues during the year than might have been expected given the evolution of metal and mineral prices. This was largely thanks to an upswing in CIT payments or from revenues deriving from other instruments whose tax base is based on income, such as Chile's special mining tax. These revenues had been severely reduced in previous years as the continual decline in international prices drove down profitability amongst the region's major producers, to the point where some reported losses. In some countries, this trend was further aggravated by large deductions for investments in fixed assets as well as the use of loss carry-forward provisions of the tax code to lower their current tax liabilities. As a result, in countries such as Argentina, Chile and Peru, mining revenues more than doubled from their 2016 levels. This was in line with an industry-wide trend, as income tax payments from the world's largest mining companies rose by an estimated 81% in 2017 (PwC, $2018_{[3]}$).

Table 2.4. **Yearly variation in hydrocarbons revenues by currency, 2016-17**

Percentage

Country	National currency	US dollar
Argentina	127	102
Bolivia (Plur. State of)	5	5
Brazil	10	20
Chile	163	174
Codelco	*39*	*45*
Private firms	*6 658*	*6 951*
Colombia	29	33
Dominican Republic	18	15
Jamaica	-81	-81
Mexico	23	21
Peru	122	130
Simple average	33	35
Memorandum		
Aluminium		*23*
Coal		*34*
Copper		*27*
Gold		*1*
Iron ore		*23*
Lead		*24*
Nickel		*8*
Tin		*12*
Zinc		*38*

Source: Economic Commission for Latin America and the Caribbean (ECLAC), based on data from ECLAC's Fiscal Revenues from Non-Renewable Natural Resources in Latin America and the Caribbean database and price data from (World Bank, 2018[3]).

StatLink https://doi.org/10.1787/888933940852

Perhaps the most emblematic of these cases is Chile, the world's largest producer of copper, where mining revenues rose from 0.38% of GDP in 2016 to 0.95% of GDP in 2017. The large increase in tax revenues, which drove this result, was due to a recovery in income tax payments by private producers as profitability improved. In 2016, receipts from these firms were essentially nil – including a net refund of taxes paid for the Special Tax on Mining, whose tax base is operating income, as pre-payments exceeded final tax liabilities. However, these revenues rose sharply in 2017, from 0.01% of GDP in 2016 to 0.45% of GDP (a 6,951% increase in US dollar terms). There was also a significant up-tick in withholding tax payments by private producers as they availed themselves of a concessional tax rate for making distributions of previously untaxed accumulated earnings before a new tax regime came into force.[2] For example, BHP Billiton Chile paid a once-off USD 2.3 billion (equivalent to 0.8% of Chile's GDP) dividend to its foreign parent, resulting in a withholding tax payment of USD 373 million (BHP, 2018[8]).

In contrast, mining revenues in Jamaica fell to nearly nil relative to GDP in 2017 (an 81% reduction in US dollar terms), reflecting the impact of the ongoing restructuring of the country's bauxite and alumina industry. The government has offered temporary waivers of up to 100% on the payment of the bauxite levy – the principal generator of mining revenues – to several of the country's largest producers to bolster investment and protect employment. In addition, in fiscal year 2017/18, the government modified the bauxite levy regime, entering into bespoke fiscal regime agreements with individual companies. The content of these arrangements differs significantly by producer, resulting in large differences in the tax treatment of companies operating in the same sector.

Projected fiscal revenues from non-renewable natural resources for 2018

Hydrocarbon revenues in 2018 are estimated to have registered their first increase since 2011, rising from 2.3% of GDP in 2017 to 2.9% of GDP (Figure 2.5). At the country level, oil and gas revenues are projected to increase by 0.5 percentage points of GDP or more in Brazil and Colombia and by 1 percentage point of GDP or more in Ecuador and Trinidad and Tobago. The impetus for this recovery was provided by a 29% increase in the annual average price for spot crude, which was supported by continued robust global growth and demand as well as limited supply from OPEC countries. Nevertheless, in the last two months of the year, there was a marked slide in the price of oil, with the year-on-year variation in spot crude falling by 12% in December, suggesting an increase in the downside risks for the medium term.

Figure 2.5. **Fiscal revenues from non-renewable natural resources, 2010-18**

Percentage of GDP

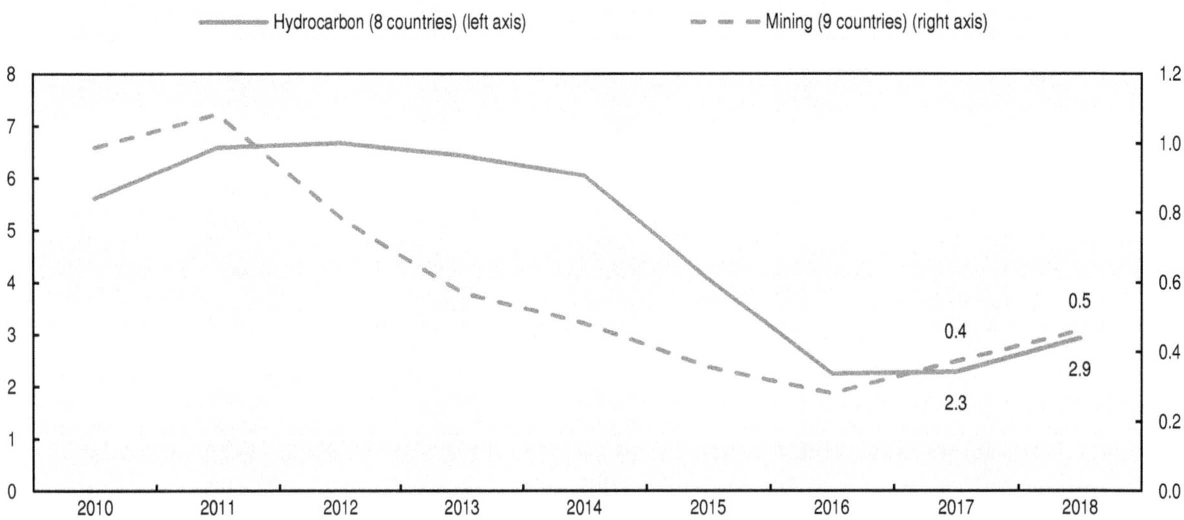

Note: Mining includes: Argentina, Bolivia (Plurinational State of), Brazil, Chile, Colombia, Dominican Republic, Jamaica, Mexico and Peru. Hydrocarbons include: Argentina, Bolivia (Plurinational State of), Brazil, Colombia, Ecuador, Mexico, Peru, and Trinidad and Tobago. Values for 2018 are based on official government estimates from 2019 budget documents or from preliminary annual figures. When figures for 2018 were not available they were estimated using monthly data (typically for the first ten months of the year). When monthly data was not available, revenues were estimated by applying the year-on-year change in the price for the most representative product – or basket of products in the case of mining – for the country, expressed in national currency terms, to 2017 revenues.

Source: Economic Commission for Latin America and the Caribbean (ECLAC), based on data from ECLAC's Fiscal Revenues from Non-Renewable Natural Resources in Latin America and the Caribbean database.

StatLink https://doi.org/10.1787/888933940643

In Brazil, a sharp rise in revenues from royalties and the government's special participation in production were responsible for a projected increase in oil and gas revenues in 2018. These were further supported by significant inflows arising from signing bonuses paid as concession contracts were established as a result of a bidding process during the year. In Colombia, CIT receipts jumped as net income of Ecopetrol – the country's principal producer – rose 154% in the first nine months of 2018 compared with the same period of the previous year. The rebound in Trinidad and Tobago reflected a normalisation of the sector in the country after several years of production disruptions that combined with falling prices to reduce CIT payments by oil companies.

Revenues from mining in the region are estimated to have posted a modest gain in 2018, rising to 0.5% of GDP from 0.4% of GDP in 2017 (Figure 2.6). As in 2017, Chile and Peru were primarily responsible for the up-tick in the regional average. Mining revenues in these countries are expected to rise over their 2017 levels by an estimated 0.5 percentage points of GDP and 0.3 percentage points of GDP, respectively. CIT receipts drove this increase, reflecting in part excellent earnings in the second half of 2017 and the first half of 2018.

The increase in mining revenues in 2018 was tempered by the evolution of prices during the year, dampening prospects for 2019. While annual average prices for many industrial metals and minerals rose in 2018 – with a concomitant increase in mining revenues[3] – this was mainly due to rapid growth in the first half of the year. Beginning in July 2018, there was a clear break in the rate of growth of international prices for several products (Figure 2.6). For example, in the second half of 2018 copper prices registered monthly year-on-year declines of roughly 10% compared to growth rates of 20% in the first half of the year. Increasing uncertainty about global growth, worries about the impact of trade tensions between the United States and China, as well as slowing growth in China, all served to put downward pressure on prices.

Figure 2.6. **Variation in international prices for selected metals and minerals**

Percentage year-on-year variation

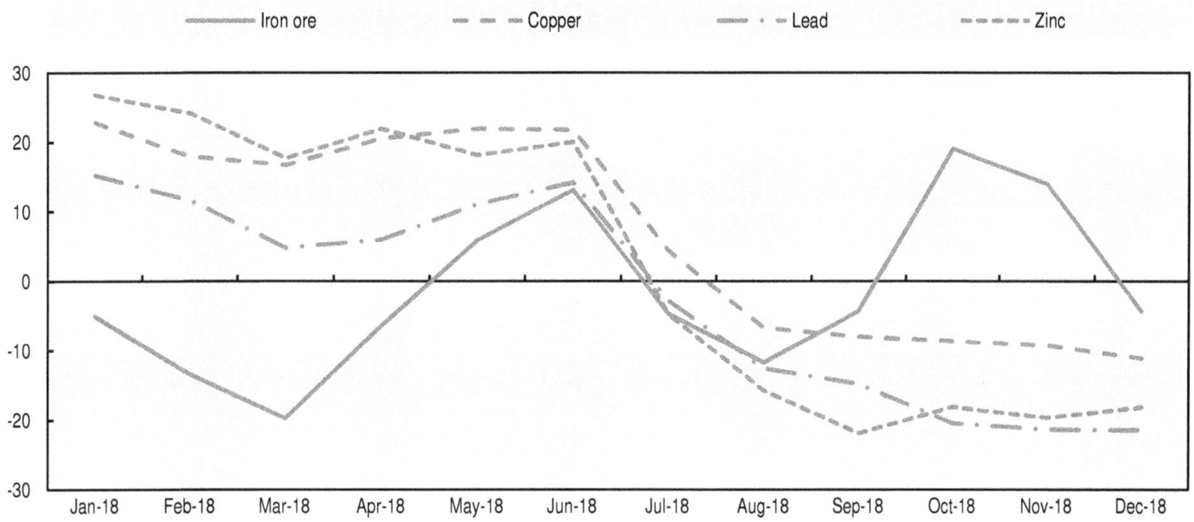

Source: Economic Commission for Latin America and the Caribbean (ECLAC), based on data from World Bank (World Bank, 2018[9]).

StatLink https://doi.org/10.1787/888933940662

Notes

1. The statistics presented in this special feature differ from those of previous editions of *Revenue Statistics in Latin America and the Caribbean*. Hydrocarbon revenues exclude those revenues deriving from taxes on the commercialization of hydrocarbons. Information for the Bolivarian Republic of Venezuela and Surinam are not included due data availability issues.
2. As part of the Chilean tax reform approved in 2014, the tax treatment of accumulated earnings held on a Retained Taxable Earnings Register was substantially changed. Under the new system foreign shareholders can avail themselves of a tax credit equal to 65% – as opposed to the 100% under the old system – of the CIT paid by the company from which they are receiving a distribution of retained earnings. As a result, the effective tax rate paid by these tax payers increased substantially.
3. The relationship between price and CIT payments is not insignificant. (Vale, 2018[6]) reports that a price reduction of USD 1 per dry metric ton unit (dmt) in the average ore price would have reduced operating income in 2017 by approximately USD 300 million. For context, during the same year the spot price for iron ore averaged USD 71.7 per dmt based on monthly data but registered a standard deviation of USD 10.

References

BHP (2018), *Annual Report*, *https://www.bhp.com/-/media/documents/investors/annual-reports/2017/bhpannualreport2017.pdf%20page%20164* (accessed on 22 February 2019). [9]

Comisión Chilena del Cobre (2018), *Anuario de Estadísticas del Cobre y Otros Minerales 1998-2017*, *https://www.cochilco.cl/Lists/Anuario/Attachments/18/Anuario%20Cochilco%202017%20final.pdf* (accessed on 14 February 2019). [7]

International Energy Agency (2018), *Oil Market Report 13 December 2018*, *https://www.iea.org/oilmarketreport/omrpublic/* (accessed on 22 February 2019). [1]

Ministerio de Economía y Finanzas de Bolivia (2018), *Memoria de la Economía Boliviana 2017*, *https://medios.economiayfinanzas.gob.bo/MH/documentos/Memorias_Fiscales/Memorias/Memoria_EB_2017.pdf* (accessed on 22 February 2019). [4]

OPEC (2018), *OPEC Annual Statistical Bulletin 2018*, *https://asb.opec.org/* (accessed on 14 February 2019). [2]

PERUPETRO (2018), *Memoria Annual de PERUPETRO S.A*, *https://www.perupetro.com.pe/wps/wcm/connect/corporativo/ba379021-14c0-4556-9893-90b6608baac0/PORTAL+MEMORIA+ANUAL+2017.pdf?MOD=AJPERES&CACHEID=ROOTWORKSPACE.Z18_N2E4HH41J8RPE0AF8M8T5Q3KQ3ba379021-14c0-4556-9893-90b6608baac0* (accessed on 22 February 2019). [5]

PwC (2018), *Mine 2018 Tempting times*, *http://www.pwc.com/mining* (accessed on 14 February 2019). [8]

Vale (2018), *Annual Report (Form 20-F)*, *http://www.vale.com/EN/investors/information-market/annual-reports/20f/20FDocs/Vale_20F_2017_i.PDF* (accessed on 22 February 2019). [6]

World Bank (2018), *World Bank Commodities Price Data*, *http://www.worldbank.org/commodities* (accessed on 22 February 2019). [3]

Capítulo 2

SECCIÓN ESPECIAL

Ingresos fiscales provenientes de recursos naturales no renovables en América Latina y el Caribe

Principales hallazgos

Ingresos fiscales provenientes de recursos naturales no renovables en 2017

Los ingresos provenientes de los hidrocarburos en América Latina y el Caribe se estabilizaron en 2017, luego de registrar una fuerte caída entre 2014 y 2016. Las condiciones favorables del mercado mundial del petróleo permitieron que estos ingresos se mantuvieran en su nivel de 2016, de 2.3% del PIB en promedio para los ocho países de la región considerados en este análisis. El incremento visto en los precios internacionales incidió en un aumento en los ingresos de instrumentos no tributarios a medida que aumentaba el valor comercial de la producción. En contraste, los ingresos tributarios disminuyeron marginalmente, ya que la rentabilidad se mantuvo débil.

Los ingresos provenientes de la minería en la región se recuperaron en 2017, respaldados por el sólido crecimiento mundial y el efecto indirecto de un estímulo fiscal y financiero significativo en China en 2016. Un aumento en los ingresos tributarios elevó los ingresos totales de un promedio del 0.28% del PIB en 2016 al 0.37% del PIB. Los ingresos por impuestos a las ganancias corporativas fueron particularmente fuertes, impulsados por los precios más altos y una disminución en los reembolsos de impuestos derivados de pérdidas financieras en años anteriores. El aumento en el promedio regional se debió principalmente a Chile (0.4% del PIB en 2016 al 0.9% del PIB en 2017) y Perú (0.3% del PIB en 2016 al 0.6% del PIB en 2017).

Ingresos fiscales proyectados en 2018

Las proyecciones de la CEPAL sugieren que los ingresos provenientes de los recursos naturales no renovables aumentaron en 2018. Un repunte en los precios del petróleo crudo se tradujo en el primer aumento en los ingresos fiscales provenientes de los hidrocarburos desde 2012, pasando de un promedio del 2.3% del PIB en 2017 al 2.9% del PIB en 2018. De manera similar, el fuerte crecimiento de los precios de los minerales y metales se mantuvo en el primer semestre de 2018, lo cual llevó consigo un aumento de los ingresos fiscales por minería del 0.4% del PIB en 2017 al 0.5% del PIB en 2018. No obstante, una fuerte corrección en el petróleo crudo y los minerales y metales en el segundo semestre del año ha puesto en duda la sostenibilidad del aumento de los ingresos fiscales provenientes de los recursos naturales registrado en 2018.

Ingresos fiscales provenientes de recursos naturales no renovables en 2017[1]

Hidrocarburos

Las tendencias del mercado mundial de petróleo y gas en 2017 fueron favorables para los productores de hidrocarburos de la región. En 2017, el mercado global del petróleo entró en déficit, ya que la demanda de petróleo – incluido el crudo, los condensados, los líquidos de gas natural (LGN) y otras fuentes de petróleo no convencional – superó el suministro (International Energy Agency, 2018$_{[1]}$). La demanda de petróleo, que aumentó de 96.4 millones de barriles por día en 2016 a 97.9 millones de barriles por día, fue impulsada en gran medida por los países de la OCDE, así como por China y la India. En contraste, hubo pocos cambios en los mercados en desarrollo y emergentes, excluyendo a Asia en desarrollo. Este patrón reflejó en gran medida las condiciones macroeconómicas globales, ya que el crecimiento económico repuntó en los países industrializados después de un 2016 particularmente débil.

En contraste, el suministro de petróleo registró un crecimiento moderado durante el año, pasando de 96.9 millones de barriles por día en 2016 a 97.5 millones de barriles por día. Como se ve en el gráfico 2.1, la producción mundial de estrictamente petróleo crudo cayó un 0.9% en 2017, el primer descenso desde la crisis económica y financiera mundial en 2009 (OPEC, 2018[2]). El factor clave detrás de esta desaceleración fue una disminución en la producción entre los miembros de la Organización de Países Exportadores de Petróleo (OPEP), reflejando la reducción de las cuotas de producción establecidas para los primeros seis meses del año y luego extendidas para cubrir todo el año mediante un acuerdo en mayo. Además, el cumplimiento de las reducidas cuotas de producción de la OPEP se vio reforzado durante el año por la vertiginosa disminución de la producción en la República Bolivariana de Venezuela. En contraste, el aumento de los precios llevó a una mayor producción en los Estados Unidos, donde se expandió la actividad de perforación.

Gráfico 2.1. **Contribuciones al crecimiento interanual de la producción mundial de petróleo crudo, 2010-17**

Porcentajes y puntos porcentuales

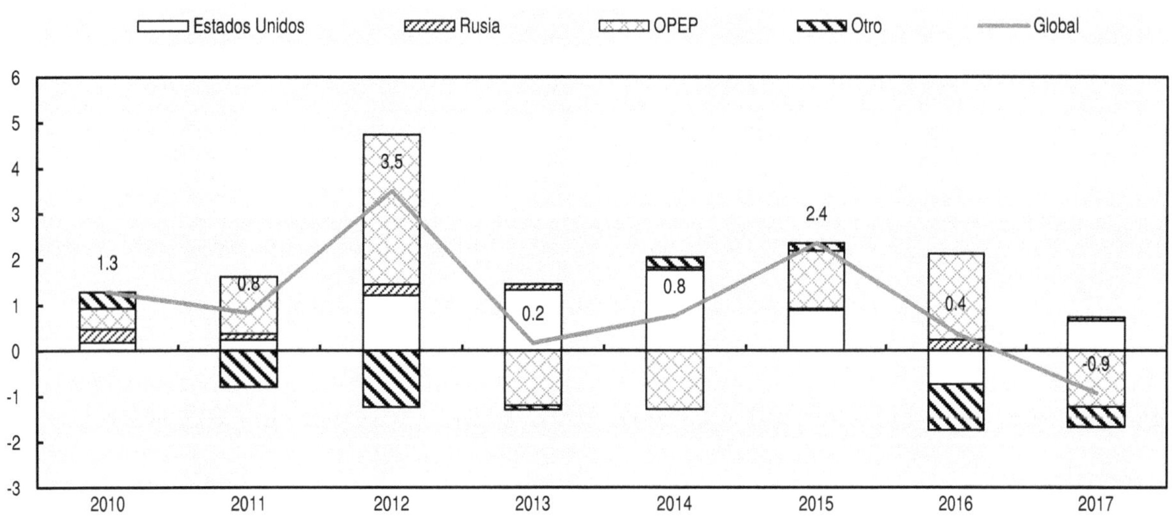

Fuente: Comisión Económica para América Latina y el Caribe (CEPAL), sobre la base de cifras de (OPEC, 2018[2]).

StatLink https://doi.org/10.1787/888933940681

Como resultado de estas tendencias globales en la oferta y la demanda, el precio promedio anual del petróleo crudo aumentó en un 23% en 2017, de USD 43 por barril a USD 53 por barril (Gráfico 2.2). A pesar de este resultado, destaca la volatilidad observada durante el año, ya que el precio prevaleciente cayó sustancialmente en el segundo trimestre del año, solo para recuperar su equilibrio en el tercer trimestre y alcanzar su máximo anual en el cuarto. Las tensiones geopolíticas y las consideraciones climáticas, como un invierno particularmente frío en América del Norte, también ayudaron a impulsar los precios durante el año.

Después de caer precipitadamente entre 2014 y 2016, en 2017 los ingresos derivados de la exploración y producción de hidrocarburos (actividades de up-stream) se estabilizaron en

América Latina y el Caribe. Para los países considerados en el cuadro 2.1, los ingresos fiscales en promedio no registraron cambios desde un nivel de 2.3% del PIB en 2016. Los ingresos tributarios asociados con el sector disminuyeron ligeramente, lo que refleja la continua débil rentabilidad de los principales productores de petróleo y gas de la región, el uso de traslados de pérdidas para reducir los pasivos corrientes y los reembolsos de los pagos anticipados del impuesto a las ganancias corporativas (CIT) que excedían los pasivos finales. Sin embargo, los ingresos no tributarios aumentaron en igual medida apoyados por rentas de propiedades más altas a medida que aumentaba el valor comercial de la producción.

Gráfico 2.2. **Precio del petróleo crudo, enero 2013 a diciembre 2017**

Dólares estadounidenses

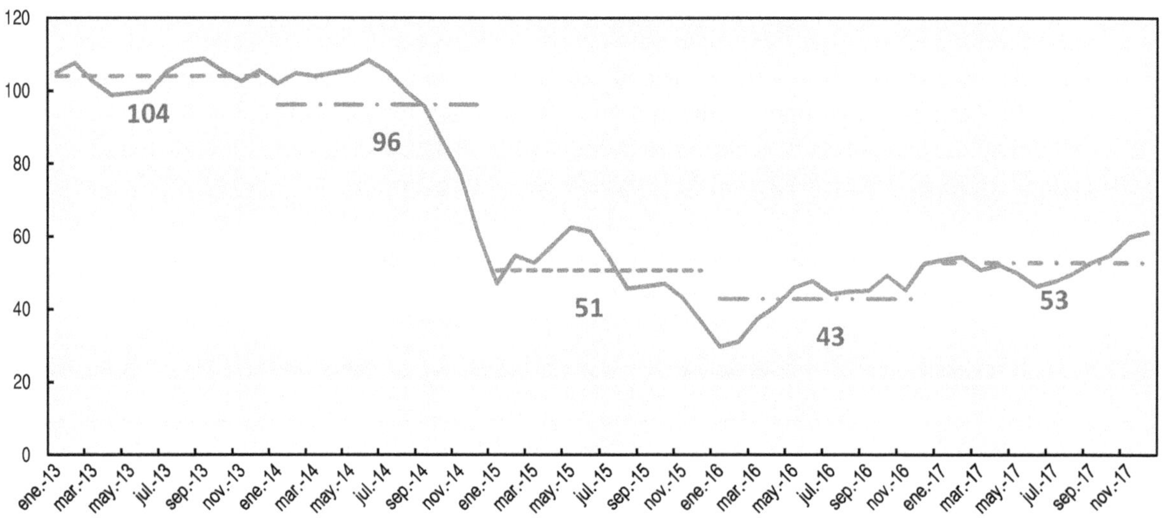

Nota: Los valores anuales corresponden a un promedio mensual.
Fuente: Comisión Económica para América Latina y el Caribe (CEPAL), sobre la base de cifras de (World Bank, 2018[3]).

StatLink https://doi.org/10.1787/888933940700

Cuadro 2.1. **Ingresos de hidrocarburos por instrumento, 2016-17**

Porcentajes del PIB

País	Total		Ingresos tributarios		Ingresos no tributarios	
	2016	2017	2016	2017	2016	2017
Argentina	0.5	0.4	0.1	0.1	0.3	0.3
Bolivia (Estado Plur. De)	4.4	4.0	0.3	0.2	4.1	3.8
Brasil	0.3	0.4	0.0	0.0	0.3	0.4
Colombia	0.6	0.7	0.3	0.2	0.3	0.6
Ecuador	5.4	5.6	0.0	0.0	5.4	5.6
México	3.9	3.8	0.0	0.0	3.9	3.8
Perú	0.4	0.5	0.1	0.1	0.3	0.4
Trinidad y Tobago	2.5	2.8	1.4	1.2	1.2	1.6
Promedio simple	*2.3*	*2.3*	*0.3*	*0.2*	*2.0*	*2.1*

Nota: Las cifras pueden no sumar debido al redondeo.
Fuente: Comisión Económica para América Latina y el Caribe (CEPAL), sobre la base de cifras de la base de datos de Ingresos fiscales de recursos naturales no renovables en América Latina y el Caribe de la CEPAL.

StatLink https://doi.org/10.1787/888933940871

A pesar de la estabilidad de los ingresos provenientes de los hidrocarburos en promedio, hubo una heterogeneidad significativa de resultados a nivel de país. Esto reflejó la interacción de la evolución de los precios, cambios en el nivel de producción y ciertos factores puntuales específicos de cada país que impactaron significativamente en los ingresos en 2016. En términos de USD, ingresos provenientes del extracción y producción de petróleo y el gas aumentaron más que el precio spot del crudo en Brasil (71% en términos de dólares estadounidenses), Colombia (28%) y Perú (52%) (Cuadro 2.2). En contraste, el crecimiento interanual en el Estado Plurinacional de Bolivia, Ecuador, México y Trinidad y Tobago fue menor, con tasas del 10% o menos.

Cuadro 2.2. **Variación interanual en los ingresos y la producción de hidrocarburos por moneda y producto, 2016-17**

Año a año, variación porcentual

País	Ingresos		Producción	
	Moneda nacional	Dólar	Petróleo crudo	Gas natural
Argentina	36	21	-6	0
Bolivia (Est. Plur. de)	0	0	n.a.	-3
Brasil	57	71	4	15
Colombia	24	28	-3	-7
Ecuador	8	8	-3	n.a.
México	5	3	-10	-12
Perú	47	52	8	-8
Trinidad y Tobago	12	10	0	1
Promedio simple	24	24	-1	-2
Memorándum				
Petróleo crudo		*23*		

Fuente: Comisión Económica para América Latina y el Caribe (CEPAL), sobre la base de cifras de la base de datos de Ingresos fiscales de recursos naturales no renovables en América Latina y el Caribe de la CEPAL, datos de producción de (OPEC, 2018[2])y datos de precios de (World Bank, 2018[3]).

StatLink https://doi.org/10.1787/888933940890

Si bien el movimiento en los precios internacionales fue el factor predominante detrás de la evolución de los ingresos por hidrocarburos, las variaciones en los niveles de producción también jugaron un papel importante. Como se ve en el cuadro 2.2, la producción promedio de petróleo crudo disminuyó en 2017, y solo Brasil y Perú registraron aumentos. Las extensas inversiones en exploración y producción en Brasil durante la década anterior se han traducido en un alza en la producción desde 2014, aunque este crecimiento se ha desacelerado recientemente. En contraste, los campos petroleros maduros y limitados niveles de inversión continúan afectando la producción de petróleo en México, que cayó un 10% en 2017.

Esta disminución en la producción registrada en varios países también condujo a una reducción en la producción de gas natural, ya que el gas es a menudo un subproducto de la producción de petróleo crudo. Este fenómeno fue especialmente evidente entre los grandes productores de petróleo como Colombia, Ecuador y México (Cuadro 2.2). En Bolivia, el mayor exportador de gas natural en América del Sur, los niveles de producción disminuyeron como resultado de una disminución en los volúmenes de exportación a Brasil (14.2%) debido a la mayor generación de energía hidroeléctrica en dicho país durante el año (Ministerio de Economía y Finanzas de Bolivia, 2018[4]). La caída de la producción de gas en Perú (8%) reflejó una disminución en la demanda interna de gas utilizado en la generación eléctrica (PERUPETRO, 2018[5]).

En Brasil, los ingresos por la extracción y producción de petróleo y gas aumentaron del 0.3% del PIB en 2016 al 0.4% del PIB en 2017, debido en gran parte a la recuperación de la participación especial del gobierno en la producción y al aumento de los ingresos provenientes del ISR. Los ingresos del pago de la participación especial – calculados sobre la base de tasas progresivas sobre los ingresos netos de producción ajustados por regalías, inversiones de exploración, costos operativos, depreciación e impuestos – casi se duplicaron en 2017 después de caer considerablemente el año anterior, ya que las empresas con contratos de concesión amortizaron excepcionalmente grandes inversiones en exploración.

Los ingresos por hidrocarburos en el Perú aumentaron del 0.4% del PIB en 2016 al 0.5% del PIB, a pesar de la disminución mencionada anteriormente en la producción de gas natural. Los mayores precios internacionales y la mayor producción de petróleo se tradujeron en un aumento en los ingresos por concepto de regalías y contratos de servicios de hidrocarburos. El incremento en los pagos de regalías fue apoyado por un aumento en las exportaciones de gas natural líquido a los mercados europeos, donde los precios son generalmente más altos que en otros mercados tradicionales de Perú, como México (PERUPETRO, 2018[5]). En particular, los ingresos del ISR provenientes del conjunto de actividades de hidrocarburos se duplicó durante el año, luego de haber alcanzado su nivel más bajo en 2016, en términos de moneda nacional, desde 2005.

En Colombia, el aumento en los ingresos de petróleo y gas, que aumentó de 0.6% del PIB en 2016 a 0.7% del PIB en 2017, fue impulsado en gran parte por una recuperación en los ingresos no tributarios. En particular, los ingresos asociados con los derechos por precios altos – que se desencadenan cuando el precio spot de un precio de referencia internacional, en este caso West Texas Intermediate (WTI), supera el nivel establecido en el contrato de exploración y producción de una empresa – se recuperaron luego de una fuerte caída el año anterior (67%) debido a los precios excepcionalmente bajos del petróleo. Los dividendos recibidos por el gobierno central de Ecopetrol también aumentaron durante el año.

En 2017, los ingresos por hidrocarburos en Trinidad y Tobago registraron su primer aumento desde 2014. Los ingresos totales aumentaron del 2.5% del PIB en 2016 al 2.8% del PIB, con una caída en los ingresos tributarios compensada por mayores ingresos no tributarios. Los ingresos tributarios se mantuvieron débiles debido en gran parte a una disminución sustancial en los ingresos por retenciones impositivas. Los ingresos no tributarios, en contraste, aumentaron de 1.2% del PIB en 2016 a 1.6% del PIB. Los ingresos por regalías registraron un fuerte aumento como resultado del aumento en el precio y la producción mayor a la esperada, que se mantuvo relativamente sin cambios entre los años en comparación con una caída proyectada. Factores similares también aumentaron los ingresos de los contratos de producción compartida.

En contraste, los ingresos del petróleo en México disminuyeron en 2017, cayendo del 3.9% del PIB en 2016 al 3.8% del PIB (aunque aumentaron ligeramente en términos de dólares estadounidenses), a pesar del impulso provocado por el repunte de los precios. Esta disminución reflejó los ingresos excepcionalmente altos registrados por Petróleos Mexicanos (Pemex) en el año anterior gracias a una serie de transacciones puntuales dentro del sector público. Excluyendo estas transferencias intergubernamentales, los ingresos totales por petróleo en 2017 habrían aumentado 20% en términos de dólares estadounidenses. A pesar de este aumento, todavía se habría quedado atrás con respecto a los precios internacionales del petróleo, reflejando el impacto de la disminución continua en la producción de hidrocarburos en México.

En el Estado Plurinacional de Bolivia, los ingresos por gas natural, especialmente los provenientes de instrumentos no tributarios, registraron una disminución significativa en 2017, descendiendo del 4.4% del PIB en 2016 al 4.0% del PIB. Los pagos de regalías y los ingresos del Impuesto Directo a los Hidrocarburos, que a pesar de su nombre es una renta de la propiedad, se vieron afectados por una disminución en las ventas a Brasil que no fue compensada por un aumento en los volúmenes de exportación a Argentina. El mecanismo de fijación de precios en los contratos de ventas de Bolivia con Argentina y Brasil también contribuyó a acotar un aumento en el valor comercial de la producción durante el año. Estos contratos estipulan que los precios se ajustan trimestralmente sobre la base del precio promedio de una canasta de productos de hidrocarburos del trimestre anterior. Por lo tanto, el aumento en los precios de los hidrocarburos registrados internacionalmente en el cuarto trimestre de 2017 solo comenzará a aplicarse en el primer trimestre de 2018. Los ingresos tributarios también tuvieron una tendencia a la baja, ya que los menores volúmenes de exportación y el modesto aumento en el precio de las exportaciones de gas boliviano arrastró las utilidades del sector y a su vez los pagos del ISR.

Minería

Los precios de los metales y minerales aumentaron en 2017 por primera vez desde 2011. Los sólidos fundamentos macroeconómicos globales incidieron en un aumento en la demanda de metales y minerales en 2017. Los factores claves detrás de esta alza incluyeron el repunte de la actividad económica en los países industrializados, especialmente en los Estados Unidos, y el efecto indirecto del estímulo fiscal y financiero en China en 2016. La mayor demanda del mineral de hierro, por ejemplo, fue impulsado en gran parte por un nivel récord de producción de acero en China derivado de la demanda mundial de productos manufacturados chinos y de grandes inversiones domésticas en infraestructura y bienes raíces (Vale, 2018[6]).

En contraste, el suministro mundial de varios metales y productos minerales clave se redujo en 2017. Por ejemplo, la producción mundial de cobre – un insumo clave para una amplia gama de actividades, incluida la construcción y la producción de componentes eléctricos – se redujo en 2017, liderado principalmente por reducciones en China y Estados Unidos, luego de registrar un fuerte crecimiento en 2015 y 2016 (Gráfico 2.3). En Chile, el productor más grande del mundo, la producción cayó en parte por una huelga de 43 días en la mina Escondida. La producción en Perú, el segundo mayor productor del mundo siguió aumentando, aunque su tasa de crecimiento se desaceleró significativamente, al igual que su contribución al crecimiento mundial de la producción de cobre.

Gráfico 2.3. **Contribuciones al crecimiento de la producción mundial de cobre, 2013-17**

Porcentajes y puntos porcentuales

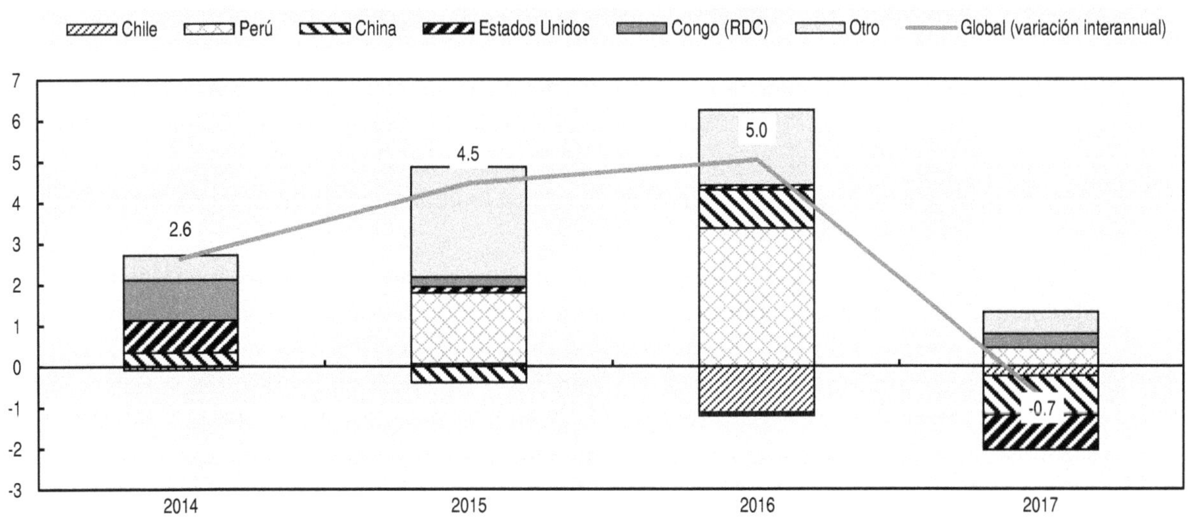

Fuente: Comisión Económica para América Latina y el Caribe (CEPAL), sobre la base de cifras de (Comisión Chilena del Cobre, 2018[7]).

StatLink https://doi.org/10.1787/888933940719

Estos factores apoyaron un repunte en los precios internacionales para una amplia gama de metales y minerales industriales (Gráfico 2.4). El aumento en los precios de estos bienes, que había mostrado un mayor dinamismo a lo largo de 2016, alcanzó su punto máximo en el primer trimestre de 2017 antes de establecerse en un crecimiento interanual relativamente estable del 20% durante el resto del año. Los precios de algunos bienes, sin embargo, experimentaron una volatilidad significativa. Los precios del mineral de hierro aumentaron en el cuarto trimestre de 2016 y en el primer trimestre de 2017 debido a un salto en la producción mundial de acero, pero comenzaron a caer a fines del año.

Gráfico 2.4. **Metales y minerales seleccionados: Variación interanual de los precios internacionales, 2015-17**

Porcentajes, por trimestre

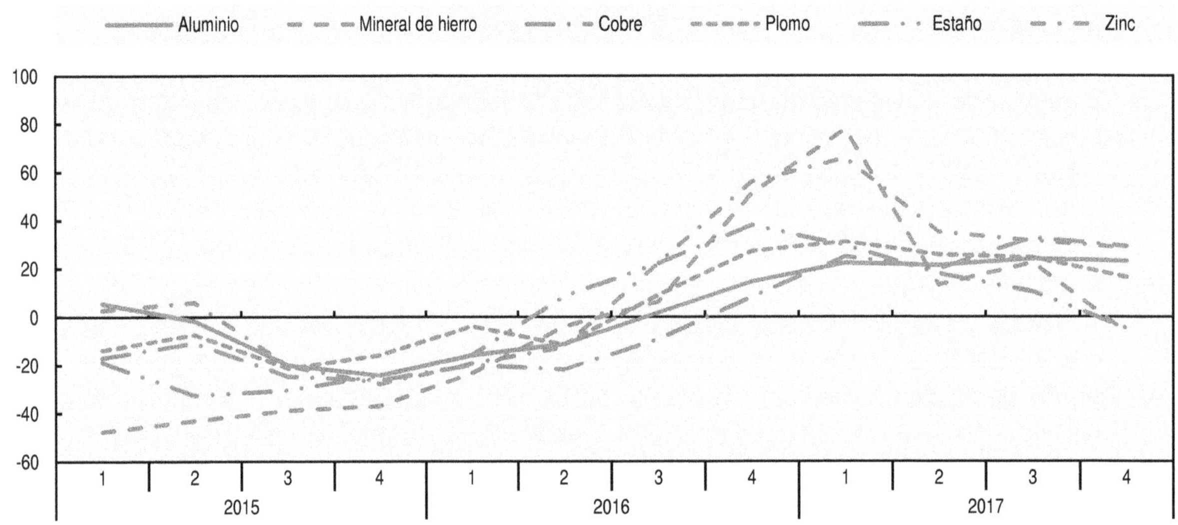

Fuente: Comisión Económica para América Latina y el Caribe (CEPAL), basada en datos de (World Bank, 2018[3]).

StatLink https://doi.org/10.1787/888933940738

Los ingresos mineros en América Latina y el Caribe se recuperaron en 2017. El aumento en los precios de los productos básicos sentó las bases para el primer aumento en los ingresos mineros en la región desde 2011. Aunque el repunte fue modesto, del 0.28% del PIB en 2016 al 0.37% del PIB en 2017, se observaron aumentos en la mayoría de los países (Cuadro 2.3). El promedio regional se vio más fuertemente afectado por los incrementos en Chile y Perú. El aumento en los ingresos totales se debió esencialmente a una mayor recaudación tributaria, que aumentó del 0.12% del PIB en 2016 a 0.20% del PIB en 2017, reflejando la alta elasticidad de los pagos del ISR a los cambios en los precios. En contraste, el promedio de los ingresos no tributarios, principalmente derivados de rentas de la propiedad como regalías, registró pocos cambios durante el período.

En términos de la variación interanual promedio en moneda nacional y en dólares estadounidenses (33% y 35%, respectivamente), el aumento en los ingresos mineros estuvo generalmente en línea con los movimientos registrados en los precios prevalecientes para los metales y minerales claves de la región (Cuadro 2.4). Sin embargo, los resultados a nivel de país fueron variados, reflejando las diferencias en la especialización de la canasta de la oferta, así como los movimientos en los tipos de cambio. A diferencia de los años anteriores, las monedas de los principales productores de la región tendieron a apreciarse en 2017, por ejemplo, en Brasil, Chile, Colombia y Perú, lo que redujo el aumento de los ingresos expresados en moneda nacional y, por lo tanto, en relación con el PIB.

Cuadro 2.3. **Ingresos mineros por instrumento, 2016-17**

Porcentaje del PIB

País	Total		Ingresos tributarios		Ingresos no tributarios	
	2016	2017	2016	2017	2016	2017
Argentina	0.02	0.04	0.01	0.03	0.01	0.01
Bolivia (Est. Plur. de)	0.79	0.75	0.34	0.26	0.45	0.49
Brasil	0.07	0.07	0.03	0.04	0.03	0.03
Chile	0.38	0.95	0.02	0.46	0.37	0.48
Codelco	0.37	0.49	0.01	0.01	0.37	0.48
Empresas privadas	0.01	0.45	0.01	0.45	0.00	0.00
Colombia	0.27	0.29	0.07	0.06	0.20	0.23
Jamaica	0.14	0.02	0.00	0.00	0.14	0.02
México	0.17	0.19	0.15	0.16	0.03	0.03
Perú	0.30	0.62	0.17	0.46	0.13	0.16
República Dominicana	0.39	0.43	0.33	0.37	0.07	0.06
Promedio simple	*0.28*	*0.37*	*0.12*	*0.20*	*0.16*	*0.17*

Nota: Puede que las cifras no sumen 100 debido al redondeo.

Fuente: Comisión Económica para América Latina y el Caribe (CEPAL), sobre la base de cifras de la base de datos de Ingresos fiscales de recursos naturales no renovables en América Latina y el Caribe de la CEPAL.

StatLink https://doi.org/10.1787/888933940909

Cuadro 2.4. **Variación interanual de los ingresos de hidrocarburos por moneda, 2016-17**

Porcentajes

País	Moneda nacional	Dólar
Argentina	127	102
Bolivia (Est. Plur. de)	5	5
Brasil	10	20
Chile	163	174
Codelco	*39*	*45*
Empresas privadas	*6 658*	*6 951*
Colombia	29	33
Jamaica	-81	-81
México	23	21
Perú	122	130
República Dominicana	18	15
Promedio simple	*33*	*35*
Memorándum		
Aluminio		*23*
Carbón		*34*
Cobre		*27*
Oro		*1*
Mineral de hierro		*23*
Plomo		*24*
Níquel		*8*
Estaño		*12*
Zinc		*38*

Fuente: Comisión Económica para América Latina y el Caribe (CEPAL), sobre la base de cifras de la base de datos de Ingresos fiscales de recursos naturales no renovables en América Latina y el Caribe de la CEPAL y datos de precios de (World Bank, 2018[3]).

StatLink https://doi.org/10.1787/888933940928

Como se puede apreciar en los cuadros 2.3 y 2.4, algunos países de la región registraron aumentos mucho mayores en los ingresos mineros durante el año de lo que podría haberse esperado dada la evolución de los precios de los metales y minerales. Esto se debió en gran parte a un aumento en los pagos del ISR, o aquellos derivados de otros instrumentos cuya base impositiva se basa en los ingresos o utilidades, como el Impuesto Especial a la Minería de Chile. Estos ingresos habían sido severamente afectados en los últimos años debido a que la continua disminución de los precios internacionales redujo la rentabilidad de los principales productores de la región, hasta el punto en que se reportaron pérdidas. En algunos países, esta tendencia se agravó aún más por las grandes deducciones por inversiones en activos fijos, así como por el uso de las disposiciones de arrastre de pérdidas del código tributario para reducir sus pasivos tributarios actuales. Como resultado, en países como Argentina, Chile y Perú los ingresos mineros aumentaron a más del doble de sus niveles de 2016. Esto estaba en línea con una tendencia en toda la industria, ya que los pagos del ISR de las empresas mineras más grandes del mundo aumentaron en un 81% en 2017 (PwC, 2018$_{[8]}$).

Quizás el más emblemático de estos casos es Chile, el mayor productor de cobre del mundo, donde los ingresos mineros aumentaron del 0.38% del PIB en 2016 al 0.95% del PIB en 2017. El gran aumento de los ingresos tributarios, que impulsó este resultado, se debió a una recuperación en el pago del ISR por los productores privados a medida que mejoraba la rentabilidad. A diferencia de 2016, cuando los ingresos de estas empresas fueron prácticamente nulos – incluido un reembolso neto de los impuestos pagados por el Impuesto Especial a la Minería, cuya base tributaria es el ingreso operativo, ya que los pagos anticipados superaron los pasivos fiscales finales – estos ingresos aumentaron considerablemente en 2017, pasando del 0.01% del PIB en 2016 al 0.45% del PIB (un aumento del 6.951% en términos de dólares estadounidenses). También hubo un aumento significativo en los pagos de impuestos de retención por parte de los productores privados, ya que se valieron de una tasa impositiva concesional para hacer distribuciones de las ganancias acumuladas no gravados antes de que entrara en vigor un nuevo régimen fiscal.[2] Por ejemplo, BHP Billiton Chile pagó un dividendo único de USD 2.3 mil millones (equivalente al 0,8% del PIB chileno) a su matriz extranjera, lo que resultó en un pago de impuestos de retención de USD 373 millones (BHP, 2018$_{[9]}$).

En contraste, los ingresos mineros en Jamaica cayeron a casi cero relativo al producto en 2017 (una reducción del 81% en términos de dólares estadounidenses), lo que refleja el impacto de la reestructuración de la industria de bauxita y alúmina del país. El gobierno ha ofrecido exenciones temporales de hasta el 100% en el pago de la tasa de bauxita, el principal generador de ingresos mineros, a varios de los mayores productores del país para reforzar la inversión y proteger el empleo. Además, en el año fiscal 2017/18, el gobierno modificó el régimen de la tasa de bauxita y firmó acuerdos de régimen fiscal específicos con empresas individuales. El contenido de estos acuerdos difiere significativamente según el productor, lo que da lugar a grandes diferencias en el tratamiento fiscal de empresas que operan en el mismo sector.

Ingresos fiscales proyectados de recursos naturales no renovables para 2018

Se estima que los ingresos por hidrocarburos en 2018 registraron su primer aumento desde 2011, pasando del 2.3% del PIB en 2017 al 2.9% del PIB (Gráfico 2.5). A nivel de país, se prevé que los ingresos del petróleo y el gas aumenten en 0.5 puntos porcentuales del PIB o más en Brasil y Colombia; y por 1 punto porcentual del PIB o más en Ecuador y Trinidad y Tobago. El ímpetu para esta recuperación fue provocado por un aumento del 29% en el precio promedio anual del crudo spot, que fue respaldado por un crecimiento solido y sostenido en la demanda mundial, así como por la oferta limitada de los países de la OPEP. Sin embargo, en los últimos dos meses del año hubo una marcada caída en el precio del petróleo, con una variación interanual del crudo spot que cayó un 12% en diciembre, lo que sugiere un aumento en el riesgo a la baja en el mediano plazo.

Gráfico 2.5. **Ingresos fiscales de recursos naturales no renovables, 2010-18**

Porcentajes del PIB

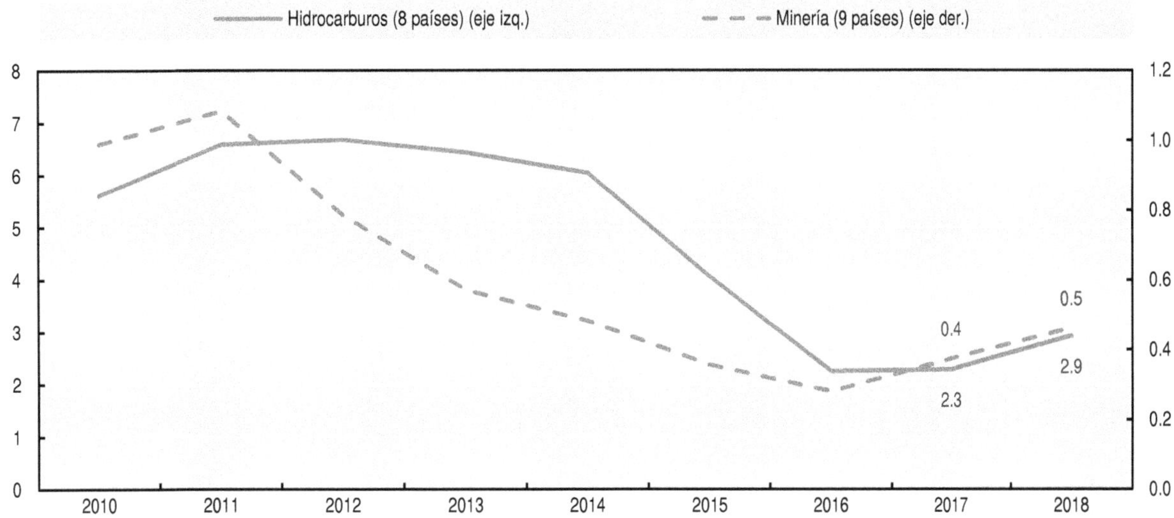

Nota: La minería incluye: Argentina, Bolivia (Estado Plurinacional de), Brasil, Chile, Colombia, República Dominicana, Jamaica, México y Perú. Los hidrocarburos incluyen: Argentina, Bolivia (Estado Plurinacional de), Brasil, Colombia, Ecuador, México, Perú y Trinidad y Tobago. Los valores para 2018 se basan en estimaciones oficiales del gobierno a partir de los documentos presupuestarios de 2019 o de cifras anuales preliminares. Cuando las cifras para 2018 no estaban disponibles, se estimaron utilizando datos mensuales (generalmente durante los primeros diez meses del año). Cuando no se disponía de datos mensuales, los ingresos se estimaron aplicando el cambio interanual en el precio del producto más representativo (o cesta de productos en el caso de la minería) para el país, expresado en términos de moneda nacional, hasta 2017 los ingresos.

Fuente: Comisión Económica para América Latina y el Caribe (CEPAL), sobre la base de cifras de la base de datos de Ingresos fiscales de recursos naturales no renovables en América Latina y el Caribe de la CEPAL.

StatLink https://doi.org/10.1787/888933940757

En Brasil, un fuerte aumento en los ingresos por regalías y la participación especial del gobierno en la producción fueron responsables de un aumento proyectado en los ingresos del petróleo y el gas en 2018. Estos fueron respaldados por importantes entradas provenientes de los bonos de suscripción pagados ya que los contratos de concesión se establecieron como un resultado de un proceso de licitación durante el año. En Colombia, los recibos de ISR aumentaron a medida que los ingresos netos de Ecopetrol, el principal productor del país, aumentaron un 154% en los primeros nueve meses de 2018 en comparación con el mismo período del año anterior. El rebote en Trinidad y Tobago reflejó una normalización del sector en el país después de varios años de interrupciones en la producción que se combinaron con la caída de los precios para reducir los pagos de ISR por parte de las compañías petroleras.

Se estima que los ingresos provenientes de la minería en la región registraron una ganancia modesta en 2018, aumentando a 0.5% del PIB desde 0.4% del PIB en 2017 (Gráfico 2.6). Al igual que en 2017, Chile y Perú fueron los principales responsables del aumento en el promedio regional. Se espera que los ingresos mineros en estos países aumenten con respecto a sus niveles de 2017 en un estimado de 0.5 puntos porcentuales del PIB y 0.3 puntos porcentuales del PIB, respectivamente. Los ingresos de ISR impulsaron este aumento, reflejando en parte excelentes ganancias en la segunda mitad de 2017 y la primera mitad de 2018.

El aumento en los ingresos mineros en 2018 se vio atenuado por la evolución de los precios durante el año, lo que frenó las perspectivas para 2019. Mientras que los precios promedio anuales de muchos metales y minerales industriales aumentaron en 2018, con un aumento consiguiente en los ingresos mineros[3], esto se debió principalmente al rápido crecimiento en la primera mitad del año. A partir de julio de 2018, hubo una clara ruptura en la tasa de crecimiento de los precios internacionales para varios productos (Gráfico 2.6). Por ejemplo, en la segunda mitad de 2018 los precios del cobre registraron descensos mensuales interanuales de aproximadamente el 10% en comparación con las tasas de crecimiento del 20% en la primera mitad del año. La creciente incertidumbre sobre el crecimiento global, las preocupaciones sobre el impacto de las tensiones comerciales entre los Estados Unidos y China, así como la desaceleración del crecimiento en China, presionaro a la baja el crecimiento de los precios.

Gráfico 2.6. **Metales y minerales seleccionados: variación interanual de los precios internacionales, enero de 2018 a diciembre de 2018**

Porcentajes

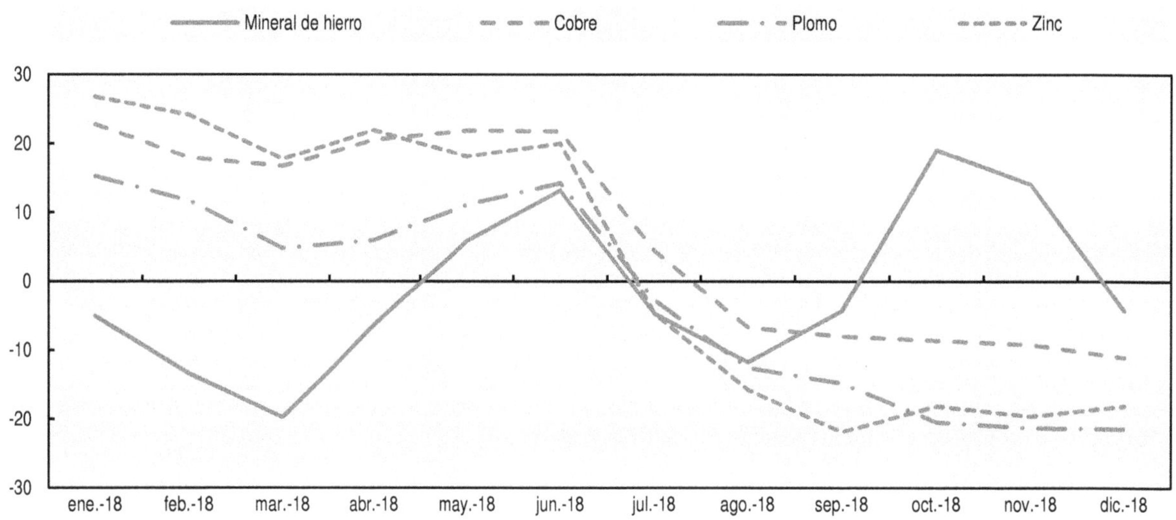

Fuente: Comisión Económica para América Latina y el Caribe (CEPAL), sobre la base de cifras de (World Bank, 2018[3]).

StatLink https://doi.org/10.1787/888933940776

Notas

1. Las estadísticas presentadas en esta sección especial difieren de las de ediciones anteriores. Los ingresos por hidrocarburos excluyen aquellos ingresos derivados de los impuestos sobre la comercialización de hidrocarburos. La información para la República Bolivariana de Venezuela y Surinam no se incluye debido a problemas de disponibilidad de datos.
2. Como parte de la reforma tributaria chilena aprobada en 2014, el tratamiento fiscal de las ganancias acumuladas mantenidas en un Fondo de Utilidad Tributaria (FUT) se modificó sustancialmente. Bajo el nuevo sistema, se grava la distribución o retiro de utilidades con el Impuesto Adicional de 35% sobre la base retirada, pero los beneficiarios no residentes solo pueden aprovechar de un crédito fiscal equivalente al 65% del impuesto de la primera categoría pagado, a diferencia del 100% bajo el sistema anterior. Como resultado, la tasa impositiva efectiva pagada por estos contribuyentes aumentó sustancialmente.
3. La relación entre el precio y los pagos de ISR no es insignificante. (Vale, 2018[6]) informa que una reducción de precio de USD 1 por unidad de tonelada métrica seca (dmt) en el precio promedio del mineral de hierro habría reducido el ingreso operativo en 2017 en aproximadamente USD 300 millones. Para pone esto en contexto, durante el mismo año, el precio del mineral de hierro promedió USD 71.7 por dmt en base a los datos mensuales, pero registró una desviación estándar de USD 10.

References

BHP (2018), *Annual Report*, *https://www.bhp.com/-/media/documents/investors/annual-reports/2017/bhpannualreport2017.pdf%20page%20164* (accessed on 22 February 2019). [9]

Comisión Chilena del Cobre (2018), *Anuario de Estadísticas del Cobre y Otros Minerales 1998-2017*, *https://www.cochilco.cl/Lists/Anuario/Attachments/18/Anuario%20Cochilco%202017%20final.pdf* (accessed on 14 February 2019). [7]

International Energy Agency (2018), *Oil Market Report 13 December 2018*, *https://www.iea.org/oilmarketreport/omrpublic/* (accessed on 22 February 2019). [1]

Ministerio de Economía y Finanzas de Bolivia (2018), *Memoria de la Economía Boliviana 2017*, *https://medios.economiayfinanzas.gob.bo/MH/documentos/Memorias_Fiscales/Memorias/Memoria_EB_2017.pdf* (accessed on 22 February 2019). [4]

OPEC (2018), *OPEC Annual Statistical Bulletin 2018*, *https://asb.opec.org/* (accessed on 14 February 2019). [2]

PERUPETRO (2018), *Memoria Annual de PERUPETRO S.A*, *https://www.perupetro.com.pe/wps/wcm/connect/corporativo/ba379021-14c0-4556-9893-90b6608baac0/PORTAL+MEMORIA+ANUAL+2017.pdf?MOD=AJPERES&CACHEID=ROOTWORKSPACE.Z18_N2E4HH41J8RPE0AF8M8T5Q3KQ3ba379021-14c0-4556-9893-90b6608baac0* (accessed on 22 February 2019). [5]

PwC (2018), *Mine 2018 Tempting times*, *http://www.pwc.com/mining* (accessed on 14 February 2019). [8]

Vale (2018), *Annual Report (Form 20-F)*, *http://www.vale.com/EN/investors/information-market/annual-reports/20f/20FDocs/Vale_20F_2017_i.PDF* (accessed on 22 February 2019). [6]

World Bank (2018), *World Bank Commodities Price Data*, *http://www.worldbank.org/commodities* (accessed on 22 February 2019). [3]

Chapter 3

SPECIAL FEATURE

Property taxation in Latin America

Capítulo 3

SECCIÓN ESPECIAL

Impuesto a la propiedad en América Latina

Chapter 3

SPECIAL FEATURE
Property taxation in Latin America

Key findings

Recurrent taxes on immovable property are a critical mechanism for local governments, allowing them to set rates at the margin to finance basic services. These needs are heightened in Latin America by extensive urbanisation, which is often accompanied by growth of informal settlements. However, administration of property taxes is complex, tracking of ownership incomplete and systems for property valuation cumbersome.

The revenues generated by recurrent taxes on immovable property in Latin America are low relative to the performance in OECD countries. Revenues from this instrument varied significantly between countries in 2016, from 0.1% of GDP in Ecuador to 0.9% of GDP in Uruguay. For the most part, revenues were equivalent to around 0.3% of GDP, versus an OECD average of 1.1% of GDP.

Responsibility for the design and administration of property taxation in Latin America varies widely. The governmental system is a critical factor behind the level of revenue generation: recurrent taxes on immovable property provide a significant part of subnational tax revenues in unitary countries, such as Chile, Costa Rica, Ecuador, Peru and Uruguay.

Case studies for Argentina, Brazil and Colombia identify the constraints and enablers of higher revenues from recurrent taxes on immovable property in greater depth.

The importance of property taxation for the sustainable development agenda is increasingly recognised even if its revenue remains relatively small in comparison with other tax categories (Ahmad, Brosio and Pablo Jiménez, 2018[1]). This chapter discusses Latin America's experiences with property taxation, identifying the challenges to higher revenue generation as well as mechanisms for overcoming these constraints. The first section explains why property taxes are important; the second discusses the evolution of property tax revenues in selected Latin American countries; and the third section includes cases studies for Argentina, Colombia and Brazil.

Why are property taxes important?[1]

Property taxes include different revenues streams: recurrent taxes on immovable property, on net wealth, estate, inheritance and gift taxes, taxes on financial and capital transactions and other taxes on property (Ahmad, Brosio and Pablo Jiménez, 2018[1]). In this section, we concentrate on revenues from recurrent taxes on immovable property, emphasising their importance for financing subnational governments.

Revenues from recurrent taxes on immovable property in developing and emerging market economies average well below 1% of GDP (Ahmad, Brosio and Gerbrandy, 2018[2]). Recent literature (Gómez Sabaini, Jiménez and Martner, 2017[3]); (OECD et al., 2018[4]) confirms that revenues from taxes on immovable property play a minor role, albeit with some variation, in terms of GDP and in relation to overall tax revenues in Latin America. (Figure 3.1). In 2016, revenues from recurrent taxes on immovable property as a percentage of GDP ranged from 0.1% in Ecuador and 0.2% in Mexico and Peru to 0.8% in Colombia and 0.9% in Uruguay. For the most part, revenues were equivalent to around 0.3% of GDP, versus an OECD average of 1.1% of GDP

Figure 3.1. **Recurrent taxes on immovable property, 1990-2016**

Percentage of GDP

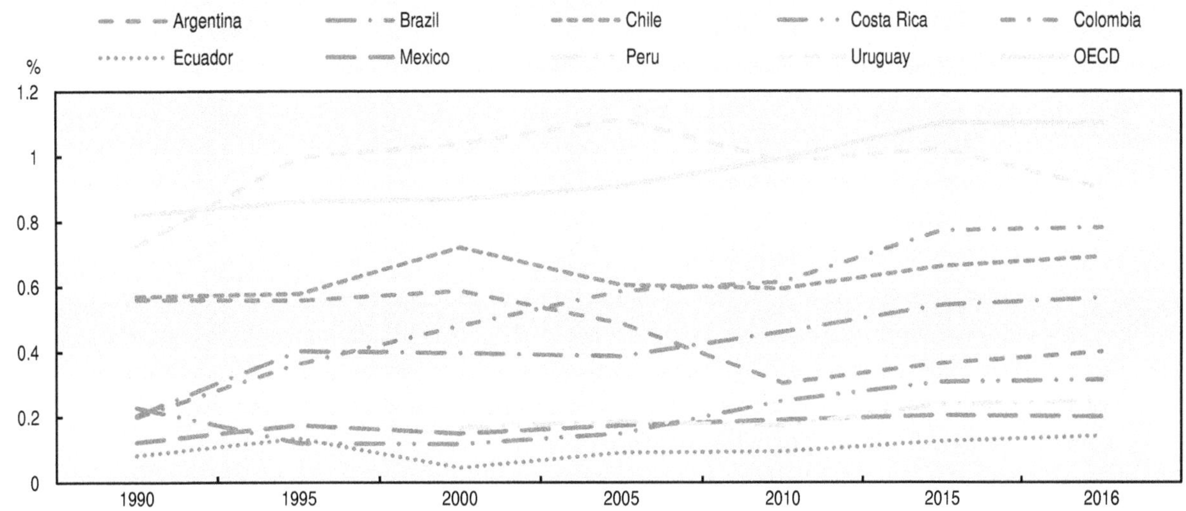

Source: (OECD/ECLAC/CIAT/IDB, 2019[6]), *https://stats.oecd.org/index.aspx?DataSetCode=RSLACT.*

StatLink *https://doi.org/10.1787/888933940947*

From an intergovernmental perspective, recurrent taxation on immovable property is an important own-source of financing for the provision of basic services for which the local government can determine rates at the margin.[2] This strengthens accountability and decision-making for local governments, as well as fiscal sustainability (Norregaard, 2013[5]). Transfers from the central government, even if untied, are not own-source as local governments cannot increase revenues when needed.[3]

The degree of efficiency and the distributive effect of property taxation depends on policy design, for example on whether poorer or liquidity-constrained households benefit from tax exemptions; or taxes are paid by owner or the occupant of the property (Blöchliger, 2015[7]); (Biderman and Camara Batista, 2018[8]).

Additionally, a system of property taxation can also provide information on assets; information from property tax valuations and transactions can be used to cross-check income tax statements by individuals.

However, property taxes have many constraints, meaning revenues fall far short of their potential and cannot meet the needs of local governments – needs exacerbated by urbanisation, migration to cities and extensive informal settlements. Moreover, the administration of property taxes is complex, tracking of ownership incomplete and systems for property valuation cumbersome (Brosio and Jiménez, 2012[9]). Assessed property values typically lag current market prices.

Evolution of revenues from recurrent taxes on immovable property

Most countries in the region rely on traditional cadastral systems for the determination of property titles and valuation. Maintaining cadasters is the bedrock of property management systems (Ahmad, Brosio and Pablo Jiménez, 2018[1]). However, maintaining cadasters and keeping them up to date is typically a difficult, complex and costly task. The situation is made more complex with communal land, and migrations leading to "informal" settlements, especially in the environs of large metropolitan areas.

Other countries have experimented with innovative ways of determining values through self-declaration (in some Colombian cities) or parametrical systems (in Bolivia) based on information about characteristics of properties provided by taxpayers

In some Latin American countries, such as Argentina, the value of real property serves as the base for determination of fees and charges for the provision of specific local services, such as garbage collection, street cleaning and lighting, and sewage systems. However, this deepens the need for accurate and updated property valuations in order to ensure adequate intergovernmental tax co-ordination.

Responsibility for the design and administration of property taxation in Latin America varies widely. In some countries, the tax rate is set by the local jurisdiction, making it an own-source of revenues. In other countries, power to set rates rests with the central government (or the state/provincial-level governments) and revenues are shared among subnational governments (either state/provincial or municipal).

For less decentralised countries, revenues from recurrent taxes on immovable property remain an important source of revenue (Figure 3.2). These provide a significant part of subnational tax revenues in unitary countries, such as Chile, Costa Rica, Ecuador, Peru and Uruguay. These countries have a different structure of financing from more decentralised countries, where the proportion of revenues from recurrent taxes on immovable property to total subnational tax revenue is much lower.

Figure 3.2. **Revenue sources by main category for subnational governments, 2016**

Percentage of subnational tax revenue

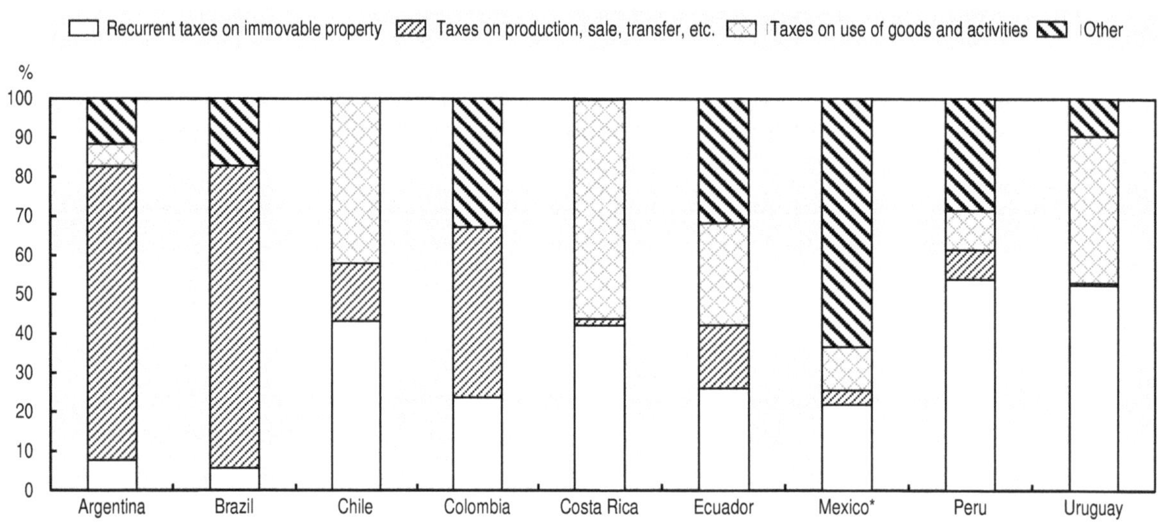

Source: (OECD/ECLAC/CIAT/IDB, 2019[6])

StatLink https://doi.org/10.1787/888933940966

Country case studies

Argentina

In Argentina, which has a federal system of government, federal and subnational jurisdictions levy taxes on real property. The federal government utilises the framework of the federal *Impuesto a los bienes personales*, which includes real property in its base as well as vehicles, financial assets and works of art. The contribution of real property to total tax collections is not identified separately in tax statistics, although some papers estimate it is 40% of the tax revenue.[4]

Provinces levy a recurrent tax on real property, both urban and rural. The immovable property tax is levied on any real property located in the relevant jurisdiction (either a province or a municipality). The taxpayer is the owner or holder of the domain and in some provinces, the occupants of the property (as in the Autonomous City of Buenos Aires.

The property tax is the third largest source of provincial revenue, equivalent to 0.4% of GDP and accounting for almost 6.9% of total provincial tax revenue. Some 88% of this revenue is generated by five of the 24 provinces, with a predominant role played by the Federal Capital (32.8%) and the province of Buenos Aires (32.2%). While in most provinces the immovable property tax is the responsibility of the provincial governments, a few (Corrientes, Chaco, Chubut, Formosa, Salta, Santa Cruz and Tierra del Fuego) have delegated the urban tax component to municipalities.

Each province is responsible for the organisation of the cadastre but municipalities also have their own cadastres. However, there exists both a National Cadastre Law and the Federal Council of Cadastre. This Council is constituted by the cadastre administrations of the 24 provinces. According to a study by (De Cesare, $2016_{[10]}$), cadastre offices usually have a relatively low hierarchy in the provincial governmental structure, and a lack of comprehensive planning prevents coordination of efforts with the corresponding tax administrations. They also note that cadastral offices often complain about a lack of staff, obsolete technology and lack of training, factors that also limit the efficiency of the property tax system.

In general, the tax base consists of both the value of the land and the construction thereupon, although in some provinces (such as Salta and Santa Fe) the value of the construction is excluded in the case of rural properties. The fiscal values of properties are typically outdated and do not correspond to their market value. Consequently, several provinces apply adjustment coefficients on the fiscal values or consider the values declared in the deeds of transfers or in Provincial Public Registries.

Another way of updating the fiscal values of property is through self-declaration by taxpayers. A self-declaration regime was recently established in Mendoza for the most valuable properties. Taxpayers covered by this regulation must declare the estimated market value of each property, including the value of the land and all improvements. The property tax for these properties is calculated by applying the aliquots provided by law to 50% of the declared market value.

Although aliquots are determined by subnational levels of government, the recent Nation-Provinces Fiscal Consensus (Consenso Fiscal) of November 2017 established that they should be within a range between 0.5% and 2% of the fiscal value of a property. In most jurisdictions, aliquots are progressive. In several cases, surcharges or higher aliquots are applied for vacant urban land.

Brazil

Brazil levies two taxes on immovable property: the tax on urban property and land (IPTU) and the rural territorial property tax (ITR). The IPTU, which generated revenue equivalent to 0.6% of GDP in 2016, is assigned to municipalities while the ITR is administered by the federal government. However, the federal government can transfer the functions of determination and collection of the ITR to municipalities if required.

The ITR is levied on the property, the productive domain or the possession of real estate located outside the urban area. Its tax base is the value of the land without improvements. Aliquots are based on the property size and degree of use, being higher for larger properties and lower degree of use; there are 30 tax rates ranging from 0.03% to 20%.

In the case of the IPTU, the calculation basis, the taxable event and the taxpayer are defined by the National Tax Code (and are thus the same for all municipalities). In contrast, aliquots, tax brackets, exemptions and other elements are established by the legislation of each municipality.

The IPTU is levied on the property, use domain or possession of real estate located in urban areas. The taxable base is the value of the property that includes the value of the land and the construction. The aliquots can be proportional (a flat rate tax), progressive or can vary according to the location and use of the property. In addition to determining the aliquots and exemptions, municipalities are responsible for activities related to tax administration, such as organisation and updating of the cadastre, the valuation of property, the determination of the tax payable and collection.

The strategies for updating cadastral data vary between municipalities. Some only update data when the taxpayer declares changes made to his property. Others carry out physical inspections and/or cross-check information with different databases, either from the same municipality or from other public or private institutions, such as the property registry, the Tax on Transmission of Real Estate, cadastre of electricity concession companies or other public services.

In 2009, the Ministry of Cities published an ordinance with guidelines for the creation, institution and updating of the Multi-Land Territorial Cadastre in municipalities (Portaria MCid nº 511). However, these guidelines are not binding. They recommend that the valuation of property be carried out through a transparent technical process and use the market value as a basis for calculating the IPTU and other property taxes. The guidelines also include minimum parameters for the level and uniformity of fiscal valuations and specify a four-year limit between valuation cycles (for small municipalities the limit is eight years).

In general, municipalities estimate the land value by the comparative method, using unitary land values for homogeneous zones and applying adjustments to reflect the characteristics of the land and its location. To estimate the value of a building, they consider the average unit costs according to the type of construction and apply an adjustment for depreciation. In general, municipalities update these values annually using an inflation index.

According to (De Cesare, 2016[10]), in addition to pressures from the population to update property values, municipalities face legal and juridical obstacles, as there is a strong political influence on inherently technical activities. The author points out that the IPTU is the only tax whose update of the taxable base needs the approval of the Legislative Power. In addition, judicial interventions have prevented the application of new fiscal values of properties that were established legally.

Colombia

Colombia, which has a unitary but decentralised system of government, is one of the countries that raise the highest proportion of revenue from recurrent taxes on immovable property. In 2016, it generated revenues equivalent to about 0.8% of GDP, making it the second-largest subnational tax instrument, with a share of almost 24% (Figure 3.2).

Revenue from the Impuesto Predial Unificado (IPU), originally under departmental jurisdiction, was assigned to municipalities by the 1991 Constitution. Municipalities are empowered to determine tax rates (within a pre-established range), exemptions and other preferential treatment.

The IPU is levied on both urban and rural properties. The taxable base in this case is determined by cadastral valuation carried out by decentralised cadastre offices in Bogotá, Antioquia, Cali and Medellín, and by the Geographic Institute Agustín Codazzi (IGAC) in other departments. Real estate values are in principle updated annually according to variation of the consumer price index.

Most municipalities in Colombia have problems updating cadastral values relative to changing market values. In general, municipal authorities can set tax rates within a certain range with respect to the cadastral valuation, using a differentiated and progressive structure depending on social stratification and land use in urban areas, which determine the taxable value of the buildings on which the property tax is levied.

The design of Colombia's property tax has contributed to an increase in revenue from recurrent taxes on immovable property from 0.2% of GDP in 1990 to 0.8% of GDP in 2016. Since 1991, there has also been a gradual adoption of modern tax administration methods, starting with Bogotá and rolled out gradually across major metropolitan areas.

Municipalities are allowed to opt for an "autoavalúo" (or self-declaration) system, subject to minimum criteria based on the IGAC Cadaster. These minimum criteria (size, location) must be approved by the Municipal Council. Particularly important in this case are the sanctions applied in case of an egregious mis-declaration.

Notes

1. Many of the developments presented in this chapter are based on an article named "An expanded role for property taxation in Latin America: adopting a simplified tax structure and digital technology" from Ahmad, Brosio and Jiménez, in print.
2. For more details about subnational own revenues, tax autonomy and intergovernmental transfers see Revenue Statistics in Latin America and the Caribbean, BID-CEPAL-CIAT-OECD, 2019) and (Jiménez and Ruelas, 2018[12]).
3. For more details about subnational own revenues and vertical gap, see (Boadway and Eyraud, 2018[11]).
4. See (Castro et al., 2014[13]).

References

Ahmad, E., G. Brosio and J. Gerbrandy (2018), *Property taxation - Economic features, revenue potential and administrative issues in a development context*, Directorate-General for International Cooperation and Development (European Commission), *http://dx.doi.org/10.2841/838791*. [2]

Ahmad, E., G. Brosio and J. Pablo Jiménez (2018), *La tributación sobre la propiedad en América Latina Adopción de una estructura tributaria simplificada y tecnología digital*, *https://www.cepal.org/sites/default/files/events/files/brosio_jimenez_ppt.pdf* (accessed on 25 February 2019). [1]

Biderman, C. and Y. Camara Batista (2018), "Is Progressive Property Tax Progressive? Evidences from São Paulo", No. WP18CB1, Lincoln Institute of Land Policy, *https://www.lincolninst.edu/sites/default/files/pubfiles/wp18cb1_biderman.pdf* (accessed on 25 February 2019). [8]

Blöchliger, H. (2015), "Reforming the Tax on Immovable Property: Taking Care of the Unloved", *OECD Economics Department Working Papers*, No. 1205, OECD Publishing, Paris, *https://dx.doi.org/10.1787/5js30tw0n7kg-en*. [7]

Boadway, R. and L. Eyraud (2018), "Designing Sound Fiscal Relations Across Government Levels in Decentralized Countries", No. WP/18/271, IMF, *https://www.imf.org/en/Publications/WP/Issues/2018/12/10/Designing-Sound-Fiscal-Relations-Across-Government-Levels-in-Decentralized-Countries-46425* (accessed on 25 February 2019). [11]

Brosio, G. and J. Jiménez (2012), *Decentralization and Reform in Latin America*, Economic Commission for Latin America and the Caribbean / Edward Elgar, *http://www.fcc.org* (accessed on 25 February 2019). [9]

Castro, L. et al. (2014), "Desafíos y potencial del impuesto inmobiliario en la Argentina LUCIO CASTRO LUCIANA DÍAZ FRERS ANA CLAUDIA ALFIERI", No. 120, CIPPEC, Buenos Aires, *https://www.cippec.org/wp-content/uploads/2017/03/1359.pdf* (accessed on 25 February 2019). [13]

De Cesare, C. (2016), "Relevancia del impuesto inmobiliario", in Cláudia M. De Cesare (ed.), *Sistemas del impuesto predial en América Latina y el Caribe*, Lincoln Institute of Land Policy, *https://www.lincolninst.edu/sites/default/files/pubfiles/sistemas-del-impuesto-predial-full-3.pdf* (accessed on 25 February 2019). [10]

Gómez Sabaini, J., J. Jiménez and R. Martner (2017), *Consensos y conflictos en la política tributaria de América Latina*, Comisión Económica para América Latina y el Caribe (CEPAL), Santiago, *http://www.cepal.org/es/suscripciones* (accessed on 25 February 2019). [3]

Jiménez, J. and I. Ruelas (2018), "Autonomía tributaria subnacional en América Latina", *Working Papers*, No. 2018-10, *https://ideas.repec.org/p/fda/fdaddt/2018-10.html* (accessed on 25 February 2019). [12]

Norregaard, J. (2013), "Taxing Immovable Property - Revenue Potential and Implementation Challenges", *Working Paper 13/129*, IMF, *https://www.imf.org/external/pubs/ft/wp/2013/wp13129.pdf* (accessed on 25 February 2019). [5]

OECD et al. (2018), *Revenue Statistics in Latin America and the Caribbean 2018*, OECD Publishing, Paris, *https://dx.doi.org/10.1787/rev_lat_car-2018-en-fr*. [4]

OECD/ECLAC/CIAT/IDB (2019), *Revenue Statistics in Latin America and the Caribbean 2019*, OECD, Paris. [6]

Capítulo 3

SECCIÓN ESPECIAL
Impuesto a la propiedad en América Latina

Principales hallazgos

Los impuestos recurrentes sobre los bienes inmuebles son un mecanismo crítico para los gobiernos locales, permitiéndoles establecer tasas en el margen para financiar servicios básicos. Estas necesidades se acentúan en América Latina por la extensa urbanización, que a menudo está acompañada por el crecimiento de asentamientos informales. Sin embargo, la administración de los impuestos a la propiedad es compleja, el seguimiento de la propiedad es incompleto y los sistemas de valoración de la propiedad no son sencillos.

Los ingresos generados por los impuestos recurrentes sobre bienes inmuebles en América Latina son bajos en relación con los de los países de la OCDE. Los ingresos de este instrumento variaron significativamente entre los países en 2016, desde el 0.1% del producto interno bruto (PIB) en Ecuador hasta el 0.9% del PIB en Uruguay. En su mayor parte, los ingresos fueron equivalentes a alrededor del 0.3% del PIB, frente a un promedio de la OCDE del 1.1% del PIB.

La responsabilidad del diseño y la administración del impuesto a la propiedad en América Latina varía ampliamente. El sistema gubernamental es un factor crítico detrás del nivel de generación de ingresos: los impuestos recurrentes sobre bienes inmuebles proporcionan una parte significativa de los ingresos tributarios subnacionales en países unitarios, como Chile, Costa Rica, Ecuador, Perú y Uruguay.

Los estudios de caso de Argentina, Brasil y Colombia identifican las restricciones y los elementos facilitadores para obtener mayores ingresos por impuestos recurrentes sobre bienes inmuebles en mayor profundidad.

La importancia de los impuestos sobre la propiedad en la Agenda para el Desarrollo Sostenible es crecientemente reconocida, aún teniendo en cuenta que sus ingresos fiscales siguen siendo relativamente pequeños en comparación con otros tipos de impuestos (Ahmad, Brosio and Pablo Jiménez, 2018[1]). En este capítulo se discute la experiencia de América Latina respecto a los impuestos a la propiedad, focalizando en aquellos recurrentes sobre bienes inmuebles. La primera sección explica por qué los impuestos a la propiedad inmueble son importantes; la segunda discute la evolución de los ingresos provenientes de estos tributos en los países de América Latina, y la tercera sección incluye estudios de caso de Argentina, Colombia y Brasil.

¿Por qué los impuestos a la propiedad son importantes?[1]

Los impuestos sobre la propiedad incluyen diferentes flujos de ingresos: impuestos recurrentes sobre bienes inmuebles, sobre patrimonio neto, impuestos sobre sucesiones, herencias y donaciones, impuestos sobre transacciones financieras y de capital y otros impuestos sobre la propiedad (Ahmad, Brosio and Pablo Jiménez, 2018[1]). En esta sección, nos concentramos en los ingresos por impuestos recurrentes sobre bienes inmuebles, enfatizando su importancia en la financiación de los gobiernos subnacionales.

Los ingresos por impuestos recurrentes sobre bienes inmuebles en economías en desarrollo y emergentes promedian muy por debajo del 1% del PIB (Ahmad, Brosio and Gerbrandy, 2018[2]). La literatura reciente (Gómez Sabaini, Jiménez and Martner, 2017[3]); (OECD et al., 2018[4]) confirma que los ingresos por impuestos sobre bienes inmuebles desempeñan un papel menor, aunque con diferencias entre países, en términos del PIB y en relación con la recaudación impositiva total en América Latina. En Colombia y Uruguay, dichos ingresos fueron equivalentes al 0.8% y al 0.9% del PIB en 2016, respectivamente, pero en su mayor parte las recaudaciones son alrededor del 0.3% del PIB (Gráfico 3.1). El promedio de la OCDE fue de 1.1% del PIB en 2016.

Visto en perspectiva intergubernamental, la imposición recurrente sobre bienes inmuebles puede ser un importante recurso subnacional propio, en la medida en que el gobierno subnacional pueda determinar las tasas y la base imponible, permitiendo la financiación de la provisión de servicios locales básicos.[2] Esto a su vez fortalece la rendición de cuentas y la toma de decisiones de los gobiernos locales, así como la sostenibilidad fiscal (Norregaard, 2013[5]).

Las transferencias del gobierno central, incluso aquellas que no están previamente asignadas, no son recursos propios en la medida en que no permiten incrementar sus ingresos a los gobiernos locales cuando sea necesario.[3] El grado de eficiencia y el efecto distributivo de la imposición a la propiedad depende del diseño de política, teniendo en cuenta, por ejemplo, si los hogares pobres, o con restricciones de liquidez, se benefician de la exenciones fiscales; o si deben ser pagados por los propietarios o por los ocupantes de la propiedad (Blöchliger, 2015[6]); (Biderman and Camara Batista, 2018[7]).

Adicionalmente, un sistema de impuestos a la propiedad puede proveer información sobre los activos; la información de transacciones y valuaciones provenientes de los impuestos a la propiedad puede ser usada para verificar las declaraciones de impuestos a la renta personal realizadas por los individuos.

Gráfico 3.1. **Impuestos recurrentes sobre bienes inmuebles en América Latina**

Porcentaje del PIB

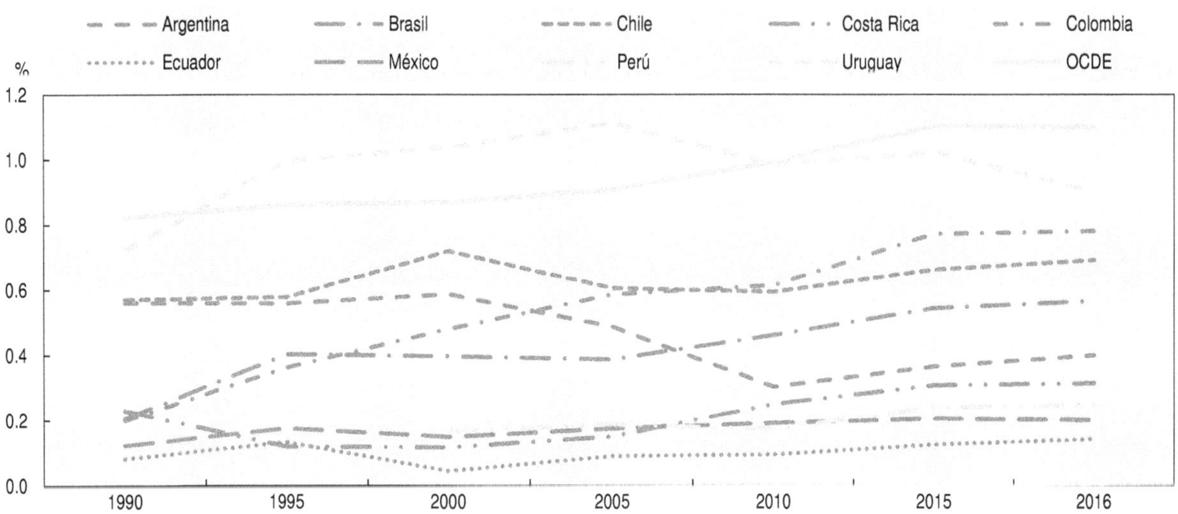

Fuente: (OECD/ECLAC/CIAT/IDB, 2019[8])

StatLink https://doi.org/10.1787/888933940985

Sin embargo, los impuestos a la propiedad tienen numerosas limitaciones, lo que se traduce en ingresos por debajo de su potencial y que no satisfacen las necesidades de los gobiernos locales – necesidades exacerbadas por la creciente urbanización, la migración a ciudades y los extensos asentamientos informales. Adicionalmente, la administración de los impuestos a la propiedad es compleja, el rastreo de propiedades incompleto, y el sistema de valoración de propiedades engorroso. Usualmente los valores estimados de las propiedades están por debajo de los precios de mercado.

Evolución y características de los ingresos por impuestos recurrentes sobre bienes inmuebles en países de América Latina

La mayoría de los países en la región dependen de los sistemas de catastro tradicionales para determinar los títulos de propiedad y sus respectivas valuaciones. El mantenimiento de los catastros suele ser la base de los sistemas de administración de propiedades (Ahmad, Brosio and Pablo Jiménez, 2018[1]). Sin embargo, mantener los catastros y actualizarlos resulta una tarea difícil, compleja y costosa. La situación se vuelve más compleja aún con la existencia de tierras comunales, y las migraciones internas que conducen a asentamientos "informales", especialmente en los alrededores de las grandes áreas metropolitanas.

Otros países han experimentado formas innovadoras, como determinar valores a través de autodeclaración (en algunas ciudades colombianas) o sistemas paramétricos (en Bolivia) basados en información sobre las características de las propiedades, proporcionadas por los contribuyentes.

En algunos países de América Latina, como Argentina, el valor de los bienes inmuebles sirve como base para la determinación de tasas y cargos por la prestación de servicios locales específicos, como la recolección de basura, la limpieza e iluminación de las calles y los sistemas de alcantarillado. Sin embargo, esto profundiza la necesidad de valoraciones de propiedad precisas y actualizadas para asegurar una adecuada coordinación fiscal intergubernamental.

La responsabilidad por el diseño y la administración del impuesto a la propiedad en América Latina varía ampliamente. En algunos países, la tasa impositiva es establecida por la jurisdicción local, lo que la convierte en una fuente de ingresos propia. En otros países, el poder para establecer tasas recae en el gobierno central (o los gobiernos intermedios) y los ingresos se comparten con los gobiernos subnacionales (intermedios o locales).

En los países menos descentralizados, los ingresos por impuestos recurrentes sobre bienes inmuebles siguen siendo una fuente importante de ingresos (Gráfico 3.2). Estos tributos proporcionan una parte significativa de los ingresos tributarios subnacionales en países unitarios, como Chile, Costa Rica, Ecuador, Perú y Uruguay. Estos países tienen estructuras de financiamiento muy diferentes de los países más descentralizados, donde la proporción de los ingresos provenientes de los impuestos recurrentes a los bienes inmuebles sobre los ingresos totales subnacionales es mucho menor.

Gráfico 3.2. **Fuentes de ingreso por categorías principales para gobiernos subnacionales, 2016**

Porcentaje del total del ingreso por impuesto

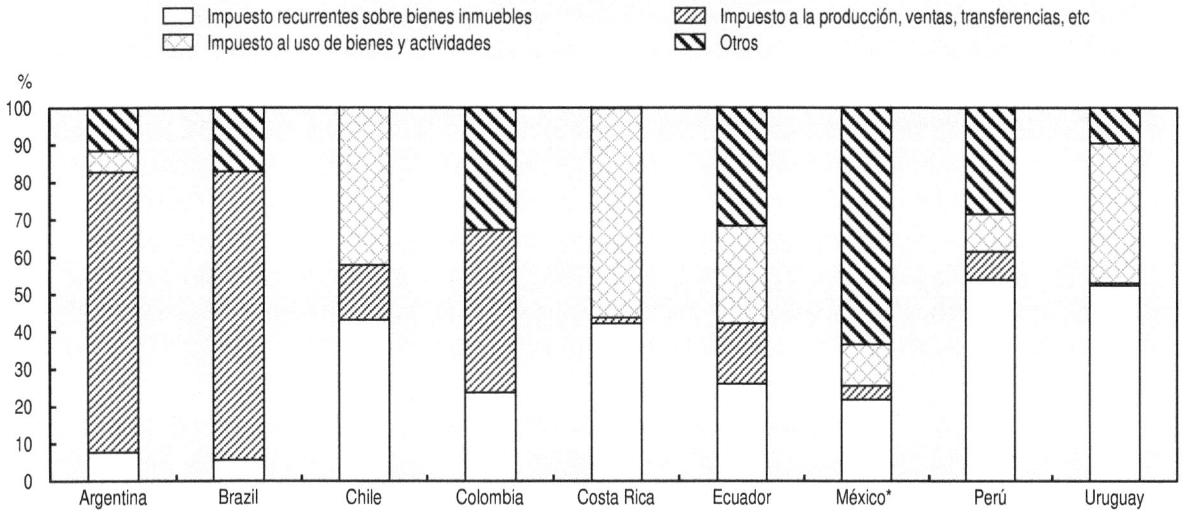

Fuente: (OECD/ECLAC/CIAT/IDB, 2019[8]).

StatLink https://doi.org/10.1787/888933941004

Estudios de caso

Argentina

En Argentina, que tiene un sistema federal de gobierno, tanto las jurisdicciones federales como las subnacionales imponen impuestos sobre bienes inmuebles. El gobierno federal utiliza el marco del impuesto federal sobre los bienes personales, que incluye bienes inmuebles en su base imponible, así como vehículos, activos financieros y obras de arte. La contribución de los bienes inmuebles a la recaudación total de impuestos no se identifica por separado en las estadísticas fiscales, si bien algunos trabajos lo estiman en el 40% del total del impuesto.[4]

Las provincias imponen un impuesto recurrente sobre bienes inmuebles, tanto urbanos como rurales. El impuesto a la propiedad es la tercera fuente de ingresos provinciales, representando el 0.4% del PIB y casi el 6.9% del ingreso tributario provincial total (Gráficos 3.1 y 3.2). Además, el 88% de este ingreso tributario se genera en cinco de las 24 provincias, con un papel predominante desempeñado por la Capital Federal (32.8%) y la provincia de Buenos Aires (32.2%).

Mientras que en la mayoría de las provincias el impuesto a la propiedad inmobiliaria sigue siendo responsabilidad de los gobiernos provinciales, algunos de ellos (Corrientes, Chaco, Chubut, Formosa, Salta, Santa Cruz y Tierra del Fuego) han delegado el componente urbano del impuesto a los municipios.

El impuesto a la propiedad inmobiliaria se aplica a cualquier propiedad real ubicada en la jurisdicción en cuestión (ya sea una provincia o un municipio). El contribuyente es el propietario o titular del dominio y en algunas provincias, los ocupantes de la propiedad (como en la Ciudad Autónoma de Buenos Aires)

Cada provincia es responsable de la organización del catastro, pero los municipios también tienen sus propios catastros. Sin embargo, existe tanto una Ley Nacional de Catastro como un Consejo Federal de Catastro. Este Consejo está constituido por las administraciones de catastro de las 23 provincias y el Gobierno de la Ciudad de Buenos Aires (GCBA). Según un estudio (Castro et al., 2014[9]), las oficinas de catastro suelen tener una jerarquía relativamente baja en la estructura gubernamental provincial, y la falta de una planificación integral impide la coordinación de esfuerzos con las administraciones tributarias correspondientes. También señalan que las oficinas catastrales a menudo se quejan de la falta de personal, tecnología obsoleta y falta de capacitación, factores que también limitan la eficiencia del sistema de impuestos a la propiedad.

En general, la base imponible consiste tanto en el valor del terreno como en la construcción del mismo, aunque en algunas provincias (como Salta y Santa Fe) el valor de la construcción se excluye en el caso de las propiedades rurales. Los valores fiscales de las propiedades suelen estar desactualizados y no corresponden al valor de mercado. En consecuencia, varias provincias aplican coeficientes de ajuste en los valores fiscales o consideran los valores declarados en las escrituras de las transferencias o en los registros públicos provinciales.

Otra forma de actualizar los valores fiscales de la propiedad es a través de la autodeclaración de los contribuyentes. Recientemente se estableció un régimen de autodeclaración en Mendoza para las propiedades más valiosas. Los contribuyentes incluidos en este régimen deben declarar el valor de mercado estimado de cada propiedad, incluido el valor de la tierra y todas las mejoras. El impuesto a la propiedad para estas propiedades se calcula aplicando las tasas determinadas en la ley correspondiente al 50% del valor de mercado declarado.

Si bien las tasas están determinadas por los niveles subnacionales de gobierno, el reciente Consenso Fiscal entre el gobierno nacional y las Provincias de noviembre de 2017 estableció que deberían estar dentro del rango entre 0.5% y 2% del valor fiscal de la propiedad. En la mayoría de las jurisdicciones, las tasas son progresivas. En muchos casos, se aplican recargos o alícuotas superiores para terrenos urbanos no utilizados.

Brasil

En Brasil existen dos impuestos que gravan los bienes inmuebles: el impuesto sobre propiedad predial y territorial urbana (IPTU) y el impuesto sobre la propiedad territorial rural (ITR). El IPTU, cuya recaudación para 2016 llegó a 0.6% del PIB, se asigna a los municipios, mientras que el ITR es administrado por el gobierno federal. Sin embargo, el gobierno federal puede transferir las funciones de determinación y recolección del ITR a los municipios, si así lo requieren.

La ITR se aplica a la propiedad, el dominio útil o la posesión de bienes inmuebles ubicados fuera del área urbana; su base imponible es el valor del terreno sin mejoras. Las alícuotas se basan en la superficie de la propiedad y su grado de utilización, siendo mayores para las propiedades más grandes y con un menor grado de utilización (hay 30 alícuotas impositivas que van del 0.03% al 20%).

En el caso del IPTU, la base de cálculo, el hecho imponible y el sujeto pasivo están definidos por el Código Tributario Nacional (y, por lo tanto, son los mismos para todos los municipios). En contraste, la legislación de cada municipio establece tasas, tramos fiscales, exenciones y otros elementos.

El IPTU se aplica a la propiedad, dominio útil o posesión de bienes inmuebles ubicados en áreas urbanas. La base imponible es el valor de la propiedad que incluye el valor del terreno y la construcción. Las tasas pueden ser proporcionales (un impuesto de tasa plana), progresivas o pueden variar según la ubicación y el uso de la propiedad. Además de determinar las tasas y las exenciones, los municipios son responsables de las actividades relacionadas con la administración del impuesto, como la organización y actualización del catastro, la valuación de la propiedad, la determinación del impuesto a pagar y las funciones de recaudación y cobranza.

Las estrategias para actualizar los datos catastrales varían entre municipios. En algunos de ellos solo se actualizan datos cuando el contribuyente declara cambios hechos en su propiedad. Otros también realizan fiscalizaciones e inspecciones físicas y/o cruzan información con diferentes bases de datos, ya sea del mismo municipio o de otras instituciones públicas o privadas (como el registro de propiedad, el Impuesto sobre la Transmisión de Bienes Inmuebles, el catastro de empresas concesionarias de electricidad o de otros servicios públicos).

En 2009, el Ministerio de Ciudades publicó una ordenanza con pautas para la creación, institución y actualización del Catastro Territorial Múltifinalitario (CTM) en los municipios (Portaria MCid nº511). Sin embargo, estas directrices no son vinculantes. Recomiendan que la valuación de los inmuebles se realice a través de un proceso técnico transparente y que utilicen el valor de mercado como base para calcular el IPTU y otros impuestos a la propiedad. Los lineamientos también incluyen parámetros mínimos para el nivel y la uniformidad de las valuaciones fiscales y especifican un límite de cuatro años entre los ciclos de valuación (para los municipios pequeños el límite es de ocho años).

En general, los municipios estiman el valor de la tierra por el método comparativo directo, utilizando valores unitarios de la tierra para zonas homogéneas y aplicando ajustes para reflejar las características de la tierra y su ubicación. Para estimar el valor del edificio, consideran los costos unitarios promedio de acuerdo con el tipo de construcción y aplican un ajuste por depreciación. En general, los municipios actualizan estos valores anualmente utilizando algún índice de inflación.

Según (De Cesare, 2016[10]), además de las presiones de la población para actualizar los valores de las propiedades, los municipios enfrentan obstáculos legales y jurídicos, ya que existe una fuerte influencia política en las actividades inherentemente técnicas. También señala que el IPTU es el único impuesto cuya actualización de la base imponible necesita la aprobación del Poder Legislativo. Además, las intervenciones judiciales han impedido la aplicación de nuevos avalúos establecidos de manera legal.

Colombia

Colombia, que tiene un sistema de gobierno unitario pero descentralizado, es uno de los países que genera la mayor proporción de ingresos por impuestos recurrentes sobre bienes inmuebles. En 2016, generó ingresos equivalentes a aproximadamente el 0.8% del PIB, lo que lo convierte en el segundo impuesto subnacional en importancia recaudatoria, con una participación de casi el 24% (Gráfico 3.2).

Los recursos provenientes del Impuesto Predial Unificado (UIP), originalmente bajo jurisdicción departamental, fueron asignados a los municipios por la Constitución de 1991. Los municipios están facultados para determinar las tasas de impuestos (dentro de un rango preestablecido), las exenciones y otros tratos preferenciales.

La UIP se aplica tanto a propiedades urbanas como rurales. La base imponible en este caso está determinada por la valoración catastral realizada por las oficinas descentralizadas del catastro en Bogotá, Antioquia, Cali y Medellín, y por el Instituto Geográfico Agustín

Codazzi (IGAC) en el resto de los departamentos. En principio, los valores inmobiliarios se actualizan anualmente de acuerdo con la variación del índice de precios al consumidor.

La mayoría de los municipios de Colombia tienen problemas para actualizar los valores catastrales en relación con los cambios en los valores de mercado. En general, las autoridades municipales pueden establecer tasas impositivas dentro de un cierto rango con respecto a la valoración catastral, utilizando una estructura diferenciada y progresiva según la estratificación social y el uso del suelo en áreas urbanas, que determinan el valor imponible de los edificios sobre los cuales se grava el impuesto a la propiedad.

El diseño del impuesto a la propiedad de Colombia ha contribuido a un aumento de los ingresos por impuestos recurrentes sobre bienes inmuebles desde el 0.2% del PIB en 1990 al 0.8% del PIB en 2016. Desde 1991, también se ha venido desarrollando una modernización gradual de la administración tributaria, comenzando con Bogotá y desplegándose gradualmente en las principales áreas metropolitanas.

Los municipios pueden optar por un sistema de "autoavalúo" (o autodeclaración), sujeto a criterios mínimos basados en el catastro del IGAC. Estos criterios mínimos (tamaño, ubicación) deben ser aprobados por el Consejo Municipal respectivo. Particularmente importantes en este caso son las sanciones aplicadas en caso de una declaración errónea grave.

Notas

1. Muchos de los desarrollos presentados en este capítulo se basan en un artículo titulado "Un rol más amplio para el impuesto a la propiedad en América Latina: adopción de una estructura tributaria simplificada y tecnología digital" de Ahmad, Brosio y Jiménez, en imprenta.
2. Para obtener más detalles sobre los ingresos propios subnacionales, la autonomía fiscal y las transferencias intergubernamentales, consulte Rev Stat en LA, BID-CEPAL-CIAT-OECD, 2017); (Jiménez and Ruelas, 2018[12]).
3. Para obtener más detalles sobre los ingresos propios subnacionales y la brecha vertical, consulte (Boadway and Eyraud, 2018[11]).
4. Véase (Castro et al., 2014[9]).

Referencias

Ahmad, E., G. Brosio and J. Gerbrandy (2018), *Property taxation - Economic features, revenue potential and administrative issues in a development context*, Directorate-General for International Cooperation and Development (European Commission), *http://dx.doi.org/10.2841/838791*. [2]

Ahmad, E., G. Brosio and J. Pablo Jiménez (2018), *La tributación sobre la propiedad en América Latina Adopción de una estructura tributaria simplificada y tecnología digital*, *https://www.cepal.org/sites/default/files/events/files/brosio_jimenez_ppt.pdf* (accessed on 25 February 2019). [1]

Biderman, C. and Y. Camara Batista (2018), "Is Progressive Property Tax Progressive? Evidences from São Paulo", No. WP18CB1, Lincoln Institute of Land Policy, *https://www.lincolninst.edu/sites/default/files/pubfiles/wp18cb1_biderman.pdf* (accessed on 25 February 2019). [7]

Blöchliger, H. (2015), "Reforming the Tax on Immovable Property: Taking Care of the Unloved", *OECD Economics Department Working Papers*, No. 1205, OECD Publishing, Paris, *https://dx.doi.org/10.1787/5js30tw0n7kg-en*. [6]

Boadway, R. and L. Eyraud (2018), "Designing Sound Fiscal Relations Across Government Levels in Decentralized Countries", No. WP/18/271, IMF, *https://www.imf.org/en/Publications/WP/Issues/2018/12/10/Designing-Sound-Fiscal-Relations-Across-Government-Levels-in-Decentralized-Countries-46425* (accessed on 25 February 2019). [11]

Castro, L. et al. (2014), "Desafíos y potencial del impuesto inmobiliario en la Argentina LUCIO CASTRO LUCIANA DÍAZ FRERS ANA CLAUDIA ALFIERI", No. 120, CIPPEC, Buenos Aires, *https://www.cippec.org/wp-content/uploads/2017/03/1359.pdf* (accessed on 25 February 2019). [9]

De Cesare, C. (2016), "Relevancia del impuesto inmobiliario", in Cláudia M. De Cesare (ed.), *Sistemas del impuesto predial en América Latina y el Caribe*, Lincoln Institute of Land Policy, *https://www.lincolninst.edu/sites/default/files/pubfiles/sistemas-del-impuesto-predial-full-3.pdf* (accessed on 25 February 2019). [10]

Gómez Sabaini, J., J. Jiménez and R. Martner (2017), *Consensos y conflictos en la política tributaria de América Latina*, Comisión Económica para América Latina y el Caribe (CEPAL), Santiago, *http://www.cepal.org/es/suscripciones* (accessed on 25 February 2019). [3]

Jiménez, J. and I. Ruelas (2018), "Autonomía tributaria subnacional en América Latina", *Working Papers*, No. 2018-10, *https://ideas.repec.org/p/fda/fdaddt/2018-10.html* (accessed on 25 February 2019). [12]

Norregaard, J. (2013), "Taxing Immovable Property - Revenue Potential and Implementation Challenges", *Working Paper 13/129*, IMF, *https://www.imf.org/external/pubs/ft/wp/2013/wp13129.pdf* (accessed on 25 February 2019). [5]

OECD et al. (2018), *Revenue Statistics in Latin America and the Caribbean 2018*, OECD Publishing, Paris, *https://dx.doi.org/10.1787/rev_lat_car-2018-en-fr*. [4]

OECD/ECLAC/CIAT/IDB (2019), *Revenue Statistics in Latin America and the Caribbean 2019*. [8]

Chapter 4

Tax levels and Tax structures, 1990-2017

Capítulo 4

Niveles impositivos y estructuras tributarias, 1990-2017

Chapter 4 / Capítulo 4

4.1. Comparative tables, 1990-2017

In all of the following tables a (..) indicates not available. The main series in this volume cover the years 1990 to 2017.

Figures referring to 1991-99, 2001-04 and 2006-09 in Tables 4.1 to 4.2 and Tables 4.15 to 4.17, figures relating to 1991-99, 2001-09 and 2011-15 in Tables 4.5 to 4.10 and figures relating to 1990-94, 1996-99 and 2001-15 in Tables 4.11 to 4.13 have been omitted because of lack of space. Complete series are, however, available on line at www.latameconomy.org and in the database OECD (2019), "Revenue Statistics in Latin America: Comparative tables", *OECD Tax Statistics*, *http://dx.doi.org/10.1787/data-00641-en.*

4.2. Cuadros comparativos, 1990-2017

En todos los cuadros siguientes, (..) indica dato indisponible. Las principales series de datos de esta sección cubren el periodo que va de 1990 a 2017.

Las cifras relativas a 1991-99, 2001-04 y a 2006-09 en Cuadros 4.1 hasta 4.2 y Cuadros 4.15 hasta 4.17 y las cifras relativas a 1991-99, 2001-09 y 2011-15 en Cuadros 4.5 hasta 4.10 y las cifras relativas a 1990-94, 1996-99 y 2001-15 en Cuadros 4.11 hasta 4.13 a se han omitido por falta de espacio. Sin embargo, las series completas están disponibles en línea en www.latameconomy.org y en la base de datos OCDE (2019), "Revenue Statistics in Latin America: Comparative tables", *OECD Tax Statistics*, *http://dx.doi.org/10.1787/data-00641-en.*

Table 4.1. **Total tax revenue as % of GDP, 1990-2017**
Cuadro 4.1. **Total de ingresos tributarios en % del PIB, 1990-2017**

	1990	2000	2005	2010	2012	2013	2014	2015	2016	2017
Argentina	13.7	19.8	24.5	29.1	30.6	31.2	31.1	31.5	30.8	30.3
Bahamas[1]	9.7	11.9	10.8	12.6	13.8	13.6	13.6	14.9	16.8	17.9
Barbados	23.2	30.8	29.3	29.8	31.0	27.5	28.1	31.0	29.6	31.8
Belize / Belice[1]	21.4	18.9	21.8	26.2	24.8	25.4	27.0	26.5	27.5	28.2
Bolivia[1]	8.3	17.6	20.1	20.7	24.6	25.5	26.2	27.6	25.9	23.9
Brazil / Brasil	25.5	29.6	32.8	32.3	32.4	32.4	31.7	31.9	32.1	32.3
Chile	16.9	18.8	20.7	19.6	21.3	19.9	19.6	20.4	20.2	20.2
Colombia	9.2	14.8	18.2	18.0	19.7	20.0	19.5	19.8	19.0	18.8
Costa Rica	22.5	21.2	21.9	22.4	22.9	23.5	23.3	23.6	24.2	24.1
Cuba	29.1	37.2	41.1	37.6	39.7	37.3	37.5	38.6	41.6	40.6
Dominican Republic / República Dominicana	8.3	12.3	13.8	12.3	13.1	13.6	13.7	13.4	13.6	13.9
Ecuador	7.2	10.3	12.1	16.6	19.8	19.6	19.3	21.3	19.9	19.9
El Salvador	10.5	13.5	16.5	17.9	18.3	19.2	18.7	19.4	20.1	20.4
Guatemala	8.3	12.4	13.1	12.4	12.9	13.0	12.7	12.4	12.6	12.4
Guyana[1]	20.6	20.8	23.0	24.2	22.5	22.9	23.9	24.2	23.6	26.2
Honduras	12.4	16.2	17.9	18.1	18.4	19.0	20.2	20.8	22.3	22.8
Jamaica	20.3	22.2	23.3	24.9	24.5	24.9	24.7	25.8	26.5	27.3
Mexico / México[2]	12.1	11.5	11.4	12.8	12.6	13.3	13.7	15.9	16.6	16.2
Nicaragua	..	13.0	17.2	19.3	20.8	21.2	21.8	22.6	23.4	23.8
Panama / Panamá	15.9	15.9	13.8	16.0	16.1	16.4	15.1	15.2	15.3	14.7
Paraguay	5.8	11.6	11.2	12.0	13.1	12.3	13.5	13.6	13.3	13.8
Peru / Perú	12.1	14.8	16.3	17.5	18.8	18.7	19.0	17.2	16.0	15.3
Trinidad and Tobago / Trinidad y Tobago[1]	24.4	22.4	28.1	28.7	27.9	28.2	30.2	29.9	23.4	22.2
Uruguay	19.9	21.9	24.0	26.3	26.9	27.6	27.4	27.3	29.0	30.9
Venezuela[3]	18.1	13.6	15.9	11.8	14.1	14.4	17.9	20.2	..	..
Unweighted average / Promedio no ponderado										
LAC / ALC[4]	**15.5**	**18.3**	**20.1**	**21.1**	**21.9**	**21.9**	**22.1**	**22.7**	**22.6**	**22.8**
OECD / OCDE[5]	**31.9**	**33.8**	**33.4**	**32.3**	**33.1**	**33.4**	**33.6**	**33.7**	**34.0**	**34.2**

Note: The figures exclude local government revenues for Argentina (but include provincial revenues), the Bahamas, Barbados, Cuba, the Dominican Republic, Honduras and Venezuela as the data are not available. The local government revenue data are available since 1994 for Bolivia, since 1998 for Jamaica and Panama, since 2000 for Peru, since 2002 for El Salvador, since 2004 for Paraguay and since 2010 for Nicaragua and since 1990 for all other countries.

1. The data include the following estimations: Bahamas (social security contributions from 2016), Belize (social security contributions from 2016), Bolivia (local tax revenues for 2017), Guyana (social security contributions from 2015), Trinidad and Tobago (local tax revenues for 2017). See the corresponding country tables for more information.
2. The data are estimated for 2017 including expected revenues for state and local governments.
3. Some tax revenue data are not available from 2014 and therefore total figures have not been included.
4. Represents the group of 24 Latin American and Caribbean countries included in this publication and excludes Venezuela due to data availability issues. Chile and Mexico are also part of the OECD (36) group.
5. Calculated by applying the unweighted average percentage change for 2017 in the 34 countries providing data for that year to the overall average tax to GDP ratio in 2016.

Nota : Las cifras excluyen los ingresos de gobiernos locales en Argentina (pero incluye ingresos de las provincias), Bahamas, Barbados, Cuba, Repúblic Dominicana, Honduras y Venezuela, ya que los datos no están disponibles. Los datos de ingresos del gobierno local están disponibles desde 1994 para Bolivia, desde 1998 para Jamaica y Panamá, 2000 para Perú, 2002 para El Salvador, 2004 para Paraguay y 2010 para Nicaragua y 1990 para todos los demás países.

1. Los datos incluyen las siguientes estimaciones: Bahamas (contribuciones a la seguridad social desde 2016), Belice (contribuciones a la seguridad social desde 2016), Bolivia (ingresos tributarios de los gobiernos locales para 2017), Guyana (contribuciones a la seguridad social desde 2015), Trinidad y Tobago (ingresos tributarios de los gobiernos locales para 2017).Véanse las tablas de país para mayor información.
2. Los datos estimados incluyen ingresos esperados a nivel estatal y local para el 2017.
3. Algunos datos de ingresos tributarios no están disponibles a partir de 2014 y, por lo tanto, no se han incluido las cifras totales.
4. Representa el grupo de 24 países de América Latina y el Caribe incluido en esta publicación y excluye a Venezuela debido a problemas de disponibilidad de datos. Chile y México son también parte del grupo OCDE (36).
5. Calculado aplicando el promedio no ponderado en el cambio porcentual para el 2017 en los 34 países con datos disponibles para ese año en el total de ingreso tributario en porcentaje del PIB en 2016.

StatLink https://doi.org/10.1787/888933941023

Table 4.2. **Total tax revenue in millions of USD at market exchange rates, 1990-2017**

Cuadro 4.2. **Total de ingresos tributarios en millones de US dólares a tipos de cambio de mercado, 1990-2017**

	1990	2000	2005	2010	2012	2013	2014	2015	2016	2017
Argentina	20 952	61 084	48 885	123 456	177 582	190 650	175 337	202 079	170 714	193 434
Bahamas[1]	505	965	1 060	1 277	1 480	1 445	1 490	1 761	1 986	2 177
Barbados	471	942	1 149	1 360	1 435	1 288	1 322	1 473	1 446	1 603
Belize / Belice[1]	90	159	248	372	393	415	464	475	503	527
Bolivia[1]	402	1 478	1 921	4 101	6 724	7 864	8 696	9 176	8 854	9 045
Brazil / Brasil	131 131	193 921	292 124	714 147	797 274	800 331	777 975	574 485	576 507	663 807
Chile	5 829	14 650	25 487	42 836	57 028	55 285	51 075	49 719	50 447	55 865
Colombia	5 136	14 614	26 477	51 582	72 786	76 225	74 274	58 169	53 739	59 020
Costa Rica	1 286	3 177	4 373	8 416	10 775	11 844	11 901	13 102	13 983	14 024
Cuba	6 265	11 367	17 528	24 201	29 068	28 804	30 236	33 591	37 277	39 072
Dominican Republic / República Dominicana	666	2 986	4 965	6 633	7 947	8 512	9 039	9 208	9 848	10 542
Ecuador	1 103	1 884	5 032	11 570	17 372	18 624	19 620	21 151	19 920	20 774
El Salvador	506	1 585	2 420	3 298	3 905	4 222	4 229	4 492	4 795	5 052
Guatemala	580	2 129	3 561	5 111	6 498	7 001	7 438	7 881	8 633	9 367
Guyana[1]	134	234	302	550	643	685	734	775	827	914
Honduras	516	1 153	1 736	2 841	3 403	3 520	3 988	4 362	4 821	5 245
Jamaica	1 076	2 054	2 619	3 286	3 621	3 543	3 427	3 650	3 721	4 026
Mexico / México	35 908	81 160	99 772	135 866	152 152	169 579	179 947	186 055	179 484	..
Nicaragua	..	664	1 084	1 693	2 193	2 332	2 586	2 846	3 092	3 288
Panama / Panamá	893	1 953	2 257	4 815	6 721	7 650	7 740	8 268	8 835	9 089
Paraguay	284	1 029	1 203	3 272	4 353	4 754	5 451	4 933	4 810	5 430
Peru / Perú	3 432	7 572	12 192	26 096	36 226	37 791	38 387	33 026	31 145	32 815
Trinidad and Tobago / Trinidad y Tobago[1]	1 184	1 748	4 300	6 139	7 133	7 392	7 945	7 253	5 159	4 855
Uruguay	2 042	4 995	4 184	10 587	13 814	15 856	15 698	14 518	15 288	18 285
Venezuela[2]	8 737	16 027	22 753	34 753	46 777	33 810	38 055	48 975	..	..

Note: The figures exclude local government revenues for Argentina (but include provincial revenues), the Bahamas, Barbados, Cuba, the Dominican Republic, Honduras and Venezuela as the data are not available. The local government revenue data are available since 1994 for Bolivia, since 1998 for Jamaica and Panama, since 2000 for Peru, since 2002 for El Salvador, since 2004 for Paraguay and since 2010 for Nicaragua and since 1990 for all other countries.

1. The data include the following estimations: Bahamas (social security contributions from 2016), Belize (social security contributions from 2016), Bolivia (local tax revenues for 2017), Guyana (social security contributions from 2015), Trinidad and Tobago (local tax revenues for 2017). See the corresponding country tables for more information.
2. Some tax revenue data are not available from 2014 and therefore total figures have not been included.

Note : Las cifras excluyen los ingresos de gobiernos locales en Argentina (pero incluye ingresos de las provincias), Bahamas, Barbados, Cuba, República Dominicana, Honduras y Venezuela, ya que los datos no están disponibles. Los datos de ingresos del gobierno local están disponibles desde 1994 para Bolivia, desde 1998 para Jamaica y Panamá, 2000 para Perú, 2002 para El Salvador, 2004 para Paraguay y 2010 para Nicaragua y 1990 para todos los demás países.

1. Los datos incluyen las siguientes estimaciones: Bahamas (contribuciones a la seguridad social desde 2016), Belice (contribuciones a la seguridad social desde 2016), Bolivia (ingresos tributarios de los gobiernos locales para 2017), Guyana (contribuciones a la seguridad social desde 2015), Trinidad y Tobago (ingresos tributarios de los gobiernos locales para 2017).Véanse las tablas de país para mayor información.
2. Algunos datos de ingresos tributarios no están disponibles a partir de 2014 y, por lo tanto, no se han incluido las cifras totales.

StatLink https://doi.org/10.1787/888933941042

Table 4.3. **Tax revenue of main headings as % of GDP, 2017**
Cuadro 4.3. **Ingresos tributarios en las principales partidas en % del PIB, 2017**

	1000 Income & profits / Ingresos y utilidades	2000 Social security / Seguridad social	3000 Payroll / Nómina	4000 Property / Propiedad	5000 Goods and services / Bienes y servicios	6000 Others / Otros
Argentina	5.3	6.9	0.0	2.9	14.5	0.7
Bahamas[1]	0.0	2.8	0.0	1.0	13.2	0.9
Barbados	8.1	3.2	0.0	1.9	18.6	0.1
Belize / Belice[1]	7.1	2.1	0.0	0.8	18.1	0.0
Bolivia[1]	4.1	4.2	0.0	0.2	13.1	2.3
Brazil / Brasil	7.0	8.4	0.8	2.0	13.1	1.0
Chile	7.0	1.5	0.0	1.1	11.0	-0.4
Colombia	6.2	1.4	0.3	1.9	7.7	1.1
Costa Rica	4.8	8.1	1.4	0.4	8.8	0.6
Cuba	8.9	5.4	1.5	0.0	22.4	2.4
Dominican Republic / República Dominicana	4.3	0.1	0.0	0.6	8.9	0.0
Ecuador	4.0	5.2	0.0	0.3	10.4	0.0
El Salvador	7.0	2.3	0.0	0.4	10.3	0.3
Guatemala	3.7	2.1	0.0	0.1	6.4	0.1
Guyana[1]	9.2	2.8	0.0	0.5	13.3	0.3
Honduras	6.1	3.2	0.0	0.6	11.7	1.2
Jamaica	8.2	1.0	0.0	0.4	16.7	0.9
Mexico / México[2]	7.2	2.1	0.4	0.3	5.8	0.1
Nicaragua	6.9	5.7	0.0	0.2	10.7	0.2
Panama / Panamá	4.0	5.8	0.2	0.4	4.2	0.2
Paraguay	2.3	3.7	0.0	0.3	7.6	0.0
Peru / Perú	5.7	2.0	0.0	0.4	7.2	0.1
Trinidad and Tobago / Trinidad y Tobago[1]	10.9	3.1	0.0	0.4	7.6	0.2
Uruguay	7.5	9.7	0.0	2.1	11.5	0.1
Venezuela[3]	..	..	0.0	0.8	5.1	0.0
Unweighted average / Promedio no ponderado						
LAC / ALC[4]	**6.1**	**3.9**	**0.2**	**0.8**	**11.4**	**0.5**
OECD / OCDE[5]	**11.3**	**9.2**	**0.4**	**1.9**	**11.0**	**0.2**

Note: The figures exclude local government revenues for Argentina (but include provincial revenues), the Bahamas, Barbados, Cuba, the Dominican Republic, Honduras and Venezuela as the data are not available. The local government revenue data are available since 1994 for Bolivia, since 1998 for Jamaica and Panama, since 2000 for Peru, since 2002 for El Salvador, since 2004 for Paraguay and since 2010 for Nicaragua and since 1990 for all other countries.

1. The data include the following estimations: Bahamas (social security contributions from 2016), Belize (social security contributions from 2016), Bolivia (local tax revenues for 2017), Guyana (social security contributions from 2015), Trinidad and Tobago (local tax revenues for 2017). See the corresponding country tables for more information.
2. Data for 2016 are used for 3000 and 4000. Federal government data are used for 5000 and 6000.
3. The data for headings 1000 taxes on income and profits and 2000 social security contributions are not available in 2017.
4. Represents the group of 24 Latin American and Caribbean countries included in this publication and excludes Venezuela due to data availability issues. Chile and Mexico are also part of the OECD (36) group.
5. Represents the unweighted average for OECD member countries. Data for 2016 are used.

Nota : Las cifras excluyen los ingresos de gobiernos locales en Argentina (pero incluye ingresos de las provincias), Bahamas, Barbados, Cuba, República Dominicana, Honduras y Venezuela, ya que los datos no están disponibles. Los datos de ingresos del gobierno local están disponibles desde 1994 para Bolivia, desde 1998 para Jamaica y Panamá, 2000 para Perú, 2002 para El Salvador, 2004 para Paraguay y 2010 para Nicaragua y 1990 para todos los demás países.

1. Los datos incluyen las siguientes estimaciones: Bahamas (contribuciones a la seguridad social desde 2016), Belice (contribuciones a la seguridad social desde 2016), Bolivia (ingresos tributarios de los gobiernos locales para 2017), Guyana (contribuciones a la seguridad social desde 2015), Trinidad y Tobago (ingresos tributarios de los gobiernos locales para 2017).Véanse las tablas de país para mayor información.
2. Se utilizan los datos de 2016 en 3000 y 4000. Datos del nivel federal se utilizan para 5000 y 6000.
3. Los datos de las partidas 1000 impuestos sobre ingresos y ganancias y 2000 contribuciones a la seguridad social no están disponibles en 2017.
4. Representa el grupo de 24 países de América Latina y el Caribe incluido en esta publicación y excluye a Venezuela debido a problemas de disponibilidad de datos. Chile y México son también parte del grupo OCDE (36).
5. Representa el promedio no ponderado para los países miembros de la OCDE. Se utilizan los datos de 2016.

StatLink https://doi.org/10.1787/888933941061

Table 4.4. **Tax revenue of main headings as % of total tax revenue, 2017**

Cuadro 4.4. **Ingresos tributarios en las principales partidas en % del total de ingresos tributarios, 2017**

	1000 Income & profits / Ingresos y utilidades	2000 Social security / Seguridad social	3000 Payroll / Nómina	4000 Property / Propiedad	5000 Goods and services / Bienes y servicios	6000 Others / Otros
Argentina	17.5	22.9	0.0	9.5	47.8	2.4
Bahamas[1]	0.0	15.6	0.0	5.5	73.7	5.2
Barbados	25.5	9.9	0.0	5.9	58.3	0.3
Belize / Belice[1]	25.2	7.6	0.0	3.0	64.2	0.0
Bolivia[1]	17.1	17.7	0.0	0.8	54.7	9.7
Brazil / Brasil	21.6	26.0	2.6	6.2	40.5	3.0
Chile	34.5	7.3	0.0	5.4	54.8	-2.0
Colombia	33.1	7.7	1.8	10.3	41.1	6.0
Costa Rica	19.8	33.5	6.0	1.8	36.4	2.5
Cuba	21.8	13.3	3.8	0.0	55.2	5.9
Dominican Republic / República Dominicana	31.0	0.5	0.0	4.6	63.9	0.0
Ecuador	19.9	26.1	0.0	1.5	52.4	0.1
El Salvador	34.3	11.3	0.0	2.1	50.6	1.7
Guatemala	30.1	16.7	0.0	1.1	51.4	0.7
Guyana[1]	35.3	10.8	0.0	1.9	50.8	1.2
Honduras	26.8	14.1	0.0	2.5	51.2	5.4
Jamaica	30.1	3.7	0.0	1.6	61.2	3.3
Mexico / México[2]	42.7	13.0	2.3	1.9	38.8	1.4
Nicaragua	28.9	24.2	0.0	0.8	45.1	1.0
Panama / Panamá	26.9	39.2	1.4	2.8	28.7	1.1
Paraguay	16.7	26.4	0.0	1.8	55.1	0.0
Peru / Perú	37.2	12.8	0.0	2.4	46.8	0.8
Trinidad and Tobago / Trinidad y Tobago[1]	49.0	14.0	0.0	1.7	34.4	1.0
Uruguay	24.4	31.2	0.0	6.8	37.2	0.4
Venezuela[3]	..	..	..	..	..	..
Unweighted average / Promedio no ponderado						
LAC / ALC[4]	**27.1**	**16.9**	**0.7**	**3.4**	**49.8**	**2.1**
OECD / OCDE[5]	**33.6**	**26.2**	**1.1**	**5.7**	**32.7**	**0.5**

Note: The figures exclude local government revenues for Argentina (but include provincial revenues), the Bahamas, Barbados, Cuba, the Dominican Republic, Honduras and Venezuela as the data are not available. The local government revenue data are available since 1994 for Bolivia, since 1998 for Jamaica and Panama, since 2000 for Peru, since 2002 for El Salvador, since 2004 for Paraguay and since 2010 for Nicaragua and since 1990 for all other countries.

1. The data include the following estimations: Bahamas (social security contributions from 2016), Belize (social security contributions from 2016), Bolivia (local tax revenues for 2017), Guyana (social security contributions from 2015), Trinidad and Tobago (local tax revenues for 2017). See the corresponding country tables for more information.
2. Data for 2016 are used as the state and local government revenue data for 2017 are not available.
3. Some tax revenue data are not available from 2014 and therefore total figures have not been included.
4. Represents the group of 24 Latin American and Caribbean countries included in this publication and excludes Venezuela due to data availability issues. Chile and Mexico are also part of the OECD (36) group.
5. Represents the unweighted average for OECD member countries. Data for 2016 are used.

Nota : Las cifras excluyen los ingresos de gobiernos locales en Argentina (pero incluye ingresos de las provincias), Bahamas, Barbados, Cuba, República Dominicana, Honduras y Venezuela, ya que los datos no están disponibles. Los datos de ingresos del gobierno local están disponibles desde 1994 para Bolivia, desde 1998 para Jamaica y Panamá, 2000 para Perú, 2002 para El Salvador, 2004 para Paraguay y 2010 para Nicaragua y 1990 para todos los demás países.

1. Los datos incluyen las siguientes estimaciones: Bahamas (contribuciones a la seguridad social desde 2016), Belice (contribuciones a la seguridad social desde 2016), Bolivia (ingresos tributarios de los gobiernos locales para 2017), Guyana (contribuciones a la seguridad social desde 2015), Trinidad y Tobago (ingresos tributarios de los gobiernos locales para 2017).Véanse las tablas de país para mayor información.
2. Se utilizan los datos de 2016 ya que los datos de ingresos del gobierno estatal y local para 2017 no están disponibles.
3. Algunos datos de ingresos tributarios no están disponibles a partir de 2014 y, por lo tanto, no se han incluido las cifras totales.
4. Representa el grupo de 24 países de América Latina y el Caribe incluido en esta publicación y excluye a Venezuela debido a problemas de disponibilidad de datos. Chile y México son también parte del grupo OCDE (36).
5. Representa el promedio no ponderado para los países miembros de la OCDE. Se utilizan los datos de 2016.

StatLink https://doi.org/10.1787/888933941080

Table 4.5. **Taxes on income and profits (1000) as % of GDP and as % of total tax revenue**
Cuadro 4.5. **Impuestos sobre la renta y las utilidades (1000) en % del PIB y del total de ingresos tributarios**

	% of GDP / % del PIB					% of total tax revenue / % del total de ingresos tributarios				
	1990	2000	2010	2016	2017	1990	2000	2010	2016	2017
Argentina	0.7	3.7	4.7	5.3	5.3	5.3	18.5	16.2	17.3	17.5
Bahamas	0.0	0.0	0.0	0.0	0.0	0.0	0.0	0.0	0.0	0.0
Barbados	6.3	9.4	8.4	8.4	8.1	27.0	30.5	28.0	28.3	25.5
Belize / Belice	4.4	4.5	8.7	7.1	7.1	20.8	23.9	33.4	25.9	25.2
Bolivia	0.4	2.3	5.0	4.6	4.1	5.3	13.2	24.3	17.9	17.1
Brazil / Brasil	4.6	5.7	6.7	7.2	7.0	18.1	19.4	20.6	22.5	21.6
Chile	3.9	4.4	7.5	6.8	7.0	23.2	23.3	38.1	33.5	34.5
Colombia	2.8	3.4	4.8	6.3	6.2	29.9	23.3	26.8	33.1	33.1
Costa Rica	2.3	2.8	3.8	4.5	4.8	10.0	13.2	17.1	18.8	19.8
Cuba	0.1	6.0	5.6	8.8	8.9	0.2	16.1	14.9	21.3	21.8
Dominican Republic / República Dominicana	2.2	2.7	2.7	4.1	4.3	25.9	22.3	22.0	29.9	31.0
Ecuador	0.9	1.6	3.4	4.4	4.0	12.6	15.7	20.4	22.0	19.9
El Salvador	2.0	3.5	5.4	6.9	7.0	18.9	25.7	30.2	34.6	34.3
Guatemala	1.6	2.5	3.1	3.9	3.7	19.5	19.9	25.1	31.4	30.1
Guyana	6.9	7.9	8.5	8.4	9.2	33.5	37.8	35.3	35.8	35.3
Honduras	2.5	2.7	4.4	6.0	6.1	20.3	16.8	24.5	26.9	26.8
Jamaica	10.3	9.9	10.3	9.0	8.2	50.9	44.8	41.3	33.9	30.1
Mexico / México[1]	4.1	4.1	5.1	7.1	7.2	34.0	36.0	39.8	42.7	42.7
Nicaragua	..	1.8	4.5	6.6	6.9	..	13.6	23.1	28.2	28.9
Panama / Panamá	3.9	3.9	4.4	4.2	4.0	24.3	24.8	27.4	27.2	26.9
Paraguay	1.2	1.5	1.6	2.2	2.3	21.1	13.1	13.5	16.2	16.7
Peru / Perú	0.7	2.9	6.5	6.1	5.7	5.7	19.2	37.1	38.4	37.2
Trinidad and Tobago / Trinidad y Tobago	12.6	12.3	19.2	11.5	10.9	51.6	55.1	67.0	49.2	49.0
Uruguay	0.9	2.0	5.5	6.5	7.5	4.8	9.3	20.8	22.5	24.4
Venezuela[2]	15.1	5.9	3.6	..	..	83.7	43.2	30.7	..	..
Unweighted average / Promedio no ponderado										
LAC / ALC[3]	**3.3**	**4.2**	**5.8**	**6.1**	**6.1**	**20.1**	**22.3**	**27.0**	**27.4**	**27.1**
OECD / OCDE[4]	**12.2**	**11.9**	**10.6**	**11.3**	..	**37.5**	**34.8**	**32.8**	**33.6**	..

Note: The figures exclude local government revenues for Argentina (but include provincial revenues), the Bahamas, Barbados, Cuba, the Dominican Republic, Honduras and Venezuela as the data are not available. The local government revenue data are available since 1994 for Bolivia, since 1998 for Jamaica and Panama, since 2000 for Peru, since 2002 for El Salvador, since 2004 for Paraguay and since 2010 for Nicaragua and since 1990 for all other countries.

1. For the figures as % of total tax revenue data for 2016 are used as the state and local government revenue data for 2017 are not available.
2. Some tax revenue data are not available from 2014 and therefore total figures have not been included.
3. Represents the group of 24 Latin American and Caribbean countries included in this publication and excludes Venezuela due to data availability issues. Chile and Mexico are also part of the OECD (36) group.
4. Represents the unweighted average for OECD member countries.

Nota : Las cifras excluyen los ingresos de gobiernos locales en Argentina (pero incluye ingresos de las provincias), Bahamas, Barbados, Cuba, República Dominicana, Honduras y Venezuela, ya que los datos no están disponibles. Los datos de ingresos del gobierno local están disponibles desde 1994 para Bolivia, desde 1998 para Jamaica y Panamá, 2000 para Perú, 2002 para El Salvador, 2004 para Paraguay y 2010 para Nicaragua y 1990 para todos los demás países.

1. Para las cifras en % del total de ingresos tributarios se utilizan los datos de 2016, ya que los datos de ingresos del gobierno estatal y local para 2017 no están disponibles.
2. Algunos datos de ingresos tributarios no están disponibles a partir de 2014 y, por lo tanto, no se han incluido las cifras totales.
3. Representa el grupo de 24 países de América Latina y el Caribe incluido en esta publicación y excluye a Venezuela debido a problemas de disponibilidad de datos. Chile y México son también parte del grupo OCDE (36).
4. Representa el promedio no ponderado para los países miembros de la OCDE.

StatLink https://doi.org/10.1787/888933941099

Table 4.6. **Social security contributions (2000) as % of GDP and as % of total tax revenue**

Cuadro 4.6. **Contribuciones a la seguridad social (2000) en % del PIB y del total de ingresos tributarios**

	% of GDP / % del PIB					% of total tax revenue / % del total de ingresos tributarios				
	1990	2000	2010	2016	2017	1990	2000	2010	2016	2017
Argentina	3.5	3.1	6.2	6.8	6.9	25.3	15.8	21.2	22.0	22.9
Bahamas[1]	1.3	1.4	1.7	2.6	2.8	13.2	11.9	13.1	15.6	15.6
Barbados	3.3	4.8	5.8	2.5	3.2	14.2	15.7	19.3	8.3	9.9
Belize / Belice[1]	1.2	1.1	2.1	2.2	2.1	5.7	5.8	8.1	8.0	7.6
Bolivia[2]	0.0	1.3	1.2	4.4	4.2	0.0	7.3	5.8	16.9	17.7
Brazil / Brasil	6.1	7.0	8.1	8.4	8.4	24.0	23.5	25.0	26.0	26.0
Chile	1.5	1.4	1.3	1.4	1.5	9.0	7.3	6.8	7.2	7.3
Colombia	0.7	2.4	2.1	1.8	1.4	7.9	16.4	11.7	9.4	7.7
Costa Rica	6.5	6.4	7.4	8.2	8.1	28.9	30.4	33.1	33.7	33.5
Cuba	3.2	3.9	4.6	5.2	5.4	11.0	10.4	12.3	12.6	13.3
Dominican Republic / República Dominicana	0.1	0.1	0.1	0.0	0.1	0.8	1.0	0.8	0.3	0.5
Ecuador	1.6	1.2	3.7	4.7	5.2	22.0	12.1	22.0	23.8	26.1
El Salvador	1.4	2.2	2.0	2.3	2.3	13.3	16.6	11.2	11.2	11.3
Guatemala	1.4	1.9	1.9	2.1	2.1	16.8	15.5	15.6	16.7	16.7
Guyana[1]	0.8	2.4	2.2	2.6	2.8	3.7	11.4	9.0	10.9	10.8
Honduras	1.0	1.6	2.9	2.9	3.2	8.5	10.0	16.0	13.1	14.1
Jamaica	0.0	0.0	0.7	1.0	1.0	0.0	0.0	2.9	3.8	3.7
Mexico / México[3]	2.0	2.1	2.1	2.2	2.1	16.8	18.0	16.2	13.0	13.0
Nicaragua	..	2.6	4.3	5.6	5.7	..	19.9	22.4	24.1	24.2
Panama / Panamá	4.8	6.0	5.4	5.8	5.8	30.4	38.0	34.0	38.3	39.2
Paraguay	0.5	3.0	2.8	3.4	3.7	8.3	25.6	22.9	25.8	26.4
Peru / Perú	0.9	1.8	1.9	2.0	2.0	7.7	12.0	10.8	12.5	12.8
Trinidad and Tobago / Trinidad y Tobago	0.9	1.4	1.9	2.9	3.1	3.6	6.4	6.8	12.4	14.0
Uruguay	6.0	6.4	6.2	8.9	9.7	30.0	29.3	23.4	30.6	31.2
Venezuela[4]	0.9	0.7	1.0	..	..	4.9	5.4	8.1	..	..
Unweighted average / Promedio no ponderado										
LAC / ALC[5]	**2.1**	**2.7**	**3.3**	**3.7**	**3.9**	**13.1**	**15.0**	**15.4**	**16.5**	**16.9**
OECD / OCDE[6]	**7.3**	**8.6**	**8.9**	**9.2**	..	**22.0**	**25.0**	**26.8**	**26.2**	..

Note: The figures exclude local government revenues for Argentina (but include provincial revenues), the Bahamas, Barbados, Cuba, the Dominican Republic, Honduras and Venezuela as the data are not available. The local government revenue data are available since 1994 for Bolivia, since 1998 for Jamaica and Panama, since 2000 for Peru, since 2002 for El Salvador, since 2004 for Paraguay and since 2010 for Nicaragua and since 1990 for all other countries.

1. The data are estimated in the following countries: Bahamas (2017), Belize (2017) and Guyana (from 2015 onward).
2. Figures for 1990-98 are estimated by the Direction General of Taxes as the methodology they use to calculate social security contributions was not employed until 1999.
3. For the figures as % of total tax revenue data for 2016 are used as the state and local government revenue data for 2017 are not available.
4. Some tax revenue data are not available from 2014 and therefore total figures have not been included.
5. Represents the group of 24 Latin American and Caribbean countries included in this publication and excludes Venezuela due to data availability issues. Chile and Mexico are also part of the OECD (36) group.
6. Represents the unweighted average for OECD member countries.

Nota : Las cifras excluyen los ingresos de gobiernos locales en Argentina (pero incluye ingresos de las provincias), Bahamas, Barbados, Cuba, República Dominicana, Honduras y Venezuela, ya que los datos no están disponibles. Los datos de ingresos del gobierno local están disponibles desde 1994 para Bolivia, desde 1998 para Jamaica y Panamá, 2000 para Perú, 2002 para El Salvador, 2004 para Paraguay y 2010 para Nicaragua y 1990 para todos los demás países.

1. Los datos son estimados en los siguientes países: Bahamas (2017), Belice (2017) y Guyana (desde 2015 en adelante).
2. Las cifras de 1990-98 son estimaciones por la Dirección General de Impuestos dado que el empleo de la metodología actual utilizada para calcular las contribuciones a la seguridad social tuvo lugar en 1999.
3. Para las cifras en % del total de ingresos tributarios se utilizan los datos de 2016, ya que los datos de ingresos del gobierno estatal y local para 2017 no están disponibles.
4. Algunos datos de ingresos tributarios no están disponibles a partir de 2014 y, por lo tanto, no se han incluido las cifras totales.
5. Representa el grupo de 24 países de América Latina y el Caribe incluido en esta publicación y excluye a Venezuela debido a problemas de disponibilidad de datos. Chile y México son también parte del grupo OCDE (36).
6. Representa el promedio no ponderado para los países miembros de la OCDE.

StatLink https://doi.org/10.1787/888933941118

Table 4.7. **Taxes on payroll (3000) as % of GDP and as % of total tax revenue**
Cuadro 4.7. **Impuestos sobre la nómina (3000) en % del PIB y del total ingresos tributarios**

	% of GDP / % del PIB					% of total tax revenue / % del total de ingresos tributarios				
	1990	2000	2010	2016	2017	1990	2000	2010	2016	2017
Argentina	0.0	0.0	0.0	0.0	0.0	0.0	0.0	0.0	0.0	0.0
Bahamas	0.0	0.0	0.0	0.0	0.0	0.0	0.0	0.0	0.0	0.0
Barbados	0.0	0.0	0.0	0.0	0.0	0.0	0.0	0.0	0.0	0.0
Belize / Belice	0.0	0.0	0.0	0.0	0.0	0.0	0.0	0.0	0.0	0.0
Bolivia	0.0	0.0	0.0	0.0	0.0	0.0	0.0	0.0	0.0	0.0
Brazil / Brasil	0.4	0.6	0.9	0.8	0.8	1.5	1.9	2.6	2.6	2.6
Chile	0.0	0.0	0.0	0.0	0.0	0.0	0.0	0.0	0.0	0.0
Colombia	0.0	0.6	0.7	0.3	0.3	0.0	4.2	4.1	1.8	1.8
Costa Rica	1.4	1.3	1.3	1.5	1.4	6.4	6.3	5.9	6.0	6.0
Cuba	0.0	3.2	6.9	2.7	1.5	0.0	8.5	18.2	6.5	3.8
Dominican Republic / República Dominicana	0.0	0.0	0.0	0.0	0.0	0.0	0.0	0.0	0.0	0.0
Ecuador	0.0	0.0	0.0	0.0	0.0	0.0	0.0	0.0	0.0	0.0
El Salvador	0.0	0.0	0.0	0.0	0.0	0.0	0.0	0.0	0.0	0.0
Guatemala	0.0	0.0	0.0	0.0	0.0	0.0	0.0	0.0	0.0	0.0
Guyana	0.0	0.0	0.0	0.0	0.0	0.0	0.0	0.0	0.0	0.0
Honduras	0.0	0.0	0.0	0.0	0.0	0.0	0.0	0.0	0.0	0.0
Jamaica	0.0	0.0	0.0	0.0	0.0	0.0	0.0	0.0	0.0	0.0
Mexico / México[1]	0.2	0.2	0.3	0.4	0.4	1.8	1.5	2.2	2.3	2.3
Nicaragua	..	0.0	0.0	0.0	0.0	..	0.0	0.0	0.0	0.0
Panama / Panamá	0.0	0.3	0.2	0.2	0.2	0.0	1.9	1.2	1.3	1.4
Paraguay	0.0	0.0	0.0	0.0	0.0	0.0	0.0	0.0	0.0	0.0
Peru / Perú	0.0	0.6	0.0	0.0	0.0	0.0	4.4	0.0	0.0	0.0
Trinidad and Tobago / Trinidad y Tobago	0.0	0.0	0.0	0.0	0.0	0.0	0.0	0.0	0.0	0.0
Uruguay	0.0	0.0	0.0	0.0	0.0	0.0	0.0	0.0	0.0	0.0
Venezuela[2]	0.0	0.0	0.0	0.0	0.0	0.0	0.0	0.0	..	..
Unweighted average / Promedio no ponderado										
LAC / ALC[3]	**0.1**	**0.3**	**0.4**	**0.2**	**0.2**	**0.4**	**1.2**	**1.4**	**0.9**	**0.7**
OECD / OCDE[4]	**0.3**	**0.4**	**0.3**	**0.4**	..	**1.0**	**0.9**	**1.0**	**1.1**	..

Note: The figures exclude local government revenues for Argentina (but include provincial revenues), the Bahamas, Barbados, Cuba, the Dominican Republic, Honduras and Venezuela as the data are not available. The local government revenue data are available since 1994 for Bolivia, since 1998 for Jamaica and Panama, since 2000 for Peru, since 2002 for El Salvador, since 2004 for Paraguay and since 2010 for Nicaragua and since 1990 for all other countries.

1. Data for 2016 are used as the state and local government revenue data for 2017 are not available.
2. The data as % of total tax revenue are not available from 2014.
3. Represents the group of 24 Latin American and Caribbean countries included in this publication and excludes Venezuela due to data availability issues. Chile and Mexico are also part of the OECD (36) group.
4. Represents the unweighted average for OECD member countries.

Nota : Las cifras excluyen los ingresos de gobiernos locales en Argentina (pero incluye ingresos de las provincias), Bahamas, Barbados, Cuba, República Dominicana, Honduras y Venezuela, ya que los datos no están disponibles. Los datos de ingresos del gobierno local están disponibles desde 1994 para Bolivia, desde 1998 para Jamaica y Panamá, 2000 para Perú, 2002 para El Salvador, 2004 para Paraguay y 2010 para Nicaragua y 1990 para todos los demás países.

1. Se utilizan los datos de 2016 ya que los datos de ingresos del gobierno estatal y local para 2017 no están disponibles.
2. Los datos en % del total de ingresos tributarios no están disponibles a partir de 2014.
3. Representa el grupo de 24 países de América Latina y el Caribe incluido en esta publicación y excluye a Venezuela debido a problemas de disponibilidad de datos. Chile y México son también parte del grupo OCDE (36).
4. Representa el promedio no ponderado para los países miembros de la OCDE.

StatLink https://doi.org/10.1787/888933941137

Table 4.8. **Taxes on property (4000) as % of GDP and as % of total tax revenue**
Cuadro 4.8. **Impuestos sobre la propiedad (4000) en % del PIB y del total de ingresos tributarios**

	% of GDP / % del PIB					% of total tax revenue / % del total de ingresos tributarios				
	1990	2000	2010	2016	2017	1990	2000	2010	2016	2017
Argentina	1.6	1.3	2.6	2.7	2.9	11.4	6.3	9.0	8.9	9.5
Bahamas	0.4	0.4	0.9	0.9	1.0	3.8	3.3	7.2	5.2	5.5
Barbados	1.0	1.5	1.2	1.9	1.9	4.2	4.9	4.2	6.5	5.9
Belize / Belice	0.7	0.8	0.8	0.9	0.8	3.5	4.2	3.0	3.1	3.0
Bolivia	0.0	0.0	0.3	0.2	0.2	0.1	0.0	1.3	0.7	0.8
Brazil / Brasil	1.7	2.4	1.9	2.0	2.0	6.5	8.1	5.9	6.2	6.2
Chile	1.0	1.3	0.8	1.0	1.1	6.2	7.0	4.1	5.1	5.4
Colombia	0.2	1.0	1.6	2.1	1.9	2.2	6.6	8.7	11.1	10.3
Costa Rica	0.3	0.2	0.3	0.4	0.4	1.3	0.9	1.5	1.8	1.8
Cuba	0.0	0.0	0.0	0.0	0.0	0.0	0.0	0.0	0.0	0.0
Dominican Republic / República Dominicana	0.1	0.2	0.7	0.6	0.6	1.2	1.4	5.5	4.6	4.6
Ecuador	0.1	0.1	0.2	0.6	0.3	1.4	0.9	1.0	3.0	1.5
El Salvador	0.5	0.1	0.1	0.4	0.4	5.1	0.7	0.5	2.2	2.1
Guatemala	0.0	0.1	0.2	0.1	0.1	0.0	1.0	1.5	0.9	1.1
Guyana	0.2	0.3	0.3	0.4	0.5	1.0	1.6	1.4	1.9	1.9
Honduras	0.1	0.3	0.3	0.5	0.6	0.7	1.5	1.8	2.1	2.5
Jamaica	0.2	0.2	0.2	0.4	0.4	0.9	0.7	0.9	1.5	1.6
Mexico / México[1]	0.2	0.2	0.3	0.3	0.3	1.9	1.8	2.3	1.9	1.9
Nicaragua	..	0.0	0.2	0.2	0.2	..	0.0	1.1	0.8	0.8
Panama / Panamá	0.8	0.5	0.7	0.4	0.4	4.9	3.2	4.4	2.4	2.8
Paraguay	0.3	0.0	0.2	0.3	0.3	4.9	0.0	1.8	2.1	1.8
Peru / Perú	1.9	0.2	0.5	0.4	0.4	15.3	1.2	3.0	2.5	2.4
Trinidad and Tobago / Trinidad y Tobago	0.7	0.6	0.3	0.4	0.4	3.0	2.5	1.1	1.6	1.7
Uruguay	1.9	2.4	2.3	2.1	2.1	9.7	10.8	8.9	7.4	6.8
Venezuela[2]	0.1	0.5	0.0	0.0	0.8	0.3	3.7	0.2	..	..
Unweighted average / Promedio no ponderado										
LAC / ALC[3]	**0.6**	**0.6**	**0.7**	**0.8**	**0.8**	**3.9**	**2.9**	**3.3**	**3.5**	**3.4**
OECD / OCDE[4]	**1.8**	**1.8**	**1.7**	**1.9**	..	**5.8**	**5.4**	**5.4**	**5.7**	..

Note: The figures exclude local government revenues for Argentina (but include provincial revenues), the Bahamas, Barbados, Cuba, the Dominican Republic, Honduras and Venezuela as the data are not available. The local government revenue data are available since 1994 for Bolivia, since 1998 for Jamaica and Panama, since 2000 for Peru, since 2002 for El Salvador, since 2004 for Paraguay and since 2010 for Nicaragua and since 1990 for all other countries.

1. Data for 2016 are used as the state and local government revenue data for 2017 are not available.
2. The data as % of total tax revenue are not available from 2014.
3. Represents the group of 24 Latin American and Caribbean countries included in this publication and excludes Venezuela due to data availability issues. Chile and Mexico are also part of the OECD (36) group.
4. Represents the unweighted average for OECD member countries.

Nota : Las cifras excluyen los ingresos de gobiernos locales en Argentina (pero incluye ingresos de las provincias), Bahamas, Barbados, Cuba, República Dominicana, Honduras y Venezuela, ya que los datos no están disponibles. Los datos de ingresos del gobierno local están disponibles desde 1994 para Bolivia, desde 1998 para Jamaica y Panamá, 2000 para Perú, 2002 para El Salvador, 2004 para Paraguay y 2010 para Nicaragua y 1990 para todos los demás países.

1. Se utilizan los datos de 2016 ya que los datos de ingresos del gobierno estatal y local para 2017 no están disponibles.
2. Los datos en % del total de ingresos tributarios no están disponibles a partir de 2014.
3. Representa el grupo de 24 países de América Latina y el Caribe incluido en esta publicación y excluye a Venezuela debido a problemas de disponibilidad de datos. Chile y México son también parte del grupo OCDE (36).
4. Representa el promedio no ponderado para los países miembros de la OCDE.

StatLink https://doi.org/10.1787/888933941156

Table 4.9. **Taxes on goods and services (5000) as % of GDP and as % of total tax revenue**

Cuadro 4.9. **Impuestos sobre bienes y servicios (5000) en % del PIB y del total de ingresos tributarios**

	% of GDP / % del PIB					% of total tax revenue / % del total de ingresos tributarios				
	1990	2000	2010	2016	2017	1990	2000	2010	2016	2017
Argentina	7.5	11.2	15.2	14.4	14.5	55.2	56.5	52.4	46.6	47.8
Bahamas	7.4	8.9	7.9	12.4	13.2	76.4	74.9	62.3	74.1	73.7
Barbados	10.3	14.9	14.3	16.8	18.6	44.3	48.4	47.9	56.6	58.3
Belize / Belice	15.0	12.5	14.5	17.3	18.1	70.0	66.1	55.5	63.0	64.2
Bolivia	6.7	12.7	12.8	14.2	13.1	80.8	72.0	61.9	55.0	54.7
Brazil / Brasil	12.2	13.7	14.0	12.7	13.1	47.7	46.3	43.2	39.6	40.5
Chile	10.6	12.0	10.0	11.0	11.0	62.9	63.8	51.2	54.6	54.8
Colombia	4.9	6.5	7.8	7.3	7.7	53.8	43.8	43.0	38.6	41.1
Costa Rica	10.2	9.9	9.0	9.0	8.8	45.5	46.7	40.3	37.1	36.4
Cuba	25.3	22.0	19.1	22.5	22.4	86.9	59.2	50.8	54.0	55.2
Dominican Republic / República Dominicana	5.8	9.1	8.8	8.9	8.9	69.6	74.2	71.8	65.1	63.9
Ecuador	4.4	7.3	9.0	10.1	10.4	61.3	71.2	54.0	50.7	52.4
El Salvador	5.4	7.7	10.1	10.0	10.3	51.3	57.0	56.2	50.1	50.6
Guatemala	5.0	7.7	7.0	6.3	6.4	59.7	62.4	56.5	50.5	51.4
Guyana	8.7	10.1	12.8	12.0	13.3	42.0	48.6	53.1	50.7	50.8
Honduras	8.2	10.7	9.7	11.9	11.7	66.2	66.1	53.5	53.2	51.2
Jamaica	7.4	11.1	13.0	15.3	16.7	36.4	50.1	52.1	57.5	61.2
Mexico / México[1]	5.3	4.8	4.9	6.4	5.8	44.0	41.7	38.0	38.8	38.8
Nicaragua	..	8.6	10.1	10.8	10.7	..	66.3	52.4	46.0	45.1
Panama / Panamá	6.0	4.7	5.0	4.6	4.2	37.6	29.4	31.4	29.8	28.7
Paraguay	3.0	6.7	7.3	7.4	7.6	51.4	58.0	61.1	55.8	55.1
Peru / Perú	7.9	9.0	8.6	7.3	7.2	65.6	60.6	49.3	45.9	46.8
Trinidad and Tobago / Trinidad y Tobago	10.0	7.8	7.1	8.4	7.6	40.8	35.0	24.7	35.9	34.4
Uruguay	11.1	11.2	12.2	11.4	11.5	55.6	51.1	46.5	39.2	37.2
Venezuela[2]	2.0	6.5	7.2	10.8	5.1	11.1	47.7	61.1	..	..
Unweighted average / Promedio no ponderado										
LAC / ALC[3]	**8.6**	**10.0**	**10.4**	**11.2**	**11.4**	**56.7**	**56.2**	**50.4**	**49.5**	**49.8**
OECD / OCDE[4]	**10.0**	**10.9**	**10.6**	**11.0**	..	**32.5**	**33.1**	**33.2**	**32.7**	..

Note: The figures exclude local government revenues for Argentina (but include provincial revenues), the Bahamas, Barbados, Cuba, the Dominican Republic, Honduras and Venezuela as the data are not available. The local government revenue data are available since 1994 for Bolivia, since 1998 for Jamaica and Panama, since 2000 for Peru, since 2002 for El Salvador, since 2004 for Paraguay and since 2010 for Nicaragua and since 1990 for all other countries.

1. In 2017, federal government data are used for the figure as % of GDP. For the figure as % of total tax revenue, data for 2016 are used as the state and local government revenue data for 2017 are not available.
2. The data as % of total tax revenue are not available from 2014.
3. Represents the group of 24 Latin American and Caribbean countries included in this publication and excludes Venezuela due to data availability issues. Chile and Mexico are also part of the OECD (36) group.
4. Represents the unweighted average for OECD member countries.

Nota : Las cifras excluyen los ingresos de gobiernos locales en Argentina (pero incluye ingresos de las provincias), Bahamas, Barbados, Cuba, República Dominicana, Honduras y Venezuela, ya que los datos no están disponibles. Los datos de ingresos del gobierno local están disponibles desde 1994 para Bolivia, desde 1998 para Jamaica y Panamá, 2000 para Perú, 2002 para El Salvador, 2004 para Paraguay y 2010 para Nicaragua y 1990 para todos los demás países.

1. En 2017, los datos del gobierno federal se utilizan para la cifra como % del PIB. Para la cifra en % del total de ingresos fiscales tributarios, se utilizan los datos de 2016, ya que los datos de ingresos del gobierno estatal y local de 2017 no están disponibles.
2. Los datos en % del total de ingresos tributarios no están disponibles a partir de 2014.
3. Representa el grupo de 24 países de América Latina y el Caribe incluido en esta publicación y excluye a Venezuela debido a problemas de disponibilidad de datos. Chile y México son también parte del grupo OCDE (36).
4. Representa el promedio no ponderado para los países miembros de la OCDE.

StatLink https://doi.org/10.1787/888933941175

Table 4.10. **Value added taxes (5111) as % of GDP and as % of total tax revenue**
Cuadro 4.10. **Impuesto al valor agregado (5111) en % del PIB y del total de ingresos tributarios**

	% of GDP / % del PIB					% of total tax revenue / % del total de ingresos tributarios				
	1990	2000	2010	2016	2017	1990	2000	2010	2016	2017
Argentina	2.1	6.2	7.0	7.1	7.2	15.6	31.1	24.1	23.1	23.9
Bahamas	0.0	0.0	0.0	5.3	5.2	0.0	0.0	0.0	31.6	29.3
Barbados	0.0	8.2	8.3	9.8	9.9	0.0	26.6	27.7	33.1	31.0
Belize / Belice	0.0	0.0	7.0	8.0	7.8	0.0	0.0	26.8	29.1	27.8
Bolivia	3.6	5.7	7.4	8.5	7.8	43.2	32.2	35.9	32.8	32.6
Brazil / Brasil	9.4	8.4	7.6	7.1	7.2	36.9	28.5	23.4	22.0	22.4
Chile	6.3	7.9	7.5	8.3	8.4	37.4	41.8	38.5	41.2	41.6
Colombia	2.1	4.1	5.3	4.8	5.5	22.6	27.7	29.4	25.5	29.1
Costa Rica	4.1	4.8	4.7	4.5	4.4	18.1	22.8	21.0	18.8	18.4
Cuba	0.0	0.0	0.0	0.0	0.0	0.0	0.0	0.0	0.0	0.0
Dominican Republic / República Dominicana	1.3	2.5	4.1	4.8	4.7	15.1	20.5	33.3	35.1	33.9
Ecuador	2.0	4.6	5.6	6.0	6.5	27.4	44.4	33.6	30.3	32.8
El Salvador	0.0	6.1	7.8	7.6	7.7	0.0	45.1	43.4	37.8	37.7
Guatemala	2.4	4.7	5.1	4.6	4.7	29.3	37.9	41.2	36.9	38.0
Guyana	0.0	0.0	5.8	5.0	5.8	0.0	0.0	24.2	21.3	22.2
Honduras	2.0	4.8	5.4	7.4	7.3	16.2	29.7	29.7	33.2	31.8
Jamaica	0.8	5.7	7.1	8.3	8.9	3.8	25.5	28.7	31.2	32.5
Mexico / México[1]	3.2	2.8	3.8	3.9	3.7	26.1	24.7	29.4	23.7	23.7
Nicaragua	..	4.5	5.5	6.0	6.2	..	34.8	28.6	25.8	25.9
Panama / Panamá	1.4	0.6	2.5	2.6	2.4	9.0	3.5	15.9	17.1	16.1
Paraguay	0.0	3.7	4.6	5.1	5.1	0.0	32.1	38.7	38.4	36.8
Peru / Perú	1.5	5.4	6.9	6.0	5.9	12.1	36.5	39.5	37.5	38.4
Trinidad and Tobago / Trinidad y Tobago	4.5	3.8	4.4	4.8	4.3	18.4	17.2	15.4	20.4	19.4
Uruguay	5.5	6.5	8.6	7.8	7.6	27.6	29.8	32.7	26.7	24.7
Venezuela[2]	0.0	4.1	5.5	8.0	3.9	0.0	30.2	46.7	..	..
Unweighted average / Promedio no ponderado										
LAC / ALC[3]	**2.3**	**4.2**	**5.5**	**6.0**	**6.0**	**15.6**	**24.7**	**27.5**	**28.0**	**27.9**
OECD / OCDE[4]	**5.2**	**6.4**	**6.5**	**6.8**	..	**16.7**	**19.4**	**20.3**	**20.2**	..

Note: The figures exclude local government revenues for Argentina (but include provincial revenues), the Bahamas, Barbados, Cuba, the Dominican Republic, Honduras and Venezuela as the data are not available. The local government revenue data are available since 1994 for Bolivia, since 1998 for Jamaica and Panama, since 2000 for Peru, since 2002 for El Salvador, since 2004 for Paraguay and since 2010 for Nicaragua and since 1990 for all other countries.

1. For the figures as % of total tax revenue data for 2016 are used as the state and local government revenue data for 2017 are not available.
2. The data as % of total tax revenue are not available from 2014.
3. Represents the group of 24 Latin American and Caribbean countries included in this publication and excludes Venezuela due to data availability issues. Chile and Mexico are also part of the OECD (36) group.
4. Represents the unweighted average for OECD member countries.

Nota : Las cifras excluyen los ingresos de gobiernos locales en Argentina (pero incluye ingresos de las provincias), Bahamas, Barbados, Cuba, República Dominicana, Honduras y Venezuela, ya que los datos no están disponibles. Los datos de ingresos del gobierno local están disponibles desde 1994 para Bolivia, desde 1998 para Jamaica y Panamá, 2000 para Perú, 2002 para El Salvador, 2004 para Paraguay y 2010 para Nicaragua y 1990 para todos los demás países.

1. Para las cifras en % del total de ingresos tributarios se utilizan los datos de 2016, ya que los datos de ingresos del gobierno estatal y local para 2017 no están disponibles.
2. Los datos en % del total de ingresos tributarios no están disponibles a partir de 2014.
3. Representa el grupo de 24 países de América Latina y el Caribe incluido en esta publicación y excluye a Venezuela debido a problemas de disponibilidad de datos. Chile y México son también parte del grupo OCDE (36).
4. Representa el promedio no ponderado para los países miembros de la OCDE.

StatLink https://doi.org/10.1787/888933941194

Table 4.11. **Tax revenues of sub-sectors of general government as % of total tax revenue**

Cuadro 4.11. **Ingresos tributarios por subsector del gobierno general, en % del total de ingresos tributarios**

	Central government / Gobierno central			State or Regional government / Gobierno estatal o regional			Local government / Gobierno local			Social Security Funds / Fondos de seguridad social		
	1995	2000	2016	1995	2000	2016	1995	2000	2016	1995	2000	2016
Federal countries / Países federales												
Argentina	59.0	66.4	61.1	17.5	17.8	16.8	..	..	..	23.4	15.8	22.0
Brazil / Brasil	44.7	47.8	43.9	26.8	25.3	24.4	3.7	3.4	5.7	24.8	23.5	26.0
Mexico / México	73.9	78.3	81.5	2.8	2.7	4.0	1.5	1.0	1.5	21.8	18.0	13.0
Venezuela[1]	94.6	94.6	..	..	..	..	..	..	..	5.4	5.4	..
Regional country / País régional												
Colombia	63.2	68.6	73.3	5.5	5.6	5.1	8.6	9.4	12.2	22.7	16.4	9.4
Unitary countries / Países unitarios												
Bahamas[2]	89.1	88.1	84.4	..	..	..	..	..	..	10.9	11.9	15.6
Barbados	85.3	84.3	91.7	..	..	..	..	..	..	14.7	15.7	8.3
Belize / Belice[2]	93.2	93.5	91.4	..	..	..	0.5	0.7	0.7	6.3	5.8	8.0
Bolivia	95.0	86.4	78.4	..	..	..	5.0	6.3	4.7	..	7.3	16.9
Chile	89.9	87.8	86.4	..	..	..	6.5	7.9	7.8	3.6	4.4	5.7
Costa Rica	65.5	63.3	59.2	..	..	..	1.6	1.9	3.0	33.0	34.8	37.8
Cuba	88.7	89.6	87.4	..	..	..	..	..	..	11.3	10.4	12.6
Dominican Republic / República Dominicana	99.3	99.0	99.7	..	..	..	..	..	..	0.7	1.0	0.3
Ecuador	70.7	86.2	73.6	..	..	..	3.8	1.7	2.6	25.6	12.1	23.8
El Salvador	85.9	83.4	86.9	..	..	..	..	..	1.9	14.1	16.6	11.2
Guatemala	83.5	83.6	82.4	..	..	..	0.6	0.9	0.9	15.9	15.5	16.7
Guyana[2]	92.6	88.6	89.0	..	..	..	..	..	0.1	7.4	11.4	10.9
Honduras	86.1	84.5	82.3	..	..	..	4.4	5.5	4.6	9.5	10.0	13.1
Jamaica	100.0	99.3	94.6	..	..	..	..	0.7	1.5	..	..	3.8
Nicaragua	84.5	80.1	69.4	..	..	..	..	..	6.5	15.7	19.9	24.1
Panama / Panamá	62.0	59.8	60.1	..	..	..	..	2.2	1.6	38.0	38.0	38.3
Paraguay	100.0	82.7	77.2	..	..	..	..	..	4.0	..	17.3	18.8
Peru / Perú	88.1	86.4	84.6	..	..	..	..	1.6	2.9	11.9	12.0	12.5
Trinidad and Tobago / Trinidad y Tobago	94.5	91.7	86.1	..	..	..	2.4	1.9	1.6	3.1	6.4	12.4
Uruguay	61.1	61.3	64.1	..	..	..	8.9	9.4	5.4	30.0	29.3	30.6

Note: The figures exclude local government revenues for Argentina (but include provincial revenues), the Bahamas, Barbados, Cuba, the Dominican Republic, Honduras and Venezuela as the data are not available. The local government revenue data are available since 1994 for Bolivia, since 1998 for Jamaica and Panama, since 2000 for Peru, since 2002 for El Salvador, since 2004 for Paraguay and since 2010 for Nicaragua and since 1990 for all other countries.

1. Some tax revenue data are not available from 2014 and therefore total figures have not been included.
2. Social security contributions are estimated for Bahamas and Belize (from 2016) and Guyana (from 2015).

Nota: Las cifras excluyen los ingresos de gobiernos locales en Argentina (pero incluye ingresos de las provincias), Bahamas, Barbados, Cuba, República Dominicana, Honduras y Venezuela, ya que los datos no están disponibles. Los datos de ingresos del gobierno local están disponibles desde 1994 para Bolivia, desde 1998 para Jamaica y Panamá, 2000 para Perú, 2002 para El Salvador, 2004 para Paraguay y 2010 para Nicaragua y 1990 para todos los demás países.

1. Algunos datos de ingresos tributarios no están disponibles a partir de 2014 y, por lo tanto, no se han incluido las cifras totales.
2. Las contribuciones a la seguridad social se estiman para Bahamas y Belice (desde 2016) y Guyana (desde 2015).

StatLink https://doi.org/10.1787/888933941213

Table 4.12. Main central government taxes as % of total tax revenues of central government, 2016

Cuadro 4.12. Impuestos principales del gobierno central en % del total de ingresos tributarios del gobierno central, 2016

	1000 Income & profits / Ingresos y utilidades	2000 Social security / Seguridad social[1]	3000 Payroll / Nómina	4000 Property / Propiedad	5000 Goods and services / Bienes y servicios	6000 Others / Otros
Federal countries / Países federales						
Argentina	28.3	0.0	0.0	10.0	54.1	7.6
Brazil / Brasil	51.3	0.0	5.8	3.9	37.3	1.6
Mexico / México	52.4	0.0	0.0	0.0	46.6	1.1
Venezuela	..	..	..	..	..	..
Regional country / País régional						
Colombia	45.1	0.0	2.5	9.6	42.4	0.4
Unitary countries / Países unitarios						
Bahamas	0.0	0.0	0.0	6.2	87.8	6.0
Barbados	30.9	0.0	0.0	7.1	61.7	0.4
Belize / Belice	28.4	0.0	0.0	2.7	69.0	0.0
Bolivia	22.9	0.0	0.0	1.0	70.2	6.0
Chile	38.8	1.6	0.0	2.0	58.0	-0.4
Costa Rica	31.8	3.3	0.0	0.9	59.8	4.3
Cuba	24.4	0.0	7.4	0.0	61.8	6.4
Dominican Republic / República Dominicana	30.0	0.0	0.0	4.6	65.4	0.0
Ecuador	29.4	0.0	0.0	2.5	67.4	0.7
El Salvador	39.8	0.0	0.0	2.6	57.6	0.0
Guatemala	38.0	0.0	0.0	0.0	61.2	0.7
Guyana	40.2	0.0	0.0	2.1	56.9	0.8
Honduras	32.7	0.0	0.0	2.6	64.7	0.0
Jamaica	35.8	0.0	0.0	0.0	60.7	3.5
Nicaragua	40.6	0.0	0.0	0.0	59.3	0.1
Panama / Panamá	45.2	0.0	2.1	3.9	48.1	0.7
Paraguay	21.0	9.1	0.0	0.0	69.9	0.0
Peru / Perú	45.4	0.0	0.0	0.2	53.7	0.8
Trinidad and Tobago / Trinidad y Tobago	57.2	0.0	0.0	0.0	41.7	1.1
Uruguay	35.2	0.0	0.0	6.9	57.9	0.0

Note: Excluding social security contributions collected by social security funds.

1. These comprise social security contributions collected by central government.

Nota : Se excluyen las contribuciones a la seguridad social que recaudados por los fondos de la seguridad social.

1. Estos comprenden contribuciones a la seguridad social recaudados por el gobierno central.

StatLink https://doi.org/10.1787/888933941232

Table 4.13. **Main state government taxes as % of total tax revenues of state government, 2016**

Cuadro 4.13. **Impuestos principales del gobierno estatal en % del total de ingresos tributarios del gobierno estatal, 2016**

	1000 Income & profits / Ingresos y utilidades	2000 Social security / Seguridad social	3000 Payroll / Nómina	4000 Property / Propiedad	5000 Goods and services / Bienes y servicios	6000 Others / Otros
Federal countries / Países federales						
Argentina	0.0	0.0	0.0	16.6	80.6	2.8
Brazil / Brasil	0.0	0.0	0.0	9.5	84.1	6.5
Mexico / México	0.0	0.0	57.7	17.8	19.5	5.1
Venezuela	..	..	..	..	..	..
Regional country / País régional						
Colombia	0.0	0.0	0.0	0.0	56.5	43.5
Unitary countries / Países unitarios						
Bahamas	..	..	..	..	..	..
Barbados	..	..	..	..	..	..
Belize / Belice	..	..	..	..	..	..
Bolivia	..	..	..	..	..	..
Chile	..	..	..	..	..	..
Costa Rica	..	..	..	..	..	..
Cuba	..	..	..	..	..	..
Dominican Republic / República Dominicana	..	..	..	..	..	..
Ecuador	..	..	..	..	..	..
El Salvador	..	..	..	..	..	..
Guatemala	..	..	..	..	..	..
Guyana	..	..	..	..	..	..
Honduras	..	..	..	..	..	..
Jamaica	..	..	..	..	..	..
Nicaragua	..	..	..	..	..	..
Panama / Panamá	..	..	..	..	..	..
Paraguay	..	..	..	..	..	..
Peru / Perú	..	..	..	..	..	..
Trinidad and Tobago / Trinidad y Tobago	..	..	..	..	..	..
Uruguay	..	..	..	..	..	..

StatLink https://doi.org/10.1787/888933941251

Table 4.14. **Main local government taxes as % of total tax revenues of local government, 2016**
Cuadro 4.14. **Impuestos principales del gobierno local en % del total de ingresos tributarios del gobierno local, 2016**

	1000 Income & profits / Ingresos y utilidades	2000 Social security / Seguridad social	3000 Payroll / Nómina	4000 Property / Propiedad	5000 Goods and services / Bienes y servicios	6000 Others / Otros
Federal countries / Países federales						
Argentina	..	..	..	..	..	..
Brazil / Brasil	0.0	0.0	0.0	38.4	47.1	14.5
Mexico / México	0.0	0.0	0.0	77.8	2.6	19.6
Venezuela	..	..	..	..	..	..
Regional country / País régional						
Colombia	0.0	0.0	0.0	33.6	38.0	28.3
Unitary countries / Países unitarios						
Bahamas	..	..	..	..	..	..
Barbados	..	..	..	..	..	..
Belize / Belice	0.0	0.0	0.0	100.0	0.0	0.0
Bolivia	0.0	0.0	0.0	0.0	0.0	100.0
Chile	0.0	0.0	0.0	43.1	56.9	0.0
Costa Rica	0.0	0.0	0.0	42.1	57.7	0.2
Cuba	..	..	..	..	..	..
Dominican Republic / República Dominicana	..	..	..	..	..	..
Ecuador	13.7	0.0	0.0	44.0	42.2	0.1
El Salvador	0.0	0.0	0.0	0.0	0.0	100.0
Guatemala	0.0	0.0	0.0	100.0	0.0	0.0
Guyana	0.0	0.0	0.0	0.0	0.0	100.0
Honduras	0.0	0.0	0.0	0.0	0.0	100.0
Jamaica	0.0	0.0	0.0	100.0	0.0	0.0
Nicaragua	0.0	0.0	0.0	12.9	74.2	12.9
Panama / Panamá	0.0	0.0	0.0	0.0	55.5	44.5
Paraguay	0.0	0.0	0.0	52.4	46.8	0.7
Peru / Perú	0.0	0.0	0.0	81.6	17.6	0.8
Trinidad and Tobago / Trinidad y Tobago	0.0	0.0	0.0	100.0	0.0	0.0
Uruguay	0.0	0.0	0.0	55.3	38.0	6.7

StatLink https://doi.org/10.1787/888933941270

Table 4.15. **Gross domestic product for tax reporting years at market prices, in millions of national currency**

Cuadro 4.15. **Producto interno bruto para los años fiscales a precios de mercado, en millones de moneda local**

		1990	2000	2005	2010	2012	2013	2014	2015	2016	2017
Argentina	ARS	74 710	308 491	582 538	1 661 721	2 637 914	3 348 308	4 579 086	5 954 511	8 188 749	10 558 497
Bahamas	BSD	5 218	8 076	9 836	10 096	10 721	10 628	10 957	11 792	11 839	12 162
Barbados	BAR	4 059	6 116	7 838	9 124	9 254	9 364	9 407	9 509	9 756	10 070
Belize / Belice	BZD	840	1 684	2 280	2 839	3 167	3 271	3 445	3 578	3 657	3 740
Bolivia	BOB	15 443	51 928	77 024	137 876	187 154	211 856	228 004	228 031	234 533	259 185
Brazil / Brasil	BRL	13	1 199 092	2 170 585	3 885 847	4 814 760	5 331 619	5 778 953	5 995 787	6 267 205	6 558 748
Chile	CLP	10 522 684	42 005 194	68 831 705	111 508 611	129 947 342	137 876 216	148 623 667	159 605 939	169 263 918	179 776 238
Colombia	COP	28 065 806	206 560 060	336 940 938	543 187 690	665 883 659	713 626 705	762 903 000	804 692 000	863 877 000	928 067 337
Costa Rica	CRC	523 319	4 607 291	9 532 875	19 596 937	23 371 406	24 860 944	27 226 884	29 281 373	31 136 211	32 799 663
Cuba	CUP	21 541	30 565	42 644	64 328	73 141	77 148	80 656	87 133	89 689	96 125
Dominican Republic / República Dominicana	DOP	77 344	393 303	1 083 445	1 983 202	2 386 016	2 619 770	2 877 528	3 099 651	3 333 419	3 613 147
Ecuador	USD	15 232	18 319	41 507	69 555	87 925	95 130	101 726	99 290	99 938	104 296
El Salvador	USD	4 818	11 785	14 698	18 448	21 386	21 977	22 586	23 166	23 912	24 805
Guatemala	GTQ	31 176	133 428	207 729	333 093	394 723	423 098	454 053	488 128	521 837	555 649
Guyana	GYD	25 432	205 128	262 250	462 910	584 784	613 653	635 377	660 227	723 581	734 150
Honduras	HNL	17 141	106 654	183 747	299 286	361 349	376 539	414 634	460 405	494 239	539 699
Jamaica	JAM	38 145	395 009	700 275	1 152 780	1 314 127	1 431 934	1 541 750	1 659 405	1 760 988	1 897 303
Mexico / México	MXN	843 623	6 693 683	9 562 648	13 366 377	15 817 755	16 277 187	17 471 467	18 536 531	20 099 594	21 766 928
Nicaragua	NIO	519	64 812	105 777	187 053	247 994	271 530	308 403	343 738	377 349	415 127
Panama / Panamá	PAB	5 632	12 304	16 374	30 150	41 648	46 718	51 228	54 316	57 821	61 838
Paraguay	PYG	6 031 160	30 874 088	66 335 828	128 989 495	147 275 542	166 714 587	179 721 609	188 230 723	204 447 278	220 641 032
Peru / Perú	PEN	5 322	177 918	247 081	420 423	508 853	546 199	574 050	610 261	657 132	699 475
Trinidad and Tobago / Trinidad y Tobago	TTD	20 619	49 250	96 425	136 271	164 654	169 039	168 403	154 626	146 995	148 570
Uruguay	UYU	12 010	276 152	425 018	808 079	1 041 211	1 178 332	1 330 508	1 455 848	1 589 195	1 697 075
Venezuela	VEF	2 279	79 656	304 087	1 016 835	1 635 450	2 245 844	3 031 242	6 025 327	23 751 849	293 407 210

Source: OECD National Accounts data for Chile and Mexico, the World Economic Outlook (IMF) for Barbados, Belize, Panama and Venezuela, and official National Accounts data for Bolivia, Ecuador, El Salvador, Guatemala, Nicaragua, Peru and Uruguay. For Argentina, Bahamas, Brazil, Columbia, Dominican Republic, Guyana, Honduras, Jamaica, Paraguay, Trinidad and Tobago, and Costa Rica, official national sources were used where available, but for some years, IMF figures, or projected figures were used instead. For Cuba, figures for 1990-2011 are provided by CEPALSTAT, while figures for 2012-17 are from the Oficina Nacional de Estadística e Información (ONEI). For Barbados, Belize, and Trinidad and Tobago, GDP figures are reported on a fiscal year basis. For Jamaica, GDP reported for 1990-2003 are reported on a fiscal year basis, while for other years, they are reported on a calendar year basis.

Fuente : Datos de Cuentas Nacionales de la OCDE para Chile y México, Perspectivas de la economía mundial (FMI) para Barbados, Belice, Panamá y Venezuela, y datos de Cuentas nacionales oficiales para Bolivia, Ecuador, El Salvador, Guatemala, Nicaragua, Perú y Uruguay. Para Argentina, Bahamas, Brasil, Colombia, República Dominicana, Guyana, Honduras, Jamaica, Paraguay, Trinidad y Tobago y Costa Rica, se utilizaron fuentes nacionales oficiales cuando estaban disponibles,alternando con cifras del FMI por temas de disponibilidad. Para Cuba, las cifras para 1990-2011 son proporcionadas por CEPALSTAT, mientras que las cifras para 2012-17 son de la Oficina Nacional de Estadística e Información (ONEI). Para Barbados, Belice y Trinidad y Tobago, las cifras del PIB se presentan sobre la base de un año fiscal. Para Jamaica, el PIB reportado para 1990-2003 se presenta sobre una base de año fiscal, mientras que para otros años, se presenta sobre una base de año calendario.

StatLink https://doi.org/10.1787/888933941289

Table 4.16. **Gross domestic product for tax reporting years at market prices, in USD**
Cuadro 4.16. **Producto interno bruto para los años fiscales a precios de mercado, en US dólares**

	1990	2000	2005	2010	2012	2013	2014	2015	2016	2017
Argentina	153 205	308 491	199 273	424 728	579 666	611 471	563 614	642 464	554 107	637 717
Bahamas	5 218	8 076	9 836	10 096	10 721	10 628	10 957	11 792	11 839	12 162
Barbados	2 029	3 058	3 919	4 562	4 627	4 682	4 704	4 754	4 878	5 035
Belize / Belice	420	842	1 140	1 420	1 583	1 635	1 723	1 789	1 829	1 870
Bolivia	4 868	8 385	9 573	19 786	27 282	30 883	33 237	33 241	34 189	37 782
Brazil / Brasil	514 004	655 453	891 633	2 208 704	2 464 053	2 471 718	2 456 055	1 800 046	1 796 014	2 055 143
Chile	34 512	77 876	122 978	218 652	267 390	278 379	260 453	243 926	250 190	277 143
Colombia	55 879	98 931	145 162	286 039	370 344	381 844	381 241	293 493	282 751	314 464
Costa Rica	5 716	14 965	19 994	37 634	46 984	50 326	51 181	55 410	57 828	58 272
Cuba	21 541	30 565	42 644	64 328	73 141	77 148	80 656	87 133	89 689	96 125
Dominican Republic / República Dominicana	7 995	24 306	35 948	53 921	60 747	62 758	66 157	68 898	72 434	76 091
Ecuador	15 232	18 319	41 507	69 555	87 925	95 130	101 726	99 290	99 938	104 296
El Salvador	4 818	11 785	14 698	18 448	21 386	21 977	22 586	23 166	23 912	24 805
Guatemala	6 950	17 187	27 211	41 338	50 388	53 851	58 722	63 767	68 663	75 620
Guyana	652	1 123	1 311	2 276	2 865	2 988	3 079	3 197	3 504	3 492
Honduras	4 169	7 104	9 672	15 730	18 529	18 499	19 757	20 980	21 644	22 979
Jamaica	5 298	9 251	11 233	13 193	14 765	14 211	13 864	14 152	14 022	14 772
Mexico / México	296 972	708 096	878 139	1 058 146	1 202 852	1 274 656	1 313 104	1 167 714	1 079 034	1 153 429
Nicaragua	519	5 109	6 321	8 759	10 532	10 983	11 880	12 611	13 184	13 814
Panama / Panamá	5 632	12 304	16 374	30 150	41 648	46 718	51 228	54 316	57 821	61 838
Paraguay	4 904	8 856	10 738	27 239	33 283	38 585	40 277	36 164	36 054	39 267
Peru / Perú	28 326	51 005	74 970	148 820	192 933	202 118	202 219	191 597	194 672	214 505
Trinidad and Tobago / Trinidad y Tobago	4 851	7 818	15 307	21 374	25 609	26 238	26 276	24 246	22 049	21 914
Uruguay	10 270	22 832	17 398	40 285	51 266	57 531	57 236	53 275	52 687	59 180
Venezuela	48 391	117 676	143 290	294 282	331 457	234 401	212 347	242 596	236 116	210 083

Source: The figures are derived by multiplying the GDP data in Table 4.15 by the exchange rate in Table 4.17.
Fuente : Las cifras se obtienen multiplicando los datos del PIB en el Cuadro 4.15 por el tipo de cambio en el Cuadro 4.17.

StatLink https://doi.org/10.1787/888933941308

Table 4.17. **Exchange rates used, national currency per US dollar at market exchange rates**
Cuadro 4.17. **Tasas de cambio utilizadas, moneda local por US dólares a precios de mercado**

		1990	2000	2005	2010	2012	2013	2014	2015	2016	2017
Argentina	ARS	0.488	1.000	2.923	3.912	4.551	5.476	8.125	9.268	14.778	16.557
Bahamas	BSD	1.000	1.000	1.000	1.000	1.000	1.000	1.000	1.000	1.000	1.000
Barbados	BAR	2.000	2.000	2.000	2.000	2.000	2.000	2.000	2.000	2.000	2.000
Belize / Belice	BZD	2.000	2.000	2.000	2.000	2.000	2.000	2.000	2.000	2.000	2.000
Bolivia	BOB	3.173	6.193	8.046	6.968	6.860	6.860	6.860	6.860	6.860	6.860
Brazil / Brasil	BRL	0.000	1.829	2.434	1.759	1.954	2.157	2.353	3.331	3.490	3.191
Chile	CLP	304.903	539.388	559.705	509.982	485.984	495.282	570.636	654.322	676.541	648.677
Colombia	COP	502.260	2 087.918	2 321.132	1 898.998	1 798.012	1 868.895	2 001.105	2 741.780	3 055.260	2 951.271
Costa Rica	CRC	91.560	307.874	476.797	520.718	497.432	493.995	531.973	528.447	538.430	562.872
Cuba	CUP	1.000	1.000	1.000	1.000	1.000	1.000	1.000	1.000	1.000	1.000
Dominican Republic / República Dominicana	DOP	9.674	16.181	30.140	36.779	39.278	41.744	43.495	44.989	46.020	47.485
Ecuador	USD	1.000	1.000	1.000	1.000	1.000	1.000	1.000	1.000	1.000	1.000
El Salvador	USD	1.000	1.000	1.000	1.000	1.000	1.000	1.000	1.000	1.000	1.000
Guatemala	GTQ	4.486	7.763	7.634	8.058	7.834	7.857	7.732	7.655	7.600	7.348
Guyana	GYD	39.000	182.625	200.000	203.375	204.125	205.375	206.375	206.500	206.500	210.250
Honduras	HNL	4.112	15.014	18.998	19.027	19.502	20.354	20.987	21.945	22.835	23.487
Jamaica	JAM	7.200	42.701	62.343	87.380	89.001	100.759	111.208	117.256	125.584	128.435
Mexico / México	MXN	2.841	9.453	10.890	12.632	13.150	12.770	13.305	15.874	18.627	18.871
Nicaragua	NIO	1.000	12.685	16.733	21.356	23.547	24.723	25.959	27.257	28.621	30.051
Panama / Panamá	PAB	1.000	1.000	1.000	1.000	1.000	1.000	1.000	1.000	1.000	1.000
Paraguay	PYG	1 229.808	3 486.353	6 177.958	4 735.462	4 424.917	4 320.674	4 462.192	5 204.910	5 670.517	5 618.933
Peru / Perú	PEN	0.188	3.488	3.296	2.825	2.637	2.702	2.839	3.185	3.376	3.261
Trinidad and Tobago / Trinidad y Tobago	TTD	4.250	6.300	6.300	6.376	6.430	6.443	6.409	6.377	6.667	6.780
Uruguay	UYU	1.169	12.095	24.429	20.059	20.310	20.482	23.246	27.327	30.163	28.676
Venezuela	VEF	0.047	0.677	2.122	3.455	4.934	9.581	14.275	24.837	100.594	1 396.622

Note: Annual average market exchange rates.
Source: World Economic Outlook (IMF), October 2018.
Nota : Se utilizan tasas de cambio de mercado promedios anuales.
Fuente : Perspectivas de la economía mundial (FMI), octubre de 2018.

StatLink https://doi.org/10.1787/888933941327

Chapter 5

Country tables, 1990-2017 – Tax revenues

Capítulo 5

Cuadros país, 1990-2017 – Ingresos tributarios

Table 5.1. **Argentina**

Details of tax revenue / Ingresos tributarios detallados

Million ARS

	1990	2000	2005	2010	2012	2013	2014	2015	2016	2017
Total tax revenue	**10 217**	**61 084**	**142 906**	**483 014**	**808 131**	**1 043 967**	**1 424 523**	**1 872 915**	**2 522 854**	**3 202 629**
1000 Taxes on income, profits and capital gains	**542**	**11 303**	**29 203**	**78 427**	**140 108**	**185 688**	**269 809**	**384 536**	**436 927**	**559 755**
1100 Of individuals	141	3 937	8 192	23 980	54 494	79 803	125 503	188 218	174 483	236 284
1110 On income and profits	130	3 854	8 151	23 858	54 279	79 449	125 067	187 663	173 721	234 117
1120 On capital gains	11	82	41	122	215	354	436	555	762	2 167
1200 Corporate	357	6 575	19 602	50 664	81 938	99 346	132 178	185 725	236 286	297 111
1210 On profits	357	6 575	19 602	50 664	81 938	99 346	132 178	185 725	236 286	297 111
Corporate income taxes	198	5 956	18 494	49 012	80 490	97 614	129 881	183 207	233 028	294 546
Tax on assets	160	19	5	4	5	3	6	4	12	5
Tax on assumed minimum income	0	600	1 102	1 648	1 443	1 728	2 291	2 513	3 246	2 560
1220 On capital gains	..	..	..	..	..	..	..	..	..	..
1300 Unallocable between 1100 and 1200	43	792	1 409	3 783	3 676	6 539	12 128	10 593	26 159	26 360
Non resident taxpayers	11	792	1 409	3 783	3 676	6 539	12 128	10 593	26 159	26 360
Other	33	0	0	0	0	0	0	0	0	0
2000 Social security contributions	**2 583**	**9 670**	**17 400**	**102 460**	**179 777**	**236 072**	**307 656**	**415 410**	**556 067**	**733 527**
2100 Employees	..	2 486	3 690	37 990	69 159	91 779	121 276	163 590	219 446	288 985
2110 On a payroll basis	..	2 486	3 690	37 990	69 159	91 779	121 276	163 590	219 446	288 985
2120 On an income tax basis	..	0	0	0	0	0	0	0	0	0
2200 Employers	..	6 069	12 557	54 713	101 114	132 999	174 965	235 610	314 628	413 212
2210 On a payroll basis	..	6 069	12 557	54 713	101 114	132 999	174 965	235 610	314 628	413 212
2220 On an income tax basis	..	0	0	0	0	0	0	0	0	0
2300 Self-employed or non-employed	98	1 115	1 153	9 757	9 504	11 293	11 416	16 210	21 994	31 330
2310 On a payroll basis	98	1 115	1 153	9 757	9 504	11 293	11 416	16 210	21 994	31 330
2320 On an income tax basis	0	0	0	0	0	0	0	0	0	0
2400 Unallocable between 2100, 2200 and 2300	2 485	0	0	0	0	0	0	0	0	0
2410 On a payroll basis	2 485	..	..	..	..	..	..	..	..	..
2420 On an income tax basis	0	..	..	..	..	..	..	..	..	..
3000 Taxes on payroll and workforce	**0**	**0**	**0**	**0**	**0**	**0**	**0**	**0**	**0**	**0**
4000 Taxes on property	**1 164**	**3 867**	**15 997**	**43 538**	**72 374**	**96 679**	**129 065**	**166 182**	**224 193**	**303 382**
4100 Recurrent taxes on immovable property	419	1 809	2 837	5 035	9 921	14 097	17 547	21 738	32 770	44 236
4110 Households	0	0	0	0	0	0	0	0	0	0
4120 Others	419	1 809	2 837	5 035	9 921	14 097	17 547	21 738	32 770	44 236
4200 Recurrent taxes on net wealth	246	1 084	1 867	5 248	7 408	10 471	14 575	18 538	19 976	22 786
4210 Individual	3	1 024	1 813	5 147	7 263	10 296	14 356	18 210	19 541	22 165
Personal assets	0	1 024	1 813	5 147	7 263	10 296	14 356	18 210	19 541	22 165
Recurrent taxes on net wealth	3	0	0	0	0	0	0	0	0	0
4220 Corporate	242	60	55	101	145	175	220	327	435	621
4300 Estate, inheritance and gift taxes	0	0	0	0	0	0	0	0	0	0
4310 Estate and inheritance taxes	..	..	..	..	..	..	..	..	..	..
4320 Gift taxes	..	..	..	..	..	..	..	..	..	..
4400 Taxes on financial and capital transactions	459	904	11 272	33 252	55 044	72 111	96 943	125 906	171 447	236 360
Immovable property transfers	0	54	116	539	721	734	912	1 256	2 052	4 091
Movable property transfers	44	0	0	0	0	0	0	0	0	0
Bank accounts' credits and debits	205	0	9 434	26 885	43 931	56 515	76 740	97 480	131 669	172 838
Stamp taxes	211	850	1 722	5 829	10 392	14 862	19 291	27 170	37 726	59 431
4500 Non-recurrent taxes	40	70	21	3	1	0	0	0	0	0
4510 On net wealth	0	0	0	0	0	..	..	..	..	..
4520 Other non-recurrent taxes	40	70	21	3	1	..	..	..	..	..
4600 Other recurrent taxes on property	0	0	0	0	0	0	0	0	0	0
5000 Taxes on goods and services	**5 636**	**34 539**	**77 959**	**253 092**	**407 716**	**517 591**	**704 677**	**889 323**	**1 176 337**	**1 529 578**
5100 Taxes on production, sale, transfer, etc	5 462	34 288	78 555	252 550	403 294	513 926	703 883	881 120	1 167 379	1 520 300
5110 General taxes	2 384	25 123	51 467	167 534	281 589	381 630	515 090	671 297	901 584	1 188 317
5111 Value added taxes	1 594	19 009	36 853	116 386	190 496	249 006	331 203	433 076	583 217	765 336
5112 Sales tax	0	0	0	0	0	0	0	0	0	0
5113 Other	791	6 114	14 613	51 148	91 093	132 624	183 887	238 221	318 367	422 981
5120 Taxes on specific goods and services	3 077	9 166	27 088	85 016	121 704	132 296	188 793	209 822	265 795	331 983
5121 Excises	1 866	5 850	10 609	26 208	40 800	49 680	69 977	92 349	129 790	182 818
Alcoholic beverages	25	36	73	238	422	525	673	985	1 163	1 591
Non alcoholic beverages	25	90	189	501	912	1 195	1 586	2 168	2 477	3 136
Beers	0	50	131	212	332	650	879	1 384	1 171	2 811
Tobacco products	425	1 875	3 460	6 884	10 310	12 343	17 432	26 152	42 183	60 249
Liquid fuel and gas	1 073	3 478	6 017	15 269	25 785	31 010	44 490	56 478	75 664	102 846
Electricity	72	205	283	591	610	547	607	590	637	1 768
Motor vehicles	59	20	0	27	153	185	121	88	265	476
Other	189	96	456	2 485	2 275	3 225	4 189	4 503	6 229	9 942
5122 Profits of fiscal monopolies	0	0	0	0	0	0	0	0	0	0

Table 5.1. **Argentina** *(cont.)*

Details of tax revenue / Ingresos tributarios detallados

Million ARS

	1990	2000	2005	2010	2012	2013	2014	2015	2016	2017
5123 Customs and import duties	219	1 976	3 877	11 428	16 640	23 551	30 058	35 512	56 365	70 635
Import duties	166	1 938	3 780	11 183	16 313	23 134	29 482	34 822	55 305	69 259
Import fees	53	38	96	246	327	416	576	691	1 060	1 376
5124 Taxes on exports	724	32	12 323	45 547	61 316	55 465	84 088	75 939	71 509	66 121
5125 Taxes on investment goods	0	0	0	0	0	0	0	0	0	0
5126 Taxes on specific services	163	1 233	150	1 429	2 227	2 677	3 533	4 420	5 782	7 792
Insurance services	42	194	8	21	35	46	65	88	118	167
Financial services	32	855	2	0	0	0	0	0	0	0
Telephone services	82	33	110	936	1 391	1 605	1 983	2 301	2 911	4 061
Other specific services	7	151	31	472	801	1 026	1 486	2 031	2 753	3 564
5127 Other taxes on internat. trade and transactions	98	74	129	404	721	924	1 136	1 601	2 349	4 616
5128 Other taxes	8	0	0	0	0	0	0	0	0	0
5130 Unallocable between 5110 and 5120	0	0	0	0	0	0	0	0	0	0
5200 Taxes on use of goods and perform activities	177	833	1 289	3 598	6 409	9 059	12 010	17 035	23 941	34 232
5210 Recurrent taxes	177	833	1 289	3 598	6 409	9 059	12 010	17 035	23 941	34 232
5211 Paid by households: motor vehicles	177	833	1 289	3 598	6 409	9 059	12 010	17 035	23 941	34 232
5212 Paid by others: motor vehicles	0	0	0	0	0	0	0	0	0	0
5213 Paid in respect of other goods	0	0	0	0	0	0	0	0	0	0
5220 Non-recurrent taxes	0	0	0	0	0	0	0	0	0	0
5300 Unallocable between 5100 and 5200	-3	-583	-1 885	-3 056	-1 987	-5 394	-11 215	-8 831	-14 983	-24 953
6000 Other taxes	**292**	**1 704**	**2 347**	**5 497**	**8 157**	**7 937**	**13 316**	**17 463**	**129 330**	**76 386**
6100 Paid solely by business	0	354	757	2 093	3 825	4 423	4 259	5 624	6 873	10 544
Simplified system for small taxpayers	0	354	757	2 093	3 825	4 423	4 259	5 624	6 873	10 544
6200 Other	292	1 351	1 590	3 404	4 332	3 514	9 056	11 839	122 457	65 842
Tax debt payments	135	24	112	293	934	-1 313	1 340	1 306	110 721	46 131
Special payments	79	6	1	0	0	0	0	0	0	0
Other national level	0	12	7	0	0	0	0	0	0	0
Other provincial level	78	1 309	1 469	3 110	3 398	4 827	7 716	10 533	11 736	19 710

Note: Year ending 31st December.
The data are on a cash basis.
The figures exclude local government tax revenues as the data are not available (but include provincial revenues).
Heading 5212: In ECLAC data, property tax on motor vehicles is classified in category 4000.
Heading 5300: The figures are negative as they represent general reimbursements of exports and specific taxes on goods and services.
Heading 6200: The tax debt payments from 2016 include revenue following the implementation of a new voluntary disclosure regime in July 2016 (Law 27260).

Source: Subsecretaría de Ingresos Públicos, Dirección Nacional de Investigaciones y Análisis Fiscal, Ministerio de Hacienda y Finanzas Públicas (Undersecretary of Public Revenue, National Direction of Research and Fiscal Analysis,

StatLink https://doi.org/10.1787/888933941346

Table 5.2. **Bahamas**

Details of tax revenue / Ingresos tributarios detallados

Million BSD

	1990	2000	2005	2010	2012	2013	2014	2015	2016	2017
Total tax revenue	**505**	**965**	**1 060**	**1 277**	**1 480**	**1 445**	**1 490**	**1 761**	**1 986**	**2 177**
1000 Taxes on income, profits and capital gains	**0**	**0**	**0**	**0**	**0**	**0**	**0**	**0**	**0**	**0**
1100 Of individuals	0	0	0	0	0	0	0	0	0	0
1110 On income and profits	..	..	..	..	..	..	..	..	..	..
1120 On capital gains	..	..	..	..	..	..	..	..	..	..
1200 Corporate	0	0	0	0	0	0	0	0	0	0
1210 On profits	..	..	..	..	..	..	..	..	..	..
1220 On capital gains	..	..	..	..	..	..	..	..	..	..
1300 Unallocable between 1100 and 1200	0	0	0	0	0	0	0	0	0	0
2000 Social security contributions	**66**	**115**	**136**	**167**	**203**	**229**	**245**	**260**	**310**	**340**
2100 Employees	..	..	..	60	74	87	91	98	..	..
2110 On a payroll basis	..	..	..	..	..	..	..	..	..	..
2120 On an income tax basis	..	..	..	..	..	..	..	..	..	..
2200 Employers	..	..	..	104	124	137	149	157	..	..
2210 On a payroll basis	..	..	..	..	..	..	..	..	..	..
2220 On an income tax basis	..	..	..	..	..	..	..	..	..	..
2300 Self-employed or non-employed	..	..	..	3	5	6	6	6	..	..
2310 On a payroll basis	..	..	..	..	..	..	..	..	..	..
2320 On an income tax basis	..	..	..	..	..	..	..	..	..	..
2400 Unallocable between 2100, 2200 and 2300	66	115	136	0	0	-1	-1	-1	310	340
2410 On a payroll basis	..	..	..	..	..	..	..	..	..	..
2420 On an income tax basis	..	..	..	..	..	..	..	..	..	..
3000 Taxes on payroll and workforce	**0**	**0**	**0**	**0**	**0**	**0**	**0**	**0**	**0**	**0**
4000 Taxes on property	**19**	**32**	**54**	**92**	**95**	**115**	**104**	**107**	**104**	**121**
4100 Recurrent taxes on immovable property	19	32	54	92	95	115	104	107	104	121
4110 Households	0	0	0	0	0	0	0	0	0	0
4120 Others	19	32	54	92	95	115	104	107	104	121
4200 Recurrent taxes on net wealth	0	0	0	0	0	0	0	0	0	0
4210 Individual	..	..	..	..	..	..	..	..	..	..
4220 Corporate	..	..	..	..	..	..	..	..	..	..
4300 Estate, inheritance and gift taxes	0	0	0	0	0	0	0	0	0	0
4310 Estate and inheritance taxes	..	..	..	..	..	..	..	..	..	..
4320 Gift taxes	..	..	..	..	..	..	..	..	..	..
4400 Taxes on financial and capital transactions	0	0	0	0	0	0	0	0	0	0
4500 Non-recurrent taxes	0	0	0	0	0	0	0	0	0	0
4510 On net wealth	..	..	..	..	..	..	..	..	..	..
4520 Other non-recurrent taxes	..	..	..	..	..	..	..	..	..	..
4600 Other recurrent taxes on property	0	0	0	0	0	0	0	0	0	0
5000 Taxes on goods and services	**386**	**723**	**736**	**795**	**1 018**	**955**	**986**	**1 203**	**1 472**	**1 604**
5100 Taxes on production, sale, transfer, etc	354	654	657	672	868	806	772	993	1 296	1 384
5110 General taxes	0	0	0	0	0	0	0	219	628	638
5111 Value added taxes	0	0	0	0	0	0	0	219	628	638
5112 Sales tax	0	0	0	0	0	0	0	0	0	0
5113 Other	0	0	0	0	0	0	0	0	0	0
5120 Taxes on specific goods and services	354	654	657	672	868	806	772	775	668	746
5121 Excises	0	0	0	188	331	246	249	262	230	287
5122 Profits of fiscal monopolies	0	0	0	0	0	0	0	0	0	0
5123 Customs and import duties	289	537	525	364	366	350	336	307	264	287
Import tax	289	435	413	348	348	332	336	307	264	287
Stamp tax from imports duties	0	102	112	15	18	18	0	0	0	0
5124 Taxes on exports	6	13	13	14	15	14	10	9	12	8
Export tax	6	13	13	14	15	14	10	9	12	8
Stamp tax from exports	0	0	0	0	0	0	0	0	0	0
5125 Taxes on investment goods	0	0	0	0	0	0	0	0	0	0
5126 Taxes on specific services	59	104	119	106	156	196	178	197	162	163
Departure tax	27	64	69	70	102	144	125	147	135	135
Gaming tax	27	20	25	10	11	10	8	25	26	27
Hotel occupancy tax	5	20	25	25	43	42	45	25	1	1
5127 Other taxes on internat. trade and transactions	0	0	0	0	0	0	0	0	0	0
5128 Other taxes	0	0	0	0	0	0	0	0	0	0
5130 Unallocable between 5110 and 5120	0	0	0	0	0	0	0	0	0	0
5200 Taxes on use of goods and perform activities	32	69	78	123	150	149	214	209	177	220
5210 Recurrent taxes	32	69	78	123	150	149	214	209	177	220
Motor vehicle tax	10	14	18	21	29	28	29	29	30	31
5211 Paid by households: motor vehicles	0	0	0	0	0	0	0	0	0	0
5212 Paid by others: motor vehicles	0	0	0	0	0	0	0	0	0	0

Table 5.2. **Bahamas** *(cont.)*

Details of tax revenue / Ingresos tributarios detallados

Million BSD

	1990	2000	2005	2010	2012	2013	2014	2015	2016	2017
5213 Paid in respect of other goods	22	55	61	102	121	121	185	180	146	189
Company fees and registration	0	5	5	5	5	5	5	5	6	7
International business companies	0	17	15	19	17	17	17	16	15	15
Others	22	33	40	78	99	99	163	159	125	167
5220 Non-recurrent taxes	0	0	0	0	0	0	0	0	0	0
5300 Unallocable between 5100 and 5200	0	0	0	0	0	0	0	0	0	0
6000 Other taxes	**33**	**95**	**135**	**223**	**163**	**145**	**155**	**191**	**100**	**112**
6100 Paid solely by business	0	0	0	0	0	0	0	0	0	0
6200 Other	33	95	135	223	163	145	155	191	100	112
All other stamp taxes	37	74	135	162	174	160	164	191	100	112
Incentive acts and other refunds	-8	14	-15	11	-11	-15	-8	0	0	0
Other taxes	4	7	15	49	0	0	0	0	0	0

Note: Fiscal year ending on 30th June.
The data for 2017 are preliminary and undertaken from the Central Bank of the Bahamas.
The figures exclude local government tax revenues as the data are not available.
Heading 2000: The data are estimated for 2016 and 2017.
Heading 2400: This heading includes refunds of social security contributions as reported by the National Insurance Board (NIB).
Heading 5111: A value added tax was enforced on 1st January 2015.
Source: The Central Bank of The Bahamas and the National Insurance Board.

StatLink https://doi.org/10.1787/888933941365

Table 5.3. **Barbados**

Details of tax revenue / Ingresos tributarios detallados

Million BAR

	1990	2000	2005	2010	2012	2013	2014	2015	2016	2017
Total tax revenue	**942**	**1 884**	**2 297**	**2 719**	**2 869**	**2 576**	**2 643**	**2 947**	**2 892**	**3 206**
1000 Taxes on income, profits and capital gains	**254**	**574**	**639**	**762**	**744**	**615**	**702**	**723**	**819**	**819**
1100 Of individuals	129	289	296	388	380	344	429	433	496	496
1110 On income and profits	129	289	296	388	380	344	429	433	496	496
1120 On capital gains	..	..	..	..	..	..	..	..	..	..
1200 Corporate	111	252	294	327	276	191	208	225	260	281
1210 On profits	111	252	294	327	276	191	208	225	260	281
1220 On capital gains	..	..	..	..	..	..	..	..	..	..
1300 Unallocable between 1100 and 1200	14	33	49	47	88	80	65	65	63	42
2000 Social security contributions	**134**	**295**	**408**	**525**	**529**	**513**	**532**	**553**	**239**	**318**
2100 Employees	..	..	..	..	..	..	..	..	..	..
2110 On a payroll basis	..	..	..	..	..	..	..	..	..	..
2120 On an income tax basis	..	..	..	..	..	..	..	..	..	..
2200 Employers	..	..	..	..	..	..	..	..	..	..
2210 On a payroll basis	..	..	..	..	..	..	..	..	..	..
2220 On an income tax basis	..	..	..	..	..	..	..	..	..	..
2300 Self-employed or non-employed	..	..	..	..	..	..	..	..	..	..
2310 On a payroll basis	..	..	..	..	..	..	..	..	..	..
2320 On an income tax basis	..	..	..	..	..	..	..	..	..	..
2400 Unallocable between 2100, 2200 and 2300	134	295	408	525	529	513	532	553	239	318
2410 On a payroll basis	..	..	..	..	..	..	..	..	..	..
2420 On an income tax basis	..	..	..	..	..	..	..	..	..	..
3000 Taxes on payroll and workforce	**0**	**0**	**0**	**0**	**0**	**0**	**0**	**0**	**0**	**0**
4000 Taxes on property	**39**	**92**	**127**	**114**	**148**	**125**	**113**	**188**	**188**	**190**
4100 Recurrent taxes on immovable property	26	60	76	98	133	109	94	173	172	174
Land tax	26	60	76	98	133	109	94	173	172	174
4110 Households	..	..	..	..	..	..	..	..	..	..
4120 Others	..	..	..	..	..	..	..	..	..	..
4200 Recurrent taxes on net wealth	0	0	0	0	0	0	0	0	0	0
4210 Individual	..	..	..	..	..	..	..	..	..	..
4220 Corporate	..	..	..	..	..	..	..	..	..	..
4300 Estate, inheritance and gift taxes	0	0	0	0	0	0	0	0	0	0
4310 Estate and inheritance taxes	..	..	..	..	..	..	..	..	..	..
4320 Gift taxes	..	..	..	..	..	..	..	..	..	..
4400 Taxes on financial and capital transactions	0	0	0	0	0	0	0	0	0	0
4500 Non-recurrent taxes	13	32	51	16	15	16	19	15	16	16
4510 On net wealth	..	..	..	..	..	..	..	..	..	..
4520 Other non-recurrent taxes	..	..	..	..	..	..	..	..	..	..
4600 Other recurrent taxes on property	0	0	0	0	0	0	0	0	0	0
5000 Taxes on goods and services	**418**	**911**	**1 101**	**1 303**	**1 436**	**1 313**	**1 284**	**1 473**	**1 637**	**1 870**
5100 Taxes on production, sale, transfer, etc	418	807	974	1 153	1 261	1 208	1 176	1 325	1 480	1 713
5110 General taxes	197	501	610	753	907	871	823	925	958	994
5111 Value added taxes	0	501	610	753	907	871	823	925	958	994
5112 Sales tax	197	0	0	0	0	0	0	0	0	0
5113 Other	0	0	0	0	0	0	0	0	0	0
5120 Taxes on specific goods and services	221	306	364	400	353	338	353	401	522	719
5121 Excises	91	173	172	209	153	150	142	169	277	477
Excises	5	159	172	148	137	129	122	169	227	311
Levies	86	14	0	61	16	21	20	0	49	166
5122 Profits of fiscal monopolies	0	0	0	0	0	0	0	0	0	0
5123 Customs and import duties	112	133	192	191	200	188	211	232	245	242
Import duties	112	133	192	191	200	188	211	232	245	242
5124 Taxes on exports	0	0	0	0	0	0	0	0	0	0
5125 Taxes on investment goods	0	0	0	0	0	0	0	0	0	0
5126 Taxes on specific services	18	1	0	0	0	0	0	0	0	0
Hotel and restaurant tax	18	1	0	0	0	0	0	0	0	0
5127 Other taxes on internat. trade and transactions	0	0	0	0	0	0	0	0	0	0
5128 Other taxes	0	0	0	0	0	0	0	0	0	0
5130 Unallocable between 5110 and 5120	0	0	0	0	0	0	0	0	0	0
5200 Taxes on use of goods and perform activities	0	104	127	150	176	105	108	148	157	157
5210 Recurrent taxes	..	104	127	150	176	105	108	148	157	157
5211 Paid by households: motor vehicles	..	0	0	0	0	0	0	0	0	0
5212 Paid by others: motor vehicles	..	0	0	0	0	0	0	0	0	0
5213 Paid in respect of other goods	..	104	127	150	176	105	108	148	157	157
5220 Non-recurrent taxes	..	0	0	0	0	0	0	0	0	0
5300 Unallocable between 5100 and 5200	0	0	0	0	0	0	0	0	0	0
6000 Other taxes	**98**	**12**	**21**	**15**	**11**	**10**	**13**	**10**	**9**	**9**
6100 Paid solely by business	0	0	0	0	0	0	0	0	0	0

Table 5.3. **Barbados** *(cont.)*

Details of tax revenue / Ingresos tributarios detallados

Million BAR

	1990	2000	2005	2010	2012	2013	2014	2015	2016	2017
6200 Other	98	12	21	15	11	10	13	10	9	9
Stamp duties	98	12	21	15	11	10	13	10	9	9

Note: Year ending 31st March.

The data are on a cash basis.

The figures exclude local government tax revenues as the data are not available.

Heading 5213: This heading includes data on tax collection levied on a recurrent basis for which the tax base is not identifiable.

Source: The Central Bank of Barbados, the Inland Revenue Department. End year figures are from the Barbados Budget Estimates 2018-19 published by the Barbados Parliament.

StatLink https://doi.org/10.1787/888933941384

Table 5.4. **Belize / Belice**

Details of tax revenue / Ingresos tributarios detallados

Million BZD

	1990	2000	2005	2010	2012	2013	2014	2015	2016	2017
Total tax revenue	**179**	**318**	**496**	**744**	**786**	**830**	**929**	**950**	**1 006**	**1 055**
1000 Taxes on income, profits and capital gains	**37**	**76**	**129**	**248**	**232**	**245**	**272**	**254**	**261**	**266**
1100 Of individuals	21	19	35	52	60	64	74	82	88	86
1110 On income and profits	21	19	35	52	60	64	74	82	88	86
Income tax (PAYE)	20	19	35	52	60	64	74	82	88	86
Income tax on individuals	1	0	0	0	0	0	0	0	0	0
1120 On capital gains	..	..	..	..	..	..	..	..	..	..
1200 Corporate	12	51	90	189	164	172	183	159	162	170
Income tax (companies)	12	1	0	51	27	18	16	1	0	0
Income tax (business tax)	0	51	90	138	132	150	167	158	162	170
Income tax (supplemental petroleum tax)	0	0	0	0	6	4	0	0	0	0
1210 On profits	..	..	..	..	..	..	..	..	..	..
1220 On capital gains	..	..	..	..	..	..	..	..	..	..
1300 Unallocable between 1100 and 1200	4	6	4	7	8	10	15	13	11	10
Income tax (arrears)	4	3	1	1	2	2	2	2	2	2
Income tax (withholding)	0	3	2	6	7	8	13	11	9	8
2000 Social security contributions	**10**	**18**	**50**	**60**	**65**	**67**	**72**	**77**	**80**	**80**
2100 Employees	..	..	..	..	..	..	..	..	..	..
2110 On a payroll basis	..	..	..	..	..	..	..	..	..	..
2120 On an income tax basis	..	..	..	..	..	..	..	..	..	..
2200 Employers	..	..	..	..	..	..	..	..	..	..
2210 On a payroll basis	..	..	..	..	..	..	..	..	..	..
2220 On an income tax basis	..	..	..	..	..	..	..	..	..	..
2300 Self-employed or non-employed	..	..	..	..	..	..	..	..	..	..
2310 On a payroll basis	..	..	..	..	..	..	..	..	..	..
2320 On an income tax basis	..	..	..	..	..	..	..	..	..	..
2400 Unallocable between 2100, 2200 and 2300	10	18	50	60	65	67	72	77	80	80
2410 On a payroll basis	..	..	..	..	..	..	..	..	..	..
2420 On an income tax basis	..	..	..	..	..	..	..	..	..	..
3000 Taxes on payroll and workforce	**0**	**0**	**0**	**0**	**0**	**0**	**0**	**0**	**0**	**0**
4000 Taxes on property	**6**	**13**	**27**	**23**	**27**	**31**	**35**	**35**	**31**	**31**
4100 Recurrent taxes on immovable property	1	2	6	7	5	6	6	5	7	6
4110 Households	1	2	6	7	5	6	6	5	7	6
4120 Others	0	0	0	0	0	0	0	0	0	0
4200 Recurrent taxes on net wealth	0	0	0	0	0	0	0	0	0	0
4210 Individual	..	..	..	..	..	..	..	..	..	..
4220 Corporate	..	..	..	..	..	..	..	..	..	..
4300 Estate, inheritance and gift taxes	0	0	0	0	0	0	0	0	0	0
4310 Estate and inheritance taxes	..	0	0	0	0	0	0	0	0	0
4320 Gift taxes	..	0	0	0	0	0	0	0	0	0
4400 Taxes on financial and capital transactions	5	11	22	16	22	25	29	29	25	25
4500 Non-recurrent taxes	0	0	0	0	0	0	0	0	0	0
4510 On net wealth	..	..	..	..	..	..	..	..	..	..
4520 Other non-recurrent taxes	..	..	..	..	..	..	..	..	..	..
4600 Other recurrent taxes on property	0	0	0	0	0	0	0	0	0	0
5000 Taxes on goods and services	**126**	**211**	**289**	**412**	**462**	**486**	**550**	**583**	**634**	**678**
5100 Taxes on production, sale, transfer, etc.	122	207	282	400	443	469	540	571	630	669
5110 General taxes	0	82	131	199	214	237	270	275	292	293
5111 Value added taxes	0	0	0	199	214	237	270	275	292	293
5112 Sales tax	..	82	131	0	0	0	0	0	0	0
5113 Other	..	0	0	0	0	0	0	0	0	0
5120 Taxes on specific goods and services	122	125	151	200	229	232	269	296	338	376
5121 Excises	35	47	57	31	34	35	38	39	159	188
Revenue replacement duty	18	39	57	7	12	13	15	15	1	1
Excise duties	17	8	0	22	20	21	22	23	157	186
Excise on locally refined petroleum products	0	0	0	0	0	0	0	1	0	0
Excise on locally extracted crude oil	0	0	0	1	2	2	1	0	1	1
5122 Profits of fiscal monopolies	0	0	0	0	0	0	0	0	0	0
5123 Customs and import duties	78	64	80	144	165	165	196	221	154	141
Import duties	50	64	80	123	141	140	167	190	123	100
Environmental tax	0	0	0	21	24	25	29	31	31	42
Imports into EPZs	0	0	0	0	0	0	0	0	0	0
Stamps duties on customs	28	0	0	0	0	0	0	0	0	0
5124 Taxes on exports	0	0	0	0	0	0	0	0	0	0
5125 Taxes on investment goods	0	0	0	0	0	0	0	0	0	0
5126 Taxes on specific services	0	0	0	0	0	0	0	0	0	0

Table 5.4. **Belize / Belice** *(cont.)*

Details of tax revenue / Ingresos tributarios detallados

Million BZD

	1990	2000	2005	2010	2012	2013	2014	2015	2016	2017
5127 Other taxes on internat. trade and transactions	8	14	15	25	30	32	35	35	24	47
Goods in transit - administration charge	3	1	1	1	1	1	1	1	1	1
Goods in transit - social fee	0	5	4	8	11	11	12	11	10	17
Taxes on foreign currency transactions	6	8	9	16	18	20	22	23	13	28
5128 Other taxes	0	0	0	0	0	0	0	0	0	0
5130 Unallocable between 5110 and 5120	0	0	0	0	0	0	0	0	0	0
5200 Taxes on use of goods and perform activities	4	4	7	13	19	17	10	12	4	9
5210 Recurrent taxes	4	4	7	13	19	17	10	12	4	9
5211 Paid by households: motor vehicles	2	3	5	3	3	4	4	4	0	4
5212 Paid by others: motor vehicles	0	0	0	0	0	0	0	0	0	0
5213 Paid in respect of other goods	2	1	2	10	16	14	6	8	4	5
5220 Non-recurrent taxes	0	0	0	0	0	0	0	0	0	0
5300 Unallocable between 5100 and 5200	0	0	0	0	0	0	0	0	0	0
6000 Other taxes	**0**	**0**	**0**	**0**	**0**	**0**	**0**	**0**	**0**	**0**
6100 Paid solely by business	..	..	..	..	..	..	..	..	..	..
6200 Other	..	..	..	..	..	..	..	..	..	..

Note: Year ending 31st March. Data are on an April(n)/March(n+1) fiscal year basis. For example, the data for 2017 represent April 2017 to March 2018.

The data are on a cash basis.

The data for 2017 represent the projected out-turn for the 2017/18 fiscal year reported in the Approved Estimates of Revenue and Expenditure for Fiscal Year 2018/2019.

Heading 2000: The data for social security contributions are estimated for 2016 and 2017.

Source: Ministry of Finance of Belize, the Social Security Board.

StatLink https://doi.org/10.1787/888933941403

Table 5.5. **Bolivia**

Details of tax revenue / Ingresos tributarios detallados

Million BOB

	1990	2000	2005	2010	2012	2013	2014	2015	2016	2017
Total tax revenue	**1 277**	**9 155**	**15 456**	**28 576**	**46 130**	**53 947**	**59 656**	**62 945**	**60 737**	**62 045**
1000 Taxes on income, profits and capital gains	**68**	**1 209**	**2 470**	**6 941**	**10 232**	**12 021**	**12 690**	**12 883**	**10 891**	**10 583**
1100 Of individuals	68	214	214	263	279	364	439	508	497	502
1110 On income and profits	68	214	214	263	279	364	439	508	497	502
RC-IVA	62	161	187	237	260	333	401	461	442	441
RC-IVA fiscal notes	6	53	28	26	19	31	38	47	55	61
1120 On capital gains	..	..	..	..	..	..	..	..	..	..
1200 Corporate	0	995	2 256	6 679	9 953	11 657	12 251	12 375	10 394	10 081
1210 On profits	..	995	2 256	6 679	9 953	11 657	12 251	12 375	10 394	10 081
Mining profits	..	0	75	473	322	283	82	67	8	572
Corporate tax	..	546	1 557	4 347	6 578	7 107	8 108	9 302	6 968	7 737
Corporate tax remittances	..	258	315	742	718	806	954	959	1 670	918
Fiscal notes on corporate tax	..	192	297	942	2 004	3 231	3 035	1 905	1 483	854
Fiscal notes on mining profits	..	0	11	174	331	229	72	143	266	0
1220 On capital gains	..	..	..	..	..	..	..	..	..	..
1300 Unallocable between 1100 and 1200	0	0	0	0	0	0	0	0	0	0
2000 Social security contributions	**0**	**666**	**936**	**1 645**	**6 339**	**7 276**	**8 694**	**9 842**	**10 251**	**10 983**
2100 Employees	..	..	..	..	..	..	..	..	..	..
2110 On a payroll basis	..	..	..	..	..	..	..	..	..	..
2120 On an income tax basis	..	..	..	..	..	..	..	..	..	..
2200 Employers	..	..	..	..	..	..	..	..	..	..
2210 On a payroll basis	..	..	..	..	..	..	..	..	..	..
2220 On an income tax basis	..	..	..	..	..	..	..	..	..	..
2300 Self-employed or non-employed	..	..	..	..	..	..	..	..	..	..
2310 On a payroll basis	..	..	..	..	..	..	..	..	..	..
2320 On an income tax basis	..	..	..	..	..	..	..	..	..	..
2400 Unallocable between 2100, 2200 and 2300	..	666	936	1 645	6 339	7 276	8 694	9 842	10 251	10 983
2410 On a payroll basis	..	666	936	1 645	6 339	7 276	8 694	9 842	10 251	10 983
2420 On an income tax basis	..	0	0	0	0	0	0	0	0	0
3000 Taxes on payroll and workforce	**0**	**0**	**0**	**0**	**0**	**0**	**0**	**0**	**0**	**0**
4000 Taxes on property	**1**	**3**	**640**	**367**	**401**	**412**	**433**	**424**	**455**	**492**
4100 Recurrent taxes on immovable property	0	0	0	0	0	0	0	0	0	0
4110 Households	..	..	..	..	..	..	..	..	..	..
4120 Others	..	..	..	..	..	..	..	..	..	..
4200 Recurrent taxes on net wealth	0	0	0	0	0	0	0	0	0	0
4210 Individual	..	..	..	..	..	..	..	..	..	..
4220 Corporate	..	..	..	..	..	..	..	..	..	..
4300 Estate, inheritance and gift taxes	1	3	7	20	23	28	32	36	15	1
4310 Estate and inheritance taxes	1	3	7	20	23	28	32	36	15	1
4320 Gift taxes	0	0	0	0	0	0	0	0	0	0
4400 Taxes on financial and capital transactions	0	0	633	347	378	384	401	388	440	491
4500 Non-recurrent taxes	0	0	0	0	0	0	0	0	0	0
4510 On net wealth	..	..	..	..	..	..	..	..	..	..
4520 Other non-recurrent taxes	..	..	..	..	..	..	..	..	..	..
4600 Other recurrent taxes on property	0	0	0	0	0	0	0	0	0	0
5000 Taxes on goods and services	**1 032**	**6 594**	**10 207**	**17 684**	**26 528**	**30 878**	**33 857**	**34 731**	**33 402**	**33 953**
5100 Taxes on production, sale, transfer, etc.	1 032	6 594	10 207	17 684	26 528	30 878	33 857	34 731	33 402	33 953
5110 General taxes	708	3 892	6 768	12 434	19 508	22 620	24 661	25 220	24 288	24 522
5111 Value added taxes	551	2 949	5 314	10 259	16 306	19 033	20 581	20 757	19 902	20 199
VAT internal market	297	1 204	1 937	4 100	6 555	7 805	9 273	9 914	10 318	9 910
VAT imports	178	1 445	2 637	5 193	7 690	8 709	9 390	9 738	8 458	9 154
VAT fiscal notes (internal market)	56	223	584	581	623	783	760	666	622	439
VAT fiscal notes (imports)	20	76	156	385	1 437	1 736	1 158	438	504	696
5112 Sales tax	0	0	0	0	0	0	0	0	0	0
5113 Other	157	943	1 455	2 174	3 202	3 587	4 081	4 463	4 386	4 323
5120 Taxes on specific goods and services	324	2 702	3 439	5 250	7 020	8 258	9 196	9 511	9 114	9 430
5121 Excises	118	2 047	2 604	3 658	4 475	5 012	5 663	5 853	6 040	6 032
Excises (Internal)	61	245	209	933	1 157	1 468	1 365	1 487	1 687	1 450
Excises (Imports)	22	298	208	379	580	719	1 051	1 109	917	953
Special tax on hydrocarbons and derivatives	0	1 348	1 529	1 070	1 144	1 681	1 998	2 581	2 696	3 105
Fiscal notes on excises	35	118	309	155	290	47	328	262	103	442
Fiscal notes on special tax on hydrocarb. and deriv.	0	40	350	1 121	1 304	1 098	921	415	638	82
5122 Profits of fiscal monopolies	0	0	0	0	0	0	0	0	0	0
5123 Customs and import duties	204	640	803	1 545	2 485	2 850	3 102	3 254	2 894	3 198
Customs and import duties	163	616	777	1 504	2 278	2 663	2 879	3 057	2 787	3 044
Fiscal notes customs and import duties	41	24	26	41	207	186	223	198	107	155
5124 Taxes on exports	0	0	0	0	0	0	0	0	0	0

Table 5.5. **Bolivia** *(cont.)*

Details of tax revenue / Ingresos tributarios detallados

Million BOB

	1990	2000	2005	2010	2012	2013	2014	2015	2016	2017
5125 Taxes on investment goods	0	0	0	0	0	0	0	0	0	0
5126 Taxes on specific services	2	15	32	47	60	91	120	127	175	200
Air departure tax	2	15	32	47	51	71	90	102	116	122
Tax on gambling	0	0	0	0	9	20	30	25	59	78
5127 Other taxes on internat. trade and transactions	0	0	0	0	0	306	311	277	6	0
5128 Other taxes	0	0	0	0	0	0	0	0	0	0
5130 Unallocable between 5110 and 5120	0	0	0	0	0	0	0	0	0	0
5200 Taxes on use of goods and perform activities	0	0	0	0	0	0	0	0	0	0
5210 Recurrent taxes	..	..	..	..	..	..	..	..	..	..
5211 Paid by households: motor vehicles	..	..	..	..	..	..	..	..	..	..
5212 Paid by others: motor vehicles	..	..	..	..	..	..	..	..	..	..
5213 Paid in respect of other goods	..	..	..	..	..	..	..	..	..	..
5220 Non-recurrent taxes	..	..	..	..	..	..	..	..	..	..
5300 Unallocable between 5100 and 5200	0	0	0	0	0	0	0	0	0	0
6000 Other taxes	**177**	**682**	**1 203**	**1 939**	**2 630**	**3 361**	**3 982**	**5 065**	**5 738**	**6 033**
6100 Paid solely by business	4	6	5	12	14	17	20	26	35	30
Simplified tax regime	3	6	4	12	14	17	20	25	35	30
Integrated tax system	1	0	0	0	0	0	0	0	0	0
6200 Other	172	676	1 199	1 927	2 615	3 344	3 961	5 040	5 703	6 003
Unified agricultural regime	0	1	5	14	22	23	23	26	27	31
Fiscal notes on transactions	15	64	250	108	56	116	53	28	39	69
Other	154	37	178	422	860	1 241	1 716	2 378	2 696	2 685
Fiscal notes on other taxes	3	0	5	3	2	9	25	23	63	8
Municipal taxes	0	575	762	1 381	1 675	1 955	2 145	2 585	2 879	3 210

Note: Year ending 31st December.

The data are on a cash basis.

Heading 2000: The figures exclude social security contributions for healthcare as historical data were not available at the time of the publication

Heading 5113: This heading includes the "Impuesto a las Transacciones", a turnover tax .

Heading 6200: The municipal taxes are estimated in 2017.

Source: Ministerio de Economía y Finanzas Públicas, Ministry of Economy and Public Finance. Unidad de Análisis de Políticas Sociales y Económicas, Social and Economic Policy Analysis Unit.

StatLink https://doi.org/10.1787/888933941422

Table 5.6. **Brazil / Brasil**

Details of tax revenue / Ingresos tributarios detallados

Million BRL

	1990	2000	2005	2010	2012	2013	2014	2015	2016	2017
Total tax revenue	**3**	**354 760**	**711 145**	**1 256 423**	**1 557 873**	**1 726 353**	**1 830 531**	**1 913 556**	**2 011 724**	**2 118 464**
1000 Taxes on income, profits and capital gains	**1**	**68 667**	**149 309**	**258 738**	**321 465**	**360 561**	**381 844**	**400 993**	**453 127**	**458 312**
1100 Of individuals	0	3 406	6 981	87 828	116 344	126 018	140 420	148 739	161 833	177 377
1110 On income and profits	0	3 406	6 981	87 828	116 344	126 018	140 420	148 739	161 833	177 377
Withholding taxes on income and profits	0	0	0	71 579	93 845	101 830	114 638	121 540	133 549	146 872
Other personal income taxes	0	0	0	16 248	22 499	24 188	25 782	27 199	28 285	30 504
1120 On capital gains	..	..	..	..	..	..	..	..	..	..
1200 Corporate	0	25 430	73 071	128 255	148 423	171 003	171 352	164 057	197 941	184 501
1210 On profits	0	25 430	73 071	128 255	148 423	171 003	171 352	164 057	197 941	184 501
Corporate income tax	0	16 680	47 832	82 474	92 589	109 316	109 020	104 910	131 181	113 815
Social contribution on net profits (CSLL)	0	8 750	25 239	45 780	55 834	61 687	62 332	59 147	66 760	70 686
1220 On capital gains	..	..	..	..	..	..	..	..	..	..
1300 Unallocable between 1100 and 1200	0	39 831	69 257	42 656	56 697	63 540	70 072	88 196	93 353	96 434
Non-residents	0	39 831	69 257	11 537	15 207	18 582	19 703	24 669	24 892	27 270
Capital	0	0	0	24 887	33 309	37 121	41 288	53 692	59 404	59 470
Others	0	0	0	6 232	8 182	7 837	9 082	9 836	9 057	9 694
2000 Social security contributions	**1**	**83 469**	**168 226**	**313 920**	**402 396**	**441 756**	**478 952**	**499 294**	**523 516**	**551 711**
2100 Employees	..	..	..	..	..	..	..	..	..	..
2110 On a payroll basis	..	..	..	..	..	..	..	..	..	..
2120 On an income tax basis	..	..	..	..	..	..	..	..	..	..
2200 Employers	0	18 709	32 248	64 271	85 813	98 045	108 782	118 323	124 713	128 743
2210 On a payroll basis	0	18 709	32 248	64 271	85 813	98 045	108 782	118 323	124 713	128 743
2220 On an income tax basis	0	0	0	0	0	0	0	0	0	0
2300 Self-employed or non-employed	..	..	..	..	..	..	..	..	..	..
2310 On a payroll basis	..	..	..	..	..	..	..	..	..	..
2320 On an income tax basis	..	..	..	..	..	..	..	..	..	..
2400 Unallocable between 2100, 2200 and 2300	1	64 760	135 978	249 650	316 583	343 712	370 171	380 972	398 802	422 968
2410 On a payroll basis	1	64 760	135 978	249 650	316 583	343 712	370 171	380 972	398 802	422 968
Social security contributions (Federal)	1	59 334	118 869	231 903	294 578	319 566	341 992	349 787	365 066	387 961
Social security contributions (State)	0	4 423	14 682	12 634	15 546	16 494	19 910	21 651	23 152	23 996
Social security contributions (Municipal)	0	1 003	2 427	5 113	6 459	7 652	8 268	9 535	10 585	11 011
2420 On an income tax basis	0	0	0	0	0	0	0	0	0	0
3000 Taxes on payroll and workforce	**0**	**6 749**	**14 468**	**33 090**	**39 206**	**43 391**	**47 724**	**50 399**	**51 550**	**54 655**
PASEP contributions	0	1 312	2 863	9 880	8 398	8 775	9 491	9 958	10 026	11 574
Payroll-based contribution to education	0	2 791	5 906	11 049	14 775	16 561	18 411	19 039	19 473	20 010
"S" System contributions	0	2 646	4 397	9 925	13 557	15 351	16 884	18 153	18 428	19 075
Other	0	0	1 302	2 236	2 477	2 704	2 938	3 248	3 623	3 996
4000 Taxes on property	**0**	**28 818**	**56 274**	**74 208**	**91 889**	**97 300**	**105 088**	**119 937**	**125 024**	**132 173**
4100 Recurrent taxes on immovable property	0	4 753	8 405	17 929	22 160	24 760	27 673	32 626	35 459	39 700
4110 Households	0	0	0	0	0	0	0	0	0	0
4120 Others	0	4 753	8 405	17 929	22 160	24 760	27 673	32 626	35 459	39 700
Tax on rural land property (ITR)	0	234	288	485	614	764	900	1 105	1 126	1 273
Tax on urban land property (IPTU)	0	4 519	8 117	17 444	21 545	23 996	26 773	31 521	34 333	38 427
4200 Recurrent taxes on net wealth	0	0	0	0	0	0	0	0	0	0
4210 Individual	..	..	..	..	..	..	..	..	..	..
4220 Corporate	..	..	..	..	..	..	..	..	..	..
4300 Estate, inheritance and gift taxes	0	329	821	2 518	3 409	4 142	4 698	6 469	7 345	7 242
4310 Estate and inheritance taxes	0	329	821	2 518	3 409	4 142	4 698	6 469	7 345	7 242
4320 Gift taxes	0	0	0	0	0	0	0	0	0	0
4400 Taxes on financial and capital transactions	0	18 442	36 587	32 393	39 291	39 166	40 263	44 586	43 126	44 722
Tax on financial operations (IOF)	0	3 096	5 974	26 571	31 002	29 417	29 756	34 681	33 645	34 660
Real estate property transfers (ITBI)	0	950	1 593	5 840	8 290	9 749	10 507	9 904	9 482	10 062
Other	0	14 396	29 021	-18	0	0	0	0	0	0
4500 Non-recurrent taxes	0	0	0	0	0	0	0	0	0	0
4510 On net wealth	..	..	..	..	..	..	..	..	..	..
4520 Other non-recurrent taxes	..	..	..	..	..	..	..	..	..	..
4600 Other recurrent taxes on property	0	5 294	10 460	21 367	27 030	29 232	32 453	36 257	39 093	40 509
5000 Taxes on goods and services	**2**	**164 144**	**317 875**	**542 258**	**665 103**	**736 671**	**766 524**	**789 753**	**796 320**	**857 250**
5100 Taxes on production, sale, transfer, etc	2	162 575	312 503	542 258	665 103	736 671	766 524	789 753	796 320	857 250
5110 General taxes	2	154 130	294 251	497 898	614 565	680 992	709 993	728 866	741 489	800 585
5111 Value added taxes	1	100 978	177 589	293 489	357 190	393 742	419 459	431 904	443 325	475 460
Tax on the circulation of goods and services (ICMS)	1	82 279	153 437	268 117	326 236	363 190	384 287	396 513	413 175	441 039
Tax on industrialised products (IPI)	0	18 699	24 153	25 372	30 954	30 552	35 172	35 391	30 150	34 421
5112 Sales tax	0	47 046	105 415	171 653	213 096	239 290	236 646	242 508	244 326	268 721
Contribution to financing social security (COFINS)	0	38 707	86 837	140 939	175 008	197 545	194 696	199 876	201 517	221 670
PIS contribution	0	8 339	18 578	30 714	38 088	41 745	41 950	42 632	42 808	47 051
5113 Other	0	6 106	11 247	32 756	44 279	47 960	53 888	54 455	53 838	56 403

Table 5.6. **Brazil / Brasil** *(cont.)*

Details of tax revenue / Ingresos tributarios detallados

Million BRL

	1990	2000	2005	2010	2012	2013	2014	2015	2016	2017
5120 Taxes on specific goods and services	0	8 445	18 252	44 360	50 538	55 679	56 531	60 887	54 831	56 665
5121 Excises	..	0	7 683	19 681	14 587	13 105	14 055	15 929	17 702	18 442
Vehicles	..	..	..	5 787	4 395	3 799	4 940	4 367	3 299	4 467
Beverages	..	..	..	2 431	3 223	3 455	3 401	2 599	2 684	2 944
Tobacco	..	..	..	3 704	4 083	5 117	5 688	5 692	5 718	5 210
Fuels	..	..	..	7 759	2 885	734	26	3 271	6 001	5 821
5122 Profits of fiscal monopolies	..	0	0	0	0	0	0	0	0	0
5123 Customs and import duties	..	8 445	8 953	21 119	31 088	36 974	36 774	38 969	31 448	32 350
5124 Taxes on exports	..	0	0	0	0	0	0	0	0	0
5125 Taxes on investment goods	..	0	0	0	0	0	0	0	0	0
5126 Taxes on specific services	..	0	983	2 349	2 883	3 367	3 204	3 005	2 741	2 862
5127 Other taxes on internat. trade and transactions	..	0	0	0	0	0	0	0	0	0
5128 Other taxes	..	0	633	1 212	1 979	2 233	2 499	2 983	2 940	3 011
5130 Unallocable between 5110 and 5120	..	0	0	0	0	0	0	0	0	0
5200 Taxes on use of goods and perform activities	0	1 569	5 372	0	0	0	0	0	0	0
5210 Recurrent taxes	0	1 569	5 372	..	..	..	..	..	..	..
5211 Paid by households: motor vehicles	0	1 569	5 372	..	..	..	..	..	..	..
5212 Paid by others: motor vehicles	0	0	0	..	..	..	..	..	..	..
5213 Paid in respect of other goods	0	0	0	..	..	..	..	..	..	..
5220 Non-recurrent taxes	0	0	0	..	..	..	..	..	..	..
5300 Unallocable between 5100 and 5200	0	0	0	0	0	0	0	0	0	0
6000 Other taxes	**0**	**2 913**	**4 993**	**34 210**	**37 814**	**46 675**	**50 398**	**53 179**	**62 188**	**64 362**
6100 Paid solely by business	0	0	277	0	0	0	0	0	0	0
Revenue service development fund (FUNDAF)	0	0	277	0	0	0	0	0	0	0
6200 Other	0	2 913	4 715	34 210	37 814	46 675	50 398	53 179	62 188	64 362
Other federal taxes	0	941	36	8 765	4 719	10 044	10 910	10 142	13 905	12 787
Other social contributions	0	1 273	1 725	0	0	0	0	0	0	0
Other state taxes	0	322	1 551	17 038	22 850	25 740	27 291	28 983	31 692	34 288
Other municipal taxes	0	377	1 404	8 406	10 245	10 891	12 198	14 054	16 591	17 287

Note: Year ending 31st December.

The data are on a cash basis.

Headings 3000, 5112 and 6200: For years prior to 2000 the PASEP (Program of Formation of the Patrimony of the Public Servants) contributions are combined with PIS (Social Integration Program) contributions in heading 5112.

Headings 5111 and 5121: From 2007 to 2011, a portion of the IPI (Industrial Products Tax) is levied separately as an excise tax on automobiles, beverages, and tobacco products.

Heading 6100: From 2008 FUNDAF (Special Fund for Development and Improvement of Auditing Activities) contributions are included in heading 6200.

Heading 5200: From 2009, taxes paid by households: motor vehicles are included in heading 5200.

Source: Secretaria da Receita Federal (Ministry of Finance) in Carga Tributária no Brasil.

StatLink https://doi.org/10.1787/888933941441

Table 5.7. **Chile**

Details of tax revenue / Ingresos tributarios detallados

Million CLP

	1990	2000	2005	2010	2012	2013	2014	2015	2016	2017
Total tax revenue	**1 777 218**	**7 901 998**	**14 265 265**	**21 845 693**	**27 714 772**	**27 381 686**	**29 145 219**	**32 532 354**	**34 129 307**	**36 238 557**
1000 Taxes on income, profits and capital gains	**412 974**	**1 841 630**	**5 171 293**	**8 329 060**	**10 803 031**	**9 520 709**	**9 628 037**	**11 840 521**	**11 444 570**	**12 516 154**
1100 Of individuals	99 154	604 100	738 620	1 492 837	1 893 620	1 964 172	2 114 296	3 199 876	2 990 653	3 500 023
Second category tax	65 552	490 980	700 150	1 449 099	1 917 675	1 981 699	2 140 345	2 350 120	2 458 249	2 585 694
Global complementary tax	33 603	113 120	38 470	43 738	-24 055	-17 527	-26 050	-36 757	-213 365	50 495
Others	0	0	0	0	0	0	0	886 513	745 769	863 834
1110 On income and profits	..	..	..	..	..	..	..	..	..	..
1120 On capital gains	..	..	..	..	..	..	..	..	..	..
1200 Corporate	219 586	882 896	3 155 480	4 448 745	7 560 906	6 041 089	6 196 077	6 839 133	7 146 657	7 658 420
First category tax	200 891	815 747	3 040 875	3 913 870	6 770 329	5 473 355	5 182 214	6 183 830	6 689 101	7 049 471
Surtax on state owned enterprises	16 074	47 634	78 267	194 203	80 084	124 220	100 851	132 352	88 362	193 058
Mining tax	0	0	0	298 558	619 150	324 577	801 647	323 507	105 653	101 970
Other	2 621	19 516	36 338	42 114	91 343	118 937	111 365	199 444	263 541	313 921
1210 On profits	..	..	..	..	..	..	..	..	..	..
1220 On capital gains	..	..	..	..	..	..	..	..	..	..
1300 Unallocable between 1100 and 1200	94 233	354 634	1 277 193	2 387 478	1 348 506	1 515 449	1 317 664	1 801 512	1 307 260	1 357 711
Additional tax	59 082	350 301	799 648	1 414 057	1 178 917	1 337 721	1 454 847	1 429 758	1 331 564	1 453 577
Other	35 151	4 332	477 545	973 421	169 589	177 727	-137 183	371 755	-24 304	-95 865
2000 Social security contributions	**159 559**	**576 758**	**931 717**	**1 493 987**	**1 802 468**	**1 968 973**	**2 110 087**	**2 252 489**	**2 441 419**	**2 627 558**
2100 Employees	154 021	553 937	893 821	1 433 159	1 742 526	1 906 340	2 044 356	2 188 575	2 373 777	2 553 915
2110 On a payroll basis	154 021	553 937	893 821	1 433 159	1 742 526	1 906 340	2 044 356	2 188 575	2 373 777	2 553 915
2120 On an income tax basis	0	0	0	0	0	0	0	0	0	0
2200 Employers	5 538	22 821	37 896	60 828	59 942	62 633	65 731	63 914	67 642	73 643
2210 On a payroll basis	5 538	22 821	37 896	60 828	59 942	62 633	65 731	63 914	67 642	73 643
2220 On an income tax basis	0	0	0	0	0	0	0	0	0	0
2300 Self-employed or non-employed	0	0	0	0	0	0	0	0	0	0
2310 On a payroll basis	..	..	..	..	..	..	..	..	..	..
2320 On an income tax basis	..	..	..	..	..	..	..	..	..	..
2400 Unallocable between 2100, 2200 and 2300	0	0	0	0	0	0	0	0	0	0
2410 On a payroll basis	..	..	..	..	..	..	..	..	..	..
2420 On an income tax basis	..	..	..	..	..	..	..	..	..	..
3000 Taxes on payroll and workforce	**0**	**0**	**0**	**0**	**0**	**0**	**0**	**0**	**0**	**0**
4000 Taxes on property	**109 319**	**554 037**	**901 776**	**898 607**	**1 180 307**	**1 133 765**	**1 228 961**	**1 421 274**	**1 731 723**	**1 950 217**
4100 Recurrent taxes on immovable property	59 968	302 244	416 565	662 368	788 919	840 842	924 062	1 056 920	1 171 399	1 229 195
4110 Households	..	..	..	..	..	..	..	..	..	..
4120 Others	..	..	..	..	..	..	..	..	..	..
4200 Recurrent taxes on net wealth	0	0	0	0	0	0	0	0	0	0
4210 Individual	..	..	..	..	..	..	..	..	..	..
4220 Corporate	..	..	..	..	..	..	..	..	..	..
4300 Estate, inheritance and gift taxes	3 444	10 906	23 184	39 338	66 719	45 550	31 340	92 236	100 490	202 376
4310 Estate and inheritance taxes	..	..	..	..	..	..	..	..	..	..
4320 Gift taxes	..	..	..	..	..	..	..	..	..	..
4400 Taxes on financial and capital transactions	45 907	240 886	462 027	196 901	324 669	247 373	273 559	272 118	459 834	518 645
4500 Non-recurrent taxes	0	0	0	0	0	0	0	0	0	0
4510 On net wealth	..	..	..	..	..	..	..	..	..	..
4520 Other non-recurrent taxes	..	..	..	..	..	..	..	..	..	..
4600 Other recurrent taxes on property	0	0	0	0	0	0	0	0	0	0
5000 Taxes on goods and services	**1 118 722**	**5 041 769**	**7 346 434**	**11 185 156**	**13 873 611**	**14 779 915**	**16 127 855**	**17 597 378**	**18 629 617**	**19 858 881**
5100 Taxes on production, sale, transfer, etc	1 074 009	4 789 827	6 952 092	10 532 904	13 052 989	13 869 529	15 131 675	16 515 485	17 449 222	18 597 179
5110 General taxes	664 421	3 306 350	5 391 285	8 399 926	10 447 374	11 170 794	12 133 710	13 273 958	14 073 050	15 069 540
5111 Value added taxes	664 421	3 306 350	5 391 285	8 399 926	10 447 374	11 170 794	12 133 710	13 273 958	14 073 050	15 069 540
5112 Sales tax	0	0	0	0	0	0	0	0	0	0
5113 Other	0	0	0	0	0	0	0	0	0	0
5120 Taxes on specific goods and services	409 588	1 483 477	1 560 807	2 132 978	2 605 615	2 698 735	2 997 965	3 241 527	3 376 172	3 527 639
5121 Excises	166 050	816 160	1 107 703	1 561 205	1 892 713	1 987 475	2 224 223	2 412 773	2 568 863	2 682 659
Cigarettes and tobacco	60 604	283 275	382 690	647 637	783 995	815 991	856 595	981 422	1 009 034	978 696
Gasoline and diesel	105 445	532 885	724 803	913 568	1 108 718	1 171 483	1 361 724	1 388 218	1 502 039	1 629 561
Oil stabilisation fund	0	0	210	0	0	0	0	0	0	0
Fisheries Law Extraction Rights	0	0	0	0	0	0	5 890	8 558	9 998	11 749
Additional tax on new motor vehicles	0	0	0	0	0	0	14	34 575	47 792	62 654
5122 Profits of fiscal monopolies	0	0	0	0	0	0	0	0	0	0
5123 Customs and import duties	222 486	548 571	286 044	267 331	314 441	303 393	337 839	343 491	308 871	321 156
5124 Taxes on exports	0	0	0	0	0	0	0	0	0	0
5125 Taxes on investment goods	0	0	0	0	0	0	0	0	0	0
5126 Taxes on specific services	21 052	118 746	167 060	304 442	398 461	407 867	435 903	485 263	498 438	523 824
5127 Other taxes on internat. trade and transactions	0	0	0	0	0	0	0	0	0	0
5128 Other taxes	0	0	0	0	0	0	0	0	0	0
5130 Unallocable between 5110 and 5120	0	0	0	0	0	0	0	0	0	0

Table 5.7. **Chile** *(cont.)*

Details of tax revenue / Ingresos tributarios detallados

Million CLP

	1990	2000	2005	2010	2012	2013	2014	2015	2016	2017
5200 Taxes on use of goods and perform activities	44 714	251 942	394 343	652 252	820 622	910 386	996 180	1 081 893	1 180 395	1 261 702
5210 Recurrent taxes	44 714	251 942	394 343	652 252	820 622	910 386	996 180	1 081 893	1 180 395	1 261 702
Motor vehicles	24 469	93 880	139 174	218 219	301 895	330 754	365 316	397 608	434 137	482 009
5211 Paid by households: motor vehicles	0	0	0	0	0	0	0	0	0	0
5212 Paid by others: motor vehicles	0	0	0	0	0	0	0	0	0	0
5213 Paid in respect of other goods	20 245	158 062	255 169	434 033	518 727	579 632	630 864	684 285	746 258	779 693
Municipal permits	18 401	136 138	234 460	396 944	468 938	527 955	578 671	630 943	692 974	725 954
Mining patents	3 374	34 730	20 094	36 213	47 899	50 094	50 448	51 767	51 641	52 254
Other	-1 530	-12 806	615	876	1 890	1 583	1 745	1 575	1 643	1 485
5220 Non-recurrent taxes	0	0	0	0	0	0	0	0	0	0
5300 Unallocable between 5100 and 5200	0	0	0	0	0	0	0	0	0	0
6000 Other taxes	**-23 356**	**-112 195**	**-85 954**	**-61 117**	**55 355**	**-21 676**	**50 279**	**-579 308**	**-118 021**	**-714 253**
6100 Paid solely by business	0	0	0	0	0	0	0	0	0	0
6200 Other	-23 356	-112 195	-85 954	-61 117	55 355	-21 676	50 279	-579 308	-118 021	-714 253

Note: Year ending 31st December.
The data are on a cash basis.
Heading 5121: In ECLAC data, figures from the Oil Prices Stabilisation Fund (FEPP) are considered as non-tax revenues.
Source: Servicio de Impuestos Internos (Chile's Tax Service).

StatLink https://doi.org/10.1787/888933941460

Table 5.8. **Colombia**

Details of tax revenue / Ingresos tributarios detallados

Million COP

	1990	2000	2005	2010	2012	2013	2014	2015	2016	2017
Total tax revenue	**2 579 426**	**30 512 910**	**61 455 845**	**97 954 930**	**130 869 983**	**142 456 786**	**148 630 814**	**159 486 587**	**164 185 912**	**174 184 722**
1000 Taxes on income, profits and capital gains	**771 694**	**7 103 525**	**17 348 618**	**26 218 852**	**43 671 856**	**47 743 096**	**50 083 349**	**52 656 876**	**54 326 726**	**57 615 236**
1100 Of individuals	47 210	1 499 345	3 594 441	5 192 384	6 841 470	7 688 346	8 517 353	9 736 861	10 404 961	11 004 827
1110 On income and profits	47 210	1 499 345	3 594 441	5 192 384	6 841 470	7 688 346	8 517 353	9 736 861	10 404 961	11 004 827
1120 On capital gains	..	..	..	..	..	..	..	..	..	..
1200 Corporate	359 758	5 119 828	13 044 361	20 405 209	35 669 308	38 546 343	40 201 967	41 070 208	42 025 176	44 491 100
1210 On profits	359 758	5 119 828	13 044 361	20 405 209	35 669 308	38 546 343	40 201 967	41 070 208	42 025 176	44 491 100
Income tax	359 758	5 119 828	13 044 361	20 405 209	35 669 308	35 606 764	27 740 492	27 144 039	27 914 442	39 644 910
Pro Equity Income Tax - CREE	0	0	0	0	0	2 939 579	12 461 475	13 926 169	14 110 734	4 846 190
1220 On capital gains	..	..	..	..	..	..	..	..	..	..
1300 Unallocable between 1100 and 1200	364 726	484 352	709 816	621 258	1 161 078	1 508 407	1 364 028	1 849 807	1 896 589	2 119 308
Income tax	364 726	484 352	709 816	621 258	1 161 078	1 508 407	1 364 028	1 849 807	1 896 589	2 119 308
Pro Equity Income Tax - CREE	0	0	0	0	0	0	0	0	0	0
2000 Social security contributions	**203 596**	**4 989 000**	**7 845 000**	**11 478 085**	**11 815 723**	**16 644 445**	**13 715 312**	**13 585 138**	**15 443 016**	**13 351 710**
2100 Employees	..	..	..	..	..	..	..	..	..	..
2110 On a payroll basis	..	..	..	..	..	..	..	..	..	..
2120 On an income tax basis	..	..	..	..	..	..	..	..	..	..
2200 Employers	..	..	..	..	..	..	..	..	..	..
2210 On a payroll basis	..	..	..	..	..	..	..	..	..	..
2220 On an income tax basis	..	..	..	..	..	..	..	..	..	..
2300 Self-employed or non-employed	..	..	..	..	..	..	..	..	..	..
2310 On a payroll basis	..	..	..	..	..	..	..	..	..	..
2320 On an income tax basis	..	..	..	..	..	..	..	..	..	..
2400 Unallocable between 2100, 2200 and 2300	203 596	4 989 000	7 845 000	11 478 085	11 815 723	16 644 445	13 715 312	13 585 138	15 443 016	13 351 710
2410 On a payroll basis	203 596	4 989 000	7 845 000	11 478 085	11 815 723	16 644 445	13 715 312	13 585 138	15 443 016	13 351 710
2420 On an income tax basis	0	0	0	0	0	0	0	0	0	0
3000 Taxes on payroll and workforce	**0**	**1 286 803**	**2 179 842**	**4 022 503**	**4 775 034**	**3 527 459**	**2 627 958**	**2 797 308**	**2 998 237**	**3 200 238**
4000 Taxes on property	**56 160**	**2 027 654**	**4 838 158**	**8 535 238**	**13 668 964**	**15 018 163**	**16 119 572**	**18 306 740**	**18 266 486**	**17 950 495**
4100 Recurrent taxes on immovable property	56 160	991 070	1 974 213	3 338 935	4 016 860	4 845 576	5 559 528	6 212 601	6 747 288	7 310 244
4110 Households	0	0	0	0	0	0	0	0	0	0
4120 Others	56 160	991 070	1 974 213	3 338 935	4 016 860	4 845 576	5 559 528	6 212 601	6 747 288	7 310 244
4200 Recurrent taxes on net wealth	0	0	462 720	1 970 530	4 183 752	4 274 832	4 118 075	5 352 940	4 440 142	3 868 595
4210 Individual	..	..	462 720	1 970 530	4 183 752	4 274 832	4 118 075	5 352 940	4 440 142	3 868 595
4220 Corporate	..	..	0	0	0	0	0	0	0	0
4300 Estate, inheritance and gift taxes	0	0	0	0	0	0	0	0	0	0
4310 Estate and inheritance taxes	..	..	..	..	..	..	..	..	..	..
4320 Gift taxes	..	..	..	..	..	..	..	..	..	..
4400 Taxes on financial and capital transactions	0	1 036 584	2 401 226	3 225 773	5 468 351	5 897 755	6 441 969	6 741 200	7 079 055	6 771 655
4500 Non-recurrent taxes	0	0	0	0	0	0	0	0	0	0
4510 On net wealth	..	..	..	..	..	..	..	..	..	..
4520 Other non-recurrent taxes	..	..	..	..	..	..	..	..	..	..
4600 Other recurrent taxes on property	0	0	0	0	0	0	0	0	0	0
5000 Taxes on goods and services	**1 388 653**	**13 367 908**	**25 866 553**	**42 156 822**	**50 795 912**	**52 393 473**	**57 894 877**	**62 378 051**	**63 375 512**	**71 537 494**
5100 Taxes on production, sale, transfer, etc	1 388 653	13 367 908	25 866 553	42 156 822	50 795 912	52 393 473	57 894 877	62 378 051	63 375 512	71 537 494
5110 General taxes	672 368	9 585 866	19 934 400	33 333 802	41 862 732	40 598 702	45 330 387	48 721 833	49 506 811	58 565 800
5111 Value added taxes	583 078	8 445 776	17 427 948	28 811 682	36 324 330	34 642 822	38 749 869	41 553 967	41 878 886	50 619 849
5112 Sales tax	89 290	1 140 090	2 506 452	4 522 121	5 538 402	5 955 879	6 580 518	7 167 866	7 627 926	7 945 951
Industry and commerce tax (State)	89 290	1 140 090	2 506 452	4 522 121	5 538 402	5 955 879	6 580 518	7 167 866	7 627 926	7 945 951
5113 Other	0	0	0	0	0	0	0	0	0	0
5120 Taxes on specific goods and services	716 285	3 782 042	5 932 153	8 823 019	8 933 180	11 794 771	12 564 490	13 656 219	13 868 701	12 971 694
5121 Excises	404 699	2 037 944	3 109 633	4 171 020	5 409 860	7 897 587	8 577 766	9 065 288	9 755 514	9 150 770
Oil	141 270	833 004	1 143 308	1 418 766	1 735 062	2 883 410	2 980 883	3 297 392	3 335 157	1 352 793
Tobacco (State)	52 898	213 410	287 379	390 472	486 282	508 089	493 868	524 357	595 476	887 534
Beer (State)	85 722	471 137	867 569	1 432 453	1 900 215	2 031 349	2 108 721	2 305 895	2 549 948	2 572 771
Liquors (State)	124 808	520 393	811 377	929 328	1 288 302	1 292 742	1 345 827	1 253 466	1 574 864	1 907 802
Restaurant, vehicles sale and mobile telephony	0	0	0	0	0	1 181 998	1 648 467	1 684 179	1 700 069	1 948 718
Carbon	0	0	0	0	0	0	0	0	0	474 596
Plastic bags	0	0	0	0	0	0	0	0	0	6 546
Medicinal cannabis	0	0	0	0	0	0	0	0	0	10
5122 Profits of fiscal monopolies	0	0	0	0	0	0	0	0	0	0
5123 Customs and import duties	311 586	1 744 097	2 822 520	4 651 999	3 523 320	3 897 184	3 986 724	4 590 931	4 113 187	3 820 924
Custom duties	180 989	1 744 097	2 822 520	4 651 999	3 523 320	3 897 184	3 986 724	4 590 931	4 113 187	3 820 924
Imports surcharge	130 597	0	0	0	0	0	0	0	0	0
5124 Taxes on exports	0	0	0	0	0	0	0	0	0	0
5125 Taxes on investment goods	0	0	0	0	0	0	0	0	0	0
5126 Taxes on specific services	0	0	0	0	0	0	0	0	0	0
5127 Other taxes on internat. trade and transactions	0	0	0	0	0	0	0	0	0	0
5128 Other taxes	0	0	0	0	0	0	0	0	0	0

Table 5.8. **Colombia** *(cont.)*

Details of tax revenue / Ingresos tributarios detallados

Million COP

	1990	2000	2005	2010	2012	2013	2014	2015	2016	2017
5130 Unallocable between 5110 and 5120	0	0	0	0	0	0	0	0	0	0
5200 Taxes on use of goods and perform activities	0	0	0	0	0	0	0	0	0	0
5210 Recurrent taxes	..	..	..	..	..	..	..	..	..	..
5211 Paid by households: motor vehicles	..	..	..	..	..	..	..	..	..	..
5212 Paid by others: motor vehicles	..	..	..	..	..	..	..	..	..	..
5213 Paid in respect of other goods	..	..	..	..	..	..	..	..	..	..
5220 Non-recurrent taxes	..	..	..	..	..	..	..	..	..	..
5300 Unallocable between 5100 and 5200	0	0	0	0	0	0	0	0	0	0
6000 Other taxes	**159 323**	**1 738 020**	**3 377 674**	**5 543 430**	**6 142 494**	**7 130 151**	**8 189 746**	**9 762 474**	**9 775 935**	**10 529 549**
6100 Paid solely by business	0	0	0	0	0	0	0	0	0	0
6200 Other	159 323	1 738 020	3 377 674	5 543 430	6 142 494	7 130 151	8 189 746	9 762 474	9 775 935	10 529 549
Stamp tax	0	401 497	633 586	357 160	58 973	58 378	72 425	105 729	97 492	75 493
Other	78 306	79 287	48 498	126 602	174 845	200 465	260 721	318 271	357 863	403 473
Other (sub-national)	81 017	1 257 236	2 695 589	5 059 668	5 908 676	6 871 308	7 856 600	9 338 474	9 320 581	10 050 583

Note: Year ending 31st December.

The data are on a cash basis.

Includes the reported consolidated revenues of the territorial entities (departments and municipalities).

Heading 2000: Before 2013, social security contributions did not include all the contributions entering FOSYGA (Solidarity and Guarantee Fund). Only the portion of the contributions used to finance the subsidised regime (up to 1.5 pp of the 12.5% of the monthly wage paid by employers and employees as an obligatory health contribution) was included. The part of the contributions entering FOSYGA to finance the contributory regime was classified in the social security sector as "other incomes". From 2013 onwards, all of the health contributions entering FOSYGA are classified as social security contributions. The portion of the contributions not entering FOSYGA that is both collected and spent by the health insurers – EPS - is not part of the fiscal accounts.

Headings 1100 and 1200: The data are estimated.

Source: Dirección de Impuestos y Aduanas Nacionales de Colombia, Ministerio de Hacienda y Crédito Público y Banco Central de Colombia. (National Tax and Customs Administration, Ministry of Finance and Public Credit and Central Bank of Colombia).

StatLink https://doi.org/10.1787/888933941479

Table 5.9. **Costa Rica**

Details of tax revenue / Ingresos tributarios detallados

Million CRC

	1990	2000	2005	2010	2012	2013	2014	2015	2016	2017
Total tax revenue	**117 711**	**978 114**	**2 084 914**	**4 382 367**	**5 359 845**	**5 851 096**	**6 330 931**	**6 923 575**	**7 528 752**	**7 893 642**
1000 Taxes on income, profits and capital gains	**11 820**	**128 805**	**324 224**	**748 093**	**891 669**	**1 014 440**	**1 091 470**	**1 247 308**	**1 416 218**	**1 562 063**
1100 Of individuals	..	..	16 438	202 849	307 489	316 894	349 139	386 241	414 247	446 519
1110 On income and profits	..	..	16 438	202 849	307 489	316 894	349 139	386 241	414 247	446 519
1120 On capital gains	..	..	..	..	..	..	..	..	..	..
1200 Corporate	..	..	288 355	450 312	461 481	545 183	574 137	659 951	742 011	843 879
1210 On profits	..	..	288 355	450 312	461 481	545 183	574 137	659 951	742 011	843 879
1220 On capital gains	..	..	..	..	..	..	..	..	..	..
1300 Unallocable between 1100 and 1200	11 820	128 805	19 430	94 932	122 699	152 363	168 194	201 116	259 961	271 664
2000 Social security contributions	**33 990**	**297 069**	**617 683**	**1 450 531**	**1 786 731**	**1 928 082**	**2 114 124**	**2 305 133**	**2 539 755**	**2 640 785**
2100 Employees	..	..	..	..	..	..	..	..	..	..
2110 On a payroll basis	..	..	..	..	..	..	..	..	..	..
2120 On an income tax basis	..	..	..	..	..	..	..	..	..	..
2200 Employers	3 447	37 313	84 988	207 206	256 593	272 706	294 486	318 652	331 124	361 161
Government contributions	3 447	37 313	84 988	207 206	256 593	272 706	294 486	318 652	331 124	361 161
2210 On a payroll basis	..	..	..	..	..	..	..	..	..	..
2220 On an income tax basis	..	..	..	..	..	..	..	..	..	..
2300 Self-employed or non-employed	..	..	..	..	..	..	..	..	..	..
2310 On a payroll basis	..	..	..	..	..	..	..	..	..	..
2320 On an income tax basis	..	..	..	..	..	..	..	..	..	..
2400 Unallocable between 2100, 2200 and 2300	30 543	259 756	532 695	1 243 325	1 530 138	1 655 376	1 819 638	1 986 481	2 208 631	2 279 624
Contributions by employees and non-government employers	30 543	249 182	497 341	1 139 265	1 399 618	1 511 383	1 648 831	1 785 522	1 985 151	2 042 620
Contributions for the special regimes	0	10 574	35 354	104 060	130 520	143 993	170 806	200 959	223 480	237 004
2410 On a payroll basis	..	..	..	..	..	..	..	..	..	..
2420 On an income tax basis	..	..	..	..	..	..	..	..	..	..
3000 Taxes on payroll and workforce	**7 575**	**61 796**	**115 730**	**260 664**	**323 957**	**352 755**	**388 869**	**423 616**	**453 369**	**471 206**
Contributions by non-government employers	7 484	59 129	112 082	248 259	309 804	337 696	372 869	406 296	435 328	453 128
Contributions by government employers	91	2 666	3 648	12 405	14 153	15 059	16 000	17 321	18 041	18 078
4000 Taxes on property	**1 566**	**8 396**	**25 110**	**63 706**	**82 007**	**99 030**	**114 313**	**123 261**	**134 332**	**145 955**
4100 Recurrent taxes on immovable property	1 200	5 390	14 264	48 963	61 057	70 785	81 613	90 003	97 869	107 156
Land tax	0	0	0	0	0	0	0	0	0	0
Additional land tax	0	0	0	0	0	0	0	0	0	0
Tax on sumptuary constructions	0	0	0	0	0	0	0	0	0	0
Immovable property tax	0	0	0	3 527	2 638	3 998	4 013	4 076	4 098	4 255
Municipal immovable property tax	1 200	5 390	14 264	45 436	58 418	66 787	77 600	85 927	93 771	102 901
4110 Households	..	..	..	..	..	..	..	..	..	..
4120 Others	..	..	..	..	..	..	..	..	..	..
4200 Recurrent taxes on net wealth	0	0	0	0	0	0	0	0	0	0
4210 Individual	..	..	..	..	..	..	..	..	..	..
4220 Corporate	..	..	..	..	..	..	..	..	..	..
4300 Estate, inheritance and gift taxes	0	0	0	0	0	0	0	0	0	0
4310 Estate and inheritance taxes	..	..	..	..	..	..	..	..	..	..
4320 Gift taxes	..	..	..	..	..	..	..	..	..	..
4400 Taxes on financial and capital transactions	366	3 007	10 846	14 743	20 950	28 246	32 700	33 258	36 462	38 799
4500 Non-recurrent taxes	0	0	0	0	0	0	0	0	0	0
4510 On net wealth	..	..	..	..	..	..	..	..	..	..
4520 Other non-recurrent taxes	..	..	..	..	..	..	..	..	..	..
4600 Other recurrent taxes on property	0	0	0	0	0	0	0	0	0	0
5000 Taxes on goods and services	**53 509**	**456 851**	**944 623**	**1 766 914**	**2 150 384**	**2 302 986**	**2 468 087**	**2 661 902**	**2 794 229**	**2 875 333**
5100 Taxes on production, sale, transfer, etc	49 867	425 713	884 453	1 600 302	1 958 415	2 092 588	2 222 962	2 388 900	2 508 186	2 575 411
5110 General taxes	21 326	222 775	485 168	920 298	1 145 403	1 212 471	1 306 110	1 368 601	1 420 938	1 466 986
5111 Value added taxes	21 326	222 775	485 168	920 298	1 122 978	1 176 745	1 266 798	1 336 075	1 414 358	1 453 348
5112 Sales tax	0	0	0	0	0	0	0	0	0	0
5113 Other	0	0	0	0	22 425	35 726	39 313	32 526	6 580	13 638
5120 Taxes on specific goods and services	28 541	202 939	399 286	680 004	813 013	880 117	916 851	1 020 299	1 087 248	1 108 425
5121 Excises	11 096	157 204	296 222	523 617	629 423	689 528	706 016	798 412	846 864	870 225
Fuels and energy	0	0	172 028	320 638	354 149	404 210	404 901	457 827	472 644	510 260
Alcohol beverages	0	8 229	20 219	28 035	35 620	35 254	36 293	43 095	43 400	43 176
Non alcoholic beverages	0	0	12 491	26 566	30 205	32 519	34 874	36 353	39 764	39 781
Soaps	0	0	573	1 317	1 487	1 989	1 493	2 562	2 912	2 332
Cement	0	0	0	227	247	291	340	304	267	311
Tobacco	0	0	0	0	19 852	38 860	32 277	33 681	32 560	30 590
Abolished specific taxes on production and consumption	0	0	0	0	0	0	0	0	0	0
Other specific taxes on consumption	11 096	148 975	90 913	146 834	187 863	176 405	195 838	224 590	255 317	243 775
5122 Profits of fiscal monopolies	0	0	0	0	0	0	0	0	0	0

Table 5.9. **Costa Rica** *(cont.)*

Details of tax revenue / Ingresos tributarios detallados

Million CRC

	1990	2000	2005	2010	2012	2013	2014	2015	2016	2017
5123 Customs and import duties	15 052	40 485	82 446	126 134	152 275	154 576	169 120	174 568	185 544	179 188
Import duties	13 977	32 336	66 598	103 851	128 358	130 634	142 226	148 666	158 559	152 756
Custom duties	1 075	8 149	15 848	22 284	23 917	23 942	26 894	25 902	26 986	26 432
5124 Taxes on exports	2 113	2 238	969	3 973	3 823	4 877	4 853	4 468	5 073	5 638
Export duties	2 113	2 088	830	3 816	3 663	4 104	3 067	2 701	3 250	3 673
Export duties Law 133	0	0	0	0	0	0	0	0	0	0
Export duties Law 5519	0	0	0	0	0	0	0	0	0	0
Tax on banana exports	0	150	139	157	160	168	176	156	184	199
Export duties on ground transportation	0	0	0	0	0	605	1 610	1 611	1 638	1 766
5125 Taxes on investment goods	0	0	0	0	0	0	0	0	0	0
5126 Taxes on specific services	280	2 929	19 555	24 767	25 579	28 571	34 081	38 687	44 934	48 290
Casinos and gambling	0	225	519	445	213	1 019	940	1 455	1 609	891
Port cargo movements	0	6	13	0	0	0	0	0	0	0
Overseas departure tax	0	0	19 022	24 322	25 366	27 552	33 141	37 232	43 325	47 399
10% on public shows	0	0	0	0	0	0	0	0	0	0
Pro-national airport's stamp tax	0	0	0	0	0	0	0	0	0	0
Stamp tax on the use of borders and ports	280	2 697	0	0	0	0	0	0	0	0
5127 Other taxes on internat. trade and transactions	0	83	94	1 513	1 913	2 565	2 782	3 093	3 512	3 695
5128 Other taxes	0	0	0	0	0	0	0	1 071	1 320	1 389
5130 Unallocable between 5110 and 5120	0	0	0	0	0	0	0	0	0	0
5200 Taxes on use of goods and perform activities	3 642	31 138	60 170	166 612	191 968	210 398	245 125	273 003	286 044	299 922
5210 Recurrent taxes	3 642	31 138	60 170	166 612	191 968	210 398	245 125	273 003	286 044	299 922
5211 Paid by households: motor vehicles	0	0	0	0	0	0	0	0	0	0
5212 Paid by others: motor vehicles	1 425	15 374	30 918	94 102	101 903	113 727	130 000	145 894	156 517	164 034
Property tax on vehicles, aircraft and boats	1 425	15 374	30 918	94 102	101 903	113 727	130 000	145 894	156 517	164 034
5213 Paid in respect of other goods	2 217	15 763	29 252	72 510	90 065	96 671	115 125	127 109	129 527	135 888
Local taxes	1 262	11 898	27 411	68 808	85 411	91 163	110 120	122 248	124 862	130 639
Hunting and fishing licences	0	0	0	0	0	0	0	0	0	0
Spirits licence	0	0	0	0	0	0	0	0	0	0
Revenue stamps	955	3 866	1 841	3 702	4 654	5 508	5 005	4 861	4 664	5 249
Sport stamp tax	0	0	0	0	0	0	0	0	0	0
5220 Non-recurrent taxes	0	0	0	0	0	0	0	0	0	0
5300 Unallocable between 5100 and 5200	0	0	0	0	0	0	0	0	0	0
6000 Other taxes	**9 251**	**25 198**	**57 545**	**92 460**	**125 097**	**153 803**	**154 069**	**162 355**	**190 850**	**198 300**
6100 Paid solely by business	0	0	0	0	0	0	0	0	0	0
6200 Other	9 251	25 198	57 545	92 460	125 097	153 803	154 069	162 355	190 850	198 300
Transfers of vehicles, aircraft and boats	497	2 530	6 357	12 311	12 947	17 177	19 099	20 999	23 022	21 872
Tax revenue from decentralised units	2 764	15 048	11 985	29 969	39 172	45 700	46 591	49 334	67 584	68 127
Other taxes	5 990	7 620	39 203	50 180	72 978	90 926	88 379	92 022	100 243	108 302

Note: Year ending 31st December.

The data are on a cash basis.

Heading 2000: The data include social security contributions paid by the governments for their employees as well as the contributions for special regimes (teachers and magistrates). In ECLAC data, social security contributions also include INA (National Institute of Apprenticeship), IMAS (Joint Social Aid Institute) and FODESAF (Social Development and Family Allowances Fund).

Heading 3000: In Costa Rica and for ECLAC, payments from decentralised institutions are classified under heading 2000.

Heading 5212: In ECLAC data, tax on ownership of vehicles, aircraft and boats is classified in category 4000.

In ECLAC data, the tax on the transfer of used vehicles Law No. 7088 of 30/11/87 is classified as a property tax.

Source: Secretaría Técnica de la Autoridad Presupuestaria, Ministerio de Finanzas y Contraloría General de la República (Technical Secretary of the Budgeting Authority, Ministry of Finance and National General Comptroller).

StatLink https://doi.org/10.1787/888933941498

Table 5.10. **Cuba**

Details of tax revenue / Ingresos tributarios detallados

Million CUP

	1990	2000	2005	2010	2012	2013	2014	2015	2016	2017
Total tax revenue	**6 265**	**11 367**	**17 528**	**24 201**	**29 068**	**28 804**	**30 236**	**33 591**	**37 277**	**39 072**
1000 Taxes on income, profits and capital gains	**14**	**1 826**	**2 451**	**3 603**	**4 535**	**5 292**	**5 995**	**6 676**	**7 937**	**8 536**
1100 Of individuals	14	291	326	554	873	1 055	1 308	1 848	2 300	2 520
1110 On income and profits	..	..	..	..	..	..	..	..	..	..
1120 On capital gains	..	..	..	..	..	..	..	..	..	..
1200 Corporate	0	1 535	2 126	3 049	3 662	4 237	4 687	4 828	5 637	6 016
1210 On profits	..	..	..	..	..	..	..	..	..	..
1220 On capital gains	..	..	..	..	..	..	..	..	..	..
1300 Unallocable between 1100 and 1200	0	0	0	0	0	0	0	0	0	0
2000 Social security contributions	**691**	**1 181**	**1 778**	**2 974**	**3 043**	**3 123**	**3 622**	**4 322**	**4 700**	**5 180**
2100 Employees	..	..	..	..	..	..	..	..	..	..
2110 On a payroll basis	..	..	..	..	..	..	..	..	..	..
2120 On an income tax basis	..	..	..	..	..	..	..	..	..	..
2200 Employers	..	..	..	..	..	..	..	..	..	..
2210 On a payroll basis	..	..	..	..	..	..	..	..	..	..
2220 On an income tax basis	..	..	..	..	..	..	..	..	..	..
2300 Self-employed or non-employed	..	..	..	..	..	..	..	..	..	..
2310 On a payroll basis	..	..	..	..	..	..	..	..	..	..
2320 On an income tax basis	..	..	..	..	..	..	..	..	..	..
2400 Unallocable between 2100, 2200 and 2300	691	1 181	1 778	2 974	3 043	3 123	3 622	4 322	4 700	5 180
2410 On a payroll basis	691	1 181	1 778	2 974	3 043	3 123	3 622	4 322	4 700	5 180
2420 On an income tax basis	0	0	0	0	0	0	0	0	0	0
3000 Taxes on payroll and workforce	**0**	**970**	**2 962**	**4 414**	**4 108**	**3 424**	**2 939**	**2 753**	**2 420**	**1 476**
4000 Taxes on property	**0**	**0**	**0**	**0**	**0**	**0**	**0**	**0**	**0**	**0**
4100 Recurrent taxes on immovable property	..	..	..	..	..	..	..	..	..	..
4110 Households	..	..	..	..	..	..	..	..	..	..
4120 Others	..	..	..	..	..	..	..	..	..	..
4200 Recurrent taxes on net wealth	..	..	..	..	..	..	..	..	..	..
4210 Individual	..	..	..	..	..	..	..	..	..	..
4220 Corporate	..	..	..	..	..	..	..	..	..	..
4300 Estate, inheritance and gift taxes	..	..	..	..	..	..	..	..	..	..
4310 Estate and inheritance taxes	..	..	..	..	..	..	..	..	..	..
4320 Gift taxes	..	..	..	..	..	..	..	..	..	..
4400 Taxes on financial and capital transactions	..	..	..	..	..	..	..	..	..	..
4500 Non-recurrent taxes	..	..	..	..	..	..	..	..	..	..
4510 On net wealth	..	..	..	..	..	..	..	..	..	..
4520 Other non-recurrent taxes	..	..	..	..	..	..	..	..	..	..
4600 Other recurrent taxes on property	..	..	..	..	..	..	..	..	..	..
5000 Taxes on goods and services	**5 443**	**6 732**	**9 844**	**12 283**	**16 232**	**15 588**	**15 911**	**17 742**	**20 135**	**21 558**
5100 Taxes on production, sale, transfer, etc	5 443	6 732	9 844	12 283	16 232	15 588	15 911	17 742	20 135	21 558
5110 General taxes	5 017	6 131	9 036	10 525	14 511	14 057	14 171	15 611	17 550	17 934
5111 Value added taxes	0	0	0	0	0	0	0	0	0	0
5112 Sales tax	5 017	6 131	9 036	10 525	14 511	14 057	14 171	15 611	17 550	17 934
5113 Other	0	0	0	0	0	0	0	0	0	0
5120 Taxes on specific goods and services	426	602	808	1 758	1 721	1 531	1 740	2 131	2 585	3 624
5121 Excises	..	..	..	..	..	..	..	..	..	..
5122 Profits of fiscal monopolies	..	..	..	..	..	..	..	..	..	..
5123 Customs and import duties	..	..	..	..	..	..	..	..	..	..
5124 Taxes on exports	..	..	..	..	..	..	..	..	..	..
5125 Taxes on investment goods	..	..	..	..	..	..	..	..	..	..
5126 Taxes on specific services	..	..	..	..	..	..	..	..	..	..
5127 Other taxes on internat. trade and transactions	..	..	..	..	..	..	..	..	..	..
5128 Other taxes	..	..	..	..	..	..	..	..	..	..
5130 Unallocable between 5110 and 5120	0	0	0	0	0	0	0	0	0	0
5200 Taxes on use of goods and perform activities	0	0	0	0	0	0	0	0	0	0
5210 Recurrent taxes	..	..	..	..	..	..	..	..	..	..
5211 Paid by households: motor vehicles	..	..	..	..	..	..	..	..	..	..
5212 Paid by others: motor vehicles	..	..	..	..	..	..	..	..	..	..
5213 Paid in respect of other goods	..	..	..	..	..	..	..	..	..	..
5220 Non-recurrent taxes	..	..	..	..	..	..	..	..	..	..
5300 Unallocable between 5100 and 5200	..	..	..	..	..	..	..	..	..	..
6000 Other taxes	**117**	**657**	**493**	**927**	**1 150**	**1 378**	**1 769**	**2 098**	**2 085**	**2 324**
6100 Paid solely by business	..	..	..	..	..	..	..	..	..	..
6200 Other	..	..	..	..	..	..	..	..	..	..

Note: Year ending 31st December.
The data are on a cash basis.
The figures exclude local government tax revenues as the data are not available.
The figures for the sub-category under the heading 5120 are not available.
Source: Oficina Nacional de Estadística e Información. Anuario Estadístico de Cuba (National Office of Statistics and Information. Annual Statistical Review of Cuba).

StatLink https://doi.org/10.1787/888933941517

Table 5.11. **Dominican Republic / República Dominicana**

Details of tax revenue / Ingresos tributarios detallados

Million DOP

	1990	2000	2005	2010	2012	2013	2014	2015	2016	2017
Total tax revenue	**6 439**	**48 310**	**149 637**	**243 942**	**312 148**	**355 314**	**393 157**	**414 245**	**453 196**	**500 583**
1000 Taxes on income, profits and capital gains	**1 670**	**10 782**	**30 042**	**53 643**	**92 850**	**108 853**	**125 098**	**119 819**	**135 705**	**155 024**
1100 Of individuals	..	4 088	7 588	17 088	21 874	27 147	31 525	35 549	40 198	43 553
1110 On income and profits	..	4 070	7 509	16 901	21 575	26 723	31 119	35 187	39 780	43 097
1120 On capital gains	..	18	79	187	299	424	406	361	418	456
1200 Corporate	..	4 679	16 222	21 475	46 921	58 923	72 865	61 695	69 362	83 047
1210 On profits	..	4 605	16 147	21 325	46 582	58 597	72 628	61 455	69 079	82 785
1220 On capital gains	..	74	75	151	339	326	238	240	283	262
Casinos	..	59	73	151	213	187	173	184	228	237
Racetracks	..	15	2	0	0	0	0	0	0	0
Phone gaming	..	0	0	0	127	139	64	56	55	25
1300 Unallocable between 1100 and 1200	1 670	2 015	6 232	15 080	24 055	22 782	20 708	22 576	26 144	28 425
2000 Social security contributions	**53**	**490**	**35**	**1 845**	**1 250**	**1 552**	**1 515**	**1 483**	**1 550**	**2 635**
2100 Employees	..	..	..	1 720	1 120	1 408	1 355	1 321	1 392	1 535
2110 On a payroll basis	..	..	..	..	..	..	..	..	..	..
2120 On an income tax basis	..	..	..	..	..	..	..	..	..	..
2200 Employers	..	..	..	125	131	144	160	163	158	1 099
2210 On a payroll basis	..	..	..	..	..	..	..	..	..	..
2220 On an income tax basis	..	..	..	..	..	..	..	..	..	..
2300 Self-employed or non-employed	..	..	..	0	0	0	0	0	0	0
2310 On a payroll basis	..	..	..	..	..	..	..	..	..	..
2320 On an income tax basis	..	..	..	..	..	..	..	..	..	..
2400 Unallocable between 2100, 2200 and 2300	53	490	35	0	0	0	0	0	0	0
2410 On a payroll basis	53	490	35	..	..	..	..	..	..	..
2420 On an income tax basis	0	0	0	..	..	..	..	..	..	..
3000 Taxes on payroll and workforce	**0**	**0**	**0**	**0**	**0**	**0**	**0**	**0**	**0**	**0**
4000 Taxes on property	**74**	**689**	**6 749**	**13 315**	**19 606**	**22 928**	**18 183**	**19 044**	**20 717**	**22 942**
4100 Recurrent taxes on immovable property	9	115	1 710	555	686	1 518	1 579	1 755	1 871	2 166
4110 Households	9	115	1 710	555	686	1 518	1 579	1 755	1 871	2 166
4120 Others	0	0	0	0	0	0	0	0	0	0
4200 Recurrent taxes on net wealth	0	0	0	2 449	7 665	8 666	3 458	3 445	3 544	4 113
Tax on assets	..	..	..	2 449	3 044	3 337	3 454	3 445	3 544	4 113
4210 Individual	..	..	..	..	0	0	0	0	0	0
4220 Corporate	..	..	..	..	4 620	5 329	4	0	0	0
4300 Estate, inheritance and gift taxes	11	96	84	231	227	315	325	418	388	455
4310 Estate and inheritance taxes	..	..	..	..	..	..	..	..	..	..
4320 Gift taxes	..	..	..	..	..	..	..	..	..	..
4400 Taxes on financial and capital transactions	40	377	4 716	8 658	9 405	11 209	11 394	12 067	13 265	13 995
Tax on checks	0	0	3 133	4 262	4 852	5 168	5 620	5 951	6 591	7 117
Real estate operations	22	217	1 413	3 864	3 872	5 236	4 876	5 169	5 668	5 802
Tax on the transfer of immovable property	18	160	170	533	682	805	898	947	1 005	1 076
4500 Non-recurrent taxes	3	32	89	488	609	412	677	591	681	711
4510 On net wealth	3	32	89	488	609	412	677	591	681	711
4520 Other non-recurrent taxes	0	0	0	0	0	0	0	0	0	0
4600 Other recurrent taxes on property	11	70	151	934	1 014	810	751	769	969	1 503
5000 Taxes on goods and services	**4 483**	**35 853**	**111 150**	**175 139**	**198 442**	**221 981**	**248 361**	**273 898**	**295 223**	**319 980**
5100 Taxes on production, sale, transfer, etc	4 414	35 135	109 432	168 641	191 369	214 540	239 526	263 435	282 288	306 680
5110 General taxes	970	9 912	40 983	81 226	92 205	112 731	130 447	147 039	159 212	169 629
5111 Value added taxes	970	9 912	40 983	81 226	92 205	112 731	130 447	147 039	159 212	169 629
5112 Sales tax	0	0	0	0	0	0	0	0	0	0
5113 Other	0	0	0	0	0	0	0	0	0	0
5120 Taxes on specific goods and services	3 444	25 224	68 449	87 415	99 164	101 809	109 080	116 396	123 076	137 051
5121 Excises	510	6 614	27 384	56 024	67 154	68 434	72 399	74 586	78 105	89 681
Alcoholic beverages	251	2 451	8 142	15 054	17 089	17 969	19 779	22 371	23 617	25 694
Tobacco products	102	469	2 879	4 529	4 470	4 356	4 382	4 532	4 117	5 120
Petroleum products	105	3 143	14 712	34 598	42 460	42 222	44 335	29 989	32 697	36 148
Other	52	551	1 651	1 843	3 136	3 887	3 904	17 694	17 674	22 719
5122 Profits of fiscal monopolies	0	0	0	0	0	0	0	0	0	0
5123 Customs and import duties	1 548	13 459	14 403	19 455	18 891	19 043	21 315	25 212	27 286	28 703
Custom duties	615	13 456	14 293	19 455	18 776	18 916	21 238	24 378	26 397	27 276
Other	933	3	110	0	115	126	76	834	889	1 426
5124 Taxes on exports	6	4	46	146	264	34	12	8	0	0
5125 Taxes on investment goods	0	0	0	0	0	0	0	0	0	0

Table 5.11. **Dominican Republic / República Dominicana** *(cont.)*

Details of tax revenue / Ingresos tributarios detallados

Million DOP

	1990	2000	2005	2010	2012	2013	2014	2015	2016	2017
5126 Taxes on specific services	344	1 590	5 609	11 411	12 516	13 863	14 956	16 245	17 361	18 287
Telecommunications	85	0	3 193	4 886	5 124	5 897	6 129	6 375	6 607	6 781
Insurance premiums	33	584	0	3 088	3 437	3 674	3 965	4 301	4 828	5 236
Travel tickets	204	809	2 414	3 428	3 951	4 283	4 839	5 535	5 892	6 252
Hotels	22	191	0	0	0	0	0	0	0	0
Others	0	7	1	9	4	9	24	35	34	18
5127 Other taxes on internat. trade and transactions	1 037	3 556	21 008	379	338	436	397	346	323	380
Exchange commission	857	3 412	19 998	70	0	0	0	0	0	0
Consular fees	77	32	271	132	130	143	142	137	149	153
Other	103	112	738	176	209	293	256	209	174	227
5128 Other taxes	0	0	0	0	0	0	0	0	0	0
5130 Unallocable between 5110 and 5120	0	0	0	0	0	0	0	0	0	0
5200 Taxes on use of goods and perform activities	69	718	1 718	6 498	7 073	7 442	8 835	10 463	12 935	13 300
5210 Recurrent taxes	69	718	1 718	2 265	2 568	2 569	2 736	2 958	3 365	3 553
5211 Paid by households: motor vehicles	45	268	977	1 277	1 271	1 073	1 289	1 558	1 932	2 081
5212 Paid by others: motor vehicles	0	0	0	0	0	0	0	0	0	0
5213 Paid in respect of other goods	24	450	742	988	1 297	1 496	1 447	1 400	1 433	1 472
Licences to carry firearms	17	237	244	296	194	240	200	171	190	176
Licences to operate gambling houses	0	114	155	211	1 076	1 229	1 221	1 208	1 210	1 250
Licences to operate slot machines	4	60	102	458	0	0	0	0	0	0
Other	4	39	240	24	28	28	26	21	34	46
5220 Non-recurrent taxes	0	0	0	4 234	4 505	4 872	6 099	7 505	9 570	9 747
Vehicle property registration	..	..	..	4 234	4 505	4 595	5 683	6 990	8 903	9 072
Ecological taxes	..	..	..	0	0	277	416	515	667	675
5300 Unallocable between 5100 and 5200	0	0	0	0	0	0	0	0	0	0
6000 Other taxes	**159**	**495**	**1 661**	**0**	**0**	**0**	**1**	**1**	**1**	**1**
6100 Paid solely by business	0	0	0	..	0	0	0	0	0	0
6200 Other	159	495	1 661	..	0	0	1	1	1	1

Note: Year ending 31st December.
The data are on a cash basis.
The figures exclude local government tax revenues as the data are not available.
Heading 2000: The data exclude social security contributions to general government managed by the private sector. An additional breakdown is available since 2015 to discern between social security contributions paid by employees and those paid by employers.
Heading 4400: The transfer tax, previously classified under heading 5121, has been reclassified under this heading.
Heading 4200: This heading includes taxes on assets and taxes on financial assets. Both taxes were previously classified under heading 4120.
Heading 5220: This heading also includes revenue from vehicle registrations, previously classified as 5121.
Source: Ministerio de Hacienda (Ministry of Finance).

StatLink https://doi.org/10.1787/888933941536

Table 5.12. **Ecuador**

Details of tax revenue / Ingresos tributarios detallados

Million USD

	1990	2000	2005	2010	2012	2013	2014	2015	2016	2017
Total tax revenue	**1 103**	**1 884**	**5 032**	**11 570**	**17 372**	**18 624**	**19 620**	**21 151**	**19 920**	**20 774**
1000 Taxes on income, profits and capital gains	**139**	**295**	**942**	**2 363**	**3 351**	**3 882**	**4 219**	**4 780**	**4 386**	**4 134**
1100 Of individuals	..	10	27	80	113	161	177	192	224	180
1110 On income and profits	..	..	..	..	..	..	..	..	..	..
1120 On capital gains	..	..	..	..	..	..	..	..	..	..
1200 Corporate	..	53	342	485	851	1 023	1 121	1 578	1 377	1 074
1210 On profits	..	..	..	..	..	..	..	..	..	..
1220 On capital gains	..	..	..	..	..	..	..	..	..	..
1300 Unallocable between 1100 and 1200	139	232	573	1 798	2 388	2 698	2 920	3 010	2 784	2 880
Unallocable income tax	139	206	859	1 873	2 466	2 784	3 034	3 109	2 817	2 992
Income tax refunds	0	27	-287	-75	-78	-86	-113	-99	-32	-112
2000 Social security contributions	**243**	**228**	**1 109**	**2 549**	**4 752**	**4 547**	**4 718**	**5 055**	**4 741**	**5 414**
2100 Employees	..	..	..	..	..	..	..	..	..	..
2110 On a payroll basis	..	..	..	..	..	..	..	..	..	..
2120 On an income tax basis	..	..	..	..	..	..	..	..	..	..
2200 Employers	..	..	..	..	..	..	..	..	..	..
2210 On a payroll basis	..	..	..	..	..	..	..	..	..	..
2220 On an income tax basis	..	..	..	..	..	..	..	..	..	..
2300 Self-employed or non-employed	..	..	..	..	..	..	..	..	..	..
2310 On a payroll basis	..	..	..	..	..	..	..	..	..	..
2320 On an income tax basis	..	..	..	..	..	..	..	..	..	..
2400 Unallocable between 2100, 2200 and 2300	243	228	1 109	2 549	4 752	4 547	4 718	5 055	4 741	5 414
2410 On a payroll basis	..	..	..	..	..	..	..	..	..	..
2420 On an income tax basis	..	..	..	..	..	..	..	..	..	..
3000 Taxes on payroll and workforce	**0**	**0**	**0**	**0**	**0**	**0**	**0**	**0**	**0**	**0**
4000 Taxes on property	**16**	**17**	**71**	**121**	**172**	**198**	**207**	**245**	**592**	**313**
4100 Recurrent taxes on immovable property	13	8	37	66	104	113	113	125	142	162
4110 Households	0	0	0	0	0	0	0	0	0	0
4120 Others	13	8	37	66	104	113	113	125	134	155
4200 Recurrent taxes on net wealth	0	0	0	0	0	0	0	0	202	16
4210 Individual	..	..	..	..	..	..	..	..	..	..
4220 Corporate	..	..	..	..	..	..	..	..	..	..
4300 Estate, inheritance and gift taxes	0	0	1	5	6	9	11	29	15	26
4310 Estate and inheritance taxes	..	..	1	5	6	9	11	29	15	26
4320 Gift taxes	..	..	0	0	0	0	0	0	0	0
4400 Taxes on financial and capital transactions	0	0	0	1	0	0	0	0	0	0
4500 Non-recurrent taxes	0	0	0	0	0	0	0	0	141	3
4510 On net wealth	..	..	..	..	..	..	..	..	..	..
4520 Other non-recurrent taxes	..	..	..	..	..	..	..	..	..	..
4600 Other recurrent taxes on property	3	9	33	50	62	76	83	91	92	106
5000 Taxes on goods and services	**676**	**1 341**	**2 856**	**6 248**	**8 984**	**9 866**	**10 374**	**11 025**	**10 104**	**10 887**
5100 Taxes on production, sale, transfer, etc	671	1 325	2 762	6 045	8 703	9 550	10 029	10 665	9 662	10 446
5110 General taxes	306	840	1 991	3 927	5 472	6 123	6 454	6 431	6 116	6 892
5111 Value added taxes	302	836	1 975	3 886	5 415	6 056	6 376	6 352	6 042	6 817
5112 Sales tax	0	0	0	0	0	0	0	0	0	0
5113 Other	4	5	16	41	57	67	78	79	74	75
5120 Taxes on specific goods and services	365	485	770	2 117	3 230	3 427	3 575	4 234	3 547	3 554
5121 Excises	90	75	221	530	685	744	803	840	803	944
Alcohol products	..	30	89	..	..	..	..	232	229	274
Soft drinks and mineral water	..	9	15	..	..	..	..	59	118	118
Cigarettes	..	24	71	..	..	..	..	195	158	126
Luxury goods and vehicles	..	11	46	..	..	..	..	213	145	185
Pipeline tax	..	0	0	..	..	..	..	0	0	0
Excise on imports	..	0	0	..	..	..	..	142	124	209
Plastic bottles	..	0	0	..	..	..	..	0	28	31
5122 Profits of fiscal monopolies	0	0	0	0	0	0	0	0	0	0
5123 Customs and import duties	227	217	547	1 152	1 261	1 352	1 357	2 026	1 633	1 468
5124 Taxes on exports	0	0	0	0	0	0	0	0	0	0
5125 Taxes on investment goods	0	0	0	0	0	0	0	0	0	0
5126 Taxes on specific services	8	18	3	435	1 285	1 331	1 415	1 288	9	10
Exit taxes	7	17	0	428	1 275	1 322	1 406	1 278	0	0
Public shows and events	1	2	3	6	8	8	7	8	8	9
Telecommunications	0	0	0	0	0	0	1	0	0	0
Construction contracts with the public sector	0	0	0	0	0	0	0	0	0	0
Disposal of livestock	0	0	0	1	1	1	1	1	1	1
Lotteries and gambling	0	0	0	0	0	0	0	0	0	0

Table 5.12. **Ecuador** *(cont.)*

Details of tax revenue / Ingresos tributarios detallados

Million USD

	1990	2000	2005	2010	2012	2013	2014	2015	2016	2017
5127 Other taxes on internat. trade and transactions	40	175	0	0	0	0	0	81	1 102	1 133
Foreign Currency Exit Tax (ISD)	0	169	..	..	..	..	..	0	1 012	1 133
On purchase of foreign exchange	22	4	..	..	..	..	..	0	0	0
On credit operations in national currency	18	2	..	..	..	..	..	81	90	0
5128 Other taxes	0	0	0	0	0	0	0	0	0	0
5130 Unallocable between 5110 and 5120	0	0	0	0	0	0	0	0	0	0
5200 Taxes on use of goods and perform activities	5	16	95	203	282	316	345	359	441	441
5210 Recurrent taxes	5	16	95	203	282	316	345	359	441	441
5211 Paid by households: motor vehicles	0	0	0	0	0	0	0	0	112	111
5212 Paid by others: motor vehicles	5	11	69	168	209	231	248	245	216	212
Annual tax on motor vehicles	3	11	60	156	194	214	228	223	195	191
5213 Paid in respect of other goods	1	5	26	35	73	85	97	115	113	118
5220 Non-recurrent taxes	0	0	0	0	0	0	0	0	0	0
5300 Unallocable between 5100 and 5200	0	0	0	0	0	0	0	0	0	0
6000 Other taxes	**29**	**2**	**54**	**289**	**112**	**132**	**102**	**45**	**97**	**26**
6100 Paid solely by business	0	0	0	0	0	0	0	0	0	0
6200 Other	29	2	54	286	105	126	102	45	97	26
Credit notes	..	..	..	0	0	0	0	0	0	0
Simplified taxation system of Ecuador (RISE)	..	..	..	6	12	15	20	20	19	22
Other reimbursements	..	..	..	0	0	0	0	0	-1	3
Others	..	..	..	280	93	111	82	25	79	0

Note: Year ending 31st December.
The data are on a cash basis.
The local data in this edition have been revised since 1990 and their classification have been improved. See Table 6.12 for more details.
Heading 2000: Social security data is recorded at the non-financial public sector level.
Source: Servicio de Rentas Internas (SRI) y Banco Central del Ecuador (Internal Revenue Service and Central Bank of Ecuador).

StatLink https://doi.org/10.1787/888933941555

Table 5.13. **El Salvador**

Details of tax revenue / Ingresos tributarios detallados

Million USD

	1990	2000	2005	2010	2012	2013	2014	2015	2016	2017
Total tax revenue	**506**	**1 585**	**2 420**	**3 298**	**3 905**	**4 222**	**4 229**	**4 492**	**4 795**	**5 052**
1000 Taxes on income, profits and capital gains	**95**	**407**	**637**	**995**	**1 250**	**1 479**	**1 522**	**1 545**	**1 659**	**1 731**
1100 Of individuals	..	..	312	571	697	578	627	739	695	758
1110 On income and profits	..	..	312	571	697	578	627	739	695	758
1120 On capital gains	..	..	..	..	..	..	..	..	..	..
1200 Corporate	..	..	356	423	555	793	693	622	763	804
1210 On profits	..	..	356	423	555	793	693	622	763	804
1220 On capital gains	..	..	..	..	..	..	..	..	..	..
1300 Unallocable between 1100 and 1200	95	407	-31	0	-2	108	201	183	202	169
Withholding income tax	95	429	0	55	66	135	204	213	232	209
Income tax refunds	0	-22	-31	-55	-68	-27	-3	-30	-31	-40
2000 Social security contributions	**67**	**263**	**282**	**369**	**404**	**425**	**445**	**488**	**539**	**572**
2100 Employees	..	75	76	99	106	112	117	130	143	152
2110 On a payroll basis	..	75	76	99	106	112	117	130	143	152
2120 On an income tax basis	..	0	0	0	0	0	0	0	0	0
2200 Employers	..	176	181	238	260	273	286	314	347	369
2210 On a payroll basis	..	176	181	238	260	273	286	314	347	369
2220 On an income tax basis	..	0	0	0	0	0	0	0	0	0
2300 Self-employed or non-employed	..	13	25	33	38	40	42	45	48	52
2310 On a payroll basis	..	13	25	33	38	40	42	45	48	52
2320 On an income tax basis	..	0	0	0	0	0	0	0	0	0
2400 Unallocable between 2100, 2200 and 2300	67	0	0	0	0	0	0	0	0	0
2410 On a payroll basis	67	..	..	..	..	..	..	..	..	..
2420 On an income tax basis	0	..	..	..	..	..	..	..	..	..
3000 Taxes on payroll and workforce	**0**	**0**	**0**	**0**	**0**	**0**	**0**	**0**	**0**	**0**
4000 Taxes on property	**26**	**12**	**16**	**16**	**20**	**21**	**24**	**107**	**107**	**108**
4100 Recurrent taxes on immovable property	0	0	0	0	0	0	0	0	0	0
4110 Households	..	..	..	..	..	..	..	..	..	..
4120 Others	..	..	..	..	..	..	..	..	..	..
4200 Recurrent taxes on net wealth	16	0	0	0	0	0	0	0	0	0
4210 Individual	16	..	..	..	..	..	..	..	..	..
4220 Corporate	0	..	..	..	..	..	..	..	..	..
4300 Estate, inheritance and gift taxes	0	0	0	0	0	0	0	0	0	0
4310 Estate and inheritance taxes	..	..	..	..	..	..	..	..	..	..
4320 Gift taxes	..	..	..	..	..	..	..	..	..	..
4400 Taxes on financial and capital transactions	10	12	16	16	20	21	24	107	107	108
Property transfers	..	..	..	..	..	..	..	20	23	23
Checks and electronic transfers of funds	..	..	..	..	..	..	..	55	54	53
Withholding for liquidity control	..	..	..	..	..	..	..	31	31	32
4500 Non-recurrent taxes	0	0	0	0	0	0	0	0	0	0
4510 On net wealth	..	..	..	..	..	..	..	..	..	..
4520 Other non-recurrent taxes	..	..	..	..	..	..	..	..	..	..
4600 Other recurrent taxes on property	0	0	0	0	0	0	0	0	0	0
5000 Taxes on goods and services	**259**	**903**	**1 447**	**1 855**	**2 155**	**2 213**	**2 147**	**2 266**	**2 400**	**2 555**
5100 Taxes on production, sale, transfer, etc	259	903	1 447	1 847	2 146	2 202	2 147	2 254	2 387	2 542
5110 General taxes	133	714	1 104	1 433	1 677	1 731	1 720	1 764	1 813	1 905
5111 Value added taxes	0	714	1 104	1 433	1 677	1 731	1 720	1 764	1 813	1 905
5112 Sales tax	0	0	0	0	0	0	0	0	0	0
5113 Other	133	0	0	0	0	0	0	0	0	0
5120 Taxes on specific goods and services	127	189	344	415	469	472	427	490	574	637
5121 Excises	65	49	162	211	253	238	224	285	355	413
Alcoholic beverages	..	..	14	18	22	19	14	22	23	24
Cigarettes	..	..	23	31	40	27	22	29	28	27
Soft drinks	..	..	33	31	40	42	43	48	49	49
Beer	..	..	26	26	42	40	32	55	61	65
Weapons, ammunition and explosives	..	..	1	1	1	1	1	1	1	1
Ad-valorem on fuels	..	..	0	0	0	0	0	7	9	8
Special contribution- Sugar	..	..	1	1	1	1	1	1	1	1
Special contribution- Public transportation	..	..	0	35	36	36	37	40	43	45
Special contribution- FOVIAL	..	..	66	69	71	72	74	80	86	79
Special contribution- Public security	..	..	0	0	0	0	0	2	56	116
5122 Profits of fiscal monopolies	0	0	0	0	0	0	0	0	0	0
5123 Customs and import duties	61	141	181	148	180	199	181	194	207	211
5124 Taxes on exports	0	0	0	0	0	0	0	0	0	0
5125 Taxes on investment goods	0	0	0	0	0	0	0	0	0	0
5126 Taxes on specific services	0	0	0	56	36	34	22	11	12	13
5127 Other taxes on internat. trade and transactions	0	0	0	0	0	0	0	0	0	0
5128 Other taxes	0	0	0	0	0	0	0	0	0	0

Table 5.13. **El Salvador** *(cont.)*

Details of tax revenue / Ingresos tributarios detallados

Million USD

	1990	2000	2005	2010	2012	2013	2014	2015	2016	2017
5130 Unallocable between 5110 and 5120	0	0	0	0	0	0	0	0	0	0
5200 Taxes on use of goods and perform activities	0	0	0	0	0	0	0	12	14	14
5210 Recurrent taxes	..	..	..	..	..	..	..	0	0	0
5211 Paid by households: motor vehicles	..	..	..	..	..	..	..	..	..	..
5212 Paid by others: motor vehicles	..	..	..	..	..	..	..	..	..	..
5213 Paid in respect of other goods	..	..	..	..	..	..	..	..	..	..
5220 Non-recurrent taxes	..	..	..	..	..	..	..	12	14	14
5300 Unallocable between 5100 and 5200	0	0	0	0	0	0	0	0	0	0
6000 Other taxes	**58**	**0**	**37**	**63**	**77**	**83**	**91**	**86**	**89**	**85**
6100 Paid solely by business	0	0	0	0	0	0	0	0	0	0
6200 Other	58	0	37	63	77	83	91	86	89	85

Note: Year ending 31st December.

The data are on a cash basis.

Heading 1000: For 2002 and from 2006 onwards sub-headings 1100 and 1200 are presented on a gross basis i.e. not including income tax refunds. The latter are classified under heading 1300.

Heading 2000: Corresponds to social security contributions paid to the Salvadoran Institute of Social Security and excludes payments to privately managed pension funds (AFPs).

Heading 5121: Special contributions to public security have been included since 2015.

Source: Dirección General de Tesorería, Ministerio de Hacienda. Banco Central de Reserva y el Instituto Salvadoreño del Seguro Social (General Treasury Directorate, Ministry of Finance, Central Reserve Bank and the Salvadoran Social Security Institute).

StatLink https://doi.org/10.1787/888933941574

Table 5.14. **Guatemala**

Details of tax revenue / Ingresos tributarios detallados

Million GTQ

	1990	2000	2005	2010	2012	2013	2014	2015	2016	2017
Total tax revenue	**2 601**	**16 531**	**27 187**	**41 185**	**50 901**	**55 002**	**57 516**	**60 329**	**65 609**	**68 829**
1000 Taxes on income, profits and capital gains	**507**	**3 295**	**6 049**	**10 319**	**13 907**	**16 093**	**17 752**	**17 534**	**20 572**	**20 693**
1100 Of individuals	25	143	645	1 225	1 477	1 246	1 784	1 826	2 082	2 468
1110 On income and profits	25	143	645	1 225	1 477	1 246	1 784	1 826	2 082	2 468
Personal income tax	25	137	642	1 225	1 477	1 246	1 784	1 826	2 082	2 468
Income from financial products	0	6	4	0	1	0	0	0	0	0
1120 On capital gains	..	..	..	..	..	..	..	..	..	..
1200 Corporate	482	3 149	3 756	6 520	9 581	11 584	12 426	11 802	14 418	13 846
1210 On profits	482	3 149	3 756	6 520	9 581	11 584	12 426	11 802	14 418	13 846
Corporate income tax	482	1 610	3 495	6 132	9 118	11 529	12 423	11 801	14 417	13 839
Income from financial products	0	248	235	386	463	52	0	0	0	0
Commercial and agricultural enterprises	0	1 291	26	2	0	3	3	0	1	6
1220 On capital gains	..	..	..	..	..	..	..	..	..	..
1300 Unallocable between 1100 and 1200	0	2	1 647	2 574	2 849	3 263	3 543	3 907	4 072	4 380
Extraordinary and temporary solidarity tax in support of peace agreements	..	0	1 647	44	4	21	9	1	1	28
Solidarity tax	..	0	0	2 530	2 845	3 243	3 533	3 906	4 070	4 352
Extraordinary and temporary solidarity tax	..	2	0	0	0	0	0	0	0	0
2000 Social security contributions	**436**	**2 569**	**4 072**	**6 408**	**7 858**	**8 617**	**8 157**	**10 034**	**10 974**	**11 523**
2100 Employees	..	..	..	..	..	..	..	..	..	..
2110 On a payroll basis	..	..	..	..	..	..	..	..	..	..
2120 On an income tax basis	..	..	..	..	..	..	..	..	..	..
2200 Employers	..	..	..	..	..	..	..	..	..	..
2210 On a payroll basis	..	..	..	..	..	..	..	..	..	..
2220 On an income tax basis	..	..	..	..	..	..	..	..	..	..
2300 Self-employed or non-employed	..	..	..	..	..	..	..	..	..	..
2310 On a payroll basis	..	..	..	..	..	..	..	..	..	..
2320 On an income tax basis	..	..	..	..	..	..	..	..	..	..
2400 Unallocable between 2100, 2200 and 2300	436	2 569	4 072	6 408	7 858	8 617	8 157	10 034	10 974	11 523
2410 On a payroll basis	436	2 569	4 072	6 408	7 858	8 617	8 157	10 034	10 974	11 523
2420 On an income tax basis	0	0	0	0	0	0	0	0	..	..
3000 Taxes on payroll and workforce	**0**	**0**	**0**	**0**	**0**	**0**	**0**	**0**	**0**	**0**
4000 Taxes on property	**0**	**165**	**350**	**630**	**743**	**791**	**843**	**713**	**587**	**739**
4100 Recurrent taxes on immovable property	..	153	341	620	735	780	829	693	565	710
4110 Households	..	0	0	0	0	0	0	0	..	..
4120 Others	..	153	341	620	735	780	829	693	565	710
Property tax	..	6	1	1	1	1	1	1	1	1
Property tax (municipal)	..	147	341	620	734	779	827	692	564	709
4200 Recurrent taxes on net wealth	..	0	0	0	0	0	0	0	0	0
4210 Individual	..	..	..	..	..	..	..	..	..	..
4220 Corporate	..	..	..	..	..	..	..	..	..	..
4300 Estate, inheritance and gift taxes	..	0	0	0	0	0	0	0	0	0
4310 Estate and inheritance taxes	..	..	..	..	..	..	..	..	..	..
4320 Gift taxes	..	..	..	..	..	..	..	..	..	..
4400 Taxes on financial and capital transactions	..	12	8	10	8	10	15	20	23	29
4500 Non-recurrent taxes	..	0	0	0	0	0	0	0	0	0
4510 On net wealth	..	..	..	..	..	..	..	..	..	..
4520 Other non-recurrent taxes	..	..	..	..	..	..	..	..	..	..
4600 Other recurrent taxes on property	..	0	0	0	0	0	0	0	0	0
5000 Taxes on goods and services	**1 554**	**10 317**	**16 402**	**23 255**	**27 514**	**29 071**	**30 405**	**31 711**	**33 105**	**35 365**
5100 Taxes on production, sale, transfer, etc	1 526	10 131	16 083	22 750	26 611	27 541	29 085	30 080	31 356	33 586
5110 General taxes	762	6 259	10 753	16 980	20 913	21 874	23 153	23 271	24 215	26 187
5111 Value added taxes	762	6 259	10 753	16 980	20 913	21 874	23 153	23 271	24 215	26 187
5112 Sales tax	0	0	0	0	0	0	0	0	0	0
5113 Other	0	0	0	0	0	0	0	0	0	0
5120 Taxes on specific goods and services	764	3 872	5 330	5 770	5 698	5 667	5 932	6 809	7 140	7 400
5121 Excises	258	1 797	1 262	3 101	3 072	3 372	3 550	4 289	4 422	4 518
Tobacco and derivatives	76	205	312	347	312	385	405	369	365	348
Beer	0	97	122	159	191	217	243	293	306	314
Alcoholic beverages	0	77	76	98	100	90	56	88	90	96
Soft drinks	0	15	172	220	263	282	300	328	348	348
Other beverages	77	12	2	2	1	1	0	0	1	0
Cement	0	0	93	99	102	100	101	312	117	114
Oil and derivatives	105	1 389	485	2 179	2 103	2 297	2 445	2 899	3 195	3 296
5122 Profits of fiscal monopolies	0	0	0	0	0	0	0	0	0	0
5123 Customs and import duties	506	1 806	3 715	2 368	2 311	1 965	2 044	2 157	2 323	2 455
5124 Taxes on exports	0	0	0	0	0	0	0	0	0	0
5125 Taxes on investment goods	0	0	0	0	0	0	0	0	0	0

Table 5.14. **Guatemala** *(cont.)*

Details of tax revenue / Ingresos tributarios detallados

Million GTQ

	1990	2000	2005	2010	2012	2013	2014	2015	2016	2017
5126 Taxes on specific services	0	269	354	301	315	330	339	363	396	427
5127 Other taxes on internat. trade and transactions	0	0	0	0	0	0	0	0	0	0
5128 Other taxes	0	0	0	0	0	0	0	0	0	0
5130 Unallocable between 5110 and 5120	0	0	0	0	0	0	0	0	0	0
5200 Taxes on use of goods and perform activities	28	186	319	505	904	1 530	1 320	1 631	1 750	1 779
5210 Recurrent taxes	28	186	319	505	904	1 530	1 320	1 631	1 750	1 779
5211 Paid by households: motor vehicles	0	0	0	0	331	694	747	914	967	953
5212 Paid by others: motor vehicles	28	186	319	505	573	836	572	717	782	826
5213 Paid in respect of other goods	0	0	0	0	0	0	0	0	0	0
5220 Non-recurrent taxes	0	0	0	0	0	0	0	0	0	0
5300 Unallocable between 5100 and 5200	0	0	0	0	0	0	0	0	0	0
6000 Other taxes	**104**	**186**	**315**	**572**	**878**	**430**	**359**	**337**	**370**	**508**
6100 Paid solely by business	0	0	0	0	0	0	0	0	..	..
6200 Other	104	186	315	572	878	430	359	337	370	508
Revenue stamps and stamped paper	104	182	313	572	877	430	359	336	370	508
Other indirect taxes	0	4	1	1	1	1	0	0	0	0

Note: Year ending 31st December.

The data are on a cash basis.

The figures exclude some local government tax revenues as the data are not available. Revenues from the municipal property tax (IUSI) are included.

Heading 2000: Corresponds to social security contributions paid to the Guatemalan Social Security Institute (IGSS) and payments by public employees to the government's pension fund.

Headings 4120 and 4400: For years prior to 2000, the property tax under heading 4120 is included in the total under heading 4400.

Heading 5121: Up to 1999, "Other beverages" contains all alcoholic and non-alcoholic beverages.

Source: Dirección de Análisis de Política Fiscal del Ministerio de Hacienda, Instituto Guatemalteco del Seguro Social y Superintendencia de la Administración Tributaria (Fiscal Policy Analysis Directorate at the Ministry of Finance, the Guatemalan Institute of Social Security and the Tax Administration Superintendency).

StatLink https://doi.org/10.1787/888933941593

Table 5.15. **Guyana**

Details of tax revenue / Ingresos tributarios detallados

Million GYD

	1990	2000	2005	2010	2012	2013	2014	2015	2016	2017
Total tax revenue	**5 232**	**42 750**	**60 319**	**111 933**	**131 350**	**140 749**	**151 550**	**160 061**	**170 779**	**192 119**
1000 Taxes on income, profits and capital gains	**1 752**	**16 179**	**23 843**	**39 561**	**44 547**	**46 587**	**51 611**	**55 011**	**61 127**	**67 880**
1100 Of individuals	333	7 734	11 139	17 816	19 530	18 506	21 389	23 300	26 773	26 515
1110 On income and profits	333	7 734	11 139	17 816	19 530	18 506	21 389	23 300	26 773	26 515
Personal	306	7 157	11 139	15 419	16 155	15 199	17 900	19 894	22 727	21 669
Self-employed	27	577	0	2 397	3 375	3 307	3 490	3 407	4 045	4 845
1120 On capital gains	..	..	..	..	..	..	..	..	..	..
1200 Corporate	1 375	8 266	12 555	21 427	24 419	27 622	29 794	31 200	33 852	41 024
1210 On profits	..	..	..	..	..	..	..	..	..	..
1220 On capital gains	..	..	..	..	..	..	..	..	..	..
1300 Unallocable between 1100 and 1200	43	179	149	317	598	459	428	511	502	341
2000 Social security contributions	**191**	**4 868**	**6 670**	**10 047**	**11 824**	**13 195**	**14 985**	**16 708**	**18 629**	**20 771**
2100 Employees	..	..	..	..	..	..	..	..	..	..
2110 On a payroll basis	..	..	..	..	..	..	..	..	..	..
2120 On an income tax basis	..	..	..	..	..	..	..	..	..	..
2200 Employers	..	..	..	..	..	..	..	..	..	..
2210 On a payroll basis	..	..	..	..	..	..	..	..	..	..
2220 On an income tax basis	..	..	..	..	..	..	..	..	..	..
2300 Self-employed or non-employed	..	..	..	..	..	..	..	..	..	..
2310 On a payroll basis	..	..	..	..	..	..	..	..	..	..
2320 On an income tax basis	..	..	..	..	..	..	..	..	..	..
2400 Unallocable between 2100, 2200 and 2300	191	4 868	6 670	10 047	11 824	13 195	14 985	16 708	18 629	20 771
2410 On a payroll basis	..	..	..	..	..	..	..	..	..	..
2420 On an income tax basis	..	..	..	..	..	..	..	..	..	..
3000 Taxes on payroll and workforce	**0**	**0**	**0**	**0**	**0**	**0**	**0**	**0**	**0**	**0**
4000 Taxes on property	**53**	**701**	**828**	**1 593**	**1 903**	**2 608**	**2 423**	**3 237**	**3 209**	**3 618**
4100 Recurrent taxes on immovable property	40	681	807	1 562	1 866	2 572	2 381	3 201	3 172	3 579
4110 Households	0	0	0	0	0	0	0	0	0	0
4120 Others	40	681	807	1 562	1 866	2 572	2 381	3 201	3 172	3 579
4200 Recurrent taxes on net wealth	0	0	0	0	0	0	0	0	0	0
4210 Individual	..	..	..	..	..	..	..	..	..	..
4220 Corporate	..	..	..	..	..	..	..	..	..	..
4300 Estate, inheritance and gift taxes	13	20	21	31	37	37	42	37	37	39
4310 Estate and inheritance taxes	..	..	..	..	..	..	..	..	..	..
4320 Gift taxes	..	..	..	..	..	..	..	..	..	..
4400 Taxes on financial and capital transactions	0	0	0	0	0	0	0	0	0	0
4500 Non-recurrent taxes	0	0	0	0	0	0	0	0	0	0
4510 On net wealth	..	..	..	..	..	..	..	..	..	..
4520 Other non-recurrent taxes	..	..	..	..	..	..	..	..	..	..
4600 Other recurrent taxes on property	0	0	0	0	0	0	0	0	0	0
5000 Taxes on goods and services	**2 200**	**20 798**	**27 940**	**59 387**	**71 368**	**76 762**	**81 272**	**84 027**	**86 500**	**97 558**
5100 Taxes on production, sale, transfer, etc	2 162	20 530	27 414	58 873	70 821	76 143	80 599	83 330	85 555	96 519
5110 General taxes	1 399	14 861	21 396	27 071	34 106	34 388	37 475	35 476	37 524	42 861
5111 Value added taxes	0	0	0	27 071	34 106	34 388	37 475	35 476	36 324	42 556
Imports	..	..	..	14 877	19 297	20 036	20 370	19 366	18 477	..
Domestic supply	..	..	..	12 194	14 809	14 352	17 105	16 110	17 847	..
5112 Sales tax	0	0	0	0	0	0	0	0	0	0
5113 Other	1 399	14 861	21 396	0	0	0	0	0	1 200	305
5120 Taxes on specific goods and services	763	5 669	6 019	31 802	36 715	41 755	43 124	47 853	48 031	53 659
5121 Excises	32	609	1 211	22 070	23 815	28 343	29 267	33 827	31 083	35 162
Imports	0	0	0	18 935	19 605	24 147	25 044	29 953	27 043	..
Domestic supply	0	0	0	2 358	3 139	3 124	3 190	3 377	4 040	..
Purchase tax - motor cars	32	475	738	0	0	0	0	0	0	..
Environmental tax	0	134	473	777	1 071	1 072	1 033	496	0	1 703
5122 Profits of fiscal monopolies	0	0	0	0	0	0	0	0	0	0
5123 Customs and import duties	544	3 943	3 635	8 302	11 561	11 866	12 167	12 357	14 887	16 273
5124 Taxes on exports	94	7	7	7	9	14	14	12	13	23
5125 Taxes on investment goods	0	0	0	0	0	0	0	0	0	0
5126 Taxes on specific services	92	1 110	1 166	1 423	1 331	1 532	1 676	1 658	2 048	2 201
Entertainment tax	12	27	2	0	0	0	0	0	0	0
Travel tax	80	1 084	1 164	1 423	1 331	1 532	1 676	1 658	2 048	2 201
5127 Other taxes on internat. trade and transactions	0	0	0	0	0	0	0	0	0	0
5128 Other taxes	0	0	0	0	0	0	0	0	0	0
5130 Unallocable between 5110 and 5120	0	0	0	0	0	0	0	0	0	0
5200 Taxes on use of goods and perform activities	38	268	525	514	547	620	673	697	945	1 039
5210 Recurrent taxes	38	268	525	514	547	620	673	697	945	1 039
5211 Paid by households: motor vehicles	27	239	274	475	513	587	637	653	868	1 039
5212 Paid by others: motor vehicles	0	0	0	0	0	0	0	0	0	0

Table 5.15. **Guyana** *(cont.)*

Details of tax revenue / Ingresos tributarios detallados

Million GYD

	1990	2000	2005	2010	2012	2013	2014	2015	2016	2017
5213 Paid in respect of other goods	12	29	251	39	34	33	35	44	78	0
Other licences	12	29	251	39	34	33	35	44	78	..
5220 Non-recurrent taxes	0	0	0	0	0	0	0	0	0	0
5300 Unallocable between 5100 and 5200	0	0	0	0	0	0	0	0	0	0
6000 Other taxes	**1 037**	**204**	**1 039**	**1 346**	**1 708**	**1 596**	**1 259**	**1 079**	**1 314**	**2 292**
6100 Paid solely by business	0	0	0	0	0	0	0	0	0	0
6200 Other	1 037	204	1 039	1 346	1 708	1 596	1 259	1 079	1 314	2 292

Note: Year ending 31st December.
The data are on a cash basis.
Heading 2000: The figures are estimated since 2015.
Miscellaneous revenues reported by the Ministry of Finance of Guyana have been excluded as these encompass interest and penalties paid on VAT and excise taxes.
Source: Ministry of Finance, the Central Bank of Guyana and the National Insurance Scheme.

StatLink https://doi.org/10.1787/888933941612

Table 5.16. **Honduras**

Details of tax revenue / Ingresos tributarios detallados

Million HNL

	1990	2000	2005	2010	2012	2013	2014	2015	2016	2017
Total tax revenue	**2 122**	**17 307**	**32 973**	**54 060**	**66 357**	**71 653**	**83 702**	**95 724**	**110 094**	**123 184**
1000 Taxes on income, profits and capital gains	**431**	**2 907**	**7 037**	**13 232**	**17 309**	**19 366**	**21 347**	**24 843**	**29 584**	**33 055**
1100 Of individuals	157	991	2 312	4 528	5 745	6 478	7 312	8 451	10 173	11 369
1110 On income and profits	157	991	2 312	4 528	5 745	6 478	7 312	8 451	10 173	11 369
1120 On capital gains	..	..	..	..	..	..	..	..	..	..
1200 Corporate	274	1 916	4 725	8 705	11 564	12 888	14 034	16 392	19 411	21 687
1210 On profits	274	1 916	4 725	8 705	11 564	12 888	14 034	16 392	19 411	21 687
Corporate income tax	274	1 916	4 121	7 400	10 088	11 523	12 756	14 742	17 746	19 832
Income tax surcharge	0	0	604	1 305	1 468	1 352	1 265	1 637	1 653	1 841
Special contribution of the cooperative sector	0	0	0	0	8	14	13	13	13	14
1220 On capital gains	..	..	..	..	..	..	..	..	..	..
1300 Unallocable between 1100 and 1200	0	0	0	0	0	0	0	0	0	0
2000 Social security contributions	**179**	**1 727**	**4 416**	**8 671**	**10 854**	**12 529**	**12 467**	**13 524**	**14 402**	**17 379**
2100 Employees	..	..	..	..	..	..	..	..	..	..
2110 On a payroll basis	..	..	..	..	..	..	..	..	..	..
2120 On an income tax basis	..	..	..	..	..	..	..	..	..	..
2200 Employers	..	..	..	..	..	..	..	..	..	..
2210 On a payroll basis	..	..	..	..	..	..	..	..	..	..
2220 On an income tax basis	..	..	..	..	..	..	..	..	..	..
2300 Self-employed or non-employed	..	..	..	..	..	..	..	..	..	..
2310 On a payroll basis	..	..	..	..	..	..	..	..	..	..
2320 On an income tax basis	..	..	..	..	..	..	..	..	..	..
2400 Unallocable between 2100, 2200 and 2300	179	1 727	4 416	8 671	10 854	12 529	12 467	13 524	14 402	17 379
2410 On a payroll basis	179	1 727	4 416	8 671	10 854	12 529	12 467	13 524	14 402	17 379
2420 On an income tax basis	0	0	0	0	0	0	0	0	0	0
3000 Taxes on payroll and workforce	**0**	**0**	**0**	**0**	**0**	**0**	**0**	**0**	**0**	**0**
4000 Taxes on property	**16**	**266**	**631**	**994**	**1 217**	**1 446**	**2 300**	**2 635**	**2 362**	**3 046**
4100 Recurrent taxes on immovable property	0	0	0	0	0	0	0	0	0	0
4110 Households	..	..	..	..	..	..	..	..	..	..
4120 Others	..	..	..	..	..	..	..	..	..	..
4200 Recurrent taxes on net wealth	0	0	0	0	0	0	0	0	0	0
4210 Individual	..	..	..	..	..	..	..	..	..	..
4220 Corporate	..	..	..	..	..	..	..	..	..	..
4300 Estate, inheritance and gift taxes	0	0	0	0	0	0	0	0	0	0
4310 Estate and inheritance taxes	..	..	..	..	..	..	..	..	..	..
4320 Gift taxes	..	..	..	..	..	..	..	..	..	..
4400 Taxes on financial and capital transactions	0	0	0	0	659	903	1 636	2 003	1 738	2 353
4500 Non-recurrent taxes	0	0	316	381	0	0	0	0	0	0
4510 On net wealth	..	..	0	0	..	..	..	..	..	..
4520 Other non-recurrent taxes	..	..	316	381	..	..	..	..	..	..
4600 Other recurrent taxes on property	16	266	315	613	558	543	664	633	624	693
5000 Taxes on goods and services	**1 405**	**11 445**	**19 032**	**28 937**	**34 764**	**35 908**	**44 945**	**52 217**	**58 611**	**63 111**
5100 Taxes on production, sale, transfer, etc	1 405	11 445	19 032	28 937	34 764	35 908	44 945	52 217	58 611	63 111
5110 General taxes	344	5 146	9 565	16 050	20 150	20 637	27 735	32 273	36 521	39 228
5111 Value added taxes	344	5 146	9 565	16 050	20 150	20 637	27 735	32 273	36 521	39 228
5112 Sales tax	0	0	0	0	0	0	0	0	0	0
5113 Other	0	0	0	0	0	0	0	0	0	0
5120 Taxes on specific goods and services	1 061	6 299	9 468	12 887	14 614	15 270	17 211	19 944	22 090	23 883
5121 Excises	256	3 600	6 322	8 458	9 490	10 119	11 588	13 349	14 953	16 405
Beer	71	376	338	376	503	503	525	668	824	974
Soft drinks	25	240	268	514	675	725	754	838	890	938
Liquors	32	48	69	121	165	165	188	195	190	192
Petroleum products	43	347	0	0	0	0	0	0	0	0
Cigarettes	57	369	437	607	633	495	610	598	564	563
Fuel tax	0	1 962	4 916	6 288	6 868	7 613	8 874	10 317	11 594	12 773
Other	28	258	295	551	646	618	638	735	890	965
5122 Profits of fiscal monopolies	0	0	0	0	0	0	0	0	0	0
5123 Customs and import duties	498	2 083	2 174	2 505	2 933	2 651	2 974	3 541	3 998	4 244
Petroleum	0	297	0	0	0	0	0	0	0	0
Other	498	1 786	2 174	2 505	2 933	2 651	2 974	3 541	3 998	4 244
5124 Taxes on exports	217	6	0	0	62	101	107	84	59	79
Bananas	39	5	..	..	0	0	0	0	0	0
Coffee	1	0	..	..	0	0	0	0	0	0
Temporary export tax	163	0	..	..	0	0	0	0	0	0
Special contribution of the mining sector	0	0	..	..	62	101	107	84	59	79
Other	15	1	..	..	0	0	0	0	0	0
5125 Taxes on investment goods	0	0	0	0	0	0	0	0	0	0

Table 5.16. **Honduras** *(cont.)*

Details of tax revenue / Ingresos tributarios detallados

Million HNL

	1990	2000	2005	2010	2012	2013	2014	2015	2016	2017
5126 Taxes on specific services	0	0	0	0	92	87	90	91	73	84
Special contribution of mobile services	..	..	..	..	75	66	67	67	51	55
Special contribution of the food and services sector	..	..	..	..	14	18	20	21	19	25
Special contribution of casino games and slot machines	..	..	..	..	3	3	3	3	2	4
5127 Other taxes on internat. trade and transactions	0	0	0	0	0	0	0	0	0	0
5128 Other taxes	90	610	971	1 924	2 038	2 312	2 451	2 880	3 007	3 070
5130 Unallocable between 5110 and 5120	0	0	0	0	0	0	0	0	0	0
5200 Taxes on use of goods and perform activities	0	0	0	0	0	0	0	0	0	0
5210 Recurrent taxes	..	..	..	..	..	..	..	..	..	..
5211 Paid by households: motor vehicles	..	..	..	..	..	..	..	..	..	..
5212 Paid by others: motor vehicles	..	..	..	..	..	..	..	..	..	..
5213 Paid in respect of other goods	..	..	..	..	..	..	..	..	..	..
5220 Non-recurrent taxes	..	..	..	..	..	..	..	..	..	..
5300 Unallocable between 5100 and 5200	0	0	0	0	0	0	0	0	0	0
6000 Other taxes	**91**	**962**	**1 858**	**2 225**	**2 214**	**2 404**	**2 644**	**2 504**	**5 136**	**6 593**
6100 Paid solely by business	0	0	0	0	0	0	0	0	0	0
6200 Other	91	962	1 858	2 225	2 214	2 404	2 644	2 504	5 136	6 593

Note: Year ending 31st December.
The data are on a cash basis.
Source: Secretaria de Finanzas (Ministry of Finance).

StatLink https://doi.org/10.1787/888933941631

Table 5.17. **Jamaica**

Details of tax revenue / Ingresos tributarios detallados

Million JAM

	1990	2000	2005	2010	2012	2013	2014	2015	2016	2017
Total tax revenue	**7 748**	**87 713**	**163 291**	**287 139**	**322 299**	**356 956**	**381 060**	**427 933**	**467 350**	**517 051**
1000 Taxes on income, profits and capital gains	**3 944**	**39 277**	**69 894**	**118 708**	**126 441**	**129 951**	**134 083**	**149 989**	**158 409**	**155 790**
1100 Of individuals	1 687	17 441	36 043	54 798	64 315	66 282	70 867	74 537	72 175	60 306
1110 On income and profits	1 687	17 441	36 043	54 798	64 315	66 282	70 867	74 537	72 175	60 306
PAYE	1 489	16 515	34 223	50 828	60 637	62 172	66 645	70 075	67 591	54 879
Other individuals	198	926	1 820	3 969	3 678	4 111	4 223	4 463	4 584	5 427
1120 On capital gains	..	..	..	..	..	..	..	..	..	..
1200 Corporate	1 280	7 627	13 134	33 091	32 706	34 539	31 991	40 198	47 530	61 401
1210 On profits	1 280	7 627	13 134	33 091	32 706	34 539	31 991	40 198	47 530	61 401
Bauxite/alumina	134	430	446	866	1	0	0	0	0	0
Other companies	1 146	7 197	12 688	32 224	32 705	34 539	31 991	39 668	46 823	60 431
Minimum business tax	0	0	0	0	0	0	0	529	707	970
1220 On capital gains	..	..	..	..	..	..	..	..	..	..
1300 Unallocable between 1100 and 1200	977	14 209	20 718	30 820	29 419	29 130	31 224	35 254	38 704	34 083
Tax on dividends	68	854	248	1 059	1 080	1 175	1 904	980	1 408	1 801
Tax on interests	605	9 535	13 277	16 970	13 437	10 706	10 103	13 518	14 451	6 417
Education tax	305	3 821	7 193	12 792	14 903	17 249	19 217	20 756	22 845	25 865
2000 Social security contributions	**0**	**0**	**4 924**	**8 199**	**11 418**	**13 875**	**15 865**	**16 449**	**17 978**	**19 249**
2100 Employees	..	..	..	..	..	..	..	..	..	..
2110 On a payroll basis	..	..	..	..	..	..	..	..	..	..
2120 On an income tax basis	..	..	..	..	..	..	..	..	..	..
2200 Employers	..	..	..	..	..	..	..	..	..	..
2210 On a payroll basis	..	..	..	..	..	..	..	..	..	..
2220 On an income tax basis	..	..	..	..	..	..	..	..	..	..
2300 Self-employed or non-employed	..	..	..	..	..	..	..	..	..	..
2310 On a payroll basis	..	..	..	..	..	..	..	..	..	..
2320 On an income tax basis	..	..	..	..	..	..	..	..	..	..
2400 Unallocable between 2100, 2200 and 2300	..	..	4 924	8 199	11 418	13 875	15 865	16 449	17 978	19 249
National Insurance Scheme (NIS) contributions	..	..	4 924	8 199	11 418	13 875	15 865	16 449	17 978	19 249
2410 On a payroll basis	..	..	..	..	..	..	..	..	..	..
2420 On an income tax basis	..	..	..	..	..	..	..	..	..	..
3000 Taxes on payroll and workforce	**0**	**0**	**0**	**0**	**0**	**0**	**0**	**0**	**0**	**0**
4000 Taxes on property	**67**	**639**	**1 592**	**2 600**	**2 427**	**5 595**	**6 138**	**7 271**	**7 101**	**8 523**
4100 Recurrent taxes on immovable property	67	639	1 592	2 600	2 427	5 595	6 138	7 271	7 101	8 523
4110 Households	67	639	1 592	2 600	2 427	5 595	6 138	7 271	7 101	8 523
Property tax	67	0	0	0	0	0	0	0	0	0
Property tax (municipal)	0	639	1 592	2 600	2 427	5 595	6 138	7 271	7 101	8 523
4120 Others	0	0	0	0	0	0	0	0	0	0
4200 Recurrent taxes on net wealth	0	0	0	0	0	0	0	0	0	0
4210 Individual	..	..	..	..	..	..	..	..	..	..
4220 Corporate	..	..	..	..	..	..	..	..	..	..
4300 Estate, inheritance and gift taxes	0	0	0	0	0	0	0	0	0	0
4310 Estate and inheritance taxes	..	..	..	..	..	..	..	..	..	..
4320 Gift taxes	..	..	..	..	..	..	..	..	..	..
4400 Taxes on financial and capital transactions	0	0	0	0	0	0	0	0	0	0
4500 Non-recurrent taxes	0	0	0	0	0	0	0	0	0	0
4510 On net wealth	..	..	..	..	..	..	..	..	..	..
4520 Other non-recurrent taxes	..	..	..	..	..	..	..	..	..	..
4600 Other recurrent taxes on property	0	0	0	0	0	0	0	0	0	0
5000 Taxes on goods and services	**2 824**	**43 907**	**77 065**	**149 544**	**171 801**	**195 143**	**212 228**	**241 055**	**268 569**	**316 562**
5100 Taxes on production, sale, transfer, etc	2 760	43 107	75 954	147 500	169 408	192 380	209 293	237 849	265 064	311 872
5110 General taxes	297	22 356	45 602	84 409	97 135	109 819	121 073	138 222	149 111	171 584
5111 Value added taxes	293	22 356	45 602	82 407	95 032	107 660	118 755	135 857	146 030	168 112
5112 Sales tax	4	0	0	0	0	0	0	0	0	0
Sales tax on used cars	4	..	..	..	..	..	..	..	..	..
5113 Other	0	0	0	2 002	2 103	2 159	2 318	2 365	3 081	3 472
Environmental levy	..	..	..	2 002	2 103	2 159	2 318	2 365	3 081	3 472
5120 Taxes on specific goods and services	2 463	20 752	30 352	63 091	72 273	82 561	88 220	99 627	115 953	140 288
5121 Excises	1 158	9 751	12 387	38 112	40 105	37 827	41 347	49 283	59 327	75 112
Excise duty	44	0	0	0	0	0	0	0	0	0
Special consumption tax	1 115	9 751	12 387	38 112	40 105	37 827	41 347	49 283	59 327	75 112
5122 Profits of fiscal monopolies	0	0	0	0	0	0	0	0	0	0
5123 Customs and import duties	782	8 498	14 999	19 959	22 905	25 938	26 281	28 960	34 033	37 737
Custom duty	782	8 498	14 999	19 959	22 905	25 938	26 281	28 960	34 033	37 737
5124 Taxes on exports	0	0	0	0	0	0	0	0	0	0
5125 Taxes on investment goods	0	0	0	0	0	0	0	0	0	0

Table 5.17. **Jamaica** *(cont.)*

Details of tax revenue / Ingresos tributarios detallados

Million JAM

	1990	2000	2005	2010	2012	2013	2014	2015	2016	2017
5126 Taxes on specific services	523	2 503	2 966	5 020	9 264	18 796	20 592	21 384	22 593	27 438
Bank and trust	204	0	0	0	0	0	0	0	0	0
Entertainment tax	11	0	0	0	0	0	0	0	0	0
Betting, gaming and lottery	50	504	1 052	1 508	1 893	2 225	2 661	2 797	2 802	2 639
Accommodation tax	87	0	0	0	265	1 636	1 900	2 050	2 254	2 598
Telephone call tax	86	0	0	0	2 342	6 405	6 687	6 559	4 810	3 543
Travel tax	86	1 999	1 914	3 512	4 763	8 531	9 344	9 979	12 726	18 659
5127 Other taxes on internat. trade and transactions	0	0	0	0	0	0	0	0	0	0
5128 Other taxes	0	0	0	0	0	0	0	0	0	0
5130 Unallocable between 5110 and 5120	0	0	0	0	0	0	0	0	0	0
5200 Taxes on use of goods and perform activities	64	800	1 111	2 045	2 393	2 763	2 934	3 206	3 505	4 690
5210 Recurrent taxes	64	800	1 111	2 045	2 393	2 763	2 934	3 206	3 505	4 690
5211 Paid by households: motor vehicles	47	751	935	1 775	2 043	2 493	2 666	2 901	3 032	3 768
5212 Paid by others: motor vehicles	0	0	0	0	0	0	0	0	0	0
5213 Paid in respect of other goods	17	49	176	270	350	270	268	305	473	922
5220 Non-recurrent taxes	0	0	0	0	0	0	0	0	0	0
5300 Unallocable between 5100 and 5200	0	0	0	0	0	0	0	0	0	0
6000 Other taxes	**914**	**3 890**	**9 816**	**8 088**	**10 212**	**12 392**	**12 747**	**13 167**	**15 293**	**16 928**
6100 Paid solely by business	0	0	0	0	0	0	0	0	0	0
6200 Other	914	3 890	9 816	8 088	10 212	12 392	12 747	13 167	15 293	16 928
Contractors levy	16	266	475	748	1 198	1 091	909	994	1 245	1 868
Stamp duty (domestic)	898	3 623	9 341	7 339	9 014	11 301	11 838	12 174	14 048	15 060

Note: Data collected by fiscal year (1st April - 31st March) for 1990-2003, then by calendar year (year ending 31st December).
The data are on a cash basis.

Source: Ministry of Finance and Planning.

StatLink https://doi.org/10.1787/888933941650

Table 5.18. **Mexico / México**

Details of tax revenue / Ingresos tributarios detallados

Million MXN

	1990	2000	2005	2010	2012	2013	2014	2015	2016	2017
Total tax revenue	**102 005**	**767 216**	**1 086 482**	**1 716 243**	**2 000 825**	**2 165 501**	**2 394 279**	**2 953 480**	**3 343 314**	**3 326 810**
1000 Taxes on income, profits and capital gains	**34 673**	**276 548**	**402 036**	**683 604**	**803 071**	**957 213**	**979 251**	**1 230 555**	**1 427 114**	**1 571 788**
1100 Of individuals	..	..	195 869	313 473	397 701	425 621	514 208	609 384	681 784	754 109
Tax on income of individuals	..	..	195 869	313 473	397 701	425 621	514 208	609 384	681 784	754 109
1110 On income and profits	..	..	..	..	..	..	..	..	..	..
1120 On capital gains	..	..	..	..	..	..	..	..	..	..
1200 Corporate	..	..	135 840	246 745	288 360	392 199	441 317	592 443	700 925	769 193
Tax on income of corporations	..	..	135 840	246 745	288 360	392 199	441 317	592 443	700 925	769 193
1210 On profits	..	..	..	..	..	..	..	..	..	..
1220 On capital gains	..	..	..	..	..	..	..	..	..	..
1300 Unallocable between 1100 and 1200	34 673	276 548	70 327	123 386	117 010	139 393	23 726	28 728	44 405	48 486
Tax on income of other individuals and corporations	..	244 841	40 780	66 937	74 042	89 028	31 076	36 268	44 225	46 004
Tax on asset	..	13 913	12 033	-624	-1 192	-1 325	-735	-502	-918	-1 069
Credit on salary	..	17 794	17 514	9 708	1 387	1 274	2 423	993	1 144	870
Oil yields tax	..	0	0	2 296	573	3 210	4 669	0	0	0
IETU	..	0	0	45 069	42 199	47 205	-13 707	-11 777	-4 039	-1 648
Imposed by Activity Exploration and extraction of hydrocarbon	..	0	0	0	0	0	0	3 746	3 994	4 330
2000 Social security contributions	**17 165**	**138 223**	**206 551**	**277 459**	**330 327**	**351 993**	**378 373**	**409 249**	**434 998**	**467 710**
2100 Employees	..	..	..	..	..	..	..	..	..	..
2110 On a payroll basis	..	..	..	..	..	..	..	..	..	..
2120 On an income tax basis	..	..	..	..	..	..	..	..	..	..
2200 Employers	..	..	..	..	..	..	..	..	..	..
2210 On a payroll basis	..	..	..	..	..	..	..	..	..	..
2220 On an income tax basis	..	..	..	..	..	..	..	..	..	..
2300 Self-employed or non-employed	..	..	..	..	..	..	..	..	..	..
2310 On a payroll basis	..	..	..	..	..	..	..	..	..	..
2320 On an income tax basis	..	..	..	..	..	..	..	..	..	..
2400 Unallocable between 2100, 2200 and 2300	17 165	138 223	206 551	277 459	330 327	351 993	378 373	409 249	434 998	467 710
2410 On a payroll basis	..	138 223	206 551	277 459	330 327	351 993	378 373	409 249	434 998	467 710
2420 On an income tax basis	..	0	0	0	0	0	0	0	0	0
3000 Taxes on payroll and workforce	**1 797**	**11 217**	**20 461**	**36 911**	**48 033**	**53 042**	**64 713**	**70 221**	**76 762**	**0**
Substitute tax on salary	..	0	0	0	0	0	0	0	0	..
Payroll tax	..	11 101	15 746	27 813	35 480	41 184	64 581	69 866	76 304	..
Tax on remuneration to the personal work	..	65	4 562	8 841	12 333	11 645	0	152	225	..
Tax on professions and fees	..	36	53	71	48	50	51	106	99	..
Tax on operations by contract	..	15	100	186	173	163	81	96	134	..
4000 Taxes on property	**1 914**	**13 964**	**26 796**	**38 955**	**45 186**	**46 238**	**54 978**	**57 673**	**63 273**	**0**
4100 Recurrent taxes on immovable property	1 036	9 948	16 641	25 724	31 544	31 338	37 751	37 961	40 357	..
4110 Households	0	0	0	0	0	0	0	0	0	..
4120 Others	1 036	9 948	16 641	25 724	31 544	31 338	37 751	37 961	40 357	..
Property tax	..	9 948	16 641	25 724	31 544	31 338	37 751	37 961	40 357	..
4200 Recurrent taxes on net wealth	0	0	0	0	0	0	0	0	0	..
4210 Individual	..	..	..	..	..	..	..	..	..	..
4220 Corporate	..	..	..	..	..	..	..	..	..	..
4300 Estate, inheritance and gift taxes	8	0	0	0	0	0	0	0	0	..
4310 Estate and inheritance taxes	8	..	..	..	..	..	..	..	..	..
4320 Gift taxes	0	..	..	..	..	..	..	..	..	..
4400 Taxes on financial and capital transactions	870	4 017	10 155	13 231	13 642	14 900	17 227	19 712	22 917	..
Alienation of immovable property	..	1 763	984	1 122	1 341	1 271	1 308	1 595	1 723	..
Transfer of ownership of real estate	..	2 236	5 528	5 027	4 575	4 518	5 008	6 671	9 593	..
Purchasing property	..	18	3 643	7 082	7 725	9 110	10 911	11 447	11 600	..
4500 Non-recurrent taxes	0	0	0	0	0	0	0	0	0	..
4510 On net wealth	..	..	..	..	..	..	..	..	..	..
4520 Other non-recurrent taxes	..	..	..	..	..	..	..	..	..	..
4600 Other recurrent taxes on property	0	0	0	0	0	0	0	0	0	..
5000 Taxes on goods and services	**44 837**	**319 612**	**418 945**	**651 915**	**737 128**	**715 811**	**880 153**	**1 141 170**	**1 295 653**	**1 254 879**
5100 Taxes on production, sale, transfer, etc	44 171	310 325	403 158	630 123	720 052	696 150	859 302	1 120 610	1 274 738	1 254 253
5110 General taxes	26 635	189 606	318 432	504 509	579 988	556 794	667 085	707 213	791 700	816 048
5111 Value added taxes	26 635	189 606	318 432	504 509	579 988	556 794	667 085	707 213	791 700	816 048
5112 Sales tax	0	0	0	0	0	0	0	0	0	0
5113 Other	0	0	0	0	0	0	0	0	0	0
5120 Taxes on specific goods and services	17 519	120 720	84 726	125 614	140 064	139 356	192 217	413 397	483 038	438 205
5121 Excises	10 072	86 163	55 286	86 098	98 490	104 111	160 754	361 538	420 448	378 537
Special tax on production and services	..	81 544	49 627	81 427	92 620	97 860	154 327	354 294	411 390	367 834
Tax on new automobiles	..	4 619	5 659	4 671	5 870	6 252	6 427	7 244	9 058	10 703
Tax on luxury goods and services	..	0	0	0	0	0	0	0	0	0

Table 5.18. **Mexico / México** *(cont.)*

Details of tax revenue / Ingresos tributarios detallados

Million MXN

	1990	2000	2005	2010	2012	2013	2014	2015	2016	2017
5122 Profits of fiscal monopolies	0	0	0	0	0	0	0	0	0	0
5123 Customs and import duties	6 998	33 285	27 512	26 602	31 161	32 324	36 841	45 366	51 889	53 793
Step customs officer	..	423	692	2 071	3 255	3 065	2 913	1 270	1 336	1 463
Import taxes	..	32 861	26 820	24 531	27 906	29 260	33 928	44 096	50 553	52 330
5124 Taxes on exports	75	4	0	0	1	1	1	1	0	0
Tax on exports	..	4	0	0	1	1	1	1	0	0
5125 Taxes on investment goods	0	0	0	0	0	0	0	0	0	0
5126 Taxes on specific services	132	1 042	1 578	10 958	7 169	-967	-7 417	1 763	5 630	-739
IDE	..	0	0	8 022	2 786	-5 988	-12 322	-3 323	-1 262	-739
Tax on lodging	..	504	798	1 384	1 702	1 890	2 067	2 561	3 009	0
Public entertainment tax	..	240	349	462	625	566	543	689	858	0
Tax on lotteries, raffles and gambling	..	267	417	923	1 329	1 213	1 218	1 416	1 828	0
Tax on commercials	..	4	15	166	16	203	216	210	906	0
Various indirect taxes	..	28	0	1	711	1 149	861	209	291	0
5127 Other taxes on internat. trade and transactions	0	0	0	0	0	0	0	0	0	0
5128 Other taxes	242	226	350	1 956	3 243	3 886	2 040	4 730	5 070	6 613
Mining fees	..	226	350	1 956	3 243	3 886	2 040	4 730	5 070	6 613
5130 Unallocable between 5110 and 5120	17	0	0	0	0	0	0	0	0	0
5200 Taxes on use of goods and perform activities	666	9 287	15 787	21 793	17 076	19 661	20 851	20 560	20 915	626
5210 Recurrent taxes	666	9 287	15 787	21 793	17 076	19 661	20 851	20 560	20 915	626
5211 Paid by households: motor vehicles	567	8 878	15 237	21 319	16 464	19 174	20 370	19 880	20 192	0
Tax on motor vehicules	..	8 878	15 237	21 319	16 464	19 174	20 370	19 880	20 192	..
5212 Paid by others: motor vehicles	0	301	357	281	370	357	367	439	503	554
Tax on federal auto transport	..	301	357	281	370	357	367	439	503	554
5213 Paid in respect of other goods	99	108	193	193	242	130	114	240	220	71
Sport fishing	..	40	80	59	55	50	65	62	68	71
Sport hunting	..	3	0	0	0	0	0	0	0	0
Tax on commercial activities	..	63	113	50	42	26	33	64	46	0
Trade in books and magazines	..	0	0	0	0	3	1	1	1	0
Tax on industrial activities	..	2	0	82	145	49	13	93	78	0
Mining	..	0	0	1	0	1	2	21	28	0
5220 Non-recurrent taxes	0	0	0	0	0	0	0	0	0	0
5300 Unallocable between 5100 and 5200	0	0	0	0	0	0	0	0	0	0
6000 Other taxes	**1 619**	**7 651**	**11 693**	**27 398**	**37 080**	**41 204**	**36 810**	**44 612**	**45 514**	**32 433**
6100 Paid solely by business	0	0	0	0	0	0	0	0	0	0
6200 Other	1 619	7 651	11 693	27 398	37 080	41 204	36 810	44 612	45 514	32 433
Accessories	..	5 504	9 543	22 206	24 077	25 301	23 717	23 211	28 480	32 153
Unallocable between 1000 and 5000 caused in exercices fiscal previous liquidation slopes or of payment	..	374	-927	30	2 260	1 618	504	4 168	329	281
Additional state and local taxes	..	1 773	3 077	5 162	10 743	14 285	12 590	17 232	16 705	0

Note: Year ending 31st December.

The data are on a cash basis.

The 2017 data for tax revenues at the state and local levels of government are not available. They comprise revenues in categories 3000, 4000, 5000 and 6000.

Heading 1000: In ECLAC data, income taxes are presented net of credit on salary figures.

Heading 2000: In ECLAC data, social security contributions are presented net of transfers from the Federal government for the payment of IMSS (Mexican Social Security Institute) pensions.

Some amounts of social security contributions are treated as non-tax revenue to align with the reporting to other international organisations.

Source: Ministry of Finance, Economic Department.

StatLink https://doi.org/10.1787/888933941669

Table 5.19. **Nicaragua**

Details of tax revenue / Ingresos tributarios detallados

Million NIO

	1990	2000	2005	2010	2012	2013	2014	2015	2016	2017
Total tax revenue	..	**8 418**	**18 353**	**36 162**	**51 626**	**57 654**	**67 119**	**77 567**	**88 482**	**98 803**
1000 Taxes on income, profits and capital gains	..	**1 144**	**3 902**	**8 351**	**13 107**	**14 832**	**18 033**	**21 313**	**24 910**	**28 557**
1100 Of individuals	..	..	..	..	..	..	..	..	..	..
1110 On income and profits	..	..	..	..	..	..	..	..	..	..
1120 On capital gains	..	..	..	..	..	..	..	..	..	..
1200 Corporate	..	..	..	..	..	..	..	..	..	..
1210 On profits	..	..	..	..	..	..	..	..	..	..
1220 On capital gains	..	..	..	..	..	..	..	..	..	..
1300 Unallocable between 1100 and 1200	..	1 144	3 902	8 351	13 107	14 832	18 033	21 313	24 910	28 557
Income tax	..	1 144	3 902	8 351	13 107	14 832	18 033	21 313	24 910	28 557
2000 Social security contributions	..	**1 678**	**3 363**	**8 090**	**11 007**	**12 805**	**15 161**	**18 194**	**21 296**	**23 868**
2100 Employees	..	..	..	..	..	..	..	..	..	..
2110 On a payroll basis	..	..	..	..	..	..	..	..	..	..
2120 On an income tax basis	..	..	..	..	..	..	..	..	..	..
2200 Employers	..	..	..	..	..	..	..	..	..	..
2210 On a payroll basis	..	..	..	..	..	..	..	..	..	..
2220 On an income tax basis	..	..	..	..	..	..	..	..	..	..
2300 Self-employed or non-employed	..	..	..	..	..	..	..	..	..	..
2310 On a payroll basis	..	..	..	..	..	..	..	..	..	..
2320 On an income tax basis	..	..	..	..	..	..	..	..	..	..
2400 Unallocable between 2100, 2200 and 2300	..	1 678	3 363	8 090	11 007	12 805	15 161	18 194	21 296	23 868
2410 On a payroll basis	..	1 678	3 363	8 090	11 007	12 805	15 161	18 194	21 296	23 868
2420 On an income tax basis	..	0	0	0	0	0	0	0	0	0
3000 Taxes on payroll and workforce	..	**0**	**0**	**0**	**0**	**0**	**0**	**0**	**0**	**0**
4000 Taxes on property	..	**0**	**211**	**403**	**497**	**577**	**627**	**682**	**744**	**808**
4100 Recurrent taxes on immovable property	..	..	211	403	497	577	627	682	744	808
4110 Households	..	..	..	..	..	..	..	..	..	..
4120 Others	..	..	..	..	..	..	..	..	..	..
4200 Recurrent taxes on net wealth	..	..	0	0	0	0	0	0	0	0
4210 Individual	..	..	..	..	..	..	..	..	..	..
4220 Corporate	..	..	..	..	..	..	..	..	..	..
4300 Estate, inheritance and gift taxes	..	..	0	0	0	0	0	0	0	0
4310 Estate and inheritance taxes	..	..	..	..	..	..	..	..	..	..
4320 Gift taxes	..	..	..	..	..	..	..	..	..	..
4400 Taxes on financial and capital transactions	..	..	0	0	0	0	0	0	0	0
4500 Non-recurrent taxes	..	..	0	0	0	0	0	0	0	0
4510 On net wealth	..	..	..	..	..	..	..	..	..	..
4520 Other non-recurrent taxes	..	..	..	..	..	..	..	..	..	..
4600 Other recurrent taxes on property	..	..	0	0	0	0	0	0	0	0
5000 Taxes on goods and services	..	**5 584**	**10 649**	**18 951**	**26 578**	**28 937**	**32 597**	**36 599**	**40 697**	**44 563**
5100 Taxes on production, sale, transfer, etc	..	5 584	10 485	18 608	26 093	28 367	31 923	35 798	39 855	43 619
5110 General taxes	..	2 931	6 359	11 932	17 490	19 332	22 265	23 787	26 273	29 201
5111 Value added taxes	..	2 931	5 599	10 353	15 151	16 736	19 385	20 714	22 822	25 551
5112 Sales tax	..	0	0	0	0	0	0	0	0	0
5113 Other	..	0	761	1 579	2 339	2 596	2 880	3 073	3 452	3 650
5120 Taxes on specific goods and services	..	2 653	4 126	6 676	8 603	9 035	9 659	12 011	13 581	14 419
5121 Excises	..	2 034	3 227	5 541	6 884	7 254	7 755	9 773	10 950	11 764
Liquor	..	84	102	198	214	253	230	264	305	355
Beer	..	203	340	645	915	1 047	1 184	1 370	1 476	1 649
Cigarettes	..	70	143	45	0	174	0	0	0	0
Soft drinks	..	123	128	248	351	389	423	501	525	545
Petroleum products	..	1 359	1 756	2 699	3 045	3 418	3 938	4 396	5 021	5 534
Excise taxes on imports	..	196	734	1 559	2 233	1 924	1 902	3 105	3 505	3 541
Other specific excises on consumption	..	-1	25	148	126	49	78	136	117	140
5122 Profits of fiscal monopolies	..	0	0	0	0	0	0	0	0	0
5123 Customs and import duties	..	619	899	1 135	1 719	1 782	1 904	2 238	2 631	2 654
Custom duties	..	452	880	1 094	1 661	1 717	1 828	2 155	2 509	2 623
Temporary protection duty	..	96	0	0	0	0	0	0	0	0
On products originating in Colombia or Honduras	..	72	18	41	58	64	76	83	123	31
5124 Taxes on exports	..	0	0	0	0	0	0	0	0	0
5125 Taxes on investment goods	..	0	0	0	0	0	0	0	0	0
5126 Taxes on specific services	..	0	0	0	0	0	0	0	0	0
5127 Other taxes on internat. trade and transactions	..	0	0	0	0	0	0	0	0	0
5128 Other taxes	..	0	0	0	0	0	0	0	0	0
5130 Unallocable between 5110 and 5120	..	0	0	0	0	0	0	0	0	0
5200 Taxes on use of goods and perform activities	..	0	163	343	485	569	674	801	842	943
5210 Recurrent taxes	..	..	18	20	21	31	41	60	59	59

Table 5.19. **Nicaragua** *(cont.)*

Details of tax revenue / Ingresos tributarios detallados

Million NIO

	1990	2000	2005	2010	2012	2013	2014	2015	2016	2017
5211 Paid by households: motor vehicles	..	..	18	20	21	31	41	60	59	59
5212 Paid by others: motor vehicles	..	..	0	0	0	0	0	0	0	0
5213 Paid in respect of other goods	..	..	0	0	0	0	0	0	0	0
5220 Non-recurrent taxes	..	..	145	323	464	539	633	741	783	884
5300 Unallocable between 5100 and 5200	..	0	0	0	0	0	0	0	0	0
6000 Other taxes	**..**	**11**	**228**	**367**	**437**	**503**	**700**	**780**	**835**	**1 007**
6100 Paid solely by business	..	0	0	0	0	0	0	0	0	0
6200 Other	..	11	228	367	437	503	700	780	835	1 007
Stamp tax	..	11	17	20	24	77	87	90	90	88
Municipal tax	..	0	212	347	413	426	614	690	745	919

Note: Year ending 31st December.

The data are on a cash basis.

Comparable statistics for 1990 cannot be shown due to the devaluation of the Nicaraguan cordoba.

The data have been revised since 1990 and the classification of some taxes has been improved. This affects headings 1300, 4400, 5111, 5123, 5213, 5220 and 6200.

Data for the years 2004-09 is now reported for headings 5113, 5211, 5213 and 6200.

Source: Banco Central de Nicaragua y Ministerio de Hacienda y Crédito Público (Central Bank of Nicaragua and Ministry of Finance and Public Credit).

StatLink https://doi.org/10.1787/888933941688

Table 5.20. **Panama / Panamá**

Details of tax revenue / Ingresos tributarios detallados

Million PAB

	1990	2000	2005	2010	2012	2013	2014	2015	2016	2017
Total tax revenue	**893**	**1 953**	**2 257**	**4 815**	**6 721**	**7 650**	**7 740**	**8 268**	**8 835**	**9 089**
1000 Taxes on income, profits and capital gains	**217**	**485**	**563**	**1 317**	**1 985**	**2 200**	**1 998**	**2 154**	**2 400**	**2 445**
1100 Of individuals	140	295	303	440	554	679	722	799	870	1 062
1110 On income and profits	140	295	303	440	554	679	722	799	870	1 062
Payroll	115	222	227	353	456	568	602	689	733	920
Personal income tax	14	20	24	35	38	52	58	45	54	54
Panama Canal Authority withholding	10	53	52	52	60	59	62	65	83	89
1120 On capital gains	..	..	..	..	..	..	..	..	..	..
1200 Corporate	66	159	213	603	1 068	970	896	938	1 036	952
1210 On profits	66	159	213	603	1 068	970	896	938	1 036	952
Colón Free Zone	5	3	4	20	51	39	43	36	36	41
Corporate income tax	61	155	208	584	1 017	931	853	902	1 000	911
1220 On capital gains	..	..	..	..	..	..	..	..	..	..
1300 Unallocable between 1100 and 1200	11	31	47	273	364	550	380	417	494	431
Dividends and complimentary tax	11	31	47	166	240	251	243	266	282	264
Capital gains	0	0	0	107	124	299	137	151	212	166
2000 Social security contributions	**271**	**742**	**827**	**1 637**	**2 186**	**2 677**	**2 794**	**3 049**	**3 380**	**3 560**
2100 Employees	..	..	..	..	..	..	..	..	..	..
2110 On a payroll basis	..	..	..	..	..	..	..	..	..	..
2120 On an income tax basis	..	..	..	..	..	..	..	..	..	..
2200 Employers	..	..	..	..	..	..	..	..	..	..
2210 On a payroll basis	..	..	..	..	..	..	..	..	..	..
2220 On an income tax basis	..	..	..	..	..	..	..	..	..	..
2300 Self-employed or non-employed	..	..	..	..	..	..	..	..	..	..
2310 On a payroll basis	..	..	..	..	..	..	..	..	..	..
2320 On an income tax basis	..	..	..	..	..	..	..	..	..	..
2400 Unallocable between 2100, 2200 and 2300	271	742	827	1 637	2 186	2 677	2 794	3 049	3 380	3 560
2410 On a payroll basis	..	..	..	..	..	..	..	..	..	..
2420 On an income tax basis	..	..	..	..	..	..	..	..	..	..
3000 Taxes on payroll and workforce	**0**	**36**	**36**	**59**	**70**	**82**	**134**	**111**	**111**	**129**
Education insurance	..	36	36	59	70	82	134	111	111	129
4000 Taxes on property	**43**	**62**	**109**	**212**	**261**	**338**	**337**	**319**	**209**	**252**
4100 Recurrent taxes on immovable property	28	34	57	108	120	181	176	151	168	208
4110 Households	28	34	56	108	120	181	176	151	168	208
4120 Others	0	0	0	0	0	0	0	0	0	0
4200 Recurrent taxes on net wealth	0	0	0	0	0	0	0	0	0	0
4210 Individual	..	..	..	..	..	..	..	..	..	..
4220 Corporate	..	..	..	..	..	..	..	..	..	..
4300 Estate, inheritance and gift taxes	0	0	0	0	0	0	0	0	0	0
4310 Estate and inheritance taxes	..	..	..	..	..	..	..	..	..	..
4320 Gift taxes	..	..	..	..	..	..	..	..	..	..
4400 Taxes on financial and capital transactions	3	9	21	30	41	49	45	48	41	44
4500 Non-recurrent taxes	0	0	0	0	0	0	0	0	0	0
4510 On net wealth	..	..	..	..	..	..	..	..	..	..
4520 Other non-recurrent taxes	..	..	..	..	..	..	..	..	..	..
4600 Other recurrent taxes on property	12	19	32	75	100	108	116	120	0	0
Commercial licences	12	19	32	75	100	108	116	120	0	0
5000 Taxes on goods and services	**335**	**573**	**692**	**1 513**	**2 124**	**2 253**	**2 384**	**2 539**	**2 636**	**2 605**
5100 Taxes on production, sale, transfer, etc	332	530	642	1 473	2 067	2 193	2 319	2 467	2 555	2 524
5110 General taxes	80	69	138	766	1 184	1 269	1 351	1 359	1 510	1 463
5111 Value added taxes	80	69	138	766	1 184	1 269	1 351	1 359	1 510	1 463
5112 Sales tax	0	0	0	0	0	0	0	0	0	0
5113 Other	0	0	0	0	0	0	0	0	0	0
5120 Taxes on specific goods and services	139	461	504	706	883	924	967	1 107	1 045	1 061
5121 Excises	0	141	106	239	356	397	452	581	519	507
Gasoline products	..	109	69	97	101	117	133	242	214	190
Beer	..	18	22	31	35	36	42	48	49	54
Wine and liquor	..	12	11	11	10	16	23	15	10	13
Soft drinks	..	2	3	6	7	7	7	7	6	11
Various products	..	0	1	95	45	53	48	53	46	31
Automobiles	..	0	0	0	133	141	176	182	172	185
Other	..	0	0	0	25	27	24	32	23	24
5122 Profits of fiscal monopolies	0	0	0	0	0	0	0	0	0	0
5123 Customs and import duties	125	298	364	390	420	409	381	391	355	350
5124 Taxes on exports	13	0	0	0	0	0	0	0	0	0
5125 Taxes on investment goods	0	0	0	0	0	0	0	0	0	0

Table 5.20. **Panama / Panamá** *(cont.)*

Details of tax revenue / Ingresos tributarios detallados

Million PAB

	1990	2000	2005	2010	2012	2013	2014	2015	2016	2017
5126 Taxes on specific services	0	17	27	65	86	96	109	111	146	180
Insurance premiums	..	17	19	47	54	60	63	48	52	86
Cable and telecommunications	..	0	6	17	31	34	45	39	41	41
Gambling	..	0	1	1	1	2	2	23	53	52
5127 Other taxes on internat. trade and transactions	1	5	7	12	21	22	25	25	25	25
Banks, financial institutions, and currency exchange	0	2	7	12	21	22	25	25	25	25
Other	1	3	0	0	0	0	0	0	0	0
5128 Other taxes	0	0	0	0	0	0	0	0	0	0
5130 Unallocable between 5110 and 5120	113	0	0	0	0	0	0	0	0	0
5200 Taxes on use of goods and perform activities	4	43	51	41	57	60	66	72	81	81
5210 Recurrent taxes	0	39	43	41	57	60	66	72	81	81
5211 Paid by households: motor vehicles	..	7	8	0	0	0	0	0	0	0
5212 Paid by others: motor vehicles	..	5	4	0	0	0	0	0	0	0
5213 Paid in respect of other goods	..	27	30	41	57	60	66	72	81	81
On commercial activities	..	25	29	38	54	57	62	69	77	77
On industrial activities	..	2	2	2	3	3	3	3	4	4
5220 Non-recurrent taxes	4	4	7	0	0	0	0	0	0	0
Building and construction	0	4	7	..	..	..	..	..	..	..
Ship registration	4	0	0	..	..	..	..	..	..	..
5300 Unallocable between 5100 and 5200	0	0	0	0	0	0	0	0	0	0
6000 Other taxes	**26**	**54**	**29**	**77**	**94**	**101**	**93**	**96**	**99**	**99**
6100 Paid solely by business	0	11	0	0	0	0	0	0	0	0
6200 Other	26	43	29	77	94	101	93	96	99	99
Legal services	17	42	28	41	45	46	41	37	35	34
Others	9	1	1	36	49	55	52	59	65	65

Note: Year ending 31st December.
The data are on a cash basis.
Heading 3000: In ECLAC data, education insurance is classified as "Other taxes" (6000).
Heading 5127: In CIAT and ECLAC data, the tax on banks, financial institutions and currency exchange is classified as a property tax (4000).

Source: Contraloría General de la República y Ministerio de Economía y Finanzas (General Comptroller of the Republic of Panama and Ministry of Economics and Finance).

StatLink https://doi.org/10.1787/888933941707

Table 5.21. **Paraguay**

Details of tax revenue / Ingresos tributarios detallados

Million PYG

	1990	2000	2005	2010	2012	2013	2014	2015	2016	2017
Total tax revenue	**348 889**	**3 587 451**	**7 434 024**	**15 496 703**	**19 261 968**	**20 540 432**	**24 324 802**	**25 677 685**	**27 272 588**	**30 511 636**
1000 Taxes on income, profits and capital gains	**73 726**	**470 388**	**938 886**	**2 096 498**	**2 902 725**	**3 100 223**	**3 678 392**	**3 922 384**	**4 429 169**	**5 086 803**
1100 Of individuals	..	41 021	82 086	184 361	254 965	283 915	398 570	409 238	396 573	526 704
1110 On income and profits	..	41 021	82 086	184 361	254 965	283 915	398 570	409 238	396 573	526 704
IRACIS - IRAGRO	..	41 021	82 086	183 211	254 458	270 540	314 649	283 401	256 019	326 555
Personal income tax	..	0	0	1 150	507	13 375	83 921	125 837	140 554	200 150
1120 On capital gains	..	0	0	0	0	0	0	0	0	0
1200 Corporate	..	429 367	856 800	1 912 137	2 647 760	2 816 308	3 279 822	3 513 146	4 032 596	4 560 099
1210 On profits	..	429 367	856 800	1 912 137	2 647 760	2 816 308	3 279 822	3 513 146	4 032 596	4 560 099
Income tax on small businesses	..	0	0	9 380	5 764	7 831	9 063	14 563	18 567	22 848
Single tax	..	4 238	5 802	715	317	32	72	5	3	2
Single tax on maquiladoras	..	0	289	3 310	4 570	4 669	9 783	10 892	12 087	20 194
IRACIS - IRAGRO	..	425 129	850 709	1 898 732	2 637 109	2 803 776	3 260 905	3 487 686	4 001 939	4 517 056
1220 On capital gains	..	0	0	0	0	0	0	0	0	0
1300 Unallocable between 1100 and 1200	73 726	0	0	0	0	0	0	0	0	0
Others	73 726	..	..	..	..	..	..	..	..	..
2000 Social security contributions	**28 882**	**919 533**	**1 591 980**	**3 552 640**	**4 844 110**	**5 158 072**	**6 336 260**	**7 044 316**	**7 048 846**	**8 052 403**
2100 Employees	..	..	..	..	..	..	..	..	..	..
2110 On a payroll basis	..	..	..	..	..	..	..	..	..	..
2120 On an income tax basis	..	..	..	..	..	..	..	..	..	..
2200 Employers	..	..	..	..	..	..	..	..	..	..
2210 On a payroll basis	..	..	..	..	..	..	..	..	..	..
2220 On an income tax basis	..	..	..	..	..	..	..	..	..	..
2300 Self-employed or non-employed	..	..	..	..	..	..	..	..	..	..
2310 On a payroll basis	..	..	..	..	..	..	..	..	..	..
2320 On an income tax basis	..	..	..	..	..	..	..	..	..	..
2400 Unallocable between 2100, 2200 and 2300	28 882	919 533	1 591 980	3 552 640	4 844 110	5 158 072	6 336 260	7 044 316	7 048 846	8 052 403
2410 On a payroll basis	28 882	919 533	1 591 980	3 552 640	4 844 110	5 158 072	6 336 260	7 044 316	7 048 846	8 052 403
2420 On an income tax basis	0	0	0	0	0	0	0	0	0	0
3000 Taxes on payroll and workforce	**0**	**0**	**0**	**0**	**0**	**0**	**0**	**0**	**0**	**0**
4000 Taxes on property	**17 162**	**0**	**0**	**272 385**	**310 254**	**350 169**	**390 102**	**429 669**	**566 117**	**559 504**
4100 Recurrent taxes on immovable property	17 162	..	..	254 306	289 510	..	..	398 251	529 479	519 325
4110 Households	17 162	..	..	254 306	289 510	..	..	398 251	529 479	519 325
Real estate tax	0	..	..	249 697	285 051	..	..	390 772	514 404	501 873
Tax on vacant lots	0	..	..	2 925	3 472	..	..	4 818	10 284	13 600
Other	17 162	..	..	1 684	987	..	..	2 661	4 792	3 852
4120 Others	0	..	..	0	0	..	..	0	0	0
4200 Recurrent taxes on net wealth	0	..	..	0	0	..	..	0	0	0
4210 Individual	..	..	..	..	..	..	..	..	..	..
4220 Corporate	..	..	..	..	..	..	..	..	..	..
4300 Estate, inheritance and gift taxes	0	..	..	0	0	..	..	0	0	0
4310 Estate and inheritance taxes	..	..	..	..	..	..	..	..	..	..
4320 Gift taxes	..	..	..	..	..	..	..	..	..	..
4400 Taxes on financial and capital transactions	0	..	..	16 316	20 061	..	..	30 987	35 259	38 417
Real estate transfer tax	..	..	..	11 766	14 704	..	..	22 406	22 978	26 263
Other	..	..	..	4 551	5 357	..	..	8 581	12 281	12 154
4500 Non-recurrent taxes	0	..	..	0	0	..	..	0	0	0
4510 On net wealth	..	..	..	..	..	..	..	..	..	..
4520 Other non-recurrent taxes	..	..	..	..	..	..	..	..	..	..
4600 Other recurrent taxes on property	0	..	..	1 762	682	..	..	431	1 378	1 762
5000 Taxes on goods and services	**179 312**	**2 080 878**	**4 309 832**	**9 460 962**	**11 081 105**	**11 808 364**	**13 919 885**	**14 272 960**	**15 220 270**	**16 804 558**
5100 Taxes on production, sale, transfer, etc	179 312	2 080 878	4 309 832	9 249 698	10 849 519	11 524 610	13 583 267	13 860 639	14 747 909	16 353 820
5110 General taxes	0	1 150 496	2 478 998	5 991 694	7 126 623	7 843 002	9 363 648	9 768 800	10 482 238	11 221 710
5111 Value added taxes	0	1 150 496	2 478 998	5 991 694	7 126 623	7 843 002	9 363 648	9 768 800	10 482 238	11 221 710
5112 Sales tax	0	0	0	0	0	0	0	0	0	0
5113 Other	0	0	0	0	0	0	0	0	0	0
5120 Taxes on specific goods and services	179 312	930 382	1 830 834	3 258 004	3 722 896	3 681 608	4 219 619	4 091 839	4 265 671	5 132 111
5121 Excises	41 087	456 561	949 962	1 710 531	2 063 020	2 048 143	2 442 895	2 404 029	2 588 912	2 889 747
Fuels	41 087	316 694	688 773	1 126 143	1 455 820	1 427 769	1 787 112	1 775 286	1 830 586	2 031 968
Other excises	0	136 194	249 239	537 887	607 200	620 374	655 783	616 342	745 189	843 123
Animal health and quality service	0	3 673	11 950	46 501	0	..	0	12 401	13 137	14 656
Livestock trade	0	0	0	0	0	0	0	0	0	0
5122 Profits of fiscal monopolies	0	0	0	0	0	0	0	0	0	0
5123 Customs and import duties	138 225	473 821	880 872	1 524 252	1 637 588	1 633 378	1 776 724	1 659 535	1 642 818	2 206 934
5124 Taxes on exports	0	0	0	0	0	0	0	0	0	0
5125 Taxes on investment goods	0	0	0	0	0	0	0	0	0	0

Table 5.21. **Paraguay** *(cont.)*

Details of tax revenue / Ingresos tributarios detallados

Million PYG

	1990	2000	2005	2010	2012	2013	2014	2015	2016	2017
5126 Taxes on specific services	0	0	0	23 221	22 288	87	0	28 274	33 942	35 430
Advertising	..	..	..	5 249	6 560	29	..	7 428	8 424	9 489
Public transport	..	..	..	4 363	4 121	1	..	4 297	4 316	4 080
Gambling	..	..	..	0	0	0	..	804	846	1 160
Other	..	0	..	13 609	11 607	57	..	15 746	20 356	20 700
5127 Other taxes on internat. trade and transactions	0	0	0	0	0	0	0	0	0	0
5128 Other taxes	0	0	0	0	0	0	0	0	0	0
5130 Unallocable between 5110 and 5120	0	0	0	0	0	0	0	0	0	0
5200 Taxes on use of goods and perform activities	0	0	0	211 027	230 890	283 754	336 618	389 482	444 952	419 704
5210 Recurrent taxes	..	..	..	211 027	230 890	283 754	336 618	389 482	444 952	419 704
5211 Paid by households: motor vehicles	..	..	..	0	0	..	..	0	0	0
5212 Paid by others: motor vehicles	..	..	..	52 365	67 399	..	..	94 393	106 200	109 084
Motor vehicle licences	..	..	..	52 365	67 399	..	..	94 393	106 200	109 084
5213 Paid in respect of other goods	..	..	..	158 662	163 491	..	..	295 090	338 752	310 620
Tax on construction	..	..	..	31 696	50 337	..	..	65 403	64 284	60 092
Licencing fees	..	..	..	126 965	113 153	..	..	229 686	274 468	250 528
5220 Non-recurrent taxes	..	..	..	0	0	0	0	0	0	0
5300 Unallocable between 5100 and 5200	0	0	0	237	696	0	0	22 838	27 409	31 034
6000 Other taxes	**49 807**	**116 652**	**593 326**	**114 219**	**123 774**	**123 603**	**163**	**8 357**	**8 186**	**8 369**
6100 Paid solely by business	0	0	0	0	0	0	0	0	0	0
6200 Other	49 807	116 652	593 326	114 219	123 774	123 603	163	8 357	8 186	8 369
Registration and stamp duties	0	71 777	192 393	332	168	179	106	91	82	143
Luxury automobile tax	0	0	3 897	91	153	218	57	54	152	7
Other	49 807	44 875	397 036	113 796	123 453	123 206	0	8 211	7 952	8 219

Note: Year ending 31st December.

The data are on a cash basis.

The figures for years up to and including 2004, as well as for 2013 and 2014, exclude local government tax revenues as the data are not available. This affects data in categories 4000, 5000 and 6000.

Heading 2000: Data on social security contributions collected by decentralised institutions are not available for 2011 to 2014, with the exception of the contributions made to the Instituto de Previsión Social (Social Security Institute).

Heading 1110: The proportion of data included in this category has been estimated from 1999 to 2014 based on the disaggregation provided in 2015.

Heading 1210: The proportion of data included in this category has been estimated from 1999 to 2014 based on the disaggregation provided in 2015.

Heading 5121: Data for animal health and quality service are not available from 2011.

Source: Subsecretaría de Estado de Tributación, Ministerio de Hacienda del Paraguay (Tax Undersecretary, Ministry of Finance of Paraguay).

StatLink https://doi.org/10.1787/888933941726

Table 5.22. **Peru / Perú**

Details of tax revenue / Ingresos tributarios detallados

Million PEN

	1990	2000	2005	2010	2012	2013	2014	2015	2016	2017
Total tax revenue	**645**	**26 413**	**40 181**	**73 723**	**95 544**	**102 126**	**108 971**	**105 192**	**105 133**	**107 005**
1000 Taxes on income, profits and capital gains	**37**	**5 078**	**11 950**	**27 317**	**39 720**	**39 357**	**43 577**	**37 772**	**40 360**	**39 846**
1100 Of individuals	3	2 117	3 327	6 518	9 462	10 570	11 423	11 137	11 760	13 008
First category	..	167	181	160	253	310	374	443	504	532
Second category	..	7	250	869	1 136	1 275	1 214	1 287	1 536	1 581
Fourth category	..	234	395	521	637	744	834	783	871	894
Fifth category	..	1 641	2 369	4 735	7 054	7 820	8 473	8 044	8 248	8 444
Tax debt payments	..	68	130	233	382	421	529	581	601	1 558
1110 On income and profits	..	..	..	..	..	..	..	..	..	..
1120 On capital gains	..	..	..	..	..	..	..	..	..	..
1200 Corporate	32	2 526	8 391	19 561	28 453	26 207	26 593	24 266	24 786	24 604
1210 On profits	32	2 526	8 391	19 561	28 453	26 207	26 593	24 266	24 786	24 604
Third category	..	2 023	5 316	14 652	20 744	19 633	18 536	16 817	16 496	15 499
Income tax on mining	..	0	0	0	442	337	372	208	236	638
Income tax special regime	..	47	55	118	202	246	275	310	335	323
Other incomes corporate	..	18	41	148	229	187	193	167	215	233
Tax debt payments	..	438	1 908	2 856	4 397	3 029	3 703	3 066	3 204	3 327
Temporary tax on net assets	..	0	1 073	1 788	2 439	2 776	3 513	3 697	4 300	4 585
1220 On capital gains	..	..	..	..	..	..	..	..	..	..
1300 Unallocable between 1100 and 1200	1	436	232	1 239	1 804	2 579	5 561	2 369	3 814	2 233
Income tax on non-residents	1	487	542	1 511	2 244	2 848	6 027	3 248	5 205	3 462
Income tax refunds	0	-51	-310	-272	-439	-269	-466	-879	-1 391	-1 228
2000 Social security contributions	**50**	**3 175**	**4 012**	**7 929**	**10 142**	**11 260**	**11 847**	**12 680**	**13 186**	**13 676**
2100 Employees	..	566	703	2 468	2 944	3 211	3 212	3 509	3 647	3 797
2110 On a payroll basis	..	566	680	1 700	2 454	2 854	3 100	3 371	3 550	3 662
2120 On an income tax basis	..	0	23	768	491	357	112	137	97	135
Solidarity contribution for pension plan	..	..	23	768	491	357	112	137	97	135
2200 Employers	..	2 515	3 285	5 454	7 194	8 044	8 631	9 170	9 536	9 878
2210 On a payroll basis	..	2 432	3 140	5 216	6 979	7 827	8 413	8 926	9 282	9 591
2220 On an income tax basis	..	83	144	238	214	217	218	244	255	287
2300 Self-employed or non-employed	..	95	25	7	4	4	4	2	3	2
2310 On a payroll basis	..	0	0	0	0	0	0	0	0	0
2320 On an income tax basis	..	95	25	7	4	4	4	2	3	2
2400 Unallocable between 2100, 2200 and 2300	50	0	0	0	0	0	0	0	0	0
2410 On a payroll basis	50	..	..	..	..	..	..	..	..	..
2420 On an income tax basis	0	..	..	..	..	..	..	..	..	..
3000 Taxes on payroll and workforce	**0**	**1 149**	**7**	**1**	**2**	**0**	**-82**	**4**	**1**	**-2**
4000 Taxes on property	**99**	**323**	**1 342**	**2 231**	**1 898**	**2 131**	**2 154**	**2 429**	**2 637**	**2 573**
4100 Recurrent taxes on immovable property	0	298	461	727	959	1 127	1 230	1 463	1 629	1 718
4110 Households	..	..	..	..	..	..	..	..	..	..
4120 Others	..	..	..	..	..	..	..	..	..	..
4200 Recurrent taxes on net wealth	61	0	0	0	0	0	0	0	0	0
4210 Individual	60	0	0	..	..	..	..	..	..	..
4220 Corporate	1	0	0	..	..	..	..	..	..	..
Revaluation of fixed assets	1	..	..	..	..	..	..	..	..	..
4300 Estate, inheritance and gift taxes	0	0	0	0	0	0	0	0	0	0
4310 Estate and inheritance taxes	..	..	..	..	..	..	..	..	..	..
4320 Gift taxes	..	..	..	..	..	..	..	..	..	..
4400 Taxes on financial and capital transactions	38	25	804	1 504	939	1 005	925	966	1 008	855
Financial transactions tax	0	0	706	944	126	134	153	161	168	175
Real estate transfer tax	0	25	98	560	813	870	772	805	840	680
Tax Law Decree 519	38	0	0	0	0	0	0	0	0	0
4500 Non-recurrent taxes	0	0	0	0	0	0	0	0	0	0
4510 On net wealth	..	..	..	..	..	..	..	..	..	..
4520 Other non-recurrent taxes	..	..	..	..	..	..	..	..	..	..
4600 Other recurrent taxes on property	0	0	76	0	0	0	0	0	0	0
5000 Taxes on goods and services	**423**	**16 011**	**22 721**	**36 353**	**42 511**	**46 264**	**49 933**	**51 102**	**48 247**	**50 061**
5100 Taxes on production, sale, transfer, etc	423	15 987	22 666	36 199	42 315	46 030	49 668	50 820	47 943	49 774
5110 General taxes	78	9 694	15 109	29 094	35 078	37 953	41 779	42 612	39 462	41 036
5111 Value added taxes	78	9 646	15 109	29 094	35 078	37 953	41 779	42 612	39 462	41 036
5112 Sales tax	0	0	0	0	0	0	0	0	0	0
5113 Other	0	47	0	0	0	0	0	0	0	0
5120 Taxes on specific goods and services	345	6 293	7 557	7 105	7 237	8 077	7 889	8 208	8 482	8 737
5121 Excises	232	3 518	4 193	4 875	5 212	5 787	5 488	5 796	6 175	6 588
Fuels	151	2 145	2 607	2 410	2 149	2 502	2 041	2 211	2 423	2 604
Gasoline sales tax	3	97	140	210	325	335	380	332	312	363
Other	78	1 304	1 459	2 258	2 769	2 978	3 094	3 284	3 479	3 711
Refunds on excise taxes	0	-28	-12	-4	-31	-28	-27	-31	-39	-91

Table 5.22. **Peru / Perú** *(cont.)*

Details of tax revenue / Ingresos tributarios detallados

Million PEN

	1990	2000	2005	2010	2012	2013	2014	2015	2016	2017
5122 Profits of fiscal monopolies	0	0	0	0	0	0	0	0	0	0
5123 Customs and import duties	64	2 741	3 143	1 803	1 529	1 706	1 790	1 775	1 606	1 448
5124 Taxes on exports	2	0	0	0	0	0	0	0	0	0
5125 Taxes on investment goods	0	0	0	0	0	0	0	0	0	0
5126 Taxes on specific services	0	34	220	427	496	585	612	637	701	702
Casinos and slot machines	..	0	49	187	219	269	279	279	298	297
Tourism tax	..	0	121	105	115	118	127	144	173	174
Municipal taxes on services	..	34	50	135	163	198	206	214	230	230
5127 Other taxes on internat. trade and transactions	48	0	0	0	0	0	0	0	0	0
5128 Other taxes	0	0	0	0	0	0	0	0	0	0
5130 Unallocable between 5110 and 5120	0	0	0	0	0	0	0	0	0	0
5200 Taxes on use of goods and perform activities	0	25	55	154	196	233	264	282	303	288
5210 Recurrent taxes	..	25	55	154	196	233	264	282	303	288
5211 Paid by households: motor vehicles	..	..	..	..	..	..	..	..	..	..
5212 Paid by others: motor vehicles	..	..	..	..	..	..	..	..	..	..
5213 Paid in respect of other goods	..	..	..	..	..	..	..	..	..	..
5220 Non-recurrent taxes	..	0	0	0	0	0	0	0	0	0
5300 Unallocable between 5100 and 5200	0	0	0	0	0	0	0	0	0	0
6000 Other taxes	**36**	**676**	**149**	**-110**	**1 272**	**3 114**	**1 542**	**1 204**	**702**	**851**
6100 Paid solely by business	0	84	73	108	133	147	158	179	185	140
Single simplified regime	..	84	73	108	133	147	158	179	185	140
University Development Fund	..	0	0	0	0	0	0	0	0	0
6200 Other	36	592	76	-218	1 139	2 967	1 384	1 025	517	711
Tax debt payments	9	543	397	714	857	893	814	922	1 068	1 109
Municipal fees	0	0	0	0	0	0	0	0	0	0
Other national level	28	20	178	254	1 372	3 133	2 034	1 771	1 091	1 771
Other local level	0	48	87	26	31	26	26	19	24	27
Other tax refund	0	-20	-587	-1 212	-1 120	-1 085	-1 490	-1 686	-1 665	-2 196

Note: Year ending 31st December.

The data are on a cash basis.

The figures for years up to 2000 exclude local government tax revenues as the data are not available. The local government tax revenue data from 2000 have been revised and their classification has been improved. See Table 6.22 for more details.

The figures for tax refunds are based on tables by date of issuance.

Heading 2000: All contributions pertaining to pensions are only made by employees and contributions to healthcare are made by employers. The exceptions are special regimes which apply to self-employed and are levied on an income basis.

Heading 5123: These are gross of tax refunds on imports. These could not be distinguished from other tax refunds classified under 6200.

Source: Superintendencia Nacional de Aduanas y de Administración Tributaria y Banco Central de Reserva del Perú (National Superintendency for Customs and Tax Administrations and Central Reserve Bank of Peru).

StatLink https://doi.org/10.1787/888933941745

Table 5.23. **Trinidad and Tobago / Trinidad y Tobago**

Details of tax revenue / Ingresos tributarios detallados

Million TTD

	1990	2000	2005	2010	2012	2013	2014	2015	2016	2017
Total tax revenue	**5 031**	**11 009**	**27 086**	**39 142**	**45 863**	**47 624**	**50 922**	**46 259**	**34 392**	**32 914**
1000 Taxes on income, profits and capital gains	**2 595**	**6 067**	**19 105**	**26 224**	**31 499**	**31 976**	**35 131**	**29 028**	**16 926**	**16 136**
1100 Of individuals	669	2 325	4 452	4 674	5 649	6 458	6 859	7 752	7 458	6 652
1110 On income and profits	669	2 325	4 452	4 674	5 649	6 458	6 859	7 752	7 458	6 652
Health surcharge	92	149	187	185	187	218	210	264	226	202
Insurance surrender tax	6	7	15	22	27	33	29	42	46	47
Individuals (Ch. 75:01)	571	2 169	4 250	4 467	5 435	6 207	6 620	7 445	7 187	6 403
1120 On capital gains	..	..	..	..	..	..	..	..	..	..
1200 Corporate	1 856	3 547	14 118	20 670	24 767	24 633	27 330	20 209	8 478	8 629
1210 On profits	1 856	3 547	14 118	20 670	24 767	24 633	27 330	20 209	8 478	8 629
Oil companies	1 439	2 441	10 806	13 834	15 827	14 772	16 970	10 513	1 036	1 078
Other companies	383	1 041	3 166	6 630	8 647	9 675	10 151	9 481	7 003	6 907
Business levy	0	65	146	206	294	187	210	215	438	644
National recovery impost	34	0	0	0	0	0	0	0	0	0
Unemployment Fund	0	157	905	989	1 259	1 163	1 240	601	131	59
1220 On capital gains	..	..	..	..	..	..	..	..	..	..
1300 Unallocable between 1100 and 1200	70	195	536	881	1 084	885	942	1 067	990	855
2000 Social security contributions	**183**	**702**	**1 173**	**2 645**	**3 086**	**3 514**	**4 137**	**4 261**	**4 252**	**4 608**
2100 Employees	..	..	..	..	..	..	..	..	..	..
2110 On a payroll basis	..	..	..	..	..	..	..	..	..	..
2120 On an income tax basis	..	..	..	..	..	..	..	..	..	..
2200 Employers	..	..	..	..	..	..	..	..	..	..
2210 On a payroll basis	..	..	..	..	..	..	..	..	..	..
2220 On an income tax basis	..	..	..	..	..	..	..	..	..	..
2300 Self-employed or non-employed	..	..	..	..	..	..	..	..	..	..
2310 On a payroll basis	..	..	..	..	..	..	..	..	..	..
2320 On an income tax basis	..	..	..	..	..	..	..	..	..	..
2400 Unallocable between 2100, 2200 and 2300	183	702	1 173	2 645	3 086	3 514	4 137	4 261	4 252	4 608
2410 On a payroll basis	..	..	..	..	..	..	..	..	..	..
2420 On an income tax basis	..	..	..	..	..	..	..	..	..	..
3000 Taxes on payroll and workforce	**0**	**0**	**0**	**0**	**0**	**0**	**0**	**0**	**0**	**0**
4000 Taxes on property	**148**	**277**	**389**	**433**	**472**	**635**	**742**	**303**	**541**	**543**
4100 Recurrent taxes on immovable property	147	277	389	433	472	635	742	303	541	543
Lands and building taxes	39	64	63	22	5	4	3	3	3	3
House rate tax	108	213	326	411	468	631	738	300	538	540
4110 Households	..	..	..	..	..	..	..	..	..	..
4120 Others	..	..	..	..	..	..	..	..	..	..
4200 Recurrent taxes on net wealth	0	0	0	0	0	0	0	0	0	0
4210 Individual	..	..	..	..	..	..	..	..	..	..
4220 Corporate	..	..	..	..	..	..	..	..	..	..
4300 Estate, inheritance and gift taxes	1	0	0	0	0	0	0	0	0	0
4310 Estate and inheritance taxes	1	..	..	..	..	..	..	..	..	..
4320 Gift taxes	0	..	..	..	..	..	..	..	..	..
4400 Taxes on financial and capital transactions	0	0	0	0	0	0	0	0	0	0
4500 Non-recurrent taxes	0	0	0	0	0	0	0	0	0	0
4510 On net wealth	..	..	..	..	..	..	..	..	..	..
4520 Other non-recurrent taxes	..	..	..	..	..	..	..	..	..	..
4600 Other recurrent taxes on property	0	0	0	0	0	0	0	0	0	0
5000 Taxes on goods and services	**2 055**	**3 852**	**6 175**	**9 667**	**10 591**	**11 253**	**10 627**	**12 264**	**12 344**	**11 312**
5100 Taxes on production, sale, transfer, etc	1 928	3 559	5 876	9 249	10 010	10 643	9 995	11 617	11 689	10 816
5110 General taxes	980	1 890	3 149	6 358	6 684	7 027	6 126	7 569	7 617	7 216
5111 Value added taxes	927	1 890	2 963	6 032	6 337	6 657	5 745	7 223	7 005	6 400
5112 Sales tax	54	0	0	0	0	0	0	0	0	1
5113 Other	0	0	186	325	347	370	381	346	612	815
Green Fund	0	0	186	325	347	370	381	346	612	791
Tax on online purchases	0	0	0	0	0	0	0	0	0	24
5120 Taxes on specific goods and services	948	1 669	2 727	2 891	3 326	3 616	3 869	4 048	4 073	3 600
5121 Excises	481	801	1 072	708	729	707	680	703	735	711
Rum and spirits	0	0	0	156	173	153	157	154	168	143
Alcohol and tobacco taxes	9	0	1	2	3	3	4	8	23	19
Beer duty	0	0	0	202	209	196	172	189	181	192
Oil (Petrol)	0	0	0	105	99	103	94	88	132	102
Cigarettes	0	0	0	241	241	236	231	235	203	227
Malt beverages	0	0	0	2	3	17	23	29	28	29
5122 Profits of fiscal monopolies	0	0	0	0	0	0	0	0	0	0
5123 Customs and import duties	260	748	1 473	1 905	2 319	2 588	2 861	3 014	3 016	2 582
5124 Taxes on exports	0	0	0	0	0	0	0	0	0	0
5125 Taxes on investment goods	0	0	0	0	0	0	0	0	0	0

Table 5.23. **Trinidad and Tobago / Trinidad y Tobago** (*cont.*)

Details of tax revenue / Ingresos tributarios detallados

Million TTD

	1990	2000	2005	2010	2012	2013	2014	2015	2016	2017
5126 Taxes on specific services	4	120	182	278	278	322	328	330	322	306
Insurance premium tax	0	56	98	167	174	194	197	191	181	162
Transaction tax on financial services	0	23	33	53	57	64	75	75	87	92
Hotel room tax	0	23	42	46	46	50	56	64	54	52
Betting and entertainment taxes	4	17	9	12	0	13	0	0	0	0
5127 Other taxes on internat. trade and transactions	202	0	0	1	0	0	0	0	0	1
5128 Other taxes	0	0	0	0	0	0	0	0	0	0
5130 Unallocable between 5110 and 5120	0	0	0	0	0	0	0	0	0	0
5200 Taxes on use of goods and perform activities	127	293	299	418	582	610	632	647	655	496
5210 Recurrent taxes	127	293	299	418	582	610	632	647	655	496
Motor vehicle taxes and duties	76	239	217	375	524	552	569	575	569	415
5211 Paid by households: motor vehicles	0	0	0	0	0	0	0	0	0	0
5212 Paid by others: motor vehicles	0	0	0	0	0	0	0	0	0	0
5213 Paid in respect of other goods	51	53	82	43	57	58	63	71	86	81
Liquor and miscellaneous business licence fees	5	10	10	10	10	11	11	11	11	10
Other taxes on the use of goods	45	44	72	33	47	47	52	61	75	71
5220 Non-recurrent taxes	0	0	0	0	0	0	0	0	0	0
5300 Unallocable between 5100 and 5200	0	0	0	0	0	0	0	0	0	0
6000 Other taxes	**49**	**111**	**245**	**172**	**214**	**246**	**285**	**403**	**329**	**315**
6100 Paid solely by business	0	0	0	0	0	0	0	0	0	0
6200 Other	49	111	245	172	214	246	285	403	329	315
Stamp duties	49	111	245	172	214	246	285	403	329	315

Note: Fiscal year ending on 30th September.
The data are on a cash basis.
This edition includes revenues from the Unemployment Fund and the Green Fund for the first time, affecting headings 1210 and 5113 respectively
Heading 4100: The local government tax revenue data (house rate tax) are estimated in 2017.

Source: Ministry of Finance and IDB-CIAT (2015), *Equivalent Fiscal Pressure for Latin America and the Caribbean*, and House of Representatives.

StatLink https://doi.org/10.1787/888933941764

Table 5.24. **Uruguay**

Details of tax revenue / Ingresos tributarios detallados

Million UYU

	1990	2000	2005	2010	2012	2013	2014	2015	2016	2017
Total tax revenue	**2 388**	**60 417**	**102 202**	**212 368**	**280 568**	**324 753**	**364 926**	**396 738**	**461 125**	**524 345**
1000 Taxes on income, profits and capital gains	**114**	**5 620**	**11 969**	**44 069**	**57 339**	**70 133**	**75 269**	**86 404**	**103 937**	**127 768**
1100 Of individuals	0	0	44	19 150	29 116	33 378	40 334	45 451	51 679	68 948
1110 On income and profits	..	..	44	16 792	25 353	29 100	35 367	39 613	44 817	60 570
Second category	..	..	..	14 644	22 534	26 048	31 365	34 881	39 883	54 327
Social security assistance	..	..	..	2 651	3 773	4 285	5 518	6 576	7 480	9 448
Tax refund	..	..	..	-504	-955	-1 233	-1 517	-1 844	-2 545	-3 204
1120 On capital gains	..	..	0	2 358	3 764	4 278	4 967	5 838	6 862	8 377
First category	..	..	..	2 358	3 764	4 278	4 967	5 838	6 862	8 377
1200 Corporate	114	5 620	11 925	23 257	26 169	34 076	31 698	37 078	47 734	53 641
1210 On profits	114	5 620	11 925	23 257	26 169	34 076	31 698	37 078	47 734	53 641
Corporate income tax (IRAE)	0	0	0	21 281	23 940	31 813	29 153	34 375	45 309	50 929
Corporate income tax (IRIC)	97	5 096	10 516	491	414	387	396	439	72	239
Small firms (minimum VAT)	0	296	457	586	631	686	741	796	850	925
Other	17	228	952	900	1 185	1 190	1 408	1 467	1 502	1 548
1220 On capital gains	0	0	0	..	..	..	..	..	..	..
1300 Unallocable between 1100 and 1200	0	0	0	1 662	2 053	2 679	3 237	3 875	4 523	5 179
Non resident taxpayers	..	..	..	1 662	2 053	2 679	3 237	3 875	4 523	5 179
2000 Social security contributions	**717**	**17 679**	**21 425**	**49 742**	**72 601**	**86 012**	**100 993**	**108 742**	**140 979**	**163 771**
2100 Employees	..	..	..	..	..	..	..	..	..	..
2110 On a payroll basis	..	..	..	..	..	..	..	..	..	..
2120 On an income tax basis	..	..	..	..	..	..	..	..	..	..
2200 Employers	..	..	..	..	..	..	..	..	..	..
2210 On a payroll basis	..	..	..	..	..	..	..	..	..	..
2220 On an income tax basis	..	..	..	..	..	..	..	..	..	..
2300 Self-employed or non-employed	..	..	..	..	..	..	..	..	..	..
2310 On a payroll basis	..	..	..	..	..	..	..	..	..	..
2320 On an income tax basis	..	..	..	..	..	..	..	..	..	..
2400 Unallocable between 2100, 2200 and 2300	717	17 679	21 425	49 742	72 601	86 012	100 993	108 742	140 979	163 771
2410 On a payroll basis	717	17 679	21 425	49 742	72 601	86 012	100 993	108 742	140 979	163 771
2420 On an income tax basis	0	0	0	0	0	0	0	0	0	0
3000 Taxes on payroll and workforce	**0**	**0**	**0**	**0**	**0**	**0**	**0**	**0**	**0**	**0**
4000 Taxes on property	**232**	**6 527**	**12 459**	**18 967**	**23 248**	**25 759**	**29 227**	**32 423**	**33 967**	**35 678**
4100 Recurrent taxes on immovable property	87	2 868	4 733	7 951	9 816	11 380	13 016	14 885	14 338	15 399
4110 Households	..	..	..	..	..	..	..	..	..	..
4120 Others	..	..	..	..	..	..	..	..	..	..
4200 Recurrent taxes on net wealth	94	2 076	4 943	8 948	11 067	11 892	13 714	14 776	16 652	17 057
4210 Individual	64	108	336	382	445	491	629	606	684	711
4220 Corporate	30	1 968	4 607	8 567	10 622	11 401	13 085	14 170	15 968	16 346
Corporate wealth	28	1 661	4 383	8 354	10 609	11 390	13 079	14 167	15 967	16 345
Other	1	307	224	213	13	11	6	3	1	1
4300 Estate, inheritance and gift taxes	0	0	0	0	0	0	0	0	0	0
4310 Estate and inheritance taxes	..	..	..	..	..	..	..	..	..	..
4320 Gift taxes	..	..	..	..	..	..	..	..	..	..
4400 Taxes on financial and capital transactions	20	476	1 212	1 740	1 898	2 007	1 994	2 241	2 439	2 662
Capital transfers	0	372	886	1 347	1 413	1 516	1 442	1 601	1 724	1 927
Capital transfers (additional)	20	104	326	393	485	491	553	639	714	735
4500 Non-recurrent taxes	0	0	0	0	0	0	0	0	0	0
4510 On net wealth	..	..	..	..	..	..	..	..	..	..
4520 Other non-recurrent taxes	..	..	..	..	..	..	..	..	..	..
4600 Other recurrent taxes on property	31	1 107	1 571	328	466	480	503	522	538	560
5000 Taxes on goods and services	**1 328**	**30 884**	**55 804**	**98 841**	**126 445**	**141 494**	**157 579**	**167 814**	**180 580**	**195 120**
5100 Taxes on production, sale, transfer, etc	1 271	28 307	52 733	95 053	122 423	136 141	151 116	160 274	171 321	184 807
5110 General taxes	660	18 009	34 641	69 365	88 338	98 758	108 260	113 651	123 262	129 663
5111 Value added taxes	660	17 995	34 601	69 365	88 338	98 758	108 260	113 651	123 262	129 663
5112 Sales tax	1	14	40	0	0	0	0	0	0	0
5113 Other	0	0	0	0	0	0	0	0	0	0
5120 Taxes on specific goods and services	611	10 298	18 092	25 688	34 085	37 383	42 857	46 623	48 059	55 144
5121 Excises	393	7 673	10 524	16 401	21 417	23 365	26 362	29 710	31 026	36 230
Fuels	203	4 067	4 900	6 551	9 147	10 269	11 816	14 096	15 222	17 129
Tobacco products	80	1 741	2 705	4 236	4 768	4 755	4 913	5 778	6 144	6 995
Alcoholic beverages	24	229	375	602	800	840	918	811	774	766
Beer	8	205	308	602	895	1 024	1 035	1 102	1 109	1 357
Non-alcoholic beverages	19	464	532	1 172	1 518	1 718	1 926	2 131	2 330	2 547
Motor vehicles	20	656	977	2 289	3 025	3 388	3 924	4 017	3 960	3 960
Sales of agricultural goods (MEVIR and INIA)	4	76	260	451	648	681	736	736	724	821
Other	35	235	468	497	616	689	1 094	1 039	761	2 656
5122 Profits of fiscal monopolies	0	0	0	0	0	0	0	0	0	0

Table 5.24. **Uruguay** *(cont.)*

Details of tax revenue / Ingresos tributarios detallados

Million UYU

	1990	2000	2005	2010	2012	2013	2014	2015	2016	2017
5123 Customs and import duties	214	1 967	5 195	8 478	11 670	13 020	15 167	15 440	15 384	17 198
5124 Taxes on exports	1	92	287	371	432	422	520	582	658	664
5125 Taxes on investment goods	0	0	0	0	0	0	0	0	0	0
5126 Taxes on specific services	3	300	1 596	438	567	576	807	892	991	1 052
5127 Other taxes on internat. trade and transactions	0	265	489	0	0	0	0	0	0	0
5128 Other taxes	0	0	0	0	0	0	0	0	0	0
5130 Unallocable between 5110 and 5120	0	0	0	0	0	0	0	0	0	0
5200 Taxes on use of goods and perform activities	57	2 576	3 071	3 788	4 022	5 353	6 463	7 540	9 259	10 313
5210 Recurrent taxes	57	2 576	3 071	3 788	4 022	5 353	6 463	7 540	9 259	10 313
5211 Paid by households: motor vehicles	0	0	0	0	0	0	0	0	0	0
5212 Paid by others: motor vehicles	57	2 576	3 071	3 788	4 022	5 353	6 463	7 540	9 259	10 313
5213 Paid in respect of other goods	0	0	0	0	0	0	0	0	0	0
5220 Non-recurrent taxes	0	0	0	0	0	0	0	0	0	0
5300 Unallocable between 5100 and 5200	0	0	0	0	0	0	0	0	0	0
6000 Other taxes	**-3**	**-292**	**546**	**749**	**935**	**1 355**	**1 857**	**1 355**	**1 663**	**2 008**
6100 Paid solely by business	-10	-596	76	0	0	214	541	0	0	0
6200 Other	7	303	470	748	935	1 141	1 316	1 355	1 663	2 008

Note: Year ending 31st December.

The data are on a cash basis.

The figures for local government tax revenues have been revised and reclassified in this edition according to the new figures from the Oficina de Planeamiento y Presupuesto de la República.

Heading 2000: Figures for 1990-98 are estimated by the Direction General of Taxes as the methodology they use to calculate social security contributions was not employed until 1999.

Headings 4000 and 5000: In ECLAC data, the tax on sales in public auctions is classified in category 4000.

Heading 5112: In ECLAC data, the tax on the sale of goods by public auctions is classified in category 4000.

Source: Dirección General Impositiva, Banco de Previsión Social e Instituto Nacional de Estadísticas (General Tax Directorate, Social Security Bank and National Statistics Institute).

StatLink https://doi.org/10.1787/888933941783

Table 5.25. **Venezuela**

Details of tax revenue / Ingresos tributarios detallados

Million VEF

	1990	2000	2005	2010	2012	2013	2014	2015	2016	2017
Total tax revenue	**412**	**10 849**	**48 285**	**120 084**	**230 803**	**323 943**	**543 226**	**1 216 386**	..	..
1000 Taxes on income, profits and capital gains	**344**	**4 686**	**18 529**	**36 836**	**70 739**	**93 694**	**187 884**	**284 786**	..	..
1100 Of individuals	..	..	..	..	..	..	..	..	..	..
1110 On income and profits	..	..	..	..	..	..	..	..	..	..
1120 On capital gains	..	..	..	..	..	..	..	..	..	..
1200 Corporate	315	3 368	11 184	8 700	22 879	25 270	67 601	47 388	..	..
1210 On profits	315	3 368	11 184	8 700	22 879	25 270	67 601	47 388	..	..
Oil	315	3 368	11 184	8 700	22 879	25 270	67 601	47 388	..	..
1220 On capital gains	..	..	..	..	..	..	..	..	..	..
1300 Unallocable between 1100 and 1200	30	1 317	7 345	28 137	47 859	68 424	120 283	237 399	733 170	3 137 851
2000 Social security contributions	**20**	**591**	**1 890**	**9 690**	**15 585**	**21 422**	..	..	..	..
2100 Employees	..	..	..	..	..	..	..	..	..	..
2110 On a payroll basis	..	..	..	..	..	..	..	..	..	..
2120 On an income tax basis	..	..	..	..	..	..	..	..	..	..
2200 Employers	..	..	..	..	..	..	..	..	..	..
2210 On a payroll basis	..	..	..	..	..	..	..	..	..	..
2220 On an income tax basis	..	..	..	..	..	..	..	..	..	..
2300 Self-employed or non-employed	..	..	..	..	..	..	..	..	..	..
2310 On a payroll basis	..	..	..	..	..	..	..	..	..	..
2320 On an income tax basis	..	..	..	..	..	..	..	..	..	..
2400 Unallocable between 2100, 2200 and 2300	20	591	1 890	9 690	15 585	21 422	..	..	..	..
2410 On a payroll basis	..	..	..	..	..	..	..	..	..	..
2420 On an income tax basis	..	..	..	..	..	..	..	..	..	..
3000 Taxes on payroll and workforce	**0**	**0**	**0**	**0**	**0**	**0**	**0**	**0**	**0**	**0**
4000 Taxes on property	**1**	**400**	**2 834**	**222**	**346**	**530**	**1 046**	**2 946**	**9 088**	**2 435 304**
4100 Recurrent taxes on immovable property	0	0	0	0	0	0	0	0	0	0
4110 Households	..	..	..	..	..	..	..	..	..	..
4120 Others	..	..	..	..	..	..	..	..	..	..
4200 Recurrent taxes on net wealth	0	0	0	0	0	0	0	0	0	0
4210 Individual	..	..	..	..	..	..	..	..	..	..
4220 Corporate	..	..	..	..	..	..	..	..	..	..
4300 Estate, inheritance and gift taxes	1	19	55	222	346	530	1 046	2 946	9 088	36 130
4310 Estate and inheritance taxes	1	19	55	222	346	530	1 046	2 946	9 088	36 130
4320 Gift taxes	0	0	0	0	0	0	0	0	0	0
4400 Taxes on financial and capital transactions	0	381	2 779	0	0	0	0	0	0	2 399 174
Bank debits	..	292	2 743	..	..	..	..	..	..	0
Registration of immovable property rights	..	89	36	..	..	..	..	..	..	0
Tax on Large Financial Transactions (IGTF)	..	0	0	..	..	..	..	..	..	2 399 174
4500 Non-recurrent taxes	0	0	0	0	0	0	0	0	0	0
4510 On net wealth	..	..	..	..	..	..	..	..	..	..
4520 Other non-recurrent taxes	..	..	..	..	..	..	..	..	..	..
4600 Other recurrent taxes on property	0	0	0	0	0	0	0	0	0	0
5000 Taxes on goods and services	**46**	**5 173**	**25 032**	**73 336**	**140 203**	**203 894**	**346 272**	**912 820**	**2 558 015**	**14 866 952**
5100 Taxes on production, sale, transfer, etc	46	5 173	25 032	73 336	140 203	203 894	346 272	912 820	2 558 015	14 866 952
5110 General taxes	0	3 272	19 513	56 101	111 102	164 737	272 187	702 743	1 907 078	11 299 017
5111 Value added taxes	0	3 272	19 513	56 101	111 102	164 737	272 187	702 743	1 907 078	11 299 017
5112 Sales tax	0	0	0	0	0	0	0	0	0	0
5113 Other	0	0	0	0	0	0	0	0	0	0
5120 Taxes on specific goods and services	46	1 901	5 519	17 236	29 101	39 157	74 085	210 077	650 937	3 567 934
5121 Excises	16	774	1 604	8 872	11 247	16 371	30 525	116 575	439 925	2 967 919
Oil	6	468	472	1 280	0	0	0	0	0	0
Alcoholic beverages	6	85	427	2 192	3 542	5 975	10 888	44 498	156 878	1 411 340
Tobacco	4	220	704	5 401	7 706	10 397	19 636	72 077	283 047	1 556 579
Matches	0	1	1	0	0	0	0	0	0	0
5122 Profits of fiscal monopolies	0	0	0	0	0	0	0	0	0	0
5123 Customs and import duties	30	972	3 652	8 133	17 750	22 656	43 398	93 260	210 352	598 648
5124 Taxes on exports	0	0	0	0	0	0	0	0	0	0
5125 Taxes on investment goods	0	0	0	0	0	0	0	0	0	0
5126 Taxes on specific services	0	155	263	230	104	130	162	242	660	1 367
Telecommunications	0	151	237	0	0	0	0	0	0	0
Casinos, bingo and slot machines	0	5	26	230	104	130	162	242	660	1 367
5127 Other taxes on internat. trade and transactions	0	0	0	0	0	0	0	0	0	0
5128 Other taxes	0	0	0	0	0	0	0	0	0	0
5130 Unallocable between 5110 and 5120	0	0	0	0	0	0	0	0	0	0
5200 Taxes on use of goods and perform activities	0	0	0	0	0	0	0	0	0	0
5210 Recurrent taxes	..	..	..	..	..	..	..	..	..	..
5211 Paid by households: motor vehicles	..	..	..	..	..	..	..	..	..	..
5212 Paid by others: motor vehicles	..	..	..	..	..	..	..	..	..	..

Table 5.25. **Venezuela** (*cont.*)

Details of tax revenue / Ingresos tributarios detallados

Million VEF

	1990	2000	2005	2010	2012	2013	2014	2015	2016	2017
5213 Paid in respect of other goods	..	..	..	..	..	..	..	..	..	..
5220 Non-recurrent taxes	..	..	..	..	..	..	..	..	..	..
5300 Unallocable between 5100 and 5200	0	0	0	0	0	0	0	0	0	0
6000 Other taxes	**0**	**0**	**0**	**0**	**3 931**	**4 403**	**8 024**	**15 833**	**26 306**	**122 517**
6100 Paid solely by business	..	..	..	..	0	0	0	0	0	0
6200 Other	..	..	..	..	3 931	4 403	8 024	15 833	26 306	122 517

Note: The figures since 2015 should be interpreted with caution as they have been affected by the high rate of inflation over this period.

The total tax revenue data are not available since 2014 due to missing data for social security contributions since 2014 and for oil revenues since 2016 (classified in heading 1210 taxes on corporate profits).

Year ending 31st December.

The data are on a cash basis.

The figures exclude state and local government tax revenues as the data are not available.

Source: Servicio Nacional Integrado de Administración Aduanera y Tributaria, Ministerio de Finanzas (National Integrated Service of Customs and Tax Administration, Ministry of Finance).

StatLink https://doi.org/10.1787/888933941802

Chapter 6

Tax revenues by sub-sectors of general government

Capítulo 6

Ingresos tributarios por sub-sectores de gobierno general

Chapter 6 / Capítulo 6

Tax revenues by sub-sectors of general government

Revenues of both the Latin American and the OECD countries have been attributed to the different levels of government according to the revised guidelines set out in to the final version of the 2008 System of National Accounts (SNA). Under this, revenues are generally attributed to the level of government that exercises the authority to impose the tax or has the final discretion to set and vary the tax rate.

Ingresos tributarios por sub-sectores de gobierno general

Los ingresos de los países latinoamericanos y de los países de la OCDE se han atribuido a los diferentes niveles de gobierno de acuerdo con lo recogido en la versión final 2008 del Sistema de Cuentas Nacionales (SCN), según el cual, los ingresos se atribuyen por lo general al nivel de gobierno que ejerce la facultad de aplicar el impuesto o que puede a su discreción establecer y modificar la tasa del impuesto.

Table 6.1. **Argentina, tax revenues by sub-sectors of government**

Million ARS

	Federal government					State/Regional				
	1990	2000	2010	2015	2017	1990	2000	2010	2015	2017
1000 Taxes on income, profits and capital gains	**542**	**11 303**	**78 427**	**384 536**	**559 755**	**0**	**0**	**0**	**0**	**0**
1100 Of individuals	141	3 937	23 980	188 218	236 284	..	..	..	..	..
1200 Corporate	357	6 575	50 664	185 725	297 111	..	..	..	..	..
1300 Unallocable between 1100 and 1200	43	792	3 783	10 593	26 360	..	..	..	..	..
2000 Social security contributions	**0**	**0**	**0**	**0**	**0**	**0**	**0**	**0**	**0**	**0**
2100 Employees	..	..	..	..	..	..	..	..	..	..
2200 Employers	..	..	..	..	..	..	..	..	..	..
2300 Self-employed or non-employed	..	..	..	..	..	..	..	..	..	..
2400 Unallocable between 2100, 2200 and 2300	..	..	..	..	..	..	..	..	..	..
3000 Taxes on payroll and workforce	**0**	**0**	**0**	**0**	**0**	**0**	**0**	**0**	**0**	**0**
4000 Taxes on property	**616**	**1 254**	**32 674**	**117 274**	**199 716**	**549**	**2 614**	**10 864**	**48 908**	**103 666**
4100 Recurrent taxes on immovable property	0	0	0	0	0	419	1 809	5 035	21 738	44 236
4200 Recurrent taxes on net wealth	246	1 084	5 248	18 538	22 786	0	0	0	0	0
4300 Estate, inheritance and gift taxes	0	0	0	0	0	0	0	0	0	0
4400 Taxes on financial and capital transactions	330	100	27 423	98 736	176 930	130	804	5 829	27 170	59 431
4500 Non-recurrent taxes	40	70	3	0	0	0	0	0	0	0
4600 Other recurrent taxes on property	0	0	0	0	0	0	0	0	0	0
5000 Taxes on goods and services	**4 669**	**27 592**	**198 346**	**634 068**	**1 072 366**	**967**	**6 947**	**54 746**	**255 256**	**457 212**
5100 Taxes on production, sale, transfer, etc	4 671	28 174	201 402	642 899	1 097 319	791	6 114	51 148	238 221	422 981
5110 General taxes	1 594	19 009	116 386	433 076	765 336	791	6 114	51 148	238 221	422 981
5120 Taxes on specific goods and services	3 077	9 166	85 016	209 822	331 983	0	0	0	0	0
5130 Unallocable between 5110 and 5120	0	0	0	0	0	0	0	0	0	0
5200 Taxes on use of goods and perform activities[1]	0	0	0	0	0	177	833	3 598	17 035	34 232
5300 Unallocable between 5100 and 5200	-3	-583	-3 056	-8 831	-24 953	0	0	0	0	0
6000 Other taxes	**214**	**395**	**2 386**	**6 931**	**56 676**	**78**	**1 309**	**3 110**	**10 533**	**19 710**
6100 Paid solely by business	0	354	2 093	5 624	10 544	0	0	0	0	0
6200 Other[2]	214	41	294	1 306	46 132	78	1 309	3 110	10 533	19 710
Total tax revenue	**6 040**	**40 544**	**311 834**	**1 142 808**	**1 888 513**	**1 594**	**10 870**	**68 720**	**314 697**	**580 588**

Million ARS

	Local government[3]					Social Security Funds				
	1990	2000	2010	2015	2017	1990	2000	2010	2015	2017
1000 Taxes on income, profits and capital gains	**..**	**..**	**..**	**..**	**..**	**0**	**0**	**0**	**0**	**0**
1100 Of individuals	..	..	..	..	..	..	..	..	..	..
1200 Corporate	..	..	..	..	..	..	..	..	..	..
1300 Unallocable between 1100 and 1200	..	..	..	..	..	..	..	..	..	..
2000 Social security contributions	**..**	**..**	**..**	**..**	**..**	**2 583**	**9 670**	**102 460**	**415 410**	**733 527**
2100 Employees	..	..	..	..	..	..	2 486	37 990	163 590	288 985
2200 Employers	..	..	..	..	..	..	6 069	54 713	235 610	413 212
2300 Self-employed or non-employed	..	..	..	..	..	98	1 115	9 757	16 210	31 330
2400 Unallocable between 2100, 2200 and 2300	..	..	..	..	..	2 485	0	0	0	0
3000 Taxes on payroll and workforce	**..**	**..**	**..**	**..**	**..**	**0**	**0**	**0**	**0**	**0**
4000 Taxes on property	**..**	**..**	**..**	**..**	**..**	**0**	**0**	**0**	**0**	**0**
4100 Recurrent taxes on immovable property	..	..	..	..	..	..	..	..	..	..
4200 Recurrent taxes on net wealth	..	..	..	..	..	..	..	..	..	..
4300 Estate, inheritance and gift taxes	..	..	..	..	..	..	..	..	..	..
4400 Taxes on financial and capital transactions	..	..	..	..	..	..	..	..	..	..
4500 Non-recurrent taxes	..	..	..	..	..	..	..	..	..	..
4600 Other recurrent taxes on property	..	..	..	..	..	..	..	..	..	..
5000 Taxes on goods and services	**..**	**..**	**..**	**..**	**..**	**0**	**0**	**0**	**0**	**0**
5100 Taxes on production, sale, transfer, etc	..	..	..	..	..	..	..	..	..	..
5110 General taxes	..	..	..	..	..	..	..	..	..	..
5120 Taxes on specific goods and services	..	..	..	..	..	..	..	..	..	..
5130 Unallocable between 5110 and 5120	..	..	..	..	..	..	..	..	..	..
5200 Taxes on use of goods and perform activities[1]	..	..	..	..	..	..	..	..	..	..
5300 Unallocable between 5100 and 5200	..	..	..	..	..	..	..	..	..	..
6000 Other taxes	**..**	**..**	**..**	**..**	**..**	**0**	**0**	**0**	**0**	**0**
6100 Paid solely by business	..	..	..	..	..	..	..	..	..	..
6200 Other[2]	..	..	..	..	..	..	..	..	..	..
Total tax revenue	**..**	**..**	**..**	**..**	**..**	**2 583**	**9 670**	**102 460**	**415 410**	**733 527**

1. In ECLAC data, tax on ownership of motor vehicles is classified in category 4000.
2. The tax debt payments from 2016 include revenue following the implementation of a new voluntary disclosure regime in July 2016 (Law 27260).
3. The figures exclude local government tax revenues as the data are not available.

StatLink https://doi.org/10.1787/888933941821

Table 6.2. **Bahamas, tax revenues by sub-sectors of government**

Million BSD

	Federal government[1]					State/Regional				
	1990	2000	2010	2015	2017	1990	2000	2010	2015	2017
1000 Taxes on income, profits and capital gains	**0**	**0**	**0**	**0**	**0**	**..**	**..**	**..**	**..**	**..**
1100 Of individuals	0	0	0	0	0	..	..	..	..	..
1200 Corporate	0	0	0	0	0	..	..	..	..	..
1300 Unallocable between 1100 and 1200	0	0	0	0	0	..	..	..	..	..
2000 Social security contributions	**0**	**0**	**0**	**0**	**0**	**..**	**..**	**..**	**..**	**..**
2100 Employees	..	..	..	..	..	..	..	..	..	..
2200 Employers	..	..	..	..	..	..	..	..	..	..
2300 Self-employed or non-employed	..	..	..	..	..	..	..	..	..	..
2400 Unallocable between 2100, 2200 and 2300	..	..	..	..	..	..	..	..	..	..
3000 Taxes on payroll and workforce	**0**	**0**	**0**	**0**	**0**	**..**	**..**	**..**	**..**	**..**
4000 Taxes on property	**19**	**32**	**92**	**107**	**121**	**..**	**..**	**..**	**..**	**..**
4100 Recurrent taxes on immovable property	19	32	92	107	121	..	..	..	..	..
4200 Recurrent taxes on net wealth	0	0	0	0	0	..	..	..	..	..
4300 Estate, inheritance and gift taxes	0	0	0	0	0	..	..	..	..	..
4400 Taxes on financial and capital transactions	0	0	0	0	0	..	..	..	..	..
4500 Non-recurrent taxes	0	0	0	0	0	..	..	..	..	..
4600 Other recurrent taxes on property	0	0	0	0	0	..	..	..	..	..
5000 Taxes on goods and services	**386**	**723**	**795**	**1 203**	**1 604**	**..**	**..**	**..**	**..**	**..**
5100 Taxes on production, sale, transfer, etc	354	654	672	993	1 384	..	..	..	..	..
5110 General taxes	0	0	0	219	638	..	..	..	..	..
5120 Taxes on specific goods and services	354	654	672	775	746	..	..	..	..	..
5130 Unallocable between 5110 and 5120	0	0	0	0	0	..	..	..	..	..
5200 Taxes on use of goods and perform activities	32	69	123	209	220	..	..	..	..	..
5300 Unallocable between 5100 and 5200	0	0	0	0	0	..	..	..	..	..
6000 Other taxes	**33**	**95**	**223**	**191**	**112**	**..**	**..**	**..**	**..**	**..**
6100 Paid solely by business	0	0	0	0	0	..	..	..	..	..
6200 Other	33	95	223	191	112	..	..	..	..	..
Total tax revenue	**438**	**849**	**1 109**	**1 500**	**1 837**	**..**	**..**	**..**	**..**	**..**

Million BSD

	Local government[3]					Social Security Funds				
	1990	2000	2010	2015	2017	1990	2000	2010	2015	2017
1000 Taxes on income, profits and capital gains	**..**	**..**	**..**	**..**	**..**	**0**	**0**	**0**	**0**	**0**
1100 Of individuals	..	..	..	..	..	..	..	..	..	..
1200 Corporate	..	..	..	..	..	..	..	..	..	..
1300 Unallocable between 1100 and 1200	..	..	..	..	..	..	..	..	..	..
2000 Social security contributions[2]	**..**	**..**	**..**	**..**	**..**	**66**	**115**	**167**	**260**	**340**
2100 Employees	..	..	..	..	..	..	..	60	98	..
2200 Employers	..	..	..	..	..	..	..	104	157	..
2300 Self-employed or non-employed	..	..	..	..	..	..	..	3	6	..
2400 Unallocable between 2100, 2200 and 2300	..	..	..	..	..	66	115	0	-1	340
3000 Taxes on payroll and workforce	**..**	**..**	**..**	**..**	**..**	**0**	**0**	**0**	**0**	**0**
4000 Taxes on property	**..**	**..**	**..**	**..**	**..**	**0**	**0**	**0**	**0**	**0**
4100 Recurrent taxes on immovable property	..	..	..	..	..	..	..	..	..	..
4200 Recurrent taxes on net wealth	..	..	..	..	..	..	..	..	..	..
4300 Estate, inheritance and gift taxes	..	..	..	..	..	..	..	..	..	..
4400 Taxes on financial and capital transactions	..	..	..	..	..	..	..	..	..	..
4500 Non-recurrent taxes	..	..	..	..	..	..	..	..	..	..
4600 Other recurrent taxes on property	..	..	..	..	..	..	..	..	..	..
5000 Taxes on goods and services	**..**	**..**	**..**	**..**	**..**	**0**	**0**	**0**	**0**	**0**
5100 Taxes on production, sale, transfer, etc	..	..	..	..	..	..	..	..	..	..
5110 General taxes	..	..	..	..	..	..	..	..	..	..
5120 Taxes on specific goods and services	..	..	..	..	..	..	..	..	..	..
5130 Unallocable between 5110 and 5120	..	..	..	..	..	..	..	..	..	..
5200 Taxes on use of goods and perform activities	..	..	..	..	..	..	..	..	..	..
5300 Unallocable between 5100 and 5200	..	..	..	..	..	..	..	..	..	..
6000 Other taxes	**..**	**..**	**..**	**..**	**..**	**0**	**0**	**0**	**0**	**0**
6100 Paid solely by business	..	..	..	..	..	..	..	..	..	..
6200 Other	..	..	..	..	..	..	..	..	..	..
Total tax revenue	**..**	**..**	**..**	**..**	**..**	**66**	**115**	**167**	**260**	**340**

1. The data for 2017 are preliminary and undertaken from the Central Bank of The Bahamas.
2. The data for social security contributions are estimated for 2016 and 2017.
3. The figures exclude local government tax revenues as the data are not available.

StatLink https://doi.org/10.1787/888933941840

Table 6.3. **Barbados, tax revenues by sub-sectors of government**

Million BAR

	Federal government[1]					State/Regional				
	1990	2000	2010	2015	2017	1990	2000	2010	2015	2017
1000 Taxes on income, profits and capital gains	**254**	**574**	**762**	**723**	**819**	..	..	..	..	..
1100 Of individuals	129	289	388	433	496	..	..	..	..	..
1200 Corporate	111	252	327	225	281	..	..	..	..	..
1300 Unallocable between 1100 and 1200	14	33	47	65	42	..	..	..	..	..
2000 Social security contributions	**0**	**0**	**0**	**0**	**0**	..	..	..	..	..
2100 Employees	..	..	..	..	..	..	..	..	..	..
2200 Employers	..	..	..	..	..	..	..	..	..	..
2300 Self-employed or non-employed	..	..	..	..	..	..	..	..	..	..
2400 Unallocable between 2100, 2200 and 2300	..	..	..	..	..	..	..	..	..	..
3000 Taxes on payroll and workforce	**0**	**0**	**0**	**0**	**0**	..	..	..	..	..
4000 Taxes on property	**39**	**92**	**114**	**188**	**190**	..	..	..	..	..
4100 Recurrent taxes on immovable property	26	60	98	173	174	..	..	..	..	..
4200 Recurrent taxes on net wealth	0	0	0	0	0	..	..	..	..	..
4300 Estate, inheritance and gift taxes	0	0	0	0	0	..	..	..	..	..
4400 Taxes on financial and capital transactions	0	0	0	0	0	..	..	..	..	..
4500 Non-recurrent taxes	13	32	16	15	16	..	..	..	..	..
4600 Other recurrent taxes on property	0	0	0	0	0	..	..	..	..	..
5000 Taxes on goods and services	**418**	**911**	**1 303**	**1 473**	**1 870**	..	..	..	..	..
5100 Taxes on production, sale, transfer, etc	418	807	1 153	1 325	1 713	..	..	..	..	..
5110 General taxes	197	501	753	925	994	..	..	..	..	..
5120 Taxes on specific goods and services	221	306	400	401	719	..	..	..	..	..
5130 Unallocable between 5110 and 5120	0	0	0	0	0	..	..	..	..	..
5200 Taxes on use of goods and perform activities	0	104	150	148	157	..	..	..	..	..
5300 Unallocable between 5100 and 5200	0	0	0	0	0	..	..	..	..	..
6000 Other taxes	**98**	**12**	**15**	**10**	**9**	..	..	..	..	..
6100 Paid solely by business	0	0	0	0	0	..	..	..	..	..
6200 Other	98	12	15	10	9	..	..	..	..	..
Total tax revenue	**808**	**1 589**	**2 194**	**2 394**	**2 888**	..	..	..	..	..

Million BAR

	Local government[2]					Social Security Funds[1]				
	1990	2000	2010	2015	2017	1990	2000	2010	2015	2017
1000 Taxes on income, profits and capital gains	..	..	..	..	..	**0**	**0**	**0**	**0**	**0**
1100 Of individuals	..	..	..	..	..	..	..	..	..	..
1200 Corporate	..	..	..	..	..	..	..	..	..	..
1300 Unallocable between 1100 and 1200	..	..	..	..	..	..	..	..	..	..
2000 Social security contributions	..	..	..	..	..	**134**	**295**	**525**	**553**	**318**
2100 Employees	..	..	..	..	..	..	..	..	..	..
2200 Employers	..	..	..	..	..	..	..	..	..	..
2300 Self-employed or non-employed	..	..	..	..	..	..	..	..	..	..
2400 Unallocable between 2100, 2200 and 2300	..	..	..	..	..	134	295	525	553	318
3000 Taxes on payroll and workforce	..	..	..	..	..	**0**	**0**	**0**	**0**	**0**
4000 Taxes on property	..	..	..	..	..	**0**	**0**	**0**	**0**	**0**
4100 Recurrent taxes on immovable property	..	..	..	..	..	..	..	..	..	..
4200 Recurrent taxes on net wealth	..	..	..	..	..	..	..	..	..	..
4300 Estate, inheritance and gift taxes	..	..	..	..	..	..	..	..	..	..
4400 Taxes on financial and capital transactions	..	..	..	..	..	..	..	..	..	..
4500 Non-recurrent taxes	..	..	..	..	..	..	..	..	..	..
4600 Other recurrent taxes on property	..	..	..	..	..	..	..	..	..	..
5000 Taxes on goods and services	..	..	..	..	..	**0**	**0**	**0**	**0**	**0**
5100 Taxes on production, sale, transfer, etc	..	..	..	..	..	..	..	..	..	..
5110 General taxes	..	..	..	..	..	..	..	..	..	..
5120 Taxes on specific goods and services	..	..	..	..	..	..	..	..	..	..
5130 Unallocable between 5110 and 5120	..	..	..	..	..	..	..	..	..	..
5200 Taxes on use of goods and perform activities	..	..	..	..	..	..	..	..	..	..
5300 Unallocable between 5100 and 5200	..	..	..	..	..	..	..	..	..	..
6000 Other taxes	..	..	..	..	..	**0**	**0**	**0**	**0**	**0**
6100 Paid solely by business	..	..	..	..	..	..	..	..	..	..
6200 Other	..	..	..	..	..	..	..	..	..	..
Total tax revenue	..	..	..	..	..	**134**	**295**	**525**	**553**	**318**

1. The data for 2017 are from the Barbados Budget Estimates 2018-19 published by the Barbados Parliament.
2. The figures exclude local government tax revenues as the data are not available.

StatLink https://doi.org/10.1787/888933941859

Table 6.4. **Belize, tax revenues by sub-sectors of government**

Million BZD

	Federal government[1]					State/Regional				
	1990	2000	2010	2015	2017	1990	2000	2010	2015	2017
1000 Taxes on income, profits and capital gains	**37**	**76**	**248**	**254**	**266**	..	..	..	..	..
1100 Of individuals	21	19	52	82	86	..	..	..	..	..
1200 Corporate	12	51	189	159	170	..	..	..	..	..
1300 Unallocable between 1100 and 1200	4	6	7	13	10	..	..	..	..	..
2000 Social security contributions	**0**	**0**	**0**	**0**	**0**	..	..	..	..	..
2100 Employees	..	..	..	..	..	..	..	..	..	..
2200 Employers	..	..	..	..	..	..	..	..	..	..
2300 Self-employed or non-employed	..	..	..	..	..	..	..	..	..	..
2400 Unallocable between 2100, 2200 and 2300	..	..	..	..	..	..	..	..	..	..
3000 Taxes on payroll and workforce	**0**	**0**	**0**	**0**	**0**	..	..	..	..	..
4000 Taxes on property	**5**	**11**	**16**	**29**	**25**	..	..	..	..	..
4100 Recurrent taxes on immovable property	0	0	0	0	0	..	..	..	..	..
4200 Recurrent taxes on net wealth	0	0	0	0	0	..	..	..	..	..
4300 Estate, inheritance and gift taxes	0	0	0	0	0	..	..	..	..	..
4400 Taxes on financial and capital transactions	5	11	16	29	25	..	..	..	..	..
4500 Non-recurrent taxes	0	0	0	0	0	..	..	..	..	..
4600 Other recurrent taxes on property	0	0	0	0	0	..	..	..	..	..
5000 Taxes on goods and services	**126**	**211**	**412**	**583**	**678**	..	..	..	..	..
5100 Taxes on production, sale, transfer, etc	122	207	400	571	669	..	..	..	..	..
5110 General taxes	0	82	199	275	293	..	..	..	..	..
5120 Taxes on specific goods and services	122	125	200	296	376	..	..	..	..	..
5130 Unallocable between 5110 and 5120	0	0	0	0	0	..	..	..	..	..
5200 Taxes on use of goods and perform activities	4	4	13	12	9	..	..	..	..	..
5300 Unallocable between 5100 and 5200	0	0	0	0	0	..	..	..	..	..
6000 Other taxes	**0**	**0**	**0**	**0**	**0**	..	..	..	..	..
6100 Paid solely by business	..	..	..	..	..	..	..	..	..	..
6200 Other	..	..	..	..	..	..	..	..	..	..
Total tax revenue	**168**	**298**	**677**	**867**	**968**	..	..	..	..	..

Million BZD

	Local government[1]					Social Security Funds[1]				
	1990	2000	2010	2015	2017	1990	2000	2010	2015	2017
1000 Taxes on income, profits and capital gains	**0**	**0**	**0**	**0**	**0**	**0**	**0**	**0**	**0**	**0**
1100 Of individuals	..	..	..	..	..	..	..	..	..	..
1200 Corporate	..	..	..	..	..	..	..	..	..	..
1300 Unallocable between 1100 and 1200	..	..	..	..	..	..	..	..	..	..
2000 Social security contributions[2]	**0**	**0**	**0**	**0**	**0**	**10**	**18**	**60**	**77**	**80**
2100 Employees	..	..	..	..	..	..	..	..	..	..
2200 Employers	..	..	..	..	..	..	..	..	..	..
2300 Self-employed or non-employed	..	..	..	..	..	..	..	..	..	..
2400 Unallocable between 2100, 2200 and 2300	..	..	..	..	..	10	18	60	77	80
3000 Taxes on payroll and workforce	**0**	**0**	**0**	**0**	**0**	**0**	**0**	**0**	**0**	**0**
4000 Taxes on property	**1**	**2**	**7**	**5**	**6**	**0**	**0**	**0**	**0**	**0**
4100 Recurrent taxes on immovable property	1	2	7	5	6	..	..	..	..	..
4200 Recurrent taxes on net wealth	0	0	0	0	0	..	..	..	..	..
4300 Estate, inheritance and gift taxes	0	0	0	0	0	..	..	..	..	..
4400 Taxes on financial and capital transactions	0	0	0	0	0	..	..	..	..	..
4500 Non-recurrent taxes	0	0	0	0	0	..	..	..	..	..
4600 Other recurrent taxes on property	0	0	0	0	0	..	..	..	..	..
5000 Taxes on goods and services	**0**	**0**	**0**	**0**	**0**	**0**	**0**	**0**	**0**	**0**
5100 Taxes on production, sale, transfer, etc	..	..	..	..	..	..	..	..	..	..
5110 General taxes	..	..	..	..	..	..	..	..	..	..
5120 Taxes on specific goods and services	..	..	..	..	..	..	..	..	..	..
5130 Unallocable between 5110 and 5120	..	..	..	..	..	..	..	..	..	..
5200 Taxes on use of goods and perform activities	..	..	..	..	..	..	..	..	..	..
5300 Unallocable between 5100 and 5200	..	..	..	..	..	..	..	..	..	..
6000 Other taxes	**0**	**0**	**0**	**0**	**0**	**0**	**0**	**0**	**0**	**0**
6100 Paid solely by business	..	..	..	..	..	..	..	..	..	..
6200 Other	..	..	..	..	..	..	..	..	..	..
Total tax revenue	**1**	**2**	**7**	**5**	**6**	**10**	**18**	**60**	**77**	**80**

1. The data for 2017 are the expected out-turn as presented by the Belize draft estimates of revenue and expenditures.
2. The data for social security contributions are estimated for 2016 and 2017.

StatLink https://doi.org/10.1787/888933941878

Table 6.5. **Bolivia, tax revenues by sub-sectors of government**

Million BOB

	Federal government					State/Regional				
	1990	2000	2010	2015	2017	1990	2000	2010	2015	2017
1000 Taxes on income, profits and capital gains	**68**	**1 209**	**6 941**	**12 883**	**10 583**	..	..	..	..	..
1100 Of individuals	68	214	263	508	502	..	..	..	..	..
1200 Corporate	0	995	6 679	12 375	10 081	..	..	..	..	..
1300 Unallocable between 1100 and 1200	0	0	0	0	0	..	..	..	..	..
2000 Social security contributions	**0**	**0**	**0**	**0**	**0**	..	..	..	..	..
2100 Employees	..	..	..	..	..	..	..	..	..	..
2200 Employers	..	..	..	..	..	..	..	..	..	..
2300 Self-employed or non-employed	..	..	..	..	..	..	..	..	..	..
2400 Unallocable between 2100, 2200 and 2300	..	..	..	..	..	..	..	..	..	..
3000 Taxes on payroll and workforce	**0**	**0**	**0**	**0**	**0**	..	..	..	..	..
4000 Taxes on property	**1**	**3**	**367**	**424**	**492**	..	..	..	..	..
4100 Recurrent taxes on immovable property	0	0	0	0	0	..	..	..	..	..
4200 Recurrent taxes on net wealth	0	0	0	0	0	..	..	..	..	..
4300 Estate, inheritance and gift taxes	1	3	20	36	1	..	..	..	..	..
4400 Taxes on financial and capital transactions	0	0	347	388	491	..	..	..	..	..
4500 Non-recurrent taxes	0	0	0	0	0	..	..	..	..	..
4600 Other recurrent taxes on property	0	0	0	0	0	..	..	..	..	..
5000 Taxes on goods and services	**1 032**	**6 594**	**17 684**	**34 731**	**33 953**	..	..	..	..	..
5100 Taxes on production, sale, transfer, etc	1 032	6 594	17 684	34 731	33 953	..	..	..	..	..
5110 General taxes	708	3 892	12 434	25 220	24 522	..	..	..	..	..
5120 Taxes on specific goods and services	324	2 702	5 250	9 511	9 430	..	..	..	..	..
5130 Unallocable between 5110 and 5120	0	0	0	0	0	..	..	..	..	..
5200 Taxes on use of goods and perform activities	0	0	0	0	0	..	..	..	..	..
5300 Unallocable between 5100 and 5200	0	0	0	0	0	..	..	..	..	..
6000 Other taxes	**177**	**107**	**558**	**2 480**	**2 823**	..	..	..	..	..
6100 Paid solely by business	4	6	12	26	30	..	..	..	..	..
6200 Other	172	101	546	2 454	2 793	..	..	..	..	..
Total tax revenue	**1 277**	**7 913**	**25 551**	**50 518**	**47 851**	..	..	..	..	..

Million BOB

	Local government[1]					Social Security Funds				
	1990	2000	2010	2015	2017	1990	2000	2010	2015	2017
1000 Taxes on income, profits and capital gains	..	**0**	**0**	**0**	**0**	..	**0**	**0**	**0**	**0**
1100 Of individuals	..	..	..	..	..	..	..	..	..	..
1200 Corporate	..	..	..	..	..	..	..	..	..	..
1300 Unallocable between 1100 and 1200	..	..	..	..	..	..	..	..	..	..
2000 Social security contributions	..	**0**	**0**	**0**	**0**	..	**666**	**1 645**	**9 842**	**10 983**
2100 Employees	..	..	..	..	..	..	..	..	..	..
2200 Employers	..	..	..	..	..	..	..	..	..	..
2300 Self-employed or non-employed	..	..	..	..	..	..	..	..	..	..
2400 Unallocable between 2100, 2200 and 2300	..	..	..	..	..	..	666	1 645	9 842	10 983
3000 Taxes on payroll and workforce	..	**0**	**0**	**0**	**0**	..	**0**	**0**	**0**	**0**
4000 Taxes on property	..	**0**	**0**	**0**	**0**	..	**0**	**0**	**0**	**0**
4100 Recurrent taxes on immovable property	..	..	..	..	..	..	..	..	..	..
4200 Recurrent taxes on net wealth	..	..	..	..	..	..	..	..	..	..
4300 Estate, inheritance and gift taxes	..	..	..	..	..	..	..	..	..	..
4400 Taxes on financial and capital transactions	..	..	..	..	..	..	..	..	..	..
4500 Non-recurrent taxes	..	..	..	..	..	..	..	..	..	..
4600 Other recurrent taxes on property	..	..	..	..	..	..	..	..	..	..
5000 Taxes on goods and services	..	**0**	**0**	**0**	**0**	..	**0**	**0**	**0**	**0**
5100 Taxes on production, sale, transfer, etc	..	..	..	..	..	..	..	..	..	..
5110 General taxes	..	..	..	..	..	..	..	..	..	..
5120 Taxes on specific goods and services	..	..	..	..	..	..	..	..	..	..
5130 Unallocable between 5110 and 5120	..	..	..	..	..	..	..	..	..	..
5200 Taxes on use of goods and perform activities	..	..	..	..	..	..	..	..	..	..
5300 Unallocable between 5100 and 5200	..	..	..	..	..	..	..	..	..	..
6000 Other taxes	..	**575**	**1 381**	**2 585**	**3 210**	..	**0**	**0**	**0**	**0**
6100 Paid solely by business	..	0	0	0	0	..	..	..	..	..
6200 Other	..	575	1 381	2 585	3 210	..	..	..	..	..
Total tax revenue	..	**575**	**1 381**	**2 585**	**3 210**	..	**666**	**1 645**	**9 842**	**10 984**

1. The figures exclude local government tax revenues for the period 1990-1993 as the data are not available. The data for 2017 are estimated.

StatLink https://doi.org/10.1787/888933941897

Table 6.6. **Brazil, tax revenues by sub-sectors of government**

Million BRL

	Federal government					State/Regional				
	1990	2000	2010	2015	2017	1990	2000	2010	2015	2017
1000 Taxes on income, profits and capital gains	**1**	**68 667**	**258 738**	**400 993**	**458 312**	**0**	**0**	**0**	**0**	**0**
1100 Of individuals	0	3 406	87 828	148 739	177 377	..	..	..	..	..
1200 Corporate	0	25 430	128 255	164 057	184 501	..	..	..	..	..
1300 Unallocable between 1100 and 1200	0	39 831	42 656	88 196	96 434	..	..	..	..	..
2000 Social security contributions	**0**	**0**	**0**	**0**	**0**	**0**	**0**	**0**	**0**	**0**
2100 Employees	..	..	..	..	..	..	..	..	..	..
2200 Employers	..	..	..	..	..	..	..	..	..	..
2300 Self-employed or non-employed	..	..	..	..	..	..	..	..	..	..
2400 Unallocable between 2100, 2200 and 2300	..	..	..	..	..	..	..	..	..	..
3000 Taxes on payroll and workforce[1]	**0**	**6 749**	**33 090**	**50 399**	**54 655**	**0**	**0**	**0**	**0**	**0**
4000 Taxes on property	**0**	**17 726**	**27 038**	**35 786**	**35 934**	**0**	**5 623**	**23 885**	**42 726**	**47 751**
4100 Recurrent taxes on immovable property	0	234	485	1 105	1 273	0	0	0	0	0
4200 Recurrent taxes on net wealth	0	0	0	0	0	0	0	0	0	0
4300 Estate, inheritance and gift taxes	0	0	0	0	0	0	329	2 518	6 469	7 242
4400 Taxes on financial and capital transactions	0	17 492	26 553	34 681	34 660	0	0	0	0	0
4500 Non-recurrent taxes	0	0	0	0	0	0	0	0	0	0
4600 Other recurrent taxes on property	0	0	0	0	0	0	5 294	21 367	36 257	40 509
5000 Taxes on goods and services	**1**	**74 190**	**241 385**	**338 785**	**359 807**	**1**	**83 848**	**268 117**	**396 513**	**441 039**
5100 Taxes on production, sale, transfer, etc	1	74 190	241 385	338 785	359 807	1	82 279	268 117	396 513	441 039
5110 General taxes[1]	1	65 745	197 025	277 898	303 142	1	82 279	268 117	396 513	441 039
5120 Taxes on specific goods and services	0	8 445	44 360	60 887	56 665	0	0	0	0	0
5130 Unallocable between 5110 and 5120	0	0	0	0	0	0	0	0	0	0
5200 Taxes on use of goods and perform activities	0	0	0	0	0	0	1 569	0	0	0
5300 Unallocable between 5100 and 5200	0	0	0	0	0	0	0	0	0	0
6000 Other taxes[2]	**0**	**2 214**	**8 765**	**10 142**	**12 787**	**0**	**322**	**17 038**	**28 983**	**34 288**
6100 Paid solely by business	0	0	0	0	0	0	0	0	0	0
6200 Other[1]	0	2 214	8 765	10 142	12 787	0	322	17 038	28 983	34 288
Total tax revenue	**1**	**169 546**	**569 016**	**836 105**	**921 496**	**1**	**89 793**	**309 040**	**468 222**	**523 078**

Million BRL

	Local government					Social Security Funds				
	1990	2000	2010	2015	2017	1990	2000	2010	2015	2017
1000 Taxes on income, profits and capital gains	**0**	**0**	**0**	**0**	**0**	**0**	**0**	**0**	**0**	**0**
1100 Of individuals	..	..	..	..	..	..	..	..	..	..
1200 Corporate	..	..	..	..	..	..	..	..	..	..
1300 Unallocable between 1100 and 1200	..	..	..	..	..	..	..	..	..	..
2000 Social security contributions	**0**	**0**	**0**	**0**	**0**	**1**	**83 469**	**313 920**	**499 294**	**551 711**
2100 Employees	..	..	..	..	..	..	..	..	..	..
2200 Employers	..	..	..	..	..	0	18 709	64 271	118 323	128 743
2300 Self-employed or non-employed	..	..	..	..	..	..	..	..	..	..
2400 Unallocable between 2100, 2200 and 2300	..	..	..	..	..	1	64 760	249 650	380 972	422 968
3000 Taxes on payroll and workforce[1]	**0**	**0**	**0**	**0**	**0**	**0**	**0**	**0**	**0**	**0**
4000 Taxes on property	**0**	**5 469**	**23 285**	**41 426**	**48 489**	**0**	**0**	**0**	**0**	**0**
4100 Recurrent taxes on immovable property	0	4 519	17 444	31 521	38 427	..	..	..	..	..
4200 Recurrent taxes on net wealth	0	0	0	0	0	..	..	..	..	..
4300 Estate, inheritance and gift taxes	0	0	0	0	0	..	..	..	..	..
4400 Taxes on financial and capital transactions	0	950	5 840	9 904	10 062	..	..	..	..	..
4500 Non-recurrent taxes	0	0	0	0	0	..	..	..	..	..
4600 Other recurrent taxes on property	0	0	0	0	0	..	..	..	..	..
5000 Taxes on goods and services	**0**	**6 106**	**32 756**	**54 455**	**56 403**	**0**	**0**	**0**	**0**	**0**
5100 Taxes on production, sale, transfer, etc	0	6 106	32 756	54 455	56 403	..	..	..	..	..
5110 General taxes[1]	0	6 106	32 756	54 455	56 403	..	..	..	..	..
5120 Taxes on specific goods and services	0	0	0	0	0	..	..	..	..	..
5130 Unallocable between 5110 and 5120	0	0	0	0	0	..	..	..	..	..
5200 Taxes on use of goods and perform activities	0	0	0	0	0	..	..	..	..	..
5300 Unallocable between 5100 and 5200	0	0	0	0	0	..	..	..	..	..
6000 Other taxes[2]	**0**	**377**	**8 406**	**14 054**	**17 287**	**0**	**0**	**0**	**0**	**0**
6100 Paid solely by business	0	0	0	0	0	..	..	..	..	..
6200 Other[1]	0	377	8 406	14 054	17 287	..	..	..	..	..
Total tax revenue	**0**	**11 952**	**64 447**	**109 935**	**122 179**	**1**	**83 469**	**313 920**	**499 294**	**551 711**

1. The PASEP (Program of Formation of the Patrimony of the Public Servants) contributions are added to the PIS (Social Integration Program) contributions in heading 5110 for the years prior to 2000.
2. The FUNDAF (Special Fund for Development and Improvement of Auditing Activities) contributions are included in heading 6200 from 2008.

StatLink https://doi.org/10.1787/888933941916

Table 6.7. **Chile, tax revenues by sub-sectors of government**

Million CLP

	Federal government					State/Regional				
	1990	2000	2010	2015	2017	1990	2000	2010	2015	2017
1000 Taxes on income, profits and capital gains	**412 974**	**1 841 630**	**8 329 060**	**11 840 521**	**12 516 154**	..	..	..	..	..
1100 Of individuals	99 154	604 100	1 492 837	3 199 876	3 500 023	..	..	..	..	..
1200 Corporate	219 586	882 896	4 448 745	6 839 133	7 658 420	..	..	..	..	..
1300 Unallocable between 1100 and 1200	94 233	354 634	2 387 478	1 801 512	1 357 711	..	..	..	..	..
2000 Social security contributions	**66 738**	**232 728**	**371 386**	**434 658**	**506 019**	..	..	..	..	..
2100 Employees	61 200	209 907	310 558	370 744	432 376	..	..	..	..	..
2200 Employers	5 538	22 821	60 828	63 914	73 643	..	..	..	..	..
2300 Self-employed or non-employed	0	0	0	0	0	..	..	..	..	..
2400 Unallocable between 2100, 2200 and 2300	0	0	0	0	0	..	..	..	..	..
3000 Taxes on payroll and workforce	**0**	**0**	**0**	**0**	**0**	..	..	..	..	..
4000 Taxes on property	**59 682**	**255 371**	**245 044**	**379 603**	**738 311**	..	..	..	..	..
4100 Recurrent taxes on immovable property	10 331	3 578	8 805	15 249	17 289	..	..	..	..	..
4200 Recurrent taxes on net wealth	0	0	0	0	0	..	..	..	..	..
4300 Estate, inheritance and gift taxes	3 444	10 906	39 338	92 236	202 376	..	..	..	..	..
4400 Taxes on financial and capital transactions	45 907	240 886	196 901	272 118	518 645	..	..	..	..	..
4500 Non-recurrent taxes	0	0	0	0	0	..	..	..	..	..
4600 Other recurrent taxes on property	0	0	0	0	0	..	..	..	..	..
5000 Taxes on goods and services	**1 063 677**	**4 719 255**	**10 330 378**	**16 181 720**	**18 227 989**	..	..	..	..	..
5100 Taxes on production, sale, transfer, etc	1 060 304	4 684 525	10 294 165	16 129 953	18 175 735	..	..	..	..	..
5110 General taxes	664 421	3 306 350	8 399 926	13 273 958	15 069 540	..	..	..	..	..
5120 Taxes on specific goods and services[1]	395 883	1 378 175	1 894 239	2 855 995	3 106 195	..	..	..	..	..
5130 Unallocable between 5110 and 5120	0	0	0	0	0	..	..	..	..	..
5200 Taxes on use of goods and perform activities	3 374	34 730	36 213	51 767	52 254	..	..	..	..	..
5300 Unallocable between 5100 and 5200	0	0	0	0	0	..	..	..	..	..
6000 Other taxes	**-23 356**	**-112 195**	**-61 117**	**-579 308**	**-714 253**	..	..	..	..	..
6100 Paid solely by business	0	0	0	0	0	..	..	..	..	..
6200 Other	-23 356	-112 195	-61 117	-579 308	-714 253	..	..	..	..	..
Total tax revenue	**1 579 715**	**6 936 788**	**19 214 751**	**28 257 194**	**31 274 220**	..	..	..	..	..

Million CLP

	Local government					Social Security Funds				
	1990	2000	2010	2015	2017	1990	2000	2010	2015	2017
1000 Taxes on income, profits and capital gains	**0**	**0**	**0**	**0**	**0**	**0**	**0**	**0**	**0**	**0**
1100 Of individuals	0	0	0	0	0	0	0	0	0	0
1200 Corporate	0	0	0	0	0	0	0	0	0	0
1300 Unallocable between 1100 and 1200	0	0	0	0	0	0	0	0	0	0
2000 Social security contributions	**0**	**0**	**0**	**0**	**0**	**92 821**	**344 030**	**1 122 601**	**1 817 831**	**2 121 539**
2100 Employees	..	..	..	..	..	92 821	344 030	1 122 601	1 817 831	2 121 539
2200 Employers	..	..	..	..	..	0	0	0	0	0
2300 Self-employed or non-employed	..	..	..	..	..	0	0	0	0	0
2400 Unallocable between 2100, 2200 and 2300	..	..	..	..	..	0	0	0	0	0
3000 Taxes on payroll and workforce	**0**	**0**	**0**	**0**	**0**	**0**	**0**	**0**	**0**	**0**
4000 Taxes on property	**49 637**	**298 666**	**653 563**	**1 041 671**	**1 211 906**	**0**	**0**	**0**	**0**	**0**
4100 Recurrent taxes on immovable property	49 637	298 666	653 563	1 041 671	1 211 906	..	..	..	..	..
4200 Recurrent taxes on net wealth	0	0	0	0	0	..	..	..	..	..
4300 Estate, inheritance and gift taxes	0	0	0	0	0	..	..	..	..	..
4400 Taxes on financial and capital transactions	0	0	0	0	0	..	..	..	..	..
4500 Non-recurrent taxes	0	0	0	0	0	..	..	..	..	..
4600 Other recurrent taxes on property	0	0	0	0	0	..	..	..	..	..
5000 Taxes on goods and services	**55 045**	**322 514**	**854 778**	**1 415 658**	**1 630 892**	**0**	**0**	**0**	**0**	**0**
5100 Taxes on production, sale, transfer, etc	13 705	105 302	238 739	385 532	421 444	..	..	..	..	..
5110 General taxes	0	0	0	0	0	..	..	..	..	..
5120 Taxes on specific goods and services[1]	13 705	105 302	238 739	385 532	421 444	..	..	..	..	..
5130 Unallocable between 5110 and 5120	0	0	0	0	0	..	..	..	..	..
5200 Taxes on use of goods and perform activities	41 340	217 212	616 039	1 030 126	1 209 448	..	..	..	..	..
5300 Unallocable between 5100 and 5200	0	0	0	0	0	..	..	..	..	..
6000 Other taxes	**0**	**0**	**0**	**0**	**0**	**0**	**0**	**0**	**0**	**0**
6100 Paid solely by business	..	..	..	..	..	..	..	..	..	..
6200 Other	..	..	..	..	..	..	..	..	..	..
Total tax revenue	**104 682**	**621 180**	**1 508 341**	**2 457 329**	**2 842 798**	**92 821**	**344 030**	**1 122 601**	**1 817 831**	**2 121 539**

1. ECLAC classifies Oil Prices Stabilisation Fund (FEPP) revenues as non-tax revenues.

StatLink https://doi.org/10.1787/888933941935

Table 6.8. **Colombia, tax revenues by sub-sectors of government**

Million COP

	Federal government					State/Regional[1]				
	1990	2000	2010	2015	2017	1990	2000	2010	2015	2017
1000 Taxes on income, profits and capital gains	**771 694**	**7 103 525**	**26 218 852**	**52 656 876**	**57 615 236**	**0**	**0**	**0**	**0**	**0**
1100 Of individuals	47 210	1 499 345	5 192 384	9 736 861	11 004 827	..	..	..	..	..
1200 Corporate	359 758	5 119 828	20 405 209	41 070 208	44 491 100	..	..	..	..	..
1300 Unallocable between 1100 and 1200	364 726	484 352	621 258	1 849 807	2 119 308	..	..	..	..	..
2000 Social security contributions	**0**	**0**	**0**	**0**	**0**	**0**	**0**	**0**	**0**	**0**
2100 Employees	..	..	..	..	..	..	..	..	..	..
2200 Employers	..	..	..	..	..	..	..	..	..	..
2300 Self-employed or non-employed	..	..	..	..	..	..	..	..	..	..
2400 Unallocable between 2100, 2200 and 2300	..	..	..	..	..	..	..	..	..	..
3000 Taxes on payroll and workforce	**0**	**1 286 803**	**4 022 503**	**2 797 308**	**3 200 238**	**0**	**0**	**0**	**0**	**0**
4000 Taxes on property	**0**	**1 036 584**	**5 196 303**	**12 094 140**	**10 640 250**	**0**	**0**	**0**	**0**	**0**
4100 Recurrent taxes on immovable property	..	0	0	0	0	..	..	..	..	..
4200 Recurrent taxes on net wealth	..	0	1 970 530	5 352 940	3 868 595	..	..	..	..	..
4300 Estate, inheritance and gift taxes	..	0	0	0	0	..	..	..	..	..
4400 Taxes on financial and capital transactions	..	1 036 584	3 225 773	6 741 200	6 771 655	..	..	..	..	..
4500 Non-recurrent taxes	..	0	0	0	0	..	..	..	..	..
4600 Other recurrent taxes on property	..	0	0	0	0	..	..	..	..	..
5000 Taxes on goods and services	**1 035 934**	**11 022 878**	**34 882 447**	**51 126 468**	**58 223 436**	**263 429**	**1 204 940**	**2 752 254**	**4 083 718**	**5 368 108**
5100 Taxes on production, sale, transfer, etc	1 035 934	11 022 878	34 882 447	51 126 468	58 223 436	263 429	1 204 940	2 752 254	4 083 718	5 368 108
5110 General taxes	583 078	8 445 776	28 811 682	41 553 967	50 619 849	0	0	0	0	0
5120 Taxes on specific goods and services	452 856	2 577 102	6 070 765	9 572 501	7 603 587	263 429	1 204 940	2 752 254	4 083 718	5 368 108
5130 Unallocable between 5110 and 5120	0	0	0	0	0	0	0	0	0	0
5200 Taxes on use of goods and perform activities	0	0	0	0	0	0	0	0	0	0
5300 Unallocable between 5100 and 5200	0	0	0	0	0	0	0	0	0	0
6000 Other taxes	**78 306**	**480 784**	**483 762**	**424 000**	**478 966**	**0**	**518 253**	**2 029 017**	**3 528 393**	**3 571 495**
6100 Paid solely by business	0	0	0	0	0	..	0	0	0	0
6200 Other	78 306	480 784	483 762	424 000	478 966	..	518 253	2 029 017	3 528 393	3 571 495
Total tax revenue	**1 885 934**	**20 930 574**	**70 803 867**	**119 098 791**	**130 158 126**	**263 429**	**1 723 193**	**4 781 271**	**7 612 111**	**8 939 603**

Million COP

	Local government[1]					Social Security Funds[2]				
	1990	2000	2010	2015	2017	1990	2000	2010	2015	2017
1000 Taxes on income, profits and capital gains	**0**	**0**	**0**	**0**	**0**	**0**	**0**	**0**	**0**	**0**
1100 Of individuals	..	..	..	..	..	..	..	..	..	..
1200 Corporate	..	..	..	..	..	..	..	..	..	..
1300 Unallocable between 1100 and 1200	..	..	..	..	..	..	..	..	..	..
2000 Social security contributions	**0**	**0**	**0**	**0**	**0**	**203 596**	**4 989 000**	**11 478 085**	**13 585 138**	**13 351 710**
2100 Employees	..	..	..	..	..	..	..	..	..	..
2200 Employers	..	..	..	..	..	..	..	..	..	..
2300 Self-employed or non-employed	..	..	..	..	..	..	..	..	..	..
2400 Unallocable between 2100, 2200 and 2300	..	..	..	..	..	203 596	4 989 000	11 478 085	13 585 138	13 351 710
3000 Taxes on payroll and workforce	**0**	**0**	**0**	**0**	**0**	**0**	**0**	**0**	**0**	**0**
4000 Taxes on property	**56 160**	**991 070**	**3 338 935**	**6 212 601**	**7 310 244**	**0**	**0**	**0**	**0**	**0**
4100 Recurrent taxes on immovable property	56 160	991 070	3 338 935	6 212 601	7 310 244	..	..	..	..	..
4200 Recurrent taxes on net wealth	0	0	0	0	0	..	..	..	..	..
4300 Estate, inheritance and gift taxes	0	0	0	0	0	..	..	..	..	..
4400 Taxes on financial and capital transactions	0	0	0	0	0	..	..	..	..	..
4500 Non-recurrent taxes	0	0	0	0	0	..	..	..	..	..
4600 Other recurrent taxes on property	0	0	0	0	0	..	..	..	..	..
5000 Taxes on goods and services	**89 290**	**1 140 090**	**4 522 121**	**7 167 866**	**7 945 951**	**0**	**0**	**0**	**0**	**0**
5100 Taxes on production, sale, transfer, etc	89 290	1 140 090	4 522 121	7 167 866	7 945 951	..	..	..	..	..
5110 General taxes	89 290	1 140 090	4 522 121	7 167 866	7 945 951	..	..	..	..	..
5120 Taxes on specific goods and services	0	0	0	0	0	..	..	..	..	..
5130 Unallocable between 5110 and 5120	0	0	0	0	0	..	..	..	..	..
5200 Taxes on use of goods and perform activities	0	0	0	0	0	..	..	..	..	..
5300 Unallocable between 5100 and 5200	0	0	0	0	0	..	..	..	..	..
6000 Other taxes	**81 017**	**738 983**	**3 030 650**	**5 810 081**	**6 479 088**	**0**	**0**	**0**	**0**	**0**
6100 Paid solely by business	0	0	0	0	0	..	..	..	..	..
6200 Other	81 017	738 983	3 030 650	5 810 081	6 479 088	..	..	..	..	..
Total tax revenue	**226 467**	**2 870 144**	**10 891 707**	**19 190 548**	**21 735 283**	**203 596**	**4 989 000**	**11 478 085**	**13 585 138**	**13 351 710**

1. The data correspond to the reported consolidated revenues of the territorial entities (departments and municipalities).
2. All of the health contributions pertaining to FOSYGA (Solidarity and Guarantee Fund) are classified as social security contributions from 2013. Prior to 2013, only the portion of the contributions used to finance the subsidised regime was included and the part to finance the contributory regime was classified in the social security sector as "other incomes".

StatLink https://doi.org/10.1787/888933941954

Table 6.9. **Costa Rica, tax revenues by sub-sectors of government**

Million CRC

	Federal government					State/Regional				
	1990	2000	2010	2015	2017	1990	2000	2010	2015	2017
1000 Taxes on income, profits and capital gains	**11 820**	**128 805**	**748 093**	**1 247 308**	**1 562 063**	..	..	..	..	..
1100 Of individuals	..	..	202 849	386 241	446 519	..	..	..	..	..
1200 Corporate	..	..	450 312	659 951	843 879	..	..	..	..	..
1300 Unallocable between 1100 and 1200	11 820	128 805	94 932	201 116	271 664	..	..	..	..	..
2000 Social security contributions[1]	**1 345**	**18 677**	**61 193**	**63 458**	**71 148**	..	..	..	..	..
2100 Employees	..	..	..	..	..	..	..	..	..	..
2200 Employers	..	..	..	..	..	..	..	..	..	..
2300 Self-employed or non-employed	..	..	..	..	..	..	..	..	..	..
2400 Unallocable between 2100, 2200 and 2300	1 345	18 677	61 193	63 458	71 148	..	..	..	..	..
3000 Taxes on payroll and workforce	**0**	**0**	**0**	**0**	**0**	..	..	..	..	..
4000 Taxes on property	**366**	**3 007**	**18 270**	**37 334**	**43 054**	..	..	..	..	..
4100 Recurrent taxes on immovable property	0	0	3 527	4 076	4 255	..	..	..	..	..
4200 Recurrent taxes on net wealth	0	0	0	0	0	..	..	..	..	..
4300 Estate, inheritance and gift taxes	0	0	0	0	0	..	..	..	..	..
4400 Taxes on financial and capital transactions	366	3 007	14 743	33 258	38 799	..	..	..	..	..
4500 Non-recurrent taxes	0	0	0	0	0	..	..	..	..	..
4600 Other recurrent taxes on property	0	0	0	0	0	..	..	..	..	..
5000 Taxes on goods and services	**52 248**	**444 870**	**1 696 593**	**2 536 562**	**2 740 999**	..	..	..	..	..
5100 Taxes on production, sale, transfer, etc	49 867	425 630	1 598 789	2 385 807	2 571 716	..	..	..	..	..
5110 General taxes	21 326	222 775	920 298	1 368 601	1 466 986	..	..	..	..	..
5120 Taxes on specific goods and services[2]	28 541	202 856	678 491	1 017 206	1 104 730	..	..	..	..	..
5130 Unallocable between 5110 and 5120	0	0	0	0	0	..	..	..	..	..
5200 Taxes on use of goods and perform activities	2 380	19 240	97 804	150 755	169 283	..	..	..	..	..
5300 Unallocable between 5100 and 5200	0	0	0	0	0	..	..	..	..	..
6000 Other taxes[3]	**9 251**	**23 956**	**92 452**	**162 200**	**198 180**	..	..	..	..	..
6100 Paid solely by business	0	0	0	0	0	..	..	..	..	..
6200 Other	9 251	23 956	92 452	162 200	198 180	..	..	..	..	..
Total tax revenue	**75 030**	**619 314**	**2 616 600**	**4 046 862**	**4 615 443**	..	..	..	..	..

Million CRC

	Local government					Social Security Funds				
	1990	2000	2010	2015	2017	1990	2000	2010	2015	2017
1000 Taxes on income, profits and capital gains	**0**	**0**	**0**	**0**	**0**	**0**	**0**	**0**	**0**	**0**
1100 Of individuals	..	..	..	..	..	..	..	..	..	..
1200 Corporate	..	..	..	..	..	..	..	..	..	..
1300 Unallocable between 1100 and 1200	..	..	..	..	..	..	..	..	..	..
2000 Social security contributions[1]	**0**	**0**	**0**	**0**	**0**	**32 645**	**278 392**	**1 389 338**	**2 241 674**	**2 569 637**
2100 Employees	..	..	..	..	..	..	..	..	..	..
2200 Employers	..	..	..	..	..	3 447	37 313	207 206	318 652	361 161
2300 Self-employed or non-employed	..	..	..	..	..	..	..	..	..	..
2400 Unallocable between 2100, 2200 and 2300	..	..	..	..	..	29 198	241 079	1 182 132	1 923 022	2 208 476
3000 Taxes on payroll and workforce	**0**	**0**	**0**	**0**	**0**	**7 575**	**61 796**	**260 664**	**423 616**	**471 206**
4000 Taxes on property	**1 200**	**5 390**	**45 436**	**85 927**	**102 901**	**0**	**0**	**0**	**0**	**0**
4100 Recurrent taxes on immovable property	1 200	5 390	45 436	85 927	102 901	..	..	..	..	..
4200 Recurrent taxes on net wealth	0	0	0	0	0	..	..	..	..	..
4300 Estate, inheritance and gift taxes	0	0	0	0	0	..	..	..	..	..
4400 Taxes on financial and capital transactions	0	0	0	0	0	..	..	..	..	..
4500 Non-recurrent taxes	0	0	0	0	0	..	..	..	..	..
4600 Other recurrent taxes on property	0	0	0	0	0	..	..	..	..	..
5000 Taxes on goods and services	**1 262**	**11 981**	**70 321**	**125 341**	**134 334**	**0**	**0**	**0**	**0**	**0**
5100 Taxes on production, sale, transfer, etc	0	83	1 513	3 093	3 695	..	..	..	..	..
5110 General taxes	..	0	0	0	0	..	..	..	..	..
5120 Taxes on specific goods and services[2]	..	83	1 513	3 093	3 695	..	..	..	..	..
5130 Unallocable between 5110 and 5120	..	0	0	0	0	..	..	..	..	..
5200 Taxes on use of goods and perform activities	1 262	11 898	68 808	122 248	130 639	..	..	..	..	..
5300 Unallocable between 5100 and 5200	0	0	0	0	0	..	..	..	..	..
6000 Other taxes[3]	**0**	**1 242**	**8**	**155**	**121**	**0**	**0**	**0**	**0**	**0**
6100 Paid solely by business	..	0	0	0	0	..	..	..	..	..
6200 Other	..	1 242	8	155	121	..	..	..	..	..
Total tax revenue	**2 461**	**18 613**	**115 765**	**211 422**	**237 356**	**40 220**	**340 187**	**1 650 002**	**2 665 291**	**3 040 843**

1. The data include social security contributions paid by the governments for their employees as well as the contributions for special regimes (teachers and magistrates). In ECLAC data, social security contributions also include INA (National Institute of Apprenticeship), IMAS (Joint Social Aid Institute) and FODESAF (Social Development and Family Allowances Fund).
2. In ECLAC data, the tax on ownership of vehicles, aircraft and boats is classified in category 4000.
3. The tax revenue of decentralised bodies is classified under the central government. In Costa Rica this revenue is classified under a separate unit (decentralised) considered to be different to the central government.

StatLink https://doi.org/10.1787/888933941973

Table 6.10. **Cuba, tax revenues by sub-sectors of government**

Million CUP

	Federal government					State/Regional				
	1990	2000	2010	2015	2017	1990	2000	2010	2015	2017
1000 Taxes on income, profits and capital gains	**14**	**1 826**	**3 603**	**6 676**	**8 536**	..	..	..	..	..
1100 Of individuals	14	291	554	1 848	2 520	..	..	..	..	..
1200 Corporate	0	1 535	3 049	4 828	6 016	..	..	..	..	..
1300 Unallocable between 1100 and 1200	0	0	0	0	0	..	..	..	..	..
2000 Social security contributions	**0**	**0**	**0**	**0**	**0**	..	..	..	..	..
2100 Employees	..	..	..	..	..	..	..	..	..	..
2200 Employers	..	..	..	..	..	..	..	..	..	..
2300 Self-employed or non-employed	..	..	..	..	..	..	..	..	..	..
2400 Unallocable between 2100, 2200 and 2300	..	..	..	..	..	..	..	..	..	..
3000 Taxes on payroll and workforce	**0**	**970**	**4 414**	**2 753**	**1 476**	..	..	..	..	..
4000 Taxes on property	**0**	**0**	**0**	**0**	**0**	..	..	..	..	..
4100 Recurrent taxes on immovable property	..	..	..	..	..	..	..	..	..	..
4200 Recurrent taxes on net wealth	..	..	..	..	..	..	..	..	..	..
4300 Estate, inheritance and gift taxes	..	..	..	..	..	..	..	..	..	..
4400 Taxes on financial and capital transactions	..	..	..	..	..	..	..	..	..	..
4500 Non-recurrent taxes	..	..	..	..	..	..	..	..	..	..
4600 Other recurrent taxes on property	..	..	..	..	..	..	..	..	..	..
5000 Taxes on goods and services	**5 443**	**6 732**	**12 283**	**17 742**	**21 558**	..	..	..	..	..
5100 Taxes on production, sale, transfer, etc	5 443	6 732	12 283	17 742	21 558	..	..	..	..	..
5110 General taxes	5 017	6 131	10 525	15 611	17 934	..	..	..	..	..
5120 Taxes on specific goods and services	426	602	1 758	2 131	3 624	..	..	..	..	..
5130 Unallocable between 5110 and 5120	0	0	0	0	0	..	..	..	..	..
5200 Taxes on use of goods and perform activities	0	0	0	0	0	..	..	..	..	..
5300 Unallocable between 5100 and 5200	0	0	0	0	0	..	..	..	..	..
6000 Other taxes	**117**	**657**	**927**	**2 098**	**2 324**	..	..	..	..	..
6100 Paid solely by business	..	..	..	..	..	..	..	..	..	..
6200 Other	..	..	..	..	..	..	..	..	..	..
Total tax revenue	**5 574**	**10 185**	**21 227**	**29 269**	**33 893**	..	..	..	..	..

Million CUP

	Local government[1]					Social Security Funds				
	1990	2000	2010	2015	2017	1990	2000	2010	2015	2017
1000 Taxes on income, profits and capital gains	..	..	..	..	..	**0**	**0**	**0**	**0**	**0**
1100 Of individuals	..	..	..	..	..	..	..	..	..	..
1200 Corporate	..	..	..	..	..	..	..	..	..	..
1300 Unallocable between 1100 and 1200	..	..	..	..	..	..	..	..	..	..
2000 Social security contributions	..	..	..	..	..	**691**	**1 181**	**2 974**	**4 322**	**5 180**
2100 Employees	..	..	..	..	..	..	..	..	..	..
2200 Employers	..	..	..	..	..	..	..	..	..	..
2300 Self-employed or non-employed	..	..	..	..	..	..	..	..	..	..
2400 Unallocable between 2100, 2200 and 2300	..	..	..	..	..	691	1 181	2 974	4 322	5 180
3000 Taxes on payroll and workforce	..	..	..	..	..	**0**	**0**	**0**	**0**	**0**
4000 Taxes on property	..	..	..	..	..	**0**	**0**	**0**	**0**	**0**
4100 Recurrent taxes on immovable property	..	..	..	..	..	..	..	..	..	..
4200 Recurrent taxes on net wealth	..	..	..	..	..	..	..	..	..	..
4300 Estate, inheritance and gift taxes	..	..	..	..	..	..	..	..	..	..
4400 Taxes on financial and capital transactions	..	..	..	..	..	..	..	..	..	..
4500 Non-recurrent taxes	..	..	..	..	..	..	..	..	..	..
4600 Other recurrent taxes on property	..	..	..	..	..	..	..	..	..	..
5000 Taxes on goods and services	..	..	..	..	..	**0**	**0**	**0**	**0**	**0**
5100 Taxes on production, sale, transfer, etc	..	..	..	..	..	..	..	..	..	..
5110 General taxes	..	..	..	..	..	..	..	..	..	..
5120 Taxes on specific goods and services	..	..	..	..	..	..	..	..	..	..
5130 Unallocable between 5110 and 5120	..	..	..	..	..	..	..	..	..	..
5200 Taxes on use of goods and perform activities	..	..	..	..	..	..	..	..	..	..
5300 Unallocable between 5100 and 5200	..	..	..	..	..	..	..	..	..	..
6000 Other taxes	..	..	..	..	..	**0**	**0**	**0**	**0**	**0**
6100 Paid solely by business	..	..	..	..	..	..	..	..	..	..
6200 Other	..	..	..	..	..	..	..	..	..	..
Total tax revenue	..	..	..	..	..	**691**	**1 181**	**2 974**	**4 322**	**5 180**

1. The figures exclude local government tax revenues as the data are not available.

StatLink https://doi.org/10.1787/888933941992

Table 6.11. **Dominican Republic, tax revenues by sub-sectors of government**

Million DOP

	Federal government					State/Regional				
	1990	2000	2010	2015	2017	1990	2000	2010	2015	2017
1000 Taxes on income, profits and capital gains	**1 670**	**10 782**	**53 643**	**119 819**	**155 024**	..	..	..	..	..
1100 Of individuals	..	4 088	17 088	35 549	43 553	..	..	..	..	..
1200 Corporate	..	4 679	21 475	61 695	83 047	..	..	..	..	..
1300 Unallocable between 1100 and 1200	1 670	2 015	15 080	22 576	28 425	..	..	..	..	..
2000 Social security contributions	**0**	**0**	**0**	**0**	**0**	..	..	..	..	..
2100 Employees	..	..	..	..	..	..	..	..	..	..
2200 Employers	..	..	..	..	..	..	..	..	..	..
2300 Self-employed or non-employed	..	..	..	..	..	..	..	..	..	..
2400 Unallocable between 2100, 2200 and 2300	..	..	..	..	..	..	..	..	..	..
3000 Taxes on payroll and workforce	**0**	**0**	**0**	**0**	**0**	..	..	..	..	..
4000 Taxes on property	**74**	**689**	**13 315**	**19 044**	**22 942**	..	..	..	..	..
4100 Recurrent taxes on immovable property	9	115	555	1 755	2 166	..	..	..	..	..
4200 Recurrent taxes on net wealth	0	0	2 449	3 445	4 113	..	..	..	..	..
4300 Estate, inheritance and gift taxes	11	96	231	418	455	..	..	..	..	..
4400 Taxes on financial and capital transactions	40	377	8 658	12 067	13 995	..	..	..	..	..
4500 Non-recurrent taxes	3	32	488	591	711	..	..	..	..	..
4600 Other recurrent taxes on property	11	70	934	769	1 503	..	..	..	..	..
5000 Taxes on goods and services	**4 483**	**35 853**	**175 139**	**273 898**	**319 980**	..	..	..	..	..
5100 Taxes on production, sale, transfer, etc	4 414	35 135	168 641	263 435	306 680	..	..	..	..	..
5110 General taxes	970	9 912	81 226	147 039	169 629	..	..	..	..	..
5120 Taxes on specific goods and services[1]	3 444	25 224	87 415	116 396	137 051	..	..	..	..	..
5130 Unallocable between 5110 and 5120	0	0	0	0	0	..	..	..	..	..
5200 Taxes on use of goods and perform activities	69	718	6 498	10 463	13 300	..	..	..	..	..
5300 Unallocable between 5100 and 5200	0	0	0	0	0	..	..	..	..	..
6000 Other taxes[2]	**159**	**495**	**0**	**1**	**1**	..	..	..	..	..
6100 Paid solely by business	0	0	..	0	0	..	..	..	..	..
6200 Other	159	495	0	1	1	..	..	..	..	..
Total tax revenue	**6 386**	**47 820**	**242 097**	**412 762**	**497 948**	..	..	..	..	..

Million DOP

	Local government[3]					Social Security Funds[4]				
	1990	2000	2010	2015	2017	1990	2000	2010	2015	2017
1000 Taxes on income, profits and capital gains	..	..	..	..	..	**0**	**0**	**0**	**0**	**0**
1100 Of individuals	..	..	..	..	..	..	..	..	..	..
1200 Corporate	..	..	..	..	..	..	..	..	..	..
1300 Unallocable between 1100 and 1200	..	..	..	..	..	..	..	..	..	..
2000 Social security contributions	..	..	..	..	..	**53**	**490**	**1 845**	**1 483**	**2 635**
2100 Employees	..	..	..	..	..	..	..	1 720	1 321	1 535
2200 Employers	..	..	..	..	..	..	..	125	163	1 099
2300 Self-employed or non-employed	..	..	..	..	..	..	..	0	0	0
2400 Unallocable between 2100, 2200 and 2300	..	..	..	..	..	53	490	0	0	0
3000 Taxes on payroll and workforce	..	..	..	..	..	**0**	**0**	**0**	**0**	**0**
4000 Taxes on property	..	..	..	..	..	**0**	**0**	**0**	**0**	**0**
4100 Recurrent taxes on immovable property	..	..	..	..	..	..	..	..	..	..
4200 Recurrent taxes on net wealth	..	..	..	..	..	..	..	..	..	..
4300 Estate, inheritance and gift taxes	..	..	..	..	..	..	..	..	..	..
4400 Taxes on financial and capital transactions	..	..	..	..	..	..	..	..	..	..
4500 Non-recurrent taxes	..	..	..	..	..	..	..	..	..	..
4600 Other recurrent taxes on property	..	..	..	..	..	..	..	..	..	..
5000 Taxes on goods and services	..	..	..	..	..	**0**	**0**	**0**	**0**	**0**
5100 Taxes on production, sale, transfer, etc	..	..	..	..	..	..	..	..	..	..
5110 General taxes	..	..	..	..	..	..	..	..	..	..
5120 Taxes on specific goods and services[1]	..	..	..	..	..	..	..	..	..	..
5130 Unallocable between 5110 and 5120	..	..	..	..	..	..	..	..	..	..
5200 Taxes on use of goods and perform activities	..	..	..	..	..	..	..	..	..	..
5300 Unallocable between 5100 and 5200	..	..	..	..	..	..	..	..	..	..
6000 Other taxes[2]	..	..	..	..	..	**0**	**0**	**0**	**0**	**0**
6100 Paid solely by business	..	..	..	..	..	..	..	..	..	..
6200 Other	..	..	..	..	..	..	..	..	..	..
Total tax revenue	..	..	..	..	..	**53**	**490**	**1 845**	**1 483**	**2 635**

1. In ECLAC data, the tax on transfer of movable goods is classified as a property tax (4000).
2. In ECLAC data, the vehicle transfer tax is classified as a property tax (4000).
3. The figures exclude local government tax revenues as the data are not available.
4. The figures exclude social security contributions to general government managed by the private sector.

StatLink https://doi.org/10.1787/888933942011

Table 6.12. **Ecuador, tax revenues by sub-sectors of government**

Million USD

	Federal government[1]					State/Regional				
	1990	2000	2010	2015	2017	1990	2000	2010	2015	2017
1000 Taxes on income, profits and capital gains	**138**	**293**	**2 348**	**4 705**	**4 063**	..	..	..	..	..
1100 Of individuals	..	10	80	192	180	..	..	..	..	..
1200 Corporate	..	53	485	1 578	1 074	..	..	..	..	..
1300 Unallocable between 1100 and 1200	138	231	1 783	2 935	2 809	..	..	..	..	..
2000 Social security contributions	**0**	**0**	**0**	**0**	**0**	..	..	..	..	..
2100 Employees	..	..	..	..	..	..	..	..	..	..
2200 Employers	..	..	..	..	..	..	..	..	..	..
2300 Self-employed or non-employed	..	..	..	..	..	..	..	..	..	..
2400 Unallocable between 2100, 2200 and 2300	..	..	..	..	..	..	..	..	..	..
3000 Taxes on payroll and workforce	**0**	**0**	**0**	**0**	**0**	..	..	..	..	..
4000 Taxes on property	**0**	**0**	**5**	**29**	**52**	..	..	..	..	..
4100 Recurrent taxes on immovable property	..	..	0	0	7	..	..	..	..	..
4200 Recurrent taxes on net wealth	..	..	0	0	16	..	..	..	..	..
4300 Estate, inheritance and gift taxes	..	..	5	29	26	..	..	..	..	..
4400 Taxes on financial and capital transactions	..	..	0	0	0	..	..	..	..	..
4500 Non-recurrent taxes	..	..	0	0	3	..	..	..	..	..
4600 Other recurrent taxes on property	..	..	0	0	0	..	..	..	..	..
5000 Taxes on goods and services	**668**	**1 330**	**6 152**	**10 800**	**10 663**	..	..	..	..	..
5100 Taxes on production, sale, transfer, etc	665	1 319	5 997	10 577	10 361	..	..	..	..	..
5110 General taxes	302	836	3 886	6 352	6 817	..	..	..	..	..
5120 Taxes on specific goods and services	363	483	2 110	4 224	3 544	..	..	..	..	..
5130 Unallocable between 5110 and 5120	0	0	0	0	0	..	..	..	..	..
5200 Taxes on use of goods and perform activities	3	11	156	223	302	..	..	..	..	..
5300 Unallocable between 5100 and 5200	0	0	0	0	0	..	..	..	..	..
6000 Other taxes	**27**	**0**	**289**	**45**	**25**	..	..	..	..	..
6100 Paid solely by business	0	..	0	0	0	..	..	..	..	..
6200 Other	27	..	286	45	25	..	..	..	..	..
Total tax revenue	**833**	**1 623**	**8 794**	**15 579**	**14 804**	..	..	..	..	..

Million USD

	Local government[1,2]					Social Security Funds[1]				
	1990	2000	2010	2015	2017	1990	2000	2010	2015	2017
1000 Taxes on income, profits and capital gains	**1**	**2**	**15**	**75**	**71**	**0**	**0**	**0**	**0**	**0**
1100 Of individuals	..	..	..	..	..	..	..	..	..	..
1200 Corporate	..	..	..	..	..	..	..	..	..	..
1300 Unallocable between 1100 and 1200	1	2	15	75	71	..	..	..	..	..
2000 Social security contributions	**0**	**0**	**0**	**0**	**0**	**243**	**228**	**2 549**	**5 055**	**5 414**
2100 Employees	..	..	..	..	..	..	..	..	..	..
2200 Employers	..	..	..	..	..	..	..	..	..	..
2300 Self-employed or non-employed	..	..	..	..	..	..	..	..	..	..
2400 Unallocable between 2100, 2200 and 2300	..	..	..	..	..	243	228	2 549	5 055	5 414
3000 Taxes on payroll and workforce	**0**	**0**	**0**	**0**	**0**	**0**	**0**	**0**	**0**	**0**
4000 Taxes on property	**16**	**17**	**116**	**216**	**261**	**0**	**0**	**0**	**0**	**0**
4100 Recurrent taxes on immovable property	13	8	66	125	155	..	..	..	..	..
4200 Recurrent taxes on net wealth	0	0	0	0	0	..	..	..	..	..
4300 Estate, inheritance and gift taxes	0	0	0	0	0	..	..	..	..	..
4400 Taxes on financial and capital transactions	0	0	1	0	0	..	..	..	..	..
4500 Non-recurrent taxes	0	0	0	0	0	..	..	..	..	..
4600 Other recurrent taxes on property	3	9	50	91	106	..	..	..	..	..
5000 Taxes on goods and services	**8**	**12**	**96**	**225**	**224**	**0**	**0**	**0**	**0**	**0**
5100 Taxes on production, sale, transfer, etc	6	6	48	89	85	..	..	..	..	..
5110 General taxes	4	5	41	79	75	..	..	..	..	..
5120 Taxes on specific goods and services	1	2	7	10	10	..	..	..	..	..
5130 Unallocable between 5110 and 5120	0	0	0	0	0	..	..	..	..	..
5200 Taxes on use of goods and perform activities	2	5	47	136	139	..	..	..	..	..
5300 Unallocable between 5100 and 5200	0	0	0	0	0	..	..	..	..	..
6000 Other taxes	**2**	**2**	**1**	**0**	**0**	**0**	**0**	**0**	**0**	**0**
6100 Paid solely by business	0	0	0	0	0	..	..	..	..	..
6200 Other	2	2	1	0	0	..	..	..	..	..
Total tax revenue	**27**	**33**	**228**	**516**	**556**	**243**	**228**	**2 549**	**5 055**	**5 414**

1. The figures from 2016 include solidarity contributions enforced in this year to finance the reconstruction efforts in the aftermath of the 2015 earthquake. These affect headings 1100, 1200, 4200, 4500, 4600 and 5111.
2. The local data have been revised since 1990 and their classification have been improved, affecting headings 1000, 4400, 5120 and 5200.

StatLink https://doi.org/10.1787/888933942030

Table 6.13. **El Salvador, tax revenues by sub-sectors of government**

Million USD

	Federal government					State/Regional				
	1990	2000	2010	2015	2017	1990	2000	2010	2015	2017
1000 Taxes on income, profits and capital gains	**95**	**407**	**995**	**1 545**	**1 731**	..	..	..	..	..
1100 Of individuals	..	..	571	739	758	..	..	..	..	..
1200 Corporate	..	..	423	622	804	..	..	..	..	..
1300 Unallocable between 1100 and 1200	95	407	0	183	169	..	..	..	..	..
2000 Social security contributions	**0**	**0**	**0**	**0**	**0**	..	..	..	..	..
2100 Employees	..	..	..	..	..	..	..	..	..	..
2200 Employers	..	..	..	..	..	..	..	..	..	..
2300 Self-employed or non-employed	..	..	..	..	..	..	..	..	..	..
2400 Unallocable between 2100, 2200 and 2300	..	..	..	..	..	..	..	..	..	..
3000 Taxes on payroll and workforce	**0**	**0**	**0**	**0**	**0**	..	..	..	..	..
4000 Taxes on property	**26**	**12**	**16**	**107**	**108**	..	..	..	..	..
4100 Recurrent taxes on immovable property	0	0	0	0	0	..	..	..	..	..
4200 Recurrent taxes on net wealth	16	0	0	0	0	..	..	..	..	..
4300 Estate, inheritance and gift taxes	0	0	0	0	0	..	..	..	..	..
4400 Taxes on financial and capital transactions	10	12	16	107	108	..	..	..	..	..
4500 Non-recurrent taxes	0	0	0	0	0	..	..	..	..	..
4600 Other recurrent taxes on property	0	0	0	0	0	..	..	..	..	..
5000 Taxes on goods and services	**259**	**903**	**1 855**	**2 266**	**2 555**	..	..	..	..	..
5100 Taxes on production, sale, transfer, etc	259	903	1 847	2 254	2 542	..	..	..	..	..
5110 General taxes	133	714	1 433	1 764	1 905	..	..	..	..	..
5120 Taxes on specific goods and services	127	189	415	490	637	..	..	..	..	..
5130 Unallocable between 5110 and 5120	0	0	0	0	0	..	..	..	..	..
5200 Taxes on use of goods and perform activities	0	0	0	12	14	..	..	..	..	..
5300 Unallocable between 5100 and 5200	0	0	0	0	0	..	..	..	..	..
6000 Other taxes	**58**	**0**	**0**	**0**	**0**	..	..	..	..	..
6100 Paid solely by business	0	0	..	..	..	..	..	..	..	..
6200 Other	58	0	..	..	..	..	..	..	..	..
Total tax revenue	**438**	**1 322**	**2 865**	**3 918**	**4 394**	..	..	..	..	..

Million USD

	Local government					Social Security Funds[1]				
	1990	2000	2010	2015	2017	1990	2000	2010	2015	2017
1000 Taxes on income, profits and capital gains	..	..	**0**	**0**	**0**	**0**	**0**	**0**	**0**	**0**
1100 Of individuals	..	..	..	..	..	..	..	..	..	..
1200 Corporate	..	..	..	..	..	..	..	..	..	..
1300 Unallocable between 1100 and 1200	..	..	..	..	..	..	..	..	..	..
2000 Social security contributions	..	..	**0**	**0**	**0**	**67**	**263**	**369**	**488**	**572**
2100 Employees	..	..	..	..	..	..	75	99	130	152
2200 Employers	..	..	..	..	..	..	176	238	314	369
2300 Self-employed or non-employed	..	..	..	..	..	..	13	33	45	52
2400 Unallocable between 2100, 2200 and 2300	..	..	..	..	..	67	0	0	0	0
3000 Taxes on payroll and workforce	..	..	**0**	**0**	**0**	**0**	**0**	**0**	**0**	**0**
4000 Taxes on property	..	..	**0**	**0**	**0**	**0**	**0**	**0**	**0**	**0**
4100 Recurrent taxes on immovable property	..	..	..	..	..	..	..	..	..	..
4200 Recurrent taxes on net wealth	..	..	..	..	..	..	..	..	..	..
4300 Estate, inheritance and gift taxes	..	..	..	..	..	..	..	..	..	..
4400 Taxes on financial and capital transactions	..	..	..	..	..	..	..	..	..	..
4500 Non-recurrent taxes	..	..	..	..	..	..	..	..	..	..
4600 Other recurrent taxes on property	..	..	..	..	..	..	..	..	..	..
5000 Taxes on goods and services	..	..	**0**	**0**	**0**	**0**	**0**	**0**	**0**	**0**
5100 Taxes on production, sale, transfer, etc	..	..	..	..	..	..	..	..	..	..
5110 General taxes	..	..	..	..	..	..	..	..	..	..
5120 Taxes on specific goods and services	..	..	..	..	..	..	..	..	..	..
5130 Unallocable between 5110 and 5120	..	..	..	..	..	..	..	..	..	..
5200 Taxes on use of goods and perform activities	..	..	..	..	..	..	..	..	..	..
5300 Unallocable between 5100 and 5200	..	..	..	..	..	..	..	..	..	..
6000 Other taxes	..	..	**63**	**86**	**85**	**0**	**0**	**0**	**0**	**0**
6100 Paid solely by business	..	..	0	0	0	..	..	..	..	..
6200 Other	..	..	63	86	85	..	..	..	..	..
Total tax revenue	..	..	**63**	**86**	**85**	**67**	**263**	**369**	**488**	**572**

1. Social security contributions are those paid to the Salvadoran Institute of Social Security (ISSS) and exclude contributions to the privately managed regime.

StatLink https://doi.org/10.1787/888933942049

Table 6.14. **Guatemala, tax revenues by sub-sectors of government**

Million GTQ

	Federal government					State/Regional				
	1990	2000	2010	2015	2017	1990	2000	2010	2015	2017
1000 Taxes on income, profits and capital gains	**507**	**3 295**	**10 319**	**17 534**	**20 693**	..	..	..	..	..
1100 Of individuals	25	143	1 225	1 826	2 468	..	..	..	..	..
1200 Corporate	482	3 149	6 520	11 802	13 846	..	..	..	..	..
1300 Unallocable between 1100 and 1200	0	2	2 574	3 907	4 380	..	..	..	..	..
2000 Social security contributions	**0**	**0**	**0**	**0**	**0**	..	..	..	..	..
2100 Employees	..	..	..	..	..	..	..	..	..	..
2200 Employers	..	..	..	..	..	..	..	..	..	..
2300 Self-employed or non-employed	..	..	..	..	..	..	..	..	..	..
2400 Unallocable between 2100, 2200 and 2300	..	..	..	..	..	..	..	..	..	..
3000 Taxes on payroll and workforce	**0**	**0**	**0**	**0**	**0**	..	..	..	..	..
4000 Taxes on property	**0**	**17**	**11**	**21**	**30**	..	..	..	..	..
4100 Recurrent taxes on immovable property	..	6	1	1	1	..	..	..	..	..
4200 Recurrent taxes on net wealth	..	0	0	0	0	..	..	..	..	..
4300 Estate, inheritance and gift taxes	..	0	0	0	0	..	..	..	..	..
4400 Taxes on financial and capital transactions	..	12	10	20	29	..	..	..	..	..
4500 Non-recurrent taxes	..	0	0	0	0	..	..	..	..	..
4600 Other recurrent taxes on property	..	0	0	0	0	..	..	..	..	..
5000 Taxes on goods and services	**1 554**	**10 317**	**23 255**	**31 711**	**35 365**	..	..	..	..	..
5100 Taxes on production, sale, transfer, etc	1 526	10 131	22 750	30 080	33 586	..	..	..	..	..
5110 General taxes	762	6 259	16 980	23 271	26 187	..	..	..	..	..
5120 Taxes on specific goods and services	764	3 872	5 770	6 809	7 400	..	..	..	..	..
5130 Unallocable between 5110 and 5120	0	0	0	0	0	..	..	..	..	..
5200 Taxes on use of goods and perform activities	28	186	505	1 631	1 779	..	..	..	..	..
5300 Unallocable between 5100 and 5200	0	0	0	0	0	..	..	..	..	..
6000 Other taxes	**104**	**186**	**572**	**337**	**508**	..	..	..	..	..
6100 Paid solely by business	0	0	0	0	..	..	..	..	..	..
6200 Other	104	186	572	337	508	..	..	..	..	..
Total tax revenue	**2 165**	**13 816**	**34 157**	**49 604**	**56 597**	..	..	..	..	..

Million GTQ

	Local government[1]					Social Security Funds[2]				
	1990	2000	2010	2015	2017	1990	2000	2010	2015	2017
1000 Taxes on income, profits and capital gains	..	**0**	**0**	**0**	**0**	**0**	**0**	**0**	**0**	**0**
1100 Of individuals	..	..	..	..	..	..	..	..	..	..
1200 Corporate	..	..	..	..	..	..	..	..	..	..
1300 Unallocable between 1100 and 1200	..	..	..	..	..	..	..	..	..	..
2000 Social security contributions	..	**0**	**0**	**0**	**0**	**436**	**2 569**	**6 408**	**10 034**	**11 523**
2100 Employees	..	..	..	..	..	..	..	..	..	..
2200 Employers	..	..	..	..	..	..	..	..	..	..
2300 Self-employed or non-employed	..	..	..	..	..	..	..	..	..	..
2400 Unallocable between 2100, 2200 and 2300	..	..	..	..	..	436	2 569	6 408	10 034	11 523
3000 Taxes on payroll and workforce	..	**0**	**0**	**0**	**0**	**0**	**0**	**0**	**0**	**0**
4000 Taxes on property	..	**147**	**620**	**692**	**709**	**0**	**0**	**0**	**0**	**0**
4100 Recurrent taxes on immovable property	..	147	620	692	709	..	..	..	..	..
4200 Recurrent taxes on net wealth	..	0	0	0	0	..	..	..	..	..
4300 Estate, inheritance and gift taxes	..	0	0	0	0	..	..	..	..	..
4400 Taxes on financial and capital transactions	..	0	0	0	0	..	..	..	..	..
4500 Non-recurrent taxes	..	0	0	0	0	..	..	..	..	..
4600 Other recurrent taxes on property	..	0	0	0	0	..	..	..	..	..
5000 Taxes on goods and services	..	**0**	**0**	**0**	**0**	**0**	**0**	**0**	**0**	**0**
5100 Taxes on production, sale, transfer, etc	..	..	..	..	..	..	..	..	..	..
5110 General taxes	..	..	..	..	..	..	..	..	..	..
5120 Taxes on specific goods and services	..	..	..	..	..	..	..	..	..	..
5130 Unallocable between 5110 and 5120	..	..	..	..	..	..	..	..	..	..
5200 Taxes on use of goods and perform activities	..	..	..	..	..	..	..	..	..	..
5300 Unallocable between 5100 and 5200	..	..	..	..	..	..	..	..	..	..
6000 Other taxes	..	**0**	**0**	**0**	**0**	**0**	**0**	**0**	**0**	**0**
6100 Paid solely by business	..	..	..	..	..	..	..	..	..	..
6200 Other	..	..	..	..	..	..	..	..	..	..
Total tax revenue	..	**147**	**620**	**692**	**709**	**436**	**2 569**	**6 408**	**10 034**	**11 523**

1. Revenues from the municipal property tax (IUSI) are recorded at the local government level.
2. Corresponds to social security contributions to the Guatemalan Social Security Institute (IGSS) and payments by public employees to the government's pension fund.

StatLink https://doi.org/10.1787/888933942068

Table 6.15. **Guyana, tax revenues by sub-sectors of government**

Million GYD

	Federal government					State/Regional				
	1990	2000	2010	2015	2017	1990	2000	2010	2015	2017
1000 Taxes on income, profits and capital gains	**1 752**	**16 179**	**39 561**	**55 011**	**67 880**	..	..	..	..	..
1100 Of individuals	333	7 734	17 816	23 300	26 515	..	..	..	..	..
1200 Corporate	1 375	8 266	21 427	31 200	41 024	..	..	..	..	..
1300 Unallocable between 1100 and 1200	43	179	317	511	341	..	..	..	..	..
2000 Social security contributions	**0**	**0**	**0**	**0**	**0**	..	..	..	..	..
2100 Employees	..	..	..	..	..	..	..	..	..	..
2200 Employers	..	..	..	..	..	..	..	..	..	..
2300 Self-employed or non-employed	..	..	..	..	..	..	..	..	..	..
2400 Unallocable between 2100, 2200 and 2300	..	..	..	..	..	..	..	..	..	..
3000 Taxes on payroll and workforce	**0**	**0**	**0**	**0**	**0**	..	..	..	..	..
4000 Taxes on property	**53**	**701**	**1 593**	**3 237**	**3 618**	..	..	..	..	..
4100 Recurrent taxes on immovable property	40	681	1 562	3 201	3 579	..	..	..	..	..
4200 Recurrent taxes on net wealth	0	0	0	0	0	..	..	..	..	..
4300 Estate, inheritance and gift taxes	13	20	31	37	39	..	..	..	..	..
4400 Taxes on financial and capital transactions	0	0	0	0	0	..	..	..	..	..
4500 Non-recurrent taxes	0	0	0	0	0	..	..	..	..	..
4600 Other recurrent taxes on property	0	0	0	0	0	..	..	..	..	..
5000 Taxes on goods and services	**2 200**	**20 798**	**59 387**	**84 027**	**97 558**	..	..	..	..	..
5100 Taxes on production, sale, transfer, etc	2 162	20 530	58 873	83 330	96 519	..	..	..	..	..
5110 General taxes	1 399	14 861	27 071	35 476	42 861	..	..	..	..	..
5120 Taxes on specific goods and services	763	5 669	31 802	47 853	53 659	..	..	..	..	..
5130 Unallocable between 5110 and 5120	0	0	0	0	0	..	..	..	..	..
5200 Taxes on use of goods and perform activities	38	268	514	697	1 039	..	..	..	..	..
5300 Unallocable between 5100 and 5200	0	0	0	0	0	..	..	..	..	..
6000 Other taxes	**1 037**	**204**	**1 233**	**1 038**	**2 094**	..	..	..	..	..
6100 Paid solely by business	0	0	0	0	0	..	..	..	..	..
6200 Other	1 037	204	1 233	1 038	2 094	..	..	..	..	..
Total tax revenue	**5 041**	**37 882**	**101 773**	**143 313**	**171 150**	..	..	..	..	..

Million GYD

	Local government					Social Security Funds				
	1990	2000	2010	2015	2017	1990	2000	2010	2015	2017
1000 Taxes on income, profits and capital gains	..	..	**0**	**0**	**0**	**0**	**0**	**0**	**0**	**0**
1100 Of individuals	..	..	..	..	..	..	..	..	..	..
1200 Corporate	..	..	..	..	..	..	..	..	..	..
1300 Unallocable between 1100 and 1200	..	..	..	..	..	..	..	..	..	..
2000 Social security contributions[1]	..	..	**0**	**0**	**0**	**191**	**4 868**	**10 047**	**16 708**	**20 771**
2100 Employees	..	..	..	..	..	..	..	..	..	..
2200 Employers	..	..	..	..	..	..	..	..	..	..
2300 Self-employed or non-employed	..	..	..	..	..	..	..	..	..	..
2400 Unallocable between 2100, 2200 and 2300	..	..	..	..	..	191	4 868	10 047	16 708	20 771
3000 Taxes on payroll and workforce	..	..	**0**	**0**	**0**	**0**	**0**	**0**	**0**	**0**
4000 Taxes on property	..	..	**0**	**0**	**0**	**0**	**0**	**0**	**0**	**0**
4100 Recurrent taxes on immovable property	..	..	..	..	..	..	..	..	..	..
4200 Recurrent taxes on net wealth	..	..	..	..	..	..	..	..	..	..
4300 Estate, inheritance and gift taxes	..	..	..	..	..	..	..	..	..	..
4400 Taxes on financial and capital transactions	..	..	..	..	..	..	..	..	..	..
4500 Non-recurrent taxes	..	..	..	..	..	..	..	..	..	..
4600 Other recurrent taxes on property	..	..	..	..	..	..	..	..	..	..
5000 Taxes on goods and services	..	..	**0**	**0**	**0**	**0**	**0**	**0**	**0**	**0**
5100 Taxes on production, sale, transfer, etc	..	..	..	..	..	..	..	..	..	..
5110 General taxes	..	..	..	..	..	..	..	..	..	..
5120 Taxes on specific goods and services	..	..	..	..	..	..	..	..	..	..
5130 Unallocable between 5110 and 5120	..	..	..	..	..	..	..	..	..	..
5200 Taxes on use of goods and perform activities	..	..	..	..	..	..	..	..	..	..
5300 Unallocable between 5100 and 5200	..	..	..	..	..	..	..	..	..	..
6000 Other taxes	..	..	**113**	**41**	**198**	**0**	**0**	**0**	**0**	**0**
6100 Paid solely by business	..	..	0	0	0	..	..	..	..	..
6200 Other	..	..	113	41	198	..	..	..	..	..
Total tax revenue	..	..	**113**	**41**	**198**	**191**	**4 868**	**10 047**	**16 708**	**20 771**

1. Social security figures are estimated since 2015.

StatLink https://doi.org/10.1787/888933942087

Table 6.16. **Honduras, tax revenues by sub-sectors of government**

Million HNL

	Federal government					State/Regional				
	1990	2000	2010	2015	2017	1990	2000	2010	2015	2017
1000 Taxes on income, profits and capital gains	**431**	**2 907**	**13 232**	**24 843**	**33 055**	..	..	..	..	..
1100 Of individuals	157	991	4 528	8 451	11 369	..	..	..	..	..
1200 Corporate	274	1 916	8 705	16 392	21 687	..	..	..	..	..
1300 Unallocable between 1100 and 1200	0	0	0	0	0	..	..	..	..	..
2000 Social security contributions	**0**	**0**	**0**	**0**	**0**	..	..	..	..	..
2100 Employees	..	..	..	..	..	..	..	..	..	..
2200 Employers	..	..	..	..	..	..	..	..	..	..
2300 Self-employed or non-employed	..	..	..	..	..	..	..	..	..	..
2400 Unallocable between 2100, 2200 and 2300	..	..	..	..	..	..	..	..	..	..
3000 Taxes on payroll and workforce	**0**	**0**	**0**	**0**	**0**	..	..	..	..	..
4000 Taxes on property	**16**	**266**	**994**	**2 635**	**3 046**	..	..	..	..	..
4100 Recurrent taxes on immovable property	0	0	0	0	0	..	..	..	..	..
4200 Recurrent taxes on net wealth	0	0	0	0	0	..	..	..	..	..
4300 Estate, inheritance and gift taxes	0	0	0	0	0	..	..	..	..	..
4400 Taxes on financial and capital transactions	0	0	0	2 003	2 353	..	..	..	..	..
4500 Non-recurrent taxes	0	0	381	0	0	..	..	..	..	..
4600 Other recurrent taxes on property	16	266	613	633	693	..	..	..	..	..
5000 Taxes on goods and services	**1 405**	**11 445**	**28 937**	**52 217**	**63 111**	..	..	..	..	..
5100 Taxes on production, sale, transfer, etc	1 405	11 445	28 937	52 217	63 111	..	..	..	..	..
5110 General taxes	344	5 146	16 050	32 273	39 228	..	..	..	..	..
5120 Taxes on specific goods and services	1 061	6 299	12 887	19 944	23 883	..	..	..	..	..
5130 Unallocable between 5110 and 5120	0	0	0	0	0	..	..	..	..	..
5200 Taxes on use of goods and perform activities	0	0	0	0	0	..	..	..	..	..
5300 Unallocable between 5100 and 5200	0	0	0	0	0	..	..	..	..	..
6000 Other taxes	**1**	**2**	**9**	**8**	**14**	..	..	..	..	..
6100 Paid solely by business	0	0	0	0	0	..	..	..	..	..
6200 Other	1	2	9	8	14	..	..	..	..	..
Total tax revenue	**1 853**	**14 620**	**43 173**	**79 704**	**99 226**	..	..	..	..	..

Million HNL

	Local government[1]					Social Security Funds				
	1990	2000	2010	2015	2017	1990	2000	2010	2015	2017
1000 Taxes on income, profits and capital gains	**0**	**0**	**0**	**0**	**0**	**0**	**0**	**0**	**0**	**0**
1100 Of individuals	..	..	..	..	..	..	..	..	..	..
1200 Corporate	..	..	..	..	..	..	..	..	..	..
1300 Unallocable between 1100 and 1200	..	..	..	..	..	..	..	..	..	..
2000 Social security contributions	**0**	**0**	**0**	**0**	**0**	**179**	**1 727**	**8 671**	**13 524**	**17 379**
2100 Employees	..	..	..	..	..	..	..	..	..	..
2200 Employers	..	..	..	..	..	..	..	..	..	..
2300 Self-employed or non-employed	..	..	..	..	..	..	..	..	..	..
2400 Unallocable between 2100, 2200 and 2300	..	..	..	..	..	179	1 727	8 671	13 524	17 379
3000 Taxes on payroll and workforce	**0**	**0**	**0**	**0**	**0**	**0**	**0**	**0**	**0**	**0**
4000 Taxes on property	**0**	**0**	**0**	**0**	**0**	**0**	**0**	**0**	**0**	**0**
4100 Recurrent taxes on immovable property	..	..	..	..	..	..	..	..	..	..
4200 Recurrent taxes on net wealth	..	..	..	..	..	..	..	..	..	..
4300 Estate, inheritance and gift taxes	..	..	..	..	..	..	..	..	..	..
4400 Taxes on financial and capital transactions	..	..	..	..	..	..	..	..	..	..
4500 Non-recurrent taxes	..	..	..	..	..	..	..	..	..	..
4600 Other recurrent taxes on property	..	..	..	..	..	..	..	..	..	..
5000 Taxes on goods and services	**0**	**0**	**0**	**0**	**0**	**0**	**0**	**0**	**0**	**0**
5100 Taxes on production, sale, transfer, etc	..	..	..	..	..	..	..	..	..	..
5110 General taxes	..	..	..	..	..	..	..	..	..	..
5120 Taxes on specific goods and services	..	..	..	..	..	..	..	..	..	..
5130 Unallocable between 5110 and 5120	..	..	..	..	..	..	..	..	..	..
5200 Taxes on use of goods and perform activities	..	..	..	..	..	..	..	..	..	..
5300 Unallocable between 5100 and 5200	..	..	..	..	..	..	..	..	..	..
6000 Other taxes	**90**	**960**	**2 216**	**2 496**	**6 579**	**0**	**0**	**0**	**0**	**0**
6100 Paid solely by business	0	0	0	0	0	..	..	..	..	..
6200 Other	90	960	2 216	2 496	6 579	..	..	..	..	..
Total tax revenue	**90**	**960**	**2 216**	**2 496**	**6 579**	**179**	**1 727**	**8 671**	**13 524**	**17 379**

1. The figures may include non-tax revenues and central government transfers but it has not been possible to distinguish the different components of local government tax revenues.

StatLink https://doi.org/10.1787/888933942106

Table 6.17. **Jamaica, tax revenues by sub-sectors of government**

Million JAM

	Federal government					State/Regional				
	1990	2000	2010	2015	2017	1990	2000	2010	2015	2017
1000 Taxes on income, profits and capital gains	**3 944**	**39 277**	**118 708**	**149 989**	**155 790**	..	..	..	..	..
1100 Of individuals	1 687	17 441	54 798	74 537	60 306	..	..	..	..	..
1200 Corporate	1 280	7 627	33 091	40 198	61 401	..	..	..	..	..
1300 Unallocable between 1100 and 1200	977	14 209	30 820	35 254	34 083	..	..	..	..	..
2000 Social security contributions	**0**	**0**	**0**	**0**	**0**	..	..	..	..	..
2100 Employees	..	..	..	..	..	..	..	..	..	..
2200 Employers	..	..	..	..	..	..	..	..	..	..
2300 Self-employed or non-employed	..	..	..	..	..	..	..	..	..	..
2400 Unallocable between 2100, 2200 and 2300	..	..	..	..	..	..	..	..	..	..
3000 Taxes on payroll and workforce	**0**	**0**	**0**	**0**	**0**	..	..	..	..	..
4000 Taxes on property	**67**	**0**	**0**	**0**	**0**	..	..	..	..	..
4100 Recurrent taxes on immovable property	67	..	..	..	..	..	..	..	..	..
4200 Recurrent taxes on net wealth	0	..	..	..	..	..	..	..	..	..
4300 Estate, inheritance and gift taxes	0	..	..	..	..	..	..	..	..	..
4400 Taxes on financial and capital transactions	0	..	..	..	..	..	..	..	..	..
4500 Non-recurrent taxes	0	..	..	..	..	..	..	..	..	..
4600 Other recurrent taxes on property	0	..	..	..	..	..	..	..	..	..
5000 Taxes on goods and services	**2 824**	**43 907**	**149 544**	**241 055**	**316 562**	..	..	..	..	..
5100 Taxes on production, sale, transfer, etc	2 760	43 107	147 500	237 849	311 872	..	..	..	..	..
5110 General taxes	297	22 356	84 409	138 222	171 584	..	..	..	..	..
5120 Taxes on specific goods and services	2 463	20 752	63 091	99 627	140 288	..	..	..	..	..
5130 Unallocable between 5110 and 5120	0	0	0	0	0	..	..	..	..	..
5200 Taxes on use of goods and perform activities	64	800	2 045	3 206	4 690	..	..	..	..	..
5300 Unallocable between 5100 and 5200	0	0	0	0	0	..	..	..	..	..
6000 Other taxes	**914**	**3 890**	**8 088**	**13 167**	**16 928**	..	..	..	..	..
6100 Paid solely by business	0	0	0	0	0	..	..	..	..	..
6200 Other	914	3 890	8 088	13 167	16 928	..	..	..	..	..
Total tax revenue	**7 748**	**87 074**	**276 340**	**404 212**	**489 280**	..	..	..	..	..

Million JAM

	Local government					Social Security Funds				
	1990	2000	2010	2015	2017	1990	2000	2010	2015	2017
1000 Taxes on income, profits and capital gains	..	**0**	**0**	**0**	**0**	..	..	**0**	**0**	**0**
1100 Of individuals	..	..	..	..	..	..	..	..	..	..
1200 Corporate	..	..	..	..	..	..	..	..	..	..
1300 Unallocable between 1100 and 1200	..	..	..	..	..	..	..	..	..	..
2000 Social security contributions	..	**0**	**0**	**0**	**0**	..	..	**8 199**	**16 449**	**19 249**
2100 Employees	..	..	..	..	..	..	..	..	..	..
2200 Employers	..	..	..	..	..	..	..	..	..	..
2300 Self-employed or non-employed	..	..	..	..	..	..	..	..	..	..
2400 Unallocable between 2100, 2200 and 2300	..	..	..	..	..	..	..	8 199	16 449	19 249
3000 Taxes on payroll and workforce	..	**0**	**0**	**0**	**0**	..	..	**0**	**0**	**0**
4000 Taxes on property	..	**639**	**2 600**	**7 271**	**8 523**	..	..	**0**	**0**	**0**
4100 Recurrent taxes on immovable property	..	639	2 600	7 271	8 523	..	..	..	..	..
4200 Recurrent taxes on net wealth	..	0	0	0	0	..	..	..	..	..
4300 Estate, inheritance and gift taxes	..	0	0	0	0	..	..	..	..	..
4400 Taxes on financial and capital transactions	..	0	0	0	0	..	..	..	..	..
4500 Non-recurrent taxes	..	0	0	0	0	..	..	..	..	..
4600 Other recurrent taxes on property	..	0	0	0	0	..	..	..	..	..
5000 Taxes on goods and services	..	**0**	**0**	**0**	**0**	..	..	**0**	**0**	**0**
5100 Taxes on production, sale, transfer, etc	..	..	..	..	..	..	..	..	..	..
5110 General taxes	..	..	..	..	..	..	..	..	..	..
5120 Taxes on specific goods and services	..	..	..	..	..	..	..	..	..	..
5130 Unallocable between 5110 and 5120	..	..	..	..	..	..	..	..	..	..
5200 Taxes on use of goods and perform activities	..	..	..	..	..	..	..	..	..	..
5300 Unallocable between 5100 and 5200	..	..	..	..	..	..	..	..	..	..
6000 Other taxes	..	**0**	**0**	**0**	**0**	..	..	**0**	**0**	**0**
6100 Paid solely by business	..	..	..	..	..	..	..	..	..	..
6200 Other	..	..	..	..	..	..	..	..	..	..
Total tax revenue	..	**639**	**2 600**	**7 271**	**8 523**	..	..	**8 199**	**16 449**	**19 249**

StatLink https://doi.org/10.1787/888933942125

Table 6.18. **Mexico, tax revenues by sub-sectors of government**

Million MXN

	Federal government					State/Regional				
	1990	2000	2010	2015	2017	1990	2000	2010	2015	2017
1000 Taxes on income, profits and capital gains[1]	**34 668**	**276 548**	**683 604**	**1 230 555**	**1 571 788**	**3**	**0**	**0**	**0**	..
1100 Of individuals	..	..	313 473	609 384	754 109	..	..	..	..	..
1200 Corporate	..	..	246 745	592 443	769 193	..	..	..	..	..
1300 Unallocable between 1100 and 1200	34 668	276 548	123 386	28 728	48 486	3	..	..	..	..
2000 Social security contributions[2]	**0**	**0**	**0**	**0**	**0**	**0**	**0**	**0**	**0**	..
2100 Employees	..	..	..	..	..	..	..	..	..	..
2200 Employers	..	..	..	..	..	..	..	..	..	..
2300 Self-employed or non-employed	..	..	..	..	..	..	..	..	..	..
2400 Unallocable between 2100, 2200 and 2300	..	..	..	..	..	..	..	..	..	..
3000 Taxes on payroll and workforce	**818**	**0**	**0**	**0**	**0**	**972**	**11 215**	**36 818**	**70 221**	..
4000 Taxes on property	**3**	**0**	**0**	**0**	**0**	**894**	**7 018**	**13 137**	**22 481**	..
4100 Recurrent taxes on immovable property	0	..	..	..	..	482	5 238	8 522	14 245	..
4200 Recurrent taxes on net wealth	0	..	..	..	..	0	0	0	0	..
4300 Estate, inheritance and gift taxes	0	..	..	..	..	7	0	0	0	..
4400 Taxes on financial and capital transactions	3	..	..	..	..	405	1 781	4 615	8 235	..
4500 Non-recurrent taxes	0	..	..	..	..	0	0	0	0	..
4600 Other recurrent taxes on property	0	..	..	..	..	0	0	0	0	..
5000 Taxes on goods and services	**44 605**	**318 065**	**645 623**	**1 116 026**	**1 254 879**	**118**	**1 346**	**5 805**	**24 355**	..
5100 Taxes on production, sale, transfer, etc	44 029	309 283	627 187	1 115 525	1 254 253	45	910	2 470	4 357	..
5110 General taxes	26 635	189 606	504 509	707 213	816 048	0	0	0	0	..
5120 Taxes on specific goods and services	17 394	119 677	122 678	408 312	438 205	30	910	2 470	4 357	..
5130 Unallocable between 5110 and 5120	0	0	0	0	0	15	0	0	0	..
5200 Taxes on use of goods and perform activities	576	8 782	18 436	501	626	73	436	3 335	19 998	..
5300 Unallocable between 5100 and 5200	0	0	0	0	0	0	0	0	0	..
6000 Other taxes	**1 340**	**5 878**	**22 236**	**27 379**	**32 433**	**165**	**907**	**2 546**	**6 489**	..
6100 Paid solely by business	0	0	0	0	0	0	0	0	0	..
6200 Other	1 340	5 878	22 236	27 379	32 433	165	907	2 546	6 489	..
Total tax revenue	**81 434**	**600 491**	**1 351 463**	**2 373 960**	**2 859 100**	**2 152**	**20 485**	**58 307**	**123 545**	..

Million MXN

	Local government					Social Security Funds				
	1990	2000	2010	2015	2017	1990	2000	2010	2015	2017
1000 Taxes on income, profits and capital gains[1]	**2**	**0**	**0**	**0**	..	**0**	**0**	**0**	**0**	**0**
1100 Of individuals	..	..	..	..	..	..	..	..	..	..
1200 Corporate	..	..	..	..	..	..	..	..	..	..
1300 Unallocable between 1100 and 1200	2	..	..	..	..	..	..	..	..	..
2000 Social security contributions[2]	**0**	**0**	**0**	**0**	..	**17 165**	**138 223**	**277 459**	**409 249**	**467 710**
2100 Employees	..	..	..	..	..	..	..	..	..	..
2200 Employers	..	..	..	..	..	..	..	..	..	..
2300 Self-employed or non-employed	..	..	..	..	..	..	..	..	..	..
2400 Unallocable between 2100, 2200 and 2300	..	..	..	..	..	17 165	138 223	277 459	409 249	467 710
3000 Taxes on payroll and workforce	**7**	**2**	**93**	**1**	..	**0**	**0**	**0**	**0**	**0**
4000 Taxes on property	**1 017**	**6 946**	**25 818**	**35 193**	..	**0**	**0**	**0**	**0**	**0**
4100 Recurrent taxes on immovable property	554	4 710	17 202	23 715	..	..	..	..	..	..
4200 Recurrent taxes on net wealth	0	0	0	0	..	..	..	..	..	..
4300 Estate, inheritance and gift taxes	1	0	0	0	..	..	..	..	..	..
4400 Taxes on financial and capital transactions	462	2 236	8 616	11 477	..	..	..	..	..	..
4500 Non-recurrent taxes	0	0	0	0	..	..	..	..	..	..
4600 Other recurrent taxes on property	0	0	0	0	..	..	..	..	..	..
5000 Taxes on goods and services	**114**	**202**	**487**	**789**	..	**0**	**0**	**0**	**0**	**0**
5100 Taxes on production, sale, transfer, etc	97	133	466	728	..	..	..	..	..	..
5110 General taxes	0	0	0	0	..	..	..	..	..	..
5120 Taxes on specific goods and services	95	133	466	728	..	..	..	..	..	..
5130 Unallocable between 5110 and 5120	2	0	0	0	..	..	..	..	..	..
5200 Taxes on use of goods and perform activities	17	69	21	61	..	..	..	..	..	..
5300 Unallocable between 5100 and 5200	0	0	0	0	..	..	..	..	..	..
6000 Other taxes	**114**	**866**	**2 616**	**10 743**	..	**0**	**0**	**0**	**0**	**0**
6100 Paid solely by business	0	0	0	0	..	..	..	..	..	..
6200 Other	114	866	2 616	10 743	..	..	..	..	..	..
Total tax revenue	**1 254**	**8 016**	**29 014**	**46 726**	..	**17 165**	**138 223**	**277 459**	**409 249**	**467 710**

Note: The 2017 data for tax revenues of the state and local levels of government are not available. They comprise revenues in categories 3000, 4000, 5000 and 6000.

1. In ECLAC data, income taxes are presented net of credit on salary figures.
2. Some amounts of social security contributions are now treated as non-tax revenue to align with reporting to other international organisations. In ECLAC data, social security contributions are presented net of transfers from the Federal government for the payment of IMSS (Mexican Social Security Institute) pensions.

StatLink https://doi.org/10.1787/888933942144

Table 6.19. **Nicaragua, tax revenues by sub-sectors of government**

Million NIO

	Federal government					State/Regional				
	1990	2000	2010	2015	2017	1990	2000	2010	2015	2017
1000 Taxes on income, profits and capital gains	..	**1 144**	**8 351**	**21 313**	**28 557**	..	..	..	..	..
1100 Of individuals	..	..	..	..	..	..	..	..	..	..
1200 Corporate	..	..	..	..	..	..	..	..	..	..
1300 Unallocable between 1100 and 1200	..	1 144	8 351	21 313	28 557	..	..	..	..	..
2000 Social security contributions	..	**0**	**0**	**0**	**0**	..	..	..	..	..
2100 Employees	..	..	..	..	..	..	..	..	..	..
2200 Employers	..	..	..	..	..	..	..	..	..	..
2300 Self-employed or non-employed	..	..	..	..	..	..	..	..	..	..
2400 Unallocable between 2100, 2200 and 2300	..	..	..	..	..	..	..	..	..	..
3000 Taxes on payroll and workforce	..	**0**	**0**	**0**	**0**	..	..	..	..	..
4000 Taxes on property	..	**0**	**0**	**0**	**0**	..	..	..	..	..
4100 Recurrent taxes on immovable property	..	..	..	..	..	..	..	..	..	..
4200 Recurrent taxes on net wealth	..	..	..	..	..	..	..	..	..	..
4300 Estate, inheritance and gift taxes	..	..	..	..	..	..	..	..	..	..
4400 Taxes on financial and capital transactions	..	..	..	..	..	..	..	..	..	..
4500 Non-recurrent taxes	..	..	..	..	..	..	..	..	..	..
4600 Other recurrent taxes on property	..	..	..	..	..	..	..	..	..	..
5000 Taxes on goods and services	..	**5 584**	**17 029**	**32 725**	**39 970**	..	..	..	..	..
5100 Taxes on production, sale, transfer, etc	..	5 584	17 029	32 725	39 970	..	..	..	..	..
5110 General taxes	..	2 931	10 353	20 714	25 551	..	..	..	..	..
5120 Taxes on specific goods and services	..	2 653	6 676	12 011	14 419	..	..	..	..	..
5130 Unallocable between 5110 and 5120	..	0	0	0	0	..	..	..	..	..
5200 Taxes on use of goods and perform activities	..	0	0	0	0	..	..	..	..	..
5300 Unallocable between 5100 and 5200	..	0	0	0	0	..	..	..	..	..
6000 Other taxes	..	**11**	**20**	**90**	**88**	..	..	..	..	..
6100 Paid solely by business	..	0	0	0	0	..	..	..	..	..
6200 Other	..	11	20	90	88	..	..	..	..	..
Total tax revenue	..	**6 739**	**25 400**	**54 128**	**68 614**	..	..	..	..	..

Million NIO

	Local government[1]					Social Security Funds				
	1990	2000	2010	2015	2017	1990	2000	2010	2015	2017
1000 Taxes on income, profits and capital gains	..	..	**0**	**0**	**0**	..	**0**	**0**	**0**	**0**
1100 Of individuals	..	..	..	..	..	..	..	..	..	..
1200 Corporate	..	..	..	..	..	..	..	..	..	..
1300 Unallocable between 1100 and 1200	..	..	..	..	..	..	..	..	..	..
2000 Social security contributions	..	..	**0**	**0**	**0**	..	**1 678**	**8 090**	**18 194**	**23 868**
2100 Employees	..	..	..	..	..	..	..	..	..	..
2200 Employers	..	..	..	..	..	..	..	..	..	..
2300 Self-employed or non-employed	..	..	..	..	..	..	..	..	..	..
2400 Unallocable between 2100, 2200 and 2300	..	..	..	..	..	..	1 678	8 090	18 194	23 868
3000 Taxes on payroll and workforce	..	..	**0**	**0**	**0**	..	**0**	**0**	**0**	**0**
4000 Taxes on property	..	..	**403**	**682**	**808**	..	**0**	**0**	**0**	**0**
4100 Recurrent taxes on immovable property	..	..	403	682	808	..	..	..	..	..
4200 Recurrent taxes on net wealth	..	..	0	0	0	..	..	..	..	..
4300 Estate, inheritance and gift taxes	..	..	0	0	0	..	..	..	..	..
4400 Taxes on financial and capital transactions	..	..	0	0	0	..	..	..	..	..
4500 Non-recurrent taxes	..	..	0	0	0	..	..	..	..	..
4600 Other recurrent taxes on property	..	..	0	0	0	..	..	..	..	..
5000 Taxes on goods and services	..	..	**1 922**	**3 874**	**4 593**	..	**0**	**0**	**0**	**0**
5100 Taxes on production, sale, transfer, etc	..	..	1 579	3 073	3 650	..	..	..	..	..
5110 General taxes	..	..	1 579	3 073	3 650	..	..	..	..	..
5120 Taxes on specific goods and services	..	..	0	0	0	..	..	..	..	..
5130 Unallocable between 5110 and 5120	..	..	0	0	0	..	..	..	..	..
5200 Taxes on use of goods and perform activities	..	..	343	801	943	..	..	..	..	..
5300 Unallocable between 5100 and 5200	..	..	0	0	0	..	..	..	..	..
6000 Other taxes	..	..	**347**	**690**	**919**	..	**0**	**0**	**0**	**0**
6100 Paid solely by business	..	..	0	0	0	..	..	..	..	..
6200 Other	..	..	347	690	919	..	..	..	..	..
Total tax revenue	..	..	**2 672**	**5 246**	**6 320**	..	**1 678**	**8 090**	**18 194**	**23 868**

Note: Comparable statistics for 1990 cannot be shown due to the devaluation of the Nicaraguan cordoba.

1. The figures exclude local government tax revenues for the period 1990-2010 as the data are not available. The data have been revised since 1990 and the classification of some taxes has been improved, affecting headings 1300, 4400, 5111, 5123, 5213, 5220 and 6200.

StatLink https://doi.org/10.1787/888933942163

Table 6.20. **Panama, tax revenues by sub-sectors of government**

Million PAB

	Federal government					State/Regional				
	1990	2000	2010	2015	2017	1990	2000	2010	2015	2017
1000 Taxes on income, profits and capital gains	**217**	**485**	**1 317**	**2 154**	**2 445**	..	..	..	..	..
1100 Of individuals	140	295	440	799	1 062	..	..	..	..	..
1200 Corporate	66	159	603	938	952	..	..	..	..	..
1300 Unallocable between 1100 and 1200	11	31	273	417	431	..	..	..	..	..
2000 Social security contributions	**0**	**0**	**0**	**0**	**0**	..	..	..	..	..
2100 Employees	..	..	..	..	..	..	..	..	..	..
2200 Employers	..	..	..	..	..	..	..	..	..	..
2300 Self-employed or non-employed	..	..	..	..	..	..	..	..	..	..
2400 Unallocable between 2100, 2200 and 2300	..	..	..	..	..	..	..	..	..	..
3000 Taxes on payroll and workforce[1]	**0**	**36**	**59**	**111**	**129**	..	..	..	..	..
4000 Taxes on property	**43**	**62**	**212**	**319**	**252**	..	..	..	..	..
4100 Recurrent taxes on immovable property	28	34	108	151	208	..	..	..	..	..
4200 Recurrent taxes on net wealth	0	0	0	0	0	..	..	..	..	..
4300 Estate, inheritance and gift taxes	0	0	0	0	0	..	..	..	..	..
4400 Taxes on financial and capital transactions	3	9	30	48	44	..	..	..	..	..
4500 Non-recurrent taxes	0	0	0	0	0	..	..	..	..	..
4600 Other recurrent taxes on property	12	19	75	120	0	..	..	..	..	..
5000 Taxes on goods and services	**335**	**530**	**1 473**	**2 467**	**2 524**	..	..	..	..	..
5100 Taxes on production, sale, transfer, etc	332	530	1 473	2 467	2 524	..	..	..	..	..
5110 General taxes	80	69	766	1 359	1 463	..	..	..	..	..
5120 Taxes on specific goods and services[2]	139	461	706	1 107	1 061	..	..	..	..	..
5130 Unallocable between 5110 and 5120	113	0	0	0	0	..	..	..	..	..
5200 Taxes on use of goods and perform activities	4	0	0	0	0	..	..	..	..	..
5300 Unallocable between 5100 and 5200	0	0	0	0	0	..	..	..	..	..
6000 Other taxes	**26**	**54**	**41**	**37**	**34**	..	..	..	..	..
6100 Paid solely by business	0	11	0	0	0	..	..	..	..	..
6200 Other	26	43	41	37	34	..	..	..	..	..
Total tax revenue	**622**	**1 167**	**3 102**	**5 088**	**5 384**	..	..	..	..	..

Million PAB

	Local government					Social Security Funds				
	1990	2000	2010	2015	2017	1990	2000	2010	2015	2017
1000 Taxes on income, profits and capital gains	..	**0**	**0**	**0**	**0**	**0**	**0**	**0**	**0**	**0**
1100 Of individuals	..	..	..	..	..	..	..	..	..	..
1200 Corporate	..	..	..	..	..	..	..	..	..	..
1300 Unallocable between 1100 and 1200	..	..	..	..	..	..	..	..	..	..
2000 Social security contributions	..	**0**	**0**	**0**	**0**	**271**	**742**	**1 637**	**3 049**	**3 560**
2100 Employees	..	..	..	..	..	..	..	..	..	..
2200 Employers	..	..	..	..	..	..	..	..	..	..
2300 Self-employed or non-employed	..	..	..	..	..	..	..	..	..	..
2400 Unallocable between 2100, 2200 and 2300	..	..	..	..	..	271	742	1 637	3 049	3 560
3000 Taxes on payroll and workforce[1]	..	**0**	**0**	**0**	**0**	**0**	**0**	**0**	**0**	**0**
4000 Taxes on property	..	**0**	**0**	**0**	**0**	**0**	**0**	**0**	**0**	**0**
4100 Recurrent taxes on immovable property	..	0	..	..	..	..	..	..	..	..
4200 Recurrent taxes on net wealth	..	0	..	..	..	..	..	..	..	..
4300 Estate, inheritance and gift taxes	..	0	..	..	..	..	..	..	..	..
4400 Taxes on financial and capital transactions	..	0	..	..	..	..	..	..	..	..
4500 Non-recurrent taxes	..	0	..	..	..	..	..	..	..	..
4600 Other recurrent taxes on property	..	0	..	..	..	..	..	..	..	..
5000 Taxes on goods and services	..	**43**	**41**	**72**	**81**	**0**	**0**	**0**	**0**	**0**
5100 Taxes on production, sale, transfer, etc	..	0	0	0	0	..	..	..	..	..
5110 General taxes	..	0	..	..	..	..	..	..	..	..
5120 Taxes on specific goods and services[2]	..	0	..	..	..	..	..	..	..	..
5130 Unallocable between 5110 and 5120	..	0	..	..	..	..	..	..	..	..
5200 Taxes on use of goods and perform activities	..	43	41	72	81	..	..	..	..	..
5300 Unallocable between 5100 and 5200	..	0	0	0	0	..	..	..	..	..
6000 Other taxes	..	**0**	**36**	**59**	**65**	**0**	**0**	**0**	**0**	**0**
6100 Paid solely by business	..	0	0	0	..	..	..	..	..	..
6200 Other	..	0	36	59	65	..	..	..	..	..
Total tax revenue	..	**43**	**76**	**131**	**145**	**271**	**742**	**1 637**	**3 049**	**3 560**

1. In ECLAC data, education insurance is classified as "Other taxes" (6000).
2. In CIAT and ECLAC data, the tax on banks, financial institutions and currency exchange is classified as a property tax (4000).

StatLink https://doi.org/10.1787/888933942182

Table 6.21. **Paraguay, tax revenues by sub-sectors of government**

Million PYG

	Federal government					State/Regional				
	1990	2000	2010	2015	2017	1990	2000	2010	2015	2017
1000 Taxes on income, profits and capital gains	**73 726**	**470 388**	**2 096 498**	**3 922 384**	**5 086 803**	..	..	..	..	..
1100 Of individuals	..	41 021	184 361	409 238	526 704	..	..	..	..	..
1200 Corporate	..	429 367	1 912 137	3 513 146	4 560 099	..	..	..	..	..
1300 Unallocable between 1100 and 1200	73 726	0	0	0	0	..	..	..	..	..
2000 Social security contributions[1]	**28 882**	**300 451**	**1 140 654**	**1 987 988**	**2 352 309**	..	..	..	..	..
2100 Employees	..	..	..	..	..	..	..	..	..	..
2200 Employers	..	..	..	..	..	..	..	..	..	..
2300 Self-employed or non-employed	..	..	..	..	..	..	..	..	..	..
2400 Unallocable between 2100, 2200 and 2300	28 882	300 451	1 140 654	1 987 988	2 352 309	..	..	..	..	..
3000 Taxes on payroll and workforce	**0**	**0**	**0**	**0**	**0**	..	..	..	..	..
4000 Taxes on property	**17 162**	**0**	**0**	**0**	**0**	..	..	..	..	..
4100 Recurrent taxes on immovable property	17 162	..	..	..	..	..	..	..	..	..
4200 Recurrent taxes on net wealth	0	..	..	..	..	..	..	..	..	..
4300 Estate, inheritance and gift taxes	0	..	..	..	..	..	..	..	..	..
4400 Taxes on financial and capital transactions	0	..	..	..	..	..	..	..	..	..
4500 Non-recurrent taxes	0	..	..	..	..	..	..	..	..	..
4600 Other recurrent taxes on property	0	..	..	..	..	..	..	..	..	..
5000 Taxes on goods and services	**179 312**	**2 080 878**	**9 226 477**	**13 833 169**	**16 319 551**	..	..	..	..	..
5100 Taxes on production, sale, transfer, etc	179 312	2 080 878	9 226 477	13 833 169	16 319 551	..	..	..	..	..
5110 General taxes	0	1 150 496	5 991 694	9 768 800	11 221 710	..	..	..	..	..
5120 Taxes on specific goods and services	179 312	930 382	3 234 783	4 064 368	5 097 841	..	..	..	..	..
5130 Unallocable between 5110 and 5120	0	0	0	0	0	..	..	..	..	..
5200 Taxes on use of goods and perform activities	0	0	0	0	0	..	..	..	..	..
5300 Unallocable between 5100 and 5200	0	0	0	0	0	..	..	..	..	..
6000 Other taxes	**49 807**	**116 652**	**109 424**	**145**	**150**	..	..	..	..	..
6100 Paid solely by business	0	0	0	0	0	..	..	..	..	..
6200 Other	49 807	116 652	109 424	145	150	..	..	..	..	..
Total tax revenue	**348 889**	**2 968 370**	**12 573 052**	**19 743 686**	**23 758 813**	..	..	..	..	..

Million PYG

	Local government[2]					Social Security Funds[3]				
	1990	2000	2010	2015	2017	1990	2000	2010	2015	2017
1000 Taxes on income, profits and capital gains	..	..	**0**	**0**	**0**	..	**0**	**0**	**0**	**0**
1100 Of individuals	..	..	..	..	..	..	..	..	..	..
1200 Corporate	..	..	..	..	..	..	..	..	..	..
1300 Unallocable between 1100 and 1200	..	..	..	..	..	..	..	..	..	..
2000 Social security contributions[1]	..	..	**0**	**0**	**0**	..	**619 082**	**2 411 987**	**5 056 327**	**5 700 094**
2100 Employees	..	..	..	..	..	..	..	..	..	..
2200 Employers	..	..	..	..	..	..	..	..	..	..
2300 Self-employed or non-employed	..	..	..	..	..	..	..	..	..	..
2400 Unallocable between 2100, 2200 and 2300	..	..	..	..	..	..	619 082	2 411 987	5 056 327	5 700 094
3000 Taxes on payroll and workforce	..	..	**0**	**0**	**0**	..	**0**	**0**	**0**	**0**
4000 Taxes on property	..	..	**272 385**	**429 669**	**559 504**	..	**0**	**0**	**0**	**0**
4100 Recurrent taxes on immovable property	..	..	254 306	398 251	519 325	..	..	..	..	..
4200 Recurrent taxes on net wealth	..	..	0	0	0	..	..	..	..	..
4300 Estate, inheritance and gift taxes	..	..	0	0	0	..	..	..	..	..
4400 Taxes on financial and capital transactions	..	..	16 316	30 987	38 417	..	..	..	..	..
4500 Non-recurrent taxes	..	..	0	0	0	..	..	..	..	..
4600 Other recurrent taxes on property	..	..	1 762	431	1 762	..	..	..	..	..
5000 Taxes on goods and services	..	..	**234 485**	**439 791**	**485 007**	..	**0**	**0**	**0**	**0**
5100 Taxes on production, sale, transfer, etc	..	..	23 221	27 470	34 269	..	..	..	..	..
5110 General taxes	..	..	0	0	0	..	..	..	..	..
5120 Taxes on specific goods and services	..	..	23 221	27 470	34 269	..	..	..	..	..
5130 Unallocable between 5110 and 5120	..	..	0	0	0	..	..	..	..	..
5200 Taxes on use of goods and perform activities	..	..	211 027	389 482	419 704	..	..	..	..	..
5300 Unallocable between 5100 and 5200	..	..	237	22 838	31 034	..	..	..	..	..
6000 Other taxes	..	..	**4 795**	**8 211**	**8 219**	..	**0**	**0**	**0**	**0**
6100 Paid solely by business	..	..	0	0	0	..	..	..	..	..
6200 Other	..	..	4 795	8 211	8 219	..	..	..	..	..
Total tax revenue	..	..	**511 664**	**877 672**	**1 052 729**	..	**619 082**	**2 411 987**	**5 056 327**	**5 700 094**

1. Data on social security contributions collected by decentralised institutions are not available from 2011, with the exception of the contributions made to the Instituto de Previsión Social (Social Security Institute).
2. The figures for years up to and including 2004, as well as for 2013 and 2014, exclude local government tax revenues as the data are not available.
3. The figures for years up to and including 1998 exclude decentralised institutions as the data are not available.

StatLink https://doi.org/10.1787/888933942201

Table 6.22. **Peru, tax revenues by sub-sectors of government**

Million PEN

	Federal government					State/Regional				
	1990	2000	2010	2015	2017	1990	2000	2010	2015	2017
1000 Taxes on income, profits and capital gains	**37**	**5 078**	**27 317**	**37 772**	**39 846**	**..**	**..**	**..**	**..**	**..**
1100 Of individuals	3	2 117	6 518	11 137	13 008	..	..	..	..	..
1200 Corporate	32	2 526	19 561	24 266	24 604	..	..	..	..	..
1300 Unallocable between 1100 and 1200	1	436	1 239	2 369	2 233	..	..	..	..	..
2000 Social security contributions	**0**	**0**	**0**	**0**	**0**	**..**	**..**	**..**	**..**	**..**
2100 Employees	..	..	..	..	..	..	..	..	..	..
2200 Employers	..	..	..	..	..	..	..	..	..	..
2300 Self-employed or non-employed	..	..	..	..	..	..	..	..	..	..
2400 Unallocable between 2100, 2200 and 2300	..	..	..	..	..	..	..	..	..	..
3000 Taxes on payroll and workforce	**0**	**1 149**	**1**	**4**	**-2**	**..**	**..**	**..**	**..**	**..**
4000 Taxes on property	**99**	**0**	**944**	**161**	**175**	**..**	**..**	**..**	**..**	**..**
4100 Recurrent taxes on immovable property	0	0	0	0	0	..	..	..	..	..
4200 Recurrent taxes on net wealth	61	0	0	0	0	..	..	..	..	..
4300 Estate, inheritance and gift taxes	0	0	0	0	0	..	..	..	..	..
4400 Taxes on financial and capital transactions	38	0	944	161	175	..	..	..	..	..
4500 Non-recurrent taxes	0	0	0	0	0	..	..	..	..	..
4600 Other recurrent taxes on property	0	0	0	0	0	..	..	..	..	..
5000 Taxes on goods and services	**423**	**15 952**	**36 064**	**50 606**	**49 543**	**..**	**..**	**..**	**..**	**..**
5100 Taxes on production, sale, transfer, etc	423	15 952	36 064	50 606	49 543	..	..	..	..	..
5110 General taxes	78	9 694	29 094	42 612	41 036	..	..	..	..	..
5120 Taxes on specific goods and services	345	6 259	6 970	7 994	8 507	..	..	..	..	..
5130 Unallocable between 5110 and 5120	0	0	0	0	0	..	..	..	..	..
5200 Taxes on use of goods and perform activities	0	0	0	0	0	..	..	..	..	..
5300 Unallocable between 5100 and 5200	0	0	0	0	0	..	..	..	..	..
6000 Other taxes	**36**	**628**	**-136**	**1 185**	**824**	**..**	**..**	**..**	**..**	**..**
6100 Paid solely by business	0	84	108	179	140	..	..	..	..	..
6200 Other	36	544	-244	1 006	683	..	..	..	..	..
Total tax revenue	**595**	**22 808**	**64 191**	**89 728**	**90 386**	**..**	**..**	**..**	**..**	**..**

Million PEN

	Local government[1]					Social Security Funds				
	1990	2000	2010	2015	2017	1990	2000	2010	2015	2017
1000 Taxes on income, profits and capital gains	**..**	**0**	**0**	**0**	**0**	**0**	**0**	**0**	**0**	**0**
1100 Of individuals	..	..	..	..	..	..	..	..	..	..
1200 Corporate	..	..	..	..	..	..	..	..	..	..
1300 Unallocable between 1100 and 1200	..	..	..	..	..	..	..	..	..	..
2000 Social security contributions	**..**	**0**	**0**	**0**	**0**	**50**	**3 175**	**7 929**	**12 680**	**13 676**
2100 Employees	..	..	..	..	..	..	566	2 468	3 509	3 797
2200 Employers	..	..	..	..	..	..	2 515	5 454	9 170	9 878
2300 Self-employed or non-employed	..	..	..	..	..	..	95	7	2	2
2400 Unallocable between 2100, 2200 and 2300	..	..	..	..	..	50	0	0	0	0
3000 Taxes on payroll and workforce	**..**	**0**	**0**	**0**	**0**	**0**	**0**	**0**	**0**	**0**
4000 Taxes on property	**..**	**323**	**1 287**	**2 268**	**2 397**	**0**	**0**	**0**	**0**	**0**
4100 Recurrent taxes on immovable property	..	298	727	1 463	1 718	..	..	..	..	..
4200 Recurrent taxes on net wealth	..	0	0	0	0	..	..	..	..	..
4300 Estate, inheritance and gift taxes	..	0	0	0	0	..	..	..	..	..
4400 Taxes on financial and capital transactions	..	25	560	805	680	..	..	..	..	..
4500 Non-recurrent taxes	..	0	0	0	0	..	..	..	..	..
4600 Other recurrent taxes on property	..	0	0	0	0	..	..	..	..	..
5000 Taxes on goods and services	**..**	**59**	**290**	**496**	**518**	**0**	**0**	**0**	**0**	**0**
5100 Taxes on production, sale, transfer, etc	..	34	135	214	230	..	..	..	..	..
5110 General taxes	..	0	0	0	0	..	..	..	..	..
5120 Taxes on specific goods and services	..	34	135	214	230	..	..	..	..	..
5130 Unallocable between 5110 and 5120	..	0	0	0	0	..	..	..	..	..
5200 Taxes on use of goods and perform activities	..	25	154	282	288	..	..	..	..	..
5300 Unallocable between 5100 and 5200	..	0	0	0	0	..	..	..	..	..
6000 Other taxes	**..**	**48**	**26**	**19**	**27**	**0**	**0**	**0**	**0**	**0**
6100 Paid solely by business	..	0	0	0	0	..	..	..	..	..
6200 Other	..	48	26	19	27	..	..	..	..	..
Total tax revenue	**..**	**430**	**1 603**	**2 784**	**2 943**	**50**	**3 175**	**7 929**	**12 680**	**13 676**

1. The figures for years up to 2000 exclude local government tax revenues as the data are not available. For this edition, the data from 2000 have been revised and exclude administrative fees considered to be non-tax revenues. The administrative fees in previous editions were classified under heading 6000 "Other taxes".

StatLink https://doi.org/10.1787/888933942220

Table 6.23. **Trinidad and Tobago, tax revenues by sub-sectors of government**

Million TTD

	Federal government					State/Regional				
	1990	2000	2010	2015	2017	1990	2000	2010	2015	2017
1000 Taxes on income, profits and capital gains	**2 595**	**6 067**	**26 224**	**29 028**	**16 136**	..	..	..	..	..
1100 Of individuals	669	2 325	4 674	7 752	6 652	..	..	..	..	..
1200 Corporate[1]	1 856	3 547	20 670	20 209	8 629	..	..	..	..	..
1300 Unallocable between 1100 and 1200	70	195	881	1 067	855	..	..	..	..	..
2000 Social security contributions	**0**	**0**	**0**	**0**	**0**	..	..	..	..	..
2100 Employees	..	..	..	..	..	..	..	..	..	..
2200 Employers	..	..	..	..	..	..	..	..	..	..
2300 Self-employed or non-employed	..	..	..	..	..	..	..	..	..	..
2400 Unallocable between 2100, 2200 and 2300	..	..	..	..	..	..	..	..	..	..
3000 Taxes on payroll and workforce	**0**	**0**	**0**	**0**	**0**	..	..	..	..	..
4000 Taxes on property	**41**	**64**	**22**	**3**	**3**	..	..	..	..	..
4100 Recurrent taxes on immovable property	39	64	22	3	3	..	..	..	..	..
4200 Recurrent taxes on net wealth	0	0	0	0	0	..	..	..	..	..
4300 Estate, inheritance and gift taxes	1	0	0	0	0	..	..	..	..	..
4400 Taxes on financial and capital transactions	0	0	0	0	0	..	..	..	..	..
4500 Non-recurrent taxes	0	0	0	0	0	..	..	..	..	..
4600 Other recurrent taxes on property	0	0	0	0	0	..	..	..	..	..
5000 Taxes on goods and services	**2 055**	**3 852**	**9 667**	**12 264**	**11 312**	..	..	..	..	..
5100 Taxes on production, sale, transfer, etc	1 928	3 559	9 249	11 617	10 816	..	..	..	..	..
5110 General taxes[1]	980	1 890	6 358	7 569	7 216	..	..	..	..	..
5120 Taxes on specific goods and services	948	1 669	2 891	4 048	3 600	..	..	..	..	..
5130 Unallocable between 5110 and 5120	0	0	0	0	0	..	..	..	..	..
5200 Taxes on use of goods and perform activities	127	293	418	647	496	..	..	..	..	..
5300 Unallocable between 5100 and 5200	0	0	0	0	0	..	..	..	..	..
6000 Other taxes	**49**	**111**	**172**	**403**	**315**	..	..	..	..	..
6100 Paid solely by business	0	0	0	0	0	..	..	..	..	..
6200 Other	49	111	172	403	315	..	..	..	..	..
Total tax revenue	**4 740**	**10 094**	**36 085**	**41 697**	**27 766**	..	..	..	..	..

Million TTD

	Local government[2]					Social Security Funds				
	1990	2000	2010	2015	2017	1990	2000	2010	2015	2017
1000 Taxes on income, profits and capital gains	**0**	**0**	**0**	**0**	**0**	**0**	**0**	**0**	**0**	**0**
1100 Of individuals	..	..	..	..	..	..	..	..	..	..
1200 Corporate	..	..	..	..	..	..	..	..	..	..
1300 Unallocable between 1100 and 1200	..	..	..	..	..	..	..	..	..	..
2000 Social security contributions	**0**	**0**	**0**	**0**	**0**	**183**	**702**	**2 645**	**4 261**	**4 608**
2100 Employees	..	..	..	..	..	..	..	..	..	..
2200 Employers	..	..	..	..	..	..	..	..	..	..
2300 Self-employed or non-employed	..	..	..	..	..	..	..	..	..	..
2400 Unallocable between 2100, 2200 and 2300	..	..	..	..	..	183	702	2 645	4 261	4 608
3000 Taxes on payroll and workforce	**0**	**0**	**0**	**0**	**0**	**0**	**0**	**0**	**0**	**0**
4000 Taxes on property	**108**	**213**	**411**	**300**	**540**	**0**	**0**	**0**	**0**	**0**
4100 Recurrent taxes on immovable property	108	213	411	300	540	..	..	..	..	..
4200 Recurrent taxes on net wealth	0	0	0	0	0	..	..	..	..	..
4300 Estate, inheritance and gift taxes	0	0	0	0	0	..	..	..	..	..
4400 Taxes on financial and capital transactions	0	0	0	0	0	..	..	..	..	..
4500 Non-recurrent taxes	0	0	0	0	0	..	..	..	..	..
4600 Other recurrent taxes on property	0	0	0	0	0	..	..	..	..	..
5000 Taxes on goods and services	**0**	**0**	**0**	**0**	**0**	**0**	**0**	**0**	**0**	..
5100 Taxes on production, sale, transfer, etc	..	..	..	..	..	..	..	..	..	..
5110 General taxes	..	..	..	..	..	..	..	..	..	..
5120 Taxes on specific goods and services	..	..	..	..	..	..	..	..	..	..
5130 Unallocable between 5110 and 5120	..	..	..	..	..	..	..	..	..	..
5200 Taxes on use of goods and perform activities	..	..	..	..	..	..	..	..	..	..
5300 Unallocable between 5100 and 5200	..	..	..	..	..	..	..	..	..	..
6000 Other taxes	**0**	**0**	**0**	**0**	**0**	**0**	**0**	**0**	**0**	..
6100 Paid solely by business	..	..	..	..	..	..	..	..	..	..
6200 Other	..	..	..	..	..	..	..	..	..	..
Total tax revenue	**108**	**213**	**411**	**300**	**540**	**183**	**702**	**2 645**	**4 261**	**4 608**

1. This edition includes revenues from the Unemployment Fund and the Green Fund for the first time, affecting headings 1200 and 5110 respectively.
2. The local government tax revenue data (house rate tax) are estimated in 2017.

StatLink https://doi.org/10.1787/888933942239

Table 6.24. **Uruguay, tax revenues by sub-sectors of government**

Million UYU

	Federal government					State/Regional				
	1990	2000	2010	2015	2017	1990	2000	2010	2015	2017
1000 Taxes on income, profits and capital gains	**114**	**5 620**	**44 069**	**86 404**	**127 768**	..	..	..	..	..
1100 Of individuals	0	0	19 150	45 451	68 948	..	..	..	..	..
1200 Corporate	114	5 620	23 257	37 078	53 641	..	..	..	..	..
1300 Unallocable between 1100 and 1200	0	0	1 662	3 875	5 179	..	..	..	..	..
2000 Social security contributions[1]	**0**	**0**	**0**	**0**	**0**	..	..	..	..	..
2100 Employees	..	..	..	..	..	..	..	..	..	..
2200 Employers	..	..	..	..	..	..	..	..	..	..
2300 Self-employed or non-employed	..	..	..	..	..	..	..	..	..	..
2400 Unallocable between 2100, 2200 and 2300	..	..	..	..	..	..	..	..	..	..
3000 Taxes on payroll and workforce	**0**	**0**	**0**	**0**	**0**	..	..	..	..	..
4000 Taxes on property	**125**	**3 709**	**11 690**	**20 674**	**20 851**	..	..	..	..	..
4100 Recurrent taxes on immovable property	0	153	1 064	3 775	1 307	..	..	..	..	..
4200 Recurrent taxes on net wealth	94	2 076	8 948	14 776	17 057	..	..	..	..	..
4300 Estate, inheritance and gift taxes	0	0	0	0	0	..	..	..	..	..
4400 Taxes on financial and capital transactions	0	372	1 350	1 601	1 927	..	..	..	..	..
4500 Non-recurrent taxes	0	0	0	0	0	..	..	..	..	..
4600 Other recurrent taxes on property	31	1 107	328	522	560	..	..	..	..	..
5000 Taxes on goods and services	**1 270**	**28 301**	**94 990**	**160 146**	**184 658**	..	..	..	..	..
5100 Taxes on production, sale, transfer, etc	1 270	28 301	94 990	160 146	184 658	..	..	..	..	..
5110 General taxes	660	18 009	69 365	113 651	129 663	..	..	..	..	..
5120 Taxes on specific goods and services	610	10 291	25 625	46 495	54 995	..	..	..	..	..
5130 Unallocable between 5110 and 5120	0	0	0	0	0	..	..	..	..	..
5200 Taxes on use of goods and perform activities	0	0	0	0	0	..	..	..	..	..
5300 Unallocable between 5100 and 5200	0	0	0	0	0	..	..	..	..	..
6000 Other taxes	**-10**	**-596**	**0**	**0**	**0**	..	..	..	..	..
6100 Paid solely by business	-10	-596	0	0	0	..	..	..	..	..
6200 Other	0	0	0	0	0	..	..	..	..	..
Total tax revenue	**1 500**	**37 034**	**150 750**	**267 224**	**333 277**	..	..	..	..	..

Million UYU

	Local government[2]					Social Security Funds				
	1990	2000	2010	2015	2017	1990	2000	2010	2015	2017
1000 Taxes on income, profits and capital gains	**0**	**0**	**0**	**0**	**0**	**0**	**0**	**0**	**0**	**0**
1100 Of individuals	..	..	..	..	..	..	..	..	..	..
1200 Corporate	..	..	..	..	..	..	..	..	..	..
1300 Unallocable between 1100 and 1200	..	..	..	..	..	..	..	..	..	..
2000 Social security contributions[1]	**0**	**0**	**0**	**0**	**0**	**717**	**17 679**	**49 742**	**108 742**	**163 771**
2100 Employees	..	..	..	..	..	..	..	..	..	..
2200 Employers	..	..	..	..	..	..	..	..	..	..
2300 Self-employed or non-employed	..	..	..	..	..	..	..	..	..	..
2400 Unallocable between 2100, 2200 and 2300	..	..	..	..	..	717	17 679	49 742	108 742	163 771
3000 Taxes on payroll and workforce	**0**	**0**	**0**	**0**	**0**	**0**	**0**	**0**	**0**	**0**
4000 Taxes on property	**107**	**2 819**	**7 277**	**11 749**	**14 827**	**0**	**0**	**0**	**0**	**0**
4100 Recurrent taxes on immovable property	87	2 715	6 887	11 109	14 092	..	..	..	..	..
4200 Recurrent taxes on net wealth	0	0	0	0	0	..	..	..	..	..
4300 Estate, inheritance and gift taxes	0	0	0	0	0	..	..	..	..	..
4400 Taxes on financial and capital transactions	20	104	390	639	735	..	..	..	..	..
4500 Non-recurrent taxes	0	0	0	0	0	..	..	..	..	..
4600 Other recurrent taxes on property	0	0	0	0	0	..	..	..	..	..
5000 Taxes on goods and services	**57**	**2 583**	**3 851**	**7 668**	**10 463**	**0**	**0**	**0**	**0**	**0**
5100 Taxes on production, sale, transfer, etc	0	7	63	128	149	..	..	..	..	..
5110 General taxes	0	0	0	0	0	..	..	..	..	..
5120 Taxes on specific goods and services	0	7	63	128	149	..	..	..	..	..
5130 Unallocable between 5110 and 5120	0	0	0	0	0	..	..	..	..	..
5200 Taxes on use of goods and perform activities	57	2 576	3 788	7 540	10 313	..	..	..	..	..
5300 Unallocable between 5100 and 5200	0	0	0	0	0	..	..	..	..	..
6000 Other taxes	**7**	**303**	**748**	**1 355**	**2 008**	**0**	**0**	**0**	**0**	**0**
6100 Paid solely by business	0	0	0	0	0	..	..	..	..	..
6200 Other	7	303	748	1 355	2 008	..	..	..	..	..
Total tax revenue	**171**	**5 705**	**11 876**	**20 772**	**27 298**	**717**	**17 679**	**49 742**	**108 742**	**163 771**

1. The figures for 1990-98 are estimated by the Direction General of Taxes as the methodology they use to calculate social security contributions was not employed until 1999.
2. The figures for local government tax revenue have been reclassified in this edition according to the new figures from the Oficina de Planeamiento y Presupuesto de la República.

StatLink https://doi.org/10.1787/888933942258

Table 6.25. **Venezuela, tax revenues by sub-sectors of government**

Million VEF

	Federal government[2]					State/Regional[3]				
	1990	2000	2010	2015	2017	1990	2000	2010	2015	2017
1000 Taxes on income, profits and capital gains[1]	**344**	**4 686**	**36 836**	**284 786**	**..**	**..**	**..**	**..**	**..**	**..**
1100 Of individuals	..	..	..	..	..	..	..	..	..	..
1200 Corporate	315	3 368	8 700	47 388	..	..	..	..	..	..
1300 Unallocable between 1100 and 1200	30	1 317	28 137	237 399	3 137 851	..	..	..	..	..
2000 Social security contributions	**0**	**0**	**0**	**0**	**0**	**..**	**..**	**..**	**..**	**..**
2100 Employees	..	..	..	..	..	..	..	..	..	..
2200 Employers	..	..	..	..	..	..	..	..	..	..
2300 Self-employed or non-employed	..	..	..	..	..	..	..	..	..	..
2400 Unallocable between 2100, 2200 and 2300	..	..	..	..	..	..	..	..	..	..
3000 Taxes on payroll and workforce	**0**	**0**	**0**	**0**	**0**	**..**	**..**	**..**	**..**	**..**
4000 Taxes on property	**1**	**400**	**222**	**2 946**	**2 435 304**	**..**	**..**	**..**	**..**	**..**
4100 Recurrent taxes on immovable property	0	0	0	0	0	..	..	..	..	..
4200 Recurrent taxes on net wealth	0	0	0	0	0	..	..	..	..	..
4300 Estate, inheritance and gift taxes	1	19	222	2 946	36 130	..	..	..	..	..
4400 Taxes on financial and capital transactions	0	381	0	0	2 399 174	..	..	..	..	..
4500 Non-recurrent taxes	0	0	0	0	0	..	..	..	..	..
4600 Other recurrent taxes on property	0	0	0	0	0	..	..	..	..	..
5000 Taxes on goods and services	**46**	**5 173**	**73 336**	**912 820**	**14 866 952**	**..**	**..**	**..**	**..**	**..**
5100 Taxes on production, sale, transfer, etc	46	5 173	73 336	912 820	14 866 952	..	..	..	..	..
5110 General taxes	0	3 272	56 101	702 743	11 299 017	..	..	..	..	..
5120 Taxes on specific goods and services	46	1 901	17 236	210 077	3 567 934	..	..	..	..	..
5130 Unallocable between 5110 and 5120	0	0	0	0	0	..	..	..	..	..
5200 Taxes on use of goods and perform activities	0	0	0	0	0	..	..	..	..	..
5300 Unallocable between 5100 and 5200	0	0	0	0	0	..	..	..	..	..
6000 Other taxes	**0**	**0**	**0**	**15 833**	**122 517**	**..**	**..**	**..**	**..**	**..**
6100 Paid solely by business	..	..	..	0	0	..	..	..	..	..
6200 Other	..	..	..	15 833	122 517	..	..	..	..	..
Total tax revenue	**391**	**10 258**	**110 394**	**1 216 386**	**..**	**..**	**..**	**..**	**..**	**..**

Million VEF

	Local government[3]					Social Security Funds[4]				
	1990	2000	2010	2015	2017	1990	2000	2010	2015	2017
1000 Taxes on income, profits and capital gains	**..**	**..**	**..**	**..**	**..**	**0**	**0**	**0**	**..**	**..**
1100 Of individuals	..	..	..	..	..	..	..	..	..	..
1200 Corporate	..	..	..	..	..	..	..	..	..	..
1300 Unallocable between 1100 and 1200	..	..	..	..	..	..	..	..	..	..
2000 Social security contributions	**..**	**..**	**..**	**..**	**..**	**20**	**591**	**9 690**	**..**	**..**
2100 Employees	..	..	..	..	..	..	..	..	..	..
2200 Employers	..	..	..	..	..	..	..	..	..	..
2300 Self-employed or non-employed	..	..	..	..	..	..	..	..	..	..
2400 Unallocable between 2100, 2200 and 2300	..	..	..	..	..	20	591	9 690	..	..
3000 Taxes on payroll and workforce	**..**	**..**	**..**	**..**	**..**	**0**	**0**	**0**	**..**	**..**
4000 Taxes on property	**..**	**..**	**..**	**..**	**..**	**0**	**0**	**0**	**..**	**..**
4100 Recurrent taxes on immovable property	..	..	..	..	..	..	..	..	..	..
4200 Recurrent taxes on net wealth	..	..	..	..	..	..	..	..	..	..
4300 Estate, inheritance and gift taxes	..	..	..	..	..	..	..	..	..	..
4400 Taxes on financial and capital transactions	..	..	..	..	..	..	..	..	..	..
4500 Non-recurrent taxes	..	..	..	..	..	..	..	..	..	..
4600 Other recurrent taxes on property	..	..	..	..	..	..	..	..	..	..
5000 Taxes on goods and services	**..**	**..**	**..**	**..**	**..**	**0**	**0**	**0**	**..**	**..**
5100 Taxes on production, sale, transfer, etc	..	..	..	..	..	..	..	..	..	..
5110 General taxes	..	..	..	..	..	..	..	..	..	..
5120 Taxes on specific goods and services	..	..	..	..	..	..	..	..	..	..
5130 Unallocable between 5110 and 5120	..	..	..	..	..	..	..	..	..	..
5200 Taxes on use of goods and perform activities	..	..	..	..	..	..	..	..	..	..
5300 Unallocable between 5100 and 5200	..	..	..	..	..	..	..	..	..	..
6000 Other taxes	**..**	**..**	**..**	**..**	**..**	**0**	**0**	**0**	**..**	**..**
6100 Paid solely by business	..	..	..	..	..	..	..	..	..	..
6200 Other	..	..	..	..	..	..	..	..	..	..
Total tax revenue	**..**	**..**	**..**	**..**	**..**	**20**	**591**	**9 690**	**..**	**..**

1. The tax revenues from taxes on income, profits and capital gains are not available from 2016 due to missing data for revenues from taxes on oil profits (classified in heading 1200 taxes on corporate profits and capital gains)
2. The figures for 2015-17 should be interpreted with caution as they have been affected by the high rate of inflation over this period.The total tax revenue data are not available since 2014 due to missing data for social security contributions (since 2014) and oil revenues (since 2016).
3. The figures exclude state and local government tax revenues as the data are not available.
4. Data on social security contributions are not available from 2014.

StatLink https://doi.org/10.1787/888933942277

Annex A

The OECD classification of taxes and interpretative guide[1]

Table of contents

A.1. The OECD classification of taxes

1. 1000 *Taxes on income, profits and capital gains*
    - 1100 Taxes on income, profits and capital gains of individuals
        - 1110 On income and profits
        - 1120 On capital gains
    - 1200 Corporate taxes on income, profits and capital gains
        - 1210 On income and profits
        - 1220 On capital gains
    - 1300 Unallocable as between 1100 and 1200
2. 2000 *Social security contributions*
    - 2100 Employees
        - 2110 On a payroll basis
        - 2120 On an income tax basis
    - 2200 Employers
        - 2210 On a payroll basis
        - 2220 On an income tax basis
    - 2300 Self-employed or non-employed
        - 2310 On a payroll basis
        - 2320 On an income tax basis
    - 2400 Unallocable as between 2100, 2200 and 2300
        - 2410 On a payroll basis
        - 2420 On an income tax basis
3. 3000 *Taxes on payroll and workforce*
4. 4000 *Taxes on property*
    - 4100 Recurrent taxes on immovable property
        - 4110 Households
        - 4120 Other
    - 4200 Recurrent taxes on net wealth
        - 4210 Individual
        - 4220 Corporate
    - 4300 Estate, inheritance and gift taxes
        - 4310 Estate and inheritance taxes
        - 4320 Gift taxes
    - 4400 Taxes on financial and capital transactions
    - 4500 Other non-recurrent taxes on property
        - 4510 On net wealth
        - 4520 Other non-recurrent taxes
    - 4600 Other recurrent taxes on property

5. 5000 *Taxes on goods and services*

5100 Taxes on production, sale, transfer, leasing and delivery of goods and rendering of services

5110 General taxes

5111 Value added taxes

5112 Sales taxes

5113 Turnover and Other general taxes on goods and services

5120 Taxes on specific goods and services

5121 Excises

5122 Profits of fiscal monopolies

5123 Customs and import duties

5124 Taxes on exports

5125 Taxes on investment goods

5126 Taxes on specific services

5127 Other taxes on international trade and transactions

5128 Other taxes on specific goods and services

5130 Unallocable as between 5110 and 5120

5200 Taxes on use of goods, or on permission to use goods or perform activities

5210 Recurrent taxes

5211 Paid by households in respect of motor vehicles

5212 Paid by others in respect of motor vehicles

5213 Other recurrent taxes

5220 Non-recurrent taxes

5300 Unallocable as between 5100 and 5200

6. 6000 *Other taxes*

6100 Paid solely by business

6200 Paid by other than business or unidentifiable

The OECD interpretative guide[1]

A.2. Coverage

General criteria

1. In the OECD classification the term "taxes" is confined to compulsory unrequited payments to general government. Taxes are unrequited in the sense that benefits provided by government to taxpayers are not normally in proportion to their payments.

2. The term "tax" does not include fines, penalties and compulsory loans paid to government. Borderline cases between tax and non-tax revenues in relation to certain fees and charges are discussed in §11–14.

3. General government consists of the central administration, agencies whose operations are under its effective control, state and local governments and their administrations, certain social security schemes and autonomous governmental entities, excluding public enterprises. This definition of government follows that of the 2008 *System of National Accounts* (SNA).[2] In that publication, the general government sector and its sub-sectors are defined in Chapter 4, paragraphs 4.117 to 4.165.

4. Extra-budgetary units are part of the general government system. These are general government entities with individual budgets that are not fully covered by the main or general budget. These entities operate under the authority or control of a central, state, or local government. Extra-budgetary entities may have their own revenue sources, which may be supplemented by grants (transfers) from the general budget or from other sources. Even though their budgets may be subject to approval by the legislature, similar to that of budgetary accounts, they have discretion over the volume and composition of their spending. Such entities may be established to carry out specific government functions, such as road construction, or the nonmarket production of health or education services. Budgetary arrangements vary widely across countries, and various terms are used to describe these entities, but they are often referred to as "extra-budgetary funds" or "decentralised agencies."

5. Compulsory payments to supra-national bodies and their agencies are no longer included as taxes as from 1998, with some exceptions. However, custom duties collected by EU member states on behalf of the European Union are still identified as memorandum items and included in overall tax revenue amounts in the country tables (Chapter 4) of the country in which they are collected. (See §99). In countries where the church forms part of general government church taxes are included, provided they meet the criteria set out in §1 above. As the data refer to receipts of general government, levies paid to non-government bodies, welfare agencies or social insurance schemes outside general government, trade unions or trade associations, even where such levies are compulsory, are excluded. Compulsory payments to general government earmarked for such bodies are, however, included, provided that the government is not simply acting in an agency capacity.[3] Profits from fiscal monopolies are distinguished from those of other public enterprises and are treated as taxes because they reflect the exercise of the taxing power of the state by the use of monopoly powers (see §65–67), as are profits received by the government from the purchase and sale of foreign exchange at different rates (see §74).

6. Taxes paid by governments (e.g. social security contributions and payroll taxes paid by governments in their capacity as an employer, consumption taxes on their purchases or taxes on their property) are not excluded from the data provided. However, where it is possible to identify the amounts of revenue involved,[4] they are shown in Chapter 4.2 of this Report.

7. The relationship between this classification and that of the System of National Accounts (SNA) is set out in Sections A.9 and A.11 below. Because of the differences between the two classifications, the data shown in national accounts are sometimes calculated or classified differently from the practice set out in this guide. These and other differences are mentioned where appropriate (e.g. in §30 below) but it is not possible to refer to all of them. There may also be some differences between this classification and that employed domestically by certain national administrations (e.g. see §12 below), so that OECD and national statistics data may not always be consistent: any such differences, however, are likely to be very slight in terms of amounts of revenues involved.

Social security contributions

8. Compulsory social security contributions, as defined in §39, and paid to general government, are treated here as tax revenues. Being compulsory payments to general government they clearly resemble taxes. They may, however, differ from other taxes in that the receipt of social security benefits depends, in most countries, upon appropriate contributions having been made, although the size of the benefits is not necessarily related to the amount of the contributions. Better comparability between countries is obtained by treating social security contributions as taxes, but they are listed under a separate heading so that they can be distinguished in any analysis.

9. The strict dividing line between tax revenues (compulsory unrequited payments to general government) and non-tax compulsory payments (NTCPs) (payments that are either requited or made to other institutions) is clearly defined. However, within the range of different compulsory payments to governments existing across countries, it is not always straightforward in practice to decide whether specific payments are either taxes or NTCPs. For example, compulsory pension savings that are controlled by general government and that accumulate on an individual account earning a market return or a rate that compensates for inflation would at first sight be categorised as NTCPs as opposed to taxes. However, even these payments might still be 'unrequited' and therefore classify as taxes instead of NTCPs (for example if these pension savings are not paid out when the taxpayer dies before reaching the pension age and the funds are then used to provide a minimum pension to all taxpayers that are insured). These issues result in the social security revenue figures reported for most countries being based on the premise that all types of compulsory payments to general government are judged to some extent to have a re-distributional element. It should be noted that this conclusion is based on a typically broad interpretation of the term 'unrequited' in the tax definition.

10. Social security contributions which are either voluntary or not payable to general government (see §1) are not treated as taxes, though in some countries, as indicated in the country footnotes, there are difficulties in completely eliminating voluntary contributions and certain compulsory payments to the private sector from the revenue figures. Imputed social security contributions are also not treated as taxes.

Fees, user charges and licence fees

11. Apart from vehicle licence fees, which are universally regarded as taxes, it is not easy to distinguish between those fees and user charges which are to be treated as taxes and those which are not, since, whilst a fee or charge is levied in connection with a specific service or activity, the strength of the link between the fee and the service provided may vary considerably, as may the relation between the amount of the fee and the cost of providing the service. Where the recipient of a service pays a fee clearly related to the cost of providing

the service, the levy may be regarded as requited and under the definition of §1 would not be considered as a tax. In the following cases, however, a levy could be considered as 'unrequited':

a. where the charge greatly exceeds the cost of providing the service;
b. where the payer of the levy is not the receiver of the benefit (e.g. a fee collected from slaughterhouses to finance a service which is provided to farmers);
c. where government is not providing a specific service in return for the levy which it receives even though a licence may be issued to the payer (e.g. where the government grants a hunting, fishing or shooting licence which is not accompanied by the right to use a specific area of government land);
d. where benefits are received only by those paying the levy but the benefits received by each individual are not necessarily in proportion to his payments (e.g. a milk marketing levy paid by dairy farmers and used to promote the consumption of milk).

12. In marginal cases, however, the application of the criteria set out in §1 can be particularly difficult. The solution adopted – given the desirability of international uniformity and the relatively small amounts of revenue usually involved – is to follow the predominant practice among tax administrations rather than to allow each country to adopt its own view as to whether such levies are regarded as taxes or as non-tax revenue.[5]

13. A list of the main fees and charges in question and their normal[6] treatment in this publication is as follows:

Non-tax revenues:	court fees; driving licence fees; harbour fees; passport fees; radio and television licence fees where public authorities provide the service.
Taxes within heading 5200:	permission to perform such activities as distributing films; hunting, fishing and shooting; providing entertainment or gambling facilities; selling alcohol or tobacco; permission to own dogs or to use or own motor vehicles or guns; severance taxes.

14. In practice it may not always be possible to isolate tax receipts from non-tax revenue receipts when they are recorded together. If it is estimated that the bulk of the receipts derive from non-tax revenues, the whole amount involved is treated as a non-tax revenue; otherwise, such government receipts are included and classified according to the rules provided in §32 below.

Royalties

15. The ownership of subsoil assets in the form of deposits of minerals or fossil fuels (coal, oil, or natural gas) depends upon the way in which property rights are defined by law and also on international agreements in the case of deposits below international waters. In some cases, either the ground below which the mineral deposits are located, the deposits themselves or both may belong to a local or central government unit.

16. In such cases, these general government units may grant leases to other institutional units that permit them to extract these deposits over a specified period of time in return for a payment or series of payments. These payments are often described as 'royalties' but they are essentially rent that accrues to owners of natural resources in return for putting these assets at the disposal of other units for specified periods of time. The rent may take the form of periodic payments of fixed amounts, irrespective of the rate of extraction, or, more commonly, they may be a function of the quantity, volume, or value of the asset extracted. Enterprises

engaged in exploration on government land may make payments to general government units in exchange for the right to undertake test drilling or otherwise investigate the existence and location of subsoil assets. Such payments are also recorded as rents even though no extraction may take place. These payments are therefore classified as non-tax revenues.

17. The same principles apply when other institutional units are granted leases that permit them to fell timber in natural forests on land owned by general government units. These payments are also classified as non-tax revenues.

18. These rents or royalties paid to general government should not be confused with taxes on income and profits, severance taxes, business licenses, or other taxes. If the payments are levied on the profits from the extraction activity, then they should be classified as taxes on incomes, profits and gains (1000). In addition, any severance payments that are imposed on the extraction of minerals and fossil fuels from reserves owned privately or by another government should be classified as taxes. Payments related to the gross value of production should be classified as other taxes on goods and services (5128). Payments for a license or permit to conduct extraction operations should be classified as taxes on use of goods and on permission to use goods or perform activities (5213).

Fines and penalties

19. In principle, fines and penalties charged on overdue taxes or penalties imposed for the attempted evasion of taxes should not be recorded as tax revenues. However it may not be possible to separate payments of fines or other penalties from the revenues from the taxes to which they relate. In this case the fines and penalties relating to a particular tax are recorded together with the revenues from that tax and fines and penalties paid with revenue from unidentifiable taxes are classified as other taxes in Category 6000. Fines not relating to tax offences (e.g. for parking offences), or not identifiable as relating to tax offences, are also not treated as tax revenues.

A.3. Basis of reporting

Accrual reporting

20. The data reported in this publication for recent years are predominantly recorded on an accrual basis, i.e. recorded at the time that the tax liability was created. Further information is provided in the footnotes to the country table in Chapter 4 of the Report.

21. However, data for earlier years are still predominantly recorded on a cash basis, i.e. at the time at which the payment was received by government. Thus, for example, taxes withheld by employers in one year but paid to the government in the following year and taxes due in one year but actually paid in the following year are both included in the receipts of the second year. Corrective transactions, such as refunds, repayments and drawbacks, are deducted from gross revenues of the period in which they are made.

22. Data on tax revenues are recorded without offsets for the administrative expenses connected with tax collection. Similarly, where the proceeds of tax are used to subsidise particular members of the community, the subsidy is not deducted from the yield of the tax, though the tax may be shown net of subsidies in the national records of some countries.

23. As regards fiscal monopolies (heading 5122), only the amount actually transferred to the government is included in government revenues. However, if any expenditures of fiscal monopolies are considered to be government expenditures (e.g. social expenditures undertaken by fiscal monopolies at the direction of the government) they are added back for the purpose of arriving at tax revenue figures (see §65 below).

The distinction between tax and expenditure provisions[7]

24. Because this publication is concerned only with the revenue side of government operations, no account being taken of the expenditure side, a distinction has to be made between tax and expenditure provisions. Normally there is no difficulty in making this distinction as expenditures are made outside the tax system and the tax accounts and under legislation separate from the tax legislation. In borderline cases, cash flow is used to distinguish between tax provisions and expenditure provisions. Insofar as a provision affects the flow of tax payments from the taxpayer to the government, it is regarded as a tax provision and is taken into account in the data shown in this publication. A provision which does not affect this flow is seen as an expenditure provision and is disregarded in the data recorded in this publication.

25. Tax allowances, exemptions and deductions against the tax base clearly affect the amount of tax paid to the government and are therefore considered as tax provisions. At the other extreme, those subsidies which cannot be offset against tax liability and which are clearly not connected with the assessment process, do not reduce tax revenues as recorded in this publication. Tax credits are amounts deductible from tax payable (as distinct from deductions from the tax base). Two types of tax credits are distinguished, those (referred to here as wastable tax credits) which are limited to the amount of the tax liability and therefore cannot give rise to a payment by the authorities to the taxpayer, and those (referred to as non-wastable tax credits) which are not so limited, so that the excess of the credit over the tax liability can be paid to the taxpayer.[8] A wastable tax credit, like a tax allowance, clearly affects the amount of tax paid to the government, and is therefore considered as a tax provision. The practice followed for non-wastable tax credits[9] is to distinguish between the 'tax expenditure component',[10] which is that portion of the credit that is used to reduce or eliminate a taxpayer's liability, and the 'transfer component', which is the portion that exceeds the taxpayer's liability and is paid to that taxpayer. Reported tax revenues should be reduced by the amount of the tax expenditure component but not by the amount of the transfer component. In addition, the amounts of the tax expenditure and transfer components should be reported as memorandum items in the country tables. Countries that are unable to distinguish between the tax expenditure and transfer components should indicate whether or not the tax revenues have been reduced by the total of these components, and provide any available estimates of the amounts of the two components. Further information is given in Chapter 1 of the Report, which illustrates the effect of alternative treatments of non-wastable tax credits on tax to GDP.

Calendar and fiscal years

26. National authorities whose fiscal years do not correspond to the calendar year show data, where possible, on a calendar year basis to permit maximum comparability with the data of other countries. There remain a few countries where data refer to fiscal years. For these the GDP data used in the comparative tables also correspond to the fiscal years.

A.4. General classification criteria

The main classification criteria

27. The classification of receipts among the main headings (1000, 2000, 3000, 4000, 5000 and 6000) is generally governed by the base on which the tax is levied: 1000 income, profits and capital gains; 2000 and 3000 earnings, payroll or number of employees; 4000 property; 5000 goods and services; 6000 multiple bases, other bases or unidentifiable bases. Where a

tax is calculated on more than one base, the receipts are, where possible, split among the various headings (see §32 and §81). The headings 4000 and 5000 cover not only taxes where the tax base is the property, goods or services themselves but also certain related taxes. Thus, taxes on the transfer of property are included in 4400[11] and taxes on the use of goods or on permission to perform activities in 5200. In headings 4000 and 5000 a distinction is made in certain sub-headings between recurrent and non-recurrent taxes: recurrent taxes are defined as those levied at regular intervals (usually annually) and non-recurrent taxes are levied once and for all (see also §47 to §50, §53, §54 and §79 for particular applications of this distinction).

28. Earmarking of a tax for specific purposes does not affect the classification of tax receipts. However, as explained in §39 on the classification of social security contributions, the conferment of an entitlement to social benefits is crucial to the definition of the 2000 main heading.

29. The way that a tax is levied or collected (e.g. by use of stamps) does not affect classification.

Classification of taxpayers

30. In certain sub-headings distinctions are made between different categories of taxpayers. These distinctions vary from tax to tax:

a. *Between individuals and corporations in relation to income and net wealth taxes*

The basic distinction is that corporation income taxes, as distinct from individual income taxes, are levied on the corporation as an entity, not on the individuals who own it, and without regard to the personal circumstances of these individuals. The same distinction applies to net wealth taxes on corporations and those on individuals. Taxes paid on the profits of partnerships and the income of institutions, such as life insurance or pension funds, are classified according to the same rule. They are classified as corporate taxes (1200) if they are charged on the partnership or institution as an entity without regard to the personal circumstances of the owners. Otherwise, they are treated as individual taxes (1100). Usually, there is different legislation for the corporation taxes and for the individual taxes.[12] The distinction made here between individuals and corporations does not follow the sector classification between households, enterprises, and so on of the System of National Accounts for income and outlay accounts. The SNA classification requires certain unincorporated businesses[13] to be excluded from the household sector and included with non-financial enterprises and financial institutions. The tax on the profits of these businesses, however, cannot always be separated from the tax on the other income of their owners, or can be separated only on an arbitrary basis. No attempt at this separation is made here and the whole of the individual income tax is shown together without regard to the nature of the income chargeable.

b. *Between households and others in relation to taxes on immovable property*

Here the distinction is that adopted by the SNA for the production and consumption expenditure accounts. The distinction is between households as consumers (i.e. excluding non-incorporated business) on the one hand and producers on the other hand. However, taxes on dwellings occupied by households, whether paid by owner-occupiers, tenants or landlords, are classified under households. This follows the common distinction made between taxes on domestic property versus taxes on business property. Some countries are not, however, in a position to make this distinction.

c. *Between households and others in relation to motor vehicle licences*

Here the distinction is between households as consumers on the one hand and producers on the other, as in the production and consumption expenditure accounts of the SNA.

d. *Between business and others in relation to the residual taxes (6000)*

The distinction is the same as in c) above between producers on the one hand and households as consumers on the other hand. Taxes which are included under the heading 6000 because they involve more than one tax base or because the tax base does not fall within any of the previous categories but which are identifiable as levyable only on producers and not on households are included under 'business'. The rest of the taxes which are included under the heading 6000 are shown as 'other' or non-identified.

Surcharges

31. Receipts from surcharges in respect of particular taxes are usually classified with the receipts from the relevant tax whether or not the surcharge is temporary. If, however, the surcharge has a characteristic which would render it classifiable in a different heading of the OECD list, receipts from the surcharge are classified under that heading separately from the relevant tax.

Unidentifiable tax receipts and residual sub-headings

32. A number of cases arise where taxes cannot be identified as belonging entirely to a heading or sub-heading of the OECD classification and the following practices are applied in such cases:

a. The heading is known, but it is not known how receipts should be allocated between sub-headings: receipts are classified in the appropriate residual sub-heading (1300, 2400, 4520, 4600, 5130, 5300 or 6200).
b. It is known that the bulk of receipts from a group of taxes (usually local taxes) is derived from taxes within a particular heading or sub-heading, but some of the taxes in the group whose amount cannot be precisely ascertained may be classifiable in other headings or sub-headings: receipts are shown in the heading or sub-heading under which most of the receipts fall.
c. Neither the heading nor sub-heading of a tax (usually local) can be identified: the tax is classified in 6200 unless it is known that it is a tax on business in which case it is classified in 6100.

A.5. Commentaries on items of the list

1000 — Taxes on income, profits and capital gains

33. This heading covers taxes levied on the net income or profits (i.e. gross income minus allowable tax reliefs) of individuals and enterprises. Also covered are taxes levied on the capital gains of individuals and enterprises, and gains from gambling.

34. Included in the heading are:

a. taxes levied predominantly on income or profits, though partially on other bases. Taxes on various bases which are not predominantly income or profits are classified according to the principles laid down in §32 and §81;
b. taxes on property, which are levied on a presumed or estimated income as part of an income tax (see also §47(a), (c) and (d));

c. compulsory payments to social security fund contributions that are levied on income but do not confer an entitlement to social benefits. When such contributions do confer an entitlement to social benefits, they are included in heading 2000 (see §39);

d. receipts from integrated scheduler income tax systems are classified as a whole in this heading, even though certain of the scheduler taxes may be based upon gross income and may not take into account the personal circumstances of the taxpayer.

35. The main subdivision of this heading is between levies on individuals (1100) and those on corporate enterprises (1200). Under each subdivision a distinction is made between taxes on income and profits (1110 and 1210), and taxes on capital gains (1120 and 1220). If certain receipts cannot be identified as appropriate to either 1100 or 1200, or if in practice this distinction cannot be made (e.g. because there are no reliable data on the recipients of payments from which withholding taxes are deducted) they are classified in 1300 as not-allocable.

Treatment of credits under imputation systems

36. Under imputation systems of corporate income tax, a company's shareholders are wholly or partly relieved of their liability to income tax on dividends paid by the company out of income or profits liable to corporate income tax. In countries with such systems,[14] part of the tax on the company's profits is available to provide relief against the shareholders' own tax liability. The relief to the shareholder takes the form of a tax credit, the amount of which may be less than, equal to, or more than the shareholder's overall tax liability. If the tax credit exceeds this tax liability the excess may be payable to the shareholder. As this type of tax credit is an integral part of the imputation system of corporate income tax, any payment to the shareholders is treated as a repayment of tax and not as expenditure (compare the treatment of other tax credits described in §25).

37. As the tax credit under imputation systems (even when exceeding tax liability) is to be regarded as a tax provision, the question arises whether it should be deducted from individual income tax receipts (1110) or corporate income tax receipts (1210). In this Report, the full amount of corporate income tax paid is shown under 1210 and no imputed tax is included under 1110. Thus, the full amount of the credit reduces the amount of 1110 whether the credit results in a reduction of personal income tax liability or whether an actual refund is made because the credit exceeds the income tax liability. (Where, however, such tax credits are deducted from corporation tax in respect of dividends paid to corporations the amounts are deducted from the receipts of 1210).

1120 and 1220 — Taxes on capital gains

38. These sub-headings comprise taxes imposed on capital gains, 1120 covering those levied on the gains of individuals and 1220 those levied on the gains of corporate enterprises, where receipts from such taxes can be separately identified. In many countries this is not the case and the receipts from such taxes are then classified with those from the income tax. Heading 1120 also includes taxes on gains from gambling.

2000 — Social security contributions

39. Classified here are all compulsory payments that confer an entitlement to receive a (contingent) future social benefit. Such payments are usually earmarked to finance social benefits and are often paid to institutions of general government that provide such benefits. However, such earmarking is not part of the definition of social security contributions and

is not required for a tax to be classified here. However, conferment of an entitlement is required for a tax to be classified under this heading. So, levies on income or payroll that are earmarked for social security funds but do not confer an entitlement to benefit are excluded from this heading and shown under personal income taxes (1100) or taxes on payroll and workforce (3000). Taxes on other bases, such as goods and services, which are earmarked for social security benefits are not shown here but are classified according to their respective bases because they generally confer no entitlement to social security benefits.

40. Contributions for the following types of social security benefits would, *inter alia*, be included: unemployment insurance benefits and supplements, accident, injury and sickness benefits, old-age, disability and survivors' pensions, family allowances, reimbursements for medical and hospital expenses or provision of hospital or medical services. Contributions may be levied on both employees and employers.

41. Contributions may be based on earnings or payroll ('on a payroll basis') or on net income after deductions and exemptions for personal circumstances ('on an income tax basis'), and the revenues from the two bases should be separately identified if possible. However, where contributions to a general social security scheme are on a payroll basis, but the contributions of particular groups (such as the self-employed) cannot be assessed on this basis and net income is used as a proxy for gross earnings, the receipts may still be classified as being on a payroll basis. In principle, this heading excludes voluntary contributions paid to social security schemes. When separately identifiable these are shown in the memorandum item on the financing of social security benefits. In practice, however, they cannot always be separately identified from compulsory contributions, in which case they are included in this heading.

42. Contributions to social insurance schemes which are not institutions of general government and to other types of insurance schemes, provident funds, pension funds, friendly societies or other saving schemes are not considered as social security contributions. Provident funds are arrangements under which the contributions of each employee and of the corresponding employer on his/her behalf are kept in a separate account earning interest and withdrawable under specific circumstances. Pension funds are separately organised schemes negotiated between employees and employers and carry provisions for different contributions and benefits, sometimes more directly tied to salary levels and length of service than under social security schemes. When contributions to these schemes are compulsory or quasi-compulsory (e.g. by virtue of agreement with professional and union organisations) they are shown in the memorandum item (refer to Chapter 4.2 of the Report).

43. Contributions by government employees and by governments in respect of their employees, to social security schemes classified within general government are included in this heading. Contributions to separate schemes for government employees, which can be regarded as replacing general social security schemes, are also regarded as taxes.[15] Where, however, a separate scheme is not seen as replacing a general scheme and has been negotiated between the government, in its role as an employer, and its employees, it is not regarded as social security and contributions to it are not regarded as taxes, even though the scheme may have been established by legislation.

44. This heading excludes 'imputed' contributions, which correspond to social benefits paid directly by employers to their employees or former employees or to their representatives (e.g. when employers are legally obliged to pay sickness benefits for a certain period).

45. Contributions are divided into those of employees (2100), employers (2200), and self-employed or non-employed (2300), and then further sub-divided according to the basis on which they are levied. Employees are defined for this purpose as all persons engaged in activities of business units, government bodies, private non-profit institutions, or other paid employment, except the proprietors and their unpaid family members in the case of unincorporated businesses. Members of the armed forces are included, irrespective of the duration and type of their service, if they contribute to social security schemes. The contributions of employers are defined as their payments on account of their employees to social security schemes. Where employees or employers are required to continue the payment of social security contributions when the employee becomes unemployed these contributions, data permitting, are shown in 2100 and 2200 respectively. Accordingly, the sub-heading 2300 is confined to contributions paid by the self-employed and by those outside of the labour force (e.g. disabled or retired individuals).

3000 — Taxes on payroll and workforce

46. These consist of taxes payable by enterprises assessed either as a proportion of the wages or salaries paid or as a fixed amount per person employed. They do not include compulsory social security contributions paid by employers or any taxes paid by employees themselves out of their wages or salaries

4000 — Taxes on property

47. This heading covers recurrent and non-recurrent taxes on the use, ownership or transfer of property. These include taxes on immovable property or net wealth, taxes on the change of ownership of property through inheritance or gift and taxes on financial and capital transactions. The following kinds of tax are excluded from this heading:

a. taxes on capital gains resulting from the sale of a property (1120 or 1220);

b. taxes on the use of goods or on permission to use goods or perform activities (5200); see §76;

c. taxes on immovable property levied on the basis of a presumed net income which take into account the personal circumstances of the taxpayer. They are classified as income taxes along with taxes on income and capital gains derived from property (1100);

d. taxes on the use of property for residence, where the tax is payable by either proprietor or tenant and the amount payable is a function of the user's personal circumstances (pay, dependants, and so on). They are classified as taxes on income (1100);

e. taxes on building in excess of permitted maximum density, taxes on the enlargement, construction or alteration of certain buildings beyond a permitted value and taxes on building construction. They are classified as taxes on permission to perform activities (5200);

f. taxes on the use of one's own property for special trading purposes like selling alcohol, tobacco, meat or for exploitation of land resources (e.g. United States severance taxes). They are classified as taxes on permission to perform activities (5200).

4100 — *Recurrent taxes on immovable property*

48. This sub-heading covers taxes levied regularly in respect of the use or ownership of immovable property.

- these taxes are levied on land and buildings;
- they can be in the form of a percentage of an assessed property value based on a national rental income, sales price, or capitalised yield; or in terms of other characteristics of real property, (for example size or location) from which a presumed rent or capital value can be derived.
- such taxes can be levied on proprietors, tenants, or both. They can also be paid by one level of government to another level of government in respect of property under the jurisdiction of the latter.
- debts are not taken into account in the assessment of these taxes, and they differ from taxes on net wealth in this respect.

49. Taxes on immovable property are further sub-divided into those paid by households (4110) and those paid by other entities (4120), according to the criteria set out in §30(*b*) above.

4200 — *Recurrent taxes on net wealth*

50. This sub-heading covers taxes levied regularly (in most cases annually) on net wealth, i.e. taxes on a wide range of movable and immovable property, net of debt. It is sub-divided into taxes paid by individuals (4210) and taxes paid by corporate enterprises (4220) according to the criteria set out in §30(*a*) above. If separate figures exist for receipts paid by institutions, the tax payments involved are added to those paid by corporations.

4300 — *Estate, inheritance and gift taxes*

51. This sub-heading is divided into taxes on estates and inheritances (4310) and taxes on gifts (4320).[16] Estate taxes are charged on the amount of the total estate whereas inheritance taxes are charged on the shares of the individual recipients; in addition the latter may take into account the relationship of the individual recipients to the deceased.

4400 — *Taxes on financial and capital transactions*

52. This sub-heading comprises, *inter alia*, taxes on the issue, transfer, purchase and sale of securities, taxes on cheques, and taxes levied on specific legal transactions such as validation of contracts and the sale of immovable property. The heading does not include:

a. taxes on the use of goods or property or permission to perform certain activities (5200);
b. fees paid to cover court charges, charges for birth, marriage or death certificates, which are normally regarded as non-tax revenues (see §11);
c. taxes on capital gains (1000);
d. recurrent taxes on immovable property (4100);
e. recurrent taxes on net wealth (4200);
f. once-and-for-all levies on property or wealth (4500).

4500 — *Other non-recurrent taxes on property*[16]

53. This sub-heading covers once-and-for-all, as distinct from recurrent, levies on property. It is divided into taxes on net wealth (4510) and other non-recurrent taxes on property (4520). Heading 4510 would include taxes levied to meet emergency expenditures, or for

redistribution purposes. Heading 4520 would cover taxes levied to take account of increases in land value due to permission given to develop or provision of additional local facilities by general government, any taxes on the revaluation of capital and once-and-for-all taxes on particular items of property.

4600 — Other recurrent taxes on property

54. These rarely exist in OECD member countries, but the heading would include taxes on goods such as cattle, jewellery, windows, and other external signs of wealth.

5000 — Taxes on goods and services

55. All taxes and duties levied on the production, extraction, sale, transfer, leasing or delivery of goods, and the rendering of services (5100), or in respect of the use of goods or permission to use goods or to perform activities (5200) are included here. The heading thus covers:

a. multi-stage cumulative taxes;
b. general sales taxes — whether levied at manufacture/production, wholesale or retail level;
c. value-added taxes;
d. excises;
e. taxes levied on the import and export of goods;
f. taxes levied in respect of the use of goods and taxes on permission to use goods, or perform certain activities;
g. taxes on the extraction, processing or production of minerals and other products.

56. Borderline cases between this heading and heading 4000 (taxes on property) and 6100 (other taxes on business) are referred to in §47, §52 and §78. Residual sub-headings (5300) and (5130) cover tax receipts which cannot be allocated between 5100 and 5200 and between 5110 and 5120, respectively; see §32.

5100 — Taxes on the production, sale, transfer, leasing and delivery of goods and rendering of services

57. This sub-heading consists of all taxes, levied on transactions in goods and services on the basis of their intrinsic characteristics (e.g. value, weight of tobacco, strength of alcohol, and so on) as distinct from taxes imposed on the use of goods, or permission to use goods or perform activities, which fall under 5200.

5110 — General taxes on goods and services

58. This sub-heading includes all taxes, other than import and export duties (5123 and 5124), levied on the production, leasing, transfer, delivery or sales of a wide range of goods and/ or the rendering of a wide range of services, irrespective of whether they are domestically produced or imported and irrespective of the stage of production or distribution at which they are levied. It thus covers value-added taxes, sales taxes and multi-stage cumulative taxes. Receipts from border adjustments in respect of such taxes when goods are imported are added to gross receipts for this category, and repayments of such taxes when goods are exported are deducted. These taxes are subdivided into 5111 value-added taxes, 5112 sales taxes, 5113 turnover and other general taxes on goods and services.

59. Borderline cases arise between this heading and taxes on specific goods (5120) when taxes are levied on a large number of goods, for example, the United Kingdom purchase tax

(repealed in 1973) and the Japanese commodity tax (repealed in 1988). In conformity with national views, the former United Kingdom purchase tax is classified as a general tax (5112) and the former Japanese commodity tax as excises (5121).

5111 — *Value-added taxes*

60. All general consumption taxes charged on value-added are classified in this sub-heading, irrespective of the method of deduction and the stages at which the taxes are levied. In practice, all OECD countries with value-added taxes normally allow immediate deduction of taxes on purchases by all but the final consumer and impose tax at all stages. In some countries the heading may include certain taxes, such as those on financial and insurance activities, either because receipts from them cannot be identified separately from those from the value-added tax, or because they are regarded as an integral part of the value-added tax, even though similar taxes in other countries might be classified elsewhere (e.g. 5126 as taxes on services or 4400 as taxes on financial and capital transactions).

5112 — *Sales taxes*

61. All general taxes levied at one stage only, whether at manufacturing or production, wholesale or retail stage are classified here.

5113 — *Turnover and other general taxes on goods and services*

62. These are multi-stage cumulative taxes and taxes where elements of consumption taxes are combined with multistage taxes. These taxes are levied each time a transaction takes place without deduction for taxes paid on inputs. Multi-stage taxes can be combined with elements of value-added or sales taxes.

5120 — *Taxes on specific goods and services*

63. Excises, profits generated and transferred from fiscal monopolies, and customs and imports duties as well as taxes on exports, foreign exchange transactions, investment goods and betting stakes and special taxes on services, which do not form part of a general tax of 5110, are included in this category.

5121 — *Excises*

64. Excises are taxes levied as a product specific unit tax on a predefined limited range of goods. Excises are usually levied at differentiated rates on nonessential or luxury goods, alcoholic beverages, tobacco, and energy. Excises may be imposed at any stage of production or distribution and are usually assessed as a specific charge per unit based on characteristics by reference to the value, weight, strength, or quantity of the product. Included are special taxes on individual products such as sugar, sugar beets, matches, and chocolates; taxes levied at varying rates on a certain range of goods; and taxes levied on tobacco goods, alcoholic drinks, motor fuels, and hydrocarbon oils. If a tax collected principally on imported goods also applies, or would apply, under the same law to comparable domestically produced goods, then the revenue from this tax is classified as arising from excises rather than from import duties. This principle applies even if there is no comparable domestic production or no possibility of such production. Taxes on the use of utilities such as water, electricity, gas, and energy are regarded as excises rather than taxes on specific services (5126). Excises exclude those taxes that are levied as general taxes on goods and services (5110); profits of fiscal monopolies (5122); customs and other import duties (5123); or taxes on exports (5124).

5122 — *Profits of fiscal monopolies*

65. This sub-heading covers that part of the profits of fiscal monopolies which is transferred to general government or which is used to finance any expenditures considered to be government expenditures (see §23). Amounts are shown when they are transferred to general government or used to make expenditures considered to be government expenditures.

66. Fiscal monopolies reflect the exercise of the taxing power of government by the use of monopoly powers. Fiscal monopolies are non-financial public enterprises exercising a monopoly in most cases over the production or distribution of tobacco, alcoholic beverages, salt, matches, playing cards and petroleum or agricultural products (i.e. on the kind of products which are likely to be, alternatively or additionally, subject to the excises of 5121), to raise the government revenues which in other countries are gathered through taxes on dealings in such commodities by private business units. The government monopoly may be at the production stage or, as in the case of government-owned and controlled liquor stores, at the distribution stage.

67. Fiscal monopolies are distinguished from public utilities such as rail transport, electricity, post offices, and other communications, which may enjoy a monopoly or quasi-monopoly position but where the primary purpose is normally to provide basic services rather than to raise revenue for government. Transfers from such other public enterprises to the government are considered as non-tax revenues. The traditional concept of fiscal monopoly is not generally extended to include state lotteries, the profits of which are usually accordingly regarded as non-tax revenues. However, they can be included as tax revenues if the prime reason for their operation is to raise revenues to finance government expenditure. Fiscal monopoly profits are distinguished from export and import monopoly profits (5127) transferred from marketing boards or other enterprises dealing with international trade.

5123 — *Customs and other import duties*

68. Taxes, stamp duties and surcharges restricted by law to imported products are included here. Also included are levies on imported agricultural products which are imposed in member countries of the European Union and amounts paid by certain of these countries under the Monetary Compensation Accounts (MCA) system.[17] Starting from 1998, customs duties collected by European Union member states on behalf of the European Union are no longer reported under this heading in the country tables (in Chapter 4 of the Report). Excluded here are taxes collected on imports as part of a general tax on goods and services, or an excise applicable to both imported and domestically produced goods.

5124 — *Taxes on exports*

69. In the 1970s, export duties were levied in Australia, Canada and Portugal as a regular measure and they have been used in Finland for counter-cyclical purposes. Some member countries of the European Union pay, as part of the MCA system, a levy on exports (see note 16 to §68). Where these amounts are identifiable, they are shown in this heading. This heading does not include repayments of general consumption taxes or excises or customs duties on exported goods, which should be deducted from the gross receipts under 5110, 5121 or 5123, as appropriate.

5125 — *Taxes on investment goods*

70. This sub-heading covers taxes on investment goods, such as machinery. These taxes may be imposed for a number of years or temporarily for counter-cyclical purposes. Taxes

on industrial inputs which are also levied on consumers [e.g. the Swedish energy tax which is classified under (5121)] are not included here.

5126 — *Taxes on specific services*

71. All taxes assessed on the payment for specific services, such as taxes on insurance premiums, banking services, gambling and betting stakes (e.g. from horse races, football pools, lottery tickets), transport, entertainment, restaurant and advertising charges, fall into this category. Taxes levied on the gross income of companies providing the service (e.g. gross insurance premiums or gambling stakes received by the company) are also classified under this heading. Tax revenues from bank levies and payments to deposit insurance and financial stability schemes are provisionally included here for the 2012 edition. The detailed classification is set out in §108.

72. Excluded from this sub-heading are:

a. taxes on services forming part of a general tax on goods and services (5110);

b. taxes on electricity, gas and energy (5121 as excises);

c. taxes on individual gains from gambling (1120 as taxes on capital gains of individuals and non-corporate enterprises) and lump-sum taxes on the transfer of private lotteries or on the permission to set up lotteries (5200);[18]

d. taxes on cheques and on the issue, transfer or redemption of securities (4400 as taxes on financial and capital transactions).

5127 — *Other taxes on international trade and transactions*

73. This sub-heading covers revenue received by the government from the purchase and sale of foreign exchange at different rates. When the government exercises monopoly powers to extract a margin between the purchase and sales price of foreign exchange, other than to cover administrative costs, the revenue derived constitutes a compulsory levy exacted in indeterminate proportions from both purchaser and seller of foreign exchange. It is the common equivalent of an import duty and export duty levied in a single exchange rate system or of a tax on the sale or purchase of foreign exchange. Like the profits of fiscal monopolies and import or export monopolies transferred to government, it represents the exercise of monopoly powers for tax purposes and is included in tax revenues.

74. The sub-heading covers also the profits of export or import monopolies, which do not however exist in OECD countries, taxes on purchase or sale of foreign exchange, and any other taxes levied specifically on international trade or transactions.

5128 — *Other taxes on specific goods and services*

75. This item includes taxes on the extraction of minerals, fossil fuels and other exhaustible resources from deposits owned privately or by another government together with any other unidentifiable receipts from taxes on specific goods and services. Taxes on the extraction of exhaustible resources are usually a fixed amount per unit of quality or weight, but can be a percentage of value. The taxes are recorded when the resources are extracted. Payments from the extraction of exhaustible resources from deposits owned by the government unit receiving the payment are classified as rent.

5200 — *Taxes on use of goods or on permission to use goods or perform activities*

76. This sub-heading covers taxes which are levied in respect of the use of goods as distinct from taxes on the goods themselves. Unlike the latter taxes – reported under 5100 –, they are

not assessed on the value of the goods but usually as fixed amounts. Taxes on permission to use goods or to perform activities are also included here, as are pollution taxes not based upon the value of particular goods. It is sometimes difficult to distinguish between compulsory user charges and licence fees which are regarded as taxes and those which are excluded as non-tax revenues. The criteria which are employed are noted in §11–12.

77. Although the sub-heading refers to the 'use' of goods, registration of ownership rather than use may be what generates liability to tax, so that the taxes of this heading may apply to the ownership of animals or goods rather than their use (e.g. race horses, dogs and motor vehicles) and may apply even to unusable goods (e.g. unusable motor vehicles or guns).

78. Borderline cases arise with:

a. taxes on the permission to perform business activities which are levied on a combined income, payroll or turnover base and, accordingly, are classified following the rules in §81;

b. taxes on the ownership or use of property of headings 4100, 4200 and 4600. The heading 4100 is confined to taxes on the ownership or tenancy of immovable property and – unlike the taxes of 5200 – they are related to the value of the property. The net wealth taxes and taxes on chattels of 4200 and 4600 respectively are confined to the ownership rather than the use of assets, apply to groups of assets rather than particular goods and again are related to the value of the assets,

5210 — *Recurrent taxes on use of goods and on permission to use goods or perform activities*

79. The principal characteristic of taxes classified here is that they are levied at regular intervals and that they are usually fixed amounts. The most important item in terms of revenue receipts is vehicle licence taxes. This sub-heading also covers taxes on permission to hunt, shoot, fish or to sell certain products and taxes on the ownership of dogs and on the performance of certain services, provided that they meet the criteria set out in §11–12. The sub-divisions of 5210 are user taxes on motor vehicles paid by households (5211) and those paid by others (5212).[19] Sub-heading 5213 covers dog licences and user charges for permission to perform activities such as selling meat or liquor when the levies are on a recurring basis. It also covers recurrent general licences for hunting, shooting and fishing where the right to carry out these activities is not granted as part of a normal commercial transaction (e.g. the granting of the licence is not accompanied by the right to use a specific area which is owned by government).

5220 — *Non-recurrent taxes on use of goods and on permission to use goods or perform activities*

80. This section covers non-recurrent taxes levied on the use of goods or on permission to use goods or perform activities and taxes levied each time goods are used. It includes taxes levied on the emission or discharge into the environment of noxious gases, liquids or other harmful substances.

- Payments for tradable emission permits issued by governments under cap and trade schemes should be recorded here at the time the emissions occur. No revenue should be recorded for permits that governments issue free of charge. The accrual basis of recording means that there can be a timing difference between the cash being received by government for the permits and the time the emission occurs. In the national accounts, this timing gives rise to a financial liability for government during the period.

- Payments made for the collection and disposal of waste or noxious substances by public authorities should be excluded as they constitute a sale of services to enterprises.

81. Other taxes falling under heading 5200 that are not levied recurrently are also included here. Thus, once-and-for-all payments for permission to sell liquor or tobacco or to set up betting shops are included provided they meet the criteria set out in §11–12.

6000 — Other taxes

82. Taxes levied on a base, or bases, other than those described under headings 1000, 3000, 4000 and 5000, or on bases of which cannot be considered to be related to any one of these headings, are included here. Where taxes are levied on a multiple base and it is possible to estimate the receipts related to each base the separate amounts are included under the appropriate headings. If separate amounts cannot be estimated and it is known that most of the receipts are derived from one base, the whole of the receipts are classified according to that base. Otherwise, they are classified here. Other revenues included here are presumptive taxes not included elsewhere in the classification system, taxes on individuals in the form of a poll tax or capitation tax, stamp taxes not related to financial and capital transactions nor falling exclusively on a single category of transaction, expenditure taxes where personal deductions or exemptions are applied and unidentifiable tax receipts. A subdivision is made between taxes levied wholly or predominantly on business (6100) and those levied on others (6200).

A.6. Conciliation with national accounts

83. This section of the tables provides a re-conciliation between the OECD calculation of total tax revenues and the total of all taxes and social contributions paid to general government as recorded in the country's National Accounts. Where the country is a member of the European Union (EU), the comparison is between the OECD calculation of total tax revenues and the sum of tax revenues and social contributions recorded in the combination of the general government and the institutions of the EU sectors of the National Accounts.

A.7. Memorandum item on the financing of social security benefits

84. In view of the varying relationship between taxation and social security contributions and the cases referred to in §39 to §45, a memorandum item collects together all payments earmarked for social security-type benefits, other than voluntary payments to the private sector. Data are presented as follows (refer Chapter 4.2 of the Report):

a. Taxes of 2000 series.

b. Taxes earmarked for social security benefits.

c. Voluntary contributions to the government.

d. Compulsory contributions to the private sector.

Guidance on the breakdown of (a) to (d) above is provided in §39 to §45.

A.8. Memorandum item on identifiable taxes paid by government

85. Identifiable taxes actually paid by government are presented in a memorandum item classified by the main headings of the OECD classification of taxes. In the vast majority of countries, only social security contributions and payroll taxes paid by government can be identified. These are, however, usually the most important taxes paid by governments (refer to Chapter 4.2 of the Report).

A.9. Relation of OECD classification of taxes to national accounting systems

86. A system of national accounts (SNA) seeks to provide a coherent framework for recording and presenting the main flows relating respectively to production, consumption, accumulation and external transactions of a given economic area, usually a country or a major region within a country. Government revenues are an important part of the transactions recorded in SNA. The final version of the 2008 SNA was jointly published by five international organisations: the United Nations, the International Monetary Fund, the European Union, the Organisation for Economic Co-operation and Development, and the World Bank in August 2009. The *System* is a comprehensive, consistent and flexible set of macroeconomic accounts. It is designed for use in countries with market economies, whatever their stage of economic development, and also in countries in transition to market economies. The important parts of the SNA's conceptual framework and its definitions of the various sectors of the economy have been reflected in the OECD's classification of taxes.

87. There are, however, some differences between the OECD classification of taxes and SNA concepts that are listed below. They arise because the aim of the former is to provide the maximum disaggregation of statistical data on what are generally regarded as taxes by tax administrations.

a. OECD includes compulsory social security contributions paid to general government in total tax revenues. Imputed and voluntary contributions plus those paid to private funds are not treated as taxes (§8 and §10 above);
b. there are different points of view on whether or not some levies and fees are classified as taxes (§11 and §12 above);
c. OECD excludes imputed taxes or subsidies resulting from the operation of official multiple exchange rates or from the central bank paying a rate of interest on required reserves that is different from other market rates;
d. there are differences in the treatment of non-wastable tax credits

88. As noted in §1 and §2, headings 1000 to 6000 of the OECD list of taxes cover all unrequited payments to general government, other than compulsory loans and fines. Such unrequited payments including fines, but excluding compulsory loans can be obtained from adding together the following figures in the 2008 SNA

- value-added type taxes (D.211);
- taxes and duties on imports, excluding VAT (D.212);
- export taxes (D.213);
- taxes on products, excluding VAT, import and export taxes (D.214);
- other taxes on production (D.29);
- taxes on income (D.51);
- other current taxes (D.59);
- social contributions (D.61), excluding voluntary contributions;
- capital taxes (D.91).

A.10. The OECD classification of taxes and the International Monetary Fund (GFS) system

89. The coverage and valuation of tax revenues in the GFS system and the 2008 SNA are very similar. Therefore, the differences between the OECD classification and that of the 2008 SNA (see §87 above) also apply to the GFS. In addition the International Monetary Fund subdivides the OECD 5000 heading into section IV (Domestic Taxes on Goods and Services) and section V (Taxes on International Trade and Transactions). This reflects the fact that while the latter usually yield insignificant amounts of revenue in OECD countries, this is not the case in many non-OECD countries.

A.11. Comparison of the OECD classification of taxes with other international classifications

90. The table below describes an item by item comparison of the OECD classification of taxes and the classifications used in the following:

i) System of National Accounts (2008 SNA);

ii) European System of Accounts (2010 ESA);

iii) IMF *Government Finance Statistics Manual* (GFSM2014).

91. These comparisons represent those that would be expected to apply in the majority of cases. However in practice some flexibility should be used in their application. This is because in particular cases, countries can adopt varying approaches to the classification of revenues in National Accounts.

OECD Classification	2008 SNA	2010 ESA	GFSM2014
1000 Taxes on income, profits and capital gains			
1100 Individuals			
1110 Income and profits	D51-8.61a	D51A	1111
1120 Capital gains	D51-8.61c, d	D51C, D	1111
1200 Corporations			
1210 Income and profits	D51-8.61b	D51B	1112
1220 Capital gains	D51-8.61c	D51C	1112
1300 Unallocable as between 1100 and 1200			1113
2000 Social security contributions			
2100 Employees	D613-8.85	D613	1211
2200 Employers	D611-8.83	D611	1212
2300 Self-employed, non-employed	D613-8.85	D613	1213
2400 Unallocable as between 2100, 2200 and 2300			1214
3000 Taxes on payroll and workforce	D29-7.97a	D29C	112
4000 Taxes on property			
4100 Recurrent taxes on immovable property			
4110 Households	D59-8.63a	D59A	1131
4120 Other	D29-7.97b	D29A	1131
4200 Recurrent net wealth taxes			
4210 Individual	D59-8.63b	D59A	1132
4220 Corporations	D59-8.63b	D59A	1132
4300 Estate, inheritance and gift taxes			
4310 Estate and inheritance taxes	D91-10.207b	D91A	1133
4320 Gift taxes	D91-10.207b	D91A	1133
4400 Taxes on financial and capital transactions	D59-7.96d; D29-7.97e	D214B, C	114114; 1161
4500 Other non-recurrent taxes on property	D91-10.207a	D91B	1135
4600 Other recurrent taxes on property	D59-8.63c	D59A	1136

OECD Classification	2008 SNA	2010 ESA	GFSM2014
5000 Taxes on goods and services			
5100 Taxes on production, sale and transfer of goods and services			
5110 General taxes on goods and services			
5111 Value-added taxes	D211-7.89	D211; D29G	11411
5112 Sales taxes	D2122-7.94a; D214-7.96a	D21224; D214I	11412
5113 Other general taxes on goods and services	D214-7.96a	D214I	11413
5120 Taxes on specific goods and services			
5121 Excises	D2122-7.94b; D214-7.96b	D21223; D214A, B, D	1142
5122 Profits of fiscal monopolies	D214-7.96e	D214J	1143
5123 Customs and other import duties	D2121-7.93	D2121; D21221, 2	1151
5124 On exports	D213-7.95a	D214K	1152-4
5125 On investment goods			
5126 On specific services	D2122-7.94c; D214-7.96c	D21225; D214E, F, G, H; D29F	1144; 1156
5127 Other taxes on international trade and transactions	D2122-7.94d D29-7.95b D29-7.97g D59-8.64d	D21226; D29D; D59E	1153; 1155-6
5128 Other taxes on specific goods and services			1146
5130 Unallocable between 5110 and 5120			
5200 Taxes on use of goods and on permission to use goods or perform activities			
5210 Recurrent taxes on use of goods and on permission to use goods or perform activities			
5211 Motor vehicle taxes households	D59-8.64c	D59D	11451
5212 Motor vehicles taxes others	D29-7.97d	D214D; D29B	11451
5213 Other recurrent taxes on use of goods and on permission to use goods or perform activities	D29-7.97c, d, f D59-8.64c	D29B, E, F; D59D	11452
5220 Non-recurrent taxes on permission to use goods or perform activities			11452
5300 Unallocable as between 5100 and 5200			
6000 Other taxes			
6100 Payable solely by business			1161
6200 Payable by other than business, or unidentifiable	D59-8.64a, b	D59B, C	1162

A.12. Attribution of tax revenues by sub-sectors of general government

92. The OECD classification requires a breakdown of tax revenues by sub-sectors of government. The definition of each sub-sector and the criteria to be used to attribute tax revenues between these sub-sectors are set out below. They follow the guidance of the 2008 SNA and GFSM 2014.

Sub-sectors of general government to be identified

a) Central government

93. The central government sub-sector includes all governmental departments, offices, establishments and other bodies which are agencies or instruments of the central authority whose competence extends over the whole territory, with the exception of the administration of social security funds. Central government therefore has the authority to impose taxes on all resident and non resident units engaged in economic activities within the country.

b) State, provincial or regional government

94. This sub-sector consists of intermediate units of government exercising a competence at a level below that of central government. It includes all such units operating independently

of central government in a part of a country's territory encompassing a number of smaller localities, with the exception of the administration of social security funds. In unitary countries, regional governments may be considered to have a separate existence where they have substantial autonomy to raise a significant proportion of their revenues from sources within their control and their officers are independent of external administrative control in the actual operation of the unit's activities.

95. At present, federal countries comprise the majority of cases where revenues attributed to intermediate units of government are identified separately. Spain is the only unitary country in this position. In the remaining unitary countries, regional revenues are included with those of local governments.

c) Local government

96. This sub-sector includes all other units of government exercising an independent competence in part of the territory of a country, with the exception of the administration of social security funds. It encompasses various urban and/or rural jurisdictions (e.g. local authorities, municipalities, cities, boroughs, districts).

d) Social security funds

97. Social security funds form a separate sub-sector of general government. The social security sub-sector is defined in the 2008 SNA by the following extracts from paragraphs 4.124 to 4.126 and 4.147:

> *"Social security schemes are social insurance schemes covering the community as a whole or large section of the community that are imposed and controlled by government units. The schemes cover a wide variety of programmes, providing benefits in cash or in kind for old age, invalidity or death, survivors, sickness and maternity, work injury, unemployment, family allowance, health care, etc. There is not necessarily a direct link between the amount of the contribution paid by an individual and the benefits he or she may receive." (Paragraph 4.124).*
>
> *"When social security schemes are separately organised from the other activities of government units and hold their assets and liabilities separately from the latter and engage in financial transactions on their own account they qualify as institutional units that are described as social security funds." (Paragraph 4.125).*
>
> *"The amounts raised, and paid out, in social security contributions and benefits may be deliberately varied in order to achieve objectives of government policy that have no direct connection with the concept of social security as a scheme to provide social benefits to members of the community. They may be raised or lowered in order to influence the level of aggregate demand in the economy, for example. Nevertheless, so long as they remain separately constituted funds, they must be treated as separate institutional units in the SNA. (Paragraph 4.126).*
>
> *"The social security funds sub-sector (of general government) consists of the social security funds operating at all levels of government. Such funds are social insurance schemes covering the community as a whole or large section of the community that are imposed by government units." (Paragraph 4.147).*

98. This definition of social security funds is followed in the OECD classification with the two following exceptions which are excluded

- Schemes imposed by government and operated by bodies outside the general government sector, as defined in §3 of this manual; and
- Schemes to which all contributions are voluntary.

Supra-national authorities

99. This sub-sector covers the revenue-raising operations of supra-national authorities within a country. In practice, the only relevant supra-national authority in the OECD area is that of the institutions of the European Union (EU). As from 1998, supra-national authorities are no longer included in the *Revenue Statistics*, to achieve consistency with the SNA definition of general government which excludes them. For example, income taxes and social security contributions collected by European Institutions and paid by European civil servants who are resident of EU member countries should not be included. However the specific levies paid by the member states of the EU continue to be included in total tax revenues and they are shown under this heading.

Criteria to be used for the attribution of tax revenues

100. When a government collects taxes and pays them over in whole or in part to other governments, it is necessary to determine whether the revenues should be considered to be those of the collecting government which it distributes to others as grants, or those of the beneficiary governments which the collecting government receives and passes on only as their agent. The criteria to be used in the attribution of revenues are set out in §101 to §104 which replicate paragraphs 3.70 to 3.73 from the 2008 SNA.

101. In general, a tax is attributed to the government unit that

a. exercises the authority to impose the tax (either as a principal or through the delegated authority of the principal),

b. has final discretion to set and vary the rate of the tax

102. Where an amount is collected by one government for and on behalf of another government, and the latter government has the authority to impose the tax, and set and vary its rate, then the former is acting as an agent for the latter and the tax is reassigned. Any amount retained by the collecting government as a collection charge should be treated as a payment for a service. Any other amount retained by the collecting government, such as under a tax-sharing arrangement, should be treated as a current grant. If the collecting government was delegated the authority to set and vary the rate, then the amount collected should be treated as tax revenue of this government.

103. Where different governments jointly and equally set the rate of a tax and jointly and equally decide on the distribution of the proceeds, with no individual government having ultimate overriding authority, then the tax revenues are attributed to each government according to its respective share of the proceeds. If an arrangement allows one government unit to exercise ultimate overriding authority, then all of the tax revenue is attributed to that unit.

104. There may also be the circumstance where a tax is imposed under the constitutional or other authority of one government, but other governments individually set the tax rate in their jurisdictions. The proceeds of the tax generated in each respective government's jurisdiction are attributed as tax revenues of that government.

Levies paid by member states of the European Union

105. The levies paid by the member states of the EU take the form specific levies which include

a. custom duties and levies on agricultural goods (5123),

b. gross monetary compensation accounts (5123 if relating to imports and 5124 if relating to exports); and

c. Steel, coal, sugar and milk levies (5128).

106. The custom duties collected by member states on behalf of the EU are recorded

- on a gross of collection fee basis;
- using figures adjusted so that duties are shown on a 'final destination' as opposed to a 'country of first entry' basis where such adjustments can be made. These adjustments concern in particular duties collected at important (sea) ports. Although the EU duties are collected by the authorities of the country of first entry, when possible these duties should be excluded from the revenue of the collecting country and be included in the revenue of the country of final destination.

107. This is the specific EU levy that most clearly conforms to the attribution criterion described in §99 above. Consequently as from 1998, these amounts are footnoted as a memorandum item to the EU member state country tables (in Chapter 4) and no longer shown under heading 5123. However the figures are included in the total tax revenue figures on the top line for all the relevant years shown in the tables.

A.13. Provisional classification of revenues from bank levies and payments to deposit insurance and financial stability schemes

108. The OECD have adopted the following interim approach to reporting revenue from bank levies plus deposit insurance and stability fees for the 2012 and subsequent editions of *OECD Revenue Statistics*. It is recommended that the amounts should be recorded under category 5126.

- Compulsory payments of stability fees, bank levies and deposit insurance should generally be treated as tax revenues where the payments are made to General Government and allocated to the governments' consolidated or general funds so that the Government is free to make immediate use of the money for the purposes that it chooses. This principle would apply regardless of whether the Government is promising to make payments to guarantee the banks' customer deposits in some future contingency.
- If the compulsory payments are made to general government and placed in funds that are earmarked to be entirely channelled back to the sector of the economy that comprises the companies that are subject to the payment, they would still generally be treated as tax revenues on the grounds that the funds would be available for the government and would reduce its budget deficit, the fee is unrequited for an individual entity and the amounts raised could be unrelated to any eventual pay out to depositors or expenditure on wider support for the financial sector.
- Payments to made to the smaller long-standing schemes for insuring 'retail' deposits, where the payment levels are consistent with the costs of insurance should be classified as fee for service.
- Any payments which involve governments realising the assets of a failed institution or receiving a priority claim on its assets in liquidation in order to fund payments of compensation to customers for their lost deposits would be treated as a fee for a service as opposed to tax revenues.
- Compulsory payments that are made to funds operated outside the government sector and non-state institutions backed by the deposit takers and all payments to voluntary schemes should not be treated as tax revenues.

Notes

1. References in this OECD Interpretative Guide to Sections or Parts of "this Report" refer to OECD (2018), *Revenue Statistics 2018*, OECD Publishing, Paris.
2. All references to SNA are to the 2008 edition.
3. See section A.12 of this guide for a discussion of the concept of agency capacity.
4. It is usually possible to identify amounts of social security contributions and payroll taxes, but not other taxes paid by government.
5. If, however, a levy which is considered as non-tax revenue by most countries is regarded as a tax — or raises substantial revenue — in one or more countries, the amounts collected are footnoted at the end of the relevant country tables, even though the amounts are not included in total tax revenues.
6. Names, however, can frequently be misleading. For example, though a passport fee would normally be considered a non-tax revenue, if a supplementary levy on passports (as is the case in Portugal) were imposed in order to raise substantial amounts of revenue relative to the cost of providing the passport, the levy would be regarded as a tax under 5200.
7. A more detailed explanation of this distinction can be found in the special feature, 'Current issues in reporting tax revenues', in the 2001 edition of the *Revenue Statistics*.
8. Sometimes the terms 'non-refundable' and 'refundable' are used, but it may be considered illogical to talk of 'refundable' when nothing has been paid.
9. A different treatment, however, is accorded to non-wastable tax credits under imputation systems of corporate income tax (§36–38).
10. This is not strictly a true tax expenditure in the formal sense. Such tax expenditures require identification of a benchmark tax system for each country or, preferably, a common international benchmark. In practice it has not been possible to reach agreement on a common international benchmark.
11. Unless based on the profit made on a sale, in which case they would be classified as capital gains taxes under 1120 or 1220.
12. In some countries the same legislation applies to both individual and corporate enterprises for particular taxes on income. However, the receipts from such taxes are usually allocable between individuals and enterprises and can therefore be shown in the appropriate sub-heading.
13. For example, "...sufficiently self-contained and independent that they behave in the same way as corporations....... (including) keeping a complete set of accounts" (2008 SNA, section 4.44).
14. In Canada — a country also referred to as having an imputation system — the (wastable) tax credit for the shareholder is in respect of domestic corporation tax deemed to have been paid whether or not a corporation tax liability has arisen. As there is no integral connection between the corporation tax liability and the credit given against income tax under such systems, these credits for dividends are treated, along with other tax credits, on the lines described in §25.
15. This may also apply where a scheme for government employees existed prior to the introduction of a general social security scheme.
16. In the 2008 SNA these are regarded as capital transfers and not as taxes (see section A.8).
17. This is the system by which the European Union adjusts for differences between the exchange rates used to determine prices under the Common Market Agricultural Policy and actual exchange rates. Payments under the system may relate to imports or exports and where these amounts are separately identifiable they are shown under the appropriate heading (5123 or 5124). In this Report, these amounts are shown gross (i.e. without deducting any subsidies paid out under the MCA system).
18. Transfers of profits of State lotteries are regarded as non-tax revenues (see also §67).
19. See §30(c) as regards this distinction.

ANEXO A

Guía de interpretación de la OCDE[1]

Índice

A.1. Clasificación de impuestos de la OCDE

1. 1000 *Impuestos sobre la renta, las utilidades y las ganancias de capital*

    1100 Impuestos sobre la renta, utilidades y ganancias de capital de personas físicas

        1110 Renta y utilidades

        1120 Ganancias de capital

    1200 Impuesto sobre la renta, utilidades y ganancias de capital de sociedades.

        1210 Renta y utilidades

        1220 Ganancias de capital

    1300 No clasificables entre 1100 y 1200

2. 2000 *Contribuciones a la seguridad social*

    2100 Empleados

        2110 Sobre la base de la nómina

        2120 Sobre la base del impuesto sobre la renta

    2200 Empleadores

        2210 Sobre la base de la nómina

        2220 Sobre la base del impuesto sobre la renta

    2300 Trabajadores por cuenta propia o no empleados

        2310 Sobre la base de la nómina

        2320 Sobre la base del impuesto sobre la renta

    2400 No clasificables entre 2100, 2200 y 2300

        2410 Sobre la base de la nómina

        2420 Sobre la base del impuesto sobre la renta

3. 3000 *Impuestos sobre la nómina y la fuerza de trabajo*

4. 4000 *Impuestos sobre la propiedad*

    4100 Impuestos recurrentes sobre la propiedad inmueble

        4110 Hogares

        4120 Otros

    4200 Impuestos recurrentes sobre la riqueza neta

        4210 Personas físicas

        4220 Sociedades

    4300 Impuestos sobre sucesiones, herencias y donaciones

        4310 Impuestos sobre sucesiones y herencias

        4320 Impuestos sobre donaciones

    4400 Impuestos sobre transacciones financieras y de capital

    4500 Otros impuestos no recurrentes sobre la propiedad

        4510 Otros impuestos sobre la riqueza neta

        4520 Otros impuestos no recurrentes

    4600 Otros impuestos recurrentes sobre la propiedad

5. 5000 *Impuestos sobre los bienes y servicios*

5100 Impuestos sobre la producción, venta, transferencia , arrendamiento y entrega de bienes y prestación de servicios

5110 Impuestos generales

5111 Impuestos sobre el valor agregado

5112 Impuestos sobre las ventas

5113 Otros impuestos generales sobre ingresos brutos y sobre bienes y servicios

5120 Impuestos sobre bienes y servicios específicos

5121 Impuestos selectivos

5122 Utilidades de los monopolios fiscales

5123 Derechos de aduanas y otros derechos de importación

5124 Impuestos sobre las exportaciones

5125 Impuestos sobre los bienes de inversión

5126 Impuestos sobre servicios específicos

5127 Otros impuestos sobre el comercio y las transacciones internacionales

5128 Otros impuestos sobre bienes y servicios específicos

5130 No clasificables entre 5110 y 5120

5200 Impuestos sobre el uso de bienes y sobre el permiso para usar bienes y realizar actividades

5210 Impuestos recurrentes

5211 Pagados por los hogares sobre vehículos automotores.

5212 Pagados por otros sobre vehículos automotores

5213 Otros impuestos recurrentes

5220 Impuestos no recurrentes

5300 No clasificables entre 5100 y 5200

6. 6000 *Otros impuestos*

6100 Pagados únicamente por empresas

6200 Pagados por otros distintos de las empresas o no identificables

Guía de Interpretación de la OCDE

A.2. Cobertura

Criterios generales

1. En la clasificación de la OCDE, el término "impuestos" se circunscribe exclusivamente a los pagos sin contraprestación efectuados al gobierno general. Los impuestos carecen de contraprestación en el sentido en que, normalmente, las prestaciones proporcionadas por el gobierno a los contribuyentes no guardan relación directa con los pagos realizados por estos.

2. El término "impuestos" no incluye las multas, sanciones pecuniarias, ni préstamos obligatorios pagados al gobierno. La delimitación entre ingresos tributarios y no tributarios en relación con ciertas tasas y cargos se abordan en los § 11–14.

3. El gobierno general comprende la Administración central y los organismos que se hallan bajo su control efectivo, los gobiernos estatales y locales y sus respectivas administraciones, y ciertos regímenes de seguridad social y entidades gubernamentales autónomas, excluidas las empresas públicas. Esta definición del gobierno proviene del *Sistema de Cuentas Nacionales* (SCN) 2008;[2] en esa publicación, el sector del gobierno general y sus subsectores se hallan definidos en el capítulo 4, párrafos 4.117 a 4.165 de la versión en inglés.

4. Las unidades extrapresupuestarias son parte del sistema de gobierno general. Estas son entidades del gobierno general con presupuestos individuales que no están completamente cubiertos por el presupuesto principal o general. Estas entidades operan bajo la autoridad o el control de un gobierno central, estatal o local. Las entidades extrapresupuestarias pueden tener sus propias fuentes de ingresos, que pueden complementarse con subvenciones (transferencias) del presupuesto general o de otras fuentes. A pesar de que sus presupuestos pueden estar sujetos a la aprobación de la legislatura, similar a la de las cuentas presupuestarias, tienen discreción sobre el volumen y la composición de sus gastos. Dichas entidades pueden establecerse para llevar a cabo funciones gubernamentales específicas, como la construcción de carreteras o la producción de servicios de salud o educación pública. Los arreglos presupuestarios varían ampliamente entre países, y se utilizan diversos términos para describir estas entidades, pero a menudo se los denomina "fondos extrapresupuestarios" o "agencias descentralizadas".

5. Los pagos obligatorios a autoridades supranacionales y a los organismos vinculados a ellas no se incluyen como impuestos desde 1998, con contadas excepciones; sin embargo, los derechos de aduana recaudados por los estados miembros de la Unión Europea en nombre de esta siguen registrándose como partidas informativas y se incluyen en los cuadros de países (Capítulo 4 de la publicación *Revenue Statistics* de la OCDE), concretamente en la recaudación tributaria total del país en el que se cobran (véase el § 99). Por otra parte, en los países en los que la Iglesia forma parte del gobierno general, se computan los impuestos eclesiásticos, siempre que reúnan los criterios establecidos en el § 1. Además, habida cuenta de que los datos hacen referencia a las entradas que recibe el gobierno general, quedan excluidos los gravámenes abonados a órganos no gubernamentales, organismos de bienestar o regímenes de seguro social externos al gobierno general, y sindicatos u organizaciones profesionales, aun cuando dichos gravámenes sean obligatorios; sin embargo, los pagos obligatorios al gobierno general asignados a esos entes sí están incluidos aquí siempre que el gobierno no actúe como mero agente de estos.[3] Las utilidades de los monopolios fiscales se diferencian de las de otras empresas públicas, y se tratan como impuestos porque reflejan el ejercicio del poder tributario del Estado mediante el uso de prerrogativas monopolísticas (véanse los §§ 65–67), al igual que las utilidades percibidas por el gobierno por la compra y la venta de divisas a diferentes tipos de cambio (véase el § 74).

6. Los impuestos pagados por el gobierno (p. ej., contribuciones a la seguridad social e impuestos sobre la nómina pagados por el gobierno en su calidad de empleador, impuestos sobre el consumo en sus compras o impuestos sobre sus propiedades) no se han excluido de los datos presentados. Sin embargo, cuando ha sido posible identificar las cantidades de ingreso implicadas,[4] se han mostrado en el Capítulo 4.2 de la publicación Estadísticas Tributarias en países de la OCDE.

7. La relación entre esta clasificación y la del Sistema de Cuentas Nacionales (SCN) se aclara en los apartados A.9 y A.11 *infra.*; dado que estas dos clasificaciones no coinciden en todos sus aspectos, en ocasiones, los datos presentados en las cuentas nacionales se calculan o clasifican de forma diferente a lo establecido en la presente guía y, aunque esas y otras diferencias se han mencionado en determinados casos (p. ej., en el § 30 *infra.*), no ha sido posible hacer referencia a todas ellas. Por otra parte, pueden darse asimismo ciertas disparidades entre la presente clasificación y la empleada internamente por algunas administraciones nacionales (véase el § 12), por lo que quizá las estadísticas de la OCDE y las nacionales no siempre concuerden; sin embargo, es más que probable que esas diferencias sean mínimas en lo que a la cuantía de ingresos se refiere.

Contribuciones a la seguridad social

8. Las contribuciones obligatorias a la seguridad social, tal y como se definen en el § 39, abonadas al gobierno general, se tratan aquí como ingresos tributarios, ya que, al tratarse de pagos preceptivos al gobierno general, se asemejan claramente a los impuestos. No obstante, pueden diferir de otros impuestos por el hecho de que la recepción de prestaciones de la seguridad social depende, en numerosos países, de que se hayan aportado las debidas contribuciones, aunque la magnitud de dichas prestaciones no tiene por qué estar supeditada obligatoriamente al importe de las contribuciones. Al tratar las contribuciones sociales como impuestos, se obtiene un mayor grado de comparabilidad entre países, aunque se han consignado en una categoría separada para poder distinguirlas en cualquier análisis.

9. La estricta distinción entre los ingresos tributarios (pagos obligatorios sin contraprestaciones directas a los gobiernos generales) y los pagos obligatorios no tributarios (NTCPs por sus siglas en inglés) (pagos que con derechos a contraprestaciones o que se realizan a otras instituciones) está claramente definida. Sin embargo, dentro del rango de diferentes pagos obligatorios realizados a los gobiernos en todos los países, no siempre es sencillo en la práctica decidir si los pagos específicos son impuestos o NTCPs. Por ejemplo, los ahorros de pensión obligatorios que son controlados por el gobierno general y que se acumulan en una cuenta individual obteniendo una rentabilidad del mercado o una tasa que compensa la inflación se clasificarían a primera vista como NTCPs en lugar de impuestos. Sin embargo, incluso estos pagos podrían no dar origen a "reembolsos" y clasificarse como impuestos en lugar de NTCPs (por ejemplo, si estos ahorros no se pagan cuando el contribuyente muere antes de alcanzar la edad de jubilación y los fondos se utilizan para proporcionar una pensión mínima a todos los contribuyentes que están asegurados). Estos problemas hacen que las cifras de ingresos de la seguridad social reportadas para la mayoría de los países se basen en la premisa de que todos los tipos de pagos obligatorios a las administraciones públicas se consideran en cierta medida como elementos de redistribución. Cabe señalar que esta conclusión se basa en una interpretación generalmente amplia del término "no correspondido" en la definición del impuesto.

10. Por el contrario, las contribuciones a la seguridad social voluntarias o no pagaderas al gobierno general (véase el § 1) no se tratan como impuestos, aunque en ciertos países, tal

y como se indica debidamente en cada caso en las notas que figuran al pie de los cuadros, plantea dificultades el eliminar tanto las contribuciones voluntarias como algunos pagos obligatorios al sector privado de las cifras de recaudo tributario. Las contribuciones a la seguridad social imputadas tampoco son considerados impuestos.

Tasas, cargos a usuarios y licencias

11. Aparte de las tasas por licencia de vehículos, universalmente consideradas como impuestos, no resulta fácil distinguir entre las tasas y cargos a usuarios que deben tratarse como impuestos y las que no, ya que, aunque toda tasa o cargo se impone en conexión con un servicio o una actividad específicos, la intensidad del vínculo entre el derecho cobrado y el servicio prestado puede variar considerablemente, al igual que puede hacerlo la relación entre la cuantía de la tasa y el costo que supone proporcionar el servicio en cuestión. En todo caso, cuando el beneficiario del servicio pague una tasa claramente relacionada con el costo que supone prestar un servicio, puede inferirse que el gravamen tiene contraprestación y, de acuerdo con la definición reseñada en el § 1, no se considerará como impuesto. En sentido contrario, puede estimarse que el gravamen "carece de contraprestación" cuando:

a. el cargo exceda con creces el costo que supone prestar el servicio;

b. el pagador o sujeto pasivo del gravamen no sea el beneficiario del servicio (p. ej., tasas recaudadas de los mataderos para financiar un servicio proporcionado a los titulares de explotaciones agropecuarias);

c. el gobierno no proporcione un servicio específico a cambio del pago del gravamen, aun y cuando se emita un permiso en beneficio del sujeto pasivo (p. ej., cuando el gobierno concede licencias de caza, pesca o tiro que no otorgan el derecho a usar una zona específica propiedad del gobierno);

d. los servicios beneficien únicamente a los pagadores del gravamen, pero las utilidades recibidas por cada persona no guarden necesariamente proporción con sus pagos (p. ej., el gravamen sobre la comercialización de la leche que recae en los criadores de ganado lechero y que se utiliza para fomentar el consumo de la leche).

12. Pese a las anteriores consideraciones, en ciertos casos excepcionales la aplicación de los criterios plasmados en el § 1 puede resultar particularmente compleja. La solución adoptada – dada la conveniencia de uniformidad internacional y las cantidades de ingreso relativamente bajas implicadas por lo general– ha consistido en seguir la práctica dominante en la mayoría de las administraciones, en lugar de permitir que cada país aplique su propia visión sobre si estos gravámenes deben considerarse como ingresos tributarios o no tributarios.[5]

13. Seguidamente, se ofrece una lista de las principales tasas y cargos en cuestión, y su tratamiento normal[6]en esta publicación:

Ingresos no tributarios:	tasas procesales, permisos de conducir, tasas portuarias, tasas por expedición de pasaportes, licencias de radio y televisión cuando las autoridades públicas proporcionan el servicio de difusión.
Impuestos de la partida 5200:	permiso para realizar actividades tales como distribución cinematográfica; caza, pesca o tiro; suministro de instalaciones para actividades recreativas o de ocio o juegos de azar; venta de bebidas alcohólicas o tabaco; posesión de animales domésticos o uso de vehículos automotores; derechos sobre la extracción.

14. En la práctica, puede que no siempre resulte posible aislar las entradas tributarias de las no tributarias cuando estas se registran conjuntamente. En ese caso, si se considera que la mayoría de las entradas proviene de ingresos no tributarios, se tratará el importe total como tal; de lo contrario, esas entradas del gobierno se incluirán y clasificarán según las normas recogidas en el § 32.

Regalías

15. La propiedad de los activos del subsuelo en forma de depósitos de minerales o combustibles fósiles (carbón, petróleo o gas natural) depende de la forma en que los derechos de propiedad están definidos por la ley y también de los acuerdos internacionales en el caso de depósitos bajo aguas internacionales. En algunos casos, ya sea en el terreno por debajo del cual se encuentran los depósitos minerales, los depósitos en sí o ambos pueden pertenecer a una unidad del gobierno local o central.

16. En tales casos, estas unidades del gobierno general pueden otorgar arrendamientos a otras unidades institucionales que les permitan extraer estos depósitos durante un período de tiempo específico a cambio de un pago o una serie de pagos. Estos pagos a menudo se describen como "regalías", pero son esencialmente rentas que se acumulan a los propietarios de los recursos naturales a cambio de poner estos activos a disposición de otros agentes durante períodos de tiempo específicos. El alquiler puede tomar la forma de pagos periódicos de cantidades fijas, independientemente de la tasa de extracción, o, más comúnmente, pueden ser una función de la cantidad, el volumen o el valor del activo extraído. Las empresas dedicadas a la exploración en tierras del gobierno pueden hacer pagos a las unidades del gobierno general a cambio del derecho a realizar perforaciones de prueba o investigar de otro modo la existencia y ubicación de los activos del subsuelo. Dichos pagos también se registran como rentas aunque no se realice ninguna extracción. Por lo tanto, estos pagos se clasifican como ingresos no tributarios.

17. Los mismos principios se aplican cuando a otras unidades institucionales se les conceden arrendamientos que les permiten talar madera en bosques naturales en tierras que son propiedad de unidades del gobierno general. Estos pagos también se clasifican como ingresos no tributarios.

18. Estas rentas o regalías pagadas al gobierno general no deben confundirse con los impuestos sobre los ingresos y las ganancias, los impuestos sobre la extracción de recursos naturales, las licencias comerciales u otros impuestos. Si los pagos se aplican a las ganancias de la actividad de extracción, entonces deben clasificarse como impuestos sobre ingresos, utilidades y ganancias (1000). Además, cualquier pago que se imponga a la extracción de minerales y combustibles fósiles de las reservas de propiedad privada o de otro gobierno se debe clasificar como impuestos. Los pagos relacionados con el valor bruto de la producción deben clasificarse como otros impuestos sobre bienes y servicios (5128). Los pagos de una licencia o permiso para realizar operaciones de extracción se deben clasificar como impuestos sobre el uso de bienes y sobre el permiso para usar bienes o realizar actividades (5213).

Multas y sanciones pecuniarias

19. En principio, las multas y sanciones pecuniarias impuestas por el pago tardío de los impuestos o por el intento de evasión de los impuestos no deben registrarse como ingresos tributarios. Sin embargo, en ocasiones no es posible distinguir y separar los pagos por multas y penalidades del recaudo del impuesto a los que estos están relacionados. En este caso, las multas y sanciones pecuniarias vinculadas a un determinado impuesto se registran con los

ingresos de ese impuesto. Las multas y penalidades pagadas sobre el recaudo de impuestos no identificados se clasifican como otros impuestos en la partida 6000. Las multas que no están relacionadas con delitos tributarios (por ejemplo, las infracciones por estacionamiento indebido), o que no puedan ser identificadas como ofensas tributarias, no serán tratadas como ingresos tributarios.

A.3. Principios de registro

Criterio de devengo

20. Los datos recogidos en esta publicación relativos a los últimos años se han registrado predominantemente según el criterio de devengo, esto es, se han computado en el momento en que nace la obligación. Se ofrece más información al respecto en las notas que figuran al pie de los cuadros de países en el Capítulo 4 del informe.

21. Sin embargo, los datos relativos a años anteriores han seguido registrándose principalmente según el criterio de caja, es decir, en el momento en que el gobierno recibió el pago. Por lo tanto, por ejemplo, los impuestos descontados por los empleadores en un año pero pagados al gobierno al año siguiente y los impuestos debidos un año pero liquidados el año después constan ambos en las entradas del segundo año. Las transacciones correctoras, tales como devoluciones, reembolsos y reintegros, se deducen de los ingresos brutos del periodo en que se realizan.

22. Los datos sobre ingresos tributarios se registran sin deducción de los gastos administrativos propios de la recaudación impositiva. De igual modo, cuando los recursos generados por un impuesto se emplean para subvencionar a miembros particulares de la comunidad, el subsidio no se descuenta del producto impositivo, aunque puede que el impuesto aparezca sin los subsidios en los registros nacionales de algunos países.

23. En lo que a los monopolios fiscales se refiere (5122), únicamente se incluye en los ingresos del gobierno el importe realmente transferido a este. Sin embargo, si cualquier gasto de los monopolios fiscales se considera gasto del gobierno (p. ej., gastos sociales emprendidos por los monopolios fiscales en beneficio del gobierno), se añadirán posteriormente con el fin de llegar a cifras de ingreso tributario (véase el § 65 *infra*.).

Distinción entre disposiciones tributarias y disposiciones relativas al gasto[7]

24. Dado que la presente publicación aborda únicamente la actividad del gobierno desde el punto de vista del ingreso, sin tener en cuenta los aspectos relacionados con el gasto, resulta preciso realizar una distinción entre las disposiciones que rigen estos dos elementos. Por lo general, no existe dificultad alguna en diferenciar ambos aspectos, ya que los gastos operan en un ámbito externo al sistema tributario y sus cuentas, y se rigen por una legislación separada de la impositiva. En los casos de difícil delimitación, se emplea el flujo de caja para distinguir entre disposiciones tributarias y disposiciones relativas al gasto. En la medida en que una disposición incida en el flujo de pagos tributarios del contribuyente al gobierno, se entenderá que reviste un carácter tributario y se tendrá en cuenta en los datos recogidos en esta publicación. Cualquier disposición que no afecte a ese flujo se reputará como relativa al gasto y no se tendrá en consideración en la información plasmada en la publicación.

25. Las desgravaciones, exenciones y deducciones tributarias sobre la base imponible afectan claramente a la cantidad transferida al gobierno y, por ende, se consideran disposiciones de naturaleza tributaria. En el extremo opuesto, los subsidios o exoneraciones que no compensen la obligación tributaria y que estén claramente desvinculados del proceso de evaluación, no

reducen los ingresos tributarios consignados en esta publicación. De particular interés en este ámbito resultan los créditos fiscales, que son cantidades deducibles del impuesto liquidable (lo que los diferencia de las deducciones sobre la base imponible). Cabe distinguir dos tipos de créditos fiscales: los créditos fiscales no exigibles (a veces denominados desaprovechables), limitados al importe de la obligación tributaria y que, por ende, no pueden generar un pago de las autoridades al contribuyente; y los créditos fiscales exigibles (o no desaprovechables), que no están sometidos a dicho límite, de forma que toda cantidad que exceda la obligación tributaria puede abonarse al contribuyente.[8] Al igual que las desgravaciones, un crédito fiscal no exigible afecta claramente a la cantidad transferida al gobierno y, por ende, se considerará como tributario. La práctica seguida para los créditos fiscales exigibles[9] consiste en distinguir entre "el componente de gasto tributario"[10] que es la porción del crédito empleada en reducir o eliminar la obligación del contribuyente" y el "componente de transferencia", constituido por la parte que excede la obligación del contribuyente y que se paga a este. Al registrar los ingresos tributarios deberá restarse la parte equivalente al componente de gasto tributario, pero no la correspondiente al componente de transferencia. Además, las cantidades de ambos componentes deberán figurar como partidas informativas en los cuadros de países. Los países que no puedan diferenciar entre estos dos componentes deberán indicar si se ha restado de los ingresos tributarios el total de ellos y presentar las evaluaciones disponibles del valor que ambos representan. Para mayor información, consúltese el Capítulo 1 de la publicación *Revenue Statistics* de la OCDE, que examina el efecto de los diversos tratamientos de los créditos fiscales exigibles en la relación impuestos sobre PIB.

Calendario y ejercicio fiscal

26. Las autoridades nacionales cuyos ejercicios fiscales no coinciden con el año calendario deben presentar los datos, siempre que sea posible, sobre la base del año calendario, a fin de permitir el mayor grado posible de comparación con la información de otros países. Subsisten algunos países en los que los datos hacen referencia a los ejercicios fiscales; para ellos, los datos relativos al PIB utilizados en los cuadros comparativos corresponden igualmente a los ejercicios fiscales.

A.4. Criterios generales de clasificación

Principales criterios de clasificación

27. El desglose de las entradas fiscales en las diversas categorías (1000, 2000, 3000, 4000, 5000 y 6000) se rige en general por la base sobre la cual recae el impuesto: 1000, renta, utilidades y ganancias de capital; 2000 y 3000, remuneraciones, nómina o número de empleados (fuerza de trabajo); 4000, propiedad; 5000, bienes y servicios; 6000, bases múltiples, otras bases o bases no identificables. Cuando un impuesto se calcula sobre más de una base, las entradas que genera se distribuyen, en la medida de lo posible, entre las diversas categorías (véanse los §§ 32 y 81). Las categorías 4000 y 5000 no sólo cubren aquellos impuestos en los que la base tributaria está constituida por la propiedad, los bienes o los servicios en sí mismos, sino también ciertos impuestos afines; y así, por ejemplo, los impuestos sobre transmisiones patrimoniales se incluyen en la partida 4400,[11] y los impuestos sobre el uso de bienes y sobre el permiso para realizar actividades, en la 5200. En las categorías 4000 y 5000, se distingue en ocasiones entre impuestos recurrentes y no recurrentes: son impuestos recurrentes los que se recaudan a intervalos regulares (por lo general, anualmente), y no recurrentes, los que se imponen una sola vez (véanse los § 47-§50, §53–§54 y §79 para profundizar en las aplicaciones particulares de esta distinción).

28. La asignación de un impuesto a fines específicos no afecta a la clasificación de las entradas fiscales que genera. Sin embargo, tal y como se explica en el § 39 en relación con la clasificación de las contribuciones a la seguridad social, el hecho de que estas confieran un derecho a recibir prestaciones sociales es decisivo para la definición de la categoría 2000.

29. La forma en que se establece o recauda un impuesto (p.ej., mediante el uso de timbres) no afecta a su clasificación.

Clasificación de los contribuyentes

30. En ocasiones, se distingue entre diversas clases de contribuyentes. Esas distinciones dependen de cada impuesto.

a. *Entre personas físicas y sociedades en relación con los impuestos sobre la renta y sobre la riqueza neta*

La distinción básica aquí es que los impuestos sobre la renta de las sociedades (impuesto de sociedades), a diferencia de los impuestos sobre la renta de las personas físicas, gravan a la sociedad como entidad y no a sus propietarios, independientemente de las circunstancias personales de estos; la misma distinción se aplica a los impuestos sobre la riqueza neta de las sociedades y de las personas físicas. Los impuestos liquidados sobre las utilidades de las asociaciones y sobre la renta de las instituciones, tales como seguros de vida o fondos de pensiones, se clasifican siguiendo la misma regla, y así, se considerarán impuestos sobre las sociedades (1200) si se cargan a la asociación o institución como persona jurídica sin tener en cuenta las circunstancias personales de sus propietarios, o impuestos sobre las personas físicas en el caso contrario (1100). Por lo general, los impuestos aplicados a las sociedades y a las personas físicas se rigen por legislaciones diferentes.[12] La distinción realizada aquí entre personas físicas y sociedades no sigue la categorización por sectores entre hogares, empresas, etcétera, del Sistema de Cuentas Nacionales para las cuentas de ingresos y desembolsos. La clasificación del SCN requiere que ciertas empresas no constituidas en sociedad[13] se excluyan del sector de los hogares y vengan a sumarse a las empresas no financieras y las instituciones financieras. Sin embargo, el impuesto sobre las utilidades de esos negocios no siempre puede separarse del impuesto sobre la renta de sus propietarios o, como mucho, puede deslindarse sólo arbitrariamente. Por ello, no se ha intentado reproducir aquí esa separación, y la totalidad del impuesto sobre la renta de las personas físicas se ha recogido en un solo bloque, independientemente de la naturaleza del ingreso imponible.

b. *Entre hogares y otros en relación con los impuestos sobre la propiedad inmueble*

Esta distinción es la misma que la adoptada por el SCN para las cuentas de gasto del consumo final de los hogares y de producción. Se trata pues de diferenciar a los hogares como consumidores (esto es, excluidas las empresas no constituidas en sociedad), por una parte, y a los productores, por otra. Los impuestos sobre las viviendas ocupadas por los hogares, tanto a cargo de los propietarios-ocupantes como de los arrendatarios o de los arrendadores, se incluyen en los hogares, lo que coincide con la diferenciación que suele hacerse comúnmente entre los impuestos sobre la propiedad doméstica y los impuestos sobre la propiedad empresarial. No obstante, algunos países no se hallan en situación de operar esta distinción.

c. *Entre hogares y otros en relación con las licencias de vehículos automotores*

Se distingue aquí entre los hogares como consumidores, por una parte, y los productores, por otra, al igual que en las cuentas de gasto del consumo final de los hogares y de producción del SCN.

d. Entre empresas y otros en relación con los impuestos residuales (6000)

La distinción es la misma que en c), esta vez, entre los productores, por una parte, y los hogares como consumidores, por otra. Los impuestos recogidos en la categoría 6000 bien porque gravan más de una base tributaria, o bien porque su base no entra dentro del ámbito de ninguna de las categorías anteriores pero es identificable como imponible sobre los productores, y no sobre los hogares, se incluyen en 'empresas'. El resto de los impuestos de la categoría 6000 se imputan a 'otros' o no identificables.

Recargos

31. Las entradas procedentes de recargos relacionados con impuestos particulares se clasifican por lo general en base al impuesto correspondiente, ya sea el recargo temporal o no. Pero si el recargo posee una característica que lo califica para ser clasificada en una categoría diferente de la lista de la OCDE, las entradas generadas por el recargo se recogen en dicha categoría, separadas de las del correspondiente impuesto.

Entradas tributarias no identificables y partidas residuales

32. En un cierto número de casos, no logra determinarse que los impuestos pertenezcan enteramente a una categoría o partida de la clasificación de la OCDE y, en esos casos, se aplican las siguientes pautas:

a. Se conoce la categoría, pero no la forma de distribuir las entradas entre las diversas subdivisiones: las entradas se clasifican en la correspondiente partida o subpartida residual (1300, 2400, 4520, 4600, 5130, 5300 o 6200).

b. Se sabe que la mayor parte de las entradas procedentes de un grupo de impuestos (normalmente, impuestos locales) proviene de impuestos de una categoría o una partida particulares, pero algunos de los impuestos del grupo cuya cuantía no puede determinarse con exactitud pueden clasificarse en otras categorías o partidas: las entradas se consignan en la categoría o partida a la que pertenezca la mayoría de ellas.

c. No puede identificarse ni la categoría ni la partida correspondiente al impuesto (normalmente, local): el impuesto se incorpora a la partida 6200, a menos que se conozca que se trata de un impuesto sobre las empresas, en cuyo caso se incluye en la partida 6100.

A.5. Comentarios sobre ítems de la lista

1000 – *Impuestos sobre la renta, las utilidades y las ganancias de capital*

33. Esta categoría cubre los impuestos aplicados a la renta o a las utilidades netas (esto es, la renta bruta menos las deducciones permitidas) de las personas físicas y las sociedades, así como los impuestos a los que se someten las ganancias de capital de esos mismos sujetos pasivos, y las ganancias obtenidas en juegos de azar.

34. Se incluyen en esta categoría:

a. los impuestos que gravan predominantemente la renta o las utilidades, aunque recaigan parcialmente sobre otras bases; los impuestos aplicados a varias bases que no sean mayoritariamente la renta o las utilidades se clasifican de acuerdo con los principios establecidos en los §§ 32 y 81;

b. los impuestos sobre la propiedad aplicados a un ingreso presunto o estimado como parte de un impuesto sobre la renta (véase el § 47(*a*), (*c*) y (*d*));

c. los pagos obligatorios al fondo de contribuciones de la seguridad social impuestos sobre la renta que no confieran un derecho a prestaciones sociales; si esas contribuciones otorgan derecho a prestaciones sociales, se incluyen en la categoría 2000 (véase el § 39);

d. el producto de los sistemas integrados de impuestos sobre la renta de régimen cedular se clasifican como un todo en esta categoría, aunque algunos de los impuestos cedulares puedan basarse en la renta bruta y no tener en cuenta las circunstancias personales del contribuyente.

35. La principal división de esta categoría se efectúa entre los gravámenes a personas físicas (1100) y aquellos a sociedades (1200). A su vez, en cada partida, se separa entre impuestos sobre la renta y las utilidades (1110 y 1210) e impuestos sobre las ganancias de capital (1120 y 1220). Si algunas entradas no pueden atribuirse pertinentemente a la partida 1100 o a la 1200, o si no puede realizarse esta distinción en la práctica (p. ej., por falta de datos fiables sobre los receptores de los pagos de los que se deducen los impuestos con retención en la fuente), las entradas se incorporan a la partida 1300 como "no clasificables".

Tratamiento de los créditos fiscales en los sistemas de imputación

36. En los sistemas de imputación del impuesto de sociedades, los accionistas están exentos, total o parcialmente, de responder en concepto del impuesto sobre la renta por los dividendos abonados por la compañía a partir de la renta o de las utilidades sometidas al impuesto de sociedades. En los países con este sistema,[14] una parte del impuesto sobre las utilidades de la sociedad está disponible para exonerar a los accionistas de su propia obligación tributaria. La exoneración del accionista reviste la forma de un crédito fiscal, cuyo importe puede ser inferior, igual o superior al pasivo tributario total del accionista. Si el crédito fiscal excede al pasivo tributario, puede que ese exceso sea pagadero al accionista. Dado que este tipo de crédito fiscal es parte integrante del sistema de imputación del impuesto sobre la renta de las sociedades, cualquier pago a los accionistas se trata como devolución tributaria, y no como gasto (compárese con el tratamiento de otros créditos fiscales descrito en el § 25).

37. Puesto que en los sistemas de imputación el crédito fiscal (incluso cuando excede la obligación tributaria) debe considerarse como disposición tributaria, se plantea la cuestión de determinar si deberá deducirse de las entradas en concepto de impuesto sobre la renta de las personas físicas (1110) o de las entradas atribuibles al impuesto sobre la renta de las sociedades (1210). En este informe, la cantidad total pagada a título del impuesto sobre la renta de las sociedades se recoge en la subpartida 1210, y el impuesto no imputado en la subpartida 1110. Por lo tanto, la cuantía total del crédito se resta de esta última subpartida, tanto si el crédito da lugar a una reducción de la obligación tributaria por renta personal, como si se realiza un reembolso porque el crédito fiscal excede el pasivo tributario por este concepto. (No obstante, si los créditos fiscales se deducen del impuesto de sociedades por dividendos repartidos a otras sociedades, las correspondientes cantidades se descuentan de las entradas registradas en la subpartida 1210.)

1120 y 1220 – Impuestos sobre las ganancias de capital

38. Como su nombre indica, estas subpartidas engloban los impuestos sobre las ganancias de capital, ya de las personas físicas (1120), ya de las sociedades (1220), siempre que las entradas procedentes de estos impuestos puedan identificarse por separado. Ese no es el caso en numerosos países, y las entradas de estos impuestos se clasifican junto con las del

impuesto sobre la renta. La subpartida 1120 contiene asimismo los impuestos sobre las ganancias obtenidas en juegos de azar.

2000 – Contribuciones a la seguridad social

39. Entran en esta categoría todos los pagos obligatorios que confieran un derecho a recibir una prestación social futura (contingente). Esos pagos suelen estar asignados al financiamiento de prestaciones sociales y, a menudo, se pagan a las instituciones del gobierno general que proporcionan dichas prestaciones. Sin embargo, esa asignación no forma parte de la definición de las contribuciones a la seguridad social y no es necesaria para que un impuesto sea clasificado en esta categoría, pero, para que un impuesto se incluya aquí, sí será preciso que confiera un derecho. Y así, los gravámenes sobre la renta o la nómina asignados a los fondos de seguridad social pero que no confieran el derecho a recibir prestaciones sociales quedan excluidos de la presente categoría y se registran bien entre los impuestos sobre la renta de las personas físicas (1100), bien junto con los impuestos sobre la nómina y la fuerza de trabajo (3000). Los impuestos aplicados sobre otras bases, como los bienes y servicios, no se consignarán aquí aunque estén asignados a prestaciones de la seguridad social, sino que se catalogarán según sus respectivas bases, ya que por lo general no otorgarán derecho alguno a prestaciones sociales.

40. Entre otras, se incluirán aquí las contribuciones a los siguientes tipos de prestaciones de la seguridad social: prestaciones y suplementos por seguro de desempleo; prestaciones por accidente, lesión o enfermedad; pensiones por jubilación, invalidez y supervivencia; ayudas familiares; reembolsos de gastos médicos u hospitalarios o prestación de servicios médicos u hospitalarios. Las contribuciones pueden recaudarse tanto de los empleados como de los empleadores.

41. Las contribuciones pueden tener como base bien las remuneraciones o la nómina ('sobre la base de la nómina'), bien la renta neta tras deducciones y exenciones por circunstancias personales ('sobre la base del impuesto sobre la renta'), y el producto de ambas bases deberá identificarse separadamente en la medida de lo posible. Cuando las contribuciones al régimen general de la seguridad social se basen en la nómina, pero las de grupos particulares (tales como los trabajadores por cuenta propia) no puedan evaluarse en función de esta base y se emplee en ese caso la renta neta como una aproximación de las remuneraciones brutas, las entradas seguirán clasificándose sobre la base de la nómina. En principio, esta categoría excluye las contribuciones voluntarias aportadas a los regímenes de seguridad social, que, cuando sea posible identificarlas de forma separada, se recogerán en la partida informativa sobre el financiamiento de las prestaciones sociales; sin embargo, en la práctica, estas aportaciones no siempre pueden desvincularse de las contribuciones obligatorias, en cuyo caso se incluirán igualmente en esta categoría.

42. Las contribuciones a los regímenes de seguro social no vinculados a instituciones del gobierno general, así como las aportaciones a otros tipos de sistemas de seguro, tales como planes de previsión o planes de pensiones, mutualidades u otros planes de ahorro, no se consideran contribuciones a la seguridad social. Los planes de previsión son acuerdos por los que las contribuciones de cada empleado y la parte correspondiente del empleador en nombre de aquél se conservan en una cuenta separada que genera interés, de la que pueden retirarse en circunstancias específicas. Por su parte, los planes de pensiones son regímenes organizados separadamente, negociados entres empleados y empleadores, que conllevan disposiciones sobre diversas contribuciones y prestaciones, a veces más directamente vinculadas a los niveles salariales y a la duración del servicio que en otros esquemas sociales.

Cuando las contribuciones a esos regímenes son obligatorias o cuasiobligatorias (p. ej., en virtud de un acuerdo con sindicatos u organizaciones profesionales), se hacen constar en la partida informativa (véase el Capítulo 4.2 de este Reporte).

43. Las contribuciones de los empleados del gobierno y de este con respecto a sus empleados a los regímenes de seguridad social incluidos en el gobierno general se clasifican en esta categoría. También se consideran impuestos las contribuciones de los empleados del gobierno a regímenes diferentes que puedan reputarse sustitutivos de los regímenes generales de seguridad social.[15] Por el contrario, cuando un régimen diferente no pueda considerarse sustitutivo de uno general y haya sido negociado entre el gobierno, en su papel de empleador, y sus empleados, no se estimará como régimen de seguridad social y, por lo tanto, las contribuciones a él no se tendrán como impuestos, aunque el régimen haya sido instaurado por la legislación.

44. Esta categoría excluye las contribuciones 'imputadas', que corresponden a las prestaciones sociales pagadas directamente por los empleadores a sus empleados, antiguos empleados o personas a cargo de estos (p. ej., cuando los empleadores están legalmente obligados a correr con las prestaciones por enfermedad durante cierto tiempo).

45. Las contribuciones se dividen en tres partidas principales – empleados (2100), empleadores (2200) y trabajadores por cuenta propia o no empleados (2300) – y se subdividen posteriormente en función de la base que gravan. A efectos de la presente publicación, se entiende por empleados todas las personas contratadas en actividades de unidades empresariales, órganos gubernamentales, instituciones privadas sin ánimo de lucro u otro tipo de empleo remunerado, con excepción de los dueños de empresas no constituidas en sociedad y de los miembros no remunerados de sus familias. También se consideran empleados los miembros de las Fuerzas Armadas, independientemente de la duración y del tipo de su servicio, siempre que coticen a regímenes de la seguridad social. Por su parte, las contribuciones de los empleadores se definen como las aportaciones que estos realizan por cuenta de sus empleados a los sistemas de seguridad social. Si los empleados o los empleadores tienen la obligación de continuar cotizando a la seguridad social en el caso de desempleo de un empleado, esas contribuciones se muestran en las partidas 2100 y 2200, respectivamente, siempre que los datos lo permitan. En consecuencia, la partida 2300 queda reservada a las contribuciones abonadas por los trabajadores por cuenta propia y por quienes no se hallan incluidos en la población activa (p. ej., incapacitados o jubilados).

3000 – Impuestos sobre la nómina y la fuerza de trabajo

46. Consiste en los impuestos pagados por las firmas o empresas, ya sea como una proporción de los salarios o la nómina, ya como una cantidad fija por persona empleada. No incluyen pagos a la seguridad social obligatorios pagados por empleadores u otros impuestos pagados por los empleados mismos de sus salarios o remuneraciones.

4000 – Impuestos sobre la propiedad

47. Esta categoría engloba los impuestos, recurrentes y no recurrentes, sobre el uso, la titularidad o la transmisión de la propiedad, lo que incluye impuestos sobre la propiedad inmueble y la riqueza neta, sobre el cambio de titularidad en la propiedad por herencia o donación, y sobre transacciones financieras y de capital. Quedan excluidas de esta categoría los siguientes tipos de impuestos:

a. los impuestos sobre las ganancias de capital procedentes de la venta de propiedad (1120 o 1220);

b. los impuestos sobre el uso de bienes y sobre el permiso para usar bienes o realizar actividades (5200): véase el § 76;

c. los impuestos sobre los bienes inmuebles gravados sobre la base de un ingreso neto presunto que tiene en cuenta las circunstancias personales del contribuyente: se clasifican como impuestos sobre la renta junto con los impuestos sobre la renta y sobre las ganancias de capital derivadas de la propiedad (1100);

d. los impuestos sobre el uso de la propiedad con fines residenciales, tanto si debe responder del impuesto el propietario como el arrendatario, siempre que la cantidad debida tenga en cuenta las circunstancias personales del usuario (ingresos, personas a cargo, etcétera): se integran en los impuestos sobre la renta (1100);

e. los impuestos sobre los edificios con una densidad máxima superior a la permitida; sobre la ampliación, construcción o modificación de ciertos edificios más allá de un valor umbral; y sobre la construcción de edificios: todos ellos se integran en los impuestos sobre el permiso para realizar actividades (5200);

f. los impuestos sobre el uso de la propiedad propia para fines comerciales especiales, tales como la venta de bebidas alcohólicas, tabaco o carne, o para la explotación de tierras (p. ej., impuestos sobre la extracción en Estados Unidos): se integran en los impuestos sobre el permiso para realizar actividades (5200).

4100 – Impuestos recurrentes sobre la propiedad inmueble

48. Esta partida comprende los impuestos con que se grava de forma regular el uso o la titularidad de bienes inmuebles.

- Estos impuestos gravan las tierras y los edificios.
- Pueden consistir en un porcentaje del valor tasado de una propiedad, basado a su vez en un ingreso por alquiler hipotético, en el precio de venta, en un rendimiento capitalizado o en otras características de la propiedad inmueble (por ejemplo, el tamaño o la ubicación) de las que quepa inferir un alquiler o un valor de capital hipotéticos.
- Estos impuestos pueden aplicarse a los propietarios, a los arrendatarios o a ambos. También pueden pagarse de un nivel de gobierno a otro en relación con los bienes bajo jurisdicción de este último.
- Para la evaluación de estos impuestos, no se tienen en cuenta las deudas y, en ese sentido, difieren de los impuestos sobre la riqueza neta.

49. Los impuestos recurrentes sobre la propiedad inmueble se subdividen a su vez en los pagados por los hogares (4110) y los abonados por otros sujetos pasivos (4120), de acuerdo con los criterios establecidos en el § 30(*b*) *supra*.

4200 – Impuestos recurrentes sobre la riqueza neta

50. Esta partida abarca los impuestos con que se grava periódicamente (por lo general, anualmente) la riqueza neta, esto es, los impuestos sobre un amplio abanico de bienes muebles e inmuebles, descontadas sus deudas. Esta partida se subdivide a su vez en los impuestos pagados por las personas físicas (4210) y los abonados por las sociedades (4220), de acuerdo con los criterios establecidos en el § 30(*a*) *supra*. Si existen cifras separadas para las entradas correspondientes a pagos realizados por instituciones, se añaden a la subpartida de las sociedades.

4300 – Impuestos sobre sucesiones, herencias y donaciones

51. Esta partida se divide entre impuestos sobre sucesiones o herencias (4310) e impuestos sobre donaciones (4320).[16] Los impuestos sobre sucesiones gravan el valor total de la sucesión o del caudal hereditario, mientras los impuestos sobre herencias se aplican a las cuotas recibidas por los causahabientes individualmente considerados o en función de la relación de estos con el difunto.

4400 – Impuestos sobre transacciones financieras y de capital

52. Esta partida incluye, entre otros, los impuestos sobre la emisión, transmisión, compra y venta de valores, sobre los cheques, y sobre transacciones legales específicas, tales como la validación de contratos o la venta de bienes inmuebles. La partida no incluye:

a. los impuestos sobre el uso de bienes y sobre el permiso para realizar ciertas actividades (5200);

b. las tasas abonadas en concepto de costos procesales o expedición de actas de nacimiento, matrimonio o defunción, que suelen considerarse como ingresos no tributarios (véase el § 11);

c. los impuestos sobre ganancias de capital (1000);

d. los impuestos recurrentes sobre la propiedad inmueble (4100);

e. los impuestos recurrentes sobre la riqueza neta (4200);

f. otros impuestos no recurrentes sobre la propiedad o la riqueza (4500).

4500 – Otros impuestos no recurrentes sobre la propiedad[16]

53. Esta partida cubre los gravámenes sobre la propiedad que, a diferencia de los impuestos recurrentes, se recaudan una sola vez. Se divide en impuestos no recurrentes sobre la riqueza neta (4510) y otros impuestos no recurrentes sobre la propiedad (4520). La subpartida 4510 contiene los impuestos que se recaudan a fin de hacer frente a gastos excepcionales o de redistribuir la riqueza. Por su parte, la subpartida 4520 comprende los impuestos que gravan los incrementos de valor de la tierra, debido, por ejemplo, a permisos para su desarrollo concedidos por el gobierno general o a la provisión por parte de este de instalaciones locales adicionales; cualesquiera impuestos sobre la reevaluación del capital; y aquellos impuestos gravados una sola vez sobre determinados tipos de propiedad.

4600 – Otros impuestos recurrentes sobre la propiedad

54. Aunque este tipo de impuestos rara vez se dan en los países miembros de la OCDE, esta partida incluye los impuestos sobre bienes tales como ganado bovino, joyas, ventanas y otros signos externos de riqueza.

5000 – Impuestos sobre los bienes y servicios

55. Se incluyen en esta categoría todos los impuestos y derechos sobre la producción, extracción, venta, transmisión, arrendamiento y entrega de bienes, así como sobre la prestación de servicios (5100), y también los impuestos aplicados al uso de bienes y al permiso para usar bienes o realizar actividades (5200). Por lo tanto, esta categoría comprende:

a. los impuestos acumulativos de etapas múltiples;

b. los impuestos generales sobre las ventas aplicados, ya sea en la fabricación/producción, ya sea en la venta al por mayor o al por menor;

c. los impuestos sobre el valor agregado;

d. los impuestos selectivos;
e. los impuestos sobre las importaciones y exportaciones de bienes;
f. los impuestos sobre el uso de bienes y sobre el permiso para usar bienes o realizar ciertas actividades;
g. los impuestos sobre la extracción, el procesamiento o la producción de minerales y otros productos.

56. Los casos de difícil delimitación entre esta categoría y la categoría 4000 (impuestos sobre la propiedad) o la partida 6100 (otros impuestos pagados únicamente por empresas) se tratan en los § 47, §52 y §78. La partida 5300 y la subpartida 5130, ambas residuales, incluyen, respectivamente, las entradas tributarias que no hayan podido clasificarse entre las partidas 5100 y 5200 o entre las subpartidas 5110 y 5120, respectivamente, veáse §32.

5100 – Impuestos sobre la producción, venta, transmisión, arrendamiento y entrega de bienes, y la prestación de servicios

57. Esta partida comprende todos los impuestos aplicados a transacciones de bienes y servicios por las características intrínsecas de estos (p. ej., valor, peso del tabaco, graduación de las bebidas alcohólicas, etcétera) a diferencia de los impuestos determinados por el uso de bienes o por el permiso para usar bienes o realizar actividades, que entran dentro del ámbito de la partida 5200.

5110 – Impuestos generales

58. En esta subpartida, se incluyen todos los impuestos, aparte de los derechos de importación y exportación (5123 y 5124, respectivamente), que gravan la producción, el arrendamiento, la transmisión, la entrega o la venta de un amplio abanico de bienes o la prestación de una gran variedad de servicios, independientemente de que sean de producción nacional o importados, o de la etapa de producción o de distribución en la que recaigan. Por ende, comprende los impuestos sobre el valor agregado, los impuestos sobre las ventas y los impuestos acumulativos de etapas múltiples. A las entradas brutas generadas, se añaden las entradas por ajustes fronterizos en concepto de esos impuestos cuando se importan bienes, y se restan las devoluciones de dichos impuestos cuando se exportan bienes. Esta subpartida se divide a su vez en los epígrafes 5111, impuestos sobre el valor agregado; 5112, impuestos sobre las ventas; y 5113, otros impuestos generales sobre los ingresos brutos y sobre bienes y servicios.

59. Suelen plantearse dificultades de delimitación entre esta subpartida y la dedicada a los impuestos sobre bienes y servicios específicos (5120) cuando los impuestos se aplican a un gran número de bienes, como, por ejemplo, en el caso del impuesto sobre las compras del Reino Unido (abolido en 1973) o el impuesto sobre mercancías de Japón (abolido en 1988). De acuerdo con las respectivas perspectivas nacionales, el antiguo impuesto sobre las compras británico se ha clasificado como impuesto general (5112), mientras el desaparecido impuesto sobre mercancías japonés se ha incluido entre los impuestos selectivos (5121).

5111 – Impuestos sobre el valor agregado

60. Todos los impuestos generales al consumo cargados sobre el valor agregado entran dentro de este epígrafe, independientemente del método de deducción y de las etapas en las que recaiga el impuesto. En la práctica, todos los países de la OCDE con este tipo de impuestos permiten que todos los intermediarios, excepto el consumidor final, se deduzcan inmediatamente los impuestos sobre las compras e imponen tributación en todas las etapas.

Para algunos países, puede que se incluyan en este epígrafe otros impuestos, tales como los aplicados sobre actividades financieras y de seguros, o bien porque las entradas que generan no pueden identificarse separadamente de las procedentes del impuesto sobre el valor agregado, o bien porque se considera que forman parte de este último, aunque esos mismos impuestos puedan clasificarse diferentemente en terceros países (p. ej., como impuestos sobre servicios específicos (5126) o impuestos sobre transacciones financieras y de capital (4400).

5112 – *Impuestos sobre las ventas*

61. Se clasifican aquí todos los impuestos generales aplicados a una sola etapa, ya sea en la fabricación/producción, o en la venta al por mayor o al por menor.

5113 – *Otros impuestos generales sobre los ingresos brutos y sobre bienes y servicios*

62. Estos son impuestos acumulativos de etapas múltiplese impuestos en los que el impuesto al consumo se combina con otros impuestos multifásicos. Estos impuestos se aplican cada vez que se realiza una transacción sin deducción del valor de los impuestos pagados sobre los insumos. Los impuestos multifásicos pueden combinarse con elementos de los impuestos sobre el valor agregado o sobre las ventas.

5120 – *Impuestos sobre bienes y servicios específicos*

63. Se incluyen en esta subpartida los impuestos selectivos, las utilidades generadas y transferidas por los monopolios fiscales, y los derechos de aduana y otros derechos de importación, así como los impuestos sobre las exportaciones, las transacciones de divisas, los bienes de inversión y las apuestas, y los impuestos especiales sobre los servicios que no formen parte de uno de los impuestos generales de la subpartida 5110.

5121 – *Impuestos selectivos*

64. Los impuestos selectivos gravan la unidad de un producto específico de una gama predefinida y limitada de bienes. Los impuestos generalmente se aplican a tasas diferenciadas sobre bienes no esenciales o de lujo, bebidas alcohólicas, tabaco y la energía. Los selectivos pueden imponerse en cualquier etapa de la producción o distribución y generalmente se aplican como un cargo específico por unidad en función de las características del bien con referencia al valor, peso, intensidad o cantidad del producto. Se incluyen impuestos especiales sobre productos como el azúcar, la remolacha azucarera, fósforos y chocolates; e impuestos que gravan a tasas variables una cierta gama de bienes; e impuestos aplicados a los productos de tabaco, bebidas alcohólicas, combustibles para motores e hidrocarburos. Si un impuesto recaudado principalmente sobre bienes importados también se aplica, o se aplicaría, bajo la misma ley a bienes comparables de producción nacional, entonces los ingresos de este impuesto se clasifican como impuestos selectivos más que de derechos de importación. Este principio se aplica incluso si no hay producción nacional comparable o no hay posibilidad de tal producción. Los impuestos sobre el uso de servicios como agua, electricidad, gas y energía se consideran como impuestos selectivos más que impuestos sobre servicios específicos (5126). Los selectivos no incluyen los gravámenes que se aplican como impuestos generales sobre bienes y servicios (5110); beneficios de los monopolios fiscales (5122); derechos de aduana y otros derechos de importación (5123); o impuestos a las exportaciones (5124).

5122 – *Utilidades de los monopolios fiscales*

65. Este epígrafe comprende la parte de las utilidades de los monopolios fiscales transferida al gobierno general o usada para financiar gastos considerados como gastos del gobierno (véase el § 23). Las cantidades implicadas se registran cuando se transfieren al gobierno general o cuando se usan para gastos considerados como gastos del gobierno.

66. Los monopolios fiscales reflejan el ejercicio del poder tributario del gobierno mediante el uso de prerrogativas monopolísticas. Se trata de empresas públicas no financieras que ejercen un monopolio, en la mayoría de los casos sobre la producción o la distribución de tabaco, bebidas alcohólicas, sal, fósforos, cartas de juego, productos derivados del petróleo y productos agrícolas (es decir, sobre el tipo de productos susceptibles de estar sometidos, alternativa o adicionalmente, a los impuestos selectivos del epígrafe 5121), con el fin de recaudar ingresos para el gobierno que en otros países se obtienen gravando las operaciones que sobre dichos bienes efectúan las unidades empresariales privadas. El monopolio del gobierno puede intervenir en la etapa de producción o, en el caso de los establecimientos de licores propiedad del gobierno o bajo control de éste, en la etapa de distribución.

67. Cabe distinguir los monopolios fiscales de los servicios públicos, tales como el transporte ferroviario, la electricidad, los servicios de correos y otras comunicaciones, que pueden gozar también de una posición monopolística o cuasi-monopolística, pero cuyo fin primero suele ser la prestación de servicios básicos y no la obtención de ingresos para el gobierno; las transferencias de esas otras empresas públicas al gobierno se consideran ingresos no tributarios. Generalmente, el concepto tradicional de monopolio fiscal no abarca a las loterías estatales, cuyas utilidades usualmente se consideran, en consecuencia, ingresos no tributarios. No obstante, se pueden considerar como ingresos tributarios si su función principal es la de recaudar para financiar gasto gubernamental. Las utilidades de los monopolios fiscales se han separado de las de los monopolios de importación y exportación (5127) transferidas de juntas de comercialización u otras empresas dedicadas al comercio internacional.

5123 – *Derechos de aduana y otros derechos de importación*

68. Se incluyen aquí los impuestos, derechos de timbre y sobrecargas limitados por ley a los productos importados, así como los gravámenes sobre los productos agrícolas importados impuestos en los países miembros de la Unión Europea y las cantidades satisfechas por algunos de esos países a tenor del sistema de montantes compensatorios monetarios (MCM).[17] Desde 1998, los derechos de aduana recaudados por los Estados miembros de la Unión Europea en nombre de ésta ya no se registran en este epígrafe en los cuadros de países (Capítulo 4 de la publicación *Revenue Statistics* de la OCDE). Quedan excluidos aquí los impuestos recaudados de las importaciones como parte de un impuesto general sobre los bienes y servicios, así como los impuestos selectivos aplicables tanto a bienes importados como a bienes de producción nacional.

5124 – *Impuestos sobre las exportaciones*

69. En los años 1970, los derechos de exportación se aplicaban en Australia, Canadá y Portugal como una medida de carácter regular, y en Finlandia se han utilizado con fines contracíclicos. Algunos países miembros de la Unión Europea pagan un gravamen sobre las exportaciones, en el marco del sistema MCM (véase la nota a pie de página §16 en el § 68). Cuando las cantidades recaudadas son identificables, se integran en este epígrafe, que no incluye, sin embargo, las devoluciones de impuestos generales al consumo, de impuestos selectivos o de derechos de aduana sobre los bienes exportados, que se deducirán de las entradas brutas de 5110, 5121 o 5123, según corresponda.

5125 – *Impuestos sobre los bienes de inversión*

70. Este epígrafe cubre los impuestos sobre los bienes de inversión, tales como la maquinaria. Estos impuestos pueden cargarse por un cierto número de años o temporalmente con fines contracíclicos. No se incluyen aquí aquellos impuestos sobre los insumos industriales que recaen también en los consumidores (p. ej., el impuesto sobre la energía en Suecia, que se clasifica en 5121).

5126 – *Impuestos sobre servicios específicos*

71. Todos los impuestos sobre el pago por servicios específicos, tales como los impuestos sobre las primas de seguro, los servicios bancarios, los juegos de azar y las apuestas (p. ej., carreras de caballos, quinielas de fútbol, lotería), el transporte, las actividades recreativas o de ocio, los restaurantes y la publicidad, entran dentro de este epígrafe. También se clasifican aquí los impuestos sobre el ingreso bruto de las empresas que prestan el servicio (p. ej., primas de seguro o apuestas brutas recibidas por una empresa). Los ingresos tributarios procedentes de gravámenes bancarios y pagos a sistemas de seguro de depósitos y de estabilidad financiera se han incluido provisionalmente en este epígrafe para la edición de 2012. La clasificación detallada figura en § 108.

72. Se excluyen de este epígrafe:

a. los impuestos sobre servicios que formen parte de un impuesto general sobre los bienes y servicios (5110);

b. los impuestos sobre la electricidad, el gas y la energía (5121, impuestos selectivos);

c. los impuestos sobre las ganancias de las personas físicas en los juegos de azar (1120, impuestos sobre las ganancias de capital de las personas físicas o de las empresas no constituidas en sociedad) y los impuestos fijos sobre la transferencia de loterías privadas o sobre el permiso para crear loterías (5200);[18]

d. los impuestos sobre los cheques y sobre la emisión, transmisión o compra y venta de valores (4400, impuestos sobre transacciones financieras y de capital).

5127 – *Otros impuestos sobre el comercio y las transacciones internacionales*

73. Este epígrafe abarca los ingresos percibidos por el gobierno por la compra y la venta de divisas a diferentes tipos de cambio. Cuando el gobierno ejerce poderes monopolísticos para obtener un margen entre los precios de compra y de venta de divisas superior al que sería necesario para cubrir los costos administrativos, el ingreso generado constituye un gravamen obligatorio impuesto en proporciones indeterminadas tanto sobre el comprador como sobre el vendedor de divisas. Es un equivalente común de los derechos de importación y exportación cargados en un sistema con tipo de cambio único o de un impuesto sobre la compraventa de divisas. Al igual que las utilidades de los monopolios fiscales o de los monopolios de importación y exportación transferidas al gobierno, representa el ejercicio de las prerrogativas monopolísticas con fines fiscales y, por lo tanto, se incluye en los ingresos tributarios.

74. El epígrafe engloba asimismo las utilidades de los monopolios de importación y exportación, que, sin embargo, son inexistentes en los países de la OCDE; los impuestos sobre la compraventa de divisas; y cualesquiera otros impuestos que recaigan sobre el comercio o las transacciones internacionales.

5128 – *Otros impuestos sobre bienes y servicios específicos*

75. Este epígrafe incluye los impuestos sobre la extracción de minerales, combustibles fósiles y otros recursos agotables de yacimientos de propieddad privada o de otro nivel de

gobierno, así como cualesquiera otras entradas no identificables procedentes de impuestos sobre bienes y servicios específicos. Los impuestos sobre la extracción de recursos agotables suelen traducirse en un importe fijo por cantidad o peso, pero también pueden adoptar un valor porcentual. Los impuestos se registran en el momento de extracción de los recursos. Los pagos por extracción de recursos agotables de yacimientos propiedad de la unidad de gobierno que recibe el pago se clasifican como alquiler.

5200 – Impuestos sobre el uso de bienes y sobre el permiso para usar bienes o realizar actividades

76. Esta partida incluye los impuestos aplicados al uso de bienes a diferencia de los impuestos sobre los propios bienes. Al contrario que los impuestos de este último tipo (registrados en la partida 5100), los impuestos considerados aquí no se basan en el valor de los bienes, sino que suelen revestir la forma de importes fijos. Los impuestos sobre el permiso para usar bienes o realizar actividades entran asimismo en esta partida, como, por ejemplo, los impuestos sobre la contaminación que no se basan en el valor de bienes particulares. En ocasiones, resulta complejo distinguir entre cargos obligatorios a los usuarios y tasas de licencia que se consideran como impuestos y aquellos que quedan excluidos por reputarse como ingresos no tributarios; los criterios de deslinde empleados se explican en los § 11 y §12.

77. Aunque el título de esta partida menciona el "uso" de bienes, es posible que sea el registro de la propiedad, y no el uso, lo que dé lugar a la obligación tributaria, y que los impuestos contenidos aquí se apliquen más al hecho de ser titular de ciertos animales o bienes (p. ej., caballos de carreras, perros y vehículos automotores) que al uso que se hace de ellos, o que recaigan incluso en bienes inutilizables (p. ej., vehículos automotores o armas inservibles).

78. Se plantean casos de difícil delimitación con respecto a:

a. los impuestos sobre el permiso para realizar actividades empresariales que parten de una base combinada de renta, nómina o volumen de ventas, que se clasifican de acuerdo con las normas del § 81;

b. los impuestos sobre la propiedad o el uso de la propiedad de las partidas 4100, 4200 y 4600; la partida 4100 se dedica exclusivamente a los impuestos sobre la titularidad o la posesión de bienes inmuebles y, a diferencia de los impuestos de la partida 5200, recaen siempre sobre el valor de la propiedad; los impuestos sobre la riqueza neta (4200) y otros impuestos recurrentes sobre la propiedad (4600) se circunscriben al hecho de ser titular de propiedades, y no al uso de activos; se aplican a grupos de activos, y no a bienes particulares; y están en todo caso relacionados con el valor de los activos en cuestión.

5210 – Impuestos recurrentes sobre el uso de bienes y sobre el permiso para usar bienes o realizar actividades

79. La principal característica de los impuestos consignados aquí es que se recaudan a intervalos regulares y se cobran por lo general según una cantidad fija. En términos de ingresos, el elemento más importante está constituido por los impuestos por licencia de vehículos, aunque también integran esta subpartida los impuestos sobre los permisos de caza, pesca o tiro o sobre la venta de ciertos productos, así como los impuestos sobre la propiedad de animales domésticos y sobre la prestación de ciertos servicios siempre que estos reúnan los criterios establecidos en los § 11 y §12. Los epígrafes en que se divide la partida 5210 son: los impuestos sobre vehículos automotores pagados por los hogares (5211)

y los satisfechos por otros sujetos pasivos (5212);[19] por su parte, el epígrafe 5213 abarca las licencias a propietarios de animales domésticos y los cargos a usuarios por el permiso de realizar actividades, tales como la venta de carne o de bebidas alcohólica cuando los gravámenes se imponen de forma recurrente, así como las licencias generales periódicas de caza, pesca y tiro cuando el derecho a emprender esas actividades no se otorga como parte de una transacción comercial normal (p. ej., la concesión de la licencia no implica el derecho a usar una zona específica propiedad del gobierno).

5220 – *Impuestos no recurrentes sobre el uso de bienes y sobre el permiso para usar bienes o realizar actividades*

80. Se incluyen aquí los impuestos no recurrentes aplicados sobre el uso de bienes y sobre el permiso para utilizar bienes o realizar actividades, así como los impuestos aplicados cada vez que se utilizan los bienes.

- Entran en esta subpartida los impuestos sobre la emisión o liberación en el medio ambiente de gases y líquidos nocivos y otras sustancias peligrosas. Los pagos por permisos negociables de emisión expedidos por los gobiernos en el marco de programas de límites máximos y comercio de emisiones deberán registrarse aquí en la fecha en que se produzcan las emisiones. No se computarán ingresos por los permisos que los gobiernos expidan a título gratuito. El registro según el criterio de devengo implica que habrá una diferencia temporal entre el momento en que el gobierno reciba el pago por los permisos y el momento en que se produzca la emisión. En las cuentas nacionales, esta diferencia genera un pasivo para el gobierno durante ese periodo.
- Se excluirán los pagos efectuados por la recogida y eliminación de desechos o sustancias nocivas por parte de los poderes públicos, ya que constituyen una venta de servicios a las empresas.

81. También se incluyen aquí otros impuestos que entren dentro del ámbito de aplicación de la partida 5200 y que no se recauden recurrentemente. Por lo tanto, quedarán comprendidos los pagos únicos por permisos para la venta de alcohol o tabaco o para la creación de centros de apuestas, siempre que cumplan los criterios de los § 11–12.

6000 – *Otros impuestos*

82. Esta categoría recoge los impuestos que reposan en una o varias bases diferentes de las descritas en las categorías 1000, 3000, 4000 y 5000, o en bases que no puedan considerarse relacionadas a ninguna de estas categorías, se incluyen aquí. Los impuestos de base múltiple, y si es posible estimar las entradas relacionadas con cada base las cantidades desglosadas se repartirán en las correspondientes categorías de acuerdo a su base. Si no pueden calcularse los valores por separado y se sabe que la mayoría de las entradas proceden de una base determinada, el total de estas se atribuirán de acuerdo con dicha base. En caso contrario, las entradas se clasificarán aquí. Otros ingresos incluidos aquí son los impuestos presuntos no incluidos en el sistema de clasificación, los impuestos a las personas en forma de impuesto de capitación, impuestos de sellos no relacionados con las transacciones financieras y de capital que no pertenecen exclusivamente a una sola categoría de transacción, impuestos a los gastos donde se aplican deducciones o exenciones personales y recibos de impuestos no identificables. Esta categoría se subdivide entre los impuestos pagados completa o principalmente por las empresas (6100) y los abonados por otros sujetos pasivos (6200).

A.6. Conciliación con las cuentas nacionales

83. Esta sección de los cuadros reconcilia el cálculo de la recaudación tributaria total realizado por la OCDE y el total de todos los impuestos y contribuciones sociales pagados al gobierno general tal y como figuran en el registro de las cuentas nacionales de cada país. Cuando el país es miembro de la Unión Europea (UE), la comparación se establece entre el cálculo de la recaudación tributaria total realizado por la OCDE y la suma de los ingresos tributarios y contribuciones sociales registrado en la combinación del gobierno general y de las instituciones de los sectores de la UE de las cuentas nacionales.

A.7. Partida informativa sobre el financiamiento de las prestaciones sociales

84. A la vista de la variedad de relaciones entre la tributación y las contribuciones a la seguridad social y de los casos mencionados en los § 39 al §45, se ha previsto una partida informativa que recopile todos los pagos asignados a las prestaciones tipo de la seguridad social, aparte de los pagos voluntarios al sector privado. Los datos se presentan de la forma siguiente (véase el Capítulo 4.2 de este Reporte):

a. Impuestos de la categoría 2000.

b. Impuestos asignados a las prestaciones de la seguridad social.

c. Contribuciones voluntarias al gobierno.

d. Contribuciones obligatorias al sector privado.

Los § 39 al §45 ofrecen las debidas orientaciones para efectuar el desglose entre las rúbricas (*a*) a (*d*).

A.8. Partida informativa sobre impuestos identificables pagados por el gobierno

85. Los impuestos identificables realmente pagados por el gobierno se presentan en una partida informativa, desglosados según las principales categorías de la clasificación de impuestos de la OCDE. En la vasta mayoría de los países, sólo pueden identificarse las contribuciones a la seguridad social y los impuestos sobre la nómina satisfechos por el gobierno, que, sin embargo, suelen ser los gravámenes más importantes liquidados por los gobiernos (véase el Capítulo 4.2 de este Reporte).

A.9. Relación de la clasificación de impuestos de la OCDE con el Sistema de Cuentas Nacionales

86. El Sistema de Cuentas Nacionales (SCN) pretende proporcionar un marco coherente para registrar y presentar los principales flujos relacionados con la producción, el consumo, la acumulación y las transacciones con el exterior de una determinada zona económica, por lo general, un país o una región destacada de un país, y, en este sentido, los ingresos del gobierno constituyen una importante parte de las transacciones registradas en todo sistema de cuentas nacionales. En agosto de 2009, la versión final del SCN 2008 se publicó conjuntamente por cinco organizaciones internacionales: la Organización de las Naciones Unidas, el Fondo Monetario Internacional, la Unión Europea, la Organización para la Cooperación y el Desarrollo Económicos, y el Banco Mundial. La publicación está diseñada para ser empleada en países con economías de mercado, sea cual sea su estadio de desarrollo económico, así como en países en transición hacia economías de mercado. Las principales partes del marco conceptual y las definiciones de los diversos sectores económicos del SCN se han plasmado en la clasificación de impuestos de la OCDE.

87. Sin embargo, existen ciertas diferencias, reseñadas seguidamente, entre la clasificación de impuestos de la OCDE y los conceptos del SCN, debidas a que la finalidad de la clasificación de la OCDE consiste en lograr la máxima desagregación posible de los datos estadísticos en relación con lo que, por lo general, las Administraciones tributarias consideran como impuestos. Y así:

a. la OCDE incluye las contribuciones a la seguridad social obligatorias, pagadas al gobierno general en la recaudación tributaria total. No se consideran como impuestos las contribuciones imputadas y voluntarias, además de aquellas pagadas a fondos privados (véanse los § 8 y §10 *supra.*);
b. los puntos de vista sobre la calificación de algunos gravámenes y tasas como impuestos son diferentes (§ 11y §12 *supra.*);
c. la OCDE excluye los impuestos imputados o los subsidios procedentes de la aplicación de múltiples tipos de cambio oficiales, o del pago de una tasa diferente a otras del mercado sobre reservas requeridas que pueda hacer el banco central;
d. los créditos fiscales exigibles se tratan de forma diferente.

88. Tal y como se ha apuntado en los § 1 y §2, las categorías 1000 a 6000 de la lista de impuestos de la OCDE cubren todos los pagos sin contraprestación al gobierno general, aparte de las multas y los préstamos obligatorios. Esos pagos sin contraprestación, incluidas las multas pero excluidos los préstamos obligatorios, pueden obtenerse añadiendo los siguientes valores del SCN 2008:

- impuestos sobre el valor agregado (D211);
- impuestos y derechos sobre las importaciones, IVA no incluido (D212);
- impuestos sobre las exportaciones (D213);
- impuestos sobre los productos, IVA e impuestos sobre las importaciones y exportaciones no incluidos (D214);
- otros impuestos sobre la producción (D29);
- impuestos sobre la renta (D51);
- otros impuestos corrientes (D59);
- contribuciones sociales (D61), excluidas las contribuciones voluntarias;
- impuestos sobre el capital (D91).

A10. Relación de la clasificación de impuestos de la OCDE con el sistema de estadísticas de finanzas públicas del Fondo Monetario Internacional

89. La cobertura y la valoración de los ingresos tributarios en el sistema de estadísticas de finanzas públicas (EFP) y en el SCN 2008 son muy similares. Por lo tanto, a excepción del tratamiento dado a los créditos fiscales exigibles, las diferencias entre la clasificación de la OCDE y la del SCN 2008 (véase el § 87 *supra.*) son de aplicación igualmente al sistema de EFP. Además, el Fondo Monetario Internacional (FMI) escinde la categoría única 5000 de la OCDE en dos categorías distintas dedicadas a los impuestos nacionales sobre bienes y servicios (114) y a los impuestos sobre el comercio y las transacciones internacionales (115). Esto refleja el hecho de que, mientras estos últimos impuestos suelen generar insignificantes cantidades de ingresos en la zona de la OCDE, ese no es el caso en la mayoría de los países no pertenecientes a la Organización.

A.11. Comparación de la clasificación de impuestos de la OCDE con otras clasificaciones internacionales

90. El cuadro siguiente recoge una comparación ítem por ítem entre la clasificación de impuestos de la OCDE y las clasificaciones empleadas en:

i) el Sistema de Cuentas Nacionales (SCN 2008);

ii) el Sistema Europeo de Cuentas (SEC 1995);

iii) el *Manual de estadísticas de finanzas públicas* del FMI (MEFP 2001).

91. Estas comparaciones representan equivalencias que podrán aplicarse en la mayoría de los casos. Con todo, deberán emplearse con cierta flexibilidad, ya que, en casos particulares, los países pueden adoptar enfoques diferentes para la clasificación de los ingresos en las cuentas nacionales.

Clasificación de la OCDE	SNA 2008	ESA 2010	GFSM2014
1000 Impuestos sobre los ingresos, utilidades y ganancias de capital			
1100 Personas			
1110 Ingresos y utilidades	D51-8.61a	D51A	1111
1120 Ganancias de capital	D51-8.61c, d	D51C, D	1111
1200 Corporaciones			
1210 Ingresos y ganancias	D51-8.61b	D51B	1112
1220 Ganancias de capital	D51-8.61c	D51C	1112
1300 No clasificables entre 1100 y 1200			1113
2000 Contribuciones a la seguridad social			
2100 Empleados	D613-8.85	D613	1211
2200 Empleadores	D611-8.83	D611	1212
2300 Auto-empleados y no empleados	D613-8.85	D613	1213
2400 No asignables entre 2100, 2200 y 2300			1214
3000 Impuestos sobre la nómina y fuerza de trabajo	D29-7.97a	D29C	112
4000 Impuesos sobre la propiedad			
4100 Impuestos recurrentes sobre la propiedad inmueble			
4110 Hogares	D59-8.63a	D59A	1131
4120 Other	D29-7.97b	D29A	1131
4200 Impuestos recurrentes sobre la riqueza neta			
4210 Hogares	D59-8.63b	D59A	1132
4220 Corporaciones	D59-8.63b	D59A	1132
4300 Impuestos sobre sucesiones, herencias y donaciones			
4310 Impuestos sobre sucesiones y herencias	D91-10.207b	D91A	1133
4320 Impuestos sobre donaciones	D91-10.207b	D91A	1133
4400 Impuestos sobre transacciones financieras y de capital	D59-7.96d; D29-7.97e	D214B, C	114114; 1161
4500 Otros impuestos no recurrentes sobre la propiedad	D91-10.207a	D91B	1135
4600 Otros impuestos recurrentes sobre la propiedad	D59-8.63c	D59A	1136
5000 Impuestos sobre los bienes y servicios			
5100 Impuestos sobre la producción, venta y transmisión de bienes y prestación de servicios			
5110 Impuestos generales sobre bienes y servicios			
5111 Impuestos sobre el valor agregado	D211-7.89	D211; D29G	11411
5112 Impuestos sobre las ventas	D2122-7.94a; D214-7.96a	D21224; D214I	11412
5113 Otros impuestos generales sobre los ingresos brutos y sobre bienes y servicios	D214-7.96a	D214I	11413
5120 Impuestos sobre bienes y servicios específicos			
5121 Impuestos selectivos	D2122-7.94b; D214-7.96b	D21223; D214A, B, D	1142
5122 Utilidades de los monopolios fiscales	D214-7.96e	D214J	1143

Clasificación de la OCDE	SNA 2008	ESA 2010	GFSM2014
5123 Derechos de aduanas y otros derechos de importación	D2121-7.93	D2121; D21221, 2	1151
5124 Sobre las exportaciones	D213-7.95a	D214K	1152-4
5125 Sobre los bienes de inversión			
5126 Sobre servicios específicos	D2122-7.94c; D214-7.96c	D21225; D214E, F, G, H; D29F	1144; 1156
5127 Otros impuestos sobre el comercio y las transacciones internacionales	D2122-7.94d D29-7.95b D29-7.97g D59-8.64d	D21226; D29D; D59E	1153; 1155-6
5128 Otros impuestos sobre bienes y servicios específicos			1146
5130 No clasificables entre 5110 y 5120			
5200 Impuestos sobre el uso de bienes y sobre el permiso para usar bienes y realizar actividades			
5210 Impuestos recurrentes			
5211 Sobre vehículos automotores: hogares	D59-8.64c	D59D	11451
5212 Sobre vehículos automotores: otros	D29-7.97d	D214D; D29B	11451
5213 Otros impuestos recurrentes en el uso de bienes y en el permiso para el uso de bienes y la realización de actividades	D29-7.97c, d, f D59-8.64c	D29B, E, F; D59D	11452
5220 Impuestos no recurrentes sobre el permiso para el uso de bienes o la realización de actividades			11452
5300 No clasificables entre 5100 y 5200			
6000 Otros impuestos			
6100 Pagados únicamente por empresas			1161
6200 Pagados por otros distintos de las empresas o no identificables	D59-8.64a, b	D59B, C	1162

A.12. Atribución de ingresos tributarios por subsectores del gobierno general

92. La clasificación de la OCDE requiere un desglose de los ingresos tributarios por subsectores del gobierno general. Seguidamente, se establecen la definición de cada subsector y los criterios que deben emplearse para atribuir los ingresos tributarios entre ellos, que siguen las orientaciones del SCN 2008 y del MEFP 2014.

Identificación de los subsectores del gobierno general

a) Gobierno central

93. El subsector del gobierno central incluye todos los departamentos, oficinas y establecimientos del gobierno, así como otros órganos que constituyen organismos o instrumentos de la autoridad central, cuya competencia se extiende a todo el territorio, con excepción de la administración de los fondos de seguridad social. En consecuencia, el gobierno central tiene la facultad de someter a tributación a todas las unidades residentes y no residentes que emprendan actividades económicas en el país.

b) Gobierno estatal, provincial o regional

94. Este subsector está compuesto por unidades intermedias del gobierno que ejercen su competencia a un nivel inferior al del gobierno central. Incluye a todas las unidades que operan independientemente del gobierno central en una parte del territorio de un país que engloba numerosas pequeñas localidades, con la excepción de la administración de los fondos de seguridad social. En los países unitarios, puede considerarse que los gobiernos regionales tienen una existencia separada, en la que cuentan con la suficiente autonomía como para recaudar sus ingresos de fuentes bajo su control, y sus funcionarios son independientes del control administrativo externo en el ejercicio de las actividades de la unidad.

95. En la actualidad, los países federales representan la mayoría de los casos en los que los ingresos atribuidos a unidades intermedias del gobierno se identifican de forma separada. España es el único país unitario en ese caso; en el resto de los países unitarios, los ingresos regionales se computan junto con los de los gobiernos locales.

c) Gobierno local

96. Este subsector incluye todas las demás unidades del gobierno que ejercen una competencia independiente en parte del territorio de un país, con excepción de la administración de los fondos de seguridad social. Engloba varios entes urbanos o rurales (p. ej., autoridades locales, municipios, ciudades, delegaciones, distritos).

d) Fondos de seguridad social

97. Los fondos de seguridad social forman un subsector separado del gobierno general. El SCN 2008 define el subsector de la seguridad social según lo expuesto en sus párrafos 4.124 a 4.126 y 4.147, citados seguidamente:

> *"Los regímenes de seguridad social son sistemas de seguros sociales que cubren a la comunidad en su conjunto o a amplios sectores de la misma, y que son impuestos y controlados por unidades del gobierno. Los sistemas abarcan una gran variedad de programas, y ofrecen prestaciones en dinero o en especie por vejez, invalidez o muerte, supervivencia, enfermedad y maternidad, accidentes de trabajo, desempleo, ayudas familiares, asistencia sanitaria, etc. No existe necesariamente una relación directa entre la cuantía de la contribución pagada por un individuo y las prestaciones que este pueda recibir." (Párrafo 4.124)*
>
> *"Cuando los sistemas de seguridad social se organizan por separado de las demás actividades de las unidades del gobierno, mantienen sus activos y pasivos separados de estas últimas, y realizan operaciones financieras por cuenta propia, se califican de unidades institucionales, que reciben el nombre de fondos de seguridad social." (Párrafo 4.125)*
>
> *"Las cantidades recaudadas y pagadas por contribuciones y prestaciones de la seguridad social pueden modificarse deliberadamente con el fin de alcanzar determinados objetivos de la política del gobierno que no tengan relación directa con el concepto de la seguridad social como sistema destinado a ofrecer prestaciones sociales a los miembros de la comunidad. Pueden aumentarse o disminuirse, por ejemplo, con el fin de influir en el nivel de la demanda agregada de la economía. No obstante, mientras se mantengan como fondos constituidos por separado, han de ser tratados, en el SCN, como unidades institucionales diferentes." (Párrafo 4.126)*
>
> *"El subsector de los fondos de seguridad social [del gobierno general] está conformado por los fondos de seguridad social que operan en todos los niveles del gobierno. Dichos fondos son sistemas de seguros sociales que cubren a la comunidad en su conjunto o a amplios sectores de la misma, y que son impuestos por unidades del gobierno." (Párrafo 4.147)*

98. La clasificación de la OCDE sigue esta definición de los fondos de seguridad social con las dos siguientes excepciones, por las se excluyen:

- los sistemas impuestos por el gobierno pero administrados por órganos externos al sector del gobierno general, tal y como se ha definido en el § 3 de este manual, y
- los sistemas en los que todas las contribuciones son voluntarias.

Autoridades supranacionales

99. Este subsector engloba las operaciones de recaudación fiscal de autoridades supranacionales dentro de un país. En la práctica, la única autoridad supranacional que cabe tener en cuenta en la zona de la OCDE es la que conforman las instituciones de la Unión Europea (UE). Desde 1998, las autoridades supranacionales no se incluyen en *Revenue Statistics*, a fin de ser coherentes con la definición que el SCN da del gobierno general, que las excluye. Por ejemplo, los impuestos sobre la renta y las contribuciones a la seguridad social recaudados por instituciones europeas y pagados a empleados públicos europeos que residen en países miembros de la OCDE no deberían incluirse. Pese a todo, ciertos gravámenes específicos pagados por los Estados miembros de la UE siguen incorporándose a la recaudación tributaria total y, en ese caso, se muestran bajo esta denominación.

Criterios de atribución de los ingresos tributarios

100. Cuando un gobierno recauda impuestos y los transfiere, en todo o en parte, a otros gobiernos, es necesario determinar si esos ingresos se imputarán al gobierno recaudador que los distribuye a otros en forma de donaciones, o si se atribuirán a los gobiernos beneficiarios para los que el gobierno recaudador actúa como mero agente, recibiendo el producto de los impuestos y transfiriéndolos posteriormente. Los criterios de atribución de los ingresos se establecen en los § 101–§104 siguientes, y siguen lo dispuesto en los puntos 3.70 a 3.73 del SCN 2008.

101. Por regla general, un impuesto se atribuye a la unidad de gobierno que:

a. ejerce la facultad de aplicar el impuesto (como entidad principal o a través de la autoridad delegada por la entidad principal), y

b. puede a su discreción establecer y modificar la tasa del impuesto.

102. Cuando un gobierno recauda impuestos para y en nombre de otro, y este último tiene la facultad de aplicar el impuesto y establecer y modificar su tasa impositiva, entonces el gobierno recaudador actúa como agente de este, y el impuesto se reasigna. Cualquier cantidad retenida por el gobierno recaudador como cargo por la recaudación deberá tratarse como pago por un servicio. Cualquier otra cantidad retenida por el gobierno recaudador, por ejemplo, en el marco de un arreglo de coparticipación de impuestos, deberá tratarse como una donación corriente. Si se delegó al gobierno recaudador la autoridad para establecer y modificar la tasa impositiva entonces las cantidades recaudadas deberán tratarse como ingresos tributarios de este gobierno.

103. Cuando diferentes gobiernos establecen conjuntamente y por igual la tasa de un impuesto y el uso de los recursos, sin que ninguno de ellos tengan la autoridad final y exclusiva, entonces los ingresos tributarios se atribuyen a cada gobierno según la proporción de recursos que le corresponda; si el acuerdo permite a una unidad del gobierno ejercer el control final y exclusivo, entonces todos los ingresos tributarios se atribuirán a dicha unidad.

104. También puede ocurrir que un gobierno tenga la autoridad constitucional o de otra índole de aplicar un impuesto, pero que otros gobiernos establezcan individualmente la tasa de ese impuesto en sus jurisdicciones; los recursos generados por el impuesto en cuestión en la jurisdicción de cada gobierno se atribuirán como ingresos tributarios a los respectivos gobiernos.

Gravámenes satisfechos por los Estados miembros de la Unión Europea

105. Los gravámenes satisfechos por los Estados miembros de la Unión Europea (UE) revisten la forma de:

a. derechos de aduana y gravámenes sobre los bienes agrícolas (5123),
b. cuentas de compensación monetaria brutas (5123 en relación con las importaciones y 5124 en relación con las exportaciones), y
c. gravámenes sobre el acero, el carbón, el azúcar y la leche (5128).

106. Los derechos de aduana recaudados por los Estados miembros de la UE en nombre de esta se registran de la siguiente forma:

- sobre la base de un coeficiente de recaudación bruta;
- ajustando los resultados, siempre que sea posible, de forma que esos derechos se muestren en relación con una base de "destino final", por oposición a la base de "país de primera entrada"; estos ajustes atañen particularmente a los derechos colectados en importantes puertos (marítimos); aunque los derechos de la UE se perciben por las autoridades del país de primera entrada, siempre que sea posible cabrá excluir esos derechos del ingreso del país recaudador e incluirlos en el ingreso del país de destino final.

107. Este es el gravamen específico de la UE que más claramente se ciñe al criterio de atribución consignado en el § 99. En consecuencia, desde 1998, las cantidades en relación con este gravamen se registran como partida informativa en los cuadros de países de los Estados miembros de la UE (en el Capítulo 4 de la publicación *Revenue Statistics* de la OCDE) y no se integran ya en la partida 5123. Sin embargo, se incluyen en las cifras de recaudación tributaria total de la línea superior para los años correspondientes mostrados en los cuadros.

A.13. Clasificación provisional de los ingresos tributarios procedentes de gravámenes bancarios y pagos a sistemas de seguro de depósitos y de estabilidad financiera

108. La OCDE ha adoptado el siguiente enfoque provisional para el registro de los ingresos procedentes de gravámenes bancarios, así como de seguro de depósitos y tasas de estabilidad para la edición 2012 y las posteriores publicaciones de *Revenue Statistics* de la OCDE. Se recomienda que los importes sean registrados bajo la subpartida 5126.

- Los pagos obligatorios de tasas de estabilidad, gravámenes bancarios y primas de seguro de depósitos se tratarán por lo general como ingresos tributarios cuando se abonen al gobierno general y se asignen a los fondos consolidados o generales de este, de forma que el gobierno pueda utilizar libre e inmediatamente el dinero para los fines que elija. Este principio se aplicará independientemente de que el gobierno prometa revertir esos pagos para garantizar los depósitos de los clientes de los bancos en caso de necesidad futura.
- Si los pagos obligatorios se abonan al gobierno general y se destinan a fondos afectados exclusivamente a volver al sector de la economía que engloba a las sociedades sujetas a dichos pagos, éstos seguirán considerándose ingresos tributarios dado que los fondos estarán disponibles para el gobierno y podrán reducir su déficit presupuestario, que la tasa no conlleva contraprestación para una entidad individual y que las cantidades recaudadas no tienen relación con cualquier pago posterior a los depositantes o cualquier gasto realizado como medio de respaldo más amplio al sector financiero.

- Se clasificarán como tasa por servicio los pagos que deban aportarse a sistemas permanentes más reducidos para garantizar los depósitos de "particulares" cuando los niveles de pago concuerden con el coste del seguro.
- También se clasificarán como tasa por servicio, y no como ingreso tributario, los pagos que impliquen que el gobierno ejecute los activos de una institución en quiebra o tenga un derecho prioritario sobre la liquidación de activos de esta con objeto de financiar los pagos de compensación a los clientes por la pérdida de sus depósitos.
- No se tratarán como ingresos tributarios los pagos obligatorios destinados a fondos externos al sector de gobierno y a instituciones no estatales respaldadas por los tomadores de depósitos, ni los pagos hechos a sistemas voluntarios.

Notas

1. Las referencias a la publicación *Revenue Statistics* de la OCDE en esta Guía Interpretativa, aluden a OECD (2018), *Revenue Statistics 2018*, OECD Publishing, Paris.
2. Todas las referencias al SCN deberán entenderse hechas a la edición de 2008.
3. Véase el apartado K de la presente guía para el análisis del concepto de agente.
4. Por lo general, es posible identificar la cuantía de las contribuciones a la seguridad social y de los impuestos sobre la nómina, pero no otros impuestos asumidos por el gobierno.
5. Sin embargo, si un gravamen considerado como ingreso no tributario en la mayoría de los países se califica de tributario –o permite recaudar sustanciales ingresos– en uno o más países, las entradas en concepto de dicho gravamen se indican en las notas que figuran al pie de los cuadros de países, pero no se incluyen en la recaudación tributaria total.
6. Obsérvese, no obstante, que los nombres pueden dar lugar a confusión. Por ejemplo, aunque una tasa sobre los pasaportes se trataría normalmente como ingreso no tributario, si se impone un gravamen suplementario sobre los pasaportes (como en el caso de Portugal) con el fin de conseguir un ingreso sustancialmente mayor que el costo que supone proporcionar el pasaporte, dicho gravamen deberá considerarse como un impuesto sobre el uso de bienes (5200).
7. Para una explicación más detallada de esta distinción, consúltese el estudio especial sobre cuestiones de actualidad en relación con el registro de los ingresos tributarios *Current issues in reporting tax revenues*, en la edición 2001 de *Revenue Statistics*.
8. En ocasiones, se emplean asimismo los términos "no reembolsable" y "reembolsable", pero puede parecer ilógico hablar de "reembolsable" cuando no se ha pagado nada.
9. Con la excepción del diferente tratamiento dado a los créditos fiscales exigibles en los sistemas de imputación del impuesto sobre sociedades (§§ 36–38).
10. No se trata aquí de verdaderos gastos tributarios en sentido formal, ya que tales gastos requieren que se identifique un sistema tributario de referencia para cada país o, mejor si cabe, una referencia internacional común y, en la práctica, no se ha logrado acuerdo sobre esta última.
11. A menos que se basen en la plusvalía obtenida con la venta, en cuyo caso se clasificarían como impuestos sobre las ganancias de capital, en las subpartidas 1120 o 1220.
12. Con todo, algunos países aplican la misma legislación a ambos en impuestos particulares sobre la renta, aunque las entradas procedentes de dichos impuestos suelen ser fácilmente atribuibles a uno u otro caso y pueden, por lo tanto, consignarse en la debida partida.
13. Por ejemplo, "[...] que son suficientemente autónomas e independientes y se comportan como si fueran sociedades [...] (incluido en el hecho de llevar) conjuntos completos de cuentas" (SCN 2008, 4.44).
14. En Canadá, país en el que se considera que rige un sistema de imputación, el crédito fiscal (no exigible) para el accionista nace en relación con el impuesto nacional sobre sociedades que se reputa haber pagado, tanto si ha surgido una obligación tributaria para la sociedad como si no. Habida cuenta de que no existe una conexión íntegra entre la obligación tributaria de la sociedad y el crédito concedido en relación con el impuesto sobre la renta en esos sistemas, los créditos por dividendos se tratan, junto con otros créditos fiscales, según lo descrito en el § 25.

15. Esto puede darse, por ejemplo, cuando ya existía un régimen para los empleados del gobierno previo a la introducción de un régimen general de seguridad social.
16. En el SCN 2008, se consideran transferencias de capital y no impuestos (véase la sección A.8.).
17. Mediante este sistema, la Unión Europea ajusta las diferencias entre los tipos de cambio empleados para determinar los precios de la política agrícola común (PAC) y los tipos de cambio reales. Los pagos realizados en este sistema pueden estar relacionados con importaciones o exportaciones y, cuando ha sido posible identificar por separado las respectivas cantidades, se han mostrado en el correspondiente epígrafe (5123 o 5124). En el presente informe, esas cantidades se han consignado en valores brutos (esto es, sin deducir ningún subsidio otorgado en el marco del sistema MCM).
18. Las transferencias de las utilidades de las loterías del Estado se consideran ingresos no tributarios (véase el § 67).
19. Véase el § 30(c) en relación con esta distinción.

OECD PUBLISHING, 2, rue André-Pascal, 75775 PARIS CEDEX – ÉDITIONS OCDE, 2, rue André-Pascal, 75775 PARÍS CEDEX 16
ISBN 978-92-64-83946-5 – 2019

www.ingramcontent.com/pod-product-compliance
Ingram Content Group UK Ltd.
Pitfield, Milton Keynes, MK11 3LW, UK
UKHW051458290926
15471UKWH00008B/1278

9 789264 839465